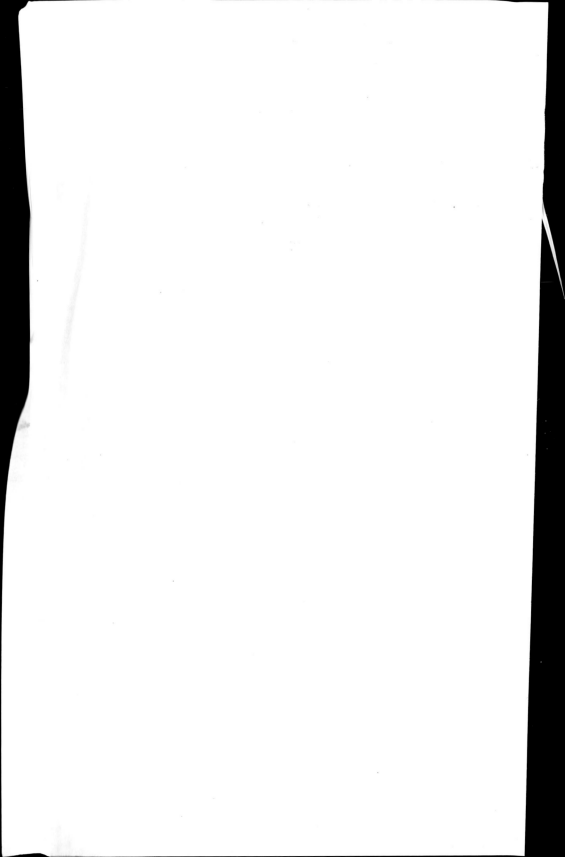

Living with Terror, Working with Trauma

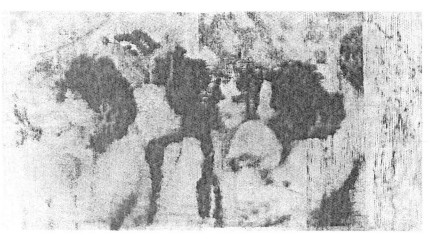
Eurydice, No. 17 *by Bracha Ettinger (1994–1996).*

Living with Terror, Working with Trauma

A Clinician's Handbook

Edited by Danielle Knafo

JASON ARONSON
Lanham • Boulder • New York • Toronto • Oxford

Published in the United States of America
by Jason Aronson
An imprint of Rowman & Littlefield Publishers, Inc.

A wholly owned subsidiary of The Rowman & Littlefield Publishing Group, Inc.
4501 Forbes Boulevard, Suite 200, Lanham, Maryland 20706
www.rowmanlittlefield.com

PO Box 317
Oxford
OX2 9RU, UK

British Library Cataloguing in Publication Information Available

Library of Congress Cataloging-in-Publication Data

Living with terror, working with trauma : a clinician's handbook / edited by
Danielle Knafo.
        p. cm.
    Includes bibliographical references.
    ISBN 0-7657-0378-5 (hardcover : alk. paper)
    1. Psychic trauma—Treatment. 2. Post-traumatic stress disorder—Treatment.
    3. Terror. 4. Victims of terrorism—Rehabilitation. 5. September 11 Terrorist
    Attacks, 2001—Psychological aspects. I. Knafo, Danielle.

    RC552.T7L55 2004
    616.85'21—dc22

                                                    2004006033

Printed in the United States of America

⊗™ The paper used in this publication meets the minimum requirements of American
National Standard for Information Sciences—Permanence of Paper for Printed Library
Materials, ANSI/NISO Z39.48-1992.

To Gavriel,
my light in times of darkness

Contents

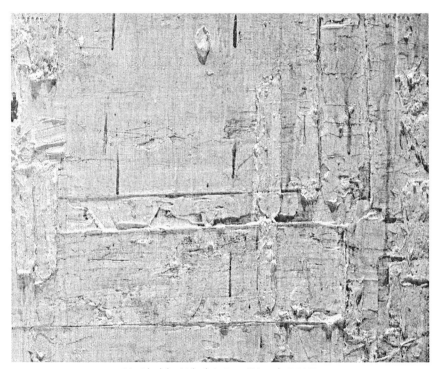

Untitled *by Wlodzimierz Ksiazek (2000).*

Acknowledgments

This book was not an easy one to complete for some obvious and some not so obvious reasons. The subject matter, although timely, is one that most prefer to distract themselves from rather than dwell on. By taking on this project, I chose to spend the past year studying the many facets of trauma, terror, and treatment of what often prove to be the most challenging cases a clinician can face. Today I am very happy that I did so. Although there were moments and days when the material affected me so profoundly that I questioned my decision, I always came back to the subject that I knew in my heart was of the utmost significance.

I am grateful to Estelle Rappoport who, following the events of September 11, asked me to give a lecture to Derner Institute's Psychoanalytic Society on what clinicians can learn from the Israeli experience. My friend and publisher, Jason Aronson, read my paper and suggested I turn it into a book. Unable to appreciate the enormity of the project at the time, I accepted. Thank you, Jason.

I am very appreciative to Bob Keisner, the chair of the graduate program in which I teach, for encouraging my intellectual pursuits. Bob has offered me tremendous support and stability during my transition back from Israel to the United States.

I am so thankful to have had the pleasure and good fortune of working with so many wonderful student assistants who helped me with all stages of preparation for the book. Jessica Lilleston was with me from the beginning of the project and has been resourceful, consistently reliable, and super efficient. Melanie Puci was equally dependable, competent, and speedy. I appreciated Lauren Scher's proficiency and organization and I am grateful to Lauren McKormick for volunteering to help edit Dr. Benyakar's chapter on Israel's five wars.

Karen Starr, although not my official assistant, assisted me both practically and emotionally. Her professional editing skills helped improve the quality and clarity of many of the book's chapters, most notably chapters 3, 4, 7, 10–12, 14, 16, 19, 21, 22, 24, and 26. Sharon Shkedi and my beloved niece, Arielle Setton, helped me organize the vast material I amassed during the course of this project. Arielle's continued encouragement was always there when I needed it. Anna Marantidis's help tracking down references and creating the index was invaluable.

I have the good luck of having friends who are also colleagues. Several of them are people I regularly turn to for questions about nearly everything I write and do. Their patience, interest, and continued support and friendship have been precious to me. They are Seymour Moscovitz, Janice Lieberman, and Morris Eagle.

My sister, Ruth Knafo Setton, is my constant emotional and intellectual companion. My parents, Rosine and Maurice Knafo, and my brother and sister, Jerry and Angelique Knafo, have always been there with emotional support and encouragement. The children of both my sisters provide constant pride and joy in me. I am fortunate to have such a wonderful family.

There are friends I would like to mention who did not help directly with the book, but their presence and indirect help was priceless. Amy Cantos was always there to help with the practical side of my life in times of chaos. Ikky Bluth, a positive force in my new surroundings, has helped me stay in shape and attend to my body when consumed with affairs of the mind. Harvey Bratt provided a home for my wandering soul.

I am very thankful to my artist friends and acquaintances, Kiki Elefant, Michal Heiman, Carolee Schneemann, Ruth Knafo Setton, Bracha Ettinger, Joshua Neustein, Wlodzimierz Ksiazek, and Karen Alkalay-Gut for allowing me to use their artwork and write about it in the book. Their ability to deal with the most difficult issues in their art has been an inspiration to me.

Finally, I would like to thank all the authors who contributed chapters to this book. I feel fortunate to have come in contact with a very special group of people. My experiences with them have proved to me that those who devote themselves to clinical work and research in the area of terror and trauma are truly extraordinary human beings.

My son, Gavriel Matan Knafo, to whom this book is dedicated, is my inspiration and joy. I will never forget his first big belly laugh. It erupted full force as he watched a television news program depicting the devastating aftereffects of a suicide bombing in a Jerusalem marketplace. While he was clearly responding to the sounds, movement, and colors in the scene, I stood silently horrified by the irony that a frenzied panorama of violence and carnage would elicit such a response from him. This book is meant to make a small difference for Gavriel and all the other children of the world, to guarantee their innocence and playfulness, and to allow them to grow in safety and without fear.

Introduction

Danielle Knafo

Human kind cannot bear very much reality.

—T. S. Eliot

What does not kill me makes me stronger.

—Nietzsche

An Israeli mother recently confessed that she had changed her mind about refusing to allow her adolescent daughter to get a tattoo. Despite the negative
association to the numbers tattooed on Jewish bodies during the Holocaust
and the taboo against tattoos under Jewish law, this mother not only acqui-
esced to her daughter's request, she insisted on it. When asked what had per-
suaded her to change her mind, she wept and said that she was tired of being
glued to the phone, the television, and the radio whenever her daughter went
out at night, praying that she was all right and hoping that she would return
home in one piece. After encountering parents who had lost their children in
bombings, this mother decided to encourage her daughter's tattoo in order to
ensure that hers would not be a body that would go unidentified—if the unspeakable were to happen.

A more extreme example of behavior in those who struggle to cope with
living a life under terror can be found in recent dramatic headlines in Middle
Eastern newspapers. Descriptions and debates surround desperate attempts on
the part of at least fifty Israeli and Palestinian couples asking to create repli-
cas of their deceased children, lost through violence, in a new and questionable cloning process (Gross, 2003).

Living a life under terror forces on us circumstances and choices like
those these parents had to face. The rupture of a sense of predictability and

1

controllability changes the way we view our place in the world. Violence breaks through one's protective armor, often without warning, and results in vast disorganization marked by social and personal dysfunction as well as psychic pain. Unfortunately, living a life under the constant threat of social violence has become more and more a reality. "Normal living" has come to consist of a subliminal awareness that at any moment our world can become a threatening, alienating, and dangerous place, replete with uncertainty and indescribable menace. In this book, an ensemble of noted experts in the field address the experience of living with terror and suggest ways of working with victims of trauma.

Psychoanalysis began with the study of trauma. Many findings in Freud and Breuer's (1893–1895) *Studies on Hysteria* are as relevant today as they were over one hundred years ago. They observed that the failure both to discharge affect following a traumatic event (i.e., to abreact it) and to place the memory of the experience in a broad associative context can lead to symptoms of conversion hysteria, also observed in war neuroses (Kardiner, 1941). According to Freud, in these disorders, strangulated affect is converted into somatic symptoms. The failure of associative correction and consequent "wearing away" of the traumatic memory results in its remaining isolated from the rest of the personality, continuing to operate like a "virus" or "parasite." Furthermore, the unintegrated memory attracts other ideas to it, thus forming a *condition seconde* (Janet) or "separate [dissociated] psychical group" in the personality.

Freud's treatment of hysteria followed directly from his conception of its causes. Abreaction of affect and recollection of the related events are needed to bring the traumatic event into associative connection with the "dominant mass of ideas," where it can be subjected to the normal "wearing-away process." Freud (1893–1895) was also the first to recognize that the effects of trauma do not always accompany the event and may emerge later—sometimes much later. He coined the term "deferred action" (*Nachträglichkeit*; *après coup*) for this clinical phenomenon.

Many of the current popular methods of working with trauma (e.g., debriefing) incorporate Freud's early ideas. Van der Kolk (1997) has noted that "the body keeps score" of traumatic memories, largely nonverbal in nature. Viewing the body as the container for traumatic memories helps explain the frequency of somatization disorders and the finding that traumatic symptoms may emerge as the result of an assault on the body. The central role of the body, bypassing mental processing (symbolization) of trauma, also explains how sensory stimuli may trigger previous traumatic memories.

Of the many contemporary approaches to trauma, Herman's formulation is particularly useful clinically: "Psychological trauma," writes Herman, is "an affliction of the powerless" in which "the victim is rendered helpless by overwhelming force." Common reactions include "intense fear, helplessness, loss of control, and threat of annihilation" (Herman, 1992, p. 32). According to Herman, intrusive thoughts and affective constriction following a trauma prevent the integration of the event. The traumatized person consequently vacillates between extreme states of reliving the trauma, with its attendant powerful feelings on the one hand and being devoid of feeling altogether, robotic "dead men walking," on the other. Behavior, too, may alternate between irritable, impulsive action and complete inhibition of action (Herman, p. 47).

Most of us are familiar with the clinical description of Post-Traumatic Stress Disorder (PTSD) in the American Psychiatric Association, *Diagnostic and Statistical Manual of Mental Disorders–Fourth Edition* (*DSM–IV*) (1994). This diagnostic category involves symptoms that emerge following exposure to an event experienced as physically or psychically life-threatening that can be subsumed under three general categories: *hyperarousal*, a state of permanent alert as if to prepare for the danger's return; *intrusion*, the reliving of the event in nightmares and flashbacks; and *psychic numbness*, resulting from the dissociation of trauma-related memories and the constriction of thought and affect. Although there exists some controversy about the relevance of PTSD as a diagnostic entity, since it refers to reactions to limited events (see chapter 3) and combines both stress and trauma reactions (see chapter 5), it continues to be the diagnostic reference for those who suffer traumatic reactions.

Although an extensive literature exists on the identification and treatment of PTSD, I felt a need to focus on the specific challenges caused by terrorist acitivities, broadly defined. In their book *Political Terrorism*, Schmid and Jongman (1984) cite 109 definitions of terrorism. Boaz Ganor, director of the International Policy Institute for Counter-Terrorism, claims that the struggle to define terrorism can be as difficult as the struggle against terrorism. Nonetheless, he defines terrorism as "the intentional use of, or threat to use violence against civilians or civilian targets, in order to attain political aims" (Ganor, 1998). Ganor's definition has three important elements: the essence of the activity is the use of, or threat to use, violence; the aim of the activity is always political; and the targets are civilians.

Terrorism has created a group of people with distinctive and uniquely contemporary therapeutic needs. In addition to the losses and stresses that occur in natural disasters or accidental trauma, volitional interpersonal violence on a large scale inevitably elicits questions regarding the meaning of human intent, good and evil, faith, basic trust, and, of course, God. Such acts cannot help but affect one's relationship to oneself; to others; to social institutions, many of which cease to function as before; and to reality itself, and create the worst prospects for recovery.

Dr. Ofra Ayalon, an Israeli psychologist and world expert on working with child victims of terrorism, claims that patients whose trauma resulted from terrorist acts demonstrate impaired social interaction and social survival due to the destruction in their basic trust. Treatment of such persons, in her view, must attempt to repair this damage in order to enable the person to live life as a social being. Ayalon offers an example:

> Three terrorists broke into an apartment in Ma'alot, Israel, and shot to death father, pregnant mother and a four-year-old boy. Then one of them approached the five-year-old girl lying in a pool of her father's blood. He gave the girl a big smile—and shot five bullets into her belly. The girl survived—to remember and tell this horrendous experience.

"One would wonder," asks Ayalon, "which psychic wounds would be more difficult to heal: the loss of her family or the total confusion in what she could expect from a smile?" (personal communication, January 14, 2002).

Acts of terror involve extreme violence and they provoke extreme reactions and defenses. When working with victims of such acts, one becomes aware of the defenses they erect as well as the defenses we have in response to them. Respect for defenses is an essential component of this work. When dealing with trauma, therapists are put in the position of determining what to open, when to open, when to close, and what to leave closed.

Common defense mechanisms to living a life under terror are avoidance, denial, numbing, somatization, and dissociation. Defenses, and the symptoms that ensue from them, represent a person's attempts to keep the world safe by warding off concerns about death, guilt, and the meaninglessness of life. It is a normal self-protective device to become oblivious to terrors of the outer and inner world in order to function. The extent to which someone constricts his or her experience, however, will determine just how much he or she is blocked from feeling, moving, deciding, and acting.

Denial is the defense of choice when one is overwhelmed by a reality that is simply too much to bear. A joke going around Israel recently illustrates this defense:

> Americans say that there is no longer danger in the United States.
> Rather, it is Israel that is dangerous.
> In Tel Aviv, they say that Jerusalem is dangerous.
> People who live in Jerusalem claim that there is only one street in Jerusalem that is dangerous.
> People who live on that street say that it is not Jerusalem that is dangerous, but the town of Gilo.
> Those from Gilo say it is not all of Gilo that is dangerous; only four homes in Gilo are dangerous.

Those living in those four homes claim that only one of the homes is dangerous.
Inhabitants of that home say that it is not the whole house that is
    dangerous, just one room: the kitchen.
Those in the kitchen say that it is not the entire kitchen, just the freezer.
And finally, the claims are that it is not the entire freezer that is
    dangerous, only the frozen chicken.

This rather humorous story captures not only the need for denial in those who live in danger from terrorism but also the absurd form such denial assumes when taken to the extreme. Humor, even black humor, is an essential coping mechanism.

A defense not often spoken or written about is the manic "high" some people feel as a result of living in a world that involves daily encounters with near-death experiences. M, the daughter of Holocaust survivors, conceded that her need to avoid boredom led her to seek strong stimulation, a need that was easily satisfied by the daily news of bombings and deaths that provide her with a sense of "living on the edge," which she craved. She added that these feelings are always followed by a deep sense of shame.

Analysts are accustomed to helping people become more grounded and improve their reality testing. Yet, in cases that involve living with terror, it is often necessary to leave defenses that distance one from a dangerous reality intact. It is often essential to help patients who are too reality bound to escape a little, indulge in fantasy, humor, and creativity. For example, one must not be too quick to undo rationalization and denial. Rationalizations, like those who live in the religious section of Jerusalem, Mea She'arim, allow them to keep their faith. After a suicide attack that took place on a Sabbath eve, religious survivors reasoned that God was testing them and proving that the Messiah is near. These defenses may constitute the only way one is able to maintain hope in an absurd world. As such, they may be necessary to sustain one's tie to life and the future. "I still believe people are good," insisted Anne Frank in her diary, denying, despite mounting evidence, the existence of evil.

Human-made violence is something that we need not only to overcome and survive but also to make sense of. By maintaining hope and creating meaning, we can determine the outcome of our survival and, more importantly, our will to live and the quality of our lives.

It is hardly a coincidence that the existentialist approach to treatment gained momentum after World War II. Frankl (1959), himself a concentration camp survivor and founder of logotherapy, noted that it was not always the physically strongest who survived the Holocaust but, more often, those who had faith and hope, those for whom meaning was not lost along with friends, family, and self-respect. As if to illustrate Frankl's point, Wiesel (2000) movingly describes the moment American soldiers liberated him and his fellow concentration camp inmates. Although they had not eaten in three days, the survivors rejected the soldiers' offer of food, says Wiesel, until "we prayed to a God who had abandoned us" (p. 98).

Wiesel's account demonstrates the extent to which the human need for meaning and faith outweighs even the physical state of starvation. As valuable a commodity as food was, it could not compete with Wiesel's God, even though he was an abandoning one. It was his God, his meaning of structure, that kept Wiesel alive and saved him from surrendering to apocalyptic nihilism by showing him that his suffering was not gratuitous.

Rank, in *The Myth and Birth of the Hero* (1932), and Becker, in *The Denial of Death* (1973), convincingly demonstrate the manner in which we all live in denial of our own death. Acts of terror, more than war, because they take place on our own soil and attack civilian populations, threaten that denial and force us to redefine the meaning of our lives. A fourteen-year-old girl wrote the following poem after an event in which terrorists raided a neighboring house on the beach of a small recreation town in the north of Israel where she lived. A father and his two small girls (aged two and four) were brutally murdered. The neighbors, who thought they were being attacked, either hid or fled from their homes.

IF THERE IS A GOD
If there is a God
And yes, many claim there is
Then how does it happen that little kids get killed?

How is it that
A girl who didn't even know
What a gunshot is
Was killed by terrorists?
And who knows if that was with God's help?

And how is it
That the children
Who had not even yet managed to do anything in
Their lives
Are the ones to be shot and the ones to die?
Yet there still are those who claim
That there is a God

If there is a God then how does this happen?
Who even needs it?
Let's get it over with.
Let's finish this matter.

If there is a God
And yes, many claim there is,
Then how does this happen
That little kids get killed?

(O. Ayalon, personal communication, January 14, 2002)

Kübler-Ross, world expert on death and dying, has suggested that loss is the price we pay for the right to love and be loved (1969). One can think of secondary traumatic stress as the cost of care for working with those who have been traumatized. Secondary stress has been given numerous names, all of which refer to the fact that trauma is contagious. "Vicarious trauma" (McCann and Pearlman, 1990) and "compassion fatigue" (Figley, 1995) were initially subsumed under the general category of countertransference or "burnout." Therapists (Shengold, 1989) and researchers (Danieli, 1994) have referred to the "via dolorosa" of psychotherapy with survivors and to ways therapists become engulfed with anguish and cope with feelings of sinking into despair. Clearly, caring for people who have experienced highly stressful events places the caregiver at risk for developing similar stress-related symptoms (Stamm, 1999). Attention to this risk is crucial, both for the therapist's own mental and physical health and for his or her patients who will not receive the best care if the professional judgment and ability to treat are adversely effected.

As with PTSD vulnerability, it should not come as a surprise to know that those therapists most susceptible to secondary trauma are those who have had a personal history of trauma (Williams and Sommer, 1995; Pearlman and Macian, 1995). Most importantly, those who work with victims of trauma are advised to be part of a supportive environment, a professional community that attends to the needs of its practitioners as well as its patients, and to balance their personal and professional life. I encountered S, a friend and colleague, several months after the World Trade Center disaster. He informed me that he had become so involved in volunteer work with victims of September 11 that he was on the verge of mental and physical collapse. He clearly did not take care of himself while he was taking care of others and, as a result, he became useless to both.

"Being a constant 'near miss' (part of the threatened society, where at any moment 'it can happen to me too') casts the therapists and victims into the same psycho-social threat zone," says Ayalon (personal communication, January 14, 2002). How can we be effective in our work with victims when we ourselves are feeling terrorized, traumatized, ridden with anxiety and fear? Ayalon (personal communication, January 14, 2002) believes that many patients trust therapists more if they are experiencing similar events. I have found that many patients resemble children in that they desire therapists to be unconnected to or untouched by these events in order to be able to direct their undivided attention and care to the patients' vast needs as well as communicate calm and stability. I am reminded of A. Freud and Burlingham (1945) who observed after World War II that many children did not become anxious during bombings unless their mothers were anxious. Either way, we are constantly challenged to be aware of the transference projections and expectations on the part of our patients as well as our own reactions that are elicited in these treatments. As a result of being "lucky," some therapists may develop rescue fantasies to compensate for their guilt at having survived unscathed.

Therapists (Brom, 2000; T. Peri, personal communication, 2002) who regularly work with trauma patients admit to the use of identification and counteridentification, rescue fantasies, denial, dissociation, humor, and other forms of psychic distancing in order to withstand the powerful emotional burden that such work poses for the care provider. Dr. Tuvia Peri, a dynamically oriented psychologist who works in Hadassah Hospital's psychiatric clinic and center for traumatic stress in Jerusalem, has treated the victims of numerous terrorist attacks. Peri, the son of Holocaust survivors, uses humor to cope with the intensity of his work: "I have a joke with my family or friends that almost every place around Jerusalem is connected to a certain terror attack that one of my patients was involved in." He explains, "I suppose that it is hard to fully identify with patients' fears and anxieties while you have to deal with similar feelings regarding yourself or your worries for your family members, who are on the same streets. . . . I suppose I am defending myself from being engaged in fear and anxiety in order to enable my routine life to go on" (T. Peri, personal communication, 2002).

Peri evaluated a police identification officer whose job of fourteen years involved the witnessing of corpses. Following a bloody terrorist attack in which twenty-two young soldiers had been brutally murdered, the man developed PTSD. In the evaluation session with Peri, he felt the need to describe in detail the exact body condition of each casualty. Peri confessed to stopping his patient in his tracks after his description of the second corpse because it was simply too much for him to handle at the moment. Peri knew he had to take care of himself and respect his own limitations if he was to be of any use to his patient. It is an important lesson for us all.

When I first arrived in Israel in 1972, my life changed dramatically. I immediately had to become accustomed to my bags being opened and checked every time I entered an official building. The omnipresence of soldiers and guns made up a new visual landscape for me. I came to regard them as signs of safety—a kind of security blanket—as well as constant reminders of the threat to my survival.

Shortly after my arrival, the Yom Kippur War broke out. I observed my cousin, an ex-army officer with whom I stayed at the time, become increasingly frustrated at not being able to fight because he had already lost his leg in the previous war. I watched his sons struggle to cope with the situation in very different ways. One tried to master and compensate for his and his father's helplessness through playful war games in which he launched repeated violent assaults on the "bad Arabs." The second son, the more "sensitive" one, found no solace in play and, instead, remained visibly terrified, rolling his eyes while standing rigid and mute whenever the sirens called us to the bomb shelter. The war took the lives of another cousin, whose wife was expecting a baby, as well as my then boyfriend's brother. I moved to Tel Aviv to study at the university after the war. My roommate woke me up nightly with bloodcurdling screams from persecutory nightmares. I had not yet learned the definition of PTSD, but I quickly identified with the fear of being killed in the dark. My best friend at the university was an artist and architect who had changed careers to psychology because he had been blinded in the war. He eventually committed suicide.

When I wrote these recollections of my first year in Israel in a paper I was invited to present at Adelphi University's Derner Institute for Psychoanalysis, I believed that they accurately portrayed my introduction to living with terror and trauma. In fact, my introduction occurred much earlier than I had written at the time. It coincided with my family's immigration from Morocco, then occupied by the French. It took me many years to realize that I had gone from Morocco, an occupied country, to Israel, a country in which I was an unwilling occupier; and that as a *juive arabe*—or Arab Jew—I was always straddling the fence between cultures that had often found themselves at war with one another.

My interest and focus on clinical issues that transcend the therapeutic four walls have always been alive in me and in my work—clinical and otherwise. The need to put together a book on terrorism and trauma clearly comes from my own background and life experiences, as I have always sought to make peace among the Jewish, Arab, French, Israeli, and American influences that reside within me. Many have mournfully commented on the end of intrapsychic work and the ways the outer world has recently invaded the clinical space. For me, the therapeutic world has never existed without its cultural overlays. At all times, wars have been fought and peace processes negotiated both in and out of the clinical setting.

After living and working in Israel for over twelve years, I recently returned to the United States. In the wake of the September 11, 2001, terrorist attacks, I, as I imagine others with similar experiences from different places around the world, have been asked by dozens of people: How do the Israelis do it?

How do they cope? How do they live under constant threat of terrorism? Psychoanalysts, in particular, confessed feelings of inadequacy and lack of expertise, wondering whether their skills and training are relevant and useful. This book represents an attempt to answer the many questions posed to me and the many more that I have found to be relevant by those who actively engage in this type of work. It provides a basic foundation in a rapidly growing field for those who wish to familiarize themselves with state-of-the-art methods with which to understand and help people overcome and even transcend potentially devastating experiences.

I am very pleased to have had such a positive response on the part of many outstanding experts in the field who graciously agreed to contribute chapters to this book. I believe that each, in his or her own way, brings a special perspective from unique experiences that when read together offer a rich multidimensional approach to understanding and treating terror-related trauma. The chapters are very different, as I believe they should be. Some write of their personal experiences with terror and trauma, while others focus on their patients' experiences; some are very theory based, while others include empirical findings; and some voice their political views, while others attempt to maintain a neutral political ground. Since terror-induced trauma is experienced within a larger sociopolitical sphere, many of my writers place their observations and clinical treatment within these contexts. Therapists should not or cannot always maintain their neutrality when working with terror-related trauma, and that in not doing so, we often learn more about ourselves and the complexities involved in situations such as those described in this book. I naturally must state that I do not necessarily espouse all the views expressed in the book.

I am a psychoanalyst. The book's contributors are primarily theoreticians and practitioners who would describe themselves as psychoanalytically oriented. Nevertheless, I invited several nonanalysts to contribute a number of chapters to this book. I believe that in order to deal effectively with trauma that has sociopolitical implications and consequences, clinicians need to be open to a variety of theoretical viewpoints and practical techniques that have proven useful. It is for this reason that the book includes humanistic, cognitive-behavioral, and neurophysiological viewpoints. I think we benefit greatly from the philosophy and experience of multiple approaches to trauma.

One of my areas of expertise is art—the psychology of art and the creative process. In my studies of artists over the years, I have learned to appreciate their ability to use their art to come to terms with tragedy and trauma. Therefore, in addition to including a variety of viewpoints in this book, it was important for me to include works of art by patients and therapists, witnesses, and survivors of trauma. Therapy, as we know (or should know) is not the only venue through which one copes with trauma. Artists have always been aware of this fact, and the myth of the mad or traumatized artist is not entirely baseless. Therefore, I introduce each part of the book with art—poems and graphic works. I hope that in doing so, the reader will appreciate what the experience of trauma as well as the work of trauma entails. Artists do not necessarily experience greater trauma than others; but they do possess a gift for communicating what these experiences are like and how one can come to terms with them in a constructive manner. It is my hope that this book will aid in providing the insights and tools with which to cope with a very frightening reality in our changing world: living with terror and working with trauma.

I have divided the chapters in the book into five parts for purposes of clarity and convenience; yet, I would like to point out that these parts are not as clear-cut as they might seem, and there are many areas of overlap. Part I, "The Meaning of Trauma," includes five chapters covering descriptions, definitions, distinctions, and clarifications of various traumatic conditions as well as the situations most likely to bring about trauma. Harold Blum opens this section with a review and update of psychoanalytic views of trauma, distinguishing between psychic trauma and traumatic object loss. Judith Herman's chapter reviews the evidence for the existence of a complex form of PTSD involving prolonged and repeated trauma that typically occurs when the victim is in captivity or under control of a perpetrator.

Marvin Hurvich argues that forms of annihilation anxiety are at the root of psychic trauma and discusses ways these forms become manifest in different psychopathologies. Henry Krystal's chapter on resilience represents a retrospective study of forty-year follow-ups of survivors of the Holocaust and other genocidal tragedies and explores the attributes that made individuals able to survive and master the potentially lethal trauma, and what characteristics favored successful resumption of "normal" life. Mordechai Benyakar and I conclude this part with a chapter on disruptive events and describe a new diagnostic category called *anxiety by disruption*. This new nosological entity addresses the problems and needs facing increasing numbers of people whose quality of life and personal experiences are severely affected by living a life under terror.

The book's second part, titled "Living with Terror," includes six chapters written by experts, each of whom has had years of experience with specialized observation and treatment within a specific population affected by extreme terror or war activities or both. Robert J. Lifton starts part II with a chapter on the manner in which Hiroshima has become our text for life in a nuclear age. David Kinzie informs us about the Cambodian genocides and describes his attempts at treating its ensuing damage. Mordechai Benyakar's chapter details

Israel's five wars and the ways in which each created different reactions as well as different treatment needs. Herbert Hendin and Ann Pollinger Haas confront us with the painful world of the Vietnam veteran both overseas and at home. Ofra Ayalon describes the effect of terrorist attacks on Israeli children, and Elia Awwad details the pervasive trauma experienced by large numbers of Palestinians during the second *intifada* (Palestinian uprising).

Some readers may wonder why Ireland, Rwanda, or other places on earth have not been included in part II. I can only respond that my purpose here was not to present a comprehensive survey of life under terror in our world but, rather, to offer several glimpses into the experiential dimension of such a life and its consequences. Authors of other chapters in the book will refer to their work in additional parts of the world. I would like to state that I chose to include Vietnam, Cambodia, Hiroshima, and the Middle East in part II because, although they involve war situations, they all include a large number of civilian casualties.

The book's third part, "Working with Trauma," covers many challenges, insights, and the most up-to-date clinical methods for conducting therapeutic interventions with patients who have been traumatized by terror. Rony Berger begins part III by addressing the immediate interventions taken with victims of terrorist attacks, in particular, the use of Traumatic Memory Restructuring (TMR) model. Bessel van der Kolk's well-known work on the neurophysiological reactions to trauma here extends to treatment recommendations that place the body at its center. Henry Krystal details the significance of working with affect in trauma victims and Nina Thomas considers the victims' need for revenge as a potent therapeutic tool toward recovery. Ilene Serlin and John Cannon bring us the humanistic perspective by focusing on the need to work with meaning in patients who have suffered terror-related trauma. The final two chapters in part III refer to therapists who work with trauma rather than their clients. John Wilson addresses the topic of countertransference and applies Heinz Kohut's concepts of empathic attunement and empathic strain to trauma work. B. H. Stamm, known for her work on secondary trauma, and her cowriters, Craig Higson-Smith and Amy Hudnall, take us to the trenches where mental health workers are often forced to assume their position.

The book's fourth part is devoted to "September 11," perhaps the most traumatic moment in the consciousness of most Americans. Martin Bergmann opens part IV with psychoanalytic reflections on the events of September 11 and discusses the ability of psychoanalysis to deal with social change. Charles Strozier and Katie Gentile recount the actual ways in which the mental health community dealt with the disaster in New York City. Bennet Roth tells us of his work leading corporate groups following the tragedy and applies large group theory to help explain the many group reactions he witnessed and worked with, including forms of resistance to group work. Maria Bergmann's chapter addresses the importance of distinguishing old trauma from new trauma when such events occur and the implication for treatment that this poses. And Isaac Tylim emphasizes the importance of allowing patients to erect memorials to their losses.

"Looking toward the Future" is the book's final part and includes five chapters that offer new directions for the understanding and treatment of terror-related trauma. These chapters highlight a number of therapeutic techniques and insights to help people repair the damage from their traumatic experiences and transcend it. Vamik Volkan speaks of the mental health practitioner's need to move beyond the individual and to diagnose entire societies as traumatized and needing care. Dan Bar-On and Fattma Kassem tell of their fascinating work that brought together second-generation Nazis and Holocaust survivors and Palestinians and Israelis, proving that one *can* speak with the enemy. Michael Eigen's chapter poignantly describes two patients whose traumatic lives enabled them to reach new places and develop in ways they would not have been able to had they not experienced them. Robert Karen addresses the very important topic of how to achieve a state of forgiveness in an age of terror and my chapter on the creative transformations of trauma brings the book to a close by showing some of the ways artists transform their private trauma in a cultural domain and discusses clinical implications for helping survivors of trauma deal creatively with their suffering.

The chapters in this book not only present a variety of perspectives, but they occasionally offer complementary and even seemingly opposing points of view. For example, Nina Thomas writes of the usefulness of revenge fantasies, while Robert Karen stresses the significance of forgiveness. Rony Berger and Ofra Ayalon tell us about the Israeli victims of Palestinian terrorist attacks, including suicide bombings, while Elia Awwad makes known the devastation and destruction caused to Palestinians by the Israeli occupation and use of military force. Some authors emphasize the importance of verbalizing their traumatic experiences and creating a meaningful narrative in which to place them (e.g., Berger, Serlin and Cannon, Knafo, Benyakar), while others (e.g., van der Kolk) stress the futility of language and the need for novel treatments that address the body directly.

It is the aim of this book to provide space for all who are affected by terror, to listen to the voices of victims and survivors, patients and therapists, witnesses and bystanders, the offspring of those who have been traumatized, and those who communicate their responses through the arts.

After one experiences a disaster like that of the Holocaust, Hiroshima, or September 11, one's world can never be viewed as it once was. In Portuguese, there is a word that has no direct translation: *saudade* (pronounced saudadje). It refers to nostalgic longing. Anyone familiar with Brazilian music knows that the word saudade is heard over and over again. The long-term mourning that survivors of such trauma become immersed in involves learning how to live with loss and grief, learning to live with a longing for the time before their lives had been so traumatically disrupted. If they are lucky, they will be able to transform their pain into something comparable to the soulful rhythmic music of Brazil, a music that never tires of singing about saudade.

I personally continue to be inspired by survivors of terror who, besides living a life that reverberates with the inevitability of loss and suffering, can show resilience of spirit and the ability to be creative once more. On September 11, Americans caught a glimpse of an apocalypse, a taste of what the end of the world might look like. It is not by chance, I believe, that the Chinese two-character image for the word crisis (*weiji*), signifies both danger and opportunity, just as the second meaning of the word "apocalypse" is to open up. The challenge we increasingly face, as we learn to live a life that incorporates greater possibilities of terror and trauma, is how to protect ourselves while remaining open to life, joy, and experience.

Holocaust survivor and Nobel Peace Prize winner Elie Wiesel reveals the wisdom of one who has lived through the worst of traumas. "When He created man," writes Wiesel, "God gave him a secret and that secret was not how to begin but how to begin again" (1976, p. 32).

My hope is not only that this book will describe the horrors of a life under terror and the challenges of clinical work with survivors of trauma, but, most of all, that it will shed light on the many ways one can heal and continue to grow from such experiences.

REFERENCES

American Psychiatric Association. (1994). *Diagnostic and statistical manual of mental disorders* (4th ed.). Washington, DC: Author.

Becker, E. (1973). *The denial of death*. New York: Free Press.

Brom, D. (2000, September 15). Shrink rap: Interview with Dr. Danny Brom. Retrieved June 19, 2004, from www.amcha.org

Danieli, Y. (1994). Countertransference, trauma, and training. In J. P. Wilson and J. D. Lindy (Eds.), *Countertransference in the treatment of PTSD*, pp. 368–88. New York: Guilford.

Figley, C. R. (1995). Compassion fatigue: Toward a new understanding of the costs of caring. In B. H. Stamm (Ed.), *Secondary traumatic stress: Self-care issues for clinicians, researchers, and educators*, pp. 3–28. Lutherville, MD: Sidran Press.

Frankl, V. (1959). *Man's search for meaning*. New York: Washington Square Press.

Freud, A., and Burlingham, D. (1945). *War and children*. New York: International Universities Press.

Freud, S., and Breuer, J. (1893–1895). *Studies on hysteria. Standard Edition*, 1. London: Hogarth Press.

Ganor, B. (1998, September 24). Defining terrorism: Is one man's terrorist another man's freedom fighter? Retrieved March 24, 2004, from www.ict.org.il

Gross, N. (2003, April 21). Keep out the clones. *The Jerusalem Report*: 24–25.

Herman, J. (1992). *Trauma and recovery: The aftermath of violence—from domestic abuse to political terror*. New York: Basic Books.

Kardiner, A. (1941). *The traumatic neuroses of war*. New York: Hoeber Publishing.

Kübler-Ross, E. (1969). *On death and dying*. New York: Macmillan.

McCann, I. L., and Pearlman, L. A. (1990). Vicarious traumatization: A framework for understanding the psychological effects of working with victims. *Journal of Traumatic Stress*, 3: 131–49.

Pearlman, L. A., and Macian, P. S. (1995). Vicarious traumatization: An empirical study of the effects of trauma work on trauma therapists. *Professional Psychology: Research and Practice*, 26: 558–65.

Rank, O. (1932). *The myth of the birth of the hero*. New York: Vintage.

Schmid, A. P., and Jongman, A. J. (1984). *Political terrorism: A research guide to concepts, theories, data bases, and literature*. Amsterdam: Transaction Books.

Schmid, A. P., Jongman, A. I., et al. (1988). *Political terrorism: A new guide to actors, authors, concepts, data bases, theories, and literature*. SWIDOC, Amsterdam: Transaction Books.

Shengold, L. (1989). *Soul murder: The effects of childhood abuse and deprivation*. New York: Fawcett Columbine.

Stamm, B. H. (Ed.). (1999). *Secondary traumatic stress: Self-Care issues for clinicians, researchers and educators* (2nd. ed.). Lutherville, MD: Sidran Press.

van der Kolk, B. A. (1997). The psychobiology of post-traumatic stress disorder. *Journal of Clinical Psychiatry*, 58 (9): 16–24.

Wiesel, E. (1976). *Messengers of God: Biblical portraits and legends* (Trans. M. Wiesel). New York: Random House.

———. (1990). In D. Knafo, and R. Setton. Madness in Jewish literature. *Academy Forum*, 34 (1 and 2): 12.

Part I

THE MEANING OF TRAUMA

Untitled *by Kiki Elefant (1985).*

Chapter One

Psychic Trauma and Traumatic Object Loss

Harold P. Blum

Psychoanalysis began with the concept of psychic trauma, which was sub-sequently not clearly differentiated from traumatic object loss or from un-conscious conflict and fantasy. Psychic trauma is investigated in relation to unconscious conflict, with and without concurrent object loss. The syn-dromes of Post-Traumatic Stress Disorder (PTSD), uncomplicated by ob-ject loss; of traumatic bereavement; and of relatively nontraumatic be-reavement are all different, yet often interwoven and inseparable. The significance of the loss, sociocultural factors, and group process influence the individual responses to trauma and traumatic bereavement. There are specific neurobiological, as well as, psychological sequelae of traumatic experience. Clinical applications are noted.

Psychoanalysis began with the study of psychic trauma, and that investigation remains altogether relevant to the contemporary scene. After the massive traumatization inflicted by the terrorist attacks of September 11, 2001, there has been widespread feeling that the country will not be the same again and awareness that traumatized individuals will not be the same again. Traumatic alteration of the personality is associated with the threat of personal injury or death or with threatened or actual injury to or the loss of loved ones. Traumatic memories concomitant with alteration of the personality persist after the im-mediate traumatic situation. In the aftermath of severe trauma, efforts at repair and mastery of traumatic injury and loss are prominent, but a "shattered self" is not reconstituted as the former personality. Integrating current research, this chapter will elaborate the interrelationship of trauma and object loss, with ref-erence to shock, strain, and cumulative trauma. Trauma with and without ob-ject loss will be differentiated from each other and from intrapsychic conflict. Neurobiological correlations will be discussed (Freud, 1916, 1917; Kris, 1956; Khan, 1963). I will also consider problems of discontinuity, dissociation, and

19

disorganization. The traumatized person lives in the three worlds of before, during, and after the trauma or traumatic loss or both.

The current elastic definition of trauma has allowed a range of intensity, from transient loss of ego regulation to the regression, helplessness, disorganization, and paralyzing panic of massive trauma. The concept of psychic trauma has been both unduly compressed and stressed beyond the confines of consensual definition. Trauma may be so narrowly defined that the ego is considered totally overwhelmed with no possibility of adequate registration of the trauma or response to the trauma. At another extreme, trauma may be loosely identified with any noxious experience or developmental interference. The classical definition of psychic trauma is that the ego has been overwhelmed and flooded by stimuli in a danger situation emanating from within or without, that is, an internal or external danger. However, this definition refers to the immediate traumatic situation, not to the persisting pathogenic internal condition that is also designated as psychic trauma. It is important to differentiate the traumatic event, the internal traumatic situation, and posttraumatic sequelae. Concurrent with massive traumatic anxiety, the ego is reduced to primitive levels of cognition and affect, but traumatic memories are registered in some form. There are tendencies to either affect numbing or affect storms and to either freezing of motility or to disorganized or frantic hyperactive motility. Freud (1917, p. 276) referred to overwhelming trauma quite differently than the narrow concept of seduction trauma of the preanalytic era, and said, "It may happen, too, that a person is brought so completely to a stop by a traumatic event which shatters the foundation of his life that he abandons all interest in the present and future and remains permanently absorbed in mental concentration upon the past." A "shattered self," that is, disorganized or fragmented personality, is a different theoretical formulation than symptoms based on ubiquitous unconscious conflict. Freud (1917, p.275) also indicated the enduring injury to the overwhelmed psyche, and asserted of trauma, "We apply it to an experience which within a short period of time presents the mind with an increase of stimulus too powerful to be dealt with or worked off in the normal way, and this must result in permanent disturbances of the manner in which the energy operates." Neurobiological findings to be referred to later support Freud's supposition. Freud (1926) later emphasized that the traumatic state was one of psychic helplessness. The experience of traumatic helplessness was quite different from anticipated danger.

The symptoms of PTSD are not those of uncontrolled regression or total disorganization of the personality. The symptoms are grouped into those that are excessive, inhibited, intrusive, or avoidant reactions. In addition to obligatory regression, there is an obligatory tendency toward repetition of the trauma in thought, feeling, and behavior. The intrusion of elements of trauma occurs in flashbacks, daydreams, nightmares, somatic reactions, and conscious preoccupation with elements of the traumatic situation. Hyperarousal, vigilance, and tendencies toward startle reactions are frequent. The avoidant or inhibitory reactions include numbing of affect and sensation, as well as avoidance of stimuli, cues, and clues that might recall or reactivate the trauma. There are immediate effects of psychic trauma, but the diagnosis of PTSD cannot be made for at least one or two months after the traumatic situation. Since PTSD is posttraumatic, it does not encompass ongoing traumatic experience without a return to safety.

Living in a war zone would be characterized by cumulative trauma with intermittent shock trauma and ongoing strain that could not be characterized as PTSD. Analysts have long understood that long-range effects and ramifications of trauma may not appear until there is a releasing stimulus or precipitating event. Fixation to severe childhood trauma is typical, but such childhood trauma may result in developmental inhibition or interference. The individual may remain developmentally retarded or deviant in areas of the personality from the time the trauma originally occurred. Such developmental fixation and retardation has also been reported and elaborated in patients who had experienced parent loss during their childhood (Fleming and Altschul, 1963; Terr, 1991).

I am skeptical of the highly questionable proposition of nonregistration of trauma or that trauma is inevitably registered in nonverbal memory. Nonregistration of trauma can hardly be the case where there are flashbacks and nightmares deriving from the traumatic experience. At the time that the psychoanalytic theories of trauma were first formulated, different forms of memory were not understood. Severe trauma may indeed be registered differently than other memories since the overwhelmed personality may be speechless and unable to reflect and the traumatic experience in whole or part repressed or dissociated or both from full conscious awareness.

Parallel to the conscious experience of trauma, psychoanalytic work supports unconscious registration of traumatic experience, not necessarily or entirely within declarative verbal memory. In my experience, such registration of traumatic experience has both verbal elements and nonverbal elements, reflected in sensory, affective, imagery, motor, acting out, and somatic phenomena. Those memory elements, which were outside of semantic representation, are not usually retrieved in psychoanalytic work through linguistic verbal expression. Verbal representation and meaning may be achieved in clinical reconstruction, which may recreate a coherent analytic version of the past traumatic experience.

Dissociation in which the traumatic experience remains in a divided or split-off consciousness is a term that has existed itself in a segregated area of psychoanalytic thought. It is not in the Lexicon (Laplanche and Pontalis, 1973) or in the American Psychoanalytic Association Glossary (Moore and Fine, 1990). Perhaps closer to the phenomena of isolation and denial, the dissociated state is reported to have a reality of its own but to be divested of attention and usual conscious awareness. Dissociation is not necessarily a product of trauma or found only in traumatic states. Denial is rarely complete, and some awareness of the disavowed reality remains. Dissociation is also the subject of considerable controversy, for example, iatrogenic dissociation. Issues of the validity of memory are quite pertinent.

Iatrogenic implanting of memories, true versus false memory, reality versus fantasy, has been periodically explored in the development of psychoanalysis. I shall only be able to comment here on the reality of the traumas under discussion, which are consequent to a terrible or horrific experience or to indisputable traumatic object loss or both. The consensual validation of the traumatic experiences of the recent terrorism is quite different from the validation of concealed traumatic experience, such as mugging or rape. An immediate multiply observed and reported traumatic situation does not evoke the same level of skepticism as a report of a traumatic experience of childhood, recalled as an adult.

Even in the immediate aftermath of trauma, distortion and dissociation of the trauma defend against overwhelming anxiety and rage. An elderly survivor may connect current nightmares and night sweats to his or her Holocaust experience. On the other hand, a parent who either is a strict disciplinarian or is unable to discipline and set appropriate limits may not be aware of the connection between his or her disturbed parenting and a history of abuse in childhood.

The effects of psychic trauma influence the way one perceives and reacts to external reality. It is stressful and confusing to live in two different unintegrated worlds, before and after sudden object loss. In traumatic bereavement the object relationship before the trauma no longer exists. The world in which the patient finds him or herself and helps to shape after the traumatic loss is significantly different. While previously discussed in terms of the splitting of the ego in relation to object loss experienced in childhood (Blum, 1983), the traumatic effect on relatives and other significant persons must also be considered. The alteration of the personality after severe trauma and object loss may entail ego splitting but may also take a variety of other forms. There may be dissociation of areas of the personality before and after the trauma, with diminished conscious awareness. Traumatic effects may be selectively retained in consciousness, may be preconscious, or may be unconscious.

The traumatic effects of object loss differ for each person within the family. The defensive maneuvers will influence the process of adaptation, the degree of clarification or confusion, and the difficulties in adaptation of the other traumatized individuals within the transformed family. In the case, for example, where a spouse has been lost, the surviving parent may acknowledge bitter truths while attempting to spare a child unnecessary pain and suffering. The surviving parent may thus help the child to deal with the reality of loss and to say goodbye over time, that is, to mourn in an age-appropriate developmental manner. On the other hand, a surviving traumatized and bereaved parent, himself or herself in grief, may foster psychopathology and fixation to trauma by avoiding talking about painful memories.

The child may not be allowed to learn about the cause and consequences of the traumatic loss. Discontinuities favor the maintenance of contradiction and confusion; for example, a child or grandparent may replace a lost parent. Object loss also affects the extrafamilial social and cultural influences impinging on a newly restructured family. The changes in the personality, the discontinuities, the inconsistencies, and the alterations that have occurred, all contribute to ongoing cumulative and strain trauma. Complex internal and external changes are frequently associated with narcissistic disturbance, denial, distrust, and doubt about perceived reality.

Splitting of the ego and the object world is anchored in the divided reality situations that are both antecedent and subsequent to traumatic loss. After the childhood loss of a parent, family life is fractured. There are changes in the surviving parent and family, as well as the social surround, with attempts to adapt to what may be radically changed circumstances. There may be greater dependence on grandparents, housekeepers, daycare, preschool, and so forth. When long-range adaptation is based on denial and dissociation or regression and repression, it is likely to be fragile and subject to later disturbance. Trauma and object loss tend to be aggregated, especially in disaster, and severe trauma may result in loss of one's former identity with associated loss of self-confidence, self-esteem, self-reliance, ideal self, and altered ego ideals. A loss of trust and confidence in others may be replaced by caution, if not suspicion. The traumatized individual may view and relate to his or her world in a very different way subsequent to the trauma, with profound doubt about the predictability and stability of the world and the self. Severe trauma may fundamentally alter one's feeling of self-regard, and being able to self-regulate, control events, or plan for a future. The uncertainty principle reigns.

While doubtful that repetitive efforts at mastery of trauma could successfully repair traumatic injury to the ego, Deutsch (1966) allowed for the possibility of later personality consolidation and mastery under favorable circumstances. The damaged ego might be strengthened to more effectively deal with new traumatic situations. Traumatic disorganization might then paradoxically permit a more favorable ego reorganization. Resilient children and adults appear to function as though they have "righting reflexes," and can change course and reverse regression. A benevolent object relationship has often provided a supportive and facilitating environment. In cases of social disaster, community support is important. Some highly traumatized children subsequently seem extraordinarily resilient, possessing unusual capacities for the resolution of conflict and recovery from trauma. Holocaust studies have also shown that while most concentration camp survivors have been severely damaged by the massive traumatic experience, some others have gone on to reconstitute their lives in remarkable ways (Klein, 1974; Krystal, 1988). As a tribute to the human spirit and capacities for recovery from trauma, such reports may not do justice to the psychic scars and vulnerabilities that may not be visible in a particular time and life situation.

No one is completely invulnerable or immune to trauma, though there is a tremendous range from coping and resilience to personality strengths and weaknesses. Pre-existing personality strengths permit more effective utilization of whatever assistance and ego support may be available after the individual is no longer in the traumatic situation. The restoration of relatively benevolent object relationships, the availability of empathic and sympathetic care, the identification with rescuing, comforting, and nurturing objects, and the social recognition and respect for the individual's identity and adaptation are very important to the gradual mastery of trauma (Pollack, 1989; Blum, 1986). The pathogenicity of trauma is balanced in degree by recovery and by possible creative solutions. The role of trauma in the genesis of art and literature has often been cited (e.g., in the creativity of Eugene O'Neil, Frida Kahlo) (Rose, 1996).

Psychic trauma is complicated and intensified by cumulative trauma and physical trauma as well as object loss. Severe injury in an accident may leave the victim with psychic wounds far more enduring than the physical injuries, which may have healed. Persistent psychic and physical traumatic injury have a co-morbidity, which impedes recovery. The nature of trauma changes not only with the individual but also with the nature and duration of the trauma and the setting in which it has occurred. Is trauma more serious if it is associated with a fabricated disaster rather than a so-called natural disaster? There are too many internal and external variables for such a clear distinction. To be traumatized by an earthquake is not likely to be the same in its conscious and unconscious meanings as to be deliberately raped, mugged, or nearly murdered by a single human assailant. There is of course tremendous overlap between the consequences of accidental trauma, self-inflicted trauma, and trauma imposed on an individual with the intent to harm or kill. One may unconsciously experience an earthquake as deliberate persecution or punishment.

The trauma may elicit intense anxiety, guilt, rage, and wishes for revenge along with fears of retaliation. Feelings of injustice and victimization trigger demands for justice and the redress of shame, humiliation, and narcissistic morti-fication. Traumatic experience may relate to the realization of unconscious dan-ger such as oedipal transgression, castration, loss of the object's love and ap-proval, object loss, or narcissistic mortification. A traumatic situation activates unconscious conflicts from multiple levels of development as well as former traumatic experience. Past traumas may telescope into a present traumatic event. Since trauma is ubiquitous in childhood, a completely isolated single adult trauma is a theoretical abstraction. However, it is highly questionable whether a "deferred action" will transform a nontraumatic event of the past into a new trauma. Rather, traumatic experience may amalgamate with related events. The ego may use a "screen trauma" as the "lesser evil," which defends against the emergence and recognition of a more repressed trauma.

In the past there was little differentiation of traumatic object loss and trauma that was not a result of, or accompanied by, object loss. Lindemann's (1944) classic paper on the symptoms of acute grief in survivors of the Boston Coconut Grove fire did not differentiate between psychic trauma without object loss and traumatic bereavement. Horowitz (1978) described the "Stress Response Syndrome" in which bereavement was not regarded as different from other traumatic or stressful experience. In his contribution Horowitz delineated the importance of cognitive functions in the capacity to cope, which applies to both trauma and bereavement. Currently, research in-terest in these syndromes has led to varied emphasis on the differences, in-terrelation and overlap, and common features (Brom and Kleber, 2000; Stroebe, Schut, and Finkenauer, 2001).

Much severe traumatic experience may involve object loss, but object loss per se may or may not be traumatic. The loss of loved ones in the recent ter-rorist attacks involved object loss associated with the shock and horror of mass murder without any anticipation or preparation. Trauma and object loss were commingled and reciprocally additive in their traumatic effects. How-ever, object loss without trauma, presents a different clinical picture. Adults expect to eventually confront the unavoidable death of an elderly parent. The death of a very elderly parent is at least inwardly anticipated and not regarded as a shocking occurrence. It is not usually associated with terror or horror un-less there is terminal agony or a predisposition to such reactions. Concerned relatives may wish for a "good death" for the very elderly, for example, to die painlessly in sleep. The conscious attitude, so commonly expressed and so-cially sanctioned, is that the parent has had a long, full life, and no one lives forever. This is different from the threat of actual death or serious injury to oneself or others as a result of totally aberrant and completely unpredictable trauma. The death of an elderly parent is not usually associated with initial disorganized or agitated behavior. Normal mourning may ensue without pathological grief or the persisting symptoms of traumatic disorder. The death of a loved child, however, is inevitably traumatic for the parents.

Acute grief may have traumatic elements, but it presents a different picture. When death of a love object is experienced, the bereaved is preoccupied with the deceased love object and may, for example, carry on imaginary conversations with him or her. Struggling with separation conflicts and searching for the lost object, there is a potent wish for reunion and restitution. This longing is in contrast to the dread of revival of the traumatic experience. Denial and protest co-exist with depression and awareness of the loss. Sobbing, tears, pining, and yearning are commonly associated with grief. In some cultures wailing, or shrieking, depending on gender role, may be common. Disbelief buys time, facilitating a more gradual acceptance of the reality of the loss. Initial panic subsides as adaptation to the loss occurs.

There is a temporal dimension to grief and mourning after object loss. Acute grief lasts from one to three months and gradually subsides. Grief and mourning are predictable and are not ordinarily associated with melancholia, with characteristic feelings of helplessness and hopelessness, or with the relative helplessness and disorganization of acute trauma. Mourning work in adults proceeds for one to two years, during which there is a disinvestment of the representation of the lost object as well as enduring identifications with the lost object. Internalization of the object attempts to compensate for the loss of the object in external reality (Freud, 1916) and promotes the acquisition of those functions which the object provided in reality. The appearance of traits of the deceased in the behavior of the bereaved (Lindemann, 1944, p. 142) is frequent, as are identifications with the interests, ideals, and values of the deceased. Anger toward the deceased for "abandonment" and narcissistic rage (Pollack, 1989), may be turned on the self, displaced or split off from the ambivalently loved lost object. With time and the progress of mourning, the survivor gradually accepts the reality of a different life without the deceased, while identifying with the lost object and maintaining the internal relationship to the lost object. Institutionalized mourning in public memorials, religious rituals with group participation, and extended community mourning usually facilitate individual mourning.

The loved one persists in memory, and emotional disinvestments in the love object are relative. Memory is subject to editing and revision at different phases of life. Pleasurable memories of the deceased, which are gratifying and supportive, may co-exist with unpleasant memories of disappointment and distress in the object relationship. The lost object may be idealized or denigrated or both. But as mourning proceeds, the mourner no longer actively seeks reunion with the loved one in pleasant or painful preoccupation or conscious fantasy. The mourner, as time passes, is less afraid of the revival of initial grief and panic associated with the loss. These predictable and temporal phenomena of grief and mourning may overlap with the effects of psychic trauma, but are quite different. In children mourning may be absent, be minimal, or be manifest differently than adult mourning. Adult psychoanalysis will likely revive a childhood loss and release a mourning process that had been long delayed. Whether this occurs spontaneously without treatment depends on the maintenance or modification of childhood defenses, such as denial and repression, and capacities for adaptive mastery and new love objects.

Trauma without object loss is a different clinical syndrome with different intrapsychic processes, though with overlap and interwoven features. The repetitive and persisting symptoms of PTSD with intrusive and distressing recollections, startle responses, and hypervigilance associated with the traumatic experience and unwanted flashbacks, are not generally found in an object loss syndrome where the traumatic elements have been of much less intensity. The revival of the traumatic experience by external cues that symbolize or resemble an aspect of the event are found in trauma but are uncommon in nontraumatic object loss. The sight of an accident, the sound of a siren or scream, and the sight and smell of smoke may precipitate a re-experiencing of the traumatic situation, as well as one's initial reactions to it. Psychic trauma is repeated in fantasy and often acted out in reality. It follows that trauma has its own metapsychology, with genetic, dynamic, economic, and structural characteristics (Rangell, 1967).

Avoidant reactions are also rather different in the syndrome of object loss versus traumatic disorder. Rather than efforts to avoid thoughts, feelings, and reminders of the trauma, the bereaved individual is predominantly concerned with preserving along with severing the relationship with the lost love object. Intense arousal and avoidance responses are far less common than thoughts and feelings about the deceased. Life will not be the same without the lost spouse, parent, and so forth, but the rest of the object world is preserved even though modified. Somatization reactions, sleep disturbance, nightmares, loss of appetite for food and sex, and lack of interest in formerly pleasurable activities may appear as part of both Bereavement Disorder or Post-Traumatic Stress Syndrome. But the central affective response to bereavement is grief while the central affect of trauma without object loss is massive anxiety. Anxiety is also a variable reaction to object loss, but this is initially separation anxiety, with other affects also activated. Though there is overlap, anniversary reactions to trauma often involve anxiety attacks, while anniversary reactions to uncomplicated object loss are more likely to be depressive responses.

Though grief is a component of posttraumatic reactions, the absence of grief and the persistence of grief are primarily pathogenic reactions to object loss. Since the self is identified with the object, all traumatic injury is on some level connected to object loss, just as object loss is connected to loss of parts of the self. The conceptual boundaries between traumatic experience without object loss and object loss syndromes are blurred and permeable. Trauma invokes loss, and loss may be traumatic. Object loss may take on traumatic proportions when it is unanticipated or untimely or both, when there is predisposition to trauma, and when the object on which the person has been dependent is no longer present. The meaning of the lost object relationship to the bereaved is crucial to whether the loss will be traumatic. Loss associated with horror and shock over the cause or mode of disappearance and death is also traumatic, as is the simultaneous loss of multiple love objects. Object loss consequent to murder or suicide is always traumatic, and the catastrophe of mass murder adds a dimension of shared shock and revulsion that tends to escalate more than to diminish anxiety and grief. Violent deaths result in both trauma and bereavement in a combined syndrome of traumatic bereavement. However, despite decades of investigation, there is no universal consensual agreement about the concept of "traumatic bereavement" (Parkes, 2001).

In the complex disturbance of traumatic object loss, there are individual variations that are not taken into account in PTSD. For example, the survivor of an accident, which killed most of his family through smoke asphyxiation, suffered from generalized anxiety. He was apprehensive about accidents as well as minor illness and injury. He had developed obsessive tormenting concerns about the safety of his children. Environmental issues were very important, and he lamented and grieved over the lack of public attention to clean air and pure water. The air, the windows, the door, and the entire environment of the analytic office were scrupulously surveyed. The analyst's physical condition was noted, and the patient would blame himself for the analyst's rhinitis and laryngitis, as though the analyst had caught the cold from the patient.

The analytic process became a protracted reliving of disguised aspects of trauma and, simultaneously, a mourning process. In a period of negative transference, the patient became depressed as his rage was directed at those who might have avoided the accident, and his rage at abandonment by his lost love objects began to surface. The internalized rage had also been a major determinant of his masochistic self-torment. Survivor guilt appeared, prominently related to his obsessive concern about his children's safety. Obsessive worries and survivor guilt may be particularly significant in some cases of traumatic bereavement.

When trauma involves an entire community, it has a public character. Group identification occurs with victims, with rescuers, and with the aggressor perpetrators. Even if one has not been directly traumatized, he or she is collectively and symbolically injured. The group trauma and losses result in communal grief and mourning as well as anxiety and anger. The World Trade Center disaster was displayed on television and discussed in the media and in personal conversations to the point of overstimulation and overdose. Children and fragile adults needed protection from overexposure to gruesome scenes. A working-through process is normally set in motion after the initial shock. Each society and culture has its own expectations of grief and mourning. There are also differences in affect expression and reactions to trauma and loss related to age and gender. In our culture in an acute traumatic situation, relative strangers may tearfully embrace. Tremulous shaking and sobbing may give way to childlike behavior with needs to be cuddled, comforted, and nurtured. The communal response may provide empathic communion and shared communication of necessary information.

Communication and relationships within the larger supportive social setting relieve a sense of helplessness and horror that define such massive traumatic loss. The numbing of affect and narrowing of thought may serve as a temporary moratorium for the traumatized ego to begin to recover its usual organization and defensive constellation. Leadership is very important in regulating regression, regaining order from chaos, clarifying confusion, and attenuating recurrent panic reactions. Given new identification with resourceful leaders, the traumatized and the wounded can begin to organize themselves and their family to mobilize the massive help needed to deal with mass traumatic loss. The panic, grief, and mourning will run their course, but traumatic injury, scarring, and vulnerability may be more or less permanent. Only the most immune or resilient or both will be left relatively unscathed.

While object loss and psychic trauma are frequently interwoven, it appears that the neurobiological reactions as well as the psychological responses are not identical. The neurobiology of object loss and the neurobiology of trauma are still the subjects of intense research and evaluation. The neurobiology of trauma involves alterations in the brain that are likely to have psychological correlates. These alterations are presumed to be more severe and lasting in infancy and childhood as the immature brain is more vulnerable to trauma.

Psychoanalysts from Freud onward have connected trauma with the activation, realization, or validation of unconscious fantasy. When one's worst nightmare of death and destruction becomes a reality, what had been a frightful fantasy may become a traumatic experience. The individual describes himself or herself as living in the nightmare or having experienced a waking nightmare, which will not go away. The worst fears may have come true as when a soldier suffering from "combat fatigue" or traumatic "shell shock" has unconsciously experienced the murder of an ambivalently loved sibling in the form of a fallen comrade in arms. Child abuse or torture may also be traumatic for the witness as well as the victim.

Trauma is much more than an intense and tenacious eruption of unconscious conflict. Unconscious psychic conflict, present before severe traumatic

experience, does not appear to have the neurobiological correlates associated
with psychic trauma. There is probably no psychic trauma after infancy,
which is not concomitant with psychic conflict, but intrapsychic conflict per
se does not account for the psychological and neurobiological sequela of
trauma. Traumatic experience cannot be currently conceptualized solely in
terms of unconscious conflict and compromise formation (Brenner, 1982).
Psychic trauma has differential effects on the psyche and soma and in infancy
on the development of psychic structure and of the brain.

The object world and internal representations change in the course of life,
and time is the great healer given a relatively normal mourning process. However, some traumatic experience may become fixed and seemingly unchanged
through later life. This fixity may be partly due to enduring traumatic memory at the core of unconscious fantasy. Subjects who experienced traumata
such as child abuse, rape, and auto accidents reported clear images connected
with the trauma, as well as intrusive flashbacks decades afterwards. (This
does not imply that the images are undistorted literal reproductions of traumatic experience.) Although there is mourning for the pre-traumatic self and
object world, the psychology and psychobiology of severe trauma are quite
different from that of "mourning and melancholia" (van der Kolk, 2000; Terr,
1991). Freud (1914, p. 78) presumed that our provisional ideas in psychology
would someday be based on organic substructure. Significant movement in
this direction has evolved in recent years. Freud (1917), cited earlier, proposed that psychic trauma caused permanent disturbance of mental energies.
Neurobiology supports the view that there are organic changes within the
central nervous system that are consequent to trauma.

Stress and protracted strain will influence cognitive and emotional development. The infant who has been exposed to excessively high levels of negative emotional arousal, or has been insufficiently stimulated and left in states
of low emotional arousal, may have permanent developmental disturbance of
the orbital frontal cortex. Trauma may also lead to kindling phenomena, perhaps related to overstimulation of the sympathetic nervous system. A tiny
trigger may elicit a traumatic response overreaction, noted long ago in shell
shock syndrome, which Kardiner (1941, p. 94) described as a physioneurosis.
In infants predisposed to anxiety, this sort of hyperreaction may ensue with
primitive merging of anxiety and rage (Weil, 1985). This is not usually associated with typical bereavement.

New evidence demonstrates that the environment influences the genes, so
that psychic trauma will have adverse affects on the central nervous system
through genetic alterations (Kandel and Kelley, 1999). The psychobiology of
trauma involves forms of perception, memory, and response to danger unknown in Freud's time. Nonconscious emotional memory involves percep-

tions of danger utilizing direct subcortical limbic system pathways through the thalamus to the amygdala, bypassing the cerebral cortex. Stress hormones are released concurrent with autonomic discharge phenomena.

The high levels of anxiety and stress hormones facilitate the possibly indelible registration of traumatic memories and their activation by the automatic, generalized reactions of the amygdala. In contrast, conscious evaluation of danger is associated with declarative explicit memory and involves pathways that include the neocortex, allowing for cognitive judgment and affect regulation (Schore, 1994; LeDoux, 1966). This suggests a neurobiological vulnerability to panic and a neurobiological impediment to transforming traumatic anxiety to signal anxiety. Damage to and shrinking of the hippocampus occurs because of trauma, which then may lead to impaired processing of memory and difficulty in placing experience in an appropriate perspective of space and time. Thought, memory, and fantasy may be confused through defense, regression, and neurobiological alteration (van der Kolk, 2000).

Trauma may have been registered in a form that is initially "unspeakable" for organic but mostly psychological reasons. Some traumatized persons may not wish to, or be able to, talk about their experience. Where there has been personality disorganization, benevolent relationships and identifications provide a foundation for reconstitution and psychotherapy. The security and safety of the analytic or therapeutic situation are necessary for concurrent attenuation of conflict and psychic trauma. Nonverbal communication is important, but the patient must eventually recover the capacity to narrate the traumatic experience in words.

It is therapeutic to communicate the sensory and affective experience of trauma and reflect about the thoughts and feelings connected with the traumatic experience (Herman, 1992). Support for the patient's ego, which has been overwhelmed, will facilitate the opportunity for later analysis of the conscious and unconscious fantasies connected with the traumatic experience. Speech is a symbolic process, which is significantly distant from the immediate psychological and somatic accompaniments of trauma. Communication with an understanding empathic object helps to clarify affective-cognitive confusion and to abreact suppressed affects. Verbalization itself has a binding effect on affect and impulse. The traumatized person is no longer isolated in the scene of panic and terror, and affects can be named and tamed. Anxiety is alleviated and can be converted to signal anxiety. The understanding object unconsciously represents the stabilizing caregiver of childhood, the parent who comes to the child's rescue, provides comfort and stability, and promotes reorganization.

Psychoanalytic therapy is also a learning and an unlearning experience, which presumably alters the neurobiological substrate, promoting ego mastery as well as the possible repair of organic brain disturbance. Psychoanalysis may prove to be an enabling treatment for the construction or reconstruction of appropriate brain pathways and processes (Slipp, 2000). The trauma is never repeated, recalled, or enacted literally, as if there has been no internal response to the trauma. There is always regression and confusion as well as efforts, however enfeebled, at mastery and integration of the traumatic experience. To reexperience, understand, abreact, and reflect on the trauma and its terrors as past rather than present requires analytic work inside and outside the transference. Memories are inexact and can be used for defensive, self-serving, and self-tormenting purposes. Because of the screening, distortion, and fragmentation of memory, the recovery of repressed memory has been incorporated into and superseded by the process of reconstruction in clinical psychoanalysis (Blum, 1994). Even in brief dynamic psychotherapy for severe psychic trauma and traumatic object loss, some superficial reconstruction of immediate cause and effect may be very helpful.

Antidepressive agents may reduce not only grief but anxiety, sleep disturbance, and startle reactions. Though psychopharmacological agents are helpful in the treatment of psychic trauma, in my opinion they are not substitutes for psychoanalysis or psychoanalytic psychotherapy. Drug treatment alone will not attenuate the internal traumatic state, with mistrust, altered defenses and object relations, narcissistic injuries, and strangulated affects.

In conclusion, psychic trauma is not equivalent to or fully explained by conflict and compromise formation. Embedded and elaborated in unconscious fantasy, psychic trauma evokes past trauma. Past trauma has its own descriptive and theoretical features and is differentiated from the consequences of object loss. However, much object loss is traumatic, and object loss frequently complicates and exacerbates psychic trauma. Psychic trauma and object loss are psychologically and neurobiologically differentiated, but clinically interweave and overlap. There is some loss, grief, and mourning with all traumatic experience and the potential for trauma with all object loss. The combination and cumulation of psychic trauma and traumatic object loss result in a very complex coalescence of conceptual and clinical issues.

REFERENCES

This chapter is reproduced from Harold P. Blum, Psychic Trauma and Traumatic Object Loss, *JAPA: The Journal of the American Psychoanalytic Association* 51 (2) (2004): 415–32. Reprinted with permission from the *Journal of the American Psychoanalytic Association*.

Blum, H. (1983). Splitting of the ego and its relation to parent loss. *Journal of the American Psychoanalytic Association*, Suppl., 31: 301–24.

———. (1986). The concept of reconstruction of trauma. In Arnold Rothstein (Ed.), *The reconstruction of trauma: Its significance in clinical work*, pp. 7–27. Madison, CT: International Universities Press.

———. (1987). The role of identification in the resolution of trauma. *The Psychoanalytic Quarterly*, 56: 609–27.

———. (1990). The effect of trauma on the opening phase of psychoanalysis. In Y. Jacobs and A. Rothstein (Eds.), *The opening phase of psychoanalysis*. New York: International Universities Press.

———. (1994). *Reconstruction in Psychoanalysis: Childhood Revisited and Recreated*. New York: International Universities Press.

Brenner, C. (1982). *The Mind in Conflict*. New York: International Universities Press.

Brenner, J., Randall, P., Scott, T. M., Bronen, R. A., Seibyl, J. P., Southwick, S. M., et al. (1995). MRI-based on measurement of hippocampal volume in patients with combat related posttraumatic stress disorder. *The American Journal of Psychiatry*, 152: 973–81.

Breuer, J., and Freud, S. (1895). Studies on hysteria. *Standard Edition*, 2. London: Hogarth Press.

Brom, D., and Kleber, R. (2000). On coping with trauma and coping with grief: similarities and differences. In R. Malkinson, S. Rubin, and E. Wilztum (Eds.), *Traumatic and post-traumatic loss and bereavement*. New York: Psychosocial Press.

Deutsch, H. (1966). Absence of grief. *The Psychoanalytic Quarterly*, 6: 12–22.

Fleming, J., and Attschul, S. (1963). Activators of mourning and growth by psychoanalysis. *International Journal of Psycho-Analysis*, 44: 419–31.

Freud, S. (1914). On narcissism. *Standard Edition*, 14, pp. 67–102. London: Hogarth Press.

———. (1916). Mourning and melancholia. *Standard Edition*, 14, pp. 237–58. London: Hogarth Press

———. (1917). Introductory lectures on psychoanalysis. *Standard Edition*, 15 and 16. London: Hogarth Press.

———. (1926). Inhibitions, symptoms and anxiety. *Standard Edition*, 20, pp. 77–175. London: Hogarth Press.

Herman, J. (1992). *Trauma and Recovery*. New York: Basic Books.

Horowitz, M. J. (1978). *Stress Response Syndromes*. New York: Aronson.

Kandel, E., and Kelley, D. (1999, Fall). Genetics, biology, and the mysteries of the mind. *The Magazine of Columbia University*, 41–47.

Kardiner, A. (1941). *The traumatic neurosis of war*. New York: P. B. Hoeber.

Khan, M. (1963). The concept of cumulative trauma. *The Psychoanalytic Study of the Child*, 18: 286–306.

Klein, H. (1974). Delayed affects and aftereffects of severe traumatization. *Israel Annals of Psychiatry*, 12: 293–303.

Kris, E. (1956). The recovery of childhood memories in psychoanalysis. *The Psychoanalytic Study of the Child*, 11: 54–88.

Krystal, H. (1988). *Integration and Self-Healing: Affect, Trauma, Alexithymia*. Hillsdale, NJ: Analytic Press.

Laplanche, J., and Pontalis, J. B. (1973). *The Language of Psycho-Analysis*. New York: Norton.

LeDoux, J. (1966). *The Emotional Brain*. New York: Simon and Schuster.

Lindemann, E. (1944). Symptomatology and management of acute grief. *The American Journal of Psychiatry*, 101: 141–49.

Moore, B., and Fine, B. (1990). *Psychoanalysis: The major concepts*. New Haven, CT: Yale University Press.

Parkes, C. (2001). *Bereavement*. London: Routledge.

Pollack, G. (1989). *The mourning-liberation process*, Vols. 1 and 2. New York: International University Press.

Rangell, L. (1967). The metapsychology of psychic trauma. In S. Furst (Ed.), *Psychic Trauma*. New York: Basic Books.

Rose, G. (1996). *Trauma and mastery in life and art*. New York: International Universities Press.

Schore, A. (1994). *Affect Regulation and the Origin of the Self*. Hillsdale, NJ: Erlbaum.

Slipp, S. (2000). Introduction to neuroscience and psychoanalysis. *The Journal of the American Academy of Psychoanalysis*, 28: 191–202.

Stroebe, M., Schut, H., and Finkenauer, C. (2001). The traumatization of grief? A conceptual framework for understanding the trauma-bereavement interface. *Israel Journal of Psychiatry and Related Sciences* (3–4): 185–201.

Terr, L. (1991). Childhood traumas: An outline and overview. *The American Journal of Psychiatry*, 148: 10–19.

van der Kolk, B. (2000). Trauma, neuroscience, and the etiology of hysteria. *Journal of the American Academy of Psychoanalysis*, 28: 237–61.

Weil, A. (1985). Thoughts about early pathology. *Journal of the American Psychoanalytic Association*, 33: 335–52.

Chapter Two

Complex PTSD: A Syndrome in Survivors of Prolonged and Repeated Trauma

Judith Lewis Herman

This chapter reviews the evidence for the existence of a complex form of posttraumatic disorder in survivors of prolonged, repeated trauma. This syndrome is currently under consideration for inclusion in the Diagnostic and Statistical Manual of Mental Disorders–Fourth Edition (DSM–IV) *under the name of Disorders of Extreme Stress Not Otherwise Specified (DESNOS). The current diagnostic formulation of Post-Traumatic Stress Disorder (PTSD) derives primarily from observations of survivors of relatively circumscribed traumatic events. This formulation fails to capture the protean sequelae of prolonged, repeated trauma. In contrast to a single traumatic event, prolonged, repeated trauma can occur only where the victim is in a state of captivity, under the control of the perpetrator. The psychological impact of subordination to coercive control has many common features, whether it occurs within the public sphere of politics or within the private sphere of sexual and domestic relations.*

The current diagnostic formulation of Post-Traumatic Stress Disorder (PTSD) derives primarily from observations of survivors of relatively circumscribed traumatic events: combat, disaster, and rape. It has been suggested that this formulation fails to capture the protean sequelae of prolonged, repeated trauma. In contrast to the circumscribed traumatic event, prolonged, repeated trauma can occur only where the victim is in a state of captivity, unable to flee, and under control of the perpetrator. Examples of such conditions include prisons, concentration camps, and slave labor camps. Such conditions also exist in some religious cults, in brothels and other institutions of organized sexual exploitation, and in some families.

Captivity, which brings the victim into prolonged contact with the perpetrator, creates a special type of relationship, one of coercive control. This is equally true whether or not the victim is rendered captive primarily by physical

force (as in the case of prisoners and hostages) or by a combination of physical, economic, social, and psychological means (as in the case of religious
cult members, battered women, and abused children). The psychological impact of subordination occurs within the public sphere of politics or within the
supposedly private (but equally political) sphere of sexual and domestic relations.

This chapter reviews the evidence for the existence of a complex form of
posttraumatic disorder in survivors of prolonged, repeated trauma. A preliminary formulation of this complex posttraumatic syndrome is currently under
consideration for inclusion in the American Psychiatric Association, *Diagnostic and Statistical Manual of Mental Disorders–Fourth Edition (DSM–IV)*
under the name of Disorders of Extreme Stress Not Otherwise Specified
(DESNOS) In the course of a larger work in progress, I have recently scanned
literature of the past fifty years on survivors of prolonged domestic, sexual,
or political victimization (Herman, 1992). This literature includes first-person
accounts of survivors themselves, descriptive clinical literature, and, where
available, more rigorously designed clinical studies. In the literature review,
particular attention was directed toward observations that did not fit easily
into the existing criteria for PTSD. Though the sources include works by authors of many nationalities, only works originally written in English or available in English translation were reviewed.

The concept of a spectrum of posttraumatic disorders has been suggested
independently by many contributors to the field. Kolb (1989), in a letter to the
editor of the *American Journal of Psychiatry*, writes of the "heterogeneity" of
PTSD. He observes that "PTSD is to psychiatry as syphilis was to medicine.
At one time or another PTSD may appear to mimic every personality disorder," and notes further that "it is those threatened over long periods of time
who suffer the long-standing severe personality disorganization." Niederland,
based on his work with survivors of the Nazi Holocaust, observes that "the
concept of traumatic neurosis does not appear sufficient to cover the multitude and severity of clinical manifestations" of the survivor syndrome (cited
in Krystal, 1968, p. 314). Tanay, working with the same population, notes that
"the psychopathology may be hidden in characterological changes that are
manifest only in disturbed object relationships and attitudes towards work,
the world, man and God" (E. Krystal, 1968, p. 221). Similarly, Kroll and his
colleagues (1989), on the basis of their work with Southeast Asian refugees,
suggest the need for an "expanded concept of PTSD that takes into account
the observations [of the effects of] severe, prolonged, and/or massive psychological and psychical traumata" (p. 1596). Horowitz (1986) suggests the
concept of a "post-traumatic character disorder" (p. 49), and Brown and
Fromm (1986) speak of "complicated PTSD."

Clinicians working with survivors of childhood abuse also invoke the need for an expanded diagnostic concept. Gelinas (1983) describes the "distinguished presentation" of the survivor of childhood sexual abuse as a patient with chronic depression complicated by dissociative symptoms, substance abuse, impulsivity, self-mutilation, and suicidality. She formulates the underlying psychopathology as a complicated traumatic neurosis. Goodwin (1988) conceptualizes the sequelae of prolonged sexual abuse as a severe posttraumatic syndrome that includes fugue and other dissociative states, ego fragmentation, affective and anxiety disorders, reenactment and revictimization, somatization and suicidality.

Clinical observations identify three broad areas of disturbance that transcend simple PTSD. The first is symptomatic: the symptom picture in survivors of prolonged trauma often appears to be more complex, diffuse, and tenacious than in simple PTSD. The second is characterological: survivors of prolonged abuse develop characteristic personality changes, including deformations of relatedness and identity. The third area involves the survivor's vulnerability to repeated harm, both self-inflicted and at the hands of others.

SYMPTOMATIC SEQUELAE OF
PROLONGED VICTIMIZATION

Multiplicity of Symptoms

The pathological environment of prolonged abuse fosters the development of a prodigious array of psychiatric symptoms. A history of abuse, particularly in childhood, appears to be one of the major factors predisposing a person to become a psychiatric patient. While only a minority of survivors of chronic childhood abuse become psychiatric patients, a large proportion (40 percent to 70 percent) of adult psychiatric patients are survivors of abuse (Briere and Runtz, 1987; Briere and Zaidi, 1989; Bryer, Nelson, Miller, and Krol, 1987; Carmen, Rieker, and Mills, 1984; Jacobson and Richardson, 1987).

Survivors who become patients present with a great number and variety of complaints. Their general levels of distress are higher than those of patients who do not have abuse histories. Detailed inventories of their symptoms reveal significant pathology in multiple domains: somatic, cognitive, affective, behavioral, and relational. Bryer and his colleagues (1987), studying psychiatric inpatients, report that women with histories of psychical or sexual abuse have significantly higher scores than other patients do on standardized measures of somatiziation, depression, general and phobic anxiety, interpersonal sensitivity, paranoia, and "psychoticism" (dissociative symptoms were not

measured specifically). Briere (1988), studying outpatients at a crisis intervention service, reports that survivors of childhood abuse display significantly more insomnia, sexual dysfunction, dissociation, anger, suicidality,
self-mutilation, drug addiction, and alcoholism than other patients do. Perhaps the most impressive finding of studies employing a "symptom checklist"
approach is the sheer length of the list of symptoms found to be significantly
related to a history of childhood abuse (Browne and Finkelhor, 1986). From
this wide array of symptoms, I have selected three categories that do not readily fall within the classic diagnostic criteria for PTSD: these are the somatic,
dissociative, and affective sequelae of prolonged trauma.

Somatization

Repetitive trauma appears to amplify and generalize the physiologic symptoms of PTSD. Chronically traumatized people are hypervigilant, anxious,
and agitated, without any recognizable baseline state of calm or comfort
(Hilberman, 1980). Over time, they begin to complain, not only of insomnia,
startle reactions, and agitation but also of numerous other somatic symptoms.
Tension headaches, gastrointestinal disturbances, and abdominal, back, or
pelvic pain are extremely common. Survivors also frequently complain of
tremors, choking sensations, or nausea. In clinical studies of survivors of the
Nazi Holocaust, psychosomatic reactions were found to be practically universal (Hoppe, 1968; H. Krystal and Niederland, 1968; De Loos, 1990). Similar observations are now reported in refugees from the concentration camps
of Southeast Asia (Kroll et al., 1989; Kinzie et al., 1990). Some survivors may
conceptualize the damage of their prolonged captivity primarily in somatic
terms. Nonspecific somatic symptoms appear to be extremely durable and
may in fact increase over time (van der Ploerd, 1989).

   The clinical literature also suggests an association between somatization
disorders and childhood trauma. Paul Briquet's initial descriptions of the disorder that now bears his name are filled with anecdotal references to domestic violence and child abuse. In a study of eighty-seven children under twelve
with hysteria, Briquet noted that one-third had been "habitually mistreated or
held constantly in fear or had been directed harshly by their parents." In another 10 percent, he attributed the children's symptoms to traumatic experiences other than parental abuse (Mai and Merskey, 1980, p. 1402). A recent
controlled study of sixty women with somatization disorder (Morrison, 1989)
found that 55 percent had been sexually molested in childhood, usually by
relatives. The study focused only on early sexual experiences; patients were
not asked about psychical abuse or about the more general climate of violence
in their families. Systematic investigation of the childhood histories of patients with somatization disorder has yet to be undertaken.

Dissociation

People in captivity become adept practitioners of the art of altered consciousness. Through the practice of dissociation, voluntary thought suppression, minimization, and sometimes outright denial, they learn to alter an unbearable reality. Prisoners frequently instruct one another in the induction of trance states. These methods are consciously applied to withstand hunger, cold, and pain (Partnoy, 1986; Sharansky, 1988). During prolonged confinement and isolation some prisoners are able to develop trance capabilities ordinarily seen only in extremely hypnotizable people, including the ability to form positive and negative hallucinations and to dissociate parts of the personality. [See first-person accounts by Elaine Mohamed in Russell (1989) and by Mauricio Rosencof in Weschler (1989).] Disturbances in time sense, memory, and concentration are almost universally reported (Allodi et al., 1985; Tennant, Gouston, and Dent, 1986; Kinzie, Fredrickson, Ben, Fleck, and Karls, 1984). Alterations in time sense begin with the obliteration of the future but eventually progress to the obliteration of the past (Levi, 1958). The rupture in continuity between present and past frequently persists even after the prisoner is released. The prisoner may give the appearance of returning to ordinary time, while psychologically remaining bound in the timelessness of the prison (Jaffe, 1968).

In survivors of prolonged childhood abuse, these dissociative capacities are developed to the extreme. Shengold (1989) describes the "mind-fragmenting operations" elaborated by abused children in order to preserve "the delusion of good parents" (p. 28). He notes the "establishment of isolated divisions of the mind in which contradictory images of the self and of the parents are never permitted to coalesce" (p. 28). The virtuosic feats of dissociation seen, for example, in multiple personality disorder (MPD) (now known as dissociative identity disorder), are almost always associated with a childhood history of massive and prolonged abuse (Putnam, Guroff, Silberman, and Barban, 1986), and in a nonclinical, college-student population (Sanders, McRoberts, and Tollefson, 1989).

Affective Changes

There are people with very strong and secure belief systems, who can endure the ordeals of prolonged abuse and emerge with their faith intact. But these are the extraordinary few. The majority experiences the bitterness of being forsaken by man and God (Wiesel, 1960). These staggering psychological losses most commonly result in a tenacious state of depression. Protracted depression is reported as the most common finding in virtually all clinical studies of chronically traumatized people (Goldstein, van Kammen, Shelley,

Miller, and van Kammen, 1987; Herman, 1981; Hilberman, 1980; Kinzie et al., 1984; E. Krystal, 1968; Walker, 1979). Every aspect of the experience of prolonged trauma combines to aggravate depressive symptoms. The chronic hyperarousal and intrusive symptoms of PTSD fuse with the vegetative symptoms of depression, producing what Niederland (1968) calls the "survivor triad" of insomnia, nightmares, and psychosomatic complaints (in E. Krystal, p. 313). The dissociative symptoms of PTSD merge with the concentration difficulties of depression. The paralysis of initiative of chronic trauma combines with the apathy and helplessness of depression. The disruptions in attachments of chronic trauma reinforce the isolation and withdrawal of depression. The debased self-image of chronic trauma fuels the guilty ruminations of depression. And the loss of faith suffered in chronic trauma merges with the hopelessness of depression.

The humiliated rage of the imprisoned person also adds to the depressive burden (Hilberman, 1980). During captivity, the prisoner cannot express anger at the perpetrator; to do so jeopardizes survival. Even after release, the survivor may continue to fear retribution for any expression of anger against all of those who remained indifferent and failed to help. Efforts to control this rage may further exacerbate the survivor's social withdrawal and paralysis of initiative. Occasional outbursts of rage against others may further alienate the survivor and prevent restoration of relationships. And internalization of rage against others may result in a malignant self-hatred and chronic suicidality. Epidemiologic studies of returned POWs consistently document increased mortality as the result of homicide, suicide, and suspicious accidents (Segal, Hunter, and Segal, 1976). Studies of battered women similarly report a tenacious suicidality. In one clinical series of one hundred battered women, 42 percent had attempted suicide (Gayford, 1975). While major depression is frequently diagnosed in survivors of prolonged abuse, the connection with the trauma is frequently lost. Patients are incompletely treated when the traumatic origins of the intractable depression are not recognized (Kinzie et al., 1990).

CHARACTEROLOGICAL SEQUELAE
OF PROLONGED VICTIMIZATION

Pathological Changes in Relationship

In situations of captivity, the perpetrator becomes the most powerful person in the life of the victim, and the psychology of victim is shaped over time by the actions and beliefs of the perpetrator. The methods that enable one human being to control another are remarkably consistent. These methods were first systematically detailed in reports of so-called brainwashing in American prisoners of war (Biderman, 1957; Farber, Harlow, and West, 1957). Subsequently, Amnesty International (1973) published a systematic review of methods of coercion, drawing on the testimony of political prisoners from widely differing cultures. The accounts of coercive methods given by battered women (Dobash and Dobash, 1979; NiCarthy, 1982; Walker, 1979), abused children (Rhodes, 1990), and coerced prostitutes (Lovelace and McGrady, 1980) bear an uncanny resemblance to those hostages, political prisoners, and survivors of concentration camps. While perpetrators of organized political or sexual exploitation may instruct each other in coercive methods, perpetrators of domestic abuse appear to reinvent them.

The methods of establishing control over another person are based on the systematic, repetitive infliction of psychological trauma. These methods are designed to instill terror and helplessness, to destroy the victim's sense of self in relation to others, and to foster a pathologic attachment to the perpetrator. Although violence is a universal method of instilling terror, the threat of death or serious harm, whether to the victim or to others close to her, is much more frequent than the actual resort to violence. Fear is also increased by unpredictable outbursts of violence and by inconsistent enforcement of numerous trivial demands and petty rules.

In addition to inducing terror, the perpetrator seeks to destroy the victim's sense of autonomy, control of the victim's body, and bodily functions. Deprivation of food, sleep, shelter, exercise, personal hygiene, or privacy are common practices. Once the perpetrator has established this degree of control, he becomes a potential source of solace as much as humiliation. The capricious granting of small indulgences may undermine the psychological resistance of the victim far more effectively than unremitting depreciation and fear.

As long as the victim maintains strong relationships with others, the perpetrator's power is limited; invariably, therefore, he seeks to isolate his victim. The perpetrator not only will attempt to prohibit communication and material support but will also try to destroy the victim's emotional ties to others. The final step in the "breaking" of the victim is not completed until she has been forced to betray her most basic attachments, by witnessing or participating in crimes against others.

As the victim is isolated, she becomes increasingly dependent on the perpetrator, not only for survival and basic bodily needs but also for information and even for emotional sustenance. Prolonged confinement in fear of death and in isolation reliably produces a bond of identification between captor and victim. This is the "traumatic bonding" that occurs in hostages, who come to view their captors as their saviors and to fear and hate their rescuers. Symonds (1982) describes this process as an enforced regression to "psychological infantilism" that "compels victims to cling to the very person who is

endangering their life" (p. 99). The same traumatic bonding may occur between a battered woman and her abuser (Dutton and Painter, 1981; Graham,
Rawlings, and Rimini, 1988) or between an abused child and an abusive parent (Herman, 1981; van der Kolk, 1987). Similar experiences are also reported by people who have been inducted into totalitarian religious cults
(Halperin, 1983; Lifton, 1987).

With increased dependency on the perpetrator comes a constriction in initiative and planning. Prisoners who have not been entirely "broken" do not
give up the capacity for active engagement with their environment. On the
contrary, they often approach the small daily tasks of survival with extraordinary ingenuity and determination. But the field of initiative is increasingly
narrowed within the confines dictated by the perpetrator. The prisoner no
longer thinks of how to escape, but rather of how to stay alive or how to make
captivity more bearable. This narrowing in the range of initiative becomes habitual with prolonged captivity and must be unlearned after the prisoner is liberated. [See, for example, the testimony of Hearst (Hearst and Moscow, 1982)
and Rosencof in Weschler, 1989]

Because of this constriction in the capacities for active engagement with the
world, chronically traumatized people are often described as passive and helpless. Some theorists have in fact applied the concept of "learned helplessness" to
the situation of battered women and other chronically traumatized people
(Walker, 1979; van der Kolk, 1987). Prolonged captivity undermines or destroys
the ordinary sense of a relatively safe sphere of initiative in which there is some
tolerance for trial and error. To the chronically traumatized person, any independent action is insubordination, which carries the risk of dire punishment.

The sense that the perpetrator is still present, even after liberation, signifies
a major alteration in the survivor's relational world. The enforced relationship, which of necessity monopolizes the victim's attention during captivity,
becomes a part of her inner life and continues to engross her attention after
release. In political prisoners, this continued relationship might take the form
of brooding preoccupation with the criminal careers of specific perpetrators
or with the more abstract concerns about unchecked forces of evil in the
world. Released prisoners continue to track their captors, and to fear them
(E. Krystal, 1968). In sexual, domestic, and religious cult prisoners, this continued relationship may take a more ambivalent form; the survivor may continue to fear the former captor and to expect that he or she will eventually
hunt him or her down; the survivor may also feel empty, confused, and worth-
less without the former captor (Walker, 1979).

Even after escape, it is not possible simply to reconstitute relationships of
the sort that existed before captivity. All relationships are now viewed through
the lens of extremity. Just as there is no range of moderate engagement of risk

for initiative, there is no range of moderate engagement of risk for relationship. The survivor approaches all relationships as though questions of life and death are at stake, oscillating between attachment and terrified withdrawal.

In survivors of childhood abuse, these disturbances in relationships are further amplified. Oscillations in attachment, with formation of intense, unstable relationships, are frequently observed. These disturbances are described most fully in patients with borderline personality disorder, a majority of whom have extensive histories of childhood abuse. A recent empirical study, confirming a past literature of clinical observations, outlines in detail the specific pattern of relational difficulties. Such patients find it very hard to tolerate being alone but are also exceedingly wary of others. Terrified of abandonment on the one hand and of domination on the other, they oscillate between extremes of abject submissiveness and furious rebellion (Melges and Swartz, 1989). Then they tend to form "special" dependent relations with idealized caretakers in which ordinary boundaries are not observed (Zanarini, Gunderson, Frankenburg, and Chauncey, 1990). Very similar patterns are described in patients with MPD, including the tendency to develop intense, highly special relationships ridden with boundary violations, conflict, and potential for exploration (Kluft, 1990).

Pathologic Changes in Identity

Subjection to a relationship of coercive control produces profound alterations in the victim's identity. All the structures of the self-image of the body, the internalized images of others, and the values and ideals that lend a sense of coherence and purpose—are invaded and systematically broken down. In some totalitarian systems (political, religious, or sexual and domestic), this process reaches the extent of taking away the victim's name (Hearst and Moscow, 1982; Lovelace and McGrady, 1980). While the victim of a single acute trauma may lose the sense that she has a self, survivors may describe themselves as reduced to a nonhuman life form (Lovelace and McGrady, 1980; Timerman, 1981). Niederland (1968), in his clinical observations of concentration camp survivors, notes that alterations of personal identity were a constant feature of the survivor syndrome. While the majority of his patients complained, "I am now a different person," the most severely harmed stated simply, "I am not a person."

Survivors of childhood abuse develop even more complex deformations of identity. A malignant sense of the self as contaminated, guilty, and evil is widely observed. Fragmentation in the sense of self is also common, reaching its most dramatic extreme in MPD. Ferenczi (1932) describes "atomization" of the abused child's personality. Rieker and Carmen (1986) describe the central pathology in victimized children as a "disordered and fragmented identity deriving from accommodations to the judgments of others." Disturbances in identity formation are also characteristic of patients with borderline and MPD, the majority of whom have childhood histories of severe trauma. In MPD, the fragmentation of the self into dissociated alters is, of course, the central feature of the disorder (Bliss, 1986; Putnam, 1989). Patients with Borderline Personality Disorder (BPD), though they lack the dissociative capacity to form fragmented alters, have similar difficulties in the formation of an integrated identity. An unstable sense of self is recognized as one of the major diagnostic criteria for BPD, and the "splitting" of inner representations of self and others is considered by some theorists the central underlying pathology of the disorder (Kernberg, 1967).

Repetition of Harm Following Prolonged Victimization

Repetitive phenomena have been widely noted to be sequelae of severe trauma. The topic has been recently reviewed in the depth by van der Kolk (1989). In simple PTSD, these repetitive phenomena may take the form of intrusive memories, somatosensory reliving experiences or behavioral reenactments of the trauma (Brett and Ostroff, 1985; Terr, 1983). After prolonged and repeated trauma, by contrast, survivors may be at risk for repeated harm, which either is self-inflicted or is at the hands of others. These repetitive phenomena do not bear a direct relation to the original trauma; they are not simple reenactments or reliving experiences. Rather, they take a disguised symptomatic or characterological form.

About 7 percent to 10 percent of psychiatric patients are thought to injure themselves deliberately (Favazza and Conterio, 1988). Self-mutilization is a repetitive behavior that appears to be quite distinct from attempted suicide. This compulsive form of self-injury appears to be strongly associated with a history of prolonged repeated trauma. Self-mutilation, which is rarely seen after a single acute trauma, is a common sequel of protracted childhood abuse (Briere, 1988; van der Kolk, Perry, and Herman, 1991). Self-injury and other paroxysmal forms of attack on the body have been shown to develop most commonly in those victims whose abuse began early in childhood (van der Kolk et al., 1991).

The phenomenon of repeated victimization also appears to be specifically associated with histories of prolonged childhood abuse. Wide-scale epidemiologic studies provide strong evidence that survivors of childhood abuse are at increased risk for repeated harm in adult life. For example, the risk of rape, sexual harassment, and battering, though very high for all women, is approximately doubled for survivors of childhood sexual abuse (Russell, 1986). One clinical observer goes so far as to label this phenomenon the "sitting duck syndrome" (Kluft, 1990).

In the most extreme cases, survivors of childhood abuse may find themselves involved in abuse of others, either in the role of passive bystander or, more rarely, as a perpetrator. Burgess, Hartman, McCausland, and Powers (1984), for example, report that children who had been exploited in a sex ring for more than one year were likely to adopt a belief system of the perpetrator and to become exploitative toward others. A history of prolonged childhood abuse does appear to be a risk factor for becoming an abuser, especially in men (Herman, 1988; Hotaling and Sugarman, 1986). In women, a history of witnessing domestic violence (Hotaling and Sugarman, 1986), or sexual victimization (Goodwin, McMarty, and DiVasto, 1982) in childhood, appears to increase the risk of subsequent marriage to an abusive mate. It should be noted, however, that contrary to the popular notion of a "generational cycle of abuse," a great majority of survivors do not abuse others (Kaufman and Zigler, 1987). For the sake of their children, survivors frequently mobilize caring and protective capacities that they have never been able to extend to themselves (Coons, 1985).

CONCLUSION

The review of the literature offers unsystematized but extensive empirical support for the concept of a complex posttraumatic syndrome in survivors of prolonged, repeated victimization. This previously undefined syndrome may co-exist with simple PTSD, but extends beyond it. The syndrome is characterized by a pleomorphic symptom picture, enduring personality changes, and high risk for repeated harm that either is self-inflicted or is at the hands of others.

Failure to recognize this syndrome as a predictable consequence of prolonged, repeated trauma contributes to the misunderstanding of survivors, a misunderstanding shared by the general society and the mental health professions alike. Social judgment of chronically traumatized people has tended to be harsh (Biderman and Zimmer, 1961; Wardell, Gillespie, and Leffler, 1983). The propensity to fault the character of victims can be seen even in the case of politically organized mass murder. Thus, for example, the aftermath of the Nazi Holocaust witnessed a protracted intellectual debate regarding the "passivity" of the Jews and even their "complicity" in their fate (Dawidowicz, 1975). Observers who have never experienced prolonged terror and who have no understanding of coercive methods of control often presume that they would show greater psychological resistance than the victim in similar circumstances. The survivor's difficulties are all too easily attributed to underlying character problems, even when the trauma is known. When the trauma is kept secret, as is frequently the case in sexual and domestic violence, the survivor's symptoms and behavior may appear quite baffling, not only to lay people but also to mental health professionals.

The clinical picture of a person who has been reduced to elemental concerns of survival is still frequently mistaken for a portrait of the survivor's underlying character. Concepts of personality developed in ordinary circumstances are frequently applied to survivors, without an understanding of the deformations of personality that occur under conditions of coercive control. Thus, patients who suffer from the complex sequelae of chronic trauma commonly risk being misdiagnosed as having personality disorders. They may be described as "dependent," "masochistic," or "self-defeating." Earlier concepts of masochism or repetition compulsion might be more usefully supplanted by the concept of a complex traumatic syndrome.

Misapplication of the concept of personality disorder may be the most stigmatizing diagnostic mistake, but it is by no means the only one. In general, the diagnostic concepts of the existing psychiatric canon, including simple PTSD, are not designed for survivors of prolonged, repeated trauma and do not fit them well. The evidence reviewed in this chapter offers strong support for expanding the concept of PTSD to include a spectrum of disorders (Brett, 1992), ranging from the brief, self-limited stress reaction to a simple acute trauma through simple PTSD to DESNOS that follows after prolonged exposure to repeated trauma.

REFERENCES

This chapter is reproduced from Judith Lewis Herman, Complex PTSD: A Syndrome in Survivors of Prolonged and Repeated Trauma, *Journal of Traumatic Stress*, 5 (3) (1992): 377–91. Reprinted with permission from Kluwer Academic/Plenum Publishers.

Allodi, F., Randall, G. R., Lutz, E., Quiroga, J., Zunzunegui, M. V., Kolff, C. A., et al. (1985). Physical and psychiatric effects of torture: Two medical studies. In E. Stover and E. Nightingale (Eds.), *The breaking of bodies and minds: Torture, psychiatric abuse, and the health professions*, 58–78. New York: Freeman.

American Psychiatric Association. (1994). *Diagnostic and statistical manual of mental disorders* (4th ed.). Washington, DC: Author.

Amnesty International. (1973). *Report on torture.* New York: Farrar, Straus, and Giroux.

Biderman, A. D. (1957). Communist attempts to elicit false confessions from Air Force prisoners of war. *Bulletin of the New York Academy of Medicine*, 33: 616–25.

Biderman, A. D., and Zimmer, H. (1961). Introduction to *The manipulation of human behavior.* New York: Wiley.

Bliss, E. L. (1986). *Multiple personality, allied disorders, and hypnosis.* New York: Oxford University Press.

Brett, E. A. (1992). Classification of PTSD in *DSM-IV* as an anxiety disorder, dissociative disorder, or stress disorder. In J. Davidson and E. Foa (Eds.), *PTSD in review: Recent research and future directions.* Washington, DC: American Psychiatric Press.

Brett, E. A., and Ostroff, R. (1985). Imagery in post-traumatic stress disorder: An overview. *American Journal of Psychiatry*, 142: 417–24.

Briere, J. (1988). Long-term clinical correlates of childhood sexual victimization. *Annals of the New York Academy of Sciences*, 528: 327–34.

Briere, J., and Runtz, M. (1987). Post sexual abuse trauma: Data and implications for clinical practice. *Journal of Interpersonal Violence*, 2: 367–79.

Briere, J., and Zaidi, L. (1989). Sexual abuse histories and sequelae in female psychiatric emergency room patients. *American Journal of Psychiatry*, 146: 1602–6.

Brown, D. P., and Fromm, E. (1986). *Hypnotherapy and hypnoanalysis.* Hillsdale, NJ: Erlbaum.

Browne, A., and Finkelhor, D. (1986). Impact of child sexual abuse: A review of the literature. *Psychological Bulletin*, 99: 55–77.

Bryer, J. B., Nelson, B. A., Miller, J. B., and Krol, P. A. (1987). Childhood sexual and physical abuse as factors in adult psychiatric illness. *American Journal of Psychiatry*, 144: 1426–30.

Burgess, A. W., Hartman, C. R., McCausland, M. P., and Powers, P. (1984). Response patterns in children and adolescents exploited through sex rings and pornography. *American Journal of Psychiatry*, 141: 656–62.

Carmen, E. H., Rieker, P. P., and Mills, T. (1984). Victims of violence and psychiatric illness. *American Journal of Psychiatry*, 141: 378–83.

Coons, P. M. (1985). Children of parents with multiple personality disorder. In R. P. Kluft (Ed.), *Childhood antecedents of multiple personality disorder*, pp. 151–66. Washington, DC: American Psychiatric Press.

Dawidowicz, L. (1975). *The war against the Jews.* London: Weidenfeld and Nicolson.

De Loos, W. (1990). Psychosomatic manifestations of chronic PTSD. In M. E. Wolf and A. D. Mosnaim (Eds.), *Posttraumatic stress disorder: Etiology, phenomenology, and treatment*, pp. 94–105. Washington, DC: American Psychiatric Press.

Dobash, R. E., and Dobash, R. (1979). *Violence against wives: A case against the patriarchy.* New York: Free Press.

Dutton, D., and Painter, S. L. (1981). Traumatic bonding: The development of emotional attachments in battered women and other relationships of intermittent abuse. *Victimology*, 6: 139–55.

Farber, I. E., Harlow, H. F., and West, L. J. (1957). Brainwashing, conditioning, and DDD (debility, dependency, and dread). *Sociometry*, 23: 120–47.

Favazza, A. R., and Conterio, K. (1988). The plight of chronic self-mutilators. *Community Mental Health Journal*, 24: 22–30.

Ferenczi, S. (1932/1955). Confusion of tongues between adults and the child: The language of tenderness and of passion. In *Final contributions to the problems and methods of psychoanalysis.* New York: Basic Books.

Gayford, J. J. (1975). Wife-battering: A preliminary survey of 100 cases. *British Medical Journal*, 1: 194–97.

Gelinas, D. (1983). The persistent negative effects of incest. *Psychiatry*, 46: 312–32.

Goldstein, G., van Kammen, V., Shelley, C., Miller, D. J., and van Kammen, D. P. (1987). Survivors of imprisonment in the Pacific theater during World War II. *American Journal of Psychiatry*, 144: 1210–13.

Goodwin, J. (1988). Evaluation and treatment of incest victims and their families: A problem oriented approach. In J. G. Howells (Ed.), *Modern perspectives in psychosocial pathology*. New York: Brunner/Mazel.

Goodwin, J., McMarty, T., and DiVasto, P. (1982). Physical and sexual abuse of the children of adult incest victims. In J. Goodwin (Ed.), *Sexual abuse: Incest victims and their families*, pp. 139–54. Boston: John Wright.

Graham, D. L., Rawlings, E., and Rimini, N. (1988). Survivors of terror: Battered women, hostages, and the Stockholm syndrome. In K. Yilo and M. Bograd (Eds.), *Feminist Perspectives on Wife Abuse*, pp. 217–33. Beverly Hills, CA: Sage.

Halperin, D. A. (1983). Group processes in cult affiliation and recruitment. In *Psychodynamic perspectives on religion, sect, and cult*. Boston: John Wright.

Hearst, P. C., and Moscow, A. (1982). *Every secret thing*. New York: Doubleday.

Herman, J. L. (1981). *Father-daughter incest*. Cambridge, MA: Harvard University Press.

———. (1988). Considering sex offenders: A model of addiction. *Signs: Journal of women in culture and society*, 13: 695–724.

———. (1992). *Trauma and recovery*. New York: Basic Books.

Hilberman, E. (1980). The "wife-beater's wife" reconsidered. *American Journal of Psychiatry*, 137: 1336–47.

Hoppe, K. D. (1968). Resomatization of affects in survivors of persecution. *International Journal of Psychoanalysis*, 49: 324–26.

Horowitz, M. (1986). *Stress Response Syndromes*. Northvale, NJ: Jason Aronson.

Hotaling, G., and Sugarman, D. (1986). An analysis of risk markers in husband to wife violence: The current state of knowledge. *Violence and Victims*, 1: 101–24.

Jacobson, A., and Richardson, B. (1987). Assault experiences of 100 psychiatric inpatients: Evidence of the need for routine inquiry. *American Journal of Psychiatry*, 144: 908–13.

Jaffe, R. (1968). Dissociative phenomena in former concentration camp inmates. *International Journal of Psychoanalysis*, 49: 310–12.

Kaufman, J., and Zigler, E. (1987). Do abused children become abusive parents? *American Journal of Orthopsychiatry*, 57: 186–92.

Kernberg, O. (1967). Borderline personality organization. *Journal of the American Psychoanalytic Association*, 15: 641–85.

Kinzie, J. D., Boehnlein, J. K., Leung, P. K., Moore, L. J., Riley, C., and Smith, D. (1990). The prevalence of posttraumatic stress disorder and its clinical significance among Southeast Asian refugees. *American Journal of Psychiatry*, 147: 913–17.

Kinzie, J. D., Fredrickson, R. H., Ben, R., Fleck, J., and Karls, W. (1984). PTSD among survivors of Cambodian concentration camps. *American Journal of Psychiatry*, 141: 645–50.

Kluft, R. P. (1990). Incest and subsequent revictimization: The case of therapist-patient sexual exploitation, with a description of the sitting duck syndrome. In

Incest-related syndromes of adult psychopathology, pp. 263–89. Washington, DC: American Psychiatric Press.

Kolb, L. C. (1989). Letter to the editor. *American Journal of Psychiatry,* 146: 811–12.

Kroll, J., Habenicht, M., Mackenzie, T., Yang, M., Chan, S., Vang, T., et al. (1989). Depression and posttraumatic stress disorder in Southeast Asian refugees. *American Journal of Psychiatry,* 146: 1592–97.

Krystal, E. (Ed.) (1968). *Massive psychic trauma.* New York: International Universities Press.

Krystal, H., and Niederland, W. (1968). Clinical observations on the survivor syndrome. In H. Krystal (Ed.). *Massive psychic trauma,* pp. 327–48. New York: International Universities Press.

Levi, P. (1958/1961). *Survival in Auschwitz: The Nazi assault on humanity* (Trans. S. Woolf). New York: Collier.

Lifton, R. J. (1987). Cults: Religious totalism and civil liberties. In *The future of immortality and other essays for a nuclear age.* New York: Basic Books.

Lovelace, L., and McGrady, M. (1980). *Ordeal.* Secaucus, NJ: Citadel.

Mai, F. M., and Merskey, H. (1980). Briquet's treatise on hysteria: Synopsis and commentary. *Archives of General Psychiatry,* 37: 1401–5.

Melges, F. T., and Swartz, M. S. (1989). Oscillations of attachment in borderline personality disorder. *American Journal of Psychiatry,* 146: 1115–20.

Morrison, J. (1989). Childhood sexual histories of women with somatization disorder. *American Journal of Psychiatry,* 146: 239–41.

NiCarthy, G. (1982). *Getting free: A handbook for women in abusive relationships.* Seattle, WA: Seal Press.

Niederland, W. G. (1968). Clinical observations on the "survivor syndrome." *International Journal of Psychoanalysis,* 49: 313–15.

Partnoy, A. (1986). *The little school: Tales of disappearance and survival in Argentina.* San Francisco, CA: Cleis Press.

Putnam, F. W. (1989). *Diagnosis and treatment of multiple personality disorder.* New York: Guilford.

Putnam, F. W., Guroff, J. J., Silberman, E. K., and Barban, L. (1986). The clinical phenomenology of multiple personality disorder: Review of 100 recent cases. *Journal of Clinical Psychiatry,* 47: 285–93.

Rhodes, R. (1990). *A hole in the world.* New York: Simon and Schuster.

Rieker, P. P., and Carmen, E. (1986). The victim-to-patient process: The disconfirmation and transformation of abuse. *American Journal of Orthopsychiatry,* 56: 360–70.

Russell, D. (1986). *The secret trauma.* New York: Basic Books.

———. (1989). *Lives of courage: Women for a new South Africa.* New York: Basic Books.

Sanders, B., McRoberts, G., and Tollefson, C. (1989). Childhood stress and dissociation in a college population. *Dissociation,* 2: 17–23.

Segal, J., Hunter, E. J., and Segal, Z. (1976). Universal consequences of captivity: Stress reactions among divergent populations of prisoners of war and their families. *International Social Science Journal,* 28: 593–609.

Sharansky, N. (1988). *Fear no evil* (Trans. S. Hoffman). New York: Random House.

Shengold, L. (1989). *Soul murder: The effects of childhood abuse and deprivation.* New Haven, CT: Yale University Press.

Symonds, M. (1982). Victim responses to terror: Understanding and treatment. In F. M. Ochberg and D. A. Soskis (Eds.), *Victims of terrorism*, pp. 95–103. Boulder, CO: Westview.

Tennant, C. C., Gouston, K. J., and Dent, O. F. (1986). The psychological effects of being a prisoner of war: Forty years after release. *American Journal of Psychiatry*, 143: 618–22.

Terr, L. C. (1983). Chowchilla revisited: The effects of psychic trauma four years after a school-bus kidnapping. *American Journal of Psychiatry*, 140: 1543–50.

Timerman, J. (1981). *Prisoner without a name, cell without a number* (Trans. T. Talbot). New York: Vintage.

van der Kolk, B. A. (1987). *Psychological trauma*. Washington, DC: American Psychiatric Press.

———. (1989). Compulsion to repeat the trauma: Reenactment, revictimization, and masochism. *Psychiatric Clinics of North America*, 12: 389–411.

van der Kolk, B. A., Perry, J. C., and Herman, J. L. (1991). Childhood origins of self-destructive behavior. *American Journal of Psychiatry*, 148: 1665–71.

van der Ploerd, H. M. (1989). Being held hostage in the Netherlands: A study of long-term aftereffects. *Journal of Traumatic Stress*, 2: 153–70.

Walker, L. (1979). *The battered woman*. New York: Harper and Row.

Wardell, L., Gillespie, D., and Leffler, A. (1983). Science and violence against wives. In D. Finkelhor, R. Gelles, G. Hotaling, and M. A. Strauss (Eds.), *The dark side of families: Current family violence research*, 69–84. Beverly Hills, CA: Sage.

Weschler, L. (1989, April 3). The great expectation: I: Liberty. *New Yorker*.

Wiesel, E. (1960). *Night* (Trans. S. Rodway). New York: Hill and Wang.

Zanarini, M. C., Gunderson, J. G., Frankenburg, F. R., and Chauncey, D. L. (1990). Discriminating borderline personality disorder from other Axis II disorders. *American Journal of Psychiatry*, 147: 161–67.

Chapter Three

Psychic Trauma and
Fears of Annihilation

Marvin Hurvich

Psychic trauma frequently triggers mortal terror, an extreme psychic danger that is reflected in experiences of annihilation anxiety. These apprehensions constitute trauma markers and are found in victims of shock and cumulative trauma as well as in cases of severe psychopathology, conditions that regularly reveal traumatic factors in the life history. Annihilation anxieties echo concerns over safety, self-preservation, and survival and are elaborated in terms of fourteen propositions. Dimensions are described as apprehensions of being overwhelmed, merged, penetrated, disintegrated, persecuted, and destroyed. Patient examples illustrate how these anxieties are manifest clinically.

Following September 11, 2001, mental health personnel in the New York City Metropolitan area were called on by the Red Cross, the NYPD, and many corporations to conduct group and individual stress management and emergency therapy sessions. Large numbers of New Yorkers, indirectly affected by the tragedy, sought emergency counseling at the Red Cross and at clinics, hospitals, and other facilities in the local area. The haunting images repeatedly shown on the television of people jumping from high floors and of others running for their lives from falling debris with smoke- and dust-filled clouds surrounding them stirred annihilation apprehensions in many local people.

From therapy patients, from supervisee reports, from discussions with colleagues, and in numerous meetings sponsored by a host of organizations, there were indications of a widespread increase in anxiety levels, especially with regard to concerns over *safety, survival, and self-preservation*. These are the apprehensions that constitute annihilation anxieties and that are the central sequelae of psychic trauma. The view that feelings of overwhelmed helplessness

51

constitute *the* psychic content of trauma (Furst, 1967, p. 37) is here extended
to the position that experiences of overwhelmed helplessness tend to include
the terror of imminent extinction and that annihilation-survival fantasies also
form a key psychic content of trauma (Hurvich, 1996). Repeatedly expressed
annihilation apprehensions of trauma victims are of being destroyed, overwhelmed, and unable to cope; of merger, intrusion, and disorganization of the
sense of self; of loss of needed support; and of expectations of additional catastrophe. This chapter will focus on delineating annihilation anxieties and will
thereby elaborate on frequently found fantasy mental contents that are associated with psychic trauma.

Patients describe feelings of being overwhelmed by the external threat as
well as by helplessness, vulnerability, and anger. They depict anticipations
and fantasies of being buried alive, smothered by debris, trapped in a burning
building, choked to death by poison gas, and blown apart by the next imminently anticipated attack. A substantial number of school children were reported in the *New York Times* to have experienced high levels of fear and
stress months after the event.

Another phenomenon was the reawakening of early traumas. It has long
been recognized that a current trauma tends to serve as a trigger for traumatic
events from one's past becoming reactivated (Winnicott, 1974; Shengold,
1989). In many cases this re-arousal of old traumatic experiences is accompanied by the activation of annihilation anxieties. One male executive in his
early forties who I saw for a consultation two days after the twin-tower collapse reported having left Tower Two soon after the first suicide plane hit. Although his office was on a high floor, he had luckily been on a lower floor at
the time and was able to escape to safety. Many of his co-workers were killed.
While grieved and shaken, he reported that since his escape, he had become
most preoccupied with an event that had occurred ten years earlier that had
not been in his awareness for some time. This related to an accident where a
friend had been killed and where he had felt some responsibility for encouraging the friend to engage with him in a somewhat risky recreational activity,
in spite of the friend's reluctance. The patient reported feeling overwhelmed
with guilt and anxiety and a heightened fear of catastrophe.

As war hysteria has grown, and Homeland Security alerts have been widely
broadcast, the World Trade Center destruction is serving as a background
trauma that gives a terrifying reality to the possibility and high likelihood of
the next strike, either from al Qaeda or Iraq, or others. These current events
are supplying the imagery for latent annihilation fears. New Yorkers are experiencing and expressing much more annihilation anxiety in anticipation of
a dreaded assault that could come from anywhere at any time. The atmosphere is entirely different from the days before the 1991 Gulf War, when di-

rect retaliation seemed remote, and before the traumatic experience of September 11, which left a feeling of anticipatory destruction and doom.

These recently triggered widespread terror experiences have much in common with responses to war, plague, flood, and famine throughout the ages (Sorokin, 1942). A number of chapters in this book delineate aspects of group terror situations. This chapter will be focused on terror experience as a component of psychic trauma in psychopathology. The hypothesis will be developed that a marker and residue of psychic trauma is annihilation anxiety.

PSYCHIC TRAUMA MARKERS

Key indicators of psychic trauma were delineated by Sigmund Freud in 1920 as a feeling of helplessness associated with sudden onset surprise, an impact that is overwhelming and an obligatory repetition in the service of mastery. In the subsequent literature, many definitions of psychic trauma have been formulated. Ferenczi (1933) added betrayal of trust, which underscores the importance of relational issues. An overall framework includes the components of a traumatic event, a traumatic process, and a traumatic effect, accompanied by painful and unpleasurable affect (Rangell, 1967, p. 79).

A broad definition of psychic trauma was provided by Greenacre (1967): "Any conditions which seem definitely unfavorable, noxious, or dramatically injurious to the developing young individual" (p. 128). A narrower definition is that psychic trauma is associated with devastating and shattering experiences that result in internal disruption as a result of putting ego functioning and ego mediation out of action (A. Freud, 1967, p. 242). Anna Freud (1967) includes as required trauma criteria, action paralysis, numbness of feeling, temper tantrums in a child, and "physical responses via the vegetative nervous system taking the place of psychical reactions" (p. 242). These indicate ego function disruption and that the person is operating with pre-ego modes. A distinction has been made between a traumatic neurosis and a traumatic event (Mahony, 1984). In the former, most of the psychopathology has been seen to result from the subject's inability to assimilate the traumatic experiences. In the latter, the major traumatic significance is seen to be based on the role of the traumatic event in activating psychopathological tendencies (p. 53). I add that there are transitional phases between unassimilability and the activation of latent psychopathological trends in the wake of traumatic experience. Both the traumatic neuroses and the traumatic event tend to arouse annihilation anxieties.

Dowling (1986) emphasizes the psychological meaning of the traumatic experience, and that this will be influenced by the person's "developmental level, prior individual experience, and instinctual, ego and superego configurations" (p. 209). The question can be raised whether accenting meaning, and the other important variables Dowling specifies, requires sidelining the criteria set forth by A. Freud, Krystal, and others.

Dowling (1986) demonstrates the importance of meaning when he writes that psychic traumas can have organizing influences on the mental sphere. "An organizing event is one which provides a nexus around which a variety of previously existing and later developmental and conflictual issues aggregate and achieve a more powerful, cohesive, and determinative meaning. An organizing event or experience has a dramatic role in shaping the further development of the individual. The residues of the past and the content of the future tend to be formulated, constructed, and reconstructed in terms of that experience" (p. 212).

As mentioned before, annihilation-survival fantasies comprise a key psychic content of trauma. Annihilation anxieties involve concerns over survival, self-preservation, and safety. Sandler (1960) pointed out that a threat to the intactness of the ego includes a lowering of feelings of safety and the experiencing of anxiety following the danger of being traumatically overwhelmed. The two key areas of concern are for the integrity of the sense of self and the intactness of the ego functions.

Specific annihilation fantasies that are residuals of the traumatic experience often serve as organizing events for the given person, centering around individually configured meanings of being overwhelmed, unable to cope, invaded, merged, and imminently destroyed. Zetzel (1949) observed that soldiers whose narcissistic defenses of invulnerability protected them from experiencing any fear prior to battle were the ones whose sense of safety in the world was compromised as a result of exposure to combat, which fragmented their specific fantasies of invulnerability.

Another concept consistent with the annihilation component of psychic trauma is what Lifton called the "death imprint": "[A] radical intrusion of an image-feeling of threat or end to life" (1979, p. 169). He elaborates: "The degree of anxiety associated with the death imprint has to do with the impossibility of assimilating the death imprint—because of its suddenness, its extreme or protracted nature, or its association with the terror of premature, unacceptable dying. Also of considerable importance is one's vulnerability to death imagery—not only to direct life threat but also to separation, stasis, and disintegration—on the basis of prior conflictual experience" (p. 169).

Annihilation anxieties can be shown to play a significant role in all the major forms of severe psychopathology, conditions that are especially found to include traumatic events in the life history: panic, nightmares, phobias, borderline, narcissistic and psychotic conditions, dissociative states, perversions, and psychosomatic disorders (Hurvich, 2000, 2003a; Pao, 1979). Karon and Vandenboss (1981) wrote, "The schizophrenic patient lives in a chronic terror state, which is so strong that other affects do not appear." Teixeira (1984) references reports in the literature of schizophrenic patients' fears of dying or being killed. He further points out that an overwhelming conscious fear of death in some schizophrenics immediately precedes the psychotic decompensation. "This extreme primitive death anxiety has been referred to as "annihilation anxiety" (p. 377).

Buie and Adler (1973) described annihilation anxieties in borderline pathology, while Kohut's (1977) theory, which emphasizes disintegration anxiety, has been characterized as employing a trauma-arrest model (Lang 1987). Weiss (1964) wrote of annihilation-type anxieties in agoraphobia, Socarides (1973) in perversions, and Max Stern (1951) and Mack (1970) in night terrors and nightmares. Gaddini (1992) and MacDougall (1989) showed the relevance of annihilation anxieties in psychosomatics, and Wurmser (1981–1982) did the same for substance abusers.

Annihilation-survival anxieties are underscored by child analysts in many important papers on severe childhood disturbance published in *The Psychoanalytic Study of the Child*. The case histories of these children are rife with examples of psychic trauma. Thus, annihilation anxieties are seen to be prominent in forms of psychopathology in which there is frequent evidence for psychic trauma.

While the narrow conception of psychic trauma has the advantage of clarity and specificity, the broader view, in the absence of clear evidence of shock, includes many phenomena widely understood as traumatic. There is clinical evidence that strain and cumulative traumas can influence personality development in ways similar to shock traumas, sans verified shock. In line with the goal of forging links between the psychoanalytic theories of psychic trauma and of anxiety, the model in figure 3.1 (Hurvich, 2003a) specifies some variables that terror and anticipatory danger have in common.

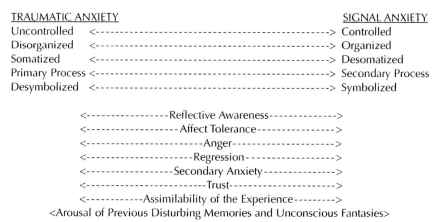

Figure 3.1.   The Relation Between Traumatic and Signal Anxieties.

When annihilation fantasies are accompanied by markers characterizing the more pathological, maladaptive, and primitive pole, the reaction is more likely to qualify as a traumatic response. Conversely, when the markers found along with annihilation content are on the more adaptive side (controlled anxiety, presence of reflective awareness, etc.), there is a greater likelihood that it is an anticipation of a traumatic situation. The important issues of time for recovery and residuals, including the possibility of a traumatic neurosis or Post-Traumatic Stress Disorder (PTSD) are relevant here. Time of onset, be it infantile, childhood, adolescence, or adulthood, is a key variable. Severe childhood trauma results in a permanent expectation of a return of the traumatic state and dread of its return. The fear of emotions develops and, thus, an impairment of affect tolerance (Krystal, 1988). More generally under debate is the contribution of psychic trauma to pathogenesis and how to distinguish pathological influences of trauma from other pathological effects. While his conception of psychic trauma changed as his theories evolved, S. Freud (1939) attributed a key role to psychic trauma in all symptom formation.

The expansion of trauma theory, and a first step toward an integration with the psychoanalytic theory of anxiety, involves the formulation that the experience of being overwhelmed, a signature of the traumatic moment, can subsequently be anticipated and associated with controlled anxiety and, hence, be included in the basic danger series (Hurvich, 2003a). Thus, issues related to being overwhelmed or annihilated (S. Freud, 1923, p. 57) may be part of a traumatic moment in present time or may constitute a danger situation that is anticipated in future time: concerns about being overwhelmed may thus be either a present or an actual or a potential threat (Schur, 1953; Hurvich, 2003a, 2003b, 2003c).

It is relevant to note the widely disseminated behavioral and symptomatic shock trauma markers, in addition to feelings of helplessness. Major ones are hyperarousal, constriction, dissociation, and denial. Additional symptoms are intrusive imagery or flashbacks, sensitivity to light and sound, hyperactivity, abrupt mood swings, reduced ability to deal with stress, and difficulty sleeping. Next come symptoms such as panic attacks and phobias; exaggerated startle, avoidant behavior; frequent crying; amnesia and forgetfulness; and inability to love, nurture, or bond with others. A set of symptoms that takes longer to develop involves problems with commitments, chronic fatigue, psychosomatic symptoms, and diminished interest in life (Levine, 1997, pp. 147–49). In the latter group, Levine mentions fear of dying, going crazy, or having a shortened life (p. 149).

The American Psychiatric Association, *Diagnostic and Statistical Manual of Mental Disorders–Fourth Edition* (*DSM–IV*) (1994) authors include behavioral symptoms such as the ones just mentioned and specify that the traumatic event is one that threatens death, serious injury, or physical integrity of self or others. The central assumption of this chapter is both consistent with, and an expansion of, the key threat delineated in the *DSM–IV* for PTSD. *Traumatic events are experiences processed by the subject as constituting a threat to psychic or physical survival or both.* A basic assumption is that shock and strain traumas decrease a sense of safety, increase a sense of vulnerability in the world, and give a heightened fear of imminent destruction— mortal terror. This threat is reflected in fantasies, conscious or unconscious or both, that have survival-annihilation content and in defensive-restitutive fantasies and behaviors directed against the fantasies and the disruptive and sometimes intolerable affects associated with them. While the *DSM-*Kraeplinian approach emphasizes descriptive, observable, symptomatic manifestations of psychic trauma, the psychodynamic approach additionally includes a focus on intrapsychic events.

These annihilation-survival-related contents and anxieties involve terror, fright, and dread. They reflect residues of, and intrapsychic reactions to, traumatic experience. The ideational aspect entails a dynamic fantasy content that is found at varying levels of symbolization and mentalization, such as fears of being overwhelmed, unable to cope, merged, invaded, and losing or being negated in one's sense of self. Such fantasy contents, uniquely elaborated by each individual, and the defenses against them, extend and particularize the utility of the concept of psychic trauma. They are amenable to psychotherapeutic inquiry as are other psychic contents (Hurvich, 2003a). This schema has been used to construct measures to assess annihilation anxieties clinically (Hurvich, 1991, 2003a; Hurvich and Simha-Alpern, 1997) and empirically (Hurvich, Benveniste, Howard, and Coonerty, 1993; Levin and Hurvich, 1995; Benveniste, Papouchis, Allen, and Hurvich, 1998).

CHARACTERISTICS OF ANNIHILATION ANXIETIES

The following propositions give the reader an overview of the characteristics of annihilation anxieties as I understood them. For a more detailed discussion, see Hurvich (2003c).

1. The danger associated with annihilation anxieties is survival threat.
2. Annihilation concerns are early dangers but can be engendered later and throughout the life cycle whenever there is a perception-fantasy of survival threat.
3. Annihilation anxieties constitute a basic danger and interlink variously with the four widely accepted basic dangers.

4. Annihilation anxieties are centrally involved in the experience of psychic trauma and comprise major traumatic residuals.
5. Excessive annihilation anxieties, especially during the developmental years, increase the likelihood of ego function weakness and self-pathology. Conversely, ego weakness and self-pathology increase the likelihood of excessive annihilation anxieties.
6. Annihilation concerns may be encoded in a concrete somatosensory, affective, presymbolic form.
7. Annihilation apprehensions, as with the four typical dangers, may be identifiable as dynamic psychic content and constitute a component in a conflict-compromise matrix.
8. Annihilation anxieties may occur with or without anticipation.
9. Annihilation-related themes and fantasies may be accompanied by uncontrolled or controlled anxiety.
10. Annihilation fantasies and affects constitute motives for defense.
11. Fears of being overwhelmed are importantly related to aggressive as well as to libidinal impulses associated with self and object representations.
12. Annihilation anxieties are found in psychotics and in nonpsychotics.
13. Anxiety and symptoms may be experienced as psychic danger and can trigger annihilation anxieties as secondary phenomena.
14. Symptoms, beliefs, affect states, and behaviors are especially resistant to change when they are defending against annihilation anxieties.

DIMENSIONS OF ANNIHILATION ANXIETIES

Annihilation anxieties can be grouped into subdimensions. They are (1) fears of being overwhelmed, of being unable to cope, and of losing control; (2) fears of merger, of being devoured, or of being entrapped; (3) fears of disintegration of self and of identity, of emptiness, of meaninglessness and nothingness, and of fears of humiliation-mortification; (4) fears of impingement, penetration, and mutilation; (5) fears of abandonment and of need for support; and (6) apprehensions over survival, persecution, and catastrophe

1. *Fears of being overwhelmed, of being unable to cope, and of losing control; fears of overstimulation, of regression including loss of control of aggressive or sexual urges, of bowel and bladder functions, of bodily equilibrium as in vertigo, and loss of control of the mind, including of going insane.* Ritvo (1981) described how sexual excitement may be associated with fantasies of "falling apart, exploding, rupture of the skin, and running out of body contents" (p. 348).

The following statement of a patient in psychoanalysis demonstrates how current concerns can trigger earlier traumatic fears of being overwhelmed:

These big worries I am having now remind me of the tonsillectomy [age 3 ¾]. It is closing in around me, suffocating me. Being restrained, held down, unable to move. This light coming toward me, I can't get away from it. It's so much more powerful than me, it's going to crush me. . . . The ether—a sense of powerlessness, fears of death and of abandonment. It's got its grip on me and I feel myself dying. It is snuffing out my life. My body feels like it is deteriorating. I need some trick or sleight of hand to slide out and get away from it.

This essentially neurotic patient, in the course of a full psychoanalytic treatment, repeatedly returns to associations of the tonsillectomy in the wake of current dangers. And as we have worked through some of the related conflictual aspects of this traumatically infused intrapsychic conflict situation, derivative fears (of cancer, heart attack, AIDS), have diminished. Steiner (1990, p. 113) reports a similar finding of fear of dying from the anesthesia mask, where the patient's career choice was related to the wish to save his own life and that of the object.

Krystal (1988) concluded, based on the long experience with victims of massive trauma, that while all manner of symptoms and diagnoses were found, the common psychopathological manifestation among these individuals was the presence of overwhelming affects, especially a mixture of depression and anxiety (p. 142).

Being overwhelmed involves an inability to establish a coherent response and can lead to disruption, disorganization, and loss of control. Some cognates are being flooded, buried, submerged, drowned, deluged, engulfed, crushed, immobilized, and overpowered.

One patient described the effect of anxiety on his ability to cope as follows:

I can't stand fear; I need comfort. Once fear steps in, I can't see anything or do anything. There are so many things I do out of fear. I'm afraid I'll fall apart, lose control, be taken over, be shot down with a machine gun. . . . The fear was always of something extreme happening. I won't get smacked; I'll get bombed. Some people fight or run away. When I'm cornered, I crumble.

And another patient, with a history of early childhood trauma stated, when faced with current issues that were triggering earlier traumatic memories: "My mind is being deluged with all sorts of frightening thoughts and images. My body is all nerves. I can't sit down for any period of time; I'm constantly up and down. I feel I'm going to crack up. At my job I can't do a thing; I just feel I can't go on." As with the other patients mentioned here, this one frequently voiced such fears, and they were accompanied by a decrease in the ability to cope with environmental requirements and challenges.

2. *Fears of merger.* These include fears of being devoured or entrapped; fears of smothering, choking, drowning, and being buried alive; and fears of being absorbed and engulfed. Related terms are fusion, engulfment, and re-engulfment. The fear of merger (re-engulfment) is described by Mahler (1968) as an age-appropriate attribute of the toddler.

What are the considerations associated with merger fears as a source of annihilation anxieties? The psychic danger is the threat of loss of the separate sense of self. A. Freud (1952) portrayed how threats to ego intactness (a regular feature of traumatic experience) can result from psychic merger with the love object and lead to loss of personal characteristics. Such merger wishes are one defensive effort that may follow traumatic experience.

3. *Fears of disintegration of self and of identity.* These are major concerns for traumatized individuals. They include apprehensions of falling apart or crumbling; apprehensions over disappearing, leaking out, evaporating, melting away; apprehensions of emptiness and of nothingness; and fears of humiliation-mortification. Disintegration involves a decrease in the level of mental organization and a decrease in structural integrity. Decreases in mental structure tend to trigger anxiety as an alarm reaction, under conditions in which they constitute a danger to the organism's capacity to cope. Arlow (1989) wrote about a borderline patient: "What disrupted the patient's psychic integrity was her fear that she might not be able to control her murderous rage toward Dr. Z and toward her mother" (p. 524).

As already mentioned, psychotic individuals have much traumatic experience in their backgrounds. Frosch (1995) holds that considerable psychotic symptomatology is understandable as a fear of psychic death through dissolution of self and object or as an attempt to preserve contact with reality and object in the interest of psychic survival. He depicted the presence of fragmentation before the formation of part self-images and part object-images and as a forerunner of splitting, and that splitting in the borderline patient is a counterpart of fragmentation in the psychotic.

4. *Fears of impingement/penetration.* Impingement fear is widely described as a posttraumatic phenomenon. Key related terms are these: being invaded, penetrated, intruded on, imposed on, encroached on, and violated. There is a significant developmental basis for this vulnerability. Winnicott (1956) held that annihilation anxiety develops in the early postnatal period, but only in response to environmental failure and as a result of excessive reaction to impingement. An undue amount of such reacting produces not frus-

tration but a threat of annihilation. ("Impingement is an intrusion on the infant at times when he is not reaching out, and the result is that he withdraws from an unwanted impact . . . [This] 'disturbs the continuity of the going on being of the new individual.'") (1958, p. 245). The essence of bad mothering has been seen as impingement on the infant, because of the mother's failure in active adaptation to the infant's needs. The likelihood is increased for premature but overly brittle ego development (Khan, 1963) and an overdeveloped false self (Winnicott, 1960b). While the centrality of developmental considerations in massive psychic trauma is under debate (Rothstein, 1986), those individuals who suffered excessive impingement during their early years are more vulnerable to intrusion experiences in psychic trauma. According to Bick (1968), a sense of being overly vulnerable to penetration by others is increased when there have been inadequate experiences of "adhesive identification" due to unsatisfactory or inadequate skin contact with the mother during earliest infancy. It leads to fantasies of the self as porous and unable to hold or contain anything.

One patient described her feelings about being impinged on this way: "I feel someone could easily violate me, mentally, physically and emotionally. And I would be shattered to pieces. Everything inside me would become like shattered glass, and couldn't come back together." This patient suffered repeated abandonment trauma with the mother and chronic, terrifying beatings and threats from the father.

Another patient who had suffered from multiple childhood psychic trauma and, importantly, from an intrusive, punishing, and blaming father spoke more rapidly and loudly in the therapy session if he anticipated that I was about to talk, and he perceived any reaction from me as an intolerable interference. These experienced intrusions triggered fears of annihilation. He could not bear to have any activity interrupted, felt that what he was doing would be completely ruined, and that interrupting and spoiling were threatening to drive him crazy. Reading an article or a chapter in a book without interruption calmed him and decreased his fear of going insane.

5. *Fears of abandonment, needing support, falling forever, and falling into a "black hole."* These issues, like the others here specified, have traumatic effects in development. For many youngsters, excessive abandonment fears result in increased vulnerability to subsequent psychic trauma and also these fears increase following psychic trauma. Needed support includes all the requirements for caretaking and dependency characteristic of the pre-object-constancy child, who is struggling with issues relevant to merger fantasies and separation-individuation issues (Mahler, Pine, and Bergman, 1975).

Childhood experiences of helplessness and of being overwhelmed are universal. It is in a person who has not yet adequately developed techniques for self-regulation, self-care, and emotional self-reliance that loss of support tends to trigger annihilation anxieties. The anxiety over loss of needed support is found in people who are overly dependent and who respond with panic and dread to the threatened loss of a significant person or when they are faced with increased responsibility, which often has the meaning to the person that he or she will lose dependent support. These individuals as a group have an increased vulnerability to the pathological aftermath of psychic trauma.

Winnicott's (1958) holding environment concept centers on the availability of needed support for the infant. It includes timely and reliable availability, attunement to factors associated with disequilibrium in the subject, and protection of the infant from overstimulation and impingement. He wrote that *being* and *annihilation* are the only options for an infant during the holding phase. Winnicott (1952; 1960a) proposed three main kinds of anxiety that result from problems in early maternal failure: unintegration, leading to a sense of disintegration; breakdown of the relationship between psyche and soma, which leads to depersonalization; and the feeling that one's center of consciousness has moved from the core to the shell.

These feelings of anxiety, which are the earliest and occur normally in the context of maternal failure, are heightened to an unmanageable degree when environmental failures occur too rapidly and too often. There is, then, a predisposition to return to a primary unintegrated state under regression. The baby, in its earliest stage lives always "on the brink of unthinkable anxiety" (Winnicott, 1962, p. 57). Where there is a weak ego organization, this experience of anxiety is persistent. Unthinkable anxiety manifests itself in later life in fears of falling to pieces, fears of falling forever, fears of having no orientation, or a fear of no sense of relationship between mind and body (Winnicott, 1958).

So, one manifestation of the fear of loss of needed support is the fear of falling. This may be found in an adult in various forms. Kernberg (1980) sees fears of darkness, silence, solitude, loneliness, and emptiness as sometimes connected with the fear of falling. Failures in the early holding function of the mothering environment are suggested when these fears are persistently found. Kernberg pointed out that the relatively high rate of suicidal attempts in six- to twelve-year-olds she observed in a psychiatric hospital frequently involved jumping out of a window. This may have the meaning of "actualizing the child's hopelessness, namely, that he is indeed falling out of maternal supports and into the arms of a black void—the absent mother" (p. 608).

6. *Apprehensions over survival/persecution and of catastrophe. Being killed, being destroyed, and having fears of world destruction; of fire and brim-*

stone, of the apocalypse, of the twilight of the gods, of doomsday, and of the death imprint. This involves a tendency to respond with a life-and-death attitude to danger, perceived threat or other situations that usually arouse some fear or anxiety. Krystal (1988) describes a "doomsday orientation" that involves a deeply pessimistic attitude, with concurrent persistent fears and a depressive lifestyle in people who suffered early psychic traumatization. A catastrophic mentality is one of the most frequent responses to psychic trauma. In those who have suffered massive psychic trauma, it has been characterized as a "doomsday orientation," a terrifying belief, even conviction, that lightning will again strike, and he or she will again be faced with a fate worse than death. (Krystal, 1988).

One patient stated:

> I feel I will explode because I can't contain the turmoil. I fear that at any moment my life will become a catastrophe. When the catastrophe happens, I will become emotionally unhinged, and it will destroy me because I can't overcome it. When I tell myself all the rational things to calm my fears, it does not help. It makes it worse because I feel I'm going insane, since I *think* one way and feel another.

CONCLUSION

As a result of the terrorist attack on the World Trade Center, New Yorkers are experiencing and expressing increased apprehensions over another unpredictable, dreaded assault. There are heightened concerns over *safety, survival, and self-preservation.* These are the apprehensions that constitute annihilation anxieties, and they are central sequelae of psychic trauma. Experiences of overwhelmed helplessness tend to include the terror of imminent extinction and annihilation-survival fantasies constitute a key psychic content of trauma. Expressed annihilation apprehensions of trauma victims are of being destroyed, overwhelmed, and unable to cope; of merger, intrusion, and disorganization of the sense of self; of loss of needed support; and of expectations of additional catastrophe. This chapter contains a description of annihilation anxieties and, thereby, underscores frequently found fantasy mental contents that are associated with psychic trauma. The position was developed that terror experience is a component of psychic trauma in psychopathology and that annihilation anxiety is a marker and residue of psychic trauma.

As clinicians, a thorough understanding of annihilation anxiety and its sequelae will allow us to better enable our clients to understand and cope with psychic trauma and the associated threat of annihilation.

REFERENCES

Adler, G. (1985). *Borderline psychopathology and its treatment*. New York: Jason Aronson.

American Psychiatric Association. (1994). *Diagnostic and statistical manual of mental disorders* (4th ed.). Washington, DC: Author

Arlow, J. (1989). Treatment of the borderline patient. *Psychoanalytic Inquiry*, 9: 517–27.

Benveniste, P., Papouchis, N., Hurvich, M., and Allen, R. (1998). Research assessment of annihilation anxiety and ego functioning. *Psychoanalytic Psychology*, 15: 536–66.

Bick, E. (1968). The experience of the skin in early object relations. *International Journal of Psychoanalysis*, 49: 484–86.

Brenner, C. (1986). Discussion of papers. In A. Rothstein (Ed.), *The reconstruction of trauma: Its significance in clinical work*. Madison, CT: International Universities Press.

Buie, D. H., and Adler, G. (1973). The uses of confrontation in the psychotherapy of borderline patients. In G. Adler and P. G. Meyerson (Eds.), *Confrontation in psychotherapy*. New York: Science House.

Dowling, S. (1986). Discussion of the various contributions. In A. Rothstein (Ed.), *The reconstruction of trauma*, pp. 205–17.

Ferenczi, S. (1933/1968). Confusion of tongues between adults and the child: The language of tenderness and passion. *Contemporary Psychoanalysis*, 24: 196–206.

Freud, A. (1952/1968). Notes on a connection between the states of negativism and of emotional surrender. In *The writings of Anna Freud* (Vol. 4, pp. 256–59). New York: International Universities Press.

———. (1967). Comments on trauma. In S. Furst (Ed.), *Psychic trauma*, pp. 235–45. New York: Basic Books.

Freud, S. (1920). Beyond the pleasure principle. *Standard Edition*, 18, pp. 7–64. London: Hogarth Press.

———. (1923). The ego and the id. *Standard Edition*, 19, pp. 12–66. London: Hogarth Press.

———. (1939). An outline of psychoanalysis. *Standard Edition*, 23, pp. 141–207. London: Hogarth Press.

Frosch, A. (1995). Preconceptually organized emotion. *Journal of the American Psychoanalytic Association*, 43: 423–47.

Furst, S. (Ed.). (1967) *Psychic trauma*. New York: Basic Books.

Gaddini, E. (1992). *A psychoanalytic theory of infantile experience: Conceptual and clinical reflections*. A. Limentani (Ed.). London: Tavistock/Routledge.

Greenacre, P. (1967). The influence of psychic trauma on genetic patterns. In S. Furst (Ed.), *Psychic trauma*, pp. 108–53. New York: Basic Books.

Hurvich, M. (1989). Traumatic moment, basic dangers and annihilation anxiety. *Psychoanalytic Psychology*, 6: 309–23.

———. (1991). Annihilation anxiety: An introduction. In H. Siegel, L. Barbanel, I. Hirsch, J. Lasky, H. Silverman, and S. Warshaw (Eds.), *Psychoanalytic reflections on current issues*. New York: New York University Press.

————. (1996, June). Annihilation anxieties and psychic trauma. Second World Conference of the International Society for Traumatic Stress, Jerusalem.

————. (2000). Fears of being overwhelmed and psychoanalytic theories of anxiety. *The Psychoanalytic Review*, 87: 615–49.

————. (2003a, January). A proposed expansion of the danger series: Annihilation as present or potential threat. Mid-winter meetings of the American Psychoanalytic Association, New York.

————. (2003b). Symbolization, desymbolization and annihilation anxieties. In R. Lasky (Ed.), *Symbolization and desymbolization: Essays in honor of Norbert Freedman*, pp. 347–65. New York: Karnac.

————. (2003c). The place of annihilation anxieties in psychoanalytic theory. *Journal of the American Psychoanalytic Association*, 51: 579–616.

Hurvich, M., and Simha-Alpern, A. (1997). Annihilation anxiety in psychosomatic disorders. In J. Schumacher Finnel (Ed.), *Mind-body problems: Psychotherapy with psychosomatic disorders*. Northvale, NJ: Jason Aronson.

Hurvich, M., Benveniste, P., Howard, J., and Coonerty, S. (1993). Assessment of annihilation anxiety from projective tests. *Perceptual and Motor Skills*, 77: 387–401.

Jacobson, E. (1967). *Psychotic conflict and reality*. New York: International University Press.

Karon, B. P., and Vandenboss, G. R. (1981). *Psychotherapy of schizophrenia: The treatment of choice*. New York: Jason Aronson.

Kernberg, P. (1980). Childhood psychosis: A psychoanalytic perspective. In S. I. Greenspan and G. H. Pollock (Eds.), *The course of life: Infancy and early childhood* (Vol. 1, pp. 603–17). Washington, DC: U.S. Government Printing Office.

Khan, M. M. R. (1963). The concept of cumulative trauma. *The Psychoanalytic Study of the Child*, 18: 286–306.

Krystal, H. (1968). *Massive psychic trauma*. New York: International Universities Press.

————. (1988). *Integration and self healing: Affect, trauma, and alexthymia*. Hillsdale, NJ: The Analytic Press.

Lang, J. A. (1987). Two contrasting frames of reference for understanding borderline patients: Kernberg and Kohut. In J. S. Grotstein, M. F. Solomon, and J. A. Lang (Eds.), *The borderline patient: Emerging concepts in diagnosis, psychodynamics, and treatment*. Hillsdale, NJ: The Analytic Press.

Levin, R., and Hurvich, M. (1995). Nightmares and annihilation anxiety. *Psychoanalytic Psychology*, 12: 247–58.

Levine, P. A. (1997). *Waking the tiger: Healing trauma*. Berkeley, CA: North Atlantic Books.

Lifton, R. J. (1979/1983). *The broken connection*. New York: Basic Books.

Loewenstein, R. M. (1964). Symptom formation and character formation. *International Journal of Psychoanalysis*, 45: 155–57.

MacDougall, J. (1989). *Theatres of the body*. New York: Norton.

Mack, J. E. (1970). *Nightmares and human conflict*. Boston: Houghton Mifflin.

Mahler, M. (1968). *On human symbiosis and the vicissitudes of individuation: Infantile psychosis* (Vol. 1). New York: International Universities Press.

Mahler, M., Pine, F., and Bergman, A. (1975). *The psychological birth of the infant.* New York: Basic Books.

Mahony, P. J. (1984). *Cries of the wolf man.* New York: International Universities Press.

Pao, P. N. (1979). *Schizophrenic disorders.* New York: International Universities Press.

Rangell, L. (1967/1986). The metapsychology of psychic trauma. In A. Rothstein (Ed.), *The reconstruction of trauma: Its significance in clinical work*, pp. 51–84. Madison, CT: International Universities Press.

Ritvo, S. (1981). Anxiety, symptom formation, and ego autonomy. *The Psychoanalytic Study of the Child*, 36: 339–64.

Rothstein, A. (Ed.) (1986). *The reconstruction of trauma: Its significance in clinical work.* Madison, CT: International Universities Press.

Sandler, J. (1960/1987). The background of safety. In *From safety to superego: Selected papers*, pp. 1–8. New York: Guilford.

Schur, M. (1953). The ego in anxiety. In R. M. Loewenstein (Ed.), *Drives, affects and behavior*, pp. 67–103. New York: International Universities Press.

Shengold, L. (1989). *Soul murder: The effect of childhood abuse and deprivation.* New Haven, CT: Yale University Press.

Socarides, C. (1973). Sexual perversion and the fear of engulfment. *International Journal of Psychoanalytic Psychotherapy*, 2: 432–48.

Sorokin, P. (1942/1968). *Man and society in calamity.* New York: Dutton.

Steiner, J. (1990). The defensive function of pathological organizations. In B. Boyer and P. Giovacchini (Eds.), *Master clinicians on the treating of the regressed patient.* Northvale, NJ: Jason Aronson.

Stern, M. (1951). Anxiety, trauma, and shock. *The Psychoanalytic Quarterly*, 20: 179–203.

Teixeira, M. A. (1984). Annihilation anxiety in schizophrenia: Metaphor or dynamic? *Psychotherapy*, 21: 377–81.

Tustin, F. (1981). *Autistic states in children.* London: Routledge and Kegan Paul.

Weiss, E. (1964). *Agoraphobia in the light of ego psychology.* New York: Grune and Stratton.

Winnicott, D. W. (1952/1958). Anxiety associated with insecurity. In *Collected Papers: Through paediatrics to psycho-analysis*, pp. 97–100. London: Tavistock.

———. (1956/1958). Primary maternal preoccupation. In *Collected papers: Through paedeatrics to psycho-analysis*, pp. 300–305. London: Tavistock.

———. (1960a/1965). The theory of the infant-parent relationship. In *The maturational processes and the holding environment*, pp. 37–55. London: Hogarth Press.

———. (1960b/1965). Ego distortion in terms of true and false self. In *The maturational processes and the holding environment*, pp. 56–63. London: Hogarth Press.

———. (1962). Ego integration in child development. In *The maturational processes and the holding environment*, pp. 56–63. London: Hogarth Press.

———. (1974). The fear of breakdown. *International Review of Psychoanalysis*, 1: 103–7.

Wurmser, L. (1981/1982). Phobic core in the addictions and the paranoid process. *International Journal of Psychoanalytic Psychotherapy*, 8: 310–35.

Zetzel, E. (1949/1970). Anxiety and the capacity to bear it. In *The capacity for emotional growth*, 33–52. New York: International Universities Press.

Chapter Four

Resilience: Accommodation and Recovery

Henry Krystal

This chapter represents a retrospective study of forty-year follow-ups of survivors of the Holocaust and other genocidal tragedies. It involves a kind of image-contrast reversal. The shift is from a clinical orientation to a retroscopic inventory: what attributes made individuals able to survive and master the potentially lethal trauma, and what characteristics favored successful resumption of "normal" life?

The adult residuals of infantile omnipotence or narcissism are a conviction of one's security, lovability, and safety. All resilience is built on it. The nature of affects, all their aspects and the ways in which they serve as signals in information processing and in alerting and preparing one for responses to danger, all are involved in the continuation of minimal essential functions, the prevention of traumatic surrender, and the prevention of abject surrender and psychogenic death when trauma cannot be prevented or avoided.

Observations of ways in which psychic reality is maintained in the constricted, traumatic state shed light on the function of signal affects, the nature of registration, and recall. Work with survivor testimonies demonstrates that unconscious and repressed memory traces are not preserved intact but are subject to complex modifications. For survivors of the Holocaust, being able to use disavowal and repudiation (primary repression) and to suspend all mourning was essential. The most severe challenge involved the ability to deal with the personal representation of God, involving one's rage, guilt, and shame, and the necessity to restore some acceptable scheme of the world order that did not depend on the traditional biblical justification of every calamity by the sins of its victims. Restoring access to benign introjects, and acquiescing to reality as justified by its causes, permits the restoration of one's capacity for love. Love is everyone's life power.

The analytic involvement with survivors of the Holocaust started with a number of leading analysts (Niederland, Schur, Eissler, Wangh, and others). We succeeded in establishing in Germany the principles of psychological damages from the persecutions. This became the legal basis for the restitution laws, which made possible psychoanalytic treatment for survivors. The insights derived from this work had widespread effects. Through conferences and joint efforts by analysts, the study of the Holocaust became a major stimulus of generalized research and treatment of posttraumatic stress disorders. Presently, there is worldwide recognition of the pioneering nature of this work.

Much of what we learned in the analytic studies of Holocaust and genocide survivors was applied directly to the treatment of survivors of natural and human-made disasters. The greatest application and further boost to this kind of exploration and care came from extending these views to the treatment of Viet Nam veterans. By now, psychoanalytic insights into trauma and its prevention and treatment have been made available throughout the world and have been applied to all ages and situations.

We are all aware that there are limitations concerning generalizations about the reactions of people during the Holocaust, because even among those who were at the very same place at the same time, each one had a different experience (Sigmund Freud's "Erlebnisse"). The variety of experiences was enormous. Depending on what challenges an individual had to face, his personal traits, assets, and patterns of behavior influenced the success of his efforts. Some choices of behaviors favored survival. I will limit my present discussion to one pattern. In some respects, the concentration camps were the epitome of the genocidal war and involved the most terrible and unique stresses. The responses in this situation are, in retrospect, most clearly classifiable. Considering these extreme conditions will illustrate some points relevant to our quest.

I feel that "healthy" infantile omnipotence is the most important asset for dealing with life's stresses and potential trauma (Krystal, 1997a; Ornstein, 1997). It is the emotional mainspring of extraordinary reserves. It provides a profound, unshakeable conviction of one's invulnerability, derived in the first place from a fortunate and harmonious pre-object, symbiotic relatedness (Kumin, 1997). The programming of the infant's sense of security is achieved by the empathic care and adoring eye-to-eye (right hemisphere to right hemisphere) communication of the mothering parent in the first three years of life (Schore, 1994).

In an adult, there is hardly any reflective self-awareness of the emotional reserves hidden deep in the soul. The availability of these emotional reserves is recognizable in a special vitality, in an optimistic and adventuresome attitude, and in social and career contacts—conveying the subject's calm conviction that he or she will be welcomed and liked. The foundation of it all is an innate, infantile, magical state, programmed, as it were, for receiving positive mothering care and thriving on it. As the infant establishes a functional self-awareness and discovers the "outside" good object, the mother is watchful for the child's distress and translates it into her affective responses. She strives to attend to the infant's needs immediately and to soothe and restore a state of well-being. Through her behavior, she conveys to the infant the message that he or she is lovable and perfect. Thus is established our sense of omnipotence that is later observed in our belief in the magical power of our wishes.

Individuals who have a healthy dose of the adult residuals of infantile narcissism can preserve their optimism in situations of stress and danger. They are able to retain initiative in their thinking, in their planning, or even just in their fantasy. Even when under severe stress, they manage to recognize the chances of improving the dangerous situation at varying degrees of risk. The ones whose risk taking worked out well treasure the memories of the actions and self-reliance that saved their own or other's lives (Krystal 1997a, 1997b; Ornstein, 1997).

Consider the opposite side of the issue: trauma is an intrapsychic phenomenon. Although certain situations can be assumed to be traumatic to all who experience them, some people can handle situations that overwhelm others. Fear is the signal of impending avoidable, manageable danger. It activates the entire organism including, and especially, the mind. In contrast, when one is confronted with danger that is estimated to be unavoidable and inescapable, one surrenders to it. Based on the subjective evaluation of the situation and with the estimation of one's own helplessness, the affect changes from fear to a catatonoid reaction. This emotion triggers surrender and initiates the traumatic state. The individual gives up all initiative and obeys orders. This state is of a cataleptic nature and has a powerful hypnotic effect. The more one obeys orders, the deeper one goes into the trance. This state starts a progression that cannot be stopped until one reaches a "robot" state. Being able to establish and maintain the constricted state is potentially a lifesaving operation.

If we have a chance to examine an individual in this condition, we find an overwhelmed, immobilized, withdrawn person, often showing derealization and depersonalization. The focus of attention is very narrow. In concentration camps, on being unloaded from the deadly cattle cars and experiencing the dehumanization, terrorization, and loss of everyone dear, potential survivors had to be able to directly block their affective responses to the fate of their families and to respond only to what needed to be done on a moment-to-moment basis with "Kadaver Gehorchsamkeit" (cadaver-like obedience—Himmler's favorite expression). Failure to achieve this feat resulted in being killed immediately. Zalman Loewenthal, while in the *Sonderkommando* (the group who was isolated from the other prisoners and whose task it was to burn the newly gassed transports in the crematoria of Auschwitz), reported, "They succeeded in blunting all emotion, all thought of any action" (Mark, 1988, p. 219).

Some prisoners instantly identified with the aggressors and imitated their behavior. Commonly, these individuals became kapos. In Auschwitz from 1942 to 1944, they had to become killers of their fellow inmates on a daily quota basis. Eventually, they expressed their sadism constantly, even in encountering newly arriving transports. A note from Zalman Gradowski written while he was in the *Sonderkommando* and buried in a scroll in the ashes around the crematorium describes the experiences of newly arriving transports:

> We endeavor to engage the more senior inmates in conversation, to learn more. But how nasty are those whom we address! How can they be so sadistic to make fun of our miserable people? How lightly, without contorting their faces, they answer questions about our families: "They are in heaven already." Has the camp caused them to lose all feelings, leaving them no better amusement then to take pleasure in the torture and suffering of others? . . . The words of such cruel statements: "Your families are buried!" Everyone is terrified. The heart recoils from the very sound of the words: "your family is no longer alive." . . . The barrack kapos . . . tell us and instruct us how to behave toward them during working hours: "Remember that you have to become robots and move at our will. Don't take a step without an order from us!" (Mark, 1988, pp. 197–98)

Our reaction to those who so thoroughly identified with the aggressor is to condemn them and to wish we could punish them. However, Lifton (1986, p. 251) reflected about a doctor in Auschwitz who was a collaborator in medical experimentation: "Samuel was a Jew, which meant a person one hundred percent condemned to death in the camp. So he had a right to prolong his life — week by week, month by month."

Returning to the process of trauma, which we left at the robot state: If the effort to arrest the progression of the traumatic state failed, the deepening of it manifested in a growing numbing of pain and painful emotions, followed by a loss of all vestiges of self-reliance, initiative, and agency. The empowerment to say "no" and to carry out self-defense was progressively lost. At a certain point, the traumatic closure reached a malignant state, with the blocking of all mental functions: cognition, registration of perceptions, recall, scanning, information processing in general, planning, and problem solving. Finally, just a vestige of these functions was retained, with some capacity for self-observation. If the traumatic process continued, all vitality was suppressed, and the individual succumbed to psychogenic death, with the heart stopping in diastole.

The following is the description Bomba (1985, p. 49) gives of his first day in Auschwitz:

> In the morning when they had the appeal to go out from the barracks, from our group I would say at least four or five were dead. I do not know how it

happened—they must have had with them some kind of poison and poisoned themselves. At least two of them were my close friends. They did not say anything. We did not even know they had poison with them.

Indeed, likely, they did not, and their death was psychogenic. Franz Suchomel, an SS man in Treblinka, stated that in a transport of five thousand Jews from France, three thousand were dead, on arrival: "Some had slashed their wrists or *just died*" (emphasis mine) (Lanzmann, 1985, p. 53). Even about shorter transports, he said that the people were "half dead and half mad."

After a couple of months of incarceration, a different kind of death made its appearance and grew in frequency: the "Musulman" process. In the early deaths, there was a direct progression of the traumatic process toward death, following a universal pattern common to the entire animal kingdom (Meerloo, 1959; Seligman, 1975). By contrast, the Musulman death pattern followed the exhaustion of all emotional resources and manifested in an observable pattern of ceasing necessary survival behavior. Sometimes, just before death, the Musulman manifested an ineffectual rage, indiscriminately lashing out at anyone who happened to be around him (Krystal, 1988). The inmates' awareness of the danger of the Musulman surrender pattern and the need to guard against it motivated many of the adjustments and behaviors in the concentration camps. For instance, the strong effort to avoid the infestation with lice getting out of hand was directly linked to this danger, because the impending Musulmen were often observed literally crawling with lice.

For those who managed to arrest the traumatic process in the robot state and had to live in this condition for a significant period, there were consequences that were to last the rest of their lives (Krystal, 1988, 1997b). Survival in the face of an impasse, a "no exit" situation, takes place in a state of "psychic closing off." Survivors undergo symbolic death in order to avoid physical or psychic death. Such cataclysms result in a permanent "death imprint," desensitization, and identification with death and with the dead (Lifton, 1976).

Many psychological functions serve the prevention of massive psychic trauma. Examples of such functions are perception, registration, and most of all, self-evaluation in a given situation. In the past, I have studied the multiplicity of functions, including ego functions, involved in trauma prevention, representing the exploration and elaboration of the idea of the "stimulus barrier," not as a passive bar, but as the totality of potentially mobilizeable defenses (Krystal, 1985). Signal affects are the essential sensory, monitoring, and regulatory signals or "switches" in information processing. They determine the choice of behavior in a given situation. They "color" the nature of the constant reinterpretation of self-representations and object representations. Signal-affects do not stop totally in the traumatic state. Indeed, as always, we have to create our mental representation of everything we behold. We must maintain our psychic reality, as it is the only knowable reality (Dorsey, 1943, 1965; Krystal 1973, 1988).

Let us consider the application of what we used to call the "stimulus barrier" to the understanding of one's functioning in the traumatic state. In my 1985 paper "Trauma and the Stimulus Barrier" I examine many aspects of the perceptive, cognitive, sensorimotor, affective, and consciousness-regulatory functions that operate unceasingly and silently in our orientation and adjustment process. I show how many mental activities serving a variety of functions are simultaneously involved in the organism's self-preservation. An example of a unique defensive operation is presented by a number of Cambodian women, who during the genocidal attack, sometimes at the instant when their loved ones were about to be killed, developed a functional blindness. This is a kind of partial blindness that persisted for years despite treatment (Wilkinson, 1994). It is quite different from conversion reaction, and it illustrates the difference between repression and repudiation (*Verwerfung* versus *Verdrängung*). From this point of view, these defensive aspects of the mind are like immunological and cellular reactions that are quietly involved in the prevention of infection and neoplasia. We become aware of them only when there is a partial failure. What can be learned about these functions from studies of the sequelae of the traumatic state?

We focus on the traumatic state, not the traumatic situation. This is why we have to look beyond ego defenses and venture into an examination of all the information processing. The contributions from experimental psychology, developmental psychology, perceptgenesis, and neuroscience have to be combined and reconciled with psychoanalytic contributions to expose the extreme complexity of factors involving attention, perception, evaluation, recall, and various memory functions. Part of the process consists of multiple "takes" of improving detail and elaboration, ending in creating a stimulus-proximate registration, on which we can obtain intersubjective agreement with others. All these operations are executed on the unconscious level.

Next, we bring in associations. We compare and confront current perceptions with accumulated memories. These memories bring in their own affect qualities that become the signal-affects directing further mental element processing (Westerlundh and Smith, 1983; Krystal and Krystal, 1994). This signal determines where and how the percept is registered in the mind. It also determines the kind and degree of consciousness and the accessibility of it for the future.

Returning to the first mental act in the chain: what could be the nature of perception in the traumatic state? From the beginning, there is a blocking of all the functions reviewed—the processes of perception and cognition on the one hand, and the affect signals on the other—that produce the particular self-evaluation in the emergency situation. In the traumatic state, the choices and breadth of references are greatly limited and the scope of attention is severely narrowed, just as in a hypnotic trance. However, some capacity for reflective self-awareness and some recognition of imminent danger may continue. Some individuals remain able to mobilize life-preserving action in dire emergencies. (For example, during "selections," some people managed to run to the "good side.") Occasionally, when they recognize an opportunity, some people in a traumatic state can mobilize themselves and act swiftly and effectively. Those decisions, such as choosing whether to go on an available transport, can have life or death consequences.

We can thus distinguish between those individuals who, when confronted with great danger, surrendered to it totally, and those who were able to ward off abject submission. Surrender also had serious consequences for the way the people acted thereafter. Traumatic constriction interfered with taking initiative on the one hand and the capacity to maintain associations and mutual-assistance group formations on the other. In the concentration camps, even though there was significant traumatization, there were individuals who, with luck and health, were able to establish a pattern of living that they accepted as being a greatly abnormal, but temporary, situation. They were able to preserve their intrapsychic resistance and initiative and to nurture the belief that they would survive and return to a condition of normality. In fact, during some temporary respites one could hear some inmates of the camps resting in their cots sharing fantasies that "when this is over" they will just show people their tattoos and receive all kinds of special compensations, favored treatment, and even honors. As long as they maintained such hope, their degree of dehumanization was moderated. Hidden vestigial optimism permitted some limited alertness and initiative, even inventiveness.

A very special combination of favorable personality assets and fortunate circumstances was required for an inmate to conceive a plan to escape and to carry it out successfully, as did Rudolf Vrba. He recounted: "The decision to escape . . . was formed immediately . . . when (he) arrived in Auschwitz." (Lanzmann, 1985, pp. 165–66) In preparing to escape, he dared to find and contact individuals who were part of the Auschwitz Resistance. As it happened, he also had a faithful comrade and collaborator "from home," and together they made preparations to escape. Vrba was dedicated to getting back to Hungary and informing the world about what was going on in Auschwitz, a goal that he was willing to die for. Thus the paralyzing power of the fear of death was suspended by his devoting himself to an objective more valued than his survival.

Members of the Auschwitz *Sonderkommando* struggled with a bitter determination to express their outrage in a suicidal rebellion. Zalman Gradowski
entered in his buried scroll:

> As for us, we have already lost all hope of living to the day of liberation. Despite
> the fact that joyful news reaches us, we have learned that the world is letting the
> barbarian destroy the remnants of the Jewish people . . . We the Sonderkom-
> mando have wanted for a long time to put an end to our terrible labor, forced on
> us on the pain of death. We wanted to do a great deed. (Mark, 1988, p. 201)

Zalman Loewenthal, a fellow inmate, who was also killed in the uprising, described the agony of defeat, as one after the other of the group members collapsed in their resolve. Some even turned informer, as did one who turned in
the leader who was preparing the rebellion and escape. Still, the preparations
continued for a few months, despite many delays, even when it was clear that
their own group would be liquidated. Two hundred of them were sent to another camp, and the conspirators learned that they were directly gassed.

The postwar discovery of the Auschwitz scrolls buried by these men gives
us a chance to observe the nature of their cognition directly. Gradowski used
an unnatural, emotional style in a vibrant and literary Yiddish with a tendency
toward Germanisms and flowery phrases. He addressed the reader directly.
He sounded as if he were giving his own eulogy. Loewenthal's manuscript
was written in a nervous, distracted style with no small degree of confusion.
It is an affectless communication. There is, in fact, no mention of any *feelings*
about the horrors and his own degradation—from being the head of a Rab-
binical court to becoming a desperate, enslaved participant in the genocide
(Mark, 1988). Both styles illustrate characteristic traumatic distortions of
memory and oral history (Krystal, 1998a).

Contemporary work with survivor testimonies still shows the characteristic cognitive styles that yield clues about the nature of registration in the traumatic state. The styles of recall and reporting are consistent with those found
in other studies of posttraumatic behavior. The stories are related in a "facts
only," constricted manner. Testimonies are given in a conflictual, painful way
and are spotty and highly distorted. Some recollections are conspicuously im-
probable and show displacements. Some can best be understood as amalgams
of dreams and fears. Some of them are screen memories, and some are found
modified in thirty-year follow-up reexaminations.

These phenomena illustrate that defensive reprocessing of memory traces
from the traumatic state continue to be operational, now serving to protect one
from the possibility of retraumatization (Krystal, 1999). Thus, a major lifesaving operation is the creation of traumatic screens and distorted memories
that function as a protection against the unthinkable. The catatonoid reaction

produces primary repression. Information incompatible with the survival of the self is not registered at all, creating a "black hole" in the information processing system. This reaction is what earlier I called repudiation (Cohen, 1985). It manifests itself in survivor testimonies, and is a major problem in attempting to do psychoanalysis with traumatized individuals (Krystal, 1999)

Another universal defensive operation is the traumatic splitting of one's self-representation. There are many splitting patterns residual from the traumatic state (Brenner, 2001). The most conspicuous of these patterns results from a fixation on the past. One has to live in the present but is not able to stop living in the past. Another major dissonance is between believing and not believing what happened—how it could have happened? This demonstrates the continuation of the defensive functions of denial and disavowal.

The splitting of identity common in other posttraumatic states is rare in Holocaust survivors. However, the following pattern is virtually universal: there is a splitting within the individual along the polarization between victim and oppressor representations. These two parasitic self-representations must be kept rigidly apart at almost any cost. Even in some analyses, they cannot be fully or carelessly exposed and discovered by the patient without causing a serious disturbance (Shaw, 1967; Krystal 1988, 1999). An eighty-year-old woman seen recently, who had many different complaints, kept complaining repetitively about pain in her left breast. My records, obtained thirty years earlier, showed that she had been bitten on the left breast by an SS man while he raped her. She was not able to make the connection between the symptom and the assault.

Repression and repudiation keep one attached to one's mental representation of the perpetrator, victim, and the primitive affect precursors generated in the traumatic state. Recall is also disturbed by the fact that in the traumatic state, registration is on a sensory-motor level that is preverbal, and therefore, no language is available for the presentation of some memory traces. Recollections are presented in an "understated" way. Memories are related in a staccato, aprosodic manner. The melody is gone out of the speech. Even though statements appear lucid, their heuristic value is like the memory of a nightmare.

Memory is unreliable. One instance: a survivor was able to recall and retell the death march from Auschwitz westward to the next camp. He could describe the circumstances of the terrible night, the frost, and the killing of everyone who could not keep on marching. There was no doubt in his mind that he recalled the whole experience, but there was never an occasion for him to tell the whole story or an audience to whom to tell it. Recently, through the "testimony" program, he started examining himself to see what he actually recalled. It turned out that he remembered only certain unconnected vignettes, isolated fragments of the event.

One of them was waiting to be marched out from Birkenau. Another was marching in the dark and beginning to hear (and see?) that people were being killed by the side of the road. Next was an image of struggling to keep marching together with two friends. One of them became weak and wanted to give up, sit down, and be killed. The two men held him up and continued marching. He does not remember how long this went on or how it stopped. In his next image he finds himself at dawn marching alone—no columns, no other prisoners. He drags himself on an empty road and encounters an old German soldier who is leaning against a fence and carrying his rifle. The soldier seems to be in as bad a shape as he is. No dialogue between them is recalled. Next, the two of them are walking through the city in which he visualizes a busy intersection with traffic regulated by military police. Somehow, he finds himself in the camp where the prisoners are "stored." Sometime later in the evening of the same or the next day he is loaded into a cattle car, and with him are the two men with whom he had been marching on the first night. They manage to get to the corner of the wagon that is a defensive position. (Also: Laub 1995.)

The spottiness of this narrative shows disturbances in registration and recall even fifty-five years later. I found in the thirty-five years of therapeutic experience and reexamination follow-ups that unconscious registrations (including repressed ones) do not remain unchanged, but are reworked perpetually (Krystal, 1998a, 1998b). This is especially conspicuous in the aging survivor as the losses of old age necessitate grieving, which in turn brings up the never accomplished or even attempted mourning. The losses occurring in aging require changes in self-representation through grieving. The capacity to grieve successfully, to a point of acceptance and acquiescence to losses, is the prerequisite for harmonious senescence. If the grieving is effective, then one can discover (in analysis) revisions of various mental contents including pathological memory traces of traumatic registrations (Krystal 1981, 1991, 1995). Dissociation and disavowal were indispensable in unbearable conditions. Denial may have been temporary or lasting, but clearly, in Auschwitz, without that kind of catastrophic reaction one would have been overwhelmed with a flood of emotions, especially grief. Mourning had to be delayed, sometimes forever.

These defenses were necessary because the imprisonment, the isolation, and the experience of sadistic killer kapos of one's own people made it most difficult to maintain loyalty and love. Love represents our life power (Dorsey 1971; Krystal, 1988, 1999). To put it in a teleological way: in order to improve one's chances of survival, one had to favor the secret preservation of love, hope, and faith under the most difficult circumstances. If one could not help one's fellow prisoners, it was sometimes an expression of love to restrain from hurting or exploiting them. The capacity for loving aided in continuing links with other people struggling for survival and providing a means of preserving hope and faith. Resilience was proportional to an individual's ability to accept unbearable conditions and persevere with at least *intrapsychic* protest, resistance, and the preservation of pre-Holocaust goals and ideals.

The preservation of some ingenuity and alertness to "what worked" in the traumatic state was a special and rare talent. In those situations in which the victims of persecution were not isolated but stayed with a group from home, preserving the capacity for socialization was perhaps the single most important resource favoring survival. In concentration camps and related experiences, no one survived without some help from others. The preservation of some capacity for social interaction was a great aid in maintaining one's own sense of humanity. The ability to form temporary alliances for survival and, when possible, to help someone, constituted a rare source of restoring a sense of being a "good person" and maintaining some self-respect.

When people were able to stay together with a group from home, they acquired a source of support to their humanity (Ornstein, 1985). The ultimate benefit of these social relations was the preservation of a viable human self-representation with some dignity. Although it was not possible to keep these principles in the forefront, it was essential to preserve the values and ideals built on the foundation of family and community life and traditions. The enduring self-view was built on a deep-seated sense of belonging in the context of a loving, sharing, and supportive family. I found an illustration of the preservation of such inner forces under the most extreme circumstances from a testimony of a *Sonderkommando* survivor: "We used to share everything. . . . When one of us was observed not sharing—we knew that he was on the way to become a Musulman" (Mark, 1988, p. 221). Under those unimaginable conditions of confrontation with death, having surrendered to the genocidal enemies and participated in their murderous design, group loyalty was the last protection against final withdrawal, surrender, and death.

Besides the traits that I have emphasized so far, which were trauma moderating, there were character traits that had survival value, with some variation according to the nature of the experiences one had. For most people, to survive, it was necessary to be flexible. The world of the Holocaust was ever changing and unpredictable. The kinds of things that people adjusted to exceed the power of our imagination. Children were separated from their parents. Those that survived had to be able to adjust to the conditions in which they found themselves—being kept alive temporarily until it was their turn to be subjected to "medical" experiments and then "sacrificed" just like laboratory animals. How could these children, who had already lost everyone they loved, function in the recognition that the doctors were not helpers but torturers and killers? They had to be capable of complete "psychic closing off." As for the children that had been in the Birkenau experimentation barrack, some managed to survive. They had bonded to each other and trusted no adults. This was still their condition after they were rescued and brought to the Hempstead Nursery (A. Freud and Dann, 1951). To this day, it is incomprehensible to the world, even though it was exposed and proven at least since 1986, that the entire German genocide program and its operation was the work of physicians (Lifton, 1986 and a movie based on his work in 1998, *Healing by Killing*).

The survival in ghettos, in camps, living on false papers—all required an extraordinary flexibility. With the sudden radical change of circumstances one had to land on both feet and forthwith use one's skills and resources. One had to be able to accept constant changeability and unpredictability, rather than stability, as the order of life.

An inner resource of enormous power was the ability to maintain some sense of continuing identification with something transcendental that would endure: God, the Jewish people—some "higher power." Robbed of their ability to trust God, many people derived emotional support from their internalized parental images or other benign introjects. The psychological regression in the infantilizing oppression and incarceration necessitated the evocation of idealized magical objects. In the absence of an actual mental representation of parents to pray to, one survivor used the image of the door handle of his home as his "survival image."

In considering concentration camp survivors' reaction to liberation, it is relevant to recall that some individuals experienced brief postliberation psychoses, for the most part persevering in continuing persecutory states. There seems to have been a need for a gradual termination of the traumatic state. Being able to monitor one's status, to regulate the rising complex feelings attending liberation, and to control the rate of increasing food intake were talents that had direct survival value. Nelly Sachs pleaded for the rescued, "Show us the sun, but gradually!" (Sachs, 1967, p. 145).

The task of psychological recovery required attaining the capacity to restore a sense of continuity and to return to an ability to anticipate the future with enthusiasm and vitality. Involved in "coming back" was the initiation of reconstruction, "piecing together of reconstructed memories, idealized childhood memories which were going to serve as inspiration, anchors and organizers" (Ornstein, 1985, p. 127). For the great majority of liberated survivors, life was totally disrupted, and all family was lost. As soon as people were well enough and had recovered from the shock of liberation, they became involved, in one form or another, in searching for the remnants of families and for fellow survivors to whom they had become attached. In general, the reestablishment of close groups and the creation of as many as possible joint activities were favorable developments.

Behind this tendency was the need to marry and reestablish families, and this was often experienced as an imperative to save the continuity of the Jewish people. This double motivation produced many hasty marriages based on some commonalities—finding someone with a familiar background, one coming from anywhere close to one's hometown or homeland. However, this behavior was, in part, problematic, because the task of reconstructing an acceptable worldview, the rebuilding of a reasonable and secure world order, had not yet been achieved. Above all, the capacity to love and feel loved was not yet restored. Symptomatic of poorly relieved regression was that inordinately many of the first pregnancies ended in miscarriages, and deliveries were often accompanied by a persecutory panic, sometimes expressed as the dread that the German doctors will kill the baby. When I speak of regression in the camps, one universal symptom of it was the cessation of menstruation by all women. Many of the same people were later in need of intervention and were identified as "numb" or "victim" families (Danieli, 1981).

For survivors, the anxiety was, at the core, derived from the question of how to deal with the (pre-persecution) notions of God. How was one to reconcile the idea of a benevolent, omniscient, and omnipotent God with what they had just witnessed? How was it going to be possible to resume a normal life pattern in a world that had betrayed the Jews and abandoned them to their destruction? How was one going to be able to experience love for a new spouse and children, when the lost ones could not be mourned? Is it any wonder that so many survivors became obsessed with the missing graves of the lost families?

The problem of survivor guilt was intensified by prewar indoctrination in a religious system that encouraged magical thinking. If neither God nor the survivor was crazy, then there was only one possible answer to the cause of the desolation: the failure of God to rescue His people meant that one's death wishes caused the devastation. To restore his fundamentalist belief in God and to avoid becoming overwhelmed with guilt, a rigid person would be driven to the one answer most survivors shunned: that the ones who perished were evil and brought the punishment on themselves. The survivors were brought up on the biblical tradition that explained all calamities that befell the Jews in this way, beginning with the story of the deluge.

Consequently, the generation of survivors who had lost their spouses and children in the Holocaust was condemned to a penitential lifestyle (Krystal, 1981). These were the kinds of emotional and moral dilemmas that plagued the survivors' families. Resilience here permitted a choice of atheism, or more commonly, of a slow and gradual return to traditional practices. Doubts and obsessions were often covered up with a driven, never-ending multiplicity of rituals (many minor ones and unrecognized as such) that accompanied every aspect of their lives.

This kind of adjustment permitted fairly good family functioning, albeit with a very common "affective anesthesia" pattern (Minkowski, 1946; Sifneos, 1967) and/or the breakthrough of symptomatic behavior such as mothers being too frightened to let their children out of their sight or vacillating from overprotectiveness to uncontrollable rages in which the children were sometimes called names like "Hitler." It would be unreasonable to expect survivors to be asymptomatic: we have been studying the various "Survivor Syndromes" ever since Niederland named them in 1961. The one thing we have learned and that we have been able to apply to a worldwide science of posttraumatic disorders is that every symptom and every problem represents creativity, a capacity for adjustment that at its genesis served to avert something worse. Most of all there is the clear indication that one's resilience is proportional to the capacity to mobilize one's love powers. Love outraged is experienced as anger or hate. Love rendered helpless manifests itself as shame. However, love represents the survivor's self-reintegrating and self-healing powers.

REFERENCES

The paper on which this chapter is based was read at the 41st International Congress of Psychoanalysis in Santiago, Chile, on July 28, 1999, and was awarded the Elisa M. Hayman Prize for research in Holocaust and Genocide. It was first published as Psychische widerständigkeit: Anpassung und Restitution bei Holocaust-Überlebenden in *Psyche Zeitschrift*, 54 (2000), Heft 9/10: 839–59. Reprinted with permission from *Psyche*.

Bomba, A. (1985). *The screenplay of SHOAH*. C. Lanzmann (Ed.). New York: Pantheon Books.
Brenner, I. (2001). *Dissociation of trauma, theory, phenomenology and technique*. Madison, CT: International Universities Press.
Cohen, J. (1985). Trauma and repression. *Psychoanalytic Inquiry*, 14: 163–89.
Danieli, Y. (1981). Differing adaptational styles in families of survivors of the Nazi Holocaust: Some implications for treatment. *Children Today*, 10: 34–35.
Dorsey, J. M. (1943). Some considerations of psychic reality. *International Journal of Psychoanalysis*, 29: 147–51.
———. (1965). *Illness or allness: Conversations of a psychiatrist*. Detroit, MI: Wayne State University Press.
———. (1971). *Psychology of emotion: Self conscious discipline by conscious emotional continence*. Detroit, MI: Wayne State University Press.
Freud, A., and Dann, S. (1951). An experiment in group upbringing. In Ruth Eissler, Anna Freud, Heinz Hartmann, and Marianne Kris (Eds.), *The psychoanalytic study of the child* (Vol. 6, pp. 127–68). New York: International Universities Press.

Krystal, H. (1973). *Psychic reality*. Paper read to the Michigan Psychoanalytic Institute. Farmington Hills, MI.

———. (1981). The aging survivor of the Holocaust. *The Journal of Geriatric Psychiatry*, 14: 165–89.

———. (1985). Trauma and the stimulus barrier. *Psychoanalytic Inquiry*, 5: 131–61.

———. (1988). *Integration and self healing*. Hillsdale, NJ: Analytic Press.

———. (1991). Integration and self healing in post traumatic states. *Journal of Geriatric Psychiatry and American Imago*, 48: 93–118.

———. (1995). Trauma and aging: A thirty-year follow-up. In C. Caruth (Ed.), *Trauma: Exploration of Memory*, pp. 76–99. Baltimore: Johns Hopkins Press.

———. (1997a). The trauma of confronting one's vulnerability and death. In C. Ellman and J. Reppen (Eds.), *Omnipotent fantasies and the vulnerable self*, pp. 149–85. Northvale, NJ: Jason Aronson.

———. (1997b, January). *Reflections on the psychology of survival and readjustment.* Address to the Second Reunion of Jewish Graduates from German Universities after World War II, Boca Raton, Florida.

———. (1997c). Late life effects of trauma: Adult catastrophic and infantile type. *Journal of Geriatric Psychiatry*, 30: 61–81.

———. (1998a). What cannot be remembered or forgotten. In J. Kauffman (Ed.), *Loss of the assumptive world: A theory of traumatic loss*, pp. 213–20. New York: Brunner-Routledge.

———. (1999, May). *Psychoanalytic approaches in posttraumatic, alexithymic, psychosomatic, and addictive patients*. Paper presented at The Michigan Psychoanalytic Society, "Milestone Program," Farmington Hills, MI.

Krystal, H., and Krystal, A. D. (1994). Psychoanalysis and neuroscience in relationship to dreams and creativity. In M. P. Shaw and M. A. Runco (Eds.), *Creativity and affect*, pp. 185–212. Norwood, NJ: Ablex Press.

Kumin, I. (1997). *Preobject relatedness: Early attachment and the psychodynamic situation*. New York: Guilford.

Lanzmann, C. (1985). *Shoah: An oral history of the Holocaust*. New York: Pantheon.

Laub, D. (1995). Truth and testimony: The process and the struggle. In C. Caruth (Ed.), *Trauma: Exploration of memory*, pp. 61–75. Baltimore: Johns Hopkins Press.

Lifton, R. J. (1976). *Life of the self.* New York: Simon & Schuster.

———. (1986). *The Nazi doctors: Medical killing and the psychology of genocide*. New York: Basic Books.

Mark, B. (1988). *The scrolls of Auschwitz*. Tel Aviv, Israel: Oved Publishing.

Meerloo, J. A. M. (1959). Shock, catalepsy, and psychogenic death. *International Record of Medicine*, 172: 384–93.

Minkowski, E. (1946). L'anesthesie affective. *Annal of Medicopsychology*, 104: 8–13.

Niederland, W. G. (1961). The problem of the survivor. *Journal of Hillside Hospital*, 10: 233–47.

Ornstein, A. (1985). Survival and recovery. *Psychoanalytic Inquiry*, 5: 99–130.

Ornstein, P. H. (1997). Omnipotence in health and illness. In C. Ellman and J. Reppen (Eds.), *Omnipotent fantasies and the vulnerable self*, pp. 117–30. Northvale, NJ: Jason Aronson.

Sachs, N. (1967). *O the chimneys*. New York: Farrar, Straus & Giroux.

Schore, A. N. (1994). *Affect regulation and the origin of the self: Neurobiology of emotional development*. Hillsdale, NJ: Erlbaum.

Seligman, M. E. P. (1975). *Helplessness: On depression, development, and death*. San Francisco: Freeman.

Shaw, R. (1967). *The man in the glass booth*. London: Chatto and Winders.

Sifneos, P. (1967). Clinical observations on some patients suffering from a variety of psychosomatic diseases. *Acta Medica Psychosomatica: Proceedings of the 7th European Conference on Psychosomatic Research, Rome*, 7: 452–58.

Westerlundh, B., and Smith, G. (1983). Perceptgenesis and the psychodymanics of perception. *Psychoanalysis and Contemporary Thought*, 6: 597–640.

Wilkinson, A. (1994, January 24). A change of the vision of God. *The New Yorker*, 69: 51–68.

Chapter Five

Disruption: Individual and Collective Threats

Mordechai Benyakar and Danielle Knafo

We enter a new century already marked by the devastating effects of ter-rorist violence. For mental health professionals, this state of affairs, of necessity, widens the scope of their focus and skills. The anxiety, help-lessness, and sense of meaninglessness that patients increasingly com-plain about are found to derive not merely from their psychic reality but, more and more, from the deterioration and collapse of their external en-vironments, environments on which they can no longer rely for security and support. In this chapter, we present a new diagnostic entity that we call the syndrome of anxiety by disruption (AbD) to address the clinical picture of growing numbers of patients and nonpatients who struggle with life under the threat of environmental violence in the form of ter-rorism and social or economic devastation. We describe the clinical manifestations, treatment implications, and imminent significance of these conditions.

Over the last fifty years, wars and combat situations have involved increasing numbers of civilian casualties (Crocq, 1997; Benyakar, 2000d). With the new realities of terror, the number of civilians who are affected has multiplied to unprecedented proportions. Today professionals in mental health as well as other disciplines are progressively made to confront the dramatic reality that surrounds them, a reality in which violence lies in the backdrop of our daily existence. There is a growing recognition that applying theoretical and clini-cal skills to one's social reality can no longer be viewed as a personal or al-truistic measure but, rather, essential for the emotional and physical preser-vation of humankind.

In this chapter, we will first describe a way of understanding how this re-ality has taken shape by clarifying the concepts of aggression and violence. Then, we will address the disruption that takes place in environments marked by violence and present the diagnostic syndrome, anxiety by disruption (AbD), we believe emerges in disruptive environments and needs to be recognized as we wrestle with new social realities. Finally, we will address treatment implications.

AGGRESSION, VIOLENCE, AND THE CHAIN OF EVIL

We would like to point to important distinctions between aggression and violence that help to highlight the changes faced by more and more people in the world today. Aggression and violence are, of course, human attitudes that provoke both physical and psychic damage (Lolas, 1991). In "Why War," Freud (1933) defined aggression as a drive, a tendency that leads man to destroy and kill and gratifies the intent to damage, upset, and humiliate others. Wars, unfair competition between companies, and enmity between political parties are only a few examples of *aggression* displayed on a massive scale.

In the case of aggression, one is aware of the identity of the aggressor, and this awareness allows one to prepare and defend oneself accordingly, both psychologically and practically. In line with Freud's second theory of anxiety that emphasizes anxiety as a signal to alert one of danger, we believe that clinical manifestations resulting from having been aggressed against belong to stress disorders. This is because that person is warned as to the identity of his or her opponent, which permits the possibility of developing defenses, facing the aggressor, fearing him, rejecting or defeating him. A good example of this is war. Soldiers go into combat knowing who their enemy is and what they need to do in order to protect themselves.

In the case of violence, on the other hand, the threat is masked, hidden, and nonspecific. It can only be foreboded and vaguely perceived (Girard, 1995). One is taken by surprise and, therefore, one feels trapped and unprotected. In addition, one is unable to discern from whence the threat comes and, therefore, cannot rely on one's judgment or perception. Most of all, it is impossible to feel one has a choice in behavior or in ways to defend oneself. Terrorism, unlike combat situations in war, has created a violent world, a world in which the enemy can be anywhere and might attack at any time. As a result, people who live in a violent world live lives pervaded with feelings of fear and helplessness (Benyakar, 2000a, 2002c; Kaës, 1979; Reinares, 1998; Gibeault, 2001; Lolas, 1991; Kernberg, 1992).

The state of defenselessness that results from living in a violent milieu is a state ripe for the propagation of hatred. We would like to illustrate this with a brief case vignette. David is a forty-five-year-old married man and a tender loving father who resides in Israel. Nevertheless, he recently surprised his family with his excessive attitudes, absurd restrictions, and risky decision making both in family matters and in matters relating to the successful business (originally his father's) he runs with his brother. His daughters do not comprehend the illogical interdictions to their activities he has implemented, especially since they contradict the more permissive parenting he displayed previously. David exclaims in his defense: "This is for everyone's good. There needs to be a little order around here. Punishment teaches the real way of life."

David's father, a man who appeared weak but had a strict attitude, taught the boys when they were young the difference between good and evil. David observed, "He would only punish us if we deserved it" in order to rationalize the brutal treatment and the beatings they received at his hands. As he was a concentration camp survivor, his legacy had been clear: "A man must know how to fight to defend himself."

David's mother, a corpulent woman, was also a Holocaust survivor. Although she had lost her entire family in the war, she never spoke about her experiences. Nonetheless, the two boys responded to her hatred that, despite its silence, was palpable. Unlike their father, she was tough inside and out, and David had no memories of intimacy or tenderness with her.

Of the two brothers, David was considered the "naughty boy." Because of his behavior, David's father administered ruthless beatings and punishments as "disciplinary" measures. Despite the harsh treatment he received, David insists, even in adulthood, that his parents were people "who sacrificed themselves for the good of the family."

When David began his compulsory army service in the Israel Defense Force, he did not wish to enlist in a combat unit, a popular choice among his friends. Instead, he accepted an administrative task. Years later, following a terrorist attack in Tel Aviv, David was heard saying, "The only solution is to kill all the Arabs."

When David was a boy, he had never come in contact with the Arab population in Israel. Along with his peers, he automatically embraced the belief that they were the enemy. His hatred toward Arabs increased and, today, he is an active member of a political party that claims the only way to achieve a peaceful life in Israel is to drive out all the Arabs. (This process has its parallel among Palestinians who state that the ones who must be expelled are the Jews.)

David, who had never physically attacked anybody, was destroying his own well-being and that of his family. We can ask: Is David an aggressive man? Is he violent? Where does his tendency to destroy what belongs to him come from? Is there a relationship between the hatred he harbors toward Arabs and his own life story? Is David an example of how the Chain of Evil functions?

Hatred is an innate human capacity; it is born of pain. Therefore, hatred is a way of relating to one's external world. Originally intended to abolish the source of pain, if it is not faced or elaborated, it can easily attach itself to another object that can, in turn, become a new source of hatred. In violent environments, individuals are unable to distinguish between their own sensations and those provoked by the external world, resulting in a situation in which blame can be spread indiscriminately. Blacks, Jews, Palestinians, women, and homosexuals all represent groups that have become such objects of hatred (Benyakar, 2000b; Aulagnier, 1979). The purpose of hatred is to put an end to one's pain, and it aims to reach this end by erasing the subjectivity of the one who feels it as well as the one to whom it is directed. The denial of subjectivity in oneself and others leads to "inhuman" attitudes and behaviors. And it is this process, a paradoxically quite human one, which nevertheless constitutes the essence of Evil (Baudrillard, 1991).

The evil that is embedded in terrorism and other violent acts causes physical pain or psychic damage or both to others by denying their subjectivity and power, and thereby inducing a sense of powerlessness and futility, what we refer to as the "traumatic experience." Thus, the repetitive cycle becomes self-perpetuating: damage, pain, and displeasure transform into diabolic action in the Chain of Evil (Benyakar, 1998).

DISRUPTION BRIDGES THE PSYCHOLOGICAL AND THE SOCIAL

Although Freud's theory of psychoanalysis began with an emphasis on external events (mostly sexual abuse) causing psychological disorders (primarily hysteria), his focus was on individual and interpersonal events rather than social or political forces that produce traumatic experiences. This, in addition to Freud's shift in attention from external to intrapsychic origins of pathology, has resulted in a theory that has, for some professionals, maintained a distinct separation between inner and outer realities and between self and other. This separation, we believe, has come at a cost because we perceive the inner and outer worlds as not possessing clear-cut boundaries, as previously hypothesized. Furthermore, we have witnessed a greater appreciation in recent decades of ways in which the external affects the internal and how the internal determines, and is affected by, the external.

Some of Freud's later writings readdress the impact of the external world on the inner world (Freud, 1925, 1940). The French school of psychoanalysis, including people like Green (1983, 1990) and Aulagnier (1977, 1979, 1994), Fain (1992), C. Botella and S. Botella (1992), and others; the English Middle School (Winnicott, 1971; Bion, 1965), Interpersonalists, and self-psychologists, as well as the relational, intersubjective, and postmodernist theories have all, in their own ways, attempted to relate the mutual influence of internal and external worlds. For example, Winnicott (1971, 1974), Ogden (1989), and Mitrani (1996) have proposed a third space to designate the overlap or meeting place of these worlds. Projective identification, a defensive operation initially postulated by Klein (1946, 1955), illustrates the mutual interaction and influence of the internal and external worlds on both self and other.

Despite these developments, which clearly bridge inner and outer worlds, they have not sufficiently extended to social or political states of threat, which include the impact of catastrophe or disaster. Disruptions caused by terrorism, one of the best examples of the threat of violence, constitute abrupt assaults to the individual and collective psyche (North et al., 1999). The question is not what is external and what is internal in these cases, but, rather, how to develop a clinical approach that treats internal wounds while taking into account their external origins and how to help those affected to survive in a disruptive environment without developing pathological forms of adaptation. Therefore, it is necessary to combine social and psychological worlds, all the while attempting to preserve what is characteristic and irreducible to each (Barton, 1969).

Social reality filters into our clinics without asking permission. Today new expressions of human suffering, resulting from disruptive social and political environments, compel us to reexamine what we think we know. They put to test established classifications (e.g., *Diagnostic and statistical manual of mental disorders [DSM–IV]*) and find them "incomplete and contradictory" because they are based solely on symptoms and oriented to the diagnosis of individual cases without heeding social elements in an important way (American Psychiatric Association, 1994; López-Ibor Aliño, 2002).

It comes as no surprise that a violent reality results in human suffering and mental illness. What features qualify a violent threat? The specific situation involving social catastrophe possesses the characteristics of (1) an atmosphere replete with unrecognizable, impalpable, and vague threats; (2) intentionally perpetrated by human actions; and (3) becoming a permanent condition in which to live. Perhaps the most paradigmatic example of this is Colombia, a country in which the military, paramilitary, and terrorists have become indistinguishable from one another as they walk the streets as part of its daily scenery. Extremist terrorism and the deleterious effects of globalization are creating maladaptive behaviors in the daily lives of increasing numbers of people worldwide. We propose to name this condition, prevalent in rising numbers of societies, *disruptive environments*. The seriousness of these situations represents an unavoidable challenge for professionals who work in the mental health field today. It is our view that this challenge needs to be met with urgency.

Disruptive environments are the result not of single events, such as a car crash or earthquake, but, rather, of a situation in which there is a constant, unidentifiable threat. Disruptive events refer to actual external events that implode the psyche, violent eruptions in social environments that threaten the inner world of its inhabitants. These changes, when persistent and unpredictable, have the power to turn a familiar surrounding into a threatening and alienated one, full of unknown, undetectable, and omnipresent menaces, and may result in mental disorders. We believe the word "traumatic" should not be used to label an event or milieu. We prefer to say that a situation is disruptive and that one's experience of that disruptive situation may or may not be a traumatic one. The word "trauma" should be reserved for internal processes—in this case, the breakdown of the articulation between affect and psychic representation.

The concepts of disruptive events and disruptive environments compel us to review the ways in which, until now, we have responded to catastrophes and their effects on people. The prevalent model has been, and remains today, that of natural disasters. This model deals with acute disasters that occur suddenly, do not last for a long time, and have devastating effects. In general, these are disruptive events. The natural disaster approach to catastrophe has prevailed even when dealing with situations like terrorist threats, situations that are unpredictable and usually last for long periods. Placing these two treatments on equal footing implies caring only for those people who have been directly injured and administering therapeutic interventions only during the short time following the event.

In fact, terrorism combines elements of "disruptive situations," that are acute, with those that are chronic and develop into disruptive environments. Terrorist acts burst into our lives violently, instantaneously, and unpredictably. They establish a state of permanent and generalized terror, a state in which people feel that although nothing might be happening at any given moment, something might happen at any moment. And although it is true that human beings possess the ability to adapt to even the most extreme conditions, as we witnessed with the Holocaust, terrorist attacks are periodic but unpredictable so as to awaken a sense of threat and perpetuate a state of fear and confusion (Kogan, 1990; Susser, Herman, and Aaron, 2002).

The pathogenic potential of disruptive situations and disruptive environments is enormous if appropriate measures are not taken before, after, and during the events. We believe that people can prepare themselves to develop resources and defend themselves from the traumatic effects of catastrophes, whether or not they are caused naturally or intentionally. This means populations need to be prepared and taught to recognize the type and magnitude of threats confronting them, know the individual or collective resources they have at their disposal, and organize themselves in order to act expeditiously and effectively during these episodes. Tadmor, Rubenstein, and Benyakar have named this ability *psychic immunity* (Tadmor et al., personal communication, 2003; Susser, Herman, and Aaron, 2002).

In this chapter, we attempt a broad approach within which to understand and address mental health problems that ensue from situations of acute and chronic disasters and catastrophes caused by human will. The characteristics of threatening and disorganizing environments, the psychological suffering they cause, and the challenges increasingly faced by therapists at the meeting point of social and individual factors present a complex and challenging task. How do we deal with the consequences that accompany implosions from the external world onto the human psyche? How can we handle a situation that casts therapists and their patients into the same psychosocial threat zone? The answers to these questions have conceptual as well as practical implications.

SYNDROME OF ANXIETY BY DISRUPTION

Terrorist threats provide the clearest example of *huis dos*, an existential condition of being trapped, so beautifully described by Jean Paul Sartre in his novel, *No Exit*. Because terrorist acts are indiscriminate, unforeseeable, spectacular, and highly symbolic, there exists no familiar mechanism to aid citizens' adaptation to disruptive environments. Fear and insecurity prevail and, above all, unpredictability renders any form of action pointless. AbD denotes symptoms generated in some people as a result of the basic challenge of living a life under such disruptive conditions.[1]

An example from a graduate class in adult psychopathology taught by me (Danielle Knafo, coauthor of this chapter) in Israel serves to illustrate our point. As a preface, Israeli students, suffice it to say, are very lively and opinionated, even when they have not read their assignments. In fact, as a teacher, one often has to interrupt them to get a word in. So, imagine my surprise when, one day, there was complete silence in response to my question, "what is stress?" I was about to speak about stress disorders, but I wanted a student to define stress first. Not one hand went up. Not one voice was heard. In fact, I looked out at a sea of puzzled faces. What was going on, I wondered. I asked again. The same thing happened for the second time. This time the silence went on for several minutes. I asked what the problem was; I asked whether anyone knew what stress was. Finally, one student offered, "But what is life without stress?" It was then that I understood that for Israelis stress is normative and therefore impossible to perceive as a disorder. An abnormal reaction to an abnormal situation can be normal behavior. Psychopathology, as other fields, must be understood within a cultural context.

In principle, we know that the syndrome AbD emerges because the psyche perceives institutions that ordinarily provide security as no longer capable of doing so. The links that associate some facts with others, and some causes with their effects, become blurred because these facts lose their prior significance. This becomes clear, for example, when an envelope containing a letter ceases to be a mode of communication and becomes, instead, a lethal weapon or when religious institutions' so-called guardians of souls offer refuge to child abusers. Parameters that hitherto supplied fixed references of meaning and safety erode and one's surroundings become distorted.

When a patient exclaims, "I am going mad because I know what is happening!" we assume that these words refer to his or her failure to develop adequate psychological and behavioral strategies to adapt to external and internal circumstances. Even though this patient may understand the threatening situation, it can still drive him or her mad. We have observed many patients in Argentina, Israel, and New York who suffer either from the inability to adapt to disruptive realities (Benyakar, Collazo, and DeRosa, 2002) or from pseudoadaptive mechanisms that they erect in response to living in disruptive environments.

"It's no longer possible to mourn the dead, because within a few hours there are more dead," says Avi Bleich, head of Tel Aviv University's Psychiatry Department (2002), commenting on the effects of routinization of terror in Israeli life. Journalist Stuart Schoffman replies to those who say to him, "I can't imagine what your life must be like right now" by detailing a typical day in Jerusalem. Among the items are these:

> Ran into a friend, we had coffee. Lighthearted conversation and did not think more than once or twice about the possibility of the café blowing up. He continues: Late lunch at friends' house, both journalists; husband made fabulous cholent [slow-cooking dish]. Wallow in the Situation, specifically the suicide bomber's head that blew off and crashed through a window of the hotel formerly called Hilton, on King David Street. *Dear All: Beyond the fear, absurdity.* What are we still doing here? we ask. I think of Gershom Sholem, pleading with his best friend Walter Benjamin to flee Hitler's Europe for Palestine, and pass the cholent (Schoffman, 2001).

Schoffman's move from anxiety and panic to domestic concerns is typical of daily coping with the Israeli "Situation" with a capital S. Doron Rosenblum recently wrote a tongue-in-cheek article in *Ha'Aretz* called "How I learned to stop worrying and find consolation in the situation: An ode to the miracle of adaptation." In it, he writes about the ironic adaptation Israelis have undergone over the last two years of the second *intifada* (Palestinian uprising) resulting in an increasingly absurd and restrictive lifestyle. Daily routines are much more calculated. Places are clearly demarcated. Many do not go to places that are not deemed absolutely necessary. Constant inventories are taken to locate where everyone in the family is at every moment. Rosenblum concludes, "each day is worse than the one before," so that people are hardly aware of the increasing adaptations they have had to make to accommodate it. At each new stage, rationalizations emerge to assuage the fears and mask the grotesque caricature of life as it has become in Israel.

The syndrome AbD, then, is a clinical entity that results from a specific relationship between the subject and his or her environment. The most important characteristic of this relationship is that disruptions cause it to be in perpetual flux. People who are psychologically affected by long-term exposure to a threatening situation over which they have no control suffer from symptoms of AbD. Psychological deterioration manifests in personal dysfunction as well as physical suffering (Benyakar, Collazo, and DeRosa, 2002).

If political, economic, and social resources cannot restructure the deterioration that takes place in commercial, educational, health, and recreational institutions, as well as the family lives of individuals, then one's quality of life becomes compromised and one's very existence threatened (Benyakar, 2002d). The so-called ghost towns in Argentina poignantly illustrate the remains of extreme social disintegration and individual pathological breakdown. Communities that suffer social disruption and crumbling institutions, as well as a total destabilization of norms, leave its citizens with nowhere to turn for assistance.

The Syndrome

Researchers, psychologists, and psychiatrists around the globe seem to agree that the following phenomena regularly appear in people subjected to social or political disruptions and life in disruptive environments:

- Cultural norms become embedded in an individual's subjectivity and regulate one's daily actions. Any sudden change in these norms can lead to the abolition of that person's symbolic resources.
- Confusion and disorientation accompany the perception that there are no opportunities available in the present. Not only is it difficult to act in the present, but it becomes impossible to set goals or lay down projects or dreams for a better future. Uncertainty with respect to the present and the future results in intense feelings of frustration and desperation.
- Personal experiences of neglect and impotence are the outcome of the breakdown of social institutions that had previously provided a framework of norms, but can no longer guarantee the rules of coexistence or fulfill the functions for which they were founded.

- Media repetition and sensationalism of terrorist events and disruptive situations perpetuate the sensation of being trapped, that no place is safe, and that there is no escape from threatening situations.
- A vague yet permanent fear, at times unrecognized, sets in as the result of living with the constant threat of danger from unidentifiable sources. This can reach a state in which the person fears leaving home, going out, or allowing one's children to be away from home.
- Fear causes feelings of suspicion, mistrust, and devaluation of others to grow deeper and more indiscriminate. These emotions may culminate in rage directed toward functionaries and politicians, people responsible for securing social norms and institutional stability.
- Distrust promotes isolation and this, in itself, exacerbates lack of confidence. A spiral is established that culminates in those affected behaving selfishly, indifferently, and hostilely toward others.
- This behavior is often quite distinct from a person's habitual behavior. Rather, these people are reacting to a bad state of affairs, to guilt feelings, and to attempts at finding ways to blame others.
- People who are unable to demonstrate their fury may fall victim to feelings of defenselessness and speechlessness, which sometimes renders them paralyzed.
- Changes in the rules of the game encourage feelings of uncertainty and impotence, which further hinder the capacity to make decisions or stick to them once taken or both. It is very common to see people who feel this way fall into states of extreme apathy or, contrarily, to resort to hyperactivity, which is wearing and ultimately without reward.
- Because people find this type of threat difficult to understand or explain, there is a need to cling to what is of absolute certainty in the midst of chaos. Alongside this need is the human tendency to find something visible and identifiable on which to place blame and vent frustration.
- States of minor confusion may appear. Some begin to doubt the validity of their feelings and perceptions, often rendering them dependent on others. These conditions are ripe for fanatic cult groups to thrive in. Such groups are usually led by charismatic leaders who offer absolute truths and a rigid structure of beliefs in which all questions are answered, doubts clarified, and decisions taken out of the hands of its followers.
- Many find it necessary to speak incessantly about what has happened and to repeatedly express their fears, insecurities, and lack of comprehension. It is as if they believe that in this manner fears can be dispelled, experiences can be validated, and people can confirm that the threat really does exist and that it is not a mere product of individual subjectivity or imagination.
- The compulsion to talk goes hand in hand with the ravenous consumption

of television news, radio, newspapers, magazines, gossip, and rumors all in the hope of obtaining information that offers clarity and peace of mind. Due to what feels like an insatiable need, some increase their consumption of such "information" to intoxicating levels, ultimately diminishing their judgment and critical abilities.

- In doing so, however, such people unconsciously transform into "chaos propagandists," those who magnify and strengthen the general ill feeling already extant in society. Therefore, fears of being personally involved in creating malaise and alarm in oneself and others—the last thing they consciously wish to do—result in identification and complicity with the very force that threatens them.
- This sensation of complicity is strengthened because it is not always possible to recognize the threat as entirely distinct or remote from the individual.
- The inability to control one's own actions is a terrifying experience frequently felt by those who live in an environment organized around terrorist threats. This is because whatever they do can end fatally by testing the terrorist's success.
- The sense that life is meaningless and behavior futile colors peoples' mood as well as motivation.

We would like to point up the phenomena with a discussion about one of Dr. Knafo's patients. Mr. A illustrates the hopelessness, irritability, and search for meaning that has become commonplace in many Americans after September 11. Although he was not directly affected by the disaster and did not lose anyone dear to him, it is clear that the events and their aftermath have had a profound and long-lasting effect on him. Mr. A, a very intelligent and professionally successful analytic patient, was the only patient of mine who remarkably failed to even mention the disaster in his sessions. Session after session, he was consumed only by his interpersonal problems. This neglect was so pronounced that the analyst's countertransference to him increased as I felt exasperated by what I perceived as his extreme narcissism and self-centeredness.

Then, one day, more than a month later, he entered the room a changed man. The usual glib, cocky, and joke-cracking Mr. A sat down saying simply that he was depressed. "What's going on in the world," he added, "makes me feel the end is near. I have to enjoy what I can. I can't take anything for granted anymore. I'm more honest and straightforward. Living day to day." Mr. A became silent for several minutes, which was very unusual for him, a man who used words and humor defensively. He broke the silence expressing dissatisfaction with his career, feeling that it was insignificant. "The big picture gets me. There is no meaning there. I feel purposeless." He expressed some envy for fundamentalists', albeit misdirected, sense of purpose after which he again fell silent.

This time, he stayed silent for the remainder of the session during which he avoided eye contact. It seemed that Mr. A was mourning his previous life, much of which he had taken for granted, and that he needed the silence. I needed to create a holding environment to contain his feelings of disillusionment and despair, to make sure he did not feel alone, and to offer continuity in a world in which everything around him was changing.

Since this session, Mr. A has continued to grapple with a growing sense of futility. He harbors fantasies of saving someone's life and dying in the process, as if he could only be a hero at the expense of his own life, clearly a manifestation of his survivor guilt. Perhaps more importantly, his fantasy represents the only way Mr. A finds hope that there is something useful and valuable he can do to battle the terror he feels and has seen.

Comparison with Other Syndromes

It may be immediately apparent that AbD possesses some features similar to disorders of general anxiety, depression, stress, and, of course, Post-Traumatic Stress Disorder. However, the symptom picture of those people with AbD does not neatly comply with the criteria that current classifications require in order to arrive at these diagnoses, and much of the phenomenology that exists in AbD does not appear in any other clinical entity. Due to environmental restrictions, people who suffer from AbD are unable to display adequate psychological or behavioral defenses. Symptoms, therefore, do not fit within the boundaries of stress or traumatic experience, even though elements of both are present (Shalev, 2000).[2] Several distinguishing features will be elaborated in the following list:

1. The disruptive situation does not cause psychic collapse and therefore should not be considered a traumatic experience.
2. The disruptive factor cannot be identified as a single threat that can be managed by the majority of people and, therefore, should not be thought of as a stress experience.
3. The syndrome AbD resembles dysthymic and anxiety disorders in that it can result in social, occupational, and family dysfunctions. Unlike these disorders, however, AbD originates in disruptions in the subjects' surrounding environment—specifically, the failure of economic and social institutions to fulfill their obligations to form and maintain individuals' norms and safety.
4. The AbD symptoms do not qualify for the classification of nonspecified anxiety disorder. In contradistinction to individuals who suffer from anxiety

disorders, known to hide or cover up their symptoms, those suffering from AbD possess a compulsive need to speak about and share their distress.

5. The most common manifestations of the syndrome are concentration difficulties; general disinterest in one's surroundings; feelings of helplessness; physical and mental asthenia; fatigue, restlessness, and impatience; lethargy or hyperactivity; occasional debilitating desperation; inability to plan for the future; the tendency toward melodrama or anhedonia; low self-esteem; sleep disruptions—insomnia or hypersomnia; and tendency to somatize and suffer from minor eating disorders.

6. The body is transformed into a receptor for anxiety in order to express what cannot be verbalized. As with somatoform disorders, physical symptoms paradoxically cause some relief. When a person's environment is severely disrupted, the body can be the sole vehicle in which a sense of continuity is found.

7. The syndrome AbD presents a unique problem for the therapeutic relationship since therapists are exposed to the same threatening environment affecting those they are in the position to assist.

At present, Dr. Benyakar is collaborating with Dr. Ezra Susser, Dr. Jack Gorman, and Dr. Carlos Collazo to validate the features that characterize the clinical manifestations of AbD in order to have it recognized within the various diagnostic systems that exist in the mental health field.

The Impact of Disruptive Environments on the Child's Ability to Plan

It is, we believe, of utmost significance to delineate not only the effects of disruption on adults but also the deleterious influence it has on child development. When social institutions deteriorate, as they do under prolonged disruptive conditions, children's ability to project into the future is severely compromised. That which permits a child to say: "When I grow up, I want to be . . . ." Or "When I grow up, I will have . . . " is no longer viable. The mass exportation of sons and daughters, which has taken place in Latin American countries, demonstrates that these societies do not offer their young valid, credible, and coherent guidelines by which to live and plan for a future. The inability to find an integrated, consistent, and coherent framework in one's environment to facilitate identification and planning results in children who are unable to look ahead or tie personal undertakings with social ventures. Instead, they feel disconnected and doomed to live out their lives in an eternal present (Benyakar and Schejtman, 1998; Critchlet, 1995; Aulagnier, 1997; Eliacheff, 1997; Pfefferbaum, 1997; Pynoos and Nader, 1993).

INTERVENTION: CHALLENGES FOR
THE MENTAL HEALTH FIELD

The general tendency to treat only those who are directly affected by disasters has potentially serious future implications. We believe that organized interventions in catastrophic situations must not only aid those who this affects directly but, also, attempt to alleviate the consequences for the general population who lives under threat and may develop maladaptive behaviors to try and cope with that threat.

What can the mental health profession do to prepare a population psychologically for calamity? Boaz Tadmor, Zohar Rubinstein, and Mordechai Benyakar (coauthor) have developed the concept of *psychic immunity* for these situations, a concept that possesses similarities to that of somatic or organic immunity. It was reasoned that one could develop adequate defenses by being exposed to the pathogenic factor in doses and during measured periods, as in the case of vaccines. From this perspective, denial is not considered an effective way to face terrorist threats. On the contrary, a person is deemed better prepared if he or she is exposed to what might take place when a terrorist attack hits.

Israelis who reside in New York were often singled out by their American brethren after September 11 because they seemed immune to the horrific events that had taken place on U.S. soil. It is as if having been exposed to terrorist threats and a life under terror in Israel had shored up their immunity to such events. Israelis themselves regarded their New York neighbors as neophytes who needed to acquire resilience in order to live a life under terrorist threat and attack. Steps that need to be taken in the process of acquiring psychic immunity are these:

1. Recognition of the external threat.
2. Recognition of the psychological capacities each individual has to face during threatening situations, stimulate them, and learn how to use them.
3. Taking of precautions and objective steps if and when the dreaded event(s) occur.

These three principles should guide programs aimed at preventative mental health care. Actions taken by mental health professionals have the power to stabilize populations' psychological health before it becomes pathological and to lessen the disruptive effects of the external world. Although we are part of that external world, we can offset the disruptive consequences by remaining consistent in our employment of containing and holding functions (Tadmor et al., personal communication).

What exactly do we treat in such situations? Initially, one should not be overly ambitious or all encompassing in an attempt to address every problem that arises. Instead, one's efforts should focus on peoples' capacity for psychological processing of events that have the potential to become distorted in their minds. Interventions should center on the human capacity to comprehend and elaborate the disruptive situation. Establishing a cathartic dialogue is very important; but in the cases we are referring to, interventions must be more precise in order to achieve their purpose. A useful dialogue acquires specificity depending on the moment and the location in which the intervention takes place as well as demographic and cultural characteristics of each population (Benyakar, 2003d).

During the Gulf War in Israel, for example, when people evacuated their homes to move to hotels, I (Benyakar) suggested that mental health professionals be the ones to provide towels, soap, and first aid supplies. In that manner, it was possible to establish a dialogue with those whose homes had been razed by missiles. Offering supplies to satisfy their basic needs opened the door to continued dialogue. This eventually allowed us to ascertain how they were processing the event as well as establish a relationship that would later evolve (Benyakar, Kretsch, and Baruch, 1994).

During a catastrophic event participation of mental health practitioners is essential. Yet, experience reveals that in catastrophic situations, the tasks related to the preservation of mental health can and must be carried out by all people involved. There are some kinds of intervention that we consider primary, or field interventions. People involved in primary interventions need to detect the degree of help needed by the affected population. Priests, neighbors, and psychiatrists can offer stability and security. But, it is best if mental health professionals are present, at least initially, to communicate what they deem important in terms of service delivery (Benyakar, 1996; 1999; 2002a).

The kind of leadership assumed in mental health interventions during catastrophic situations is also important. We would like to distinguish between structural and functional leadership. Structural leadership refers to the hierarchy of power and decision making in times of peace. This hierarchy may not, however, be the most useful in disruptive times. Therefore, a functional leadership, one that serves a function in a specific place and time, may be better suited to take over the assessment and care of those people most affected and in need of assistance (Benyakar, 2000b).

When the urgent phase subsides, specific treatment for those people who were directly affected commences. Keep in mind that although primary care is administered to those who are wounded and grieving, this is also a stage during which efforts at cultivating and maintaining psychic immunity must continue. Catastrophes continue to have direct and indirect repercussions over long periods.

Therapeutic interventions may be conducted individually, with families, or in groups. In catastrophic situations, it is advisable for mental health professionals to relinquish inflexible and dogmatic postures. They do not need to put aside their theoretical frameworks, which can guide their actions in these difficult moments; but they need to accommodate the reality to the theory rather than adjusting the theory to fit in with reality (Benyakar, 2002b, 2002c).

In addition to known cognitive-behavioral or psychodynamic treatments, clinical involvement during catastrophes requires a different type of intervention, what we call "intervention through presence." The implication here is that mental health professionals should be present at the moments and in the locations in which disasters take place. This presence permits the assessment of pathological clinical manifestations that will necessitate clinical interventions.

One must not forget that for every casualty or injured party in a given situation there are, in some cases, as many as two hundred people who are psychologically affected. Furthermore, most people who survive disasters develop psychological dysfunctions or symptoms that if not adequately attended to can turn into forms of chronic disorders. In sum, disruptions caused by terrorist attacks and terrorist threats confront mental health professionals with myriad complex challenges. If we do not heed these challenges, we run the risk of transforming AbD into the malady of the twenty-first century.

NOTES

1. Additional people deserving credit for advancing and conceptualizing this syndrome are Dr. Carlos Collazo, Dr. E. de Rosa, Dr. Alvaro Lezica, Dr. Jorge Garzarelli, Ines Hercovich, Dr. Nestor Perrone, Dr. Maria Teresa Herrera, Dr. Gustavo Tafet, and Susana Jallinsky.

2. At this time, the research department of the International Center for Mental Health in Disasters is evaluating and researching this syndrome in different environments and situations. Some teams, coordinated by the first author, are working at the Salvador University and the Buenos Aires University, along with Dr. C. Collazo, Dr. A. Lezica, I. Hercovich, M. T. Herrera, Dr. N. Perrone, Dr. J. Garzarelli, and Dr. G. Tafet; in the United States at Columbia University, the Mount Sinai Hospital, and Pace University; in New York, with Dr. E. Susser, Dr. C. Hoven, Dr. J. Gorman, Dr. J. Cancelmo, and Dr. H. Krauss; in Israel at Tel Aviv University, with Dr. B. Tadmor, Z. Rubenstein, and Dr. J. Zohar; in Spain at the Complutense University in Madrid, with Dr. J. J. Lopez Ibor and Dr. J. L. Carrasco.

REFERENCES

American Psychiatric Association. (1994). *Diagnostic and statistical manual of mental disorders* (4th ed.). Washington, DC.

Aulagnier, P. (1977). *Violence of interpretation*. Buenos Aires, Argentina: Amorrortu.
——. (1979/1994). *The destinies of pleasure: Alignment, love, passion*. Buenos Aires, Argentina: Editorial Paidós.
——. (1994). *An interpreter looking for sense*. México: Siglo XXI.
Barton, A. H. (1969). *Communities in disasters: A sociological analysis of collective stress situation*. New York: Doubleday.
Baudrillard, J. (1991). *La transparencia del mal*. Barcelona, Spain: Anagrama.
Benyakar, M. (1996). *Human resources in catastrophes: The psychiatrist's role*. Paper presented at the meeting of the X Congreso Mundial de Psiquiatría, Asociación Mundial de Psiquiatría (WPA). Simposio Internacional, Madrid, España.
——. (1998, octobre–diciembre). Agreslón y violencia en el milenio. La caden del mal (The Chain of Evil). Revista de Psicoanálisis, *Asociación Psicoanalítica Argentina*, 55 (4): 875–92.
——. (1999, agosto 6–11). *Disasters and catastrophes: A challenge for the assistance of civilians in peacetime*. Paper presented at meeting of the XI Congreso Mundial de Psiquiatría, Asociación Mundial de Psiquiatría (WPA), Hamburgo, Germany.
——. (2000a). Aggression of life and violence of death: The infant and environment. Buenos Aires, Argentina. Retrieved March 30, 2004, from www.winnicott.net
——. (2000b). Combat reaction facing traumatic experiences and stress. Buenos Aires, Argentina. Retrieved March 30, 2004, from www.psychoway.com
——. (2000c). *About certainties and uncertainties at the present time*. Paper presented at the meeting of the Preparatory Encounter for the Spanish Federal Congress of Teachers in Hearing and Language (FEPAL), Montevideo, Uruguay.
——. (2000d). *Combatant and civilian PTSD, stress and traumatic experiences*. Paper presented at the meeting of the International Jubilee Congress (WPA), Paris, France.
——. (2002a, January–March). Mental health and disasters new challenges. *Neurology, Neurosurgery and Psychiatry*, 34 (1), México.
——. (2002b). The frame and psychoanalytic space in the face of war and terror. In J. Cancelmo, I. Tylim, J. Hoffenberg, and Hattie Myers (Eds.), *Terrorism and the psychoanalytic space: International perspectives from Ground Zero*. New York; Pace University Press.
——. (2002c). Frame in social disasters, war and terrorism. In J. Raphael-Leff, *Behind the couch, between the sessions*, pp. 126–30. Colchester, UK: CPS Psychoanalytic Publication Series, University of Essex.
——. (2002d). *Human factors in mental health in disasters*. Lecture given at the XII World Psychiatry Congress, Yokohama, Japan.
——. (2002e). *Anxiety by disruption: A clinic reality*. Paper presented at the meeting of the Clinic Symposium. The 9th International Psychiatric Congress of the Argentine Association of Psychiatrists, Buenos Aires, Argentina.
——. (2003a). *Disruptive individual and collective threats: The psyche facing wars, terrorism and social catastrophes*. Buenos Aires, Argentina: Editorial Biblos.
——. (2003b, March 19–22). *Basic conceptualisations and interventions in disasters*. Paper presented at the LXIV Annual Reunion and International Congress on Neurosciences: Individual, Family and Society, Puebla, Mexico.

Benyakar, M., Collazo, C., and De Rosa, E. (2002). Anxiety by disruption. In *Interpsiquis*. Retrieved March 30, 2004, from www.psiquiatria.com

Benyakar, M., Kretsch, R., and Baruch, E. (1994). Mental health work with Gulf War evacuees: The use of a transitional therapeutic space. *Israel Journal of Psychiatry and Related Sciences*, 31 (2): 78–85.

Benyakar, M., and Schejtman, C. (1998, November). Mental health of children in wars, terrorist attacks and natural disasters. *Postdata Magazine of Psychoanalysis*. Homo Sapiens Edition. Fundación Estudios Clínicos en Psicoanálisis, 2 (3): 9–20.

Bion, W. (1965). *Transformations*. New York: Basic Books.

Bleich, A. (2002, June). Intercessory prayer for health: A matter of faith, science or both. *Harefuah*, 141 (6): 522–3.

Botella, C., and Botella, S. (1992). Néurose traumatique et cohérence psychique. *Revue Française de Psychosomatique*, 2: 25–36.

Critchlet, S. (1995). A theory of ethical experience. An entailment of a notion of the subject and possible implications for politics. In J. Raphael-Leff (Ed.), *Ethics of psychoanalysis*. London: Psychoanalytic Publication Series.

Crocq, L. (1997). The emotional consequences of war fifty years on: A psychiatrist's perspective. In L. Hunt, M. Marshall, and C. Rowlings (Eds.), *Past trauma in late life: European perspectives on therapeutic work with older people*, chap. 4, 39–48. London: J. Kingsley.

Eliacheff, C. (1997). *From child king to child victim: Familiar and institutional violence*. Buenos Aires, Argentina: Nueva visión.

Fain, M. (1992). La vie opératoire et les potentialités de néurose traumatique. *Revue Française de Psychosomatique*, 2: 5–24.

Freud, S. (1925/1926). Inhibitions, symptoms and anxiety. *Standard Edition*, 20, pp. 77–175. London: Hogarth Press.

———. (1933). Why War? *Standard Edition*, 22, pp. 197–215. London: Hogarth Press.

———. (1940 [1938]). An outline of psycho-analysis. *Standard Edition*, 23, pp. 104–207. London: Hogarth Press.

Gibeault, A. (2001). Violence, représentation et élaboration. Introduction to *Violence et destructivité*. Psychoanalyse et Psychose. Paris, France.

Girard, R. (1995). La violencia y lo sagrado. Barcelona, Spain: Anagrama.

Green, A. (1983). *Narcissism of life, narcissism of death*. Buenos Aires, Argentina: Amorrortu.

———. (1990). *The new psychoanalytic clinic and the theory of Freud*. Buenos Aires, Argentina: Amorrortu.

Kaës, R. (1979). *Crisis, breaking-off and overcoming: Transitional analysis, in individual and group psychoanalysis*. Buenos Aires, Argentina: Ediciones Cinco.

Kernberg, O. (1992). *Aggression in personality disorders and perversions*. New Haven, CT: Yale University Press.

Klein, M. (1946). Notes on some schizoid mechanisms. *International Journal of Psychoanalysis*, 27: 99–110.

———. (1955/1975). *On identification. In envy and gratitude and other works: 1946–1963*, pp. 141–75. London: Hogarth Press.

Kogan, I. (1990). A journey to pain. *International Journal of Psychoanalysis*, 71: 629–40.

Kohut, H. (1977). *The restoration of the self*. Madison, CT: International Universities Press.

Lolas, F. (1991). *Aggression and violence*. Buenos Aires, Argentina: Editorial Losada.

López-Ibor Aliño, J. (2002, August 24–29). *The psico(patho)logy of disasters*. Paper presented at the Plenary Conference of the World Congress of Psychiatry, Yokohama, Japan.

Mitrani, J. L. (1996). *A framework for the imaginary: Clinical explorations in primitive states of being*. Northvale, NJ: Jason Aronson.

North, C. S., Nixon, S. J., Shariat, S., Mallonee, S., McMillen, J. C., Spitznagel, E. L., et al. (1999). Psychiatric disorders among survivors of the Oklahoma City bombing. *JAMA*, 282: 755–62.

Ogden, T. (1989). *The primitive edge of experience*. Northvale, NJ: Jason Aronson.

Pfefferbaum, B. (1997). Post-traumatic stress disorder in children: A review of the past 10 years. *Journal of the American Academy of Child and Adolescent Psychiatry* 36 (11): 1503–11.

Pynoos, R. S., and Nader, K. (1993). Issues in the treatment of post-traumatic stress in children and adolescents. In J. P. Wilson and B. Raphael (Eds.), *International handbook of traumatic stress syndromes*. New York: Plenum Press.

Reinares, F. (1998). *Terrorism and antiterrorism*. Barcelona, Spain: Editorial Paidós.

Schoffman, S. (2001, December 31). A private peace. *Jerusalem Report*, p. 50.

Shalev, A. Y. (2000). Post-traumatic stress disorder: Diagnosis, history and life course. In D. Nutt, J. R. T. Davison, and J. Zohar (Eds.), *Post-traumatic stress disorder. Diagnosis, management and treatment*, chap. 1. London: Martin Dunitz.

Susser, E. S., Herman, D. B., and Aaron, B. (2002, Agosto). Combating the terror of terrorism. *Scientific American*, 287 (2): 70–77.

Winnicott, D. (1971). Transitional objects and transitional phenomena. In *Playing and Reality*. London: Tavistock.

Winnicott, C., Shepherd, R., and Dans, M. (Eds.). (1989). *Psycho-analytic explorations* by D. W. Winnicott. Cambridge, MA: Harvard University Press.

Part II

LIVING WITH TERROR

Dead Engineer–Kosovo *by Carolee Schneemann (1999).*

Between Bombardments

Karen Alkalay-Gut

I

Unable to move
waiting to be sprung
into action, we anticipate the sirens:
remembering the missiles of last night
targeting the people we love—
missing, missing, yet striking the heart:
the child choking on her vomit in her mask,
the old woman suffocating in unavoidable ignorance,
the psychotic whose nightmares came true.

II

We sit in the sealed kitchen with the dog,
the children all grown yet unschooled
in the blind hatred of aimed explosives.
We need each other, stroke each other,
the dog licks the rubber mask, nuzzles
the strange inhuman faces.
And then, when terror ebbs,
we remember the others,
reach for the phone:
are comforted
by comforting

III

False alarms spring us from our beds
fitting masks to our faces
still asleep. Someone must be enjoying
our terror, I think,
as we will learn
to enjoy theirs.

V

I think of Rena in Canada,
chewing her nails and screaming
when she recognizes the neighborhood of a hit
in Tel Aviv. Somehow her heart
reaches me, even here, even
hiding under the kitchen table with a quaking dog.

VI

Sleeping with a radio and a shivering dog
while my one-eyed man
scans the skies for missiles. Somehow

this is not the front I had imagined,
and all those handsome heroes
are missing.

VIII
"Think of the children in Baghdad"
the radio announcer tells the kids,
"how frightened they must be
—hiding in their shelters—
by the unrelenting bombing."
The news is on next—celebrations
high on Palestinian roofs
that our time to die has come.

XIII
My brother from New Jersey reminds me on the phone—
in the middle of a missile-ridden night—
of the metal table in the kitchen—the one
we would dive under when we heard
a loud noise in London
years after the blitz.
Where is that table
now?

XVI
CUSTOM
Tonight we wait for the alarm.
Who wants to get caught in the shower
or the toilet or in the middle of love?
You say, "I"ll wash my hair after
the attack" and I decide to put off
lacquering my nails, read
short poems about decadence instead
into the night—And it doesn't come—
And we take off our shoes and lie down
fully clothed, alert, prepared
for the sudden race to the shelter.
Even towards morning while the radio clock
shines out 3 and 4, illuminating
the passing minutes, we wait,
remember the shock of the 7:00 a.m. surprise.
Although I try to weary us with chapters from Jeremiah,
"I need my nightly missile," you say, "to fall asleep."

XVII
THE MOTHER OF ALL WARS
Oedipus tries to get to

the heart of all wombs
with 400 pound missiles
and we sit here, breathless
waiting for the next
thrust.

XVIII

"No, no sex," Eyal says. What man
can compete? This missile
gives it to all of us at once.
A war with no heroes, every man
for himself, every woman
fearing her own life,
everyone divided
from the others,
and with so many faulty options—
everyone divided against themselves.
"Even jerking off
can't do it."

XX

We hear what we fear—
listen for similar noises—
in particular the whirring motorcycles
that zoom down empty streets
as evening falls
and we begin to anticipate the sirens.
But even our names called aloud
anticipate adrenaline,
an alarm
to seek shelter.

XXII

Mike and his wife can't stop
fighting. Why does she leave
him every night to sleep
in some distant village?
Why can't she trust her husband
to protect her?
Our phone conversation is interrupted by a siren.
Two hours later, back in place, he calls to gloat:
the missile fell near her village.

XXIII

Instead of his leash
the dog brings my mask
to remind me of his walk.

XXIV

Nights without bombs are suddenly empty
Still alert, waiting at home—
remembering passionate friends in cafes
involved in each other
without thought of the skies.

XXVI

My sanest friend is sure a target
has been painted on her chest,
that the Iraqis with eagle vision
seek her out each night,
each missile aimed at her,
and only standard deviation
keeps her alive.

XVII

Some people terrified for their lives cut
themselves off in times like these. Even I
spent hours in my room, unable to face the rest
of the family those first days of war. Weeks
later we meet our friends like wary dogs,
sniffing from behind, asking about sex
and digestion before we can kiss and smell
the sweat that emerges now from deep inside.

XXVIII

"The next missile will be chemical,"
my gay friend predicts, "But who knows?
Maybe Zyclon 2 cures AIDS." For weeks
he has been alone, his lover torn from his arms,
hiding from him and the anguish outside wrapped
in rubber.

XXIX

And the voice of that man that always warms me more
than I expect is frost-bit now. I hear his control
on the answering machine and long
to rub that voice with ice the way my brother
would rub my hands reviving the blood
after long afternoons playing in the snow.

XXX

"Man like the generous vine supported lives,
The strength he gains is from the embrace he gives."
How often Pope's words return to me—that lonely outcast
who knew how much was needed and how much it cost.

XXXII

The morning after a three alarm night
I smell my mother in my bath
that acrid bloody woman-smell
filling the bath and becoming,
suddenly, sensual—a sign
the womb continues its tasks
when all outside is destruction.

XXXIII

Little Smadar gets an evening pep talk
from her British mother, about her fear
of extinction. "We must show that nasty man
we don't care. That is the part we Israelis play
in this war."
And in the morning Smadar asks, tentatively:
"Do you think Saddam will notice
that one little girl is frightened?"

XXXV

"Who do you think you are?
A post-modern Anna Frank?"
a friend remarks when he sees
I keep a journal. She
died when I was born,
I reply, why not continue
the keeping of accounts.

XXXVII

Fluttering between war and Purim,
the little fairy princess watches
the latest SCUD victims evacuated
from the Army compound in Riyadh,
takes both her masks, waves
her magic wand, and goes off
to school.

XXXVIII

And now it seems it will go away, this
threat that has hung over our skies
like Joe Bl*$*#&%#$'s cloud for so many days—
thirty nine missiles. But my daughter just now
is engulfed in terror for the first time,
seeing how she has changed
irrevocably.

XXXIX
So we begin to plan
our adult purim costumes
as if back into the swing of things.
Diane paints formulas on her face
to parade with me down the street
as a chemical warhead, and I can't think
of how to conceal what I have become
even though I expect to drink
until I can't distinguish.

PARDESS
The floor of the orchard is green,
orange and yellow. All the fruit
that wasn't picked
in time, victims
of the war, slowly returns
to the earth—emitting
an acrid smell like all
the days we have wasted
waiting for missiles
to shatter our windows
our lives.

Chapter Six

Is Hiroshima Our Text?

Robert J. Lifton

I was recently told that a prominent Zen Buddhist leader in this country has made a vow to himself that in any conversation he enters into he must bring up the subject of nuclear threat. That includes—so the story goes—the most casual social conversations, talks with taxi drivers, brief exchanges with strangers, whatever. The vow did not sound strange to me. Without being quite aware of it, I had, in effect, made a similar, if much more modest, vow to myself: that in any public statement I make on nuclear threat, I will bring up the subject of Hiroshima.

My strong impulse is to convey to everyone Hiroshima's indelible impact on me. And I also have come to sense, as both psychiatrist and antinuclear activist, the special power of specific Hiroshima or Nagasaki images for those able to receive them. Images that extreme are best described in relatively quiet, understated tones that encourage reflection on our contemporary situation. The themes put forward in this chapter (originally from a chapter of mine in a book coauthored with Richard Falk, Indefensible Weapons*) are meant to portray Hiroshima not as an event of the past but as a source of necessary knowledge for the present and the future.*

Those Hiroshima images continue their insistent claim on me: the searing details of survivors' experiences; the moving scenes, collective pain, and ultimate inadequacy of the August 6 day of commemoration; and our own bittersweet family celebration, with a few Hiroshima friends, of our son's first birthday. Put most simply, the six months spent in Hiroshima in 1962 have formed in me a special constellation of truth that when I am wise enough to draw on it, informs everything I have to say about nuclear threat and much else.

I arrived in Hiroshima in the early spring of 1962. I intended no more than a brief visit. But very quickly I made a discovery that I found almost incomprehensible. It had been seventeen years since the dropping of the first atomic weapon on an inhabited city—surely one of the tragic turning points in human history—and no one had studied the impact of that event. There had of course been research on the physical aftereffect of the bomb, and there had been brief commentaries here and there on some of the survivors at the time of the bomb and afterward. But there had been no systematic examination of what had taken place in people's lives, of the psychological and social consequences of the bomb.

I came to a terrible, but I believed essentially accurate, rule of thumb: the more significant an event, the less likely it is to be studied. Again, there are reasons. One reason, certainly relevant to Hiroshima, has to do with the fear and pain the event arouses—the unacceptable images to which as an investigator one must expose oneself. To this anxiety and pain I can certainly attest.

But another source of avoidance is the threat posed to our traditional assumptions and conventional ways of going about our studies. We would rather avoid looking at the events that by their nature must change us and change our relation to the world. We prefer to hold on to our presumptions and habits of personal and professional function. And we may well sense that seriously studying such an event means being haunted by it from then on, taking on a lifelong burden of responsibility to it.

I was able to stay in Hiroshima and conduct interview research with people there over a six-month period. The best way I know of how to describe a few of my findings that might be of use to us now is to look at the Hiroshima experience as taking place in four stages.

The first stage was the immersion in the sea of the dead and near dead at the time the bomb fell. This was the beginning of what I have called a permanent encounter with death. But it was not just death: it was grotesque and absurd death, which had no relationship to the life cycle as such. There was a sudden and absolute shift from normal existence to this overwhelming immersion in death.

Survivors recalled not only feeling that they themselves would soon die but experiencing the sense that *the whole world was dying*. For instance, a science professor who had been covered by falling debris and temporarily blinded remembered: "My body seemed all black. Everything seemed dark, dark was all over. Then I thought, 'The world is ending.'" And a Protestant minister, responding to scenes of mutilation and destruction he saw everywhere, told me: "The feeling I had was that everyone was dead. The whole city was destroyed. . . . I thought all of my family must be dead. It doesn't matter if I die. . . . I thought this was the end of Hiroshima, of Japan, of humankind." And a writer later recorded her impression:

> I just could not understand why our surroundings changed so greatly in one instant. . . . I thought it must have been something, which had nothing to do with

the way, the collapse of the earth, which was said to take place at the end of the world, which I had read about as a child. . . . There was a fearful silence, which made me feel that all people . . . were dead (Lifton, 1967, pp. 22–23).

As psychiatrists, we are accustomed to look on imagery of the end of the world as a symptom of mental illness, usually paranoid psychoses. But here it may be said that this imagery is a more or less appropriate response to an extraordinary external event.

In referring to themselves as "walking ghosts," or as one man said of himself: "I was not really alive," people were literally uncertain about whether they were dead or alive, which was why I came to call my study of the event *Death in Life: Survivors of Hiroshima* (1967).

Indicative of the nature of the event is the extraordinary disparity in estimates of the number of people killed by the bomb. These vary from less than 70,000 to more than 250,000, with the city of Hiroshima estimating 200,000. These estimates depend on whom one counts and how one goes about counting, and they can be subject at either end to various ideological and emotional influences. But the simple truth is that nobody really knows how many people the Hiroshima bomb has killed, and such was the confusion at the time that nobody will ever know.

The second stage was associated with what I call "invisible contamination." Within hours or days or weeks after the bomb fell, people—even some who had appeared to be untouched by the bomb—began to experience grotesque symptoms: severe diarrhea and weakness, ulceration of the mouth and gums with bleeding, bleeding from all the body orifices and into the skin, high fever, extremely low white blood cell counts when these could be taken, and, later, loss of scalp and body hair—the condition often following a progressive course until death. These were symptoms of acute radiation effects. People did not know that at the time, of course, and even surviving doctors thought it was some kind of strange epidemic. Ordinary people spoke of a mysterious "poison."

But the kind of terror experienced by survivors can be understood from the rumors that quickly spread among them. One rumor simply held that everyone in Hiroshima would be dead within a few months to a few years. The symbolic message here was this: none can escape from the poison; the epidemic is total—all shall die. But there was a second rumor, reported to me even more frequently and with greater emotion: the belief that trees, grass, and flowers would never again grow in Hiroshima; that from that day on, the city would be unable to sustain vegetables of any kind. The meaning here was that nature was drying altogether. Life was being extinguished at its source— an ultimate form of desolation that not only encompassed human death but also went beyond it.

These early symptoms were the first large-scale manifestation of the invisible contamination stemming from the atomic particles. The symptoms also gave rise to a special image in the minds of the people of Hiroshima—an image of the force that not only kills and destroys on a colossal scale but also leaves behind in the bodies of those exposed to it deadly influences that may emerge at any time and strike down their victims. That image has also made its way to the rest of us, however we have resisted it.

The third stage of Hiroshima survivors' encounter with dead occurred not weeks or months but years after the bomb fell, with the discovery (beginning in 1948 and 1949) that various forms of leukemia were increasing in incidence among survivors sufficiently exposed to irradiation. That fatal malignancy of the blood-forming organs became the model for the relatively loose but highly significant term "A-bomb disease." Then, over decades, there have been increases in various forms of cancer—first thyroid cancer and, then, cancer of the breast, lung, stomach, bone, bone marrow, and other areas. Since the latent period for the radiation-induced cancer can be quite long and since for many forms it is still not known, the results are by no means in. Researchers are still learning about increases in different kinds of cancers, and the truth is that the exposure to radiation can increase the incidence of virtually any form of cancer.

An additional array of harmful bodily influences either have been demonstrated, or are suspected, to be caused by radiation exposure—including impaired growth and development, premature aging, various blood diseases, endocrine and skin disorders, damage to the central nervous system, and a vague but persistently reported borderline condition of general weakness and debilitation. Again, the returns are not in. But on a chronic level of bodily concern, survivors have the feeling that the bomb can do anything, and that anything it does is likely to be fatal. Moreover, there are endless situations in which neither the survivors themselves nor the most astute physicians can say with any certainty where physical radiation effects end and psychological manifestations begin. There is always a "nagging doubt." For instance, I retain a vivid memory of a talk I had in Hiroshima with a distinguished physician who, despite injuries and radiation effects of his own, had at the time of the bomb courageously attempted to care for patients around him. He spoke in philosophical terms of the problem of radiation effects as one that "man cannot solve"; but when I asked him about general anxieties he smiled uneasily and spoke in a way that gave me the strong sense that a raw nerve had been exposed:

Yes, of course, people are anxious. Take my own case. If I am shaving in the morning and I should happen to cut myself very slightly, I dab the blood with a piece of paper—and then, when I notice that it has stopped flowing, I think to myself, "Well, I guess I am all right." (Lifton, 1967, p. 54)

Nor does the matter end with one's own body or life. There is the fear that this invisible contamination will manifest itself in the next generation, because we know scientifically that radiation can cause such abnormalities. There is medical controversy here about whether genetic abnormalities have occurred: they have not been convincingly demonstrated in studies on comparative populations, but abnormalities in the chromosomes of exposed survivors have been demonstrated. People, of course, retain profound anxiety about the possibility of transmitting this deadly taint to subsequent generations. For instance, when I visited Hiroshima in 1980, people said to me, " Well, maybe this generation is okay after all, but what about the third generation?" The fact is that, scientifically speaking, no one can assure them with certainty that subsequent generations will not be affected. Again, nobody knows. So there is no end point for the possible damage or for anxiety.

No wonder, then, that a number of survivors told me that they considered the dropping of the bomb a "big experiment" by the United States. It was a new weapon; its effects were unknown; American authorities wanted to see what those effects would be. Unfortunately, there is more than a kernel of truth in that claim, at least in its suggestion of one among several motivations. More important for us now is the idea that any use of nuclear warheads would still be, in related sense, "experimental."

The fourth stage of the Hiroshima experience is its culmination in a lifelong identification with the dead—so extreme in many cases as to cause survivors to feel "as if dead" and to take on what I spoke of as an "identity of the dead." Hiroshima and Nagasaki survivors became, in their own eyes as well in those of others, a tainted group, one whose collective identity was formed around precisely the continuous death immersion and the invisible contamination I have been discussing. The identity can include what we think of as a paradoxical guilt—the tendency of survivors to berate themselves inwardly for having remained alive while others died and for not having been able to do more to save others or to combat the general evil at the time of the bomb. In connection with the latter, the sense of "failed enactment" (Lifton, 1979, p. 174) can have little to do with what was possible at the time or with what one actually did or did not do.

More than that, survivors underwent what can be called a second victimization in the form of significant discrimination in two fundamental areas of life: marriage and work. The "logic" of the discrimination was the awareness of potential marriage partners (or families and go-betweens involved in making marriage arrangements) and prospective employers that survivors are susceptible to aftereffects of the bomb, making them poor bets for marriage (and healthy children) and employment. But the deeper, often unconscious, feeling about atomic bomb survivors was that they were death tainted, that they were reminders of a fearful event people did not want to be reminded of, and that they were "carriers," so to speak, of the dreaded A-bomb disease.

At the end of my study of these events, I spoke of Hiroshima, together with Nagasaki, as a last chance, a nuclear catastrophe from which one could still learn. The bombs had been dropped; there was an "end of the world" in ways I have described; and yet the world still exists. And precisely in this end-of-the-world quality of Hiroshima lies both its threat and its potential wisdom.

Is Hiroshima, then, our text? Certainly as our only text, it would be quite inadequate. We know well that what happened there could not really represent what would happen to people if our contemporary nuclear warheads were used. When the Hiroshima and Nagasaki bombs were dropped, they were the only two functional atomic bombs in the world. Now there are about fifty thousand nuclear warheads, most of them having many times—some a hundred or a thousand or more times—the destructive and contaminating (through radiation) power of those first "tiny" bombs. While those early bombs initiated a revolution in killing power, we may speak of another subsequent technological revelation of even greater dimensions in its magnification of that killing power. The scale of Hiroshima was difficult enough to grasp; now the scale is again so radically altered that holding literally to Hiroshima images misleads us in the direction of extreme understatement.

Yet despite all that, Hiroshima and Nagasaki hold out important nuclear-age truths for us. The first of these is the *totality of destruction*. It has been pointed out that Tokyo and Dresden were decimated no less than was Hiroshima. But in Hiroshima, it was one plane, one bomb, one city destroyed. And incalculable death and suffering was the result of that single bomb.

A second Hiroshima truth for us is that of the weapon's unending lethal influence. Radiation effects were (and are) such that the experience has had no cutoff point. Survivors have the possibility of experiencing delayed but deadly radiation effects for the rest of their lives. That possibility extends to their children and to their children's children, indefinitely into the future—over many generations; no one knows. And we have seen how the psychological blends in relation to these continuing effects.

A third truth, really derived from the other two, has to do with Hiroshima and Nagasaki survivors' identification of themselves as *victims of an ultimate weapon*—of a force that threatens to exterminate the species. This sense had considerable impact on Hiroshima survivors, sometimes creating in them an expectation of future nuclear destruction of all of humankind and most of the earth.

And there is still something more to be said about Hiroshima and Nagasaki regarding our perceptions of nuclear danger. The two cities convey to us a sense of *nuclear actuality*. The bombs were really used there. We can read, view, and, if we allow ourselves, *feel* what happened to the people in them. In the process we experience emotions such as awe, dread, and wonder (at the extent and nature of killing, maiming, and destruction)—emotions that can surely transform our intellectual and moral efforts against nuclear killing into a personal mission—one with profound ethical, spiritual, and sometimes religious overtones. Hiroshima, then, is indeed our text, even in miniature.

The argument is sometimes extended to the point of claiming that this sense of nuclear actuality has prevented full-scale nuclear war; that in the absence of restraining influence of Hiroshima and Nagasaki, the United States and the Soviet Union would have by now embarked on nuclear annihilation. The claim is difficult to evaluate, and while I feel some of its persuasiveness, I do not quite accept it. In any case, one must raise a countervailing argument having to do with another dimension of Hiroshima and Nagasaki's nuclear actuality; namely, the legitimating of a nation using atomic bombs on human populations under certain conditions (in this case, wartime). Once a thing had been done, it is psychologically and, in a sense, morally easier for it to be done again. That legitimating can then combine with an argument minimizing the effects of the Hiroshima bomb: the claim that one has unfortunately heard more than once from American leaders that Hiroshima's having been rebuilt as a city is evidence that one can fight and recover from a limited nuclear war.

Here I may say that a part of Hiroshima's value as a text is in its contrasts with our current situation. One crucial contrast has to do with the existence of an outside world to help. Hiroshima could slowly recover from the bomb because there were intact people who came in from the outside and brought healing energies to the city. Help was erratic and slow in arriving, but it did become available: from nearby areas (including a few medical teams); from Japanese returning from former overseas possessions; and, to some extent, from the American Occupation. The groups converging on Hiroshima in many cases contributed more to the recovery of the city as such than to that of individual survivors (physically, mentally, or economically). But they made possible the city's revitalization and repopulation.

In Hiroshima there was a total breakdown of the social and communal structure—of the web of institutions and arrangements necessary for the function of any human group. But because of the existence and intervention of an intact outside world, that social breakdown could be temporary.

Given the number and power of our current nuclear warheads, can one reasonably assume that there will be an intact outside world to help? I do not think so.

Like any powerful text, Hiroshima must be read, absorbed, and recreated by each generation searching for its own truths.

REFERENCES

This chapter is reproduced from Robert J. Lifton (1983), *Indefensible Weapons.* New York: Basic Books. Reprinted by permission of Basic Books, a member of Perseus Books, L.L.C.

Lifton, R. J. (1967/1982). *Death in life: Survivors of Hiroshima.* New York: Basic Books.
Lifton, R. J. (1979/1983). *The broken connection: On death and the continuity of life.* New York: Basic Books.

Chapter Seven

Cambodians and Massive Trauma: What We Have Learned after Twenty Years

J. David Kinzie

One of the major tragedies of the last fifty years was the rise of the brutal Pol Pot regime in Cambodia from 1975 to 1979. This regime was responsible for a terrible genocide of the Cambodian people. Out of this mass killing emerged some very traumatized refugees, a number of whom came to the United States. This report summarizes clinical and therapeutic experiences with Cambodian patients who lived in Portland, Oregon. I describe the Intercultural Psychiatric Program (formerly the Indochinese Psychiatric Program), the results of studies with Cambodian refugees by our own group and others, and the clinical guidelines for treatment. First, I provide a brief history of Cambodia and the Pol Pot experience.

CAMBODIA AND POL POT

The history of ancient Cambodia with its center, Angkor ("holy city," in Sanskrit), reveals a vibrant culture in the early Iron Age (500 B.C.–A.D. 400). Beginning in about A.D. 600, a central government was formed, and a series of powerful kings expanded the kingdom and began the construction of temples at Angkor (Higham, 2001). In the 1100s, seventy thousand people allegedly constructed the most famous temple, Angkor Wat. Angkor was abandoned in 1431 after a Thai invasion. It was "found" again by Portuguese visitors between 1550 and 1600. The Angkor complex near the city of Siem Reap is now a large tourist attraction.

In this century, the kingdom of Cambodia was pulled into the Indochina War. The Lon Nol government replaced Prince Sihanouk. After the fall of Vietnam in 1975, the radical Marxist government of Pol Pot led the Khmer Rouge to gain control of the country. Through its brutal Communist regime, the Khmer Rouge isolated the country and cut it off from the outside world. The regime attempted to remove all traces of previous influence. People representing traditional and Western values were systematically killed, including teachers, Buddhist monks, businesspersons, military leaders, and doctors. Contemporary writings well document the death and destruction (Hawk, 1982; Becker, 1986). Between one and three million of the population of seven million Cambodians died under this regime. Hundreds of thousands were executed. Most died of starvation and disease brought about by the forced urban evacuation to brutal labor camps. In these crude camps, husbands were separated from wives, and children above the age of six were placed in age-related camps away from their families' influence. The very fabric of Cambodian life was destroyed—contact with the past, with religion, with the educational system, and with the family was completely eliminated.

In 1979, Vietnam invaded Cambodia and Pol Pot and his followers fled to the hills. Many Cambodians were fortunate enough to cross into Thailand, a difficult and dangerous trip, where they remained in refugee camps until some became legal refugees in the United States and other countries in the 1980s.

The Intercultural Psychiatric Program (IPP) was originally established to serve refugees from the Indochina War in 1977. The primary patients were Vietnamese refugees. It has operated on the same principles for the past twenty years. The treatment is implemented by a faculty psychiatrist at Oregon Health & Science University, assisted by a mental health counselor who is of the same culture as the patient. The counselor, trained especially for mental health assessment, also serves as interpreter and case manager. Currently, the senior Cambodian counselor has been with the program for over twenty years, as have the two Cambodian psychiatrists, J. David Kinzie and J. K. Boehnlein.

In 1980, the program began treating its first Cambodian patients. They were different from the Vietnamese, not only in culture, but also in their clinical presentations. They seemed frightened, guarded, and reticent to talk. When they did, they revealed profoundly disturbing stories, sometimes with a muted affect.

The catastrophic genocide, with its appalling human suffering, has given us the opportunity to work with these gracious people for over twenty years. It has also given us the opportunity to study the effects of massive psychological and physical trauma and to try to develop effective treatment. The following is a summary of our efforts so far.

CLINICAL PHENOMENOLOGY

The trauma suffered by the Cambodians was catastrophic. Table 7.1 shows a summary of the experiences under Pol Pot. The American Psychiatric As-

Table 7.1.   Summary of Trauma Experiences Under the Pol Pot Regime Reported by
35 Adult Patients and 40 Adolescents (N=75)

	N	%
1. Forced labor, often 15 hours a day, 7 days a week for 4 years	69	92%
2. Separation from family	59	79%
3. Long periods of starvation	51	81%
4. Family members lost through execution or starvation or whose whereabouts are unknown	63	84%
For the adolescents, N=40:		
5. "Lost" and presumed dead fathers	25	63%
6. "Lost" and presumed dead mothers	15	38%

sociation, *Diagnostic and Statistical Manual of Mental Disorders–Third Edition* (*DSM–III*) was published in 1980 and gave the first operational description of Post-Traumatic Stress Disorder (PTSD). It became apparent that that was what our patients were suffering from. We devised a scale and a structured interview based on the PTSD criteria and interviewed patients using these methods. The first thirteen patients all qualified for the PTSD diagnosis (Kinzie, Frederickson, Ben, Fleck, and Karl, 1984). To our knowledge, this was the first diagnosis of PTSD using operational criteria in a non-Western population. Most of the patients were also diagnosed with depression. Twelve of the thirteen were given the same structured interview one year later (Boehnlein, Kinzie, Ben, and Fleck, 1985), and five had improved so that they no longer qualified for the diagnosis. This improvement showed predominantly in a reduction of nightmares, insomnia, and startle reactions.

There was little improvement in avoidance behavior, sense of shame, or poor concentration. Improvement was attributed to supportive, consistent psychotherapy, and the administration of tricyclic antidepressants. This moderately optimistic outlook has been tempered over time, because all members of this group subsequently suffered many relapses. As described in the proceeding, PTSD among Cambodians is a chronic, relapsing disorder. In the first hundred traumatized Cambodian patients with PTSD, seven also were found to have severe, persistent psychotic symptoms indistinguishable from schizophrenia (Kinzie and Boehnlein, 1989). This group did not differ from the nonpsychotic group in the severity of trauma experienced, but its symptoms were extremely disruptive. Several patients required hospitalization. It is apparent that psychosis can result from massive trauma among Cambodians, and we also have evidence that it exists in other traumatized refugee groups.

COMMUNITY STUDIES

In the 1980s, we became aware of some difficulties Cambodian adolescents were having in school. We performed a psychiatric evaluation on forty Cambodian students using structured interviews and *DSM-III* criteria. From the age of eight to twelve, these children had endured separation from their parents, forced labor, and starvation and had witnessed many deaths during the Pol Pot regime. Fifty percent of this group had PTSD, and 53 percent had a depressive disorder, usually of an intermittent type (Kinzie, Sack, Angell, Clark, and Ben, 1986). Information was also gathered from their families and from their schools.

The students subjectively and privately reported more distress than was observed by their caretakers. Those with a psychiatric diagnosis were more likely to be rated by their teachers as withdrawn rather than disruptive (Sack, Angell, Kinzie, Manson, and Rath, 1986). Twenty-seven students were reevaluated three years later and thirteen (48 percent) were diagnosed with PTSD using the *DSM–III–R* (American Psychiatric Association, 1987) (Kinzie, Sack, Angell, Clarke, and Ben, 1989). Sixty-one percent of those who were originally diagnosed with PTSD still met the criteria for diagnosis. There were new cases as well as remissions. In a six-year follow-up of this group, nineteen were reexamined and 32 percent had PTSD (Sack et al., 1993). It was found that depressive symptoms greatly decreased over time in contrast to PTSD, which remained relatively constant.

In a large study of other Cambodian adolescent survivors of Pol Pot (Sack et al., 1994), a structured interview (Diagnostic Interview for Children and Adolescents [DICA]) was given to 209 subjects about thirteen years after exposure to trauma. Of these, 18.2 percent were diagnosed with PTSD, and a high rate of PTSD was found in the parents of those youths— 55 percent in the mothers and 30 percent in the fathers. There was a strong relationship between the diagnosis of PTSD in the parents and in the children. When neither parent had PTSD, only 12.9 percent of the children met the diagnostic criteria. When one parent had PTSD, the rate rose to 23.3 percent. With both parents diagnosed, the adolescent rate increased to 41.2 percent.

To determine the incidence of war-related PTSD as separate from the stress of resettlement, ninety-nine Khmer youths in refugee camps in Thailand were administered the DICA, *DSM-III-R* version. Of these, 26.3 percent met the criteria for Pol Pot-related PTSD (Savin, Sack, Clarke, Meas, and Richart, 1996). In another study of refugees on the Thai border, symptoms of depression were present in two-thirds and PTSD in one-third of the population (Mollica, Pool, and Tor, 1998).

THE CAMBODIAN FAMILY

The refugee Cambodian family has been and continues to be under an enormous amount of stress. Traditional Cambodian values include a strong family identity, which provides a foundation for personal identity and self-worth (Boehnlein, Kinzie, and Leung, 1997). Children, even adult children, are expected to carry out parental decisions. Elders are revered for their age and experience. Eighty-five percent of Cambodians are Buddhist, and the teachings influence familial and social norms of behavior. In addition to the effects of trauma, acculturation to a new environment puts stress on both generation and gender roles. Elder refugees have a diminished status in the family and society because of their lack of language skills and of employment opportunities.

A major source of conflict is generational, with parents (often only a single mother) expecting obedience from children. There is increased pressure from parents who lost other children and have a need for closeness, which they interpret as respect and obedience. The children increasingly feel "American," independent about dating, employment, and moving away from home. All these pressures place a strain on the Cambodian families, who find themselves isolated and without extended family and societal support. We are increasingly aware of domestic violence, delinquency, rising school dropout rates, early pregnancy, and elder abuse occurring in Cambodian families. Massive trauma clearly has intergenerational effects on Cambodian as well as other groups (Kinzie, Boehnlein, and Sack, 1998).

STUDY OF NIGHTMARES

One of the persistent complaints of Cambodians has been the experience of nightmares of terrifying events, which often occur every night. They are severely disturbing as well as disruptive to sleep. To evaluate treatment options, we performed all-night polysomnographs on four untreated Cambodian women (Kinzie, Sack, and Riley, 1994) (figure 7.1). Two consecutive all-night recordings were done in each of the patient's homes with four patients and a research assistant observing them. The sleep record as well as the observations of reported nightmares was obtained. The process was then repeated after two weeks' treatment with clonidine. Clonidine is an antihypertensive agent, which acts by blocking the release of norepinephrine in the central nervous system. Lowering norepinephrine is thought to be the mechanism of reducing PTSD symptoms. Sleep patterns improved and nightmares markedly diminished after the clonidine treatment. These results added to the empirical evidence for the value of clonidine in reducing some PTSD symptoms. Symptoms of depression were not improved.

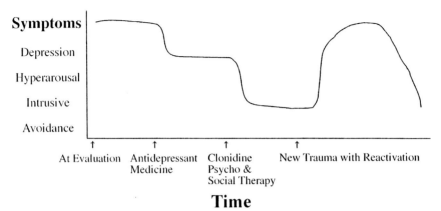

Figure 7.1.   Course of Trauma-Related Symptoms

REACTIVATION STUDIES

Another consistent finding in PTSD is the reactivation of symptoms with reminders or symbols of the actual events of the original trauma. Indeed, many
Cambodians who have been relatively asymptomatic will show a full return
of symptoms with an assault, car accident, disturbing news from home (especially requests by relatives for money), and the televised war in the Persian
Gulf or Bosnia. We wanted to determine if this hyperarousal state was specific to Cambodian or similar traumas or a more generalized reaction. We
showed five videotapes depicting a hurricane, an auto accident, a Cambodian
refugee camp, domestic violence, and Vietnam combat scenes. In overt behavior as well as heart rate increase, the Cambodians showed the greatest
number of reactions to all scenes. A Vietnam War veterans group surprisingly
showed the fewest reactions, while the control group was in between. The results indicate that physiological reactivation is a phenomenon among Cambodians, who tend to generalize to all emotionally arousing material (Kinzie,
Denny, Riley, Boehnlein, McFarland, and Leung, 1998).

An almost universally disturbing event was the World Trade Center bombing on September 11, with massive television coverage. Our refugee patients
from all cultures immediately reported a marked increase in their symptoms,
especially nightmares and intrusive memories of their own traumas. We administered a brief clinically oriented questionnaire to our clinic population of
Vietnamese, Cambodian, Laotian, Bosnian, and Somali patients. The
strongest reaction to this television coverage was among the newest groups,
the Bosnian and Somali PTSD patients. The Somalis have the greatest deterioration of subjective sense of safety. The Cambodians reported some change

in nightmares and flashbacks and depression but not as much as the Bosnians and Somalis. They showed the least effect of all groups in feeling safe. It is likely that enough time in the United States, twenty years for most, has passed, so that they do not feel as threatened as the more recent arrivals from Bosnia and Somalia (Kinzie, Boehnlein, Riley, and Sparr, 2002).

TREATMENT ISSUES

The effects of the severe trauma and loss suffered by the Cambodian refugees are shown in a diagnosis of 110 patients currently in treatment as of August 2002:

PTSD plus depression	79%
Depression alone	6%
PTSD plus schizophrenia	4%
Schizophrenia alone	7%
Alcohol abuse	2%

The psychiatric diagnosis is only one part of the issue that needs to be addressed. Housing, employment, medical coverage, and especially socialization to remove a sense of isolation in a foreign country are major unmet needs. Our program for Cambodians includes the following components (Kinzie, 1986):

1. Treat major diagnoses as listed in the preceding.
2. Address the language issues.
3. Meet the cultural expectations of treatment.
4. Provide easy access to services.
5. Establish credibility within the Cambodian community.
6. Provide clear linkage with emergency outpatient and inpatient services.
7. Provide social support and education to help the adjustment to the American community.

These services have been provided with the aid of a Cambodian mental health counselor who serves as interpreter for the psychiatrists and, after training, as case manager and socialization group leader. As we are part of a general medical facility, all services are linked, and our program is accessible to the emergency room and inpatient units. After patients were successfully treated, credibility within the community was established and referrals increased.

Medicine is a major component of treatment as it can reduce symptoms and suffering, often quite rapidly. This is not straightforward, as our first attempts with tricyclic medication resulted in a high rate of noncompliance (Kinzie, Leung, Boehnlein, and Fleck, 1987). When we checked patients' blood levels, only 22 percent of the patients' levels were in the therapeutic range and 39 percent had no medication in their blood. The Cambodians complained of the side effects, saying that American medicine was "too strong." After education about the benefits and side effects of the medicine, compliance improved greatly, with 44 percent of the patients' levels being in the therapeutic range and only 22 percent being undetectable.

Antidepressants have proven to be useful not only for depressive symptoms but also for some PTSD symptoms. There have been both benefits and side effects in the use of tricyclics, such as imipramine and doxepin, and the Selective Serotonin Reuptake Inhibitors (SSRIs), like fluoxetine and sertraline. As discussed previously, clonidine has been especially valuable for nightmares and hyperarousal (Kinzie and Leung, 1989). For most patients with PTSD and depression, a combination of antidepressants and clonidine is useful.

For psychotic symptoms, the atypical antipsychotics olanzapine and risperidone have been useful, however, the side effects of olanzapine, weight gain and a tendency toward diabetes, are a problem in a group in which the prevalence of diabetes is about 10 percent. Both olanzapine and risperidone have also been used with clonidine for PTSD symptoms.

We have found that group therapy of a special type has been very helpful (Kinzie et al., 1988). The therapy, which uses ethnic mental health counselors, sometimes in conjunction with American therapists, emphasizes socialization and education. Socialization often involves traditional activities such as cooking and preparing for celebrations, both American and Cambodian. Practical education about health, medicine, raising children, and transportation are common themes. There is no attempt to review losses or past traumas. The primary goal has been to create a community by sharing experiences and reducing isolation.

INDIVIDUAL PSYCHOTHERAPY

The devastating effect of trauma on Cambodians leads to a PTSD-depression complex, which is often chronic, with remissions and exacerbations often produced by memories of past trauma. Therapy must be guided by these realities.

Many problems occur in therapy with Cambodians, often centering on the different expectations about the therapeutic process held by the patient and the American doctor. The Cambodian patient usually expects the doctor to be actively involved in diagnosis, to focus on symptoms, and to prescribe medication to rapidly reduce these symptoms. The therapist, on the other hand, may be passive and may expect psychological treatment to be a long process without immediate results. These are conflicting expectations and can lead to disappointment on both sides. Often the Cambodian patient leaves treatment. A second problem can be the rigid therapeutic bias of the therapist.

Some therapists have the need to go over the trauma repeatedly in a hope that exposure will lead to a cure. Not only is this countertherapeutic for patients who are reexperiencing the trauma every day in intrusive memories and nightmares, but it works against the Cambodian concept of karma in which events are to be accepted rather than controlled or even understood. An equally destructive bias on the part of Cambodians is the belief that Western psychiatry has nothing to offer them and that their own native healers should treat them. Their refusal of current treatments and medicines does them a severe disservice.

The most useful approach (with a competent interpreter) is to present a friendly, open, flexible interpersonal style. The therapist needs to be active in taking a history, paying serious attention to the chief complaint, usually somatic symptoms such as headache and poor sleep (Kinzie, 1981). It is important to go through the symptoms of major depression and PTSD. A few screening questions about psychosis are asked, and more if there is indication of psychosis. Then a history of the patient's life is taken, including the psychosocial life before the trauma. Many Cambodians had a difficult life even before Pol Pot. Only after going through that does the interviewer go into the traumatic events. These are often remembered incompletely with "gaps" in either actual memory or reporting. This is extremely difficult for patients, as they often have been avoiding these very memories. Sometimes the death of important people in their lives has not been "remembered." It is to be expected that the interviewing will make the patients "worse and worse," that is, reactivate past memories and increase nightmares for a time.

The interview continues, following the continuity of the patient's life. What was the escape process like? What was the experience in the refugee camp? What has life been like in the United States? A history of medical problems and current stressors including domestic and financial issues is taken.

The patients are asked if they have any questions—concerns about mental illness are usually unspoken. Before negotiating treatment, it is important to give a formulation to the patient that makes sense and fits with her own understanding of her life. A common concluding remark is:

You are a strong person but even a strong person breaks down under severe stress. You have had severe stress. You went through four years without enough food, were beaten, and saw many people die including two of your own children. Your husband was taken away and never seen again. After that, you lived in a refugee camp before you came to the United States. When you came here, you didn't know the language and had very little money to raise your children. Now your mind and body are showing the effects of these stresses. You have pains, you can't sleep, feel sad, and all the bad things keep coming back to you in nightmares and in your thoughts. This makes it hard for you to learn and causes you to sometimes feel frustrated and angry.

This review of events and symptoms provides a current story to which most patients can agree. It also sets the stage for follow-up treatment.

I usually take blood pressure and perform some physical exam of an affected part. Hypertension is a common disorder and this "laying on of hands" helps to establish a relationship. Clonidine is useful for treating hypertension as well as symptoms of PTSD.

To negotiate treatment I review many of the patient's symptoms and ask which one or two are the most important to treat—for example, poor sleep, headache, or anger. I can usually prescribe medicine that alleviates these symptoms as well as more generally treat PTSD and depression.

At the close I explain the desired effects and side effects of the medicine and the frequency of future visits. This usually occurs after an hour-and-a-half interview, the time it usually takes to do this evaluation. At the end, sometimes I tell the patient the following: "You have three things to do. Take your medicine, keep your appointments, and you can't kill yourself." Suicide is not a high risk, but I mean to imply that I take the patient's life and treatment seriously. This authoritative stance seems to resonate with the patient's expectation of the authority figure taking care of them.

Follow-up appointments are regular, predictable, and occur in a calm, friendly atmosphere. We ask about the symptoms, as well as ongoing pressures and stresses. Raising children is a common issue. Other themes include financial pressures, relatives, and medical problems, and these themes carry over from session to session, providing continuity. Medicine adjustments are made based on treatment response. These adjustments are often minor during quiescent periods but can require major changes during exacerbation.

There is no attempt to urge or force a patient to recount the traumatic events again. However, two conditions are necessary in order for this to occur. One is that the intrusive symptoms are reduced, and the second is that the patient wants to talk about her experiences.

Unlike current technique-driven therapies, such as exposure or behavioral therapy, our experience indicates that the important aspect of a therapeutic relationship is a safe and predictable setting (Kinzie, 2001). Four aspects of the therapist need to be emphasized:

1. The ability of the therapist to listen to the horrific stories without over- or underreaction.

2. The ability of the therapist to stay over time with a variable course of treatment. This provides constancy and prevents premature termination over temporary improvement.
3. The ability to react appropriately to the giving of gifts by the Cambodian patients. Small gifts are commonly given to healers and teachers as a sign of respect. Accepting these gifts aids in the healing process.
4. The ability of the therapist to help patients find meaning in a world of evil. This involves the therapist's own personal quest for the sacred, the belief in the value of human relationships, the unity of humankind, and the possibility of the transformation of patients and ourselves. The therapist needs to have faced these problems herself in order to help the patients answer some of these very difficult and at times impossible questions.

Clearly, the process of psychotherapy is a long and complicated one, assisted in the reduction of symptoms by medication and the supportive, constant presence of the therapist. It is important to be ethically grounded and therapeutically competent to guard against countertransference feelings. At the very early stages of treatment, fidelity (being true to the patient) and nonmalfeasance (do no harm) should be the guiding principles (Kinzie and Boehnlein, 1993). As trust and confidence develops, beneficence, that is, providing competent care, becomes the primary ethical principle. Later, encouraging autonomy and pursuing justice come into play. It is important that the therapist maintain self-interest by monitoring his own needs and finding ways outside of the patient's therapy to cope with the intense emotions aroused.

CASE EXAMPLE: PHAT

Phat, a Cambodian female, began treatment over ten years ago. At that time, she was thirty-four years old and had come to the United States nine years previously. She was self-referred because, she stated, "I feel sad. I've lost everything." The patient had a very traumatic past and a difficult marital situation. Her husband left her four years prior, and she had developed symptoms since that time. Her symptoms included little sleep, difficulty enjoying anything, being tired much of the time, and irritability. She had nightmares one or two times a week of gory, bloody scenes of killing. These were the reexperiencing of actual events in Cambodia. She had intrusive thoughts of her life in Cambodia. When she heard traumatic events on the news, she had marked reexperiencing of other phenomena. She felt as if she was constantly on guard and had much difficulty relaxing. Her marital history was complicated. She was forced to marry a man in 1976 during the Pol Pot regime. They had spent only a brief time together but were reunited in 1979. At that time, her husband had a new girlfriend. They had frequent separations, and when they came to the United States, they were finally parted for good, four years before this visit. She had a child through an affair with another man. That man left her in 1988, and she felt abandoned again.

Phat was born in a rural area of Cambodia, had three years of education, and was separated from her family at the age of twenty against her will, when Pol Pot came to power. She underwent four years of forced labor, during which time her captors beat her several times on the legs. One night she heard shots fired, and the next day she saw a large number of corpses. One of her siblings was killed by the Pol Pot regime, but her other siblings and her parents made it out alive. Subsequently, she had four children, including the last one from her affair with the other man. Since then, she has been raising the children alone.

She presented herself as a very sad-appearing woman, crying frequently throughout the interview and getting very anxious while she discussed the events of the past. Her diagnosis was PTSD and Major Depressive Disorder.

During her ten years of treatment, she has been seen both in individual therapy and in a socialization group. She has experienced multiple social pressures, which have affected her treatment. Later she reconciled with her boyfriend, who was quite abusive, especially when he was drinking heavily. Her eight-year-old daughter developed some permanent brain damage secondary to a ruptured cerebral aneurysm and had to spend several weeks in a nursing home. Her daughter became oppositional ever since that time, with a short attention span and periodic outbursts. There were stresses from calls from Phat's relatives in Cambodia and from refusals of several of her children to attend school. In addition, her boyfriend periodically was picked up for drinking and was sent to jail. During this time, she developed hypertension and was placed on lisinopril, an ACE inhibitor, to control her blood pressure. Periodically, the difficulties with her brain-damaged daughter would worsen and cause her to have ongoing pressures. The daughter saw a child psychiatrist on several occasions but did not follow through on treatment. Phat developed phlebitis in her left leg and had to be on coumadin for a time. She continued to have ongoing problems with her children. All of this left her with multiple symptoms of PTSD and depression.

For a time, things improved, with the children going to school and much less pressure at home. However, some pressures remained that caused symptoms to increase, for example, when there were calls for money from her relatives in Cambodia. Apparently she had been more involved with her boyfriend than she let us know. Again he was arrested, but this time he was sent to a federal penitentiary for multiple violations. Once more she became extremely sad and felt very alone raising her children. Ultimately she went back to her husband who beat and robbed her and who she said lied to her. She felt brokenhearted about this and became very angry, experiencing increased nightmares and increased depression. The boyfriend in jail continued to ask for financial support. He promised to change and not to drink again.

She became very sad following the September 11 bombing in New York. It brought back some memories to her, and soon after that her hypertension greatly increased and she had marked increased symptoms of PTSD.

At the last visit she had improved a great deal, feeling more optimistic about her future. Her children seemed to be going to school, and she felt she would be able to maintain an equal relationship with her boyfriend once he returned from prison. Her blood pressure was also under control.

This patient continued her treatment and showed both the effect of acute trauma and the ongoing stresses. Throughout this, the group and the individual therapy provided constancy, support, and reassurance. It helped her through the despairing moments and gave her symptomatic as well as medical relief for her multiple symptoms. Clearly, the treatment is not over, as her life continues to evolve with both current stresses and past memories.

Comments on Phat

For myself as the treating psychiatrist, this patient represents the problems and joys of treating Cambodians. It is clear that treatment is long term, and it is important for the therapist to have a long-term perspective. This requires not getting too excited by the patient's improvements or too discouraged about the inevitable setbacks. The therapist represents a stable continuity in the chaotic world of the refugee patient. I did not go into the past Pol Pot traumas but rather provided clarification and support around ongoing "traumas"—her child's severe illness, the abusive relationships with men, and her hope that her jailed boyfriend had reformed. Her past losses and severe traumas left her alone, vulnerable, and desperately seeking affection and companionship. I did not interpret this but reflected with her on the difficulties of life and the problems of being alone. I mildly cautioned her that her boyfriend may find change difficult and that she may be disappointed in the future. We (the counselor and I) say directly and indirectly that we will be there for her regardless of what happens. Medicine to control her psychiatric symptoms and blood pressure provides not only symptomatic relief but also a daily reminder of her doctor, which is reassuring to her.

I saw my roles as physician, advisor, friend, and support fulfilling some roles that were missing in her life. The weekly socialization groups formed social activities, which decreased her sense of isolation. Her major symptoms of nightmares, poor sleep, depression, and anger significantly diminished over the past ten years, but she remains vulnerable and has exacerbations of symptoms with increased stressors in her life.

My own reactions are typical—admiration of how she has carried on with enormous trauma and ongoing stress and anger about the human condition that allows this to happen to people. My reflections on the evil in the world are frequent (I also treat patients from Somalia and Central America). These reflections are probably not apparent to Phat since our sessions are relaxed (no matter how difficult her life is), supportive, and usually injected with touches of humor sometimes directed at myself, for example, mispronouncing Cambodian words. I think she knows I like her, which I do, and I feel she appreciates my efforts and me. Perhaps this is the core of a therapeutic relationship.

CONCLUSION

We now know from the experience with Cambodians as well as other refugees that severe trauma can produce symptoms of a PTSD-depression complex. This can be differentially treated in the context of a therapeutic relationship with antidepressant medicine and clonidine as shown earlier in figure 7.1. Socialization group therapy further reduces social isolation and avoidance behavior. A subjective sense of shame (or survivor guilt) remains. Under new stress, traumas, or reminders, all symptoms can return, although with continued treatment they are not as severe or last as long. The PTSD-depression syndrome is a chronic-relapsing disorder, which may require lifetime therapy.

REFERENCES

American Psychiatric Association. (1980). *Diagnostic and statistical manual of mental disorders* (3rd ed.). Washington, DC: Author.

———. (1987). *Diagnostic and statistical manual of mental disorders* (Rev. ed.). Washington, DC: Author.

Becker, E. (1986). *When the war was over*. New York: Simon & Schuster.

Boehnlein, J. K., Kinzie, J. D., and Leung, P. K. (1997). *Cambodian American families*. In E. Lee (Ed.), *Working with Asian Americans: A guide for clinicians*. New York: Guilford.

Boehnlein, J. K., Kinzie J. D., Ben, R., and Fleck, J. (1985). One year follow up study of post traumatic stress disorder among survivors of Cambodian concentration camps. *American Journal of Psychiatry*, 142 (8): 956–59.

Hawk, D. (1982). The killing of Cambodia. *New Republic*, 198: 17–21.

Higham, C. (2001). *The civilization of Angkor*. Berkeley: University of California Press.

Kinzie, J. D. (1981). Evaluation and psychotherapy of Indochinese refugee patients. *American Journal of Psychotherapy*, 35: 251–61.

——. (1986). The establishment of outpatient mental health services for Southeast Asian refugees. In C. L. Williams and J. Westermeyer (Eds), *Refugee mental health in resettlement countries*, chap. 14, pp. 217–31. Washington, DC: Hemisphere Publishing.

——. (2001). Psychotherapy for massively traumatized refugees: The therapist variable. *American Journal of Psychotherapy*, 55 (4): 475–90.

Kinzie, J. D., and Boehlein, J. K. (1989). Post traumatic psychosis among Cambodian refugees. *Journal of Traumatic Stress*, 2 (2): 185–98.

——. (1993). Psychotherapy of the victims of massive violence: Countertransference and ethical issues. *American Journal of Psychotherapy*, 47 (1): 90–102.

Kinzie, J. D., Boehnlein, J. K., Riley, M. A., and Sparr, L. (2002). The effects of September 11 on traumatized refugees: Reactivation of posttraumatic stress disorder. *Journal of Nervous and Mental Disease*, 190 (7): 437–41.

Kinzie, J. D., Boehnlein, J. K., and Sack, W. H. (1998). The effects of massive trauma on Cambodian parents and children. In Y. Danieli (Ed.), *International handbook of multigenerational legacies of trauma*, 221–21. New York: Plenum Press.

Kinzie, J. D., Denny, D., Riley, C., Boehnlein, J. K., McFarland, B., and Leung, P. (1998). A cross-cultural study of reactivation of post traumatic stress disorder symptoms. *Journal of Nervous and Mental Disease*, 186: 670–76.

Kinzie, J. D., and Fleck, J. (1987). Psychotherapy with severely traumatized refugees. *American Journal of Psychotherapy*, 41 (1): 82–99.

Kinzie, J. D., Frederickson, R. H., Ben, R., Fleck, J., and Karl, W. (1984). Post traumatic stress syndrome among survivors of Cambodian concentration camps. *American Journal of Psychiatry*, 141: 645–50.

Kinzie, J. D., and Leung, P. K. (1989). Clonidine in Cambodian patients with post traumatic stress disorder. *Journal of Nervous and Mental Disease*, 177 (9): 546–50.

Kinzie, J. D., Leung, P., Boehnlein, J., and Fleck, J. (1987). Anti-depressant blood levels in Southeast Asians: Clinical and cultural implications. *Journal of Nervous Mental Disease*, 175 (8): 480–85.

Kinzie, J. D., Leung, P. K., Bui, A., Ben, R., Keopraseuth, K. O., Riley, C., et al. (1988). Group therapy with Southeast Asian refugees. *Community Mental Health Journal*, 24 (2): 157–66.

Kinzie, J. D., Sack, W., Angell, R., Clarke, G., and Ben, R. (1989). A three-year follow-up of Cambodian young people traumatized as children. *Journal of American Academy of Child and Adolescent Psychiatry*, 28 (4): 501–5.

Kinzie, J. D., Sack, W., Angell, R., Manson, S., and Rath, B. (1986). The psychiatric effects of massive trauma on Cambodian children. *Journal of American Academy of Child Psychiatry*, 25 (3): 370–76.

Kinzie, J. D., Sack, R. L., and Riley, C. M. (1994). The polysomnographic effects of clonidine on sleep disorders in post traumatic stress syndrome: A pilot study with Cambodian patients. *Journal of Nervous and Mental Disease*, 182: 585–87.

Mollica, R. F., Poole, C., and Tor, S. (1998). Symptoms, functioning, and health problems in massively traumatized populations: The legacy of Cambodian tragedy. In

B. P. Dohrenwend (Ed.), *Adversity, stress, and psychopathology*, 34–51. New York: Oxford University Press.

Sack, W., Angell, R., Kinzie, J. D., Manson, S., and Rath, B. (1986). The psychiatric effects of massive trauma on Cambodian children: II. The family, the home and the school. *Journal of American Academy of Child Psychiatry*, 25 (3): 377–83.

Sack, W. H., Clarke, G., Him, C., Dickason, D., Goff, B., Lanham, K., et al. (1993). A six-year follow-up study of Cambodian adolescents. *Journal of the American Academy of Child Psychiatry*, 32: 431–37.

Sack, W. H., McSharry, S., Clarke, G. N., Kinney, R., Seeley, J., and Lewinsohn, P. (1994). The Khmer adolescent project: I. Epidemiological findings in two generations of Cambodian refugees. *Journal of Nervous and Mental Disease*, 182: 387–95.

Savin, D., Sack, W. H., Clarke, G. N., Meas, N., and Richart, I. (1996). The Khmer adolescent project: III. A study of trauma from Thailand's site two refugee camp. *Journal of the American Academy of Child and Adolescent Psychiatry*, 35: 384–91.

Chapter Eight

Five Wars, Five Traumas: Experience and Insight from Clinical Work in Israel's Trenches

Mordechai Benyakar

This chapter presents a nosological and clinical approach to understanding and coping with trauma and stress. Experiences from the mental health interventions during Israel's five wars will be discussed. Clinical and theoretical implications are presented.

During World War I, 20 percent of the people who died were civilians. That proportion increased to 50 percent in World War II. Today civilians represent 90 percent of those affected by war disasters and terrorism. We mental health professionals must gaze at these numbers and wonder, "What can we do about it?" But this portrait is incomplete. We need to recognize the portions of the canvas that are obscured by statistics, for every casualty, injured person, or refugee represents at least three close relatives or friends who have been psychically injured. After the attack on New York's World Trade Center, it has been estimated that for each dead or seriously injured person, up to two hundred people were affected either directly or indirectly. As mental health professionals, we must do our best to consider *and implement* plans "for addressing these psychic wounds . . . to intervene at the epicenter of human hatred and destruction: the human mind" (Benyakar, 1996a; Crocq, 1997).

What follows is an account of what I have gleaned from my experience working as a mental health professional in Israel through five wars. As I will explain, each war was unique in its boundaries, nature, and effects. Each war also had something different to offer the mental health professional in developing a working model of how stress and trauma can affect a population differently and how citizens, the state, and the media can (or cannot) offer buffers that help prevent the manifestation of mental illness (Benyakar, 2000b). Most important, I will address how we as mental health professionals must tailor our treatments to the unique demands of each disruptive situation (Benyakar,

2003). Although I will discuss five wars, I will focus mostly on the Gulf War. It is from these experiences that I will relate how I developed a differential nosological and clinical approach to the treatment of trauma and stress, perhaps best described as "mental health care in the trenches."

The approaches I will describe offer as many questions as they do answers, questions that we will have to answer as situations arise and morph with the ever-changing human experience of war (Benyakar, 1994).

MY INITIATION TO THE WAR EXPERIENCE: THE SIX-DAY WAR

As a participant in the Six-Day War, I had the opportunity to observe the dynamics of emotions both within myself and in others. Only after a few years, as a therapist and researcher, was I able, together with my colleagues, to conceptualize and draw some conclusions about the characteristics of this war, such as the following:

1. *The army was very well prepared.* The army was mobilized early. Most of the soldiers were reservists who lived with the expectation that they might be asked to leave their daily activities and wear a uniform.
2. *The battle units were integrated.* The soldiers already knew each other, since they had previously trained together.
3. *The goal was clear.* The Israeli army itself established the guidelines in the battlefield. The war was ended in only six days, as if the soldiers had deliberately wanted to keep the seventh day for the Sabbath rest.
4. In spite of the emotional impact of there being casualties, *the feeling of victory was profound.* The army completed its tasks in a few days, and the country was almost manic with excitement. Every citizen felt like a national hero.

We mental health professionals came to understand that several protective elements were integral to successful processing of traumatic states and stress experiences. In this particular war, there were three support frameworks: the cohesiveness of each soldier unit; the cohesiveness of the army itself; and, later, the single, unwavering, authoritative guidance of the State (Kaës 1979; Benyakar and Rubinstein, 1984a, 1984b).

Of the five wars I will describe, the circumstances of this particular war were ideal in many respects for buffering the population from the worst effects of war. The joint performance of these three support groups worked as a stabilizing factor, and there were few cases of the so-called posttraumatic

neuroses (Brüll, 1969; Moses, 1978). Soldiers presented with adaptation issues or character disorders or both, but not symptoms typically connected
with the disruptive situation of the war, what is popularly called war trauma.

THE WAR OF ATTRITION

Young Israelis joined the mandatory military service inspired by the triumphant aura of the previous war. Unlike the Six-Day War, the armed battle
was not generalized in this war, nor was there an official state of war. A well-
trained army participated in this conflict, fighting sudden and intermittent attacks of the enemy, primarily in the border region. Many Israeli soldiers were
lost, but the Israeli people continued to feel triumphant.

At that time, the Mental Health Assisting Corps of the Israeli army was
very small, but it was not overwhelmed by people presenting with symptoms
related to the disruptive situation of the war. Most of our work was with the
impoverished and with the chronically mentally ill.

THE YOM KIPPUR WAR

Different in several respects from the two previous wars, the Yom Kippur War
demonstrated the possible effects of not having time for preparation and not
having unit cohesion within the army (Benyakar, 1973).

To understand the circumstances surrounding the Yom Kippur War, consider a country that, on this holy day, completely ceases its activities from
5:00 P.M. until 7:00 P.M. the following day. Private and public transportation
is not available. Radio and television stations are closed. Most of the citizens
are secluded either in their homes or in synagogues, and the observant fast
throughout. On this holy day, October 6, 1973, for the first time since the creation of the State of Israel, the army was caught off-guard and was forced to
retreat from its previous position. There were many casualties. From a serene,
almost lethargic environment, reserve soldiers were suddenly called to the
battlefront. Soldiers were forced by circumstance to fight alongside other soldiers who were complete strangers. The absence of group cohesion was palpable from the very beginning.

The different nature of this war experience was reflected in the types of
cases we were treating. There were soldiers who sought treatment for serious
symptoms such as partial amnesia, hypo-orexia (lack of appetite), inability to
concentrate, hypo-bulia (lack of interest in their surroundings), and inability to
reintegrate with their families. Many of the patients I treated wished to return

to battle with their fellow soldiers, but were psychically unable to do so. The incapacity to express verbally what had happened to them was a common feature. For the first time in Israel's history, the Israel Defense Force was dealing with serious psychopathology, apparently induced by war psychic damage (Benyakar and Noy, 1975).

The cases of two soldiers I treated in the Mental Health Corps exemplify some of the effects that a lack of preparation before battle and an absence of group cohesion during battle can have on soldiers. One of my patients, Mr. X, explained that in less than twelve hours he had gone from relaxing in an armchair at home to commanding a tank. He had been unable to bring himself to say goodbye to his children. With the ominous feeling that he would never see them again, he went to battle. After a short time, he was unable to perform his duty. During his treatment, he admitted that he had been overcome with a feeling of walking to his own death, and this was probably one of the reasons that he could no longer command his tank. This reserve officer came to us in a withdrawn state, suffering from nightmares, insomnia, agitation, and overwhelming feelings of guilt for his failure to perform (Benyakar, 2000a).

Abandonment was the main theme of his sessions. While he felt guilt for having abandoned his family, it soon became obvious that his deepest feeling was that he had felt abandoned. He was facing great difficulties integrating back into his family and his social environment. The surprise of having to act in a group with which he could never identify himself and his abrupt confrontation with death activated a pendular sequence of abandoning and being abandoned that had totally overcome him. He was psychologically frozen, and this led to a rupture between his inner world and his environment (Krystal, 1993; H. Krystal and J. H. Krystal, 1988; Levine, 1997; Winnicott, 1974).

A second patient, Mr. Z, said that while he was driving a tank he was attacked by a "shoulder missile," a weapon not very well known at the time. The impact blew up the tank as well as some of his fellow soldiers. While he could hear their screams for help, he realized that this was unlike his former experience in combat: he did not know the soldiers' names or their families. Amid the bombing, instead of helping his partners, he ducked and hid. When he came for treatment, he was paralyzed from the waist down. In this case, the unknown and the threatening were not only the enemy's weapons. His own group did not provide him with the necessary support with which to face the surrounding danger.

The Development of Posttraumatic Neuroses

In examining the singular aspects of this war, we were able to formulate some general concepts that we hypothesize contributed to the development of what we now refer to as "posttraumatic neuroses":

1. There were a great number of casualties.
2. Soldiers were unable to carry out their duties in the manner that they had been trained to do.
3. The enemy was attacked by surprise, and the fighting was almost constant.
4. The army units lacked cohesion because the soldiers often did not know each other beforehand.
5. The enemies used unfamiliar weapons.
6. Soldiers were forced to stay in the desert for long periods of time, away from their families.

These were all sources of stress that had not been present in the previous two wars. Given the absence of buffering effects that had operated in the previous war, we suspected that these stresses might have increased the impact of war experience for many soldiers.

Assistance Frameworks

Another factor that we believe might have contributed to the perpetuation of the soldiers' inability to reintegrate and return to service had to do with the location of intervention. At the beginning of the war, we assisted soldiers near the battlefield in the mountains of the desert. Therapists made efforts to find places to sit that offered a different ambience from the surrounding environment. We attempted to achieve an intimacy during treatment in which both patient and therapist were exposed to the same threat. We felt it was important to establish that healing was possible, even with the specter of war looming. A tree or a stone, became our referential place to meet. I called this situation "from the couch to the rocks" (Benyakar, 1994).

In a second stage, we installed the "mental health assistance team" in a comfortable and relatively luxurious hotel in the center of a city at a distance from the fighting. At this hotel, we assisted the cases that we considered too severe to be treated near the battlefield (Benyakar, Dasberg, and Plotkin, 1978; Benyakar, Dasberg, and Plotkin, 1982). Though the decision to treat some soldiers in the hotel had been for the sake of speeding the patients' recoveries, we later realized that the secondary benefits of remaining in the hotel (the many comforts offered by the hotel and the relative absence of stress) made reintegration into their units and the daily activities at home more difficult for them. On this realization, my colleagues and I agreed that the most suitable location for the soldiers' treatment should be as close as possible to the battlefield and in the same physical environment as the rest of the soldiers.

This led to the creation of an intervention model based on what we had observed and on a nearly forgotten treatment plan developed by Salmon (1919) for soldiers who had been exposed to traumatogenic or stressogenic events in World War I. According to Salmon, immediate assistance carried out as close to the battlefield as possible is ideal. He advised that therapists encourage patients to return to the activity they were performing up to the moment of disruption as soon as possible. It was based on this philosophy that we began developing the concept of the "combat assistance unit," which is a type of "campaign psychiatric hospital." This hospital was organized and implemented twenty-four hours after the war began, as close to the battlefield as possible. We set up an assistance unit with reserve professionals. The purpose of this unit was to create a transitional space with a nonfighting group culture that maintained the cohesiveness of the army as an institution. Combining the concepts of Bion and Winnicott, we can say that this cohesiveness allowed for the development of containment with an attitude of holding (Bion, 1965, 1980).

CONSENSUS AND DISCREPANCIES
ON STRESS AND TRAUMA

I have offered some of our thoughts on the environment that laid fertile ground for the development of Post Traumatic Neurosis in many soldiers and the frameworks developed to prevent some harmful effects of intervention. I will now address two conflicting theories that were proposed by my colleagues regarding the etiology of the illness. Some of my colleagues thought that the symptoms of the so-called Post Traumatic Neurosis were a direct consequence of exposure to disruptive events and that there was a relationship between the severity of the symptoms and the intensity of the disruptive conditions of the event (Horowitz, 1976; Horowitz, 1993; H. Selye, 1950, 1956, 1980). This stance was also taken by North American clinicians and adopted by the *DSM* in several editions (American Psychiatric Association 1980, 1987, 1994; Davidson and Foa, 1993).

On the other hand, there were those, including myself, who believed that the traumatic experience was rooted where there are no words, where experience cannot be verbalized or explained since it cannot be represented. This means that the relationship between the external and internal world is severed. I will say more about this later.

LEBANON: UNITED IN BATTLE
AND INTERNAL DISAGREEMENTS

The conclusions of the Yom Kippur War seemed clear, and, unfortunately, we had another opportunity to apply them soon after during the Lebanon War.

During this war, however, a different set of conditions led us to once again question the findings we had reached (Benyakar, 1978). In the Lebanon War there were more cases of psychiatric symptoms than in the previous one. There was also a lack of political consensus in most of the population regarding Israel's role in the war. The army had been established in the enemy's lands for a long time, and Israeli soldiers were constantly exposed to terrorist attacks in those lands. The Israelis did not fight to conquer more lands but to protect the security of Israel (Neumann and Levy, 1984).

We had all the necessary conditions to treat the patients: the teams were trained, and the hospitals had been set up based on established criteria. The cases that presented, however, were different from those we had encountered in previous wars. We were amazed to see that what we had thought to be a typical symptomatology in war situations was assuming a different form. In this war, the stressogenic situation lasted for a long time. Apathy and fatigue were predominant, symptoms reminiscent of what had been reported by the North American army during the Vietnam War. It is notable that both the Vietnam War and the Lebanon War were opposed by large numbers of citizens (Benyakar, Yadlin, and Zifman, 1983; Friedman, 1981; Külka et al., 1990; Mellman and Davis, 1985; Strange and Brown, 1970).

We were constantly questioning ourselves about whether it was adequate to treat cases caused by stress in the same manner as those derived from psychic trauma. We wondered if we were in fact facing two different nosological entities. These questions have persisted ever since, and I believe this is still a central issue. I think it is not by chance that in scientific literature in English there are at least eleven different ways of naming this kind of phenomena, among them are *posttraumatic neuroses*, *shell shock*, *battle fatigue*, *war neurosis*, *war trauma*, and so forth. I wonder whether this difference in nomenclature indicates that we are really talking about different kinds of phenomena (Milgram, 1993; van der Kolk, 1988). During the Lebanon War, it was clear to some of us that this was the case, and we consoled ourselves, thinking that we had at least advanced by establishing a framework with which to deal with both kinds of cases (Benyakar, 1997a, 1997b, 1997c).

THE GULF WAR

The citizens of the State of Israel, long familiar with war, were nonetheless on unfamiliar ground during the Gulf War. Since the State had been created, this was the first time its civilian population that did not live on the border was attacked. It was also the first time Israel did not counterattack. Moreover, for many citizens, the Iraqi threat of using lethal gas reopened emotional scars that had been left by the Nazis. A new threatening beast was born whose characteristics were a combination of the unknown and the familiar.

On August 1, 1990, Iraq invaded Kuwait. Because of this, Iraq received an ultimatum from the United Nations: they would have to leave Kuwait before January 15, 1991, or face war. During this waiting period, Israelis lived in great anxiety. That awful day was anticipated and dreaded at the same time. If the ultimatum were not observed, it would mean war. Mass extermination through lethal gas was a genuine threat that had horrific significance for Jewish Israelis. Fortunately for us, this did not happen. Iraq attacked Tel Aviv and Ramat-Gan with Scuds, conventional guided missiles.

Amazingly, there were no casualties from the Scuds' impact. Nonetheless, hundreds of houses were destroyed during the forty-two day war. Forty missiles fell on Israeli territory, severely upsetting the civilian population's sense of security. The Israeli authorities did not declare a state of war or emergency. The Israeli army did not fight back, even though all their combat troops and all the assisting professionals were adequately trained. A strange new dynamic existed, and I realized that all our previous intervention frameworks would prove to be misapplications in this situation.

Of the three basic reactions to threat—fight, flight, and freeze—Israelis were forced by circumstance to develop the latter. It was as if a common consensus to play dead had been arrived at. Israelis wore gas masks everywhere, unsure of where they might encounter attack. It was as if they had turned into a very peculiar army, required to resist aggression without defending themselves.

All of the population secluded in their own homes had transformed into a large cohesive group on the one hand and an amorphous entity on the other. Telephone, radio, and television communication were employed in an attempt to dissipate the feeling of paralysis caused by domestic immobilization.

We changed strategies, and an option that had been used and considered faulty in previous wars was chosen in this one: hotels were used as treatment sites. Civilians whose homes had been badly damaged or destroyed were evacuated to hotels, which functioned as temporary shelters (Benyakar, Kretsch, and Baruch, 1994).

When working with evacuees, we could see that, unlike the soldiers' reactions, the civilians' symptoms were more diffuse and less acute, but this did not mean they were less serious.

We, the professionals who had experience with these kinds of cases, gathered spontaneously as multidisciplinary and multifunctional teams (Benyakar, 1996a, 1997a). As soon as the Scuds hit, we were recognized by the national and the town council authorities, and we had to temporarily work as a stable team, performing in an integrated manner during all the time the "temporary assistance center" functioned. I personally directed the "evacuee mental health assistance" in Ramat-Gan and supervised the team in charge of Tel Aviv (Benyakar, 1998).

It was clear to us that the evacuees had been deeply affected by the impact of the event. Intervention was about helping individuals, families, and groups find their own resources to get through the situation. Any kind of contact with the evacuees was considered a therapeutic encounter. During the assistance process, the mental health team had to deal with all sorts of problems, even the need to supply towels and soap, telephone tokens, bed sheets, and other types of necessities.

Preserving the Home, in Spite of the Destroyed Houses

Our first step in helping the evacuees was to address their basic needs, such as estimating loss, searching for lost documents in the debris, recycling houses, demolishing and reconstructing those houses that could be recycled, buying appliances that had been broken, and so forth. In order to do this, it was not only necessary to have all the material resources the national and city council authorities granted but also the most suitable psychological resources. Although evacuees were unable to express their loss, they had to face the evaluation and repair of the loss (Solomon et al., 1991).

On one hand, the situation evoked anger in many, causing some to act out. On the other hand, there were people who preferred to seclude themselves and withdraw from the environment. A framework had to be created to provide a support; it could not be a bureaucratic, sterile environment. One of the basic concepts developed during the wars was the creation of a framework that was stable but able to adapt itself to meet the needs of the situation as it changed. This situation was not an easy one with which to cope; we received citizens, our neighbors or relatives, arriving in pajamas or half-dressed, absolutely disoriented by what had happened. Among them there were native Israelis as well as recent immigrants from Russia and Ethiopia, immigrants for whom the loss of home was still palpable.

The process of distributing necessities was interpreted on two levels. One level was the specific content. The other was the underlying message. The intrasubjective and the intersubjective were expressed in the therapeutic contact, as well as the trans-subjective repercussions. The therapeutic relationship was developed in a special reality, where both the patient and the therapist were exposed to the same threat, an already familiar situation for us from previous wars (Benyakar, 1994; Puget and Wender, 1982). I am reminded of a colleague who, after spending the day helping refugees at the hotel, returned to her home only to find it damaged by a missile.

The immediate reaction many evacuees had to the event was that of shock; in others, it was a weakening of the defenses, which prevented them from facing the situation. Once their initial shock was over, the evacuees started facing their loss.

The ravages of war were not only limited to the buildings; the destruction of the buildings undermined the stability and strength they had represented. The damage produced a deep feeling of helplessness and disorientation in many of the evacuees. Many also had feelings of loss from previous wars that they had never fully processed. Naturally, their current loss activated these feelings, adding to their suffering. We often addressed these issues in the therapeutic process, helping them express and process their painful feelings in words. The assistance service did its best to create a context of stability, trying to preserve for now homeless families a sense of "home."

The Wars That Have Not Occurred

It is very important to emphasize that two active forces were at work in the minds of many evacuees. One was a narcissistic retraction fleeing by means of affective isolation, cutting oneself off from an external world that from moment to moment became threatening and extremely disruptive. The other was a tendency toward "acting," avoiding the world of emotions. Both are, of course, variables of the same situation, which consists of denying a constant relation between one's inner and outer worlds. In this case, if the evacuees had accepted the external reality, they would also have accepted the predominant situation: in the face of aggression and damage, the State's decision had been not to counterattack and defend (Baudrillard, 1991).

This freezing or paralyzing in the face of danger played a large role in the manifestation of pathology, activating unprocessed memories and feelings of past loss or disruptive situations that had lain dormant. The case of Yoel, a fifty-six-year-old family man, exemplifies this process. Yoel came to our team with psychosomatic chest pains. He and his family were not in their home when it was bombed. Like other citizens, they had left the country's center (because it was the most frequent target of the bombings) and had moved to the border areas. This was one of the many amazing and paradoxical situations: being next to the frontier with the enemy offered many citizens a greater sense of safety than being in the center of the country. When a missile fell on Yoel's house, the neighbors telephoned him and told him his house had been completely razed. A few hours later, Yoel and his family arrived at the site of their former home and found a bulldozer taking away the last of the debris. Yoel broke down in tears. He was "frozen" and "petrified" standing in front of the empty lot. He told us he felt paralyzed. It started raining but he remained there, stock-still and perplexed. He does not recall how long he stood there, and he realized he was soaking and cold. Dizzy, he had felt a sharp pain in his chest and was taken to the general hospital emergency room.

Once he was discharged from the hospital, the feeling of being paralyzed recurred, mostly at night. Yoel's volition had abandoned him. He lost his temper easily, and things that used to be trivial for him now made him very tense and angry. He was impatient, and he could no longer concentrate to perform his daily duties. When he talked about the destruction of his house, he could only describe where his daughter used to play as a child. This scene he described was warm. Every time he tried to recall the event of finding his house destroyed, he turned pale; he said he felt very cold, but he could not find the words to express what had happened or his feelings about it.

Yoel remembered that during World War II in Yugoslavia, his home country, he went out with his father and saw people running frantically everywhere. He then noticed an enemy plane in the sky. He remembered exactly where he was and how he began running wildly. He felt the plane was catching up with him. He slipped and fell on weeds. There he remained frozen or petrified during the bombing. When he was telling us all this, he said he did not know why he was doing it, since he felt it had nothing to do with what had happened to him in Israel.

We came to realize that in several areas of his life, Yoel had developed adaptation behavior in new environments or, to be more accurate, an overadaptation, as Liberman, et al. (1982) would call it. He developed very clear rules of conduct, particularly in his business habits. Yoel said all the responsibilities fell on his shoulders. He was very pleased with his enterprising capacity. He did not show his feelings in his social interactions with us or during the recounting of his story (Fain, M. 1992; Marty, de M'Uzan, and David, 1963; Marty and de M'Uzan, 1968; Sifneos, Apfel-Savitz, and Frankel, 1977).

Whenever he was overwhelmed with pain, action was the only possible balm. In the Gulf War, he had once again managed to save his life, escaping from a bombing. But when he found his physical habitat had been destroyed, he became paralyzed so that he would not be annihilated, just as he had done successfully in the past. Yoel was able to show his pain and anger for what had happened to him only through his symptoms and body language, unable to put his feelings into words, just as when he was a child.

During our therapeutic meetings, Yoel eventually managed to express what was happening to him. The ghostly and sinister contents of his accounts began to diminish his symptoms to find relief. The fact that he could begin to express his ailments opened a new world to him, one that had eluded him until then.

Yoel came to understand that what had happened could be put into words and that what had once felt like an isolating and threatening environment became a world that was open and communicative. Our aim was to help other people who were affected by the Gulf War to take their first steps toward facing the affective world, relating past experiences with present ones, only after internalizing the feeling of safety and stability provided by the therapeutic framework. Lifton's (1979) concept of continuity and H. Krystal and J. H. Krystal's (1988) elaboration of affective processes during disruptive situations were applied by us in this manner to help people face the pain produced by the destruction of their homes.

The case of another evacuee I treated during this war illustrates Lifton's (1991) claim that people tend to experience a break between the past, present, and future after exposure to disruptive situations. Jana had been born in Poland and survived the Holocaust, in which most of her family had died. The different blows suffered by Jana during her life led her to develop a harsh, rigid attitude and an air of invulnerability. She had that familiar "hardening" we often observe in survivors of trauma.

Jana set up her home in Israel. She was a widow at that time, and her children no longer lived with her. She had a very active social life. When her house was bombed, all of its contents were destroyed. After a long search through the debris, Jana managed to find two things: an invitation card to a meeting at a charity society to which she belonged and a silver teaspoon that she had brought from Poland. During the first days of her stay at the hotel, she carried these two items with her everywhere.

At that time, Jana visited the place where her house had been several times. Every time she came back from those visits, she referred to the destruction as something transient and not very significant. During our conversations, she emphasized that one had to be strong and that one should not give up and be defeated by such situations. She told us this had been her attitude all her life. Throughout all our meetings the teaspoon and the invitation card were in her hands. To us, they represented the emotional contents about which she was not willing to talk. All of this changed one day when she went with a friend to see the debris that had been her friend's house. Jana broke down in tears. The concealed feelings finally unleashed because she had allowed herself to identify with her friend. This was the only way she could get in touch with her own feelings.

From this event onward, Jana allowed us to help her express the meaning of the teaspoon (it represented her past), and the invitation card, her social activity (it represented her present). They were a past and a present that had remained under the debris until then. What we tried to do in this case was to help Jana recognize her tendency to live for the future, avoiding past and present experiences, a very common attitude in many Holocaust survivors known as "hardening." I think it is extremely important to consider that whatever the intensity of the threat for each individual, it will always be specific, and each person will react to it in his or her own way. We must always recognize that people's reactions to disruptive situations may seem strange, but we must be very careful to avoid diagnosing these phenomena as pathological, as bizarre as they may seem.

The roof that the temporary shelter offered gave the evacuees the feeling of refuge and protection they required, and this enabled us to access some of their emotional needs. What allowed them to confront the external destruction during the assistance process was the integration of three elements: being in touch with their relatives, accepting their external reality just as it really was, and facing their new internal reality in a special containing and holding situation. One of the assistance goals was to succeed in having the evacuees perform a complementary process: on one hand, to walk out into the external world that surrounded them, and on the other, to express their emotional world (Benyakar 1991; Benyakar, Kretsch, and Baruch 1994).

As therapists, the reality we had to face during this war taught us that our experience only helped as long as we were able to accept the constant threat of unforeseeable events. We had to face it as a group of professionals and not allow ourselves to become paralyzed by fear.

Virtual Therapeutic Structures

Unfortunately, it appears that disasters and wars will always be with us. While we may hope that they will not take place, we need to prepare ourselves for the worst of situations. As mental health professionals, we must do our best to help people cope with the devastation in a way that incorporates what we have learned from the past. "Virtual therapeutic structures teams" (Benyakar, 2002) are organizing tools designed to carry out appropriate interventions. This kind of organization is virtual in that members must be trained to work as a team only when a disaster or catastrophe occurs. This implies a *potential presence* of its members, beyond a specific time and space.

I would like to elucidate some of the distinctions I see between different situations with which members of virtual therapeutic structures teams must learn to cope (Benyakar, 1997a).

Disruptive situations refer to actual external events that implode the psyche, violent eruptions in social environments that threaten the inner world of its inhabitants. These changes turn a familiar surrounding into a threatening and alienated one, full of unknown, undetectable, and omnipresent menaces and may result in mental disorders (see chapter 5 in this book). I think the term traumatic is insufficiently useful as a term for labeling an event. Let us instead say that a situation is disruptive and that one's experience of that disruptive situation may or may not be a traumatic one. The word "trauma" should be reserved for internal processes; in this case, the breakdown of the articulation between affect and psychic representation (Benyakar, 2003). Therefore, it is better to speak of environments in which a threat is chronic and continuous as distruptive rather than traumatic.

I have, along with several colleagues, proposed another diagnostic category, anxiety by disruption syndrome (AbD), to address the disorder caused not by an inner conflict or dynamic but, rather, by deterioration or collapse of the external environment or both. Because reactions to catastrophic events may be either stressful or traumatic, the designation of Post-Traumatic Stress Disorder (PTSD), which combines both, is a misnomer and should not be used. We must pay attention to the ways in which persons react to environmental disruptions and observe the differentiation in our treatment plans (Benyakar, Collazo, and De Rosa, 2002).

When a disruptive event is experienced as a threat, the psyche may process it in one of two ways. On one hand, it might erect defense mechanisms, the result of signal anxiety, which produce a *stress* experience. Events are stressogenic when a person reacts by mobilizing defensive structures that may or may not contribute to phobic or anxiety symptoms. On the other hand, feelings of helplessness may emerge because of autonomic anxiety and unsymbolized affect that cause an experience to be traumatic. That is, a traumatic experience represents a collapse of the structural and functional relations represented in the psyche (Benyakar et al., 1989). Experiences become traumatic when affect emerges with no concomitant representation. It is for this reason that traumatic experiences result in a defenseless and helpless psyche.

Yet, manifestation of traumatized individuals is their inability to put experience into words. Although they have already achieved symbolization through language, the traumatic experience is one that remains unstructured. This distinguishes it from psychosis, for example, in which a destructuring process takes place. The trauma, on the other hand, is not structured to begin with. In treatment, then, the traumatized person needs help to transform his or her nameless pain into suffering that can be communicated, thereby bringing about an emotional metabolic process. In this manner, I distinguish pain from suffering.

I believe that the *DSM* category of PTSD filled an important gap in the mental health nosological systems, as it gave special emphasis to the impact that the external world may have on the psyche. This was an innovative perspective that was enormously important for the clinical treatment of patients. On the other hand, I wish to argue that the PTSD diagnosis fails to distinguish between two psychic phenomena: stress and trauma. This presents a situation that poses significant obstacles to both diagnostic and clinical areas (López-Ibor Aliño, 2002). A specific event, depending on its intensity and duration, is thought to directly cause a set of symptoms. As I stated earlier, I believe that one expression of the traumatic experience is rooted where there are no words, where it cannot be verbalized or explained, since it cannot be represented. Therefore, what is concealed by the symptom of traumatic experience is the lack of representation of an emerging intense affect (Benyakar, 1996b).

It is also helpful to clarify the concept of *experience* (erlebnis), which is related to a subjective component rather than an external, objective fact. More specifically, experience is the articulation between affect and representation. Some languages do not have two different words for experience; this often leads to the subjective and the objective being confused. Not everyone who experiences an objective disruption in his or her environment responds with a subjective traumatic reaction. The English language uses the word "experience" to denote both subjective and objective occurrences, even though happening and experience might better distinguish them from one another. Other languages possess words that specifically denote the subjective connotation of experience: in Hebrew, the word chavaya, in Spanish, vivencia, in German, erlebnis. In French, although the same word is generally used, Jean Paul Sartre proposed the expression *fait vecu* when referring to the subjective component of what has been experienced by the individual. When I use the term "traumatic experience," I refer solely to its subjective connotation (Benyakar, 1996c).

The traumatic experience, then, is one of the ways in which the "negative" (Green, 1990) arises in the psyche. There is a paradox in trauma; the traumatic experience, because it goes unrepresented and unstructured, is the experience of non-experience, which is precisely what renders it so traumatic (Benyakar, 1997c; Green, 1990).

Another distinction I would like to emphasize, which I observed from the experiences I had in Israel's five wars as well as that treating the psychological impact of terrorism in Argentina and Israel, is the difference that exists between "aggression" and "violence." With aggression, one is aware of one's opponent, and this awareness allows one to prepare and defend oneself accordingly, both psychologically and concretely. A good example of this is war. Soldiers go into combat knowing whom their enemy is and what they need to do in order to protect themselves. The situation is different when we speak of "violence" (Benyakar 2000b). In this case, one is taken by surprise and, therefore, cannot defend oneself properly. One does not know when and from where the harm will come; this situation leaves a person feeling both helpless and frightened. Terrorism, unlike combat situations in war, has created a violent world, a world in which the enemy can be anywhere and might attack at any time. The defenselessness that results from this situation more often leads to trauma or, to be more precise, to traumatic experiencing (Benyakar and Lezica, 2001).

Finally, I believe it is necessary to maintain the psychoanalytic frame and the stability of psychotherapeutic settings when treating those who suffer from disruptive situations. In a world of violence, a world that lacks stability and predictability, it is all the more critical for the therapeutic setting to remain stable and constant without becoming dogmatic or rigid (Benyakar, 2002). The frame provides containment for the patient's most malignant thoughts and feelings, holding so that the patient does not feel alone in his or her encounter with violence, and figurative interpretations to aid in the translation of affects into verbal representation (Benyakar, 2002). In this manner, the frame and setting of the treatment impart stability and a sense of safety to the therapeutic relationship and the patient's inner world, all of which help bolster the self that has no choice but to survive in a society that risks losing its sense.

NOTE

I would like to highlight the important and arduous work carried out by Danielle Knafo, who invested great effort in transforming my experiences into something comprehensible for the readers. It is to be hoped this rich and important labor represents an opportunity for future collaborations aimed at developing a clinical and theoretical common ground.

REFERENCES

American Psychiatric Association. (1980). *Diagnostic and statistical manual of mental disorders* (3rd ed). Washington, DC.: Author.

———. (1987). American Psychiatric Association. (1980). *Diagnostic and statistical manual of mental disorders* (3rd ed., rev.).Washington, DC: Author.

———. (1994). *Diagnostic and statistical manual of mental disorders* (4th ed.). Washington, DC: Author.

Baudrillard, J. (1991). *La transparencia del mal*. Barcelona: Anagrama.

Benyakar, M. (1973). *Reevaluation of the theory and therapy of acute Post-Traumatic War Neurosis*. Tel Aviv, Israel: Defense Forces Publications.

———. (1978). *Clinical indications for treatment of cases of combat reactions*. Tel Aviv, Israel: Defense Forces Publications.

———. (1994). Trauma y neurosis post-traumática: De la vivencia a la reflexión teórica. *Actualidad Psicológica*, 211: 26–32.

———. (1996a). *Human resources in catastrophes: The psychiatrist's role*. Paper presented at the Tenth International Symposium of the World Congress of Psychiatry, Madrid, Spain.

———. (1996b). Juego, palabra y sublimación, en Mesa Redonda "Trauma, duelo y juego," Asociación Psicoanalítica Argentina, XVI Jornadas anuales del departamento de Niños y Adolescentes, Buenos Aires, Argentina.

———. (1996c). *Trauma, La Construcción mítica del campo Psicoanalítico*. Asociación Psicoanalítica Argentina. IV Simposio Internacional sobre Mitos y sus ámbitos de expresión interpretación psicoanalítica e interdisciplinaria, Buenos Aires, Argentina.

———. (1996d). *La vivencia traumática*. Vicisitudes en la Clínica Psicoanalítica. Conferencia presentada para la categoría de miembro titulad de la Asociación Psicoanalítica Argentina.

———. (1997a). *Principios clínicos para formación de equipos profesionales de salud mental en desastres*. Conferencia magistral en el coloquio sobre intervención psiquiátrica en catástrofes. Hospital Militar Central "Gomez Ulla," Madrid, España.

———. (1997b). Trauma y estrés, perspectivas clínicas. In H. R. Fischer (Ed.), *Conceptos Fundamentales de Psicopatología* II, capítulo 10. Buenos Aires, Argentina: Centro Editor.

———. (1997c, diciembre). Definición, diagnóstico y clínica del estrés y el trauma. Psiquiatría COM (revista electrónica) 1(43). Retrieved June 30, 2004, from www .psiquiatria.com/psiquiatria/vol1num4/art_5.htm

———. (1998, enero–febrero). Salud Mental de los evacuados de la Guerra del Golfo: Los Espacios Terapéuticos de una guerra peculiar. *Monografías de Psiquiatría*. Año X.

———. (2000a). *Lo traumático y lo ominoso*. Cuestionamientos teórico-clínicos acerca del procesamiento de las amenazas, en Revista del Departamento de Psicosomática, 1, Buenos Aires, Argentina.

———. (2000b). *Combatant and Civilian PTSD, Stress and Traumatic Experiences*. International Jubilee Congress, París.

———. (2002). The frame and psychoanalytic space in the face of wars and terror. In J. A. Cancelmo, J. Hoffenberg, I. Tylim, and H. Myers (Eds.), *Terrorism and the psychoanalytic space: International perspective from Ground Zero*. New York: Pace University Press.

———. (2003). *The disruptive individual and collective threats: The psyche facing wars, terrorism and social catastrophes*. Buenos Aires, Argentina: Editorial Biblos.

Benyakar, M., Collazo, C., and De Rosa, E. (2002). Ansiedad por Disrupción, in Interpsiquis. Retrieved in June 23, 2004, from www.psiquiatria.com

Benyakar, M., Dasberg, H., and Plotkin, I. (1978). Group therapy in two different approches to War Neuroses. *Israel Annals of Psychiatry and Related Disciplines*, 16: 183–95.

———. (1982). The influence of various therapeutic milieus on the course of group treatments in two groups of soldiers with combat reaction. In Milgram, N. A., Spielgerberg, C. D., and Sarason, I. G. (Eds.), *Stress and Anxiety*, Vol. 8. New York: McGraw-Hill International Book Company.

Benyakar, M., and Lezica, A. (2001, noviembre). *La vivencia traumática en la clínica psicoanalítica*. Psicoanálisis en la clínica y prácticas actuales, XXIII Simposio de la Asociación Psicoanalítica de Buenos Aires, Argentina, t. I.

Benyakar, M., and Rubinstein, Z. (1984a). *The military therapeutic milieu in war time*. Tel Aviv, Israel: Defense Forces Publications.

———. (1984b). *Group psychotherapy in a military unit in war time*. Tel Aviv, Israel: Defense Forces Publications.

Benyakar, M, Yadlin, N., and Zifman, N. (1983). *Ongoing individual and group psychotherapy of civilians in wartime*. Paper presented at the Third International Conference on Psychological Stress and Adjustment in Time of War and Peace, Tel Aviv, Israel.

Bion, W. (1965). *Transformations*. New York: Basic Books.

———. (1980). *Experiencias en Grupos*. Buenos Aires, Argentina: Paidos.

Brüll, F. (1969). The trauma-theoretical considerations. *The Israel Annals of Psychiatry and Related Disciplines*, 7: 96–108.

Crocq, L. (1997). The emotional consequences of war 50 years old. A psychiatric perspective. In L. Hunt, M. Marshall, and Ch. Rowlings (Eds.), *Past trauma, in late life*, pp. 39–48. London: Jessica Kingsley Publishers.

Davidson, J. R., and Foa, E. (1993). *Posttraumatic stress disorder: DSM-IV and beyond*. Washington, DC: American Psychiatric Press.

Fain, M. (1992). La vie opératoire et les potentialités de néurose traumatique. *Revue Française de Psychosomatique*, 2: 5–24.

Friedman, M. J. (1981), Post-Vietnam Syndrome: Recognition and Management. *Psychosomatics*, 22: 931–943.

Green, A. (1990). *La nueva clínica psicoanalítica y la teoría de Freud*. Buenos Aires: Amorrortu.

Horowitz, M. J. (1976). *Stress response syndromes*. New York: Jason Aronson.

———. (1993). Stress-response syndromes: A review of posttraumatic stress and adjustment disorders. In J. P. Wilson and B. Raphael (Eds.), *International handbook of traumatic stress syndromes*. New York: Plenum Press.

Kaës, R. (1979). *Crisis, ruptura y superación: análisis transicional en psicoanálisis individual y grupal*. Buenos Aires, Argentina: Ediciones Cinco.

Krystal, H. (1993). Beyond the DSM-III-R: Therapeutic considerations in posttraumatic stress syndome. In J. P. Wilson and B. Raphael (Eds.), *International handbook of traumatic stress syndrome*, pp. 841–54. New York: Plenum Press.

Krystal, H., and Krystal, J. H. (1988). *Integration and self-healing: Affect, trauma, alexithymia*. Hillsdale, NJ: The Analytic Press.

Külka, R. A., Schlenger, W. E., Fairbank, J. A., Hough, R. L., Jordan, B. K., Marmar, C., et al. (1990). *Trauma and the Vietnam War generation: Report of findings from the National Vietnam Veterans Readjustment Study*. New York: Brunner/Mazel.

Levine, P. A. (1997). How biology becomes pathology: Freezing. In *Waking the tiger: Healing trauma*. Berkeley, CA: North Atlantic Book.

Liberman, D., de Aisenberg, E. R., D'Avila, R., Dunayevich, J. B., Fernández Moujn, O., Galli, V., et al. (1982). Sobreadaptación, trastornos psicosomáticos y estados tempranos del desarrollo. *Revista de Psicoanálisis*, 5: 845.

Lifton, R. J. (1979). *The broken connection*. New York: Simon & Schuster.

———. (1991). *Death in life: Survivors of Hiroshima*. Chapel Hill: University of North Carolina Press.

López-Ibor Aliño, J. (2002, agosto). *The psycho(patho)logy of disasters*. In Plenary Lectures, XII World Congress of Psychiatry, 24–29, Yokohama, Japan.

Marty, P., and de M'Uzan, M. (1968). La pensée opératoire. *International Journal of Psychoanalysis*, p. 49.

Marty, P., de M'Uzan, M., and David, C. (1963). L' investigation psychosomatique. *Revue Française de Psychanalyse*, 27: 1345–56.

Mellman, T. A., and Davis, G. C. (1985). Combat-related flashbacks in posttraumatic stress disorder: Phenomenology and similarity to panic attacks. *Journal of Clinical Psychiatry*, 46: 379–82.

Milgram, N. (1993). War-related trauma and victimization. In J. P. Wilson and B. Raphael (Eds.), *International handbook of traumatic stress syndromes*, pp. 811–80. New York: Plenum Press.

Moses, R. (1978). Adult psychic trauma: The question of early predisposition and some detailed mechanisms. *International Journal of Psychoanalysis*, 59: 353–63.

Neumann, M., and Levy, A. A. (1984). Specific military installation in Lebanon. *Military Medicine*, pp. 196–99.

Puget, J., and Wender, L. (1982). Analista y paciente en mundos superpuestos. *Psicoanálisis*, 4: 503–36.

Salmon, T. W. (1919). The war neuroses and their lessons. *New York State Journal of Medicine*, 59: 993–94.

Selye, H. (1950). *Stress*. Montréal, Canada: Acta.

———. (1956). *The Stress of Life*. New York: McGraw-Hill.

———. (1980). The stress concept today. In I. L. Kutash and L. B. Schlesinger (Eds.), *Handbook of stress and anxiety*. San Francisco: Jossey-Bass.

Sifneos, P. E., Apfel-Savitz, R., and Frankel, F. H. (1977). The phenomenon of "alexithymia": Observations in neurotic and psychosomatic patients. In W. Brautigam and M. von Rad (Eds.), *Toward a theory of psychosomatic disorders*. Basel, Switzerland: Karger.

Solomon, Z., Laor, N., Weiler, D., Muller, U., Hadar, O., Waysman, M., et al. (1991). The psychological impact of the Gulf War: A study of acute stress in Israeli evacuees. *Archives of General Psychiatry*, 50: 320–21.

Strange, R. E., and Brown, D. E., (1970), Home from the war: A study of psychiatric problems in Vietnam returnees. *American Journal of Psychiatry*, 127: 130–34.

van der Kolk, B. A. (1988). The trauma spectrum: The interaction of biological and social events in the genesis of the trauma response. *Journal of Traumatic Stress*, 1: 273–90.

Winnicott, D. (1974). Fear of breakdown. *Review of Psychoanalysis*, 1 (1–2): 103–7.

Chapter Nine

Wounds of War: The Aftermath of Combat in Vietnam

Herbert Hendin and Ann Pollinger Haas

The unique nature of combat in Vietnam, in particular the opportunities provided for behaviors by soldiers that could induce guilt (such as the killing of civilians), made veterans of that war particularly likely to develop Post-Traumatic Stress Disorder (PTSD). Our studies have found suicidal behavior and preoccupation with suicide to be disproportionately frequent among Vietnam combat veterans with PTSD and to be related not so much to having engaged in nonmilitary combat behavior as to feeling out of control due to fear or rage while doing so. The combat histories of veterans who did not develop PTSD show a common cluster of affective and behavioral traits that appear to have been protective. The military policies that shaped the way war was fought in Vietnam, the reception many soldiers faced on their return home, and clinicians' frequent failure to recognize and effectively treat PTSD, all contributed to the long-term difficulties experienced by so many Vietnam veterans.

Post-Traumatic Stress Disorder (PTSD) is likely to be frequent among soldiers exposed to combat in any war. Indeed, historical and literary accounts from at least as far back as the U.S. Civil War provide striking examples of former combatants who suffered severe and debilitating stress reactions, long before the disorder became the subject of clinical interest (Hendin and Haas, 1984a). Our work with large numbers of Vietnam combat veterans has made clear, however, the special nature of the Vietnam experience and its aftermath.

The meanings of combat for each individual who fought in Vietnam were singularly personal, deriving from a complex meshing of factors related both to his prewar life and to what he encountered in Vietnam (Hendin, Pollinger-Haas, Singer, and Ulman, 1981). But they were also a function of experiences that were widely shared. The shared experience in Vietnam derived largely from the unstructured and often chaotic nature of combat in that war. In contrast to previous American wars, combat in Vietnam frequently included killing women, children, and the elderly who were sometimes the enemy and sometimes not. Not knowing which they were added to the terror of the experience and to the reactions that followed. These killings were at times inadvertent, at times committed out of necessity, and at times done wantonly or vengefully.

The psychological consequences of a war where the number killed rather than the territory won was the prime objective were enormous. Military strategies gave our soldiers little guidance as to the proper use of force. As a Marine captain and holder of the Navy Cross put it, "The senior officers in Vietnam appeared to have no conception of the country, the culture, or the people they were dealing with. If they ordered the evacuation of an area, they felt justified in subsequently declaring it a free-fire zone. But the Vietnamese, particularly the elderly, often knew no other way to live than to go back to their homes and their land. If they were found by young troops too caught up in war to use their own judgment, the results were disastrous." One can add that they were disastrous as well to the young men who were involved.

The average American combatant in Vietnam was only nineteen compared to an average of over twenty-five in World War II, and their youth was no doubt a contributing factor to their vulnerability. Many were not mature enough to deal effectively with the seemingly purposeless nature of combat in Vietnam, and policies that emphasized body counts and declared free-fire zones did not contribute to the maintenance of discipline by combat officers. Officers who had a second combat tour in Vietnam in the early 1970s, after tours between 1966 and 1968, confirmed the demoralization of the troops in the last years of the war due to their sense of the futility of their mission. The demoralization was reflected in drug abuse, crime, and racial difficulties, which made discipline problematic. The combat officers found themselves as much the victims of political and military policy made on higher levels as the men did.

The role officers played in undisciplined killing in Vietnam was as variable as that of the soldiers. Some participated in it, some condoned it, some ignored it, and many tried to stop it, with limited success. A typical example was that of a captain who radioed a message to his men in an armored personnel carrier that he wished to interrogate a man they had captured. When the men came back, they told him the prisoner had fallen off the carrier and had been crushed under the tracks. He believed they were lying, but he felt it was futile to press the point. The same captain, however, was able to tell men in his company who had made trophies of the ears of enemy soldiers that he would not accept such behavior.

The unique context of the war in Vietnam determined that many combat soldiers would develop PTSD. In a significant percentage, guilt contributed to the development of a particularly self-destructive expression of the disorder.

THE AFTERMATH OF GUILT

Although the nature of the war in Vietnam provided ample opportunities for guilt-inducing behaviors among combat soldiers, among veterans whose stress disorders center on guilt, we have found the individual meanings and the defenses against awareness of it to vary considerably. The following case is illustrative:

Tom Bradley was a thirty-four-year-old Vietnam veteran who had served in an infantry unit and saw extensive combat in the Iron Triangle region north of Saigon. At the time we met him in the early 1980s, he had spent many years attempting to suppress *his* PTSD with drugs. Eventually, the destructive effects of the drugs led him to seek help. Initially, he was not in touch at all with the guilt at the core of his disorder. His nightmares reflected specific combat experiences: setting off a Claymore mine that killed an armed Vietcong woman; being wounded when he entered a booby-trapped hut; and watching his squad torch a Buddhist monastery, killing the "monks" inside. In relating the last dream, Tom described how his men had felt betrayed by the monks who had not revealed the presence of tunnels under the monastery that had been used by the Vietcong to infiltrate his squad's position and cut the throats of several of their men. From his position on an armored personnel carrier, Tom could see the monastery go up in smoke. He seemed not to want to know for certain what occurred, but indicated he understood the anger that triggered it and acted as though he was not bothered by the event.

It was another event in which he was a passive participant that proved to be the most troublesome and guilt inducing for him. He reported a recurrent nightmare that "scares the hell out of me it's so real." In the dream he is carrying the dead body of a young woman and trying to hide it. On waking up he would sense that he had some involvement in the girl's death but would be unable to recall what it was. In therapy, he was asked if he had ever raped a Vietnamese woman. He replied that he had not but added casually that he had once witnessed a rape. His squad had been assigned to secure the entrance to a tunnel complex while four men from another squad explored the tunnels. This squad reported by radio finding a hospital complex with a French doctor, two French nurses, and a Vietnamese assistant. There was an explosion and the four came out dragging the body of one of the nurses who was bleeding from arm wounds. Each of the four raped the nurse while Tom's squad watched. When the last man was finished he pulled out his knife and killed the woman. When this happened, Tom and his squad departed; he never knew how they disposed of the nurse's body. He did know that when the four soldiers reported the incident, they made no mention of taking anyone alive. When asked if he had been sexually excited watching the rapes, he freely admitted that he had.

Although Tom had never consciously connected his nightmare of trying to bury a dead girl to this experience, he was able to understand that it was the stimulus for the dream. He realized that he had "participated" in the rape and in the cover-up of what had occurred. Just as in the dream he was trying to find a place to bury the dead girl's body, he had tried for years to bury the entire event. Although he had succeeded on a conscious level, the burden of guilt he was nonetheless carrying was evident in the dream (Hendin and Haas, 1984b).

As Tom's case suggests, treatment of guilt-centered stress disorders requires determining the specific events to which the guilt is linked. Doing so provides leverage in treatment, since uncovering and talking about the actual event serves to reduce the guilt, and any reduction in guilt is accompanied by a reduction in trauma-induced symptoms.

SUICIDE

One of the most virulent expressions of guilt in Vietnam veterans with PTSD is suicide. Since the late 1970s, there have been frequent reports of a disproportionate rate of suicide among Vietnam veterans (U.S. Congress, 1978; Baker, 1984; Hearst, Neuman, and Hulley, 1986; Centers for Disease Control, 1987; Pollock, Rhodes, Boyle, Decoufle, and McGee, 1990). Our own studies as well as the other reports (Bullman and Kang, 1994; Kramer, Lindy, Green, Grace, and Leonard, 1994; Bullman and Kang, 1996) suggest that the suicide rate for Vietnam veterans would be much higher if the figures were restricted to combat veterans and that it would be higher still if they included only veterans with *a diagnosis* of PTSD.

In our study of one hundred Vietnam combat veterans with PTSD, nineteen had made postwar suicide attempts and fifteen more were preoccupied with suicide. During the course of our study, three of the thirty-four suicidal veterans did kill themselves. None of the veterans we studied had made a suicide attempt or showed evidence of preoccupation with suicide before his combat experience (Hendin and Haas, 1991).

Among these veterans, we found guilt over actions in combat to be the most significant predictor of both suicide attempts and preoccupation with suicide. Although combat-related guilt, usually related to having killed prisoners of war, was previously identified as an important factor in the stress disorders of American veterans studied several years after their combat experiences in World War II (Futterman and Pumpiam-Mindlin, 1951), the linkage between guilt and suicide had not been previously described.

To explore this linkage, we examined the combat histories of these men for the presence of five specific combat actions likely to have been guilt-inducing:

inadvertent or deliberate killing of civilians, mutilation or torture of the enemy, wounding or killing other Americans, rape, and passively witnessing nonmilitary actions by fellow soldiers. Somewhat unexpectedly, such combat behavior was sufficiently frequent in the histories of the nonsuicidal as well as the suicidal veterans that it did not distinguish the two groups. The most frequent such action, the killing of civilians, was found among 68 percent of the suicide attempters and 58 percent of the nonsuicidal veterans. In the majority of cases in both groups, women and children were among those killed, which was particularly disturbing to the veterans.

Although the overt combat behavior of the suicidal and nonsuicidal veterans was quite similar, further analysis revealed significant differences between the two groups in the affective states under which the nonmilitary killing of civilians occurred. Over 90 percent of the suicide attempters who had killed civilians had felt out of control when they did so, compared to only 42 percent of the nonsuicidal veterans.

In most of the suicidal cases, the actions that had been committed made the postservice guilt and nightmares of punishment seem understandable and almost inevitable. A typical experience was that of a forward artillery spotter who after witnessing friends killed by Vietcong called for artillery fire on a nearby village that had been classified as friendly. Through his binoculars he saw an old woman with betel nut stains on her teeth blown up by a shell while she was running toward the fire as if trying to stop it. At the time, he was laughing, but later he could not believe he had become so callous. In his most repetitive postservice nightmare, he is captured, tied to a pole, and spat on by the villagers, led by the old woman with the stained teeth.

Although survivor guilt has been described as an almost omnipresent symptom in the traumatic stress disorders of concentration camp survivors (Niederland, 1968; Eitinger, 1969) and survivors of the atomic explosion at Hiroshima (Lifton, 1968), among our Vietnam veterans we did not find survivor guilt to be as frequent as guilt about combat actions (Hendin and Haas, 1991). Most probably this is because virtually all survivors of the concentration camps and Hiroshima lost someone close to them, whereas not all our Vietnam veterans lost close friends in combat. Among the seventy-two who did, 53 percent had marked survivor guilt compared to only 29 percent of the twenty-eight veterans who did not lose close friends. This difference was found to be statistically significant.

Statistical analysis did not identify survivor guilt as a significant predictor of suicide attempts, suggesting that its effect overlaps to a considerable degree with that of guilt concerning combat actions. Forty of the one hundred veterans studied showed both marked guilt about combat actions and marked survivor guilt. Among this group, 35 percent had made a suicide attempt. In contrast, none of the thirty veterans without marked combat guilt or survival guilt had attempted suicide.

Research interest has increasingly focused on understanding why some patients in high-risk diagnostic categories are suicidal while most are not. Among depressed patients, intense affective states such as desperation, hopelessness, rage, and anxiety have been found to be significant in distinguishing those who are suicidal from those who are not (Beck, Steer, Beck, and Newman, 1993; Fawcett, Clarke, and Busch, 1993; Hendin, Maltsberger, Lipschitz, Haas, and Kyle, 2001). In the case of veterans with PTSD, our findings indicate that intense combat-related guilt is the most significant explanatory affect. Interestingly, we did not have a single case in which a veteran who was depressed but did not show combat-related guilt had made a suicide attempt.

The suicidal veterans, like other veterans, varied considerably in the degree to which they were in touch with their combat-related guilt and its relation to their self-destructive behavior. For them too, dreams often provided the first indication of their lingering guilt about combat actions. One veteran who had killed prisoners of war stated that everyone had done it and that he was not troubled by his behavior. However, he dreamed repetitively of being killed in the same way he had killed the prisoners.

WHAT PROTECTS SOME

Given the trauma of intense combat in Vietnam, it is not difficult to understand the high incidence of PTSD among men who fought in that war. It seems almost more challenging to attempt to explain what protected some who saw intense combat from developing this type of disorder. With this goal, we undertook a detailed analysis of the combat experiences of a group of eleven veterans who, ten to fifteen years after intense combat experiences, had experienced no symptoms of PTSD (Hendin and Haas, 1984c). Through this analysis we were able to identify certain consistent qualities in these veterans.

Ability to Function Calmly under Pressure

Veterans in this group regarded the ability to stay calm under pressure as a good soldier's most important attribute. All seemed to see impulsiveness as a threat to individual and group survival. One described experiencing a momentary break in his emotional control when his squad's machine gun did not fire, and he angrily took grenades from the other men, virtually single-handedly making a success of an ambush. His subsequent reaction to what he regarded as reck-lessness and his determination not to repeat such behavior were striking.

Another veteran reported a comparable experience, which he also described as the only time while in Vietnam that he felt real anger. His platoon had been called in to help another that had been ambushed and had suffered heavy ca-sualties. Enemy fire from a nearby bunker was preventing helicopters from landing to evacuate the wounded, among whom the veteran recognized a close friend, and the platoon sergeant had "flipped out." In a mood of frustration and anger the veteran told everyone nearby to clear out. Standing up and grabbing a large antitank M79 bazooka that was seldom used because of its dangerous recoil, he began firing and succeeded in wiping out the enemy behind the bunker. Although, like the first veteran, he was decorated for his actions, he also said that for several days afterward he felt foolish for having put himself in such danger and admonished himself never to do anything like that again.

In this group, another veteran, who had taken pride in his competence as a professional soldier, his ability to deal calmly with life-threatening situations, and the respect given to him by the men in his squad and by his superiors, volunteered for a second tour of duty in Vietnam, convinced that his skill as a soldier would prevent anything from happening to him. After six months of his second tour, a close friend whom he had regarded as just as skilled and professional a soldier as himself was killed in action. This changed his feel-ing about his own vulnerability, and he took the first available opportunity to get out of combat, a response that reflected his recognition that the emotional balance essential for functioning in combat might be deserting him.

Ability to Find Purpose and Exercise Judgment

Consistent with the emphasis these men placed on emotional control for proper decision making was their ability to deal with the war in terms of the limited objectives of each day's mission. As soldiers, they strove to find purpose in their combat actions, even when the situation appeared highly chaotic and un-structured. Those who developed PTSD, on the other hand, commonly felt that the conflict was utterly meaningless and that they were out of control in it, a sense that seems to have been expressed in the phrase frequently used by com-bat soldiers in Vietnam that whatever was going on, "don't mean nothing."

Having a sense of purpose allowed those who did not develop PTSD to ex-ercise judgment in regard to combat actions. Sometimes this required these men to take responsibility for countermanding orders from their superior of-ficers. One veteran, for example, described an incident in which his squad was out on ambush and about sixty Vietcong came by. Realizing that the Claymore mines they had set would have killed only about half of the enemy, which would have left his squad at the mercy of the other thirty soldiers, he went against standing orders and directed his men not to activate the mines. After the Vietcong passed by, he called in to request artillery fire in the direction they appeared to be headed.

Another veteran told of a similar incident in which his squad had been instructed to make a body count at night in an unsafe area. Considering it foolish to go out before daybreak, he lied and told his officer that the count had been completed. In no case did such disobedience appear to express defiance or a need simply to challenge authority. Rather, these men trusted their own values and judgment and made choices that were consistent with both effectiveness and survival.

Acceptance of Fear in Self and Others

One veteran had "the shakes" for a few days after he was fired at from point-blank range. He accepted his fear as an appropriate reaction to what had happened, was not ashamed of what he felt, and was able to talk about his feelings with his comrades.

As a group, those who did not develop postcombat stress disorders also accepted signs of fear in their comrades. Rather than condemning others' expression of fear, they tended to explain it as due to a man's inexperience or momentary lapse. This was reflected in the episode one veteran related of witnessing a comrade shoot and kill a young Vietcong boy who was swimming in a bomb crater filled with water. Recognizing the youth was not a threat since his gun was lying some yards away, this veteran felt that the boy should have been taken prisoner and reacted with sorrow to the boy's death. However, he did not condemn the other man, saying, "That guy didn't act out of a feeling of hatred, and he wasn't into killing. He was just frightened." Such a reaction sharply contrasted with those of the significant number of veterans with PTSD who denied or felt humiliated by their own fear in combat and were prone to condemn what they saw as cowardice in others.

Lack of Excessive Violence

Virtually all Vietnam combat veterans in our study reported some excitement during engagements in which they killed the enemy. Some, however, developed a lust for killing. Among veterans with PTSD, a high percentage were stimulated by violence or driven by hatred of the enemy; however, we have not found this to be true of any of those who did not develop the disorder.

Although most combat soldiers felt social pressure to repress fear and guilt, the military in Vietnam was more ambivalent toward rage and a proclivity for violence. Many thought such feelings made men into better soldiers. In our experience, although such emotions may occasionally have led some to perform heroic acts, when sustained they were more likely to lead to behavior that was self-destructive both to the individual and his comrades. As a group the veterans who did not develop PTSD tended to believe that rage and violence clouded judgment and led to dangerous mistakes. One of the veterans in this group told of a man in his squad who spent hours sharpening his long hunting knife and talking about how he was planning to sneak up on unsuspecting Vietcong and slit their throats. Feeling this man was a danger to the unit, the veteran arranged with his squad leader to get him transferred out.

Each of the veterans in this group was able to resist expressing frustration through enraged behavior toward the Vietnamese, even when others in their units were doing so, and did not dehumanize the enemy in their attitudes, speech, or behavior. Several in this group related incidents that suggested not only the absence of rage and dehumanization but also a strong sense of humanity and compassion. One man, for example, had been with another soldier when they saw at some distance people carrying litters who appeared to be part of a Vietcong hospital unit. Although they felt they could have been able to kill at least some of the group from their concealed position behind the tree line, they decided not to fire.

Absence of Guilt

The high degree of emotional control that these soldiers exhibited during combat contributed to an absence of actions over which they felt, or needed to deny, guilt. Veterans without PTSD tended to regard killing enemy soldiers in battle as an unfortunate necessity and to experience relatively little guilt afterward. None of these veterans had engaged in nonmilitary killings of civilians, prisoners, or other Americans; in sexual abuses; or in mutilation of enemy dead. As we have discussed, such actions, and subsequent guilt, were seen in a significant proportion of the veterans who developed PTSD.

Another striking factor seen among the veterans without posttraumatic stress was an absence of guilt over having survived while others died or over actions required to survive. With the exception of one veteran who did not lose any of his closest friends or squad members during his combat tour, each of the men in this group witnessed the deaths of others they felt close to in Vietnam. In spite of the sorrow this evoked, none were preoccupied with these deaths or felt guilty they were alive. For this group, in contrast to veterans whose stress disorders are centered on survival guilt, relationships developed before or after the war seemed to have greater primacy in their lives than those formed during combat.

The cluster of traits seen among veterans who did not develop PTSD—calmness under pressure, the ability to find purpose and exercise judgment, acceptance of their own and others' emotions and limitations, and a lack of excessively violent or guilt-arousing behavior—constituted an adaptation that was uniquely suitable for the preservation of emotional stability in situations that were often unstructured and unstable. These veterans experienced combat in Vietnam as a dangerous challenge to be met effectively while attempting to stay alive. In contrast to many of those who developed PTSD, they did not perceive combat as a test of their worth as men, as an opportunity to express anger or vengeance, or as a situation in which they were powerless victims.

Certainly, the combat adaptations of these men reflected their prewar character structure and emotional stability. Although some of the veterans who handled combat particularly well came from warm, supportive families who gave them a sound beginning in life and played a significant role in their postwar readjustment, others virtually raised themselves, led relatively isolated lives before going to Vietnam, and had few structured forms of support during the postwar years. In spite of their circumstances, all had had a stable precombat adjustment that was reflected in the way they dealt with combat and with the challenges they faced in the postwar years.

Our findings suggest the importance of looking more closely at perceptual and adaptive factors rather than simply at objective aspects of the combat experience in seeking to explain why some veterans have been severely distressed after their return from Vietnam while others have not. It is not so much what the individual experienced in Vietnam but how those events and situations were perceived, integrated, and acted on that bears the primary relationship to the postcombat response.

SOCIAL IMPLICATIONS

Whether or not Vietnam veterans developed PTSD, virtually all were affected to one degree or another by the social context they encountered on their return home. Policies that rotated most soldiers in and out of Vietnam as individuals rather than units and that moved them from the heart of combat back to the United States in as little as twenty-four hours frequently compounded the combat soldier's adjustment. Some men reenlisted in noncombat areas to give themselves more time to "decompress" after their combat experience. Delayed or not, the return home for most was a difficult encounter.

The mixture of terror, horror, shame, guilt, and rage that were part of combat in Vietnam made it difficult for most veterans to communicate what had happened to them, while causing family and friends to feel reluctant to share their experience. Repeatedly, veterans have told us that their families, including fathers who were often veterans of World War II, were too uncomfortable to listen when they talked of Vietnam. And families were usually more sympathetic than outsiders, who often treated the veterans as villains for having fought or as failures for not having won. For many Vietnam veterans, the attempt to come to terms with their combat experiences has been complicated by a sense that no worthwhile purpose was served by their sacrifices and those of their comrades. The alienation of most men who fought in Vietnam from the institutions and leaders responsible for U.S. policy in that war is profound and has contributed to their sense, which some continue to feel, of living in a hostile environment.

Scholarship that appeared many years after the Vietnam War largely confirmed the shared wisdom of the men in the field that those directing policy had little knowledge of the people they were fighting and that the policies they were committed to had little chance of success (Karnow, 1982; Summers, 1982). The distinguished historian, Barbara Tuchman, perhaps put it best, stating in her 1985 book, *The March of Folly: From Troy to Vietnam*, "The folly in Vietnam consisted not in pursuit of a goal in ignorance of its obstacles but in persistence despite accumulating evidence that the goal was unattainable, and the effect disproportionate to the American interest and eventually damaging to American society, reputation, and disposable power in the world."

Greater understanding of posttraumatic stress on the part of mental health professionals would likewise have had a significant impact on the lives of countless veterans whose work, marital problems, substance abuse, or antisocial behavior were often seen and responded to without awareness of the underlying presence of a combat-related disorder. Prior to our seeing him, Tom Bradley, whose PTSD centered on guilt over his passive observation of a rape and murder, had been treated in individual and marital therapy for several years with no discussion of his combat experiences or recognition of their impact on his life. His experience was common among the veterans we have seen.

In past work we have shown how understanding the meaning of the combat experience is central to treating PTSD (Hendin and Haas, 1984b). The veteran whose PTSD has a paranoid quality must be helped to change his perception of civilian life as an extension of combat. The depressed veteran must be moved away from making his life a memorial to his loss. The guilty veteran needs to see that he has already punished himself more than enough. No matter what form the disorder takes, stress-oriented psychotherapy must be modified to deal with how combat-related problems have merged with problems of the veteran's postcombat life. In our experience, such treatment can be remarkably effective, even with veterans whose PTSD is complicated by substance abuse, suicidal behavior, or criminal activity. It appears most effective, however, in cases where these problems are clearly secondary to traumatic stress and do not predate combat experience.

Understanding the meaning of the traumatic experience for the individual is equally important in treating posttraumatic stress in civilian life. Work with civilian victims of trauma has shown us that the victim's behavior during a traumatic situation is a significant factor in causing guilt that contributes to and complicates posttraumatic disorder. Elizabeth Barnes, a flight attendant, was one of thirty who survived a plane crash in which several hundred had died. Although many of the survivors had developed PTSD, Elizabeth's disorder was complicated by guilt that was linked to her behavior during the trauma. In her panicked rush to escape from the burning plane, she had not stopped to help another attendant who was trapped by the wreckage. The other attendant was rescued, but Elizabeth's guilt over her behavior made her recovery much more difficult than that of the other attendant who had been more seriously injured. The flight attendant who had been trapped was eventually able to resume flying; Elizabeth was not, and the fear of heights she developed extended to bridges and elevators.

Posttraumatic stress appears to be the inevitable price of war for a high percentage of those exposed to sustained combat. Is there anything we can learn from the Vietnam experience that can, if not prevent, at least mitigate the effects of PTSD in those exposed to life-threatening experiences in combat?

Our tradition has been to insist on civilian determination as to when and if men are to be used in combat, but how they are to be used and how they are to be trained have always been considered military prerogatives. Society becomes involved after particularly egregious wartime events become known and public pressure requires someone to blame for the particular tragedy.

There is an understandable fear on the part of the military that civilian interference might lead to a lack of discipline or toughness in recruits. Shortly after the Vietnam War ended, however, critics began questioning the methods by which soldiers were prepared for combat, based on their actual effectiveness (Eisenhart, 1975). Not preparing soldiers to expect to be afraid during combat or to feel shock and horror on seeing the mutilated bodies of dying and dead comrades, appears to have created a sense of false bravado that frequently crumbled in the face of the realities of combat in Vietnam.

One of our veterans told a story of seeing a training film of combat in Vietnam in which wounded South Vietnamese soldiers were being evacuated. The sergeant showing the film was making the point that stupid soldiers are the ones who get hit. At that moment the commanding officer came in and ordered the film stopped because he objected to the medical evacuation scenes. The implication that only foolish soldiers are wounded or killed is itself questionable preparation for combat. The fact that the officer felt it necessary to hide from the recruits the reality that combat soldiers get injured and die likely made them more uneasy than the film itself would have done.

The military in Vietnam also ignored the need for soldiers exposed to sustained combat to discuss their experiences with skilled professionals who would not use the information in a judgmental or punitive way. Had this opportunity occurred, warning signs of posttraumatic stress—insomnia, outbreaks of rage, or episodes of uncontrollable anxiety—would have likely been detected in many soldiers before their discharge. Helping these men to understand their combat and postcombat reactions would have made them far better prepared to deal with their stress symptoms. As it was, many were so unprepared for the emotional aftereffects of combat that they feared for their sanity and withdrew into a shell of their own making.

Neither the soldier nor his family and friends back home are prepared for the full consequences of combat. Most assume that the risks of war are short term, with the odds of survival in one's favor. If a son, husband, brother, or friend returns home from combat, those who are close to him are likely to feel pride, relief, and gratitude over his survival. Many undoubtedly expect that the growth and confidence gained from the experience will be reflected in a better future than might otherwise have been possible.

But even before Vietnam, experience had shown us that the tragic effects of combat often only begin with the end of war. The combat soldiers described by Erich Maria Remarque in *All Quiet on the Western Front* (1929) who had spent years killing and seeing comrades killed in the trenches of World War I, suspected that their lives were over whether or not they survived. The hero of the novel suggests that one man, slightly older than the rest, who had operated a farm and had a clear sense of who he was before the war, might be able to resume his life. For the rest of the group who were just beginning to find themselves, death had so permeated their lives that they were destined to remain what Remarque referred to as "a generation of men who even though they may have escaped its shells were destroyed by the war." Awareness of the human price paid by the combat soldier who has fought and survived, while not an argument against war under any circumstances, is a factor that must be included in assessing the costs of war.

Not only the individual veteran and those close to him but the country as a whole has suffered from the lingering effects of combat on Vietnam veterans. With rare exceptions, these men came home with a sense of bitterness toward their country stemming from a feeling that their lives were dealt with carelessly by a government that had no clear sense of what it wanted from them. As one veteran put it, "In Vietnam I lost my feelings for God, for my family, and for my country. My feelings for my family and for God are returning, but I don't think I'll ever get over my anger toward the United States." One veteran who handled extensive combat well, who did not develop PTSD, and whose postwar work and family life did not show scars of the war, has never voted in a national election. His refusal to vote is an expression of his belief that presidents of both parties waged the war for which his friends died needlessly, and therefore no political leadership can be trusted. The disaffection of a large proportion of young men, most of whom went to Vietnam eager to serve their country, is one of the many sad legacies of that war.

What the Vietnam veteran needs from his country is not praise or gratitude but empathy. This entails a willingness to enter into his experience. Still today, more than thirty years after the end of the war, the demands of such an encounter are painful, and the urge to avoid it is great.

The time lag is not so surprising. It took forty years for the story of the horror of the Bataan Death March to be fully told (Knox, 1981). The fact that the fall of the Bataan peninsula to the Japanese in World War II was a major military defeat signaling our eventual loss of the Philippine Islands; that our men suffered unspeakable horrors as prisoners of war; that some of those horrors were inflicted by desperate, starving, and dying Americans on one another; and that almost two-thirds of the ten thousand American prisoners died made us reluctant to explore what had happened. The soldiers who did survive, interviewed in their sixties, experienced a painful satisfaction in telling their story. Reading about, or watching the television documentary based on, the survivors' accounts permits a painful but moving empathy with those men that leaves one feeling better for knowing. Vietnam veterans were particularly moved by the story of Bataan, though many wondered why the experience had not been brought to the public's attention long before.

Interest in the political and military history of the Vietnam War has been an encouraging first sign, but an intellectual concern with that war needs to be accompanied by a human concern with the experience of the fighting men during and after combat. For the Vietnam experience was not simply a matter of military or political policies or mistakes. It was a devastating emotional encounter with fear, violence, guilt, death, and mourning. The country that asked its young men to fight the war that was fought in Vietnam needs to be willing to share the pain that knowledge of the experience entails. Understanding is coming unfortunately late in the lives of these veterans, but better late than not at all.

REFERENCES

Baker, J. (1984). Monitoring of suicidal behavior among patients in the VA health care system. *Psychiatric Annals*, 14: 272–75.

Beck, A. T., Steer, R. A., Beck, J. S., and Newman, C. F. (1993). Hopelessness, depression, suicidal ideation, and clinical diagnosis of depression. *Suicide and Life-Threatening Behavior*, 23: 139–45.

Bullman, T. A., and Kang, H. K. (1994). Posttraumatic stress disorder and the risk of traumatic deaths among Vietnam veterans. *Journal of Nervous and Mental Disease*, 182: 604–10.

———. (1996). The risk of suicide among wounded Vietnam veterans. *American Journal of Public Health*, 86: 662–67.

Centers for Disease Control. (1987). Postservice mortality among Vietnam veterans. *Journal of the American Medical Association*, 257: 790–95.

Eisenhart, R. W. (1975). "You can't hack it little girl": A discussion of the covert psychological agenda of modern combat training. *Journal of Social Issues*, 31: 13–23.

Eitinger, L. (1969). Psychosomatic problems in concentration camp survivors. *Journal of Psychosomatic Research*, 13: 183–89.

Fawcett, J., Clarke, D. C., and Busch, K. A. (1993). Assessing and treating the patient at risk for suicide. *Psychiatric Annals*, 23: 244–55.

Futterman, S., and Pumpiam-Mindlin, E. (1951). Traumatic war neurosis five years later. *American Journal of Psychiatry*, 108: 401–8.

Hearst, N., Neuman, T. B., and Hulley, S. B. (1986). Delayed effects of the military draft on mortality: A randomized natural experiment. *New England Journal of Medicine*, 314: 620–24.

Hendin, H., and Haas, A. P. (1984a). Posttraumatic stress disorders in veterans of early American wars. *The Psychohistory Review*, 12: 25–30.

———. (1984b). What protects some? Combat adaptations of veterans without posttraumatic stress disorders. *American Journal of Psychiatry*, 141: 956–60.

———. (1984c). *Wounds of war: The psychological aftermath of combat in Vietnam*. New York: Basic Books.

———. (1991). Suicide and guilt as manifestations of posttraumatic stress disorder in Vietnam veterans. *American Journal of Psychiatry*, 5: 586–91.

Hendin, H., Maltsberger, J. T., Lipschitz, A., Haas, A. P., and Kyle, J. (2001). Recognizing and responding to a suicide crisis. *Suicide and Life-Threatening Behavior*, 31: 115–28.

Hendin, H., Pollinger-Haas, A., Singer, P., and Ulman, R. (1981). Meanings of combat and the development of posttraumatic stress disorder. *American Journal of Psychiatry*, 138: 1490–93.

Karnow, S. (1982). *Vietnam: A history*. New York: Viking Press.

Knox, D. (1981). *Death march: The survivors of Bataan*. New York: Harcourt, Brace, and Jovanovich.

Kramer T. L., Lindy, J. D., Green, B. L., Grace, M. C., and Leonard, A. C. (1994). The comorbidity of post-traumatic stress disorder and suicidality in Vietnam veterans. *Suicide and Life-Threatening Behavior*, 24: 58–67.

Lifton, R. J. (1968). *Death in life: Survivors of Hiroshima.* New York: Random House.

Niederland, W. (1968), Clinical observations on the "survivor syndrome." *International Journal of Psychoanalysis*, 49: 313–15.

Pollock, D. A., Rhodes, P., Boyle, C. A., Decoufle, P., and McGee, D. L. (1990). Estimating the number of suicides among Vietnam veterans. *American Journal of Psychiatry*, 147: 772–76.

Remarque, E. M. (1929). *All quiet on the Western Front.* Boston: Little, Brown.

Summers, H. G. (1982). *On strategy: A critical analysis of the Vietnam War.* Navato, CA: Presidio Press.

Tuchman, B. W. (1985). *The march of folly: From Troy to Vietnam.* New York: Random House.

U.S. Congress. House. Committee on Veterans Affairs. *Presidential review memorandum on Vietnam-era veterans*, House Report 38, October 10, 1978.

Chapter Ten

Children's Responses
to Terrorist Attacks

Ofra Ayalon

This chapter deals with the plague of terrorism and its impact on a great number of people who are caught up in the traumatic ripple effects, forming ever-widening "circles of vulnerability," including families, friends, peers, eyewitnesses, rescuers, and mental health workers. Based on thirty-five years of research, the author analyzes the impact of terrorism on child victims or survivors in terms of the main feature of trauma: the rupture of continuity in time, in relations and attachments, in perceptions of self and others, in basic assumptions about the world, in future expectations, and, above all, in ruptures in one's fabric of meaning and belief systems. The growing number of children involved in terrorist victimization in Israel and other countries prompted the formation of new, age-appropriate methods that focus on the need to establish the survivor's sense of continuity of experience. This chapter describes the author's internationally used Community Oriented Preventive Education (COPE) program for dealing with disaster and trauma by enhancing six channels of coping resources. It advocates the children's right to grow and to actualize their full potential in a safe environment.

PROLOGUE

On September 11, 2001, I was scheduled for a San Francisco television interview as part of a media tour that I conducted together with Dr. Boaz Ganor, head of the International Policy Institute for Counter-Terrorism (ICT). The idea behind this tour was to discuss the issues faced by a society coping with terrorism—specifically, how Israeli society copes with the perpetual threat of suicide bombing. Our wake-up call on that particular morning was the attack on the World Trade Center and the Pentagon. During the next few frantic days, the demand for our public presentations on this particular brand of terrorism grew enormously. As part of the rising interest in our work, I have been asked how I came to be involved in the area of trauma induced by war and terrorism and its impact on children. Here is the story.

MA'ALOT MASSACRE

It all started for me on the morning of May 15, 1974. Driving my car to the child guidance clinic where I had been employed as a family therapist, I heard over the radio a trembling voice announcing that 105 children, who were on their spring school outing, were captured in a school building in Ma'alot and held hostage by three Palestine Liberation Organization (PLO) gunmen. I froze in my seat, hardly breathing, flooded by horrific images of recently hijacked planes, the Japanese terrorist's attack on Ben-Gurion International Airport, and the kidnapping and murder of the eleven Israeli athletes in the Munich Olympics. Only one month earlier, four terrorists from across the Lebanese border stormed a residential home in a small town in the north of Israel and killed all eighteen neighbors. The sole survivor was a ten-year-old girl. The bullet aimed at her killed the little dog she was clasping.

Sixteen hours later, as the terrorists' deadline expired, they shot and killed twenty-two children and wounded many more just before an army rescue squad entered the school and managed to save the remaining hostages. The following day I drove to the hospital where many of the wounded children were being treated. The matron pointed me to a small room where a five-year-old girl lay motionless, white as a sheet. She had been found in a house near the attacked school, lying wounded in a pool of blood next to the mutilated bodies of her father, her pregnant mother, and her four-year-old brother. When I arrived at the emergency room, she had been diagnosed as "clinically dead," with no pulse and no blood pressure. Emergency surgery saved her life. She was still in a critical stage, dozing in and out of consciousness. I stayed by her bedside a long time before turning to the other wounded survivors of what has been known since as the "Ma'alot massacre."

For the following eighteen years I stayed in touch with these brave young people, most of whom had been between fifteen and sixteen years old at the time of this event, trying to learn how they were coping as time passed. Over the years I returned to the same group of survivors with the following questions: "What did you think, what did you feel, what did you do during the hostage event that either upset you or helped you?" I asked about the time period shortly after the event and also about the long range: "What helped you and what distressed you in the long run?" One other question asked about the behavior of other people, such as terrorists, friends, teachers, parents, medical staff, and therapists: "What did others do during the event or in the aftermath that either helped you or disturbed you?"

This method of inquiry introduces a new research paradigm, specially suited for people who have been traumatized. It approaches the victims or survivors with full consideration for the disempowering effects of their ordeal and seeks to empower them. At the same time, it seeks to collect the most credible information about their immediate and long-range trauma-related responses (Ayalon and Soskis, 1986). This method of inquiry is based on the assumption that every person, adult or child, is furnished with coping resources and uses them for his or her physical and psychological survival.

The questions are geared toward identifying the existing coping resources as well as the instances when the existing coping patterns are overwhelmed by the traumatic experience, causing detrimental effects on the survivors. This diagnostic process, which turns the survivor into an active collaborator in assessing both the helpful and nonhelpful patterns of dealing with the trauma, becomes the first step in the rehabilitative therapy process. It fulfills the person's need to regain identity and mastery, whether in a symbolic or tangible fashion. This method enables survivors to view the event in a new light, not only as helpless victims, but also as active survivors capable of choosing and shaping their own fate.

Thus began my fascination with the strength and stamina of the human spirit. I was puzzled and curious to learn how people, especially young ones in their formative years, handled devastating life events and coped in the face of great adversity. Out of my own personal horror in the face of terrorism, I needed to understand what goes on in the minds of victims during and after their face-to-face nightmarish encounter with the perpetrator. I needed to understand how one can endure such an experience as that of the little girl (who survived to become a lovable and competent young woman), who disclosed to me her last memory of the terrorist, "He was bending over me with a nice smile on his face, as he emptied his cartridge into my belly." And then, she said, "I pretended to be dead so he would not come back and kill me completely." I am writing this chapter in memory of the victims and in honor of the survivors.

TERRORISM: THE VICIOUS ART OF INFLICTING TERROR

The actions of the terrorist—murder, sabotage, blackmail—may be identical to those of the common criminal. However, for the terrorist, these are all a means to achieve broader goals, whether ideological, religious, social or economic. The way to the terrorist's ultimate political goal runs through a vital interim objective—the creation of an unremitting paralyzing sensation of fear in the target community. Thus, modern terrorism is a means of instilling in every individual the feeling that the next terror attack may have his name on it (Ganor, 2002).

The nature of terrorist activity is such that it calculatedly and systematically wreaks terror on random, defenseless civilian populations. The arbitrary choice of victims conveys that terror can victimize anyone, anywhere, anytime. Terrorism is targeted to demoralize the population, to win a psychological and political war, and to gain public awareness through publicity in the media. (On September 11, 2002, memorial day, a sharp observation was made in the news, stating that Bin Laden never needs to launch another attack on America, as every media exposure of the collapsing World Trade Center replicates his outstanding achievement and its consequent horror.) Politically, terrorism tries to extort something from a third party, such as a government or an organization, by using random people as pawns (Ochberg, 1978). Randomizing and maximizing the number of casualties is a method of creating fear of danger that is always impending and unpredictable.

It is obvious that this method is effective only against societies that place a high value on human life, as the act of terrorism is intended to make them give in to protect their people. It is rendered ineffective in a culture where there is no reverence for individual lives. It cannot work against a culture that enlists young people to become suicide bombers and promises them sexual and other gains in heaven if they sacrifice their lives by killing others, either for political or for religious purposes. Consequently, it is no wonder that terrorists target children, who are the most precious and vulnerable members of society. That is especially true in a society of survivors such as Israel, which lives under the shadow of the Holocaust. In Israeli society, children are precious, not only to their parents, which is self-evident, but to the community as a whole. Children are the future. Children are the proof that the Holocaust genocide is no longer there and that there is hope for a national resurrection.

Palestinian terrorism has sharply cut into this collective wound by targeting infants and schoolchildren (Ayalon and Waters, 2002). The last century, as well as the beginning of the current one, has been marked by terrorists assaulting Israeli nurseries and schools, seizing hostages, hijacking airplanes, participating in drive-by shootings, and booby-trapping and suicide bombing the civilian population. In some cases, the victims were murdered at the onset of the attack; in others, they were held as hostages until rescued by the army. The victims varied in age and kinship, including babies, children, teenagers, and their parents. In certain cases, the attacks were directed toward an entire family, and in others, the victims were hit in the company of peers, friends, or strangers, as schools were ambushed and bombs exploded in buses, in shopping centers, and on street corners. On top of the death and injury toll, each attack spreads horror among the direct eyewitnesses and the rest of the population through the media.

CIRCLES OF VULNERABILITY: RIPPLE EFFECTS OF THE TRAUMATIC EXPERIENCE

When a terrorist attack hits direct victims, an immeasurable number of people are caught up in the traumatic ripple effects, forming ever-widening "circles of vulnerability." Families who lose their "dear ones," friends and peers, are all victimized, and so are the rescue workers who come in close contact with the horrors of death and injury. The circles of vulnerability include the medical staff, social workers, teachers, and psychologists who are exposed vicariously to the trauma of their students and clients. Eyewitnesses are also traumatized.

Many children are actual survivors and many more become "near miss" victims, by their physical or psychological proximity to the dead, injured, or orphaned peers. The near miss traumatic ideation is formed in the child's mind by the indelible realization that "it could have happened to me." Many of them are hidden victims who carry hidden scars. Often neither they nor their parents realize how wounded they are. They are often neglected by posttrauma health services as well. The trauma of being an eyewitness to a lethal terrorist attack is mainly determined by the imposed passivity of having to watch or listen helplessly to the sights and sounds of death and destruction. The eyewitness is unprotected from the impact of the violence and may suffer from vicarious traumatic disorder. Like a stone cast into a pool of water, the ripples of the disaster spread throughout the pool and affect the entire community. The great risk lies in the fact that family, school, law enforcement agencies, and mental health professionals commonly neglect the needs of the witnesses. In planning victim services, it is important to identify the high-risk individuals who are vicariously affected by their geographical proximity to the site of the incident, by their social proximity to the victims, or by the psychological proximity of the victims or both (Ochberg and Soskis, 1982). At the same time, it is paramount to identify those agents in the community who are available to give support, who range from professional caretakers to volunteers and peers.

PSYCHOLOGICAL IMPACT OF TERRORISM ON THE COMMUNITY

What are the threats inflicted by terrorism that disrupt children's social and psychological balance? The impending threat to life and to bodily integrity, the danger of losing limbs and becoming crippled, which is the plight of a great many survivors of terrorist attacks, permeates every level of daily routine—it can strike everywhere. When airplanes, buses, and trains are targeted and when shops and restaurants are exploding, daily mobility can no longer be taken for granted. The threat is contagious—there is a lurking danger that any train or bus can become a death trap. Yet another source of threat is the dread of losing dear ones, beloved spouses, parents, children, and friends. Young people fear for their parents. Parents often say, "A child's pain or injury is even worse than my own. I wish it would have happened to me instead of my child." Another threat involved in terrorism is the threat to the home, to the alleged security within it, as terrorists burst into homes and kill people in their beds.

During the Gulf War in 1991, in which Israel was on the receiving end of an assault on its civilian population, the rockets sent from Iraq hit over two thousand homes. On top of the rocket bombings, the whole population was under threat of biochemical terrorism for forty days and nights, consequently wearing gas masks and being confined to sealed rooms during each attack (Ayalon, 1997b).

Terrorism imposes a threat to our value system, damaging the ability to trust others and the assumption that we live in a relatively safe world. Our culture places a lot of emphasis on "attachment" in childhood and tries to instill in babies and small children a sense of "basic trust" that is considered a psychological foundation for healthy development. When encountering the viciousness and violence of terrorism, one gets in touch with something so destructive in the other person that it destroys this basic trust. When trust in other human beings turns out to be misleading, any stranger may potentially be perceived as an enemy. Exposure to cruelty, the proximity of an attacker who seems to enjoy causing suffering, destroys the victim's basic comprehension of what is acceptable human behavior.

Exposure to terrorist brutality evokes the danger of emotional leakage or contagion of aggression from perpetrator to victim. The surging aggression in the victim is fed by utter frustration and is reinforced by perceiving the aggressor as an authority, whose power is derived from absolute physical advantage. The damaging outcome of the perpetual encounter with such destructive aggression may shake or even break the acquired fragile psychological barrier against our innate aggressive drives, the shield that serves to safeguard our civilization. This process is especially dangerous for children who may identify with the aggressor and, in a paradoxical way, cast the terrorists into their role models (Ayalon and Waters, 2002).

THE IMPACT OF TERRORISM ON
CHILD VICTIMS OR SURVIVORS

Childhood is an unquestionably impressionable period. Overwhelming and stressful events may imprint a permanent stamp on the developing personality in ways that are not easy to measure by existing psychological measurements. In some cases, patterns of repetitive maladaptive behaviors may be set in motion following the traumatic event, but in other cases, these patterns, dormant for years, may be triggered later by additional trauma. Child survivors of past events often report heightened anxiety, anger, sadness, and flashbacks following repetitive terrorist attacks (Desivilya, Gal, and Ayalon, 1996).

Children in various phases of development, who have immature coping styles and are dependent on adults for understanding the external events, are even more vulnerable. The loss of family, caretakers, and friends may shatter their world and put them at high risk. Children tend to regress, suffer from sleeping and eating disorders, lose trust in others, have impaired concentration, and neglect their schoolwork. Some become aggressive and violent. Small children keep reenacting the trauma in their games and have recurrent nightmares (Terr, 1990).

In all instances of child survivors of current terrorist attacks, one of the most prominent stressful elements of the traumatic experience is the perceived failure of their meaningful adults to shield their children or themselves from danger. Toddlers who survived a whole night's terrorist captivity in their Kibbutz nursery, watching an infant being shot to death, expressed a great deal of anger and resentment at their parents for having "abandoned" them. These desperate accusations signify a breach in the developing ability of the three-year-old children to trust adults and to bond securely with their parents (Ayalon, 1982). In many cases, children endured long periods of separation from their parents. In other cases, children went through the harrowing experience of watching their parents being injured or killed.

Adolescents are particularly susceptible to stress that involves disfiguration and humiliation. Being reduced to total helplessness and exposed to violence for hours during the hostage situation resulted in the aftermath in prolonged periods of regressive dependency, which clashed with their loss of trust in others and with their age-appropriate struggle for independence. Regression was enhanced by the fact that terrorists held control over toilet procedures and the privilege of moving, talking, or eating enhanced the regression. Their isolation from any source of support increased the tendency to cling to supernatural rescue fantasies (Ayalon, 1983a).

IMMEDIATE REACTIONS DURING ATTACK

The encounter with someone whose intention is to kill, wherein the victim is totally unable to protect himself or others, involves many elements that are conducive to prolonged trauma. The range of immediate reactions reported by survivors reflected the whirlpool of drives, fears, attitudes, and norms of behavior, wherein every possible solution seemed to lead to an even greater catastrophe. The severity of the trauma is measured, among other factors, by the duration of the event, which varied from a few moments to a number of days, and by the death toll. The trauma of the young hostages stemmed from a combination of physical pain and mental anguish created by the following elements:

The *brush with death* shattered the illusion of invulnerability that usually shields us against existential anxiety (Lahad and Ayalon, 1995). Years later, one boy who survived with an injury, says, "I feel dead. I go every day to the cemetery to visit my dead friends" (Ayalon and Horowitz, 1996). The *arbitrariness* of the attack intensified the fear of the victims and degraded them to a subhuman level, badly shaking their sense of personal identity. *Uncertainty* about the duration and seriousness of the situation and the chances of being rescued had destructive consequences (Ayalon and Lahad, 2000). Loss of the ability to defend oneself and others and the obstruction of escape routes increased *frustration*. Frustration is known to breed *aggression*, which has no way of being diffused and is consequently directed inward and turned into *desperation* (Seligman, 1975). *Ambivalent attachment to the aggressor* occurred when some hostages felt totally dominated and dependent on the terrorists for the most basic and private daily functions, such as mobility, speech, nourishment, and toilet functioning.

In our survey six years later, one girl disclosed that initially she had felt helped by her effort to communicate with her captor, believing she could influence him to change his mind and retract from the murderous plan. Later, however, she criticized her own behavior, "Today, when I look back and think that I actually spoke with the terrorists, with those murderers, I feel awful. How could I even speak to them?" (Ayalon and Soskis, 1986, p. 271) Research on hostages provides some evidence showing that communicating with the terrorists might delay or prevent their murderous intentions. Yet, in retrospect, this activity may have damaged the survivors' self-image and burdened them with guilt and self-disgust, as reported by one girl, who shared some bread with one of the captors. After her rescue from the bloody attack, in which many of her peers were killed and injured, she developed an aversive reaction to eating bread, which for her became contaminated and repulsive (Ayalon, 1983a, 1983b).

In the group of Israelis who were held hostage in Entebbe, communication with the captors seems to have saved lives. When the Israelis and Jews were separated from the rest of the hostages, one of the Jewish passengers exposed the number that had been tattooed on his arm in a German concentration camp in the Holocaust, accusing the German terrorist of being a Nazi. Later, the same terrorist, during the rescue operation by the Israeli army, hesitated to shoot him and the man was saved (Schreiber, 1979). In this case, communication with the captor seemed a heroic stance and helped in the rehabilitation of the survivor from his traumatic experience.

PALLIATIVE COPING STYLES

From hostages' reports of what helped them during their ordeal, it seems that denial and dissociation abated the unbearable anxiety. Daydreams about hearth and home, fantasizing about a beloved person, and ruminating over childhood memories seemed to have helped the children to hold on (Ayalon and Soskis, 1986). Survivors of terrorism use dissociation as a coping mechanism against severe trauma. "The dissociation mechanisms are probably sophisticated methods that survivors of trauma developed in order to cope with unbearable experiences. The ability to imagine, fantasize, and experience oneself in a different time and space saved these survivors from unbearable painful experiences." (Megged, 2001, pp. 23–24) The "invisible bubble" is an example of such a mechanism:

Shula was almost sixteen when she became a hostage in a terrorist attack on her group of classmates. She describes the many hours in captivity surrounded by wired explosives and guns pointed by the terrorists. She said, "They could dictate to us to sit or to stand, to speak or to keep quiet, to eat or drink, to go the toilets or to wait for hours on end, but they could not control my imagination . . . I remember sitting for hours as if I were in an invisible bubble. I actually had the sensory experience of sitting at the Sabbath evening dinner table, hearing my father make the blessings and my brothers singing the Sabbath songs, seeing the lit candles and smelling the food." (Saban, 1990, p. 47) The girl stated that this was what had kept her alive and sane. Magical thinking, taking vows, and bargaining with fate ("If I survive, I will always be good") reinforced hope in some of the hostages, who also found consolation in prayer and religious rituals. Prayers and faith in God were strategies aimed at maintaining meaning and hope.

The cost of trauma in human suffering and distress is very high both to victims and to those surrounding them. Shock, anxiety, pain, rage, guilt, and despair continue to hurt as "thorns in the spirit" (James, 1898). The traumatic experiences need to be acknowledged, expressed, listened to, witnessed by caring others, tolerated, contained, treated, and healed. Major obstacles block the ability of victims and survivors to voice their emotional turmoil and to be heard by others. A very helpful strategy mentioned by a survivor was the effort to record and bear witness: "In the hospital, with bandaged hands, I kept writing my diary" (Ayalon and Soskis, 1986, pp. 263).

ACTIVE COPING STYLES

Activity has been recorded as one of the most effective manners of psychological coping (Janis, 1958; Gal and Lazarus, 1975). In quite a few researched terrorist events, we found that young children showed initiative in calling for support or rescuing themselves. A five-year-old wounded girl clung to her dead father and pretended to be dead, while the terrorists were shooting her mother and younger brother. Another girl, six years old, captured by a terrorist on a dark stairway, kicked the captor in the leg, managed to free herself and hide under a piece of furniture while the terrorist was pacing the room for hours looking for her. An eleven-year-old girl used a secret code language to fool her captors and call the military for help. A twelve-year-old girl, who ran for her life among bullets and explosions in the middle of the night, stopped on her way to pick up a younger child who seemed panicked and lost (Ayalon, 1983a; 1988). In spite of the children's immediate resourcefulness, their ordeal took its toll, reflected in the recovery period by symptoms such as excessive fears, nightmares, bedwetting, retaliatory fantasies, aggressive acting out, withdrawal, school refusal, clinging to parents, and compulsive engagement in ritualistic games. In one case, the ritualistic game took the form of breaking, fixing, and then breaking again different symbolic objects. In another case, it took the form of mimicking medical procedures and imposing them on just about everyone in sight.

Coping reactions that were adaptive at one phase of the traumatic experience could have deleterious effects in the aftermath. A few adolescents, who managed to escape from the besieged school at the onset of the previously mentioned Ma'alot attack, suffered most severely from long-lasting unrelieved guilt at having abandoned their friends and having been saved at their expense (Ayalon, 1983a). Apparently, survivor guilt torments a great number of children who survived suicide attacks on their school bus or were the only survivors of their families in some recent suicide bombings of homes and shops.

LONG-TERM RESPONSES

Long-term effects of a world shattered by a massive act of terrorism may result in perpetual disruption of the sense of self, integration, and continuity of one's personal history. The main feature of trauma is "rupture"—it ruptures continuity in time, in relations and attachments, in perceptions of self and others, in basic assumptions about the world, in future expectations, and above all—it ruptures the fabric of meaning (Gordon and Wraith, 1993). Victims are unable to grasp the full implications of the loss or come to terms with the reality of the situation: it is inexplicable, unbelievable, and incomprehensible. The imagery of terrorist violence can become an unconscious organizing principle, determining how people see the world and how they choose to act. Some may develop a militaristic coping strategy, tinted with paranoid suspicions that may precipitate a new round of violence.

Violent and militaristic responses may, for some people, constitute a response to trauma—an attempt to overcome one's worst inner fears, to awaken a sense of feeling in an otherwise "frozen" psyche, or to find a legitimate outlet for massive grief and anger (Lumsden, 1997). One of the hostages who, by volunteering to carry the terrorists' messages out of the building, was spared several hours of the ordeal and its harrowing termination, described a perpetual preoccupation with his guilt and a great need to act out his hostility. During a military action against terrorist bases in Lebanon, in which he participated as a regular soldier, it became well known that he was "carrying out a private war of revenge for his murdered mates." According to him, he succeeded in releasing an enormous personal pressure by being able to participate in this military operation. But he is still considered an "angry young man" (Ayalon, 1983a).

Some survivors suffer guilt, become chronically suspicious or angry, or turn their unspent aggression inward, damaging themselves mentally or physically. Some emerge with a bleak outlook on life, with feelings of depression, anhedonia, and helplessness. Others adopt a heroic attitude, trying to become "saviors." Finally, some shift toward forgiveness and altruism, a feature that is reflected dramatically in the case of a woman film director, wounded as a teenager by a terrorist, who has made it her life mission to fight for his release from jail, risking being considered a "traitor" by other survivors (Desivilya, Gal, and Ayalon, 1996).

THE SURVIVOR SYNDROME

One major change that was prominent across the group of the young survivors was the emergence of a "survivor identity" that became the subjective measure of all subsequent life experiences. Some began their life narrative from the day of the attack, as if all previous experiences were wiped out. An examination of the personal meaning associated with retaining "survivor identity" revealed that it converged with two distinct outlooks on life, one generally optimistic and the other predominantly pessimistic. The former has generated a belief in the survivors that through their traumatic experience and rescue they have been chosen for life by supreme powers, and hence they feel protected and immune. In contrast, their pessimistic counterparts viewed their ordeal as a proof of guilt, condemnation, or punishment and nurtured catastrophic expectations for the future (Ayalon and Soskis, 1986).

Seventeen years after the events, well into their young adulthood, more than half of the survivors still suffered from the following moderate- to low-frequency symptoms: hyperalertness, sleep disturbances and recurrent dreams, intrusive images and thoughts, catastrophe relived through fantasy, avoidance of objects and places that reminded them of the event, startle reactions to abrupt noises, and nervousness. A small minority complained about depressive reactions, numbing of sensations (psychic numbing), social withdrawal, memory blocks, and problems of concentration. A few continued to feel persecution, expectation of the recurrence of the event, the need to search for prophetic signs (omens and portents), regret and guilt toward the victims who perished, a lack of social support, suspicion and alienation ("A stranger could never understand what I've been through"). A subgroup of survivors showed a great drive for excellence, achievement, and altruistic contribution to society, while some took great pains to hide their past predicament even from their own children (Ayalon, 1983a; Desivilya, Gal, and Ayalon, 1996). The fact that different individuals adopt different survival strategies explains that we cannot easily predict adult behavior from childhood trauma.

On a positive note, cognitive factors such as faith and a sense of social responsibility were found to be conducive to coping with the stressful situation (Soskis and Ayalon, 1985).

SUPPORT NETWORKS

Social support has been identified as both a buffer against stress and an enhancer of the ability to cope. Creating a small cohesive group of victims with reliable leadership, efficient role allocation, and a high degree of interpersonal communication contributed much to the power of the victims to cope with stress, both at the time of the attack and during the period of rehabilitation (Ayalon, 1983a, 1983b.). The proximity, immediacy, and expectancy

(PIE) principle, coined by Salmon during World War I for combat stress treatment (Salmon, 1919), is employed within the active community and self-help groups. Geographic *proximity* is exercised when the children are not evacuated or displaced from their home community. The natural scene of the school or community center is preferred to a clinical setting. It prevents stigmatization and reestablishes the pre-trauma connotation of the place where the traumatic events occurred. *Immediacy* is advocated whenever possible, to prevent the posttraumatic symptoms from setting in. In cases involving the death of parents, siblings, or peers, short-term intervention and bereavement rituals become part of the healing. *Expectancy* includes providing accurate information about the event, explaining the context, insisting on redeeming the survivors from guilt feelings, and explaining the process of grieving and delivering messages of hope for personal and group recuperation.

We can identify two distinct circles of support for children traumatized by terrorism. The first is composed of family members, friends, neighbors, and colleagues. The second is composed of children who share the same fate, in which the giving and receiving of support takes place on equal ground, with the tacit understanding that "only someone who has gone through a similar experience can understand my suffering." The "shared fate" support provides a sense of group cohesiveness and different models of individual coping strategies.

THE TRANSITIONAL SPACE WHERE HEALING TAKES PLACE

Between the external world that harbors violence and atrocities and the internal vulnerable sense of self that is uniquely individual lies the "transitional space," the domain of imagination, play, and creativity. Borrowed from Winnicott's concept (Winnicott, 1971), this intermediate psychic zone offers the opportunity for healing and growth. According to Winnicott, in the process of learning to individuate from the mother figure, children often attach themselves to a transitional object such as a blanket or doll. This object possesses symbolic power, simultaneously acting as a reminder of the absent mother and the comforting breast. The symbolic value of the primary transitional objects gradually spreads and becomes an ever-growing transitional space for the child's play, linking inner needs and external realities. This transitional space can serve as a bridge between the situational terrorist events and the psychological traumatic experience. In this arena, the child's natural activity of play and creativity can have a cathartic effect. It is the space for internal conflict resolution and healing of the trauma, a place in which to create order out of uncertainty and chaos, and to heal the wounds inflicted by the terrorist violence (Ayalon, 1998a).

CREATIVE METHODS IN DEBRIEFING
AND EARLY CRISIS INTERVENTION

The primary requirement for child survivors of all ages is to experience physical and psychological safety. What young children need most of all following a traumatic experience is to restore their sense of a secure "home base"
and to reestablish their trust in their parents and caretakers. This requires that
significant others be involved and supportive. When safety is restored, the
children's natural coping skills can begin to emerge. It is only at this point
that the debriefing technique may be considered (Wraith, 2000; Gurwithch,
Sitterle, Young, and Pfefferbaum, 2002).

Debriefing and early crisis intervention seek to enhance and broaden natural resilience and teach new coping skills, to work through perceptions and
responses to the disaster so that the event may be integrated into the fabric of
life and remembered—without reawakening traumatic reactions. Debriefing
is geared toward engaging victims and helpers in integrating their bizarre and
shattering experience into a cohesive, cognitive, emotional, and social frame.
In other words, the goal is to help group members find meaning and order in
a chaotic and unexpected life experience (Dyregrov, 1999).

Debriefing is offered as a structured way to elicit the personal story of the
experience with an emphasis on the sensory perceptions (sight, smell, sound,
touch, and taste), thoughts, feelings, and behaviors experienced during and
shortly after the event. These are shared with others in the "shared fate" small
group, composed of children with similar experiences, under the premise that
any response to the disaster is accepted and normalized through the group-
sharing process. By using a variety of creative techniques and tools, children's group debriefings offer a safe space for ventilation and validation of
painful experiences. Creative methods enhance coping resources and provide
cognitive learning experience by contributing to the children's knowledge
about trauma and its aftermath.

The growing number of children involved in terrorist victimization
prompted the formation of age-appropriate methods of debriefing that focus
on the need to establish the survivors' sense of "continuity of experience."
(Ayalon and Soskis, 1986; Ayalon and van Tassel, 1987; Ayalon and Lahad,
2000; Galliano and Lahad, 2000). In order to anchor the children to their pre-
disaster stability, a time when their world seemed familiar and predictable,
the initial questions posed to an individual or a group focus on activities and
experiences during the hours prior to the incident. Similarly, sessions end
with the expectation of returning to some level of routine and normalcy. Another revision, pertinent to children but recommended for adults as well, is to
invite family members and relatives to participate in the debriefing process

for support and nurturance, either in the session or just outside the room where the debriefing takes place (Lahad and Cohen, 1998).

A further adaptation was made for very young children who have limited ability to process information cognitively and verbally but can engage spontaneously in imaginative play and "make believe" with toy figures and puppets. This debriefing procedure is carried out on a metaphoric level, using the language of children and projective play techniques. Toys as well as imaginary figures in games and in stories provide a safe distance from which children can access their own frightening experience (Ayalon, 1993a, 1993b). To ensure a successful process, it is highly recommended that the facilitators be people known to and trusted by the children. The following is an example of using a metaphoric debriefing card game with very young children.

METAPHORIC TELLING OF THE TRAUMA STORY AND FINDING THE COPING RESOURCES

COPE CARDS is a package of eighty-eight illustrated cards devised to help process trauma and enhance coping (Ayalon, Lukyanova, and Egetmeyer, 2002). When children feel "trapped in the trauma," and are unable to recall or recount the event without fear of overpowering emotion, the cards may provide triggers for personal story making. Work with COPE CARDS provides the opportunity to tell the personal recollections of the traumatization within a safe environment. The purpose of hearing the details of the trauma story is to revisit the scene and, in so doing, remove the grip of terror and horror. "Metaphoric stories triggered by the visual images of the cards are one step removed from the anguished reality. This 'creative distance' facilitates the recall and working through of traumatic experiences" (Ayalon and Egetmeyer, 2002, p. 18). Employing images and the imagination serves as a protective screen against becoming overwhelmed by intense emotions. When memories become too much to bear, one can return to the imagined story or look for other cards that may serve as anchors for a sense of thriving, surviving, and healing (Ayalon, 1993b; Lahad, 1999).

TELLING THE TRAUMA STORY

1. The child is offered a choice of one card, and then he or she introduces himself to the helper or the group via this card. (The group must not include more than five or six children.)
2. The card is given "a voice" to tell the story. The child tells how the figure in the card felt during the event, and then tells how it feels in the present.

3. There is an exchange of suggestions of how to "cope" with the figure's story (e.g., how to sleep better, how to push away fears and bad dreams, how to express anger). The discussion remains within the metaphor.

This method was used with kindergarten children (four- to five-year-olds) following a terrorist attack on a small village. Most of the children heard shooting and shouts throughout the night. They were told the basic facts surrounding the events by their parents and older siblings. The teacher reported that in a previous similar event, the children had expressed their experience mostly through aggressive play and spontaneous drawing but had very limited recourse to verbal processing. Given the COPE CARDS, the teacher encouraged the group of children to pick one card each. Next, the teacher described the rules of the new game: each child tells the story of his or her card, talking only when his or her turn comes. The teacher's card was a bear. The teacher's bear modeled the process for the children.

Bear said, "Good morning. I am a bear and my name is Dobi. I live in the woods. Last night I was napping as I heard loud noises of shooting and immediately I went into my cave and peeped outside to see what was going on. I felt my heart beat and I was trembling. Did any of you hear these noises?"

The children told their individual stories of the sequence of events through their own cards. "Dobi" expressed her feelings and fears and all the others used their cards to tell their reactions and feelings. Then Dobi chose a new card to show what helped. Each cardholder added a new card—the card that helped and then shared "what helped" with the rest of the group. At the end, each child put the "fear" card on the floor and covered it with the "help" card. The fear was not denied or made "all better" but was balanced by the images of coping.

Within a few days following the metaphorical game-like debriefing, parents reported a marked reduction in the children's fears and other disturbing behaviors (Ayalon and Egetmeyer, 2002, p. 16).

MODELING METAPHORIC AND CREATIVE
METHODS WITH A TRAUMATIZED FAMILY

A young couple with two daughters, aged five and seven, living on the fifth floor of a high-rise building, awakened one night to the terrible sounds of gunshots and screaming: three armed men were raiding their building. Rushing out of their flat to run and hide, the family was separated, and the parents lost sight of their daughters. Until they were reunited many hours later, each believed the others to be dead. They found out later that their next-door neighbors, a father and two daughters, were brutally murdered. Following the horrid event, each member of the family suffered severe stress reactions: the parents felt guilty and depressed, and the girls manifested phobic fears and catastrophic expectations of the ordeal repeating itself once again. They clung to their parents as they moved around the house, had nightmares, refused to sleep anywhere except in the parents' bedroom, and were afraid to leave the house.

The therapist paid a home visit and decided on crisis intervention strategies that engaged the parents as co-therapists in their daughters' treatment. This strategy was meant to empower the parents and to help them regain the parental accountability that was lost. The therapist assumed that the parents would gain from vicarious learning and guidance by helping the girls. In order to work in this manner, the therapist assumed different roles and modeled them to the parents, who were expected to carry on accordingly on a daily basis. The therapist, in guiding the parents, used a variety of metaphorical intervention methods combined with behavioral and cognitive techniques. The girls were given "paradoxical instructions" that would confirm their clinging reactions as normal and implement a change at the same time: "It's absolutely impossible for you to leave your parents' bedroom at the moment. It will take a very long time before you'll be able to do so, maybe even a whole month!"

Behavioral and cognitive desensitization was used to reduce their fears and gain control. This included rating each room in the apartment according to how frightening it was on a scale from one to ten and keeping a "fear diary" noting whenever nocturnal fears reoccurred and enactments of "jumping out of bed in a panic" to strange noises made by the therapist or parents. Creative methods included drawing in detail frightening fantasies, with an emphasis on small inappropriate details, such as a monster with a wristwatch. To help them change roles from "victim" to "caregiver," the girls were encouraged to "mother" and comfort their "frightened dolls." Finally, they got a "fear award," "fear" being reframed as a sign of ingenuity necessary for their survival (Alon, 1985).

In a period of two weeks, the girls' phobic reactions gradually subsided, and there were marked decreases in the parents' fears as well.

SCHOOL-BASED INTERVENTIONS

Following is a case of an intervention process with a group of school children exposed to terrorist persecution and the murder of their neighbors. Three Palestinian terrorists raided a house on the beach in a coastal town in the north of Israel. A father and his daughter (aged four) were brutally murdered on the shore and a two-year-old child suffocated to death, while neighbors, under the impression of being attacked, either hid or fled from their houses. A survey of the schools the next morning indicated that fifty-four children were absent. When the school bus crisis team brought them back, it became apparent that the night's events severely traumatized them. Initial assessment showed acute symptoms of bewilderment, anxiety, startle response to noises, flashbacks, fear of the dark, and avoidance of such reminders as the beach (the scene of the crime). There were crying spells, headaches, and stomachaches. The children clung to their parents. Most children in this high-risk group haunted by images of the murdered girls found concentration in the classroom impossible. The school crisis team started a small-group brief intervention within the school premises that lasted for five consecutive days. School staff had daily short debriefing and counseling sessions while they carried on with their normal routine (Ben Eli and Sela, 1980).

BEYOND WORDS

The traumatic experiences were so horrendous that words were not sufficient to describe the indescribable or to express the unexpected severe mental pain, the sights, the sounds, and the haunting memories. Drawing and finger painting conveyed the frightening images long before personal narratives were formed. All expressions, even the most idiosyncratic, were granted full legitimization by the facilitators and explained as "normal" for processing the trauma. Then the traumatic events of the night—the shouts, the flights from home to safer hiding places, the sights and sounds—were reenacted with detailed descriptions of every move, thought and feeling of self, and others. Some children chose to play the victims' roles while others played the role of the perpetrators, imitating the terrorists' shouts and even letting themselves be "captured" and "killed." As violent emotions surged, they were channeled into scenarios of vengeance and retaliation against the aggressors and acted out through dramatic reenactment and puppet shows. The first signs of relief were noticed when the children mimicked an execution of the "puppet terrorists."

As chaotic expressions settled down, children regained their age-appropriate communication skills and managed to make maps and clay models of the scene, with detailed reconstruction of the sequence of events. At this stage, most of them were able to reassess their behaviors and realize the survival value they held. Parents became involved in helping with a procedure of extinction of the "beach phobia" by holding their children as they performed relaxation exercises on the beach. One fourteen-year-old stated, "My father took me to the sea shore. I saw the terrorists' boat and the rocks on which they smashed the head of the little girl. I regret having seen the boat. It haunts me in my dreams. But I am not afraid of the sea any longer."

In the last phase of this brief intervention, children wrote and exchanged poems that they eventually collated and handed over to the bereaved mother who lost her husband and two daughters. Some of the writing was pure expression of grief and mourning, and some was quite defiant, venting the shock, rage, and collapse of trust in a "just world," as is evident in the following example written by a child survivor:

> There are rocks on the shore where the sun used to set
> The rocks are not white, now they are red
> Their hearts are bleeding inside
>
> Because they witnessed a horrible sight
> They saw vicious terrorists with all their might
>
> Smashing the heads of Danny and his daughter Einat . . .
> The rocks are red with the blood that was shed
> Dear Danny, sweet Einat - now you are dead!
> My heart cries for you and I am so sad.

(Written by a twelve-year-old survivor. Unpublished memorial manuscript for the victims of Naharya, 1979)

On the last day, the group assembled pieces of broken glass and erected a memorial that they captioned, "So Life Was Broken." Building the memorial signified the beginning of acceptance of the loss (Ayalon, 1987). During this period, families were counseled on how to respond to their children. The parents were encouraged to share their own feelings with their children and work through the difficult period of recuperation together. Most symptoms subsided gradually, and the children resumed their daily activities. The follow-up surveys, at two months and at eight months later, found a lot of grief, but no persistence of symptoms, with a few exceptions for whom posttraumatic intervention was resumed.

A SPECIAL TECHNIQUE IN THE WAKE OF A TERRORIST ATTACK ON SCHOOL CHILDREN

Specialized short-term techniques for dealing with acute trauma have become prominent over the last decade. Research on the effectiveness of posttraumatic therapies falls short of providing definitive information; therapists, therefore, must rely on clinical evidence in their choice and assessment of interventions. One of the better-researched new methods is Eye Movement Desensitization and Reprocessing (EMDR) therapy.

EMDR therapy is intended to process, integrate, and resolve the elements of the traumatic experience so that it no longer results in distress. Research has found that such treatment helps people who have gone through extremely stress-ful experiences (Shapiro and Silk-Forrest, 1997). It has been suggested that eye movement may be connected to the brain's processing system. It is important to remember that the brain retains the trauma as well as does the healing.

The following is a case of posttraumatic EMDR intervention with trauma-tized children. In spring 1997, a class of twelve-year-old girls on a school trip to "The Island of Peace" on the border between Israel and Jordan were attacked by a Jordanian armed soldier, who suddenly opened fire and murdered seven girls and wounded many more by shooting them from short range in front of the other children and teachers. The devastated community used the local psy-chosocial services for initial debriefing and crisis intervention. Screening for traumatic reactions of all the school's teachers and students by local mental health workers three months later revealed a number of pupils and staff who manifestly suffered from symptoms of Post-Traumatic Stress Disorder (PTSD).

Three teachers and five girls were offered a series of EMDR sessions (Sil-ver and Rogers, 2001). Each individual in this high-risk group received three or four consecutive individual sessions of EMDR. The traumatic imagery that was focused on was different for each participant. One injured girl focused on her wounded legs and her damaged appearance. The empty classroom seat where her dead friend used to sit perturbed another girl. Not all of those who received EMDR treatment were actually present at the disaster. Two girls who had missed the trip suffered from nightmares about what they imagined had happened and guilt at not having been there with their friends. The teachers ag-onized that they could have done more to protect their students. One teacher was haunted by the gory images of the massacre and by her own feeling of ut-ter helplessness. One male teacher was completely distraught and guilt ridden, on top of being blamed by the bereaved parents. He could not benefit from the EMDR sessions in the given format (too short, too late, lack of time to develop rapport, and lack of motivation to get well under the circumstances).

Reported results for all the girls were positive according to EMDR criteria. Two teachers were referred for further treatment, one for EMDR and the other for a traditional type of therapy. An informal follow-up conducted on the an-niversary of the disaster corroborated the initial results.

THE DANGER OF CHOOSING AN
INAPPROPRIATE TREATMENT METHOD

Methods that re-create an intensive reexperience of the trauma, such as de-sensitization, operant shaping, flooding (implosion), prolonged exposure, and paradoxical intention, intend to redeem the victim from emotionally stuck situations, repressed memories, and avoidance behaviors. Saigh (1992) recommends flooding and reports many cases of positive outcomes with children. It is a powerful method, but not without risks (Keane and Kaloupel, 1982). For example, flooding as a method of trauma therapy may be inappropriate for children who use high levels of avoidance as their coping strategy (Brown and Fromm, 1986). Therefore, flooding, and other methods that focus on the victim reexperiencing the trauma, needs to be used only by highly experienced and supervised helpers.

Following is a description of a failure of flooding in posttrauma therapy. At the age of five, a girl survived a terrorist attack in which she witnessed the brutal murder of her whole family. She herself was badly wounded. Thirteen years later, after a period of relative rehabilitation and normal functioning (during which she avoided memories of the traumatic event as well as her life prior to it), she approached a therapist to deal with the loss of a meaningful relationship. At the same time, her initial trauma was reactivated by exposure to gunshots. The girl, then in her teens, withdrew into severe depression.

Her situation was exacerbated as a result of the wrong choice of therapeutic method: she was flooded by repressed memories and encouraged to re-live the initial circumstances of her traumatic event. She was overwhelmed with unbearable pain and guilt for having survived the trauma that killed her family. In his review of the therapeutic procedure, the therapist admitted that in this case the method of therapy was insensitive to the survivor's psychological defenses and coping style (Levin-Bar-Yosef and Alon, 2000). A corrective experience outside the clinical process, which involved a symbolic mourning and atonement ritual, helped the girl to regain her emotional balance.

COPE PROJECT—BRIDGING THE GAP

The toll of violence and terrorism on Israeli society has created major stresses on the educational system. During the early days of trauma research when there was little expert knowledge or awareness of the plight of children in dangerous environments and of the role of the community in providing large-scale trauma relief, Community Oriented Preventive Education (COPE) was a pioneering project (Ayalon, 1978, 1979). Developed during 1974–1977, when the Israeli community was badly shaken by the eruption of an unpredicted war (known as the Yom Kippur War) and beleaguered by a series of atrocious terrorist attacks (Ayalon, 1983a), the COPE model was a breakthrough in disaster response and management, with a special focus on children. It was published as an emergency kit called "Rescue!" and subsequently implemented first in the Israeli educational system and later in other societies caught up in the throes of human-made or natural disasters (Rowe, 1985; Hundeide, 1994; Lahad and Cohen, 1998; Lahad, 2000; Gurwithch, Sitterle, Young, and Pfefferbaum, 2002).

COPE includes four major components that are considered seminal in enhancing children's coping resources. To begin with, COPE informs helpers about children's traumatic sequelae, their need for help, and the responsibility of the community (especially the educational community) to respond to these needs. Second, it provides training for community personnel, including mental health and education professionals as well as paraprofessionals and volunteers, who learn how to deal with traumatic events and their consequences. The third component involves targeting three intervention strategies: anticipatory, buffering, and recuperation, roughly corresponding to the three stages of a crisis (Caplan, 1974). This classification helps in planning preventive stress inoculation (before), crisis intervention (during), and rehabilitative treatment (in the aftermath) of large-scale terrorist attacks. The fourth component integrates structure and content. COPE provides an open-ended trauma-recovery curriculum for creative group activities, using the child's language of imagination and play. It assumes the existence of coping resources, either active or dormant, in every individual and in every system.

These interdependent resources, identified through observations and research of traumatized populations (Lahad, 1997), were grouped into an integrative cluster; namely, Belief, Affect, Social Interaction, Imagination, Cognition, and Physiology (BASIC-Ph). The BASIC-Ph multidimensional approach, inspired by the ideas of multimodal therapy (Lazarus, 1981), relates to six dimensions of coping. It suggests that each individual's coping style comprises an idiosyncratic combination of these six dimensions, which act as input and output channels in the person–world interaction. Everyone has the potential to use all six channels for coping. Children, like adults, respond to traumatic stress in more than one of these channels. The cognitive channel (C) uses strategies such as information gathering, problem solving, and positive thinking. The affective channel (A) processes the wide range of emotions triggered by the trauma and their verbal or nonverbal expression. The social channel (S) contains group belonging, role fulfillment, and the mutual function of receiving and giving support. The imaginative channel (I) enables the amelioration of stress through denial and fantasy, but is also responsible for creative solutions to the problems using imagery, dreams, and intuitions. The spiritual channel (B) sustains religious beliefs and value systems, and the search for meaning. The physical channel (Ph) is broadly responsible for the neurochemical and motor responses to stress, as well as behavioral ways of handling stress, which may range from relaxation to excessive physical activity.

This holistic channel approach became the major denominator for assessing resilience and enhancing the coping resources of individuals and large population groups (Lahad, Shacham, and Niv, 2000). It is important to note that the BASIC-Ph holistic model is not a clinical tool. The model is used to investigate strength and indicates which coping modalities should be enhanced. It is sensitive to cultural norms and expectations and enables us to promote indigenous activities that contain therapeutic elements as natural ingredients in everyday life, such as social and religious rituals and collective challenges that confirm each person's place in the community.

The techniques offered by COPE are varied, flexible, and amenable to change by the program facilitator. An extensive use is made of in vivo exposures, bibliotherapy with metaphoric stories and poems, and simulation games. The child's language of play and fantasy, creative as well as communicative, is used. Children are encouraged to work through a wide range of emotions using a variety of modes of expression and activities. They also receive cognitive training in conflict resolution and problem solving under stress. The practice of relaxation and guided fantasy techniques has been proven a highly effective tool for handling fear cues. Producing a vigilant approach is a delicate art involving a balance of downgrading threatening cues without becoming callous and staying alert without being overwhelmed by anxiety. The COPE program provides many opportunities for children to develop an active attitude toward stress, either as a direct attempt at reducing the threat or using distracting activity in periods of uncertainty. The program has gained international acknowledgment and been published in several languages (Ayalon, 1978, 1991, 1995a, 1995b, 1995c).

These orientations were adopted and further developed by the Israeli Community Stress Prevention Center (CSPC), established on the northern border in 1981 following a prolonged exposure of the civilian population to massive bombardments from over the border and terrorist attacks on homes and schools (Lahad and Cohen, 1998).

CAMPAIGN FOR ACCEPTANCE OF THE COMMUNITY APPROACH TO TRAUMA STRESS

Initially, professional groups viewed the community approach with much ambivalence and skepticism. Mental health experts found it difficult to exchange the security of the clinic for the undefined "field work" in the places where the traumatic experiences occurred. It was difficult to change the attitudes of school authorities, who tended to shun the need to deal with traumatic events or invest in stress prevention. Agencies of welfare and health services tended toward competitive intervention rather than cooperation in the face of disaster (Ayalon, 1997a). These difficulties were exacerbated by the lack of acceptable treatment methods or protocols for such disasters as mass killings of school children, for children who become terrorists' hostages, or children who are forced to spend long periods of time in air-raid shelters, separated from their parents. To confound the issue even further, the psychosocial team members were themselves part of the beleaguered community, exposed to the very same risks, anxieties, and traumas. This "shared fate" had contributed a great deal to the empathic understanding of their clients' plight but, at the same time, increased burnout and compassion fatigue (Figley, 1995; Knafo, Introduction to this book).

It seems, looking back, that the campaign for community stress intervention, which is still going on in many societies has won global approval (Capewell, 2003). The Israeli CSPC's model of work with communities, schools, families, and individuals has been adopted by many local urban municipalities and Kibbutz rural communities within Israel and is now in much demand in many countries (Ayalon, Lahad, and Cohen, 1998, 1999).

CAN WE LIVE WITHOUT AN ENEMY?

This provocative question, posed by Dorothy Rowe (1985), touches on the greatest danger both to the individual and to the collective, emanating from a continuing exposure to violence, namely, perpetuating the cycle of violence in a split between "good" and "evil" and the projection of all evil characteristics onto the other. Depth psychology maintains that the "enemy" image is constructed from denied aspects of the self (Volkan, 1990). "In the beginning we create the enemy. Before the weapon comes the image. We are driven to fabricate an enemy as a scapegoat to bear the burden of our denied enmity" (Keen, 1986, p. 1). When we project our denied aspects of personality onto others, we try to destroy the other as a way of unknowingly getting rid of what we hate in ourselves. The interface between external hostile encounters, such as war and terrorism-induced violence, and projections of inner rejected parts generates a persistent psychosocial fear–hate combination that is very resistant to change.

While the trauma caused by terrorist attacks is real and needs to be tended to, prolonged exposure to terrorism as a psychosocial phenomenon harbors long-range dangers for the moral development of the attacked society and its value system. It creates an overriding atmosphere of suspicion and demonization of the "other" that may permeate all levels of development and contaminate a basic humanist value of society. Massive projection becomes a developmental danger for children, because it is too absolute, too final, too irreversible," says child psychiatrist Alan Flashman (Flashman, 2003).

He maintains that it damages all aspects of emotional balance and behavior. It is reflected in impaired moral judgment, social irresponsibility, lack of empathy, constriction of creative imagination, and invasion of demonic frightening fantasies. When intolerance for the "other" is increased by massive projection, aggression and hatred may spread, contaminating vast areas of human relations inside and outside the family and peer group.

There exist two levels of dealing with the danger of massive projection within a responsible educational policy: On one level, attention should be turned inward in a soul-searching process, through which both individuals and the collective acknowledge and own those inner "rejected" aspects. The second level deals with encounters with representatives of the "other side," in order to transcend stereotypical and biased perceptions of those regarded as "enemies." Admittedly, it is difficult enough to conduct encounters between antagonistic groups in the aftermath of hostilities, but it is usually deemed impossible to do it during active hostile acts of war and terror (Ayalon, 1988, 1999). The COPE holistic coping model, using all BASIC-Ph channels, includes suggestions for such a program (Ayalon and Lahad, 2000) that have been practiced in mixed national groups who suffered the atrocities of war in the former Yugoslavia (Ayalon, Lahad, and Cohen, 1998, 1999) and in a limited number of encounters with Israeli and Palestinian teachers who are struggling against all odds to implement these principles in the education of their pupils.

Flashman (2003) states, "Nothing gives children more hope than understanding that children of the enemy side are very much like themselves—also growing up in times of pain, solitude and silence." A Palestinian child psychiatrist, a delegate in the peace talks, believes in breaking the cycle of violence and states, "I believe strongly that there is God in every child—Jewish, Muslim or Christian—and no one has the right to kill that God, particularly in the name of God" (El-Sarraj and Meldrum, 2002, p. 132).

CHILDREN'S EMPOWERMENT:
THE FIGHT FOR CHILDREN'S RIGHTS

War and other human-made disasters deeply affect children. The bad news is that they are vulnerable, they suffer, and they need protection. The good news is that children seem to be resilient. The word "resilience" has come to describe the human being's ability to survive, recover, and persevere against various obstacles and threats. Studies of children in war zones around the world have found that a great many children maintain an active and positive attitude in the face of adversity (Garbarino, 1993; Garbarino, Kostelny, and Dubrow, 1993). Lahad (1997), as an advocate of children's innate resilience, offers to maintain it by systematically enhancing both intrapsychic and action-oriented coping resources. Furman (1997) insists that people can be taught to identify their resilient elements, those that had sustained them through life's hardships. Quoting a study of World War II survivors, he shows that a majority of the "war children" had, contrary to the generally held belief, survived their trials well. Many of them thought they had even learned from their trials, and that their difficulties had only made them stronger.

A more radical child advocacy emerging in the international community fights to eliminate or at least reduce the factors that jeopardize children's lives, whether or not children can learn to cope with them (and some cannot). This advocacy seeks to empower children by protecting their "bill of rights." This movement toward empowering children is controversial, as it fundamentally questions adults' authority and the social structure that depends on exercising power and control (Dubrow, 1997). Being caught up in violent conflict is a reality for millions of children in the world, a reality that consistently robs them of justice and human rights and constitutes a violation of the Geneva Convention on the Rights of the Child. This bill of rights includes the child's right to life; the right to a name, a home, and a family; the right to a nationality; the right to education and recreation; the right to freedom of expression; and the right to dignity and special protection and care in situations of armed conflict. All of these are violated.

To reverse this situation, Goodwin-Gill and Cohn, in their book *Child Soldiers* (1994), sum up the efforts of the General Assembly of the United Nations to protect children from being actively involved in warfare: "Children, particularly if deprived of their liberty, shall be accorded the respect due to them on account of their age. They must never be compelled or encouraged to take part in acts of violence" (Goodwin-Gill and Cohn, 1994, p. 150). Likewise, Graca Machel's project (Machel, 1996) promotes the active involvement of children in breaking the cycle of violence and traumatization, thus looking at children as a "zone of peace." Out of these intensive activities, a new hope is rising that different community interventions that focus on detraumatizing adults will also benefit children.

EPILOGUE

These lines are written on the anniversary in 2002 of the horrendous terrorist attack on America. School children in Jerusalem, badly shaken by a bloody sequence of suicide bombings of their city over the last two years, wrote letters of compassionate identification to their peers in the United States. A sixteen-year-old girl wrote:

> Thirty-three times during the last year terrorists targeted us in my hometown, Jerusalem. The danger here is lurking everywhere. My friends and I light candles for our friends who were murdered and we sit Shiva. But we go on with our studies, with our social life, our music and traveling. We cry and we laugh. The shock of what you went through in New York is still with me. I hope you were not personally hurt. Don't give up. Brace yourself as we do. We should not allow the terrorist to win by intimidating us.

REFERENCES

Alon, N. (1985). An Ericksonian approach to treatment of chronic post traumatic patients. In J. K. Zeig (Ed.), *Ericksonian hypnotherapy*, pp. 307–26. New York: Brunner/Mazel.

Ayalon, O. (1978). *Emergency kit*. Haifa, Israel: University of Haifa Press. (Hebrew).

———. (1979). Community oriented preparation for emergency: C.O.P.E. *Death Education*, 3: 222–44.

———. (1982). Children as hostages. *The Practitioner*, 226:1771–73.

———. (1983a). Face to face with terrorists. In A. Cohen (Ed.), *Education as encounter*, 81–102. Haifa, Israel: University of Haifa Press.

———. (1983b). Coping with terrorism: The Israeli case. In D. Meichenbaum and M. Jaremko (Eds.), *Stress reduction and prevention*, pp. 293–339. New York: Plenum Publications.

———. (1987/1992). *Rescue!: Community oriented prevention education for coping with stress*. Ellicott City, MD: Chevron Publishing.

———. (1988). Community care for victims of terrorist activities. In M. Lahad and A. Cohen (Eds.), *Community stress prevention series* (Vol. 1, pp. 98–126). Kiriat Shmona, Israel: Community Stress Prevention Center.

———. (1991). *Rescue: Coping with stress in Thailand*. Bangkok: Paribatra. (Thai).

———. (1993a). Post traumatic stress recovery. In J. Wilson and B. Raphael (Eds.), *International handbook of traumatic stress syndromes*, 855–66. New York: Plenum Press.

———. (1993b). Death in literature and bibliotherapy. In R. Malkinsom, S. Rubin, and E. Vitztum (Eds.), *Loss and bereavement in Israeli society*, pp. 155–75. Jerusalem: Ministry of Defense. (Hebrew).

———. (1995a). *I can cope*. Helsinki, Finland: Mannerheim Children's League. (Finnish).

———. (1995b). *Help our children*. Zagreb, Croatia: UNICEF. (Croatian).

———. (1995c). *Enfrentando situatioes de estres*. Jerusalem: Ministry of Education. (Spanish).

———. (1997a). A community from crisis to change. In M. Lahad and A. Cohen (Eds.), *Community stress prevention series* (Vol. 2, pp. 177–90). Kiryat Shmona, Israel: Community Stress Prevention Center.

———. (1997b). Sealed rooms and gas masks. In M. Lahad and A. Cohen (Eds.), *Community stress prevention series* (Vol. 2, pp. 191–98). Kiryat Shmona, Israel: Community Stress Prevention Center.

———. (1998a). Community healing for children traumatized by war. *International Journal of Psychiatry*, 10: 224–33.

———. (1998b). Reconciliation: Changing the face of the enemy. In O. Ayalon, M. Lahad, and A. Cohen (Eds.), *Community stress prevention series* (Vol. 3, pp. 62–66). Jerusalem: Ministry of Education and Kiryat Shemona, Israel: Community Stress Prevention Center.

———. (1999). Reconciliation: A holistic peace curriculum. In M. Iverson and D. Broen (Eds.), *Reconciliation anthology*. Copenhagen, Denmark: Danish Refugee Council. (Danish).

Ayalon, O., and Egetmeyer, M. (2002). *COPE CARDS for trauma and healing handbook*. Kirchzarten, Germany: OH Ferlag.

Ayalon, O., and Horowitz, M. (1996). *Survivors of Ma'alot: A Handbook*. Tel Aviv: The Israeli Educational Television. (Hebrew).

Ayalon, O., and Lahad, M. (2000). *Life on the edge/2000: Stress and coping in high risk situations and uncertainty*. Haifa, Israel: Nord Publications (Hebrew).

Ayalon, O., Lahad, M., and Cohen, A. (Eds.). (1998). *Community stress prevention series*, Vol. 3. Jerusalem: Ministry of Education and Kiryat Shemona: Community Stress Prevention Center.

———. (1999). *Community stress prevention series*, Vol. 4. Jerusalem: Ministry of Education and Kiryat Shemona, Israel: Community Stress Prevention Center.

Ayalon, O., Lukyanova, M., and Egetmeyer, M. (2002). *COPE CARDS (therapeutic card game)*. Kirchzarten, Germany: OH Ferlag.

Ayalon, O., and Soskis D. (1986). Survivors of terrorist victimization. In N. A. Milgram (Ed.), *Stress and coping in time of war: Generalizations from the Israeli experience*, pp. 257–74. Philadelphia: Brunner-Routledge.

Ayalon, O., and van Tassel, E. (1987). Living in a dangerous environment. In M. Brassard, R. Germain, and S. Hart (Eds.), *Psychological maltreatment of children and youth*, pp. 171–82. New York: Pergamon Press.

Ayalon, O., and Waters, F. (2002). The impact of terrorism on Jews in Israel. *The Journal of Trauma Practice*, 1: 133–54.

Ben Eli, Z., and Sela, M. (1980). Terrorism in Nahariya. *Journal of Psychology and Counseling in Education*, 13: 94–101. (Hebrew).

Brown, D. P., and Fromm, E. (1986). *Hypnotherapy and hypnoanalysis*. Hillside, NJ: Lawrence Erlbaum.

Capewell, E. (2003). Community care in the wake of terror in Ireland. In O. Ayalon, M. Lahad, and A. Cohen, *Community stress prevention series*, Vol. 5. Kiryat Shmona, Israel: Community Stress Prevention Center.

Caplan, G. (1974). *Support systems and community mental health*. New York: Behavioral Publications.

Desivilya, S. H., Gal, R., and Ayalon, O. (1996). Long-term effects of trauma in adolescence. *Anxiety, Stress and Coping*, 913: 135–50.

Dubrow, N. (1997) Children's human rights: The equation of justice and peace. *Palestine-Israel Journal*, 4: 6–11.

Dyregrov, A. (1999). Helpful and hurtful aspects of psychological debriefing groups. *International Journal of Emergency Mental Health*, 1: 175–81.

El-Sarraj, E., and Meldrum, L. (2002). The impact of terrorism on Palestinians in Israel. *The Journal of Trauma Practice*, 1: 125–32.

Flashman, A. (2003). Children and trauma: security, connection, meaning. In O. Ayalon, M. Lahad, and A. Cohen (Eds.), *Community stress prevention series*, Vol. 5. Kiryat Shmona, Israel: Community Stress Prevention Center.

Figley, C. (Ed.). (1995). *Compassion fatigue: Coping with secondary traumatic stress disorder in those who treat the traumatized.* New York: Brunner/Mazel.

Furman, B. (1997). *It's never too late to have a happy childhood.* Helsinki, Finland: Vastapaino.

Gal, R., and Lazarus, R. (1975). The role of activity in anticipation and confronting stressful situations. *Journal of Human Stress*, 1: 36–42.

Galliano, S., and Lahad, M. (2000). *Manual for practice of critical incident processing and recovery.* London: Independent Counseling and Advisory Services (ICAS).

Ganor, B. (2002). Terror as a strategy of psychological warfare? In *The international policy institute for counter-terrorism (ICT) papers.* Herzlia, Israel: The Interdisciplinary Center. Retrieved April 5, 2004, from www.ict.org.il

Garbarino, J. (1993). Developmental consequences of living in dangerous and unstable environments. In M. McCallin (Ed.), *Research, practice and policy issues.* Geneva, Switzerland: Geneva, International Catholic Child Bureau.

Garbarino, J., Kostelny, K., and Dubrow, N. (1993). *No place to be a child: Growing up in a war zone.* Lexington, MA: D. C. Heath & Co.

Goodwin-Gill, G., and Cohn, I. (1994). *Child Soldiers.* Oxford, England: Clarendon Press.

Gordon, R., and Wraith, R. (1993). Responses of children and adolescents to disaster. In P. Wilson and B. Raphael (Eds.), *International handbook of traumatic stress syndromes*, pp. 561–75. New York: Plenum Press.

Gurwitch, Sitterle, Young, and Pfefferbaum. (2002). The aftermath of terrorism. In A. M. La Greca, W. K. Silverman, E. M. Vernberg, and M. Robert (Eds.), *Helping children cope with disaster and terrorism*, pp. 327–57.Washington, DC: American Psychological Association.

Hundeide, K. (1994). *Children's life-world and their reaction to war.* Oslo International Child Development Programs.

James, W. (1898). *Psychological Review*, 1: 199.

Janis, I. (1958). *Psychological stress.* New York: Willey.

Keane, T. M., and Kaloupel, D. G. (1982). Imaginal flooding in the treatment of post traumatic stress disorder. *Journal of Consulting and Clinical Psychology*, 50: 138–40.

Keen, S. (1986). *The faces of the enemy.* New York: Harper & Row.

Lahad, M. (1997). BASIC-Ph: The story of coping resources. In M. Lahad and A. Cohen (Eds.), *Community stress prevention* series (Vols. 1 and 2, pp. 117–45). Kiryat Shmona, Israel: Community Stress Prevention Center.

———. (1999). The use of drama therapy with crisis intervention groups, following mass evacuation. *The Arts in Psychotherapy*, 26: 27–33.

———. (2000). *Creative supervision.* London: Jessica Kingsley Publishers.

Lahad, M., and Ayalon, M. (1995). *On life and death.* Haifa, Israel: Nord Publications.

Lahad, M., and Cohen, A. (1998). Eighteen years of community stress prevention. In O. Ayalon, M. Lahad, and A. Cohen (Eds.), *Community stress prevention series*, Vol. 3, pp. 1–9. Kiryat Shmona, Israel: Community Stress Prevention Center.

Lahad, M., Shacham, Y., and Niv, S. (2000). Coping and community resources in children facing disaster. In A. Shalev and R. Yehuda (Eds.), *International handbook of human response to trauma*, pp. 389–95. New York: Kluwer Academic/Plenum Press.

Lazarus, A. (1981). *The practice of multimodal therapy.* New York: Springer.

Levin-Bar-Yosef, T., and Alon, N. (2000). Therapeutic approaches for PTSD. In A. Klingman, A. Raviv, and B. Stein (Eds.), *Children in stress and emergencies*, pp. 215–37. Jerusalem: Ministry of Education. (Hebrew).

Lumsden, M. (1997). Breaking the cycle of violence: Are communal therapies a means of healing shattered selves? *Journal of Peace Research*, 34: 377–83.

Machel, G. (1996). *Impact of armed conflict on children.* New York: United Nations Childrens Fund.

Megged, A. (2001). *Fairies and witches.* Haifa, Israel: Nord Publications. (Hebrew).

Ochberg, F. (1978). The victims of terrorism: Psychiatric considerations. *Terrorism: An International Journal*, 1: 147–67.

Ochberg, F., and Soskis, D. (Eds.). (1982). *Victims of terrorism.* Boulder, CO: Westview.

Rowe, D. (1985). *Living with the Bomb.* London: Routledge and Kegan.

———. (1988, July 19). A matter of death and life. *The Guardian*, p. 16.

Saban, S. (1990). *To live again.* Tel Aviv, Israel: Ministry of Defense Publications.

Saigh, P. A. (1992). The behavioral treatment of child and adolescent post traumatic stress disorder. *Advances in Behavioral Research and Therapy*, 14: 247–75.

Salmon, T. W. (1919). The war neuroses and their lessons. *New York Journal of Medicine*, 59: 993–94.

Seligman, M. E. P. (1975). *Helplessness on depression, development and death.* San Francisco: W. H. Freeman.

Silver, S. M., and Rogers, S. (2001). *Light in the heart of darkness: EMDR and the treatment of war and terrorism survivors.* New York: Norton.

Shapiro, F., and Silk-Forrest, M. (1997). *EMDR: The breakthrough therapy for overcoming anxiety, stress, and trauma.* New York: Basic Books.

Soskis, D., and Ayalon, O. (1985). A six-year follow-up of hostage victims. *Terrorism*, 7: 411–15.

Terr, L. (1990). *Too scared to cry.* New York: Harper & Row.

Volkan, V. (1990). Psychoanalytic aspects of ethnic conflicts. In J. V. Montville (Ed.), *Conflict and peacemaking in multiethnic societies*, 81–92. Lexington, MA: Lexington Books.

Winnicott, D. W. (1971). *Playing and reality.* London: Tavistock.

Wraith, R. (2000). Children and debriefing: Theory, interventions and outcomes. In B. Raphael and J. P. Wilson (Eds.), *Psychological debriefing: theory, practice, and evidence*, pp. 195–212. Cambridge, England: University Press.

Chapter Eleven

Defeated Dreams:
The Tragedy of Survivors

Elia Awwad

The history of the Arab/Palestinian-Israeli conflict goes back more than one hundred years. From a Palestinian perspective, this conflict has been characterized by catastrophe and bloodshed, pain and suffering, loss, hate, and revenge. This perspective is blended with a bitter feeling passed from one generation to the next that the Palestinians are the victims and the Israelis are the perpetrators. This inherited dichotomy of victim and victimizer will continue as long as the historical responsibility and truth regarding injustice and violence toward the Palestinian people remain unacknowledged.

Both recovery and reconciliation require remembering and sharing of experiences and coming to terms with one's own suffering and pain. In this chapter, I document stories of survivors in the aftermath of the forty-day Israeli military siege of the Nativity Church in Bethlehem, which took place from April 1 to May 9, 2002. In addition, I analyze the images drawn by a group of Bethlehem's Palestinian children depicting the reality of their lives. Finally, I share my own professional experience in working with traumatized Palestinians in the last two years of the violence. Based on this experience, I present current efforts for working with human-made disasters in Palestine and Israel and propose future directions of interventions designed to guide both Palestinian professionals who are providing services and international organizations that are supporting psychosocial projects in Palestine.

In general terms, the psychosocial consequences of Israeli soldier and settler violence against Palestinians are better understood if we take into consideration the following variables (Awwad, 2002):

1. Compared with other countries in the region in particular, and the world in general, where there is a wealth of material and human resources, Palestine

suffers from a severe lack of psychosocial services and qualified and trained mental health professionals to deal with nationwide trauma and human tragedy. Palestinian professionals have no formal training in assessing, conceptualizing, or treating trauma-related disorders.

2. In contrast to other disasters that may take place as discrete traumatic experiences known as Type I traumas (Terr, 1991), the more than one-hundred-year history of the Arab-Israeli conflict is characterized by bloodshed and ongoing human suffering. The effects of the latter are passed from one generation to the next and are classed as Type II traumas (1991). The repeated and long-standing disturbance and the chronicity of the Palestinians' traumatic experiences make healing extremely difficult, if not impossible.

3. Seeking professional assistance is still regarded by the Palestinian community as a stigma. Therefore, Palestinians are caught between their psychological needs and losing their sense of belonging and inclusion in community life (Awwad, 1999). Stigmatization of victims makes healing more problematic.

4. Poverty, political instability, uncertainty about the future, high unemployment, accumulated loss, lack of security and protection, and the severity and intensity of exposure to violence, all make Palestinians more vulnerable to trauma and to the effects of disaster.

5. Culture and religion in Palestine influence the meaning and the subjective experience, perception of symptoms, and subsequent expression of trauma and loss. For example, the killing of a Palestinian by the Israeli army or the death of a suicide bomber is a traumatic event causing a terrifying experience, but the deceased is perceived by the family as a "martyr" and not a victim. The "martyr phenomenon" produces emotional numbness, therefore psychological pain is repressed (a form of affective avoidance).

6. In a nation with a history of repeated trauma and loss, the impact of a disaster includes not only the primary victims of violence but also the secondary victims, such as those who witnessed the traumatic events. This includes, but is not restricted to, relief workers, volunteers, rescue personnel, and mental health professionals. People who work with victims may experience profound psychological effects. These effects can be disruptive and painful for the helpers and persist for months or even years after their work with traumatized people.

According to Vrijlandt (2001, p. 8), "The results of vicarious traumatization (VT) can be disastrous when organizations have no respite for their staff, have high case loads, inadequate supervision, fail to identify signs of VT, and fail to provide vacations and continuing education and psychotherapy for their employees."

Following a disaster, up to 90 percent or more of victims may exhibit some psychological symptoms in the hours immediately following. Though such symptoms may disappear over the succeeding weeks, still 20 percent to 50 percent or more may exhibit signs of psychological distress. For many survivors, long-term or delayed responses may continue to appear for years after the disaster. Moreover, "in the absence of well-designed interventions, up to 50% or more of the victims of a disaster may develop lasting depression, pervasive anxiety, post-traumatic stress disorder and other emotional disturbances" (Ehrenreich, 2001, p. 5).

Litz and Gray (2002) reviewed a number of studies conducted to examine early intervention for trauma survivors. The authors stated that these studies have shown that those survivors reveal a range of Post-Traumatic Stress Disorder (PTSD) responses in the first weeks after a traumatic event, but most of them adapt effectively within approximately three months. Those who fail to recover by that time are at risk of chronic PTSD. Furthermore, Kessler et al. (1995, cited in Litz and Gray, 2002) found that "one third of people with PTSD fail to recover after many years, in many cases after years of mental health treatment."

It is difficult to arrive at a working definition of trauma that grasps the unique features of traumatic experiences and correctly places them in the context of a wider Palestinian narrative. I agree with Carlson (1997, p. 27) that

> While no theory may be able to explain the effect of every possible traumatic event, a theory that could explain [various traumatic events] would be very broadly applicable. It is also worth noting here that defining the features of potentially traumatic events will not provide an adequate explanation for their effects. Whereas some events may be so powerful that they would traumatize anyone, most potentially traumatic events are not so powerful. This means that the framework must also explain why a potentially traumatic event evokes a traumatic response in some people but not in others.

I use as a point of departure the experiences of Palestinian women, men, and children who have experienced events that have involved "actual or threatened death or serious injury or a threat to the physical integrity of self or others" (American Psychiatric Association, 1994, p. 427). This is a standard defining feature of PTSD. I am also aware that the Palestinian response to these events has been "intense fear, helplessness, or horror" (1994, p. 428) on a national scale.

I do not reject Carlson's point that the long-standing DSM diagnostic criterion for PTSD used by the American Psychiatric Association may be of limited use (1997). The reader should also note that I am not arguing that Palestinians as a nation or as a people suffer from PTSD. However, this diagnostic criterion does need to be measured against actual unfolding events on the ground in Palestine as a complex Palestinian narrative emerges. Carlson's point that traumatic events rest on three composite elements (1997) must also be measured against the Palestinian reality and can be used to correctly grasp the Palestinian narrative in its entirety.

Using Carlson's framework (1997), we can examine case histories of apparently traumatized Palestinians and decide based on rational criteria if indeed Palestinians are experiencing traumatic events. Let us ask ourselves the following questions as we read these case histories and examine the emerging Palestinian narrative:

1. Can we say that Palestinians perceive, or have logical reason to perceive, that what is taking place around them has a highly negative valence?
2. Can we also say that Palestinians have experienced sudden "actual or threatened psychological pain" or should we instead say that this pain, if it indeed exists, has risen gradually? We can ask as well how much time may be needed for Palestinians to escape from traumatic events if indeed such events have occurred.
3. Can we say that Palestinians have felt or experienced, with or without just cause, an inability to control events affecting them and subsequent threats to their "physical safety and psychic integrity?" If we can indeed agree that such feelings and experiences do exist as part of a logical chain of events, we should also ask if traumatized Palestinians are preoccupied with their own (lack of) control over traumatic events.

Finally, I ask the reader to consider Carlson's points (1997) that most potentially traumatic events are not powerful enough to result in actual trauma and that fear and trauma cannot be quantified in equal measures among people who have experienced potentially traumatic events. Carlson was writing before the *Second Intifada* developed and did not consider the political and social corollaries that can be more readily grasped in present-day Palestine. I ask the reader to attempt, at least in a general way, to draw such corollaries and in effect step beyond one's social comfort zone when examining the Palestinian narrative.

Carlson's framework (1997), taken in whole or in part, helps us to determine the extent to which Palestinians may have been traumatized by events taking place in Palestine-Israel since 2000. Each element suggested by Carlson raises a number of clinical questions and observations and suggests a series of social and political comparisons that are beyond the scope of this chapter.

To more specifically examine the psychological consequences of violence and trauma on Palestinians, I present in this chapter the cases of individuals and groups affected by an Israeli military action in spring 2002. On April 1, 2002, the Israeli army invaded the Bethlehem District for the fourth time since the beginning of the Second Intifada against the Israeli occupation. This invasion lasted until May 9, 2002. The army imposed a curfew on the Bethlehem District where 152,000 people were forced into house arrest for thirty-nine days. During the first day of the Israeli invasion of Bethlehem, three hundred youths took refuge in the Nativity Church. A strict military siege on the church followed. Of the three hundred youths, thirty-nine were deported; twenty-six to Gaza City and thirteen to different European countries. During the siege eight young people were killed inside the church by Israeli snipers and thirty-two were physically injured.

SAMPLE CASE HISTORIES

The information in this section is drawn from primary sources (i.e., the victims tell their own stories of current traumatic experiences). Though the recollections are from a subjective point of view, they are an essential tool for assessing and understanding the victims' trauma responses.

Sami

Sami is a forty-six-year-old married Palestinian male who came for counseling. Sami is suffering from symptoms of acute stress reactions resulting from Israeli Apache helicopter attacks on his home. The attacks began at approximately 8:00 A.M. on April 2, 2002, during the forty-day siege of the Nativity Church in Bethlehem. His home is located five hundred meters from the Nativity Church. A group of Palestinians was hiding from Israeli soldiers inside the church after a fight took place between Palestinians and the soldiers during the fourth Israeli invasion of Bethlehem.

The attack on Sami's home resulted in part of the house, including the children's room, being burned and the electricity being cut off. Sami ran from the house with his six children and wife to a downstairs apartment. There they found his brother, sister-in-law, and two of their children in his mother's bedroom shaking from fear. After almost one hour after the attack, Israeli soldiers came to his neighbors' homes and started to shout at them to open their doors. They heard screaming and shooting at the water tanks located on the top of the houses but were too afraid to go to the first floor to look at the damage.

The Israeli soldiers reached the door of Sami's home and attached an explosive, blowing open the door. A group of soldiers entered the home. The thirteen-member family was in the mother's bedroom where the mother was hiding the children in the bathroom. As the soldiers came down the stairs, they started to fire at the family. The mother, aged sixty-four, and Sami's brother, aged thirty-seven, were immediately killed. Sami explained that before the shooting took place, he and his brother and mother were holding hands and were standing against the wall since there was not enough space in his mother's room. Children were screaming and begging the soldiers for mercy. The soldiers left the home and Sami stayed there for twenty-seven hours holding his mother's hand. Sami reported he felt lucky that the telephone line was not cut. A few hours after this incident Sami received several calls. During his conversations he asked for help to remove the two dead bodies. Sami discovered later that ambulances had tried to reach his home, but they had been ordered by Israeli soldiers atop of tanks and military vehicles to leave the area because of the imposed curfew and the military operation. Some of the ambulances were shot at in order to scare them into leaving. Sami said that for all this time "we kept silent and we didn't breathe. We were praying to God that the soldiers would not enter the home again or discover us." He said that the first twenty-seven hours were "the most awful hours in all my life. They were full of horror, pain and grief." He said, "Each of these hours represents a year of my life."

Sami described the events and his feelings in the following words:

> There was no water, electricity, or food. However, 27 hours after the killing of my mother and brother passed, mass media people suddenly came down to talk to us. I started to tell my story. After 25 hours of coordination between the Palestinian authorities, the Israeli military District Coordination Office (DCO), the Red Cross, and the Palestine Red Crescent Society (PRCS) Emergency Medical Services Department in Bethlehem, the ambulance was allowed to reach my home and carry the two bodies to a nearby hospital.
>
> The second painful memory of this tragedy was when we tried to leave our destroyed home and move out to stay in a safe place. We were 11 people and we needed another similar coordination between all parties concerned to get us all out. After 10 hours of negotiations, we were carried by two ambulances toward my sister's home. It was only on the 6th of April that we heard on a local television station that families who had members who were killed would be allowed to bury them.

Sami explained that when he went with his sister to the hospital to receive the two bodies they were shot at several times. He believes it was a miracle that they were not killed. Sami's sister collapsed and was transferred to an emergency room at the hospital after viewing the bodies.

When Sami returned from the cemetery, he learned that his sister had had a miscarriage. She was permitted to leave the hospital the following day. Several days later, when the curfew was lifted for a few hours and people could get out to buy food and medicine, Sami returned to his destroyed home. He found the door open and discovered that soldiers were staying in his home. Furniture and kitchen items were destroyed. Bullets were all around the house. On the second visit to his home during a lift in the curfew, Sami noticed more damage. The pictures on the wall were all shot; cameras, a radio, and a stereo had been stolen; and the television and the video player were broken. His Audi automobile, which he had parked behind his home, had been completely destroyed.

At the end of his third counseling session, Sami said, "I hope the occupation of Bethlehem will continue so I can stay more days in my sister's home. If the occupation ends then I have to move to my destroyed home with my wife and children, my brother's wife and her children." He added, "I know I am selfish to think this way but I can't sleep while thinking how can we all survive in a destroyed home without food and money. On the other hand, I hate to see myself depending on my sister to feed all of us daily, especially during the siege and the continued curfew when no money is left for her and her husband."

Before the event, Sami had a diploma in business administration and enjoyed a happy marriage. During his work he also developed a good relationship with a number of prominent people working as owners of souvenir shops in Bethlehem and Jerusalem. He worked for sixteen years in a souvenir shop near the Nativity Church before the Second Intifada. After the violence started on September 29, 2000, tourism to Bethlehem stopped. Sami lost his job and could not find other employment. He was unable to take care of his wife, his mother, and six children.

During the event, Sami suffered the following experiences in the period of violence:

1. Losing his mother and brother violently.
2. Feeling his own life and existence threatened.
3. Staying with two dead bodies, screaming and terrified children, and barely functioning adults, for a long period of time in one room with no electricity.
4. Exposing children to extremely terrifying events including hearing shooting, seeing and smelling the dead bodies of relatives, and experiencing severe fear, horror, and disorientation.
5. Lacking social support, either during the violent incident or during the funeral and after, because of the forty-day curfew imposed on Bethlehem. He buried his mother and brother alone, under extremely dangerous conditions, while tanks, military vehicles, gunmen, and snipers were in the city.

After the event, Sami experienced the following traumatic feelings and experiences:

1. The trauma and loss felt by all the surviving members of his family.
2. The sadness for his sister's miscarriage during the crisis.
3. The shame of becoming dependent, along with his immediate family, on his sister and brother-in-law and the subsequent feelings of low self-esteem and loss of his caregiver status.
4. The feelings of helplessness and hopelessness in the face of an uncertain future with no sense of protection or security.

Jamila

Jamila is a forty-eight-year-old female from Deheisha Refugee Camp near Bethlehem. During her interview she talked about what happened to her two sons, Jad (twenty-six years old) and Zaid (eighteen years old). She also has an older married son and a younger unmarried daughter. Jad was assassinated, along with four of his friends, by an Israeli Apache helicopter. Zaid was deported to the Gaza Strip as part of a deal between the Israeli government and Palestinian Authority after the forty-day siege of Nativity Church.

According to Jamila, a collaborator[1] who was with her son Jad and his friends suddenly decided to leave them and informed the Israeli intelligence service about their location in the camp. They were hiding in a place in the camp that would have been difficult for anyone to find. While Jad was sleeping in a car after three consecutive days with no rest, an Israeli Apache suddenly appeared and hit his car with a rocket. Jad was killed and only a few pieces of his burnt body were found. His four friends were also killed in the attack.

One of his hands was found on the window of his car while his legs were found outside. Jamila said that she could not look at the remains, nor could she participate in the funeral. When asked why, she replied, "I want to keep remembering his beautiful face when he hugged me the last time he was at home, saying to me that he was going to be a martyr."

Two weeks after the assassination of Jad, Jamila's youngest son Zaid took refuge in the Nativity Church. This action, the siege on the church and the subsequent agreement between the Israeli and Palestinian authorities, led to Zaid's deportation.

When asked about which of the two events was more painful for her, the assassination of her second son or the deportation of her youngest son, Jamila replied that the deportation was more painful. Jad, she said, is now in heaven with God while Zaid is alive, "but his suffering is like a fire burning me. I am now preoccupied with Zaid's survival." Jamila talked about how she spent hours watching television waiting to hear what happened to Zaid in the church. When the electricity was cut off during the curfew and she heard that Israeli snipers had killed several people hiding in the church, she wept continuously and could not sleep until a physician prescribed tranquilizers for her.

Jamila heard that Zaid left the church while it was under siege by Israeli tanks and vehicles. Two days later, she learned that Zaid was without food and water. He returned to the church through a secret tunnel and called her from inside via mobile phone to let her know that he was still alive.

Her son was in the midst of a severe conflict. During the fourth week of the siege, Jamila asked Zaid by telephone to surrender to the Israeli soldiers. She hoped that he would be imprisoned and not killed. She dreamed that he was married, and when she awoke, she had a premonition that he might have been killed. Zaid had decided to continue his struggle against the Israeli army. After the assassination of his older brother, he wanted revenge.

Many residents near the building in Gaza City where her deported son and other deportees are staying have left their homes. They fear Israeli planes will strike and shell the building. The only communication between Jamila and her son in Gaza City is by telephone.

During our interview, Jamila wept and said angrily, "I need to see my son!" But she also added, "If I were asked to choose between seeing him or my son being a martyr, I will accept not seeing him anymore." His sister, she added, writes his name on her school bag and on the inner walls of the home. She is depressed. Jamila ended the interview by saying, "I am frustrated and wish I had no feeling."

Before the event:

1. The family was living a normal life, though they were refugees living under difficult circumstances.
2. The assassinated son, Jad, was a worker in Israel, while the deported son, Zaid, was a university student.
3. The mother showed love and care for her two sons.
4. The mother hoped that Jad would marry and Zaid would continue his education.

During the event:

1. The mother suffered from the loss of her two sons.
2. The mother was always afraid for the safety of her deported son.
3. The family, especially the mother, lacked social support to cope with their anxieties and fears, especially during the siege of the Nativity Church when Bethlehem was under a strict curfew.

4. The mother experienced feelings of frustration and depression as a result of being unable to help her deported son during the siege and before deportation took place.

After the event:

1. The mother's loss of her two sons has been devastating and overwhelming.
2. The mother fears that her deported son will continue to be in danger and under threat of death by the Israeli army.
3. The mother perceives that deportation may be for an unlimited time. Her uncertainty about the future is disruptive to her life.
4. The mother experiences the painful emotional and perceptual fear that she may never see her son again.
5. The mother is torn between wishful thinking—wanting to see her son—and the reality that renders the wish impossible at this point.
6. The mother still practices wishful thinking that her son will graduate and marry, which is unlikely due to his present condition.

WIVES OF THE DEPORTEES

Two social workers from the PRCS Mental Health Department conducted two group sessions with twenty-five wives of the deportees, aged twenty to forty. Two other social workers conducted two group sessions with thirty mothers of the deportees, aged forty-five to seventy-two.

The following is a summary of the main issues raised by the wives of the deportees during these sessions:

These women expressed their daily suffering after the deportation of their husbands. The deportation itself was both a shock and an unexpected traumatic event. They could not believe that their husbands were deported without Israeli soldiers allowing them to say goodbye. One of the wives, Ola, stated that she cannot breathe when she thinks of the deportation day. She lived just a few meters from the church, yet she could not even see her husband when he was deported. What is more painful is that the deportation is for an unlimited time. The women in the group talked about their feelings of frustration, sadness, despair, and oppression against them and against their families. The group was troubled by the high price their husbands paid because, as they stated, "They loved their country and they're fighting the Israeli military occupation that is denying them their legitimate right for an independent state." They have also strongly criticized the Palestinian leadership for signing with the Israeli government what they call, "a shameful agreement against the will of their deported husbands and their families." Zaina stated, "I wish I asked my husband to stay home the day the Israeli army invaded Bethlehem."

The wives shared the following problems:

Psychological Suffering

The wives feel a sense of loss and deprivation as a result of the absence of their husbands. They feel lonely, helpless, and disabled. They are crying continuously in despair because they have intrusive thoughts, insomnia, and lack of appetite. These women stressed that their children are suffering from similar symptoms as a result of losing the emotional bond with their fathers. Some children ask their mothers about their fathers at mealtime, the usual time for Palestinian families to get together. The children remember their father's favorite foods. They ask about when their fathers will come back home and where they are now. And they ask when their fathers will bring them a toy that they promised to buy.

Social Suffering

This includes social restrictions imposed by the community on the deportees' wives' personal freedom. For example, the wife cannot leave her home alone or with her children unless there is an urgent need. If a woman would like to leave her home, she needs to ask permission from her husband's family. If she is permitted to leave, she cannot be late because she is afraid that people in her neighborhood may think she has a relationship with another man.

Therefore, it was found that some members of the group had left their homes and are now residing in their parents' homes or with the parents of their husbands. Another burden is created because there is not enough space, and often they and their children must live in one room. Though they feel more protected now, they suffer from a lack of stability in their lives because their parents often interfere in their private lives.

Financial Problems

These result from the absence of their husbands who covered their living costs and medical and school expenses for their children. Furthermore, no financial support was given to these women from other social institutions though a few stated that sometimes they receive food. All these financial stressors have led to a feeling among these women that they have become a burden to their families and their community.

Emotional Deprivation

The deportees' wives and their children have unmet emotional needs. It is the right of the child, as one woman said, to live in, "a complete family," with the mother and the father. Some women stated that they delivered during this period, and the newborn child needs the emotional presence of his father. However, some women were afraid that their husbands may have a second marriage since the deportation has not been given an end date. All agreed that the idea of their husbands marrying another woman is the most upsetting and painful stressor.

Before the event:

1. The wives of the deportees, their children and their husbands, were living as stable a life and as normal a marriage as one can have under occupation.
2. Their aspirations and wishes for a happy marriage and family life were like those of other Palestinian married wives.

During the event:

1. The wives suffered from severe psychotrauma as a result of the continued anxieties and fears about the lives of their husbands who were at high risk under siege.
2. The wives experienced an unpredicted change in family life accompanied by insomnia and intrusive thoughts about the security of their husbands who were just a few hundred meters from them.
3. The wives felt emotional pain because of their inability to reach, see, or meet their husbands.
4. The wives felt horror whenever there was shooting at the church, and they imagined their husbands injured or killed.

After the event:

1. They feel loss, anger, and depression, particularly because they could not meet or say goodbye to their husbands before deportation took place to either the Gaza Strip or Europe.
2. They continue to endure emotional, financial, and social stressors.
3. They fear what might happen to their husbands if the Israeli army attacks them in the Gaza Strip or if Israeli intelligence tries to assassinate them in Europe.
4. They feel uncertainty about the future since no one can tell them when their husbands will come home again. This fact creates a distressing emotional feeling for them and their children.

5. They feel that they are repressing their true feelings from their husbands when they call each other and that their husbands are doing the same.
6. They fear that their husbands may marry other women, leading to their husbands' emotional bonds being connected to someone else. (Some members of the group raised this issue when their husbands told them that they feel bored and that they have to do all the housework by themselves.)

EXAMINING PALESTINIAN CHILDREN'S PERCEPTIONS OF THE AL-AQSA INTIFADA

Palestinian children have suffered greatly from the current conflict. Many still remember, and do not fully deal with, the stress and trauma of the previous intifada. This cumulative and constant exposure to conflict increases the risk of stress and trauma-related symptoms and disorders. In every society there is a desire to protect children, even in times of conflict. Yet it is often an impossible task, especially when the crisis is widespread and long lasting. Children and youth are at a disadvantage, as they often have not developed the ability to express themselves concerning the stress and personal conflict they feel. Instead of talking about their problems, they act out against the world. The resulting behavioral changes affect both the family and classroom dynamic. Common behavioral changes include increased aggression, loss of concentration, inattentiveness, separation anxiety (clinging to parents), nervousness, negativity, and carelessness. Other symptoms include nightmares, anger, fear, changes in appetite, psychosomatic complaints, and bed-wetting. As words are not the most effective tool for children and youths to use to express themselves, an alternative is the use of pictorial representations through illustration. Drawing a picture can reveal the perceptions and internal conflict the child may be experiencing. Pictures can also be used as a vehicle to guide discussion and counseling.

In this current study, twenty-one sample drawings were obtained from eighth grade Palestinian students from the Bethlehem district. The original sample included 423 drawings from school-aged children representing governmental, private, and UNRWA schools in the Bethlehem district. The age range of these children is from twelve to fourteen years. Though the sample size is small, it gives a brief insight into the perceptions and internal conflict experienced by Palestinian children due to the current intifada. This sample could very easily be applied in general terms, as similar results are expected across Palestine. It should be noted that the images were drawn only one month after the siege on the church began. Now nine months later, manifestations from the conflict have become a part of daily life. The cumulative effects

of daily violence and trauma that are witnessed have serious long-term implications. It must also be kept in mind that nine months from a child's perspective is much longer than that of an adult. These events have occupied a whole
school year. The impact on education and development has yet to be studied.

The children were given a full class period to produce their images. The
following themes and results were seen. Please refer to the following full description of each image and the accompanying table of present elements and
themes (table 11.1).

Overall, five reoccurring and underlying themes were noted: (1) Personification, (2) Violence and Aggression against People, (3) Destruction of
Houses or Property, (4) Symbolic Elements, and (5) Chosen Artistic Characteristics. Most drawings included multiple elements, with twelve being the
mean average of elements present. Violence and Aggression against People
proved to be the largest category, with ninety-four elements depicted.

1. *Personification*: In this category we see a strong tendency to perceive the
   conflict from the point of view of how it influences the Palestinian people.
   Death and injury to Palestinians is repeatedly illustrated. The graphic and
   symbolic image of the killing of Mohammed Al-Durra, the child shot dead
   by Israeli soldiers while in his father's arms, is a recurrent theme. The perception by the child that he or she cannot be protected, even by a parent,
   from Israeli aggression has serious implications. Mohammed represents
   every school-aged child. His image and his death have become a symbol of
   the Second Intifada and have been shown constantly since his death. The
   children are very aware of the incident because they have seen it repeatedly.
   Many children fear that they could themselves suffer the same fate.

   Other ways that the conflict is personified are through the illustrated
   acts of violence, killing, and injury. Many images depict graphic scenes of
   people being shot or having been killed. The most graphic of these images
   are those of people having been shot in the head and bleeding from their
   wounds. Blood is often used to emphasize the death and suffering of the
   victim. Children's exposure and witnessing of violent events is clearly indicated by these images. In addition, the graphic nature of television coverage of violence further traumatizes and exposes children to the conflict.

   Another element of personification is that of Israeli aggression and violence in terms of soldiers. Soldiers appear in 57 percent of the images.
   This is significant in the diagnosis of posttraumatic stress and other related
   disorders, which are intensified or more likely when trauma is inflicted or
   perceived on a human level (American Psychiatric Association, 1994, pp.
   424–29). Not only are Israeli soldiers the perceived aggressors but they are
   also seen as the cause of death and injury to Palestinian people.

Table 11.1. Present Elements

Picture #	1	2	3	4	5	6	7	8	9	10	11	12	13	14	15	16	17	18	19	20	21	T
1. Personification																						**65**
People Present	*	*			*	*		*	*	*	*			*	*	*	*	*	*	*	*	16
Soldiers		*			*	*		*	*					*	*	*	*		*	*	*	12
Mohammed Al-Durra	*	*			*	*				*	*											6
Injury to Person	*	*			*	*				*	*					*	*	*	*	*	*	12
Shot in the Head	*	*				*											*					4
Facial Expression (clearly indicated)	*	*			*	*		*		*					*	*	*		*			10
Crying	*	*	*	*						*				*		*						5
2. Violence and Aggression against People																						**94**
Blood	*	*			*			*		*	*			*		*		*	*		*	10
Shooting	*	*	*		*	*		*	*	*	*		*	*		*	*	*	*	*	*	18
Killing (Active)	*	*	*		*	*			*	*	*				*	*	*	*	*		*	11
Stone Throwing					*	*				*				*	*	*	*			*		8
Death	*	*	*						*	*	*		*	*		*	*	*	*	*	*	11
Military Force	*	*	*		*	*		*	*	*		*	*	*	*	*	*	*	*	*	*	18
Conflict (Exchange)					*	*				*				*	*	*	*			*	*	8
Bullet Wounds	*				*	*		*		*	*		*			*	*	*		*	*	10
3. Destruction of Houses and Property																						**13**
Damage to Houses								*					*					*	*			4
Displacement (Tents)													*						*	*		2
Bullet or Shell Damage (to Buildings)	*						*	*		*	*		*							*	*	7

(continued)

Table 11.1.   Present Elements (*continued*)

Picture #	1	2	3	4	5	6	7	8	9	10	11	12	13	14	15	16	17	18	19	20	21	T
4. Symbolic Elements																						**46**
Flags		*	*	*	*			*		*				*	*	*	*	*			*	12
Ambulance					*									*			*					3
Al-Aqsa Mosque			*	*	*	*															*	5
Fire (Explosion)													*					*	*			3
Settlements								*	*									*				3
Sign of Peace							*															1
Demonstration								*						*							*	3
Churches and/or Mosques								*	*													2
Sun									*						*	*		*				4
Trees			*	*	*	*		*		*					*	*	*	*				10
5. Chosen Artistic Characteristics																						**35**
Red Blood	*							*	*	*	*			*			*			*		9
Red Weapons and/or Ammunition		*	*														*	*			*	5
Red Victims			*																			1
No Color	*				*		*	*	*			*										6
Written Words		*	*	*	*	*	*	*	*	*	*	*						*			*	14
TOTALS	14	16	14	5	16	15	3	13	9	18	11	3	7	11	11	15	17	15	9	13	18	253

The child also uses facial expressions to express the human element and emotions that he or she feels and perceives. They are clearly indicated in many examples. Some examples illustrate the expected scenario of "happy-smiling" Israeli soldiers and "sad-frowning" Palestinians. Yet there are also examples of "smiling" Palestinians engaged in conflict. In several examples, Israeli soldiers are purposefully drawn with no facial emotion while shooting at Palestinians, thus demonstrating a perception of carelessness in the acts of violence. Furthermore, the tears of the victims express crying, sadness, and helplessness. These facial expressions reflect the children's perception of the emotional states of both parties.

2. *Violence and Aggression against People*: Violence and aggression are represented in depictions of soldiers, shooting, active killing, death, military force, stone throwing, conflict exchange, blood, weapons, and ammunition. The images demonstrate that children fear that they can be attacked by violence from all directions. They illustrate being attacked from both land and sky by helicopters, tanks, and soldiers. The children are acutely aware of the strong Israeli military force and that they are virtually defenseless against these military attacks. In several examples of the representation of Israeli-Palestinian clashes, the comparison of stone throwing with the use of military weapons is clearly depicted. These scenes of violence and aggression, including the resulting death and injury, suggest the fear, vulnerability, nervousness, and anxiety the children are experiencing.

3. *Destruction of Houses and Property*: The destruction of houses and property is a clear theme in the drawings. The number of children in the sample that have been, directly or indirectly, affected by house demolition remains to be determined. Within the Bethlehem area, many families (over three hundred in Beit Sahour alone) have lost their homes to the conflict. With the home symbolizing a place of family, safety, and security, the destruction of these homes also implies the destruction of the child's sense of personal security. Displacement is clearly indicated in two examples by the inclusion of tents beside damaged houses. The need to leave one's home and seek refuge elsewhere is a clear concern. Images of house demolition imply that the children are experiencing fear and vulnerability.

4. *Symbolic Elements*: Numerous symbolic elements are present in the drawings. These include the killing of Mohammed Al-Durra, the Al-Aqsa Mosque, the flags, the use of red to depict blood, the death and killing; the dove as the sign of peace; the demonstrations, the churches or mosques, the sun, the trees, the fire and explosions, the settlements, and the military forces. Though these symbols hold different meanings for each child, they give insight into the key elements of the conflict, as they perceive them.

As mentioned in the section on personification, the killing of Mohammed Al-Durra is symbolic of the vulnerability of all children. The theme of the Al-Aqsa Mosque shows their awareness of the intifada, what it stands for, and why it is taking place. Al-Aqsa has become the symbol of the intifada. The children are displaying their national pride and expressing their desire to have their own nation. Related to the pride displayed within the theme of Al-Aqsa, flags are also used to represent pride in their culture, nation, and people. Often Palestinian flags are shown flying on Palestinian land, other times they are shown being carried. Israeli flags, as with the Palestinian flags, are often used to emphasize the sides of the conflict and whose land is being depicted. The Israeli flag is most commonly associated with Israeli military forces such a tanks, helicopters, and jeeps. The Star of David is also clearly indicated on the soldiers' uniforms. Interestingly, no representations of damage to the Israeli or Palestinian flags are present, as might be expected in relation to the conflict.

Furthermore, the use of red to depict blood, death, and injury (and its causes such as ammunition and weapons) represents the reality and outcome of the violence. The sign of peace (be it only one example) symbolizes the hope for a better future. Churches or mosques or both symbolize religious faith, especially the need for it in times of conflict. Fire and explosions symbolize the strong impact of military weapons and the extensive damage they cause. Settlements symbolize the conflict, the occupation of Palestinian land, and the vast differences in quality of living between the two peoples. Military forces symbolize the violence and aggression witnessed and experienced on a daily basis. Sun and trees are frequently depicted; their symbolic meaning is more abstract but may imply a sense of normalcy in the midst of the crisis. Symbolism in children's drawing is often used to represent larger concepts that are not otherwise expressible.

5. *Chosen Artistic Characteristics*: Noticeable artistic characteristics that have been either included or excluded give insight into possible internal reflections. The following characteristics were noted in the sample: the use of written words, lack of color, and the prominent use of red to illustrate death. The use of written words to further emphasize the child's perspective is used in 67 percent of the examples. Three categories of words and phrases that were dominant include: (1) pride and faith, (2) blame for the conflict, (3) identification. There is frequent reference to both Islamic and Christian faith as a source of strength and symbolism. Lack of color suggests that the child feels withdrawn and emotionally distant from the conflict (or subject of the image). The strong, abundant, and frequent use of red to represent blood and injury comes across clearly (62 percent of the examples).

Interestingly, in five examples, red is also used to represent the weapon or ammunition or both as the cause of death and injury. The child's perception that weapons are used to kill is clearly represented. The use of color is also a significant indicator of internal feelings and perceptions. Some images are completely void of color while others are full of it. In one image the whole scene is void of color except for the emphasized red blood of Mohammed Al-Durra's fatal wounds. What the blood represents to the child must be considered. It may represent the fear of death, the obvious amount of blood spilled, or the violence they have witnessed. The examples with no color may suggest lack of emotion toward the conflict. These artistic characteristics are all an important part of the analysis.

All the images outline the underlying concerns the children have concerning the current conflict. Each child is affected individually and each child has been exposed to different aspects and intensity of the violence and conflict. Overall, the following concerns can be identified:

1. *Fear of death or injury or both to oneself, family, or friend.* These are represented in the images of Mohammed Al-Durra as well as the killing, injury, and deaths of Palestinians, especially children.
2. *Fear of damage to one's house and resulting displacement.* This is evident in the images of the houses being destroyed and fired on by Israeli forces. The examples of tents beside the houses illustrate the forced displacement of families. For every child, "home" is a place of security and comfort. If "home" is destroyed, so is the child's sense of security.
3. *Blame for the conflict on Israel and the United States.* This is evident in the drawings and words related to a Unites States and Israeli partnership in the conflict. These negative words and illustrations demonstrate anger and frustration toward the aggressors and occupiers who are killing their people.
4. *Frustration with Israeli military force in comparison with the limited means of resistance for Palestinians.* This is frequently expressed by the confrontations between Israeli soldiers and Palestinians. Palestinians are always shown throwing stones while the soldiers shoot back at them with guns, tanks, and helicopters. There are no examples showing Palestinians with guns or anything more than stones to defend themselves.
5. *View of the aggressor.* Israeli soldiers and military force, in addition to settlements, are the only clear representation of Israel. Therefore, it is likely that the perception of the occupier and the aggressor is seen purely in a military and political light as opposed to the overall perception of Israel as a people.

6. *Settlements as a source of conflict.* In the Bethlehem area there are several settlements, which are a constant source of conflict. Shooting and attacks surrounding the settlements are common occurrences. A child's perception that their removal would end the conflict is a reasonable interpretation.

TRAUMA AND STRESS: SYMPTOMS AND DISORDERS

Children suffering from posttraumatic symptoms may be suffering from numerous symptom classes including phobias, separation anxiety, adjustment and panic disorders, major depression, and acute stress. Both Type I (single event) and Type II (ongoing) trauma can result in PTSD (American Psychiatric Association, 1994, pp. 424–29). Yet due to the long-lasting nature of the conflict, Palestinian children are seen to be suffering from Type II trauma. Children with posttraumatic stress symptoms must be given serious attention to reduce the impact of trauma.

Symptoms of stress and trauma are especially visible in the school environment. Loss of concentration, increased aggression, fear of going to school, distractibility, and wetting accidents are common in the classroom. These symptoms indicate stress-related disorders such as Acute Stress Disorder (ASD) and PTSD. At the time of these drawings, the intifada had only been going on for one month, which would be sufficient only to classify symptoms of ASD (lasting only one month [American Psychiatric Association, 1994, p. 427]). Yet the symptoms of PTSD (symptoms lasting longer than one month and inclusive of those symptoms displayed in ASD) are certainly applicable given the current duration of the intifada. Many Palestinian children are currently displaying these symptoms.

Various factors strengthen the likelihood that PTSD will result, including intensity and physical proximity to the trauma, whether the trauma is based on single or multiple incidents and whether the trauma is of human design (American Psychiatric Association, 1994, p. 424). Characteristic symptoms resulting from extreme trauma include (1) persistent reexperiencing of the traumatic event, (2) persistent avoidance of event-related stimuli and numbing of general responsiveness, and (3) persistent symptoms of increased arousal and intentional problems (p. 424).

CONCLUSION

The interpretation of children's drawings as related to the underlying causes of stress and trauma gives an insight into their perception of the conflict. It is a valuable tool for assessing the resulting trauma in children. Because few children are able to express themselves in words, drawing allows them an opportunity to let out their feelings in a creative and expressive way. Though interpretation of these drawings alone cannot replace an in-depth interview with the child, a window to his or her view of the world is opened. When discussing children's perceptions of the current situation, it is important to get an understanding of why they are perceiving what they are and how these perceptions are affecting them.

The children are all very aware of the intifada. Their perceptions are shaped by how the events have been directly and indirectly seen by them. They are exposed to the situation on a daily basis through the media as well as by witnessing the events firsthand. Within the Bethlehem area, where the sample of drawings came from, shelling, shooting, and conflict can be heard echoing through the hills daily. This has a huge impact on children who continually feel the effects of stress and trauma. Working to reduce the effects of conflict-related trauma on Palestinian children should be a priority for schools and local psychosocial programs. This chapter has shown that the intifada is a constant preoccupation of these children. The exposure to conflict will have long-lasting effects that must be addressed as soon as possible.

DEVELOPING A PALESTINIAN MODEL OF INTERVENTION DURING THE CONFLICT

Over the last two years, the PRCS Mental Health Department has had to react to a sharp rise in the psychosocial needs of the population. To be effective and to continue to provide a high level of services, it has been necessary to find new ways in which to access, assist, and treat target groups living under extreme and complex circumstances.

The reality in Palestine has meant that health care providers have had to adapt to increasingly unstable and changeable circumstances. For the Mental Health Department, the closures have made our ability to function increasingly difficult, and we have had to react to the circumstances imposed on us in order to continue to provide support to the population. As director, I have had to manage the teams on the ground and ensure that they are able to perform effectively in their respective communities. Rapid needs assessments have been conducted in all areas to determine what services are needed, where they are needed, and who needs them. Programs are then devised and implemented that are specifically structured to support the target groups. Due to the stress and pressures involved, staff members have had to develop flexibility and versatility in their attitudes toward the environment and working practices so they can continue to function.

SUMMARY OF ACTIVITIES—MEETING
IMMEDIATE EMERGENCY NEEDS

• *Working with the Emergency Medical Services (EMS)*: The staff members have been placed with EMS crews to provide immediate emotional support to injured people, with an emphasis on youth and children. Working in the ambulance, the staff members remain with the patients from the time they are collected by the EMS until reaching the hospital. They then stay until family members arrive. This has helped to reduce the shock and trauma associated with violent injury.

• *Outreach crisis intervention services*: The PRCS has set up field hospitals and clinics throughout the West Bank and Gaza Strip to facilitate urgent treatment for the public. Many cases have been victims of bombing and shelling attacks; therefore, the need to train staff in close proximity to areas of danger has been paramount. Staff members working in the hospitals and clinics provide psychosocial support at an early point in the victims' exposure to a traumatic incident, enabling them to better understand and cope with their feelings and fears.

• *Group sessions for surviving women*: Aimed at women who have suffered emotional distress through home demolition and destruction, small groups have been brought together and encouraged to share their experiences. These group sessions have been vital in allowing women to express their fears and anxieties as a result of losing their homes.

• *Group sessions for the EMS (Bethlehem Branch)*: EMS staff members, in particular, are vulnerable. Working in extreme and adverse conditions where their personal safety is at high risk, being removed from familiar and secure surroundings for long periods of time, and providing critical support for communities suffering ongoing trauma and violence—all have an impact on the well-being of EMS staff. Group sessions have been vital in encouraging staff to talk about their experiences and have provided a support network to which they can turn. In addition, a psychosocial intervention program has been developed to support the EMS staff and their families. A comprehensive study highlighting the effects of working in violent conditions and the ways in which to alleviate the pressures has recently been submitted to the European Union.

• *Psychological and emotional support for school children and youth and the education of teachers and parents about trauma in children*: Children are at the highest level of risk from emotional trauma and consequently suffer from many psychosocial problems. Training has been provided to teachers and parents to help them to recognize manifestations of stress in children and to find ways in which to provide support to the children.

- *Workshops for school counselors*: School counselors are untrained and unprepared for situations where children have suffered and experienced violence and bereavement through violence. Training courses were implemented to enable them to understand the symptoms of stress and trauma as well as to develop strategies and techniques for effective intervention. The courses given covered crisis intervention, basic counseling skills, evacuations, and grief counseling.
- *Public awareness campaign*: Increasing awareness in the public has been vital to enable them to better understand the effects they are suffering and to help them learn self-help techniques or to encourage them to seek help from trained professionals. Two types of media have been used. First, local media have been utilized in a general way to reach a wide and diverse audience, encouraging dialogue and understanding in the community. Second, pamphlets have been produced where social workers visit target groups, such as women, children, and refugee camps, and use these information leaflets at a more specific and direct level to provide education.
- *Training professionals who are on the front line*: Many health care professionals have not had formal training in the field of trauma. Training has been provided to strengthen the ability of staff in crisis intervention and trauma management.
- *Education for pregnant women*: Due to difficulties in transporting women in labor to maternity hospitals, many suffer anxiety and fear before the delivery. In cooperation with maternity hospitals, expectant mothers attended sessions showing them how to deal with and overcome these fears.
- *Workshops—Stress Management for West Bank Caregivers*: International experts have been invited to implement training and workshops to help improve skills and to learn new techniques for stress management.
- *Training of social work students from local universities*: Students have been placed in the field to gain clinical experience, under direct staff supervision. Their academic courses cannot adequately cover the realities of working with a severely traumatized population. By getting hands-on experience, they are able to gain a better understanding and are well equipped when they complete their studies and start to work in the community.

PROJECTS IN ACTION

- *Children's Human Rights Education Project*: This project, funded by UNICEF, aims to educate students about their rights. A training course was conducted for schoolteachers to educate them about children's rights in order that they may assist their students in expressing these rights. Schoolchildren

were encouraged to express their rights through artistic expression, for example, drawings, photography, and short stories.

- *Youth Violence Prevention Program in the West Bank and Gaza Strip*: The
  goal of this project, funded by the Canadian International Development
  Agency and the Quebec Government through Medical Aid for Palestine, is
  to assist Palestinian youth to deal in a nonviolent way with seven issues
  with which they are struggling as a result of the current conflict. These are
  political violence, poverty and unemployment, loss, lack of respect of the
  civil law, domestic violence, school violence, and anxiety and frustration.
  A multimedia center has been established in both Bethlehem and Khan
  Younis. It offers training programs for youth affected by violence and creates job opportunities and counseling services for them.
- *Trauma Management—A Recovery Program for Palestinian Emergency
  Medical Services and Emergency Response Teams*: This project, which is
  funded by the European Union through the German Red Cross, has been
  created to respond to the psychosocial needs of the PRCS EMS teams and
  their families during the Second Intifada. These teams are overworked and
  underpaid. In the course of their work, they have been exposed to violent
  events such as shootings, killings, and detentions by the Israeli army. The
  main objective of this project is to offer psychological support services to
  the EMS teams working in thirty stations in the West Bank and Gaza Strip.
  Other components of this project include a program conducting studies to
  assess their exposure to violent events and its impact on their emotional well-
  being; a psychological support program for these EMS teams and their families; an awareness program to educate them about how to respond to the traumatic reactions of victims; and a training program for the intervention team.
- *A Community-Based Prevention Program for Children and Youth*: A project, funded by USAID through the Save the Children Fund, was established
  to provide a prevention program for traumatized children in the Hebron district in the southern West Bank. The main goal of this project is to conduct
  a series of workshops and activities in eight marginalized areas. The themes
  of these workshops center around children's developmental needs, psychosocial needs, and security needs. Ten messages were developed to express these needs and various tools were created to implement them.
- *Deportee's families*: There are many families who are suffering from the
  effects of loss and separation. A total of thirty-nine men were exiled by
  the Israeli army from the Bethlehem district during the Nativity Church
  siege to either the Gaza Strip or abroad. The families need a great deal of
  support to help cope with this. In an effort to provide psychological support services to these families, group sessions have been offered for the
  wives and mothers of the deportees.

FUTURE DIRECTIONS OF INTERVENTION

Although Palestinians have not been exposed to natural disasters, they have suffered for more than three decades from the impact of other traumatic events, specifically wars, violence, and persistent aggression of military occupation. However, it should be noted that not all Palestinians respond in the same way to the same event; what may be traumatic to one individual may have little or no impact on another, due to individual differences in coping style.

Nevertheless, in order to provide effective intervention to a high-risk population, such as the Palestinians who are suffering from chronic, severe, and intense exposure to traumatic events, local Palestinian professional and international organizations working to support the West Bank and Gaza Strip field projects should first take the following directions into consideration:

1. Mental health professionals need to deal with the barriers to providing psychosocial services mentioned earlier. This is in addition to a lack of a national mental health plan.

2. The socioeconomic, political, and cultural contexts of this nation should be carefully taken into consideration before intervention takes place. Well-designed Western approaches to treat trauma victims may not work if imposed on intended beneficiaries without understanding these contexts. For example, how can a clinician intervene to assist a traumatized mother after her child was killed by the Israeli army or a wife whose husband was assassinated without understanding the way survivors perceive and subjectively experience expressed symptoms of trauma and react to traumatic events? As I mentioned earlier, the deceased are perceived as martyrs and not victims. The suicide bomber is also perceived as a martyr. The family of the suicide insists on calling him a martyr and not a suicide. A suicide, in the family's perception, is a desperate person, but a martyr is killed for the following "legitimate" motives:

   • A religious motive: The person is fighting the enemy, that is, the Israeli occupation that is the enemy of God since the Israeli army causes suffering and destruction to his followers, occupying their land and holy places. The martyr, therefore, will be alive with God in heaven.

   • A national motive: Fighters are sacrificing themselves to free the nation from the oppression of a military occupation.

   • A humanistic motive: They will fight the occupier and die to free the Palestinians from their occupier.

   • A social motive: The families of the martyrs get sympathy and social support from people regardless of their socioeconomic status.

- A financial motive: Freedom fighters know that if the Israeli army kills them, their families will receive financial assistance.

    Furthermore, the underlying philosophy behind martyrdom has a greater goal—to cause death to a large number of people among the people of the enemy and to cause losses in all aspects of the enemy's life. This includes the economy, security, and changing the attitude of the enemy about the ability of their leaders to protect them. Therefore, causing horror and interruption in the routine life of the enemy is perceived as a "legitimate" justification for their acts.

3. Clinicians, especially those working in the West Bank and to a lesser degree in the Gaza Strip, often live as do the rest of the Palestinians, under a military curfew (house arrest). Therefore, providing outreach services to those needing professional assistance is extremely difficult. Initial screening of victims—whenever these victims seek help or when services are accessible to them (when the curfew is lifted)—and an inquiry about prior trauma and a history of severe psychological problems may be problematic under these "war" conditions. Therefore, proper diagnosis and effective treatment seem to be limited, particularly if the treatment is long term. Even brief screening is usually impossible to conduct in the immediate aftermath of trauma. Similarly, providing effective early intervention and secondary prevention is difficult.

4. The provision of social support for the victims and their families under prolonged periods of curfews and repeated military invasions becomes difficult, too, especially in the immediate aftermath of exposure to a violent event.

5. The intense exposure to violent events and living in a hostile environment where killing, bombing, shooting, home demolition, intimidation, surprise attack, and so on, are daily practices of the Israeli army, helping the victims to return to a routine or normal life is difficult. It must be achieved, however, in order to enhance predictability and to enable them to gain safety, stability, and control over their lives.

6. In a country that is suffering from a mass disaster and where trained and qualified clinicians in the trauma field are rare, ethical issues arise. These include obtaining informed consent from victims of trauma before intervention, informing victims about the credentials of the helpers prior to intervention, and supervising helpers. These are requisite conditions for therapy to take place.

7. It follows that implementing a certain framework of therapy to fit all trauma survivors may fail as a result of the complexities of the issues of pre- and posttrauma experience and the harsh and negative conditions on the ground, which all work against recovery.

8. Clinicians may find that Palestinian survivors have histories that require multimodal intervention, which needs to be applied over a longer period of time.
9. There is a lack of a referral system in Palestine. Clinicians who work in Palestine should be aware of the consequences of such a weakness in their daily work with Palestinian survivors.
10. Literature suggests that traumatized individuals have a high risk of developing medical illness. Trauma survivors as compared with nontraumatized individuals "report more medical symptoms, use more medical services, have more medical illnesses detected during a physical examination, and display higher mortality" (Foa, Keane, and Friedman, 2002, p. 8).

In this context, Palestinian physicians often prescribe psychoactive medication for patients they believe are suffering from mental health problems. They often lack accurate information about the chemical components of psychoactive medications, and a variety of local and foreign medications on the market differs in quality and effectiveness (Awwad, 1999). In addition, an increasing number of Palestinians suffer from traumatic reactions because of their daily exposure to or witnessing of traumatic events. They seek medical advice from nonmental health professionals, particularly physicians, to relieve them from symptoms of traumatic reactions. However, these general practitioners are not trained to provide treatment. Therefore, diagnosis and treatment of PTSD not only represents an ethical concern but may complicate the healing process. For the just-mentioned reason, training and education in the diagnosis and treatment of trauma-related disorders for Palestinian general practitioners—particularly for those working in emergency medical clinics and hospitals as well as primary health care clinics in remote areas—is a priority.

NOTE

1. This informer was working at the fire department. He was apprehended by the Palestinian intelligence service and confessed to being an informer four months later.

REFERENCES

American Psychiatric Association (1994). *Diagnostic and statistical manual of disorders* (4th ed.). Washington, DC: Author.
Awwad, E. (1999). "Between trauma and recovery: Some perspectives on Palestinian's vulnerability and adaptation." In K. Nader, N. Dubrow, and B. Hudnall

Stamm (Eds), *Honoring differences: Cultural issues in the treatment of trauma and loss*. New York: Francis and Taylor.

———. (2002). *Assessment of exposure to violent events on Palestinian emergency medical services: Learning to survive through pain*. ECHO FPA grant No. 99/1000.

Carlson, E. B. (1997). *Trauma assessments: A clinician's guide*. New York: The Guilford Press.

Ehrenreich, J. H. (2001). *Coping with disaster: A guidebook to psychosocial intervention* (Rev. ed.). New York: Center for Psychology and Society, State University of New York.

Foa, E. B., Keane, T. M., and Friedman, M. J. (2002). *Effective treatments for PTSD: Practice guidelines from the International Society for Traumatic Studies*. New York: Guilford.

Litz, B., and Gray, M. (2002). Early intervention for trauma: Current status and future directions. National Center for Post-Traumatic Stress Disorder, Department of Veterans Affairs. Retrieved April 7, 2004, from www.ncptsd.org

Terr, L. C. (1991). Childhood traumas: An outline and overview. *American Journal of Psychiatry*, 148: 10–20.

Vrijlandt, J. (2001, September 6–8). Vicarious traumatization. In a report on the working conference, *Managing stress of the humanitarian aid worker: Towards an integrated approach*. Amsterdam, The Netherlands: Centers for Disease Control and Prevention and The Antares Foundation.

Part III

WORKING WITH TRAUMA

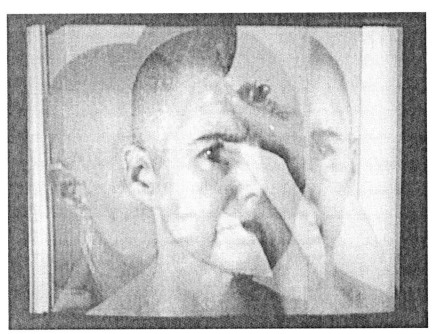

Untitled *by Kiki Elefant (2003).*

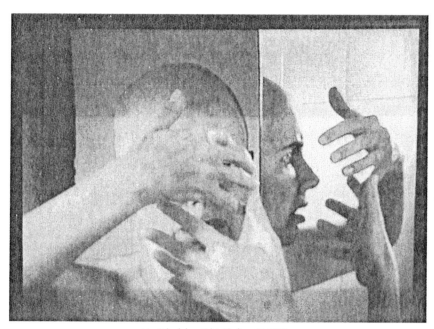

Untitled *by Kiki Elefant (2003).*

Chapter Twelve

Early Interventions with Victims of Terrorism

Rony Berger

This chapter summarizes the major dilemmas in the field of early interventions with survivors of terrorism, including the complexity of their immediate reactions and the phenomenological nature of the terror threat. I further delineate the various stages survivors undergo in coping with the aftermath of terror attacks and the concurrent psychological tasks facing professionals. Then, I outline the principles of the initial clinical evaluation utilized with survivors of terrorism. Finally, but perhaps most importantly, I describe my approach to prevent adverse posttraumatic reactions: the Traumatic Memory Reconstruction (TMR) model. TMR's rationale, principles, and individual and group applications are presented and illustrated with case material.

The recent terror attacks against the United States on September 11, 2001, have profoundly affected the lives of Americans as well as millions around the Western world and have drawn unprecedented attention to the phenomenon of international terrorism. Professionally, they have further accelerated the already growing interest in the study of trauma survivors and the pursuit of effective early interventions in the aftermath of traumatic events.

While these hideous terror attacks have sharply awakened public awareness regarding the danger of terrorism, we in Israel, unfortunately, have been too familiar with this phenomenon since (and perhaps even before) the inception of the State of Israel. To illustrate the magnitude of the Israeli public's exposure to terrorism, according to the official Israeli Defense Force's website (www.idf.il) between September 2000 and February 16, 2003, 419 terror attacks (including suicide bombing, car bombs, mortar bombings, shootings, and lynching) were documented, 655 of them were within the "green-line." In terms of Israeli casualties,[1] 506 civilians were killed and 3,595 were injured in the last two and a half years. To grasp the significant toll on the Israeli society, translated proportionally to the size of the American population, the number of those killed would have been the equivalent of 23,000 Americans and the number of those injured would have been the equivalent of 163,000. Indeed, this unprecedented ongoing exposure to terror attacks was reflected in a recent study (A. Bleich, Z. Solomon, and M. Gelkof, personal communication, January 2003) indicating that 44 percent of Israelis either were directly involved (16 percent) or knew of a relative or a friend who were involved in a terror attack.

Thus, there is no surprise that in this trauma-ridden society established in the ashes of the Holocaust, a society that has known numerous wars and countless hostilities, one would find mental health professionals who have always been interested in studying the long-term effects of trauma and loss. However, the unremitting terror attacks during the past two years forced Israeli professionals to explore effective methods in handling the acute stress reactions of the growing number of terror victims.

Research has shown that most survivors exhibit posttraumatic reactions following a traumatic event, reactions that generally dissipate within the first year (Blanchard et al., 1996; Koren, Arnon, and Klein, 1999; Rothbaum, Foa, Riggs, Murdock, and Walsh, 1992; Riggs, Rothbaum, and Foa, 1995). However, between 10 percent and 30 percent of those who develop early acute symptoms fail to recover, manifesting Post-Traumatic Stress Disorder (PTSD) symptoms years after the traumatic event (Green, Grace, and Gleser, 1985; Kessler, Sonnega, Bromet, Hughes, and Nelson, 1995; Solomon, 1993). Unfortunately, studies predicting PTSD have not yet been able to sort out those survivors who are at risk of developing long-term stress disorders from those who manifest temporary acute "symptoms."

Consequently, two types of early intervention approaches have emerged: the generic approach and the selective approach. The generic approach, best exemplified by Critical Incident Stress Debriefing (CISD) (Mitchell and Everly, 1995), offers psychological assistance to all exposed survivors relatively soon after the trauma, whereas the second approach provides more specialized intervention (most recently in the form of cognitive behavior therapy [Bryant, Harvey, Dang, Sackville, and Basten, 1998; Bryant and Harvey, 2000]), or Eye Movement Desensitization and Reprocessing (Silver and Rogers, 2002), to a selected at-risk group weeks or months after exposure. Both approaches have advantages and shortcomings.

The advantage of the first model lies in the fact that it casts a wide net, thus presuming to mitigate acute reactions of many survivors in a relatively short period of time. Furthermore, its proponents claim that by intervening soon after the traumatic event, they are in a better position to normalize survivors' reactions and to support their natural coping strategies (Mitchell and Everly,

2000). Unfortunately, despite its widespread popularity, recent studies have challenged the efficacy of this model, suggesting that one-session psychological debriefing might even cause harm to some survivors (Bisson, McFarlane, and Rose, 2000; Elklit, 2001; Neria and Solomon, 1999; Raphael, Meldrum, and McFarlane, 1995; Rose, Bisson, and Wessely, 2001; Van Emmerick, Kamphuis, and Hulsbosch, 2002).

The primary advantage of the second approach rests on the fact that it targets only those individuals who are likely to develop PTSD, while respecting those who are able to utilize their natural resources. Hence, it has the potential of being not only more cost-effective but also less harmful. The pitfalls of the selective model, however, are twofold. First, it adopts a "wait and see" posture, thereby wasting valuable time during which some biological processes may be crystallized (Shalev, 2002). Second, and perhaps more importantly, it simply misses too many survivors who are not formally diagnosed as suffering from acute stress-related disorders

We at Natal, the Israel Center for the Victims of War and Terror, attempted to integrate these two approaches by developing an alternative approach, the Traumatic Memory Restructuring (TMR) model. On the one hand, we agree with the selective approach and feel that early interventions should not be forced on all survivors; rather, they should primarily address those who manifest severe and uncontrollable acute reactions or who are at risk of developing stress-related disorders. On the other hand, at the current state of knowledge in the field, we believe that psychological assistance should not be limited to survivors with formal diagnoses such as Acute Stress Disorder (ASD) or PTSD and should be rendered before the three-month cut point suggested by some experts in the field (see the guidelines proposed by Foa, Hembree, Riggs, Rauch, and Franklin, 2001).

This chapter is divided into two parts. The first part briefly summarizes major dilemmas regarding acute reactions of terror-attack survivors and outlines the principles of early interventions. It elucidates the phenomenological nature of the terror threat, the complexity of the acute reactions, and the various phases survivors undergo in the aftermath of terror attacks. The second part starts by presenting our initial assessment and follows by outlining our TMR model, namely, its rationale, basic principles, and application using a clinical case. It ends by drawing conclusions regarding the future of the TMR model and by pointing to empirical research needed in this area. It is our belief that the TMR approach has the potential not only for ameliorating the initial adverse reactions of terror attack survivors but, hopefully, for preventing the development of PTSDs, at least in some of the survivors. While our extensive clinical experience shows promise, this methodology clearly needs further empirical evidence.

THE PHENOMENOLOGY OF TERROR SURVIVORS

In his book *Fighting Terrorism*, Benjamin Netanyahu, former Israeli prime minister, defines terrorism as "the systematic assault on civilians to inspire fear for political ends" (Netanyahu, 1997, p. 8). He goes further to suggest that the terrorist's underlying message is that "every member of the society is 'guilty,' that anyone can be a victim and therefore no one is safe" (p. 9). This definition indeed captures the strategic aim of terrorism, namely, to spread fear and panic and to demoralize the targeted population. When a society is exposed to an ongoing wave of terror assaults, like the one we have experienced in Israel during the past two years, an insidious and corrosive "terror spiral" (Berger, 2002) emerges, affecting its citizens both personally and collectively.

The terror spiral (see figure 12.1) shows that terrorism simultaneously elicits the survival threat and the sense of uncertainty. It often seems that the terrorists capitalize on this knowledge by changing their modus operandi.

This situation leads to a significant decline in personal and collective security, shaking the tenuous "illusion of safety" (i.e., the belief that we are in-

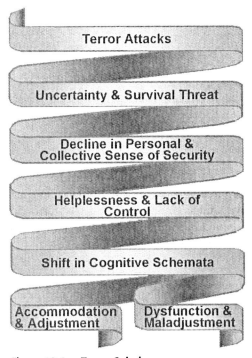

Figure 12.1.   Terror Spiral.

vulnerable), which is a belief we have all gradually adopted during our formative years. We then seem to be infected with what Robert Lifton (1967) termed "traces of death" and are forced to confront our fragile sense of human vulnerability. This experience is universally unpleasant, and for some, it may even be rather disturbing.

Should we continue to experience the perceived threat of terrorism, a sense of helplessness and lack of control gradually emerges, a feeling that may be intolerable. In order to regain control over these feelings, we tend to use a variety of coping mechanisms including: denial, dissociation, numbing, distraction, avoidance, rationalization, withdrawal, and overdoing. Nonetheless, the most effective way to overcome these feelings is to directly fight terrorism. However, since this task is formidable, individuals as well as nations often resort to aggressive and hostile reactions to demonstrate to themselves or to their citizens that they are in control of this situation. Unfortunately, these types of actions frequently lead to counterreactions, further escalating the situation.

Helplessness and lack of control may also lead to a state of chronic anxiety and despair, gradually shifting our internal cognitive schemata. We then tend to see the world as uninviting and dangerous, ourselves as being more vulnerable or self-righteous, and others as either friends or foes. Colors of uncertainty tint our future, and a sense of hopelessness begins to surface. This cognitive shift coupled with the feelings of helplessness, anxiety, and despair may result in both personal and national adaptation and adjustment or may lead to dysfunction and maladjustment.

Our clinical experience suggests that almost all terror survivors are struggling with two phenomenological and isomorphic dilemmas: one is assimilating the new and often frightening worldview with the old and familiar one, and the other is integrating the newfound fragile sense of self with the relatively secure one of the past. Overcoming these challenging psychological tasks is necessary for all survivors in order to achieve adaptive functioning, to maintain their well-being, and, in the final analysis, to transcend their traumatic experience.

THE COMPLEXITY OF ACUTE REACTIONS IN THE AFTERMATH OF A TERROR ATTACK

Several researchers have recently pointed to the complex and multidimensional nature of acute reactions in the aftermath of traumatic events (Bryant and Harvey, 2000; Litz, Gray, Bryant, and Adler, 2001; Shalev, 2002; Shalev and Ursano, 2003). Their observations suggest that early intervention with survivors of terrorism is a rather complex and demanding endeavor.

First, they observe that survivors' early reactions represent an attempt to handle the chaotic situation rather than a mental condition. Hence, "pathologizing" these responses by characterizing them as "symptoms" not only ignores their adaptive function but may also be harmful. Since there is some evidence that early interventions may reduce the long-term adverse effects on survivors (Solomon, 1993), it seems necessary to accurately differentiate between those whose initial reactions represent adaptation and those whose reactions may lead to future maladjustment. However, because studies regarding predictors of PTSD have shown inconsistent results (for review see Berwin, Andrews, and Valentine, 2000), the task of the clinician appears rather challenging.

Second, they note that the variability and inconsistency in the presentation of acute stress reactions further complicates the early treatment of trauma survivors. Empirical studies of survivors, particularly among combatants, showed that early stress reactions are "polymorphous and labile" consisting of a variety of symptoms including: irritability, restlessness, stupor, startle reactions, insomnia, nausea, vomiting, abdominal pain, numbing, anxiety, depression, and aggressive outbursts (Bartmeir, 1946; Grinker and Spiegel, 1945; Solomon, 1993). Clinicians should therefore be cautious in assessing the nature of acute reactions to terror attacks. In this context, it may be important to remember Shalev and Ursano's (2003) observation that morphology of acute reactions is less important than their functionality.

Third, they emphasize the role of concurrent stressors (like medical procedures, injuries, ongoing threats of terror attacks, relocation or separation from "loved ones") in shaping survivors' early responses. This point is particularly relevant to Israeli survivors of terror attacks who are continuously confronted with the threat of terrorism. It is, therefore, difficult to ascertain whether responses in the aftermath of a terror assault result from the traumatic experience (are posttraumatic) or from the anticipation of further hostilities (are pre-traumatic).

Fourth, they remind us that survivors have multiple needs which vary among individuals, which change rapidly, and which are often not psychologically based. For instance, many survivors seek reassurance, soothing, contact with family and friends, and even information regarding the event before they consider their psychological well-being. Conservation of Resources (COR) theorists also highlight a similar view, maintaining that mental health professionals often ignore the lack of nonpsychological resources of survivors (Hobfoll, 1989). Hence, clinicians should be prepared to abandon their traditional role and either serve as liaison between survivors and significant others or render themselves the empathic humane support that is often all that is needed by survivors. In so doing, clinicians who provide early intervention (particularly to survivors of terror attacks where identification with them is embedded in our national identity) are not only exposed themselves to extremely distressful conditions (as often is the case with terror attacks) but also find themselves stripped of their natural coping resource, their professional role. It is therefore imperative that they be prepared for this demanding task as well as receive emotional support.

Another important issue that pertains to early intervention following a terror attack is the complex phenomenology of human trauma. While it is professionally accepted that the survival threat is at the core of the trauma, Shalev and Ursano (2003) pointed to other traumatizing elements as playing a role in constructing survivors' experiences and, therefore, in shaping their acute reactions. Indeed, our experience working with survivors corroborates this observation. Traumatizing aspects of the terror attack such as the incongruence of the experience ("One minute I was drinking tea with my wife in a coffee shop, the next I was in the middle of a battle zone."), the survival guilt ("It could have easily been me rather than her."), or the exposure to the grotesque ("I cannot forget the picture of this decapitated baby.") should be thoroughly explored by the clinician to fully understand the survivor's experience.

Finally, clinicians, particularly those with an exclusive psychological orientation, should not overlook the multiple biological mechanisms involved in shaping the early experience of the survivor. Although few pharmacological interventions during the early phases of trauma have so far shown to be effective (Shalev, 2002), understanding the biological aspects of the traumatic experience (as we shall later illustrate) is crucial not only for designing future medical interventions but also for psychological body-oriented interventions.

THE PHASES OF EARLY INTERVENTION FOLLOWING A TERROR ATTACK

The complexity of acute reactions described in the preceding suggests that the temporal dimension is essential not only in dictating who will be the recipients and providers of early interventions, but also in establishing the goals and the nature of these interventions. Adopting the National Institute of Mental Health's (NIMH's) guidance for early interventions (2002), we divided the sequence of reactions in the aftermath of a terror attack into four phases: preimpact, impact, early postimpact, and early recovery. Table 12.1 summarizes the progression of these phases, outlining the major stressors faced by survivors, their changing needs, and characteristic behaviors in each phase.

Table 12.1. Phases of Early Intervention in the Aftermath Terror Attack

Phase	Preimpact Months Before	Impact (Hours)	Early Postimpact (0–Week)	Early Recovery (1–8 Weeks)
Stressors	Impending threat Uncertainty Government Briefing Rumors Lack of preparedness Being overprepared Risk assessment	Survival threat Threat to body integrity Losses Grotesque images Human cruelty *Secondary stressors* injuries, medical procedures pain, continued threats, etc.	Primary & secondary Stressors as in previous phase Hospitalization Police interrogation Separation Initial reactions Media exposure Retelling the story	Painful memories Uncontrollable behaviors Planning the return to normal activities Financial burdens Withdrawal of support systems
Survivor's Needs	Risk assessment Reliable information regarding the threat Existence of emergency system Trained services providers	Safety & security Food & shelter Orientation Contact with loved ones Communication with others Information about the event	Empathy & understanding Acceptance of injuries and pain Accept psychological limitations Affect modulation	Reestablish previous "assumptive world" Process the traumatic experience & construct Acceptance of losses
Goals	Preparation, improve coping	Survival, communication	Adjustment	Process experience Appraisal & planning
Behavior	Preparation vs. denial	Fight/flight, freeze, surrender, etc.	Resilience vs. exhaustion	Grief, reappraisal, intrusive memories, narrative formation

Role of Helpers	Organize emergency system Train personnel Set up community support system Gain & disseminate knowledge	Rescue & protect Ensure food & shelter Assess the environment for ongoing threat Provide medical assistance Inform family & relatives	Provide concrete needs Financial assistance	Respond with sensitivity
Role of Mental Health Professonals	Assist in preparation and training Inform and influence policy Create collaborations Disseminate knowledge Identify groups at risk	Provide safety & security Reassure & soothe Assist in negotiating practical needs Facilitate communication with family & friends Provide information & education to families & the community Monitor the impact on the environment Keep families together & facilitate reunion with loved ones	Provide a "holding environment" Normalize initial reactions Ventilate and debrief survivors & families Screen for vulnerable high-risk individuals and groups Refer when indicated Reach out to survivors who may need assistance Set up community support systems Look after the bereaved Provide spiritual support	Assist in rebuilding survivors' previous "assumptive world" Help construct a nontraumatizing narrative Identify at-risk survivors & families Provide treatment Monitor services that are being provided

In addition, it delineates the role of helpers and mental health professionals and the techniques they frequently utilize. It should be noted that while
these phases are presented as separate, in reality, they are overlapping for
many of the survivors. Since this chapter focuses on early interventions, we
will not elaborate on the phase of long-term recovery.

The Preimpact Phase

People in general are exposed to impending threats because of personal traumatic experiences, media coverage, government briefings, and local rumors.
The anticipation of future terror attacks coupled with the uncertainty of when
and where they will strike creates a rather stressful environment that significantly affects the public. In order to deal with this situation, individuals need
reliable sources of information that will help them properly assess the risk as
well as the knowledge they need to protect them. At times like this, most people adopt one of two styles: they either take a hypervigilant stance and avoid
potential risks (engage in "controlled avoidance") or deny the presence of the
impending danger.

The role of helpers is to organize and maintain an emergency system that
will be operative on demand (i.e., to set up community support system), to
prepare, train, and gain knowledge, and to disseminate that knowledge to the
community. The role of mental health professionals is to consult in building
these systems based on psychological knowledge and to assist in preparing
the public to deal with the threat of terror attacks. The people at Natal, Israel
Trauma Center for Victims of Terror and War, have developed several
community-based resilience programs to deal with the ongoing threat of terrorism (Berger, 2001). In addition, professionals should be involved in identifying groups at risk by using risk-assessment methods and help in setting up
community support services. Finally, the mental health community itself
should prepare to deal with survivors by utilizing specialized training that
combines both experiential and didactic features.

The Impact Phase

The most imminent stressors at this stage are naturally the threat to one's life
or to one's body integrity and to those who are close to the survivor. However, many terror attack survivors also report experiencing extreme distress
by being exposed to horrifying images of severely injured people or body
parts as well as to the human cruelty of the terrorists. Following these ad-
versities, survivors often face immediate secondary stressors such as continued danger (the potential for another assault), medical procedures, pain if

they are injured, and evacuation to hospitals (which is in and of itself a rather stressful ordeal).

Despite the frequent occurrence of terror attacks, the initial shock is usually overwhelming, resulting in a great deal of confusion and bewilderment. Survivors thus often need a sense of orientation and organization. Another important need at this stage is to reassure relatives and friends regarding their well-being. Unfortunately, many survivors fail to do this, because the communication system often collapses due to overuse immediately following a terror attack.

Behaviors of survivors at this stage (fight, flight, or freeze) seem to be predicated by archaic survival mechanisms and are often powerful, automatic, and uncontrollable. Consequently, some survivors are surprised and upset by their own stress reactions, reactions that have the potential to be the most overwhelming and distressing aspect of the event.

The role of helpers at this phase is primarily to rescue and protect survivors, establish contact with their relatives, evacuate them, and provide medical assistance if needed. The role of mental health professionals is to reassure and soothe survivors and to provide them with a sense of safety and security. In addition, they can assist in negotiating the survivors' practical needs. Shalev and Ursano (2003) succinctly described that role, stating, "The main role of helpers at this stage can be equated with 'primary organizer,' that is, a person who, by his or her stable presence, reduces the randomness of both external and internal realities" (p. 4).

The Early Postimpact Phase

At this stage, survivors have been rescued and are no longer at risk. Nonetheless, many of them are faced with a new reality of being evacuated to a hospital, being separated from family and friends, being interrogated by police officers, or being accosted by the media. Others simply have to adjust to the fact that they have been a "near miss" and to endless questions posed by concerned relatives and friends. Most survivors begin the process of digesting their psychological and physical newfound reality. As indicated in the preceding, the majority of survivors initially exhibit emotional and behavioral reactions such as recurrent memories and flashbacks, sympathetic arousal, avoidant behaviors, or anxiety reactions that may be both distressing and disabling.

One of the major psychological tasks of survivors, at this stage, is to accept and tolerate these initial responses. If they are able to do so, most of these temporary reactions dissipate, and they experience a sense of resilience. However, some survivors, particularly those with very acute reactions, tend to negatively view their initial reactions, a process that may gradually affect their self-esteem. Furthermore, there is some evidence that the negative self-evaluation of the early responses may contribute to the development of PTSD (Ehlers and Steil, 1995).

Social support, at this phase, is extremely important as it provides survivors with a much-needed "holding environment" and reconnects them to their previous reality. Those who are lacking adequate social support tend to become isolated and withdrawn.

Needs of survivors vary significantly, though most of them, at this point, seem to require empathy and understanding. Some prefer to incessantly share their experience with almost anyone who is willing to listen, while others tend to withdraw and reflect on it by themselves.

The role of helpers at this stage is to supply concrete needs such as physical and financial assistance, as well as to orient survivors. The role of mental-health professionals, on the other hand, is to provide survivors with a warm holding environment that is capable of containing the often extreme reactions of this phase. The clinician also extends this support to the larger holding environment (i.e., family and friends), which allows them to express their distress, comforts them, and provides them with information regarding early responses. Aside from normalizing survivors' behavior, the clinician also screens for extreme uncontrollable reactions that require immediate intervention.

The Early Recovery Phase

At this phase, both survivors and their families often expect a full recovery from the trauma and a return to normal activities. Unfortunately, many survivors experience intermittent periods of "symptomatic" behavior that affects their normal functioning (e.g., periods of insomnia). Those who accept these temporary "dysfunctional" behaviors and normalize them seem to fare rather well, whereas others who are unable to resign themselves to their new reality, manifest adjustment difficulties. Family, relatives, and friends can also influence the survivor either by tolerating his or her behavior or by criticizing it.

This is the stage when survivors begin to assimilate fully the traumatic experience into their previous "assumptive world" (Parkes, 1975) and to construct and reconstruct their traumatic narrative. They also engage in appraising the meaning of their experience and learning from it. Existential questions about the nature of the world ("Is the world meaningful and dangerous?"), the motivation of people ("How could people be so cruel?") and the meaning of oneself ("Why did it happen to me and why was I spared?") often surface. Most survivors revisit the traumatic event directly by recalling their experiences or indirectly through intrusive thoughts and flashbacks. Some tend to obsess over each detail of their experience while others tend to distance themselves by avoiding potential reminders and by attempting to focus on daily routines.

Grief is also prevalent among survivors, not only due to loss of life but also due to the loss of their naiveté and previous sense of security. It is important that survivors allow themselves to experience mourning over these losses and that loved ones show them support.

The role of helpers in this phase is to assist in fulfilling their concrete needs, to accommodate their physical and emotional temporary limitations, to provide encouragement, and to respond with sensitivity. Mental health professionals' primary goal is to assist survivors in rebuilding their previous assumptive world and to construct their traumatic narrative. Importantly, they also need to identify survivors who are at risk (i.e., those who experience significant uncontrollable distress, depression, dissociation, generalized anxiety, or ASD) and either to provide them with or to refer them to specialized therapy. It is in this phase that TMR seems to be useful in ameliorating their initial adverse reactions and in preventing the development of PTSDs. Additional techniques used by clinicians are Psychological Debriefing (Mitchell and Everly, 2000), Cognitive Behavior Therapy (Bryant and Harvey, 2000), and Eye Movement Desensitization and Reprocessing (Shapiro, 1995).

ASSESSMENT OF SURVIVORS IN THE AFTERMATH OF TERROR ATTACKS

The heterogeneity and complexity of early responses and the rapidly fluctuating reactions following a terror attack necessitate a comprehensive assessment of survivors. The primary goal of clinicians is to separate survivors who exhibit stress-related symptoms that have the potential of eventually becoming chronic and disabling from those with temporary reactions that dissipate over time. In order to perform this complicated task successfully, clinicians need to evaluate the emergence of current "dysfunctional symptoms" and the development of symptoms (strength, frequency, and duration) over time. In addition, it is beneficial to assess the presence of secondary stressors, the existence of pre-traumatic risk factors, the efficacy of the survivor's coping strategies, and the viability of their support systems. Perhaps most importantly, clinicians should evaluate the phenomenological nature of the trauma in an effort to understand the underlying traumatizing elements unique for each survivor.

Before outlining the particular domains that instruct us in performing an initial evaluation of terror attack survivors, we would like to raise several issues pertinent to the process of early assessment: Primarily, as indicated before, survivors of terror attacks experience a great deal of upheaval and distress during the initial phases. They often fluctuate between periods of incessant telling of their "story" and periods of avoiding confrontation with the traumatic experience. Awareness of the potential for sensitization and re-traumatization due to the initial evaluation should not be overlooked. Thus, exercising caution, respecting the boundaries of the survivor, prolonging the period of the assessment, or delaying it altogether (see clinical case in this chapter) is of paramount importance.

Timing of the initial assessment is also critical. In the first few days following an assault, concerned relatives and friends as well as government dignitaries (including the president, the prime minister, and other ministers) often visit the survivor to support, comfort, or express condolences when appropriate. Furthermore, secondary stressors such as medical procedures and pain from injury or loss of life and property may limit the availability of the survivor for such an evaluation. The clinician should consider the appropriateness of the timing for the assessment.

Another issue common to terror attack survivors is the attempt of either government officials or the media to use their stories for propaganda against terrorist organizations or for internal political purposes. Such an encounter, particularly when it is not directly articulated, may leave the survivor rather upset and distrustful. Mental health professionals should be aware of such an experience on the part of the survivor and attempt to rectify it by accurately clarifying the purpose of their assessment.

Related to the previous dilemma is the issue of conflict of interest and secondary gains. While performing the assessment, clinicians ought to be cognizant of whose interests they represent (i.e., the interest of the organizations, who often explore the survivor's level of competency or eligibility for compensation) or the interests of the survivor. Being direct and upfront with the survivor is necessary.

Finally, any significant and meaningful evaluation is predicated on establishing a safe and secure environment and on creating a good rapport between the survivor and the clinician. Since for many survivors this may be their first encounter with mental health professionals, it is essential that they be left with a positive experience.

Table 12.2 summarizes seven areas that require thorough exploration. The first area relates to the phenomenology of the survivors and is perhaps the most delicate and sensitive aspect of the initial evaluation. Identifying with the survivor's story, clinicians sometimes assume or project the most traumatizing part of the experience rather than ask about it. A direct question such as, "What is the most painful or disturbing part of the experience?" can help in identifying that aspect of the trauma.

Table 12.2.   Early Assessment of Survivors in the Aftermath of a Terror Attack

1. Evaluation of traumatizing elements in the experience
   - Threat to one's life/body integrity or to those of loved ones
   - Witnessing death and injury of others
   - Uncertainty
   - Loss
   - Survival guilt
   - Exposure to the grotesque
   - Human cruelty
   - Others
2. Presence of secondary stressors
   - Continued threat of terror attacks
   - Injuries and pain
   - Medical procedures
   - Police interrogation
   - Loss of occupation
   - Financial difficulties resulting from the trauma
3. Evaluation of posttraumatic reactions
   - Intrusive phenomena
   - Severity and generalizabilty of avoidant behavior
   - Persistent and uncontrollable arousal (including high heart beat rate)
   - Dissociative symptoms
   - Significant and debilitating depression
   - Full syndrome of Acute Stress Disorder
4. Development of posttraumatic reactions over time
   - Severity
   - Frequency
   - Duration
5. Efficacy of coping strategies in the aftermath of the experience
   - Level of subjective distress
   - Efficiency of performing daily activities
   - Capacity for affect modulation
   - Maintenance of positive self-esteem
   - Quality of interpersonal relationships
6. Assessment of pretraumatic risk factors
   - Exposure to past traumatic experiences
   - Traumatic family history
   - Psychiatric and psychological difficulties
   - Difficulties with early attachment
7. Quality of support system
   - Family
   - Friends
   - Community
   - Society

Occasionally, however, survivors are unable to articulate the most disturbing features of their experiences either because they are unwilling to reveal
those burdensome aspects or because they are unaware of them. Clinicians
should carefully listen with their "third ears" to the survivors' traumatic narratives and note these "traumatizing voices," but avoid confronting them in
the very early phases.

The second area for assessment is the presence of concurrent stressors and
the degree to which they affect early reactions. Clinicians who fail to identify
these stressors may attribute dysfunctional features to behaviors that are actually survival driven. For instance, a settler who was injured in a shooting
terror attack and developed a driving phobia requested the clinician to assist
him in coping with the anxiety of driving his car in the West Bank. When the
clinician asked us to help him teach the man relaxation and guided imagery
techniques, we suggested that he reconsider this approach because we felt the
client behavior was appropriate to the circumstances he was in (it is rather
dangerous to drive in the West Bank). We believe that in areas inundated with
terror activities, such as some parts of Israel, working with survivors who
manifest avoidant behavior should be limited. One should also be aware of
the practical burdens faced by terror survivors whose occupational ability is
impaired and who sometimes suffer significant property and financial losses.

The third domain is rather self-evident as it follows the American Psychiatric
Association, *Diagnostic and Statistical Manual of Stress Disorders–Fourth
Edition*'s diagnosis for ASD (1994). However, it is our experience as well as
that of others (Bryant and Harvey, 2000; Shalev, 2002) that survivors who exhibit severe and uncontrollable reactions (symptoms that do not necessarily fit
the full diagnosis of ASD) are still at risk of developing chronic stress-related
disorders. Special attention should be given to peri-traumatic symptoms that
have been shown to predict PTSD such as avoidant behaviors (Harvey and
Bryant, 1998, 1999), depressive symptoms (Shalev, Freedman, et al., 1998),
and initial high heart rate (Shalev, Sahar, et al., 1998).

The fourth domain pertains to the fact that early responses are "labile and
polymorphous" (Solomon, 1993). It is thus more important to evaluate the development of acute posttraumatic reactions over time rather than to exclusively focus on its severity. Clinicians should, therefore, phrase their questions
in a temporal dimension, attending to the changes in frequency and duration.
For instance, if the assessment of survivors' intrusive phenomena is done two
weeks following the assault, they should ask how these recurring memories or
flashbacks manifest days after the event, a week later, and at the present time
before making judgments as to the nature of these experiences. Alternatively,
if clinicians perform this assessment shortly after the event, they should consider repeating these evaluations at least twice before they make their final di-

agnosis. Survivors who exhibit similar or worse posttraumatic symptoms in terms of severity and frequency over the first few weeks and months are more likely to develop PTSD than those whose symptoms gradually decline.

The fifth domain of the assessment extends its scope beyond the immediate reactions of survivors and focuses on the manner in which survivors cope with their new reality. Although some studies indicate that certain coping strategies are more effective than others are in dealing with stress symptoms (Harvey and Bryant, 1999; Warda and Bryant, 1998; Solomon, Mikulincer, and Arad, 1991), our clinical experience suggests efficacy depends more on the characteristic style of the survivor as well as on the nature of his or her experience.

First, we evaluate survivors' perceived level of discomfort by using Wolpe's Subjective Units of Distress (for further discussion see Shapiro, 1995). This measure allows us to track the subjective experiences of survivors following the traumatic event. Second, following Shalev and Ursano's (2003) recommendation, we also use Pearlin and Schooler's (1978) coping model to evaluate the efficacy of survivors' coping strategies. We start by evaluating survivors' ability to perform daily activities such as self-care, parental duties, and work obligations. We then examine their quality of affect modulation by asking them to describe how they reduce their arousal level and handle intense feelings like panic or rage. We continue by inquiring if there were any changes in their self-image following the event. Finally, we appraise the quality of their interpersonal relationships and monitor changes in their social practices.

In the sixth area of assessment involving risk factors, we consider survivors' previous traumatic experiences, their family history, their preexisting psychological problems, and their difficulties with early-attachment figures, factors that were associated with the development of PTSD.

The last area we evaluate is survivors' social resources, because they have shown to serve as a protective factor against the development of PTSD. We consider different levels of involvement from the most immediate contact of the family through the assistance of friends and the community. Survivors of terror attacks in Israel are also supported by the society, not only in terms of moral support (they are often portrayed as heroes by the media) but also in terms of financial support given by the government.

TRAUMATIC MEMORY RESTRUCTURING

Background

The preventive method, TMR, was designed to deal with survivors who are at risk of developing chronic stress-related disorders in the early phases following a traumatic event. It was originally proposed as an alternative approach to the psychological debriefing model, which in our experience in the past two years showed mixed results in alleviating the often volatile and uncontrollable early reactions exhibited by survivors of terror attacks. Despite our earnest attempt to improve the psychological debriefing procedure (both Mitchell's CISD model [1983] and Dyregrov's debriefing procedure [1989]) by using selection criteria, small groups, and follow-up sessions, we observed that many survivors who participated in these sessions failed to fully process their traumatic experiences. Furthermore, it was our impression that a select group of survivors became more distressed following this procedure, forcing us to seek other strategies to overcome their sensitization.

TMR is an integrative multimodal approach that facilitates simultaneous processing of traumatic memories on somatic, emotional, and cognitive levels during the first weeks and months following a traumatic event. Its aims are twofold: (1) to reduce the intensity and shorten the duration of highly distressful and uncontrollable acute reactions in the early phases and (2) to prevent the long-term effects of trauma, particularly the development of PTSD and other stress-related disorders.

This approach rests on the premise that survivors who develop ASD or are at risk of developing PTSD are unable to fully metabolize and integrate their traumatic experiences and thus are continually re-living their past memories and react toward them as if they are part of their present reality. These survivors can be likened to people who are stuck in a time warp, unable to learn from, or properly respond to, the present.

Unlike some other early interventions, TMR is a highly specialized method that should be offered by experienced clinicians who are specifically trained to use it. Since occasionally there are situations that require generic approaches like group debriefing (i.e., when the survivor is a part of a cohesive group such as a police unit or when there is a large number of survivors relative to the number of clinicians), we recommend that clinicians incorporate the TMR principles within the structure of the psychological debriefing. Our experience in using group debriefing with survivors of terror attacks, while accommodating this procedure to the TMR model, has been rather successful. However, since it prolongs the debriefing procedure, we tend to offer it to relatively small groups of survivors (six to eight).

Rationale

The rationale of TMR is based on current studies of traumatic memory formation, cognitive theory of information processing, clinical studies of survivors with PTSD, and narrative psychotherapy.

Contemporary research differentiates between two basic memory systems: "explicit" memory and "implicit" memory. Explicit memory, also known as "declarative" or "episodic" memory, refers to conscious recollection of facts and events that are constructed in a narrative form. Implicit memory, also termed "procedural" or "iconic" memory, refers to unconscious recollections of motor skills, habits, reflexes, emotional experiences, and conditioned responses. Memories of ordinary and mildly stressful events, considered explicit memories, are integrated within one's previous learning experiences and are transformed into a narrative autobiographical memory. Conversely, unprocessed memories characteristic of traumatized individuals are considered implicit memories. These memories are retrieved in a nonlinguistic form as images, sensations, affects, and somatic states. They appear to be disorganized and fragmented, thus, remain vivid and stable for a long period of time following the traumatic event. Furthermore, while ordinary memories require conscious effort for their retrieval, traumatic memories seem uncontrollable and are easily reexperienced by a variety of triggers.

Clinical observations of survivors who are diagnosed with PTSD suggest that they are engulfed in their traumatic experiences, failing to integrate them into their past experiences. These observations have led trauma experts to postulate that survivors with PTSD encode their traumatic memories differently than those who do not exhibit this pathology. Indeed, extreme adrenergic responses mediated via the amygdala during the early phases of trauma may affect memory consolidation (McGaugh, 1989), resulting in greater accessibility of these memory traces. Furthermore, neuroanatomical research (Rauch et al., 1996) suggests that subcortical brain structures (the brain stem and the limbic system) are implicated in memory formation and storage of traumatized individuals, altering their ability to organize and integrate them with new experiences.

If, as suggested by the just-mentioned evidence, implicit memory indeed plays a significant role in the evolution of survivors' stress-related psychopathology, then facilitating the transformation of their traumatic memory (using TMR) into a more organized, linguistic, and narrative form (explicit memory) may inhibit or prevent its formation.

Contemporary theory of information processing, profoundly influenced by recent neuroscience studies (Damasio, 1999; LeDoux, 1996; Panksepp, 1998; Schore, 1994), proposes three independent and interconnected systems for organizing human experience: sensorimotor processing, emotional processing, and cognitive processing.

These three levels of mental functions are associated with different brain structures such that sensorimotor and emotional processing emerges from "lower-level" brain systems (the brain stem and the limbic system), while cognitive processing evolves from "higher-level" structures (the neocortex). Though these systems are considered hierarchically organized, higher-level structures seem to be dependent on the development and functioning of lower functions (Fisher and Murray, 1991).

Under normal conditions, high-level cortical functions control lower-level subcortical functions, a phenomenon known as "top-down processing" (LeDoux, 1996, p. 272). Conversely, during highly stressful conditions (trauma) lower-level processing becomes predominant, often overriding and regulating higher-level functioning. This phenomenon is known as "bottom-up processing" (Hobson, 1994, p. 174). Ogden and Minton (2000) suggested that the relationship between top-down and bottom-up processing is at the core of both the phenomenology and the treatment of traumatized individuals. They observe that while traditional psychotherapy models "harnessed top-down techniques to manage disruptive bottom-up processes" (p. 6), sensorimotor psychotherapy (a model developed by them) offers "support rather than manage sensorimotor processing" (p. 7). Furthermore, they suggest that effective information processing necessitates a certain range of arousal level (i.e., "optimum arousal zone"). Traumatized individuals who are either hyperaroused or hypoaroused (i.e., exhibit freezing and numbing responses) tend to dissociate, thereby impeding their ability to use higher-level processing.

TMR emphasizes the role of sensorimotor experiences in processing traumatic memories. However, unlike sensorimotor psychotherapy, it does not presuppose the predominance of somatic processes in shaping the experience of all trauma survivors, nor does it see sensorimotor processing as a primary entry point of trauma treatment. TMR attributes equal importance to cognitive, emotional, and somatic processing, seeking to tailor the processing "ingredients" to the survivor's needs.

Clinical studies regarding the characteristics of traumatic recollections further elucidate the differences between individuals who were exposed to trauma and were diagnosed with PTSD and survivors who did not develop PTSD. For example, a longitudinal study of World War II veterans (Lee, Valliant, Torrey, and Elder, 1995) demonstrated the immutability of PTSD patients' traumatic memories. While war memories of veterans diagnosed with PTSD remained relatively intact for almost fifty years after the war, memories of veterans without PTSD were significantly altered.

Foa and her colleagues also pointed to unique characteristics of rape recollections recounted by survivors diagnosed with PTSD. Foa, Molnar, and Cashman (1995) showed that trauma stories of rape survivors consisted of thoughts that were more organized following effective exposure therapy. They also found that decreased fragmentation in the rape narrative predicted a better prognosis. Similar results were obtained by Amir, Stafford, Freshman, and Foa (1995) who found a significant correlation between the level of traumatic narrative organization and PTSD symptoms. Finally, Tromp, Koss, Figueredo, and Tharan (1995) compared rape memories to either pleasant or unpleasant intense memories, indicating that the most powerful discriminator was the degree of clarity, vividness, and temporal organization.

The findings of Foa and her colleagues seem to be consistent with Pennebaker's studies regarding verbal and written disclosure of traumatic events (Pennebaker, 1993; Pennebaker and Beall, 1986; Pennebaker and Francis, 1996). These researchers suggest that narratives of individuals with improved health were marked by their organization and connectedness as well as reflected insight and causality.

Considering all the evidence discussed in the preceding, it appears that facilitating the transformation of trauma memories from a confusing, fragmented, and disorganized narrative into a coherent, logical, and organized story may indeed reduce initial adverse reactions and perhaps even prevent the development of PTSD.

We finally want to also acknowledge the contribution of narrative psychotherapy (Gustafson, 1992; Omer and Stenger, 1992; Schafer, 1982; White and Epston, 1990) in shaping our TMR model. While it is beyond the scope of this chapter to describe this therapeutic modality, many trauma experts alluded to the negative and often distorted meaning that survivors attach to their experience. It is therefore important to identify these traumatizing voices and to alter them, particularly during the early phases when survivors are rather suggestive and the neurological system is still flexible (Shalev, 2003).

The TMR Procedure

Before we present the TMR procedure, we would like to emphasize that this is a set of principles and strategies that guide us in restructuring survivors' traumatic memories rather than a manualized procedure that should be "religiously" followed. While we strongly consider these guidelines important in facilitating survivors' early recovery and protecting them from unnecessary sensitization, we also believe clinicians should be allowed to adjust their therapeutic style and previous knowledge according to the TMR principles.

Since TMR primarily addresses survivors who are at risk of developing stress-related disorders, a careful early assessment (see preceding) is required before processing survivors' traumatic memories. We are cognizant of the fact that any assessment of survivors in the early phases will unavoidably elicit their traumatic narratives and, thus, have the potential for reactivation. Hence, we also recommend that clinicians who are involved in the initial intake of survivors to follow the TMR guidelines and avoid intrusive "prodding" into their traumatic stories. In our experience, it is highly recommended that the clinician who does the initial intake also process the survivor's traumatic memory as it sustains the continuity of care, a condition that facilitates recovery.

The first step in processing traumatic memories of survivors is rather obvious, namely, establishing a good rapport, fostering a trustful relationship, and engaging survivors in the process of recalling their traumatic experiences (see table 12.3). Several theoreticians have recently alluded to the importance of what some called a "regulatory dyad" (van der Kolk, 1996a) or "social engagement system" (Porges, 1995) in modulating physiological arousal and fostering completion of defensive responses. The concept we tend to favor is that of "parental attunement" (Stern, 1985) that describes the synchronized mother–child relationship. Similarly, we believe that the clinician needs to be attuned to the rhythm, tone, body gestures, and breathing, as well as the language and metaphors, used by the survivor in order to fully join his or her experience.

We further use Neuro-Linguistic Programming concepts of "pacing" and "leading" (Bandler and Grinder, 1975) to emphasize the dual role of the clinician—following the survivor's horrid and painful journey into their traumatic inferno and leading them back to safe shores. Thereafter, we provide survivors with the rationale for our intervention and attempt to increase their motivation for participation. Clinicians should not ignore the often-excruciating emotional pain survivors (and also they) experience in revisiting traumatic memories; hence, they need to adopt a rather empathic and supportive attitude toward survivors.

An experienced explorer undertaking a dangerous mission into uncharted terrain knows that he or she needs to invest time and effort in preparation for the journey. Likewise, survivors (and for that matter, also clinicians) should be equipped with ample resources before they recollect their traumatic experiences (see table 12.3). We therefore investigate what external and internal resources are available for survivors by examining survivors' past history of coping with difficult situations. Depending on the unique experiences and preferences of survivors, we then introduce them to somatic resources (grounding, felt sense, and sensorimotor amplification), breathing methods (diaphragmatic breathing), relaxation techniques (progressive or all-body relaxation) or imagery exercises (the "safe place"). The reason to provide these extra resources is to ensure that survivors are capable of modulating uncontrollable physiological arousal and high-intensity emotions, not only when the clinicians are present, but also when memories are spontaneously evoked (as is often the case after TMR sessions).

We begin restructuring survivors' memories by asking survivors to recall experiences before the event. This is done to foster continuity of the experience (for further discussion see Omer and Alon, 1994). The principle of fos-

Table 12.3. Principles of Traumatic Memory Restructuring

1. Joining the survivor
   - Become attuned to the survivor
   - Pace and lead survivor
   - Provide rationale and increase motivation
2. Resourcing the survivor
   - Somatic resources—grounding, "felt sense," amplification
   - Breathing
   - Relaxation
   - Imagery—"safe place"
3. Establishing temporal continuity
4. Modulating arousal level
   - Enhancing somatosensory awareness
   - Labeling somatosensory experiences
   - Connecting emotions to sensations
   - Modeling or probing of feelings
5. Fostering causality
6. Narrative modification
   - Didactic methods
   - Reframing
   - Socratic questioning
   - Externalization
   - Cognitive interweave
7. Retelling the traumatic story by the clinician
8. Re-authoring the newly processed traumatic narrative
9. Developing a future orientation

tering temporal continuity (see table 12.3) helps to process the story and provides it with a logical sequence. Accordingly, we process the traumatic memory beyond the impact phase and even the early recovery phase. We have also found that extending the processing period past the impact stage is helpful as some survivors encounter the most traumatizing experience after the event. For instance, one of the survivors of the terror attack on Israeli tourists in Mombasa, Kenya, related to us that the most painful experience for him was the way his family greeted him on his return to Israel.

Though table 12.3 presents TMR principles in a sequence, this sequence does not imply either order of importance or order of use within the therapeutic process.

The next set of techniques is of paramount importance as they assist survivors in processing the somatic aspects of their experiences and in modulating their arousal levels. Furthermore, they also serve as distraction strategies. These techniques can be used throughout the processing and restructuring sessions; however, they are best used under two conditions: when survivors exhibit physiological signs of hyperarousal or hypoarousal (in Foa and Roth-baum's [1998] terms: "over-engagement" or "under-engagement") or when the narrative is stuck.

In order to enhance the survivor's somatosensory awareness, the clinician monitors bodily changes in the survivor as she recounts her traumatic experience. Then, the clinician either draws the survivor's attention to these shifts ("What do you experience in your body right now?") or relates these observations to her ("Notice the changes in your breathing!"). In tracking the survivor's somatic reactions, the clinician focuses on both subtle bodily changes (i.e., breathing rate and patterns, muscular tensions, pallor, eye dilation, facial movements, trembling, etc.) and more gross movements (i.e., lifting of the shoulder, tapping one's leg, stretching, etc.).

The next task of the clinician is to assist survivors in transforming their somatosensory experiences into linguistic categories, namely, labeling them (see table 12.3). It is our observation that survivors tend to use evaluative categories ("I feel regular in my body.") or affective language ("I sense extreme fear in my body.") in describing their sensorimotor experiences. Thus, we help them to develop a sensory vocabulary by cueing them ("Do you feel tense, warm, calm, etc.?"), by inquiring regarding the space and shape of their sensations ("Do you sense it throughout your chest or is it only in the center?"), and sometimes by encouraging them to employ bodily metaphors ("I feel like my knees are going to buckle."). This is a rather difficult task for many survivors, particularly those who are dissociated. However, with time and patience, they learn to recognize their bodily sensations and to articulate them.

In addition, we recommend two other somatosensory techniques: connecting emotions with sensations and modeling or probing feelings (see table 12.3). After survivors become aware of and articulate their somatosensory experiences, we reflect these descriptions and ask them to identify the feelings that they represent. Following the classic experiment of Schachter and Singer (1962) and the new research in neuroscience (Damasio, 1999), we think that somatosensory input is often a precursor of emotional and cognitive processing; hence, we encourage survivors to make the connection between them. Moreover, our experience suggests that this can be an effective technique to deal with alexithymia, often observed in traumatized individuals. Finally, we use modeling ("What I feel when you recount this story is . . .") or probing ("Do you feel frustrated, angry, enraged, etc.?") for survivors who exhibit dissociation, physiological or psychological numbing, or diminished muscular tonicity.

Throughout the recounting of their stories, we facilitate better organization of traumatic narratives by asking survivors to make logical connections between fragments of their stories and using cause and effect reasoning when we deem it is necessary ("Can you better explain to me what happened there?"). We also encourage survivors to complete traumatic narratives (narratives with "black holes" due to amnesia), because often these unfinished stories tend to haunt survivors. They are therefore asked to fill up those gaps ("What could have happened?") and are assisted in reauthoring their complete stories.

Many trauma experts alluded to the tendency of trauma survivors to misinterpret the circumstance of their traumatic experiences, to attribute negative meaning toward their immediate reactions and toward their coping efforts, or to dramatically shift their view about the world, others, and themselves (Foa and Rothbaum, 1998; Janoff-Bulman, 1992; McCann and Pearlman, 1990; van der Kolk, 1996b). It has been our experience with terror attack survivors that many of them are inclined to blame themselves, accuse the Israeli authorities, experience intense survival guilt, or become engrossed in a victim or hero narrative. As we pointed out previously, during the very early stage, survivors often seem to be in a trance-like state and are therefore rather suggestible. Sensitive and experienced clinicians who recognize survivors' traumatizing voices (i.e., faulty attributions and misinterpretations) can effectively facilitate reconstruction of these "pathological" narratives. In table 12.3 we suggest several techniques for assisting survivors in reauthoring their narratives and imbuing them with more constructive meaning. Though we have found these techniques to be helpful for us, there are certainly other methods that can be similarly effective. Full exposition of these techniques is certainly beyond the scope of this chapter. Instead, we opted to give brief examples of each of the interventions.

We often use didactic methods to reinterpret intense sympathetic reactions suggesting to survivors that their reactions are not just normal but also necessary. Thus, for a woman who told us she stood frozen in front of a terrorist's decapitated head for twenty minutes (at least in her subjective sense of time), we normalized this reaction by explaining to her how bodily freezing reflexes work in mammals as well as in humans.

Reframing was used, for example, with a terror survivor who was initially shocked when a terrorist bomb exploded in a restaurant, rendering him immobile for several minutes before he was able to assist his young children. We gave him the message that we were impressed by his ability to perfectly contain himself, conserve his energies, and approach his children in a rather calm and collected manner. Unlike the other people whom he described as acting "hysterically," he was the only one who did not lose his cool, sparing his children from witnessing parents who seemed out of control. Thus, instead of viewing himself as a weak and irresponsible father who cannot protect his children "under fire," we reframed his behavior as a sign of unique strength and self-sacrifice.

Socratic questioning was employed with an elderly woman who felt tremendous guilt feeling for not stopping a terrorist who attacked a group of soldiers, two of whom were later killed. During her recollection, she constantly made comments about the "missed opportunity" to stop the assailant by reaching for help or alerting the soldiers. Through a series of leading questions, she eventually acknowledged that had she taken action against the terrorist, things would have been much worse, not only for her, but also for many other civilians who were present at the scene.

Finally, we used externalization (White and Epston, 1990) to reconstruct the narrative of an adolescent who exhibited a great deal of anxiety bordering on panic attacks, an intense physiological arousal, and worst of all from his perspective, the inability to stay home by himself. These symptoms were manifested several days after two terrorists entered the settlement where he lived, murdering the family next door. Being an extremely intelligent individual who despised any physical activities, this adolescent was able to accept our proposal that he could outsmart his weak body and control it with his sharp brain. Thus, we externalized his physical symptoms suggesting he was actually involved in a war against his body and not just Palestinian terrorists.

After survivors fully process their traumatic experiences on all levels and after we help them transform their narratives into more coherent, logical, organized, and constructive stories, we retell them the newly constructed traumatic narratives (see table 12.3). Following Memory Structuring Intervention (MSI), an intervention that was developed by Gidron, Gal, Freedman, Twister, Lauden, Snir, et al. (2001), we also find it useful to retell the entire processed narrative to the survivors. This technique helps us clarify misunderstandings regarding the survivors' stories and further facilitate the processing of the complete narrative. It is important, however, that the clinician stay with the level of processing achieved in the session and resist re-packaging of the narrative by embellishing or interpreting the survivor's story.

We also encourage survivors to write their trauma stories and to read them, not only to us but also to others with whom they feel comfortable. Unlike Cognitive Processing Therapy (Resick and Schnicke, 1992), which first asks survivors to write a detailed account of their trauma, we prefer survivors to do it after the experience is fully processed. It has been our experience that sharing traumatic stories with close family and friends can break the "conspiracy of silence" and further support survivors' recovery.

Toward the later TMR sessions, we introduce survivors to a future orientation (see table 12.3) by asking them to place their traumatic experience within the overall context of their lives ("What have you learned from this experience?" and "What lessons can you draw from this experience about yourself, about life, etc.?"). We then ask them to go to the future (several months or a year from now) and describe a day in their lives. We process that experience using the same techniques. Occasionally, we also encourage them to envision gratifying experiences that may provide them with a sense of mastery and pleasure. In so doing, they begin to develop what van der Kolk, McFarlane, and van der Hart term "restitutive emotional experiences" (1996, p. 433).

THE NURSE WHO COULD NOT RESCUE HER CHILD: A CLINICAL CASE USING TMR WITH A SURVIVOR OF A TERROR ATTACK

A physician referred Dina to TMR four weeks after her three-year-old daughter and she survived a suicide terror attack on a public bus in Israel. Although this horrific assault left three people dead and scores wounded, both Dina and her young daughter miraculously escaped the attack with only mild burns and bruises.

Dina was initially reluctant to seek any professional help, feeling that as a head nurse in a major hospital she ought to handle this situation by herself. However, recurrent distressing thoughts and haunting memories of the event, physiological symptoms of hyperarousal, irritability, difficulties with attention, and, most of all, a sense of estrangement from fellow workers began to interfere with her work and threatened her position in the hospital. It was only then that she was convinced she may need professional assistance and agreed "to give it a try."

Being an independent and cautious individual who had a rather negative attitude toward psychologists, Dina, a thirty-two-year-old attractive, married woman, approached our first session with much hesitance and trepidation. She "laid down the rules" from the onset, stating three conditions: First, she was not sure whether therapy, in general, and I, in particular, was suitable for her needs. Second, she did not think she needed long-term therapy. Third, she wanted to take an active role in the therapeutic process and did not want "a passive therapist who will engage in constantly reading my mind." Dina seemed a bit surprised when I happily consented to all her rules. In fact, I told her that I usually do not espouse a long-term therapy model and that I actually expect most of my clients to take a collaborative role. Furthermore, I congratulated her for being so attuned to her own needs and for being straightforward with me.

Instead of performing a thorough initial assessment (see the preceding), I decided to first get acquainted with Dina and asked her to briefly tell me her "life story." Again, she was a bit hesitant but was able to share some details regarding her family of origin. However, when I expressed my genuine awe coupled with my curiosity as to how she, who came from a large and disadvantaged family, managed to overcome all these obstacles and accomplish so much, Dina seemed to change her mood and began to be rather cooperative. Only then did the joining begin to form, and it strengthened by my insistence to learn more about her job, an area that was undoubtedly her major strength. When she seemed more relaxed and engaged, I decided to introduce the assessment and she readily complied. At this point, I moved from pacing to leading. She was able to reveal that since the terror attack, she suffered from debilitating symptoms such as panic attacks, insomnia, severe anger outbursts directed toward both her husband and daughter, and avoidant behavior that began to be generalized in many situations. Dina also reported suffering from severe gastric pain and a slight paralysis in her right arm (that seriously interfered with her ability to adequately function at home and on her job), for which no medical causes were discovered. These symptoms clearly worsened since the attack, both in frequency and in duration.

After disclosing these facts, Dina appeared rather embarrassed and shameful, admitting to being scared of alienating her family and friends and compromising her career. Most importantly, she asserted, "I hate the way I'm becoming" and added that she would not be able to live with "being out of control and dependent on others."

As far as her trauma history is concerned, she reported two major incidents: the first was the drowning of her beloved young brother when she was a teenager, and the second was a recent car accident in which both she and her husband were injured. Though she reported adequately coping with these traumatic experiences, during the interview, she still seemed rather upset when sharing these experiences.

When asked to recount very briefly her current traumatic experience, Dina readily complied. However, as she proceeded relating the story, she became so overwhelmed by intense physical arousal and terror that we mutually decided she temporarily postpone sharing her traumatic experience until her body was ready for it. Instead, I taught her progressive muscular relaxation (a technique that usually gives survivors some relief).

We ended the first session after two hours (we strongly suggest that the traditional one therapy hour is insufficient to do this work), with the full description of the TMR procedure and its rationale. Although I truly believed she was a good candidate for TMR, I urged her to take few days and to seriously reconsider the appropriateness of this intervention for her (a paradoxical intervention geared to increase her motivation). Dina, who was rather assertive, insisted immediately that we schedule another session.

I devoted the following session exclusively to identifying and building resources. Dina reported that she was immensely satisfied and proud of herself for being successful in applying the relaxation technique. She was congratulated for being a fantastic learner and was told that this might be an indication that unlike my original impression she was indeed capable of effectively using TMR (again, building motivation and expectation).

Then, I introduced her to the safe place technique, a resource that we found popular among our survivors. This is an imagery exercise in which the individuals are traveling in their minds to a safe haven (we prefer a real place), where their loved ones, including favorite pets and objects, join them. We anchor this experience using somatic cues ("Focus on bodily sensations that represent for you this safe place and amplify their strength.") or visual cues ("Take a snapshot of the place and see it as a postcard."). These cues are often utilized later during the processing sessions to modulate physiological arousal and intense affective states, as indeed was the case with Dina.

It was only during the third session that we started processing the traumatic event. As Dina approached this point, she seemed rather frightened, exhibiting shallow breathing, minor heart palpitations, tension in her spine and chest (as if getting prepared for imminent danger), and tremors in her limbs. I gently stopped her story and asked her to pay attention to her body. She immediately smiled and bashfully apologized for being nervous. I invited her to remain quiet, take her time, and continue to monitor her bodily sensations ("developing body awareness"). She related that though she was anxious, she felt comfortable with me and wanted to proceed with her trauma account. I slowed her down (we call this technique "stretching the moment") and asked her to verbalize her present somatic experiences ("labeling sensations"). Dina could not distinguish specific sensations and could only report that she was a bit nervous but otherwise "normal." Being an intellectual person, it was clear that she had difficulties staying in her body. During the session, I stopped her whenever I noticed the slightest bodily changes (pallor, eye dilation, breathing, minor muscular tensions, and micromovements) and made her aware of them. It took her a long time before she was able to recognize her bodily experiences and to articulate them.

In addition, I invited her to translate sensations into feelings by reflecting on her somatosensory descriptions and asking what feelings they represented. For instance, when she described how she saw the severely injured terrorist being evacuated to a hospital, she could not report any feelings, though she clearly exhibited intense bodily reactions. After she described her sensations, I asked, "When you tell me that you have a throbbing headache, your jaws are tightly clenched, and your back feels like it is on the verge of breaking, what do you feel?" What feelings go along with these sensations?" She took some time, but eventually recognized that she was enraged with both the terrorist and the emergency medical staff for treating him. The thought that she could really strangle the terrorist, rather than offer him first aid, bothered her. Being a nurse, she felt this experience conflicted with her medical belief system, forcing her to hold back these natural aggressive impulses. Later, we will demonstrate how we helped Dina to constructively express these murderous feelings, thereby allowing completion of these aggressive impulses.

I asked Dina to recount her trauma story from the night before the incident (establishing temporal continuity). She described with much pleasure how she and her daughter snuggled in bed and how she told her daughter one of her favorite childhood stories. The next morning, she reported, waking up experiencing "bad vibes." She remembered being puzzled by her experience, yet she did not know how to interpret these feelings. She told me that later she recognized that this experience might have been "a warning sign from above" that she had ignored. (We find these omens to be prevalent among survivors). She contemplated taking a day off, but could not bring herself to call work, for fear of disappointing her coworkers. She took the public bus with her daughter as she does daily, except on that day they sat in the back of the bus, as no empty seats were available in front where they usually sit. Luckily, this mundane fact saved both of them, because ten minutes later a suicide terrorist detonated an explosive belt, killing and injuring most of the passengers who sat in the front rows of the bus.

As Dina related the story, her body tensed, her breathing almost stopped, her pupils dilated, and her upper body shuddered. Though she wanted to continue telling the story, I asked her to follow her sensorimotor reactions, focusing on different areas in her body. As she articulated these bodily sensations, her breathing became much more belabored, her teeth chattered, and her upper body to her lower limbs experienced waves of shaking. She seemed stunned by her intense responses, pleading for me to explain what was going on. I normalized these reactions and asked her to "let her body follow its course." I also got physically closer to her, and after asking permission, held my hand between her shoulder blades (a bioenergetic support move). After several minutes of extreme shaking coupled with violent sobbing, her body slowly began to relax. Since she still seemed overwhelmed by her emotions, I attempted to ground her by asking her to focus her eyes on objects in the therapy room and describe them to me. That slowed her down a bit, yet she still seemed rather distressed. I then asked her to go to her safe place by using both somatic and visual anchors that had been previously established. Gradually, Dina's body softened, her breathing deepened, and she seemed more relaxed. This somatosensory process was repeated several times during the sessions until she learned to better self-regulate her own body.

Going back to her story, Dina related how she jumped out of the bus window and then realized that her daughter was still trapped in the burning bus.

For a brief period of time, seemingly forever, she became totally paralyzed and could not move or ask for help. She felt as if she had fainted and could not remember anything until someone handed her her daughter, who had only a few minor burns. Later she found out that a bystander had entered the burning bus, literally sacrificing his life, and rescued her daughter. We attempted to process this moment slowly and painstakingly, to no avail. She did not recall anything that had happened, nor was she able to tap into her somatosensory experience. Nonetheless, after going through this story several times, I noticed a strange look on her face as if she was no longer present in the moment. When asked to share her thoughts, Dina painfully whispered in my ear, "My husband would never have let that happen to my daughter!" to which I spontaneously responded, "But he was never there." As I made this rather simplistic comment, I noticed her skin color becoming rosier and her overall musculature relaxed. A painful yet more compassionate look spread over her face. I pointed out these changes and asked her to "follow her body." As she articulated her body experiences to me, she seemed saddened and began to softly weep (emotional processing). When she relaxed, I asked her to relate what had happened to her. Dina shared with me that she has always had questions about her competency as a mother and that she has never forgiven herself for not rescuing her daughter. She added that when I mentioned her husband was not there, it finally dawned on her that maybe she judges herself too harshly.

I then decided to relate to her the facts regarding biological defense mechanisms and shock responses (didactic method) and to see if she could apply them to her situation. As we talked thereafter, she appeared more self-accepting, yet still maintained that she would rather have been more active in rescuing her daughter. She was also concerned as to whether she would be able to defend her child during extreme situations in the future. I was worried about her concerns, emphatically suggested that we should further explore her freezing reactions next session. After retelling her the experiences she had processed, we finished the session with my recommendation that she share this story with her husband.

When she came to the next session, she appeared much more cheerful and energetic. She related that many of her symptoms decreased, including her anxiety, anger outbursts, and insomnia. She was particularly happy with the fact that for the first time she did not experience any gastric pain or paralysis in her right arm. We again reprocessed the entire traumatic event, taking it this time to completion. In this session, we focused on two scenes that were particularly difficult.

First, we revisited the scene where she could not help her daughter. Since she seemed more in control, I asked her to close her eyes and talk in the present tense as if she was actually there. This time, Dina was much more capable of embodying the experience and expressed both her terror and guilt feelings.

As she processed her bodily sensations, she became aware of her desire to un-freeze her body and rescue her child. She reported that her throat was ex-tremely constricted, her chest collapsed, and her legs were "heavy like marble stone." By amplifying those sensations ("Close your eyes, focus on these sen-sations, and make them feel stronger!") and facilitating her breathing, she was able to gradually melt the constriction in her throat and spontaneously released a loud scream. This was followed by tapping her feet on the floor and stretch-ing her arms as if she were reaching for her child. It should be emphasized that Dina, who probably needed to gain back control over her bodily functions, spontaneously orchestrated this experience with minimal guidance.

The last scene we processed related to her rage toward the terrorist and toward the medical personnel who treated him on the scene. It turned out that after Dina recovered from her initial shock, she managed to find a female bystander who took care of her child while she rushed to help the injured people from the bus. As described in the preceding, when we processed this scene, Dina realized she became rather enraged, but could not express these feelings. I asked her if she still needed to express those feelings, and she thought it might be a good idea. Bringing her back to the scene and having her somatically experience the rage in her arms, back, and jaws, I handed her a soft pillow and suggested she let her hands "do what they need to do." She began to squeeze and punch the pillow fu-riously until she had had enough and then kicked it away.

After Dina completed to reprocess and to restructure her traumatic experi-ence, I asked her to tell me what she had learned from this horrible experi-ence. Dina reflected for a while, and to my surprise, said that this incident taught her that "not everything is in my control, and perhaps this is for the better!" She then related that before the terror attack she used to be very over-protective of her daughter, refusing to let others babysit for her. "Maybe, I need to relax and let her be a bit more independent," she added. Dina also said that both her traumatic experience and the work with me taught her to be less suspicious of others and to give people more credit ("I never thought some-one would sacrifice his life to save my daughter!").

I saw Dina for two additional sessions where we did more emotional and cognitive processing and discussed ways to deal with some of her avoidant behavior and triggers. Then, we mutually agreed to terminate our work. At the end of our treatment (six sessions), almost all the symptoms she initially pre-sented dissipated. She reported her functioning at home and on her job re-turned to the level it had been before the traumatic event and in some ways even improved (she reported being more sensitive and compassionate). In two follow-up sessions, three and six months after termination, no evidence of stress-related symptoms was detected and her functioning continued to im-prove. A similar picture was obtained a year later.

CONCLUSION

In this chapter we explored the phenomenological nature of the terror threat and outlined the major dilemmas facing the practitioner who is involved in providing early intervention for trauma survivors and, particularly, survivors of terror attacks. We emphasized the phases survivors undergo in the aftermath of terror attacks, thereby placing early intervention within a temporal context. Then we proposed a procedure for initial assessment and a model (TMR) for early intervention. We pointed out that the TMR approach is based on memory formation and information-processing theory, current neuroscience research, and studies with survivors diagnosed with PTSD. Our aim in presenting the TMR approach is to provide an alternative model to the psychological debriefing model; a model that can alleviate acute adverse reactions of trauma survivors, but, more importantly, prevent PTSD and other stress-related disorders.

Several other early intervention models have recently been proposed, including Cognitive Behavioral Therapy (CBT), Eye Movement Desensitization and Reprocessing (EMDR), and Memory Structuring Intervention (MSI). While all these models (effective as they may be) focus on processing traumatic memories of survivors, we would suggest that they have primarily focused on cognitive processing, ignoring, to some degree, emotional and certainly somatic processing. In other words, it seems that these models have emphasized "top-down" processing at the expense of "bottom-up" processing. TMR, as we demonstrated in the preceding, synergistically processes the somatosensory, emotional, and cognitive aspects of traumatic memories and, hence, has a potential to be more effective for a larger group of survivors.

Though we have successfully applied this early intervention for survivors of terrorism (and several survivors of car accidents and rapes), we see no reason why this approach would not yield positive results with other groups of survivors.

In this chapter we did not emphasize selection criteria for TMR aside from survivors who showed significant distress and uncontrollable behavior as well as full-blown ASD. However, we feel some survivors with severe mental health disorders may not be appropriate for this model (i.e., survivors with a psychosis, severe dissociative disorders, or brain damage). We would also like to stress that clinicians who work with suicidal or homicidal survivors should exercise due caution in applying any trauma-processing intervention, TMR included.

Our clinical data in using TMR with survivors of terror is rather promising. To date, we have been monitoring twenty-four survivors who have been exposed to TMR, nine males (37.5 percent) and fifteen females (62.5 percent).

Our ages ranged from nine to seventy-six, with the majority of survivors in their early thirties and forties. All our survivors exhibited various degrees of ASD and PTSD symptoms and were considered (according to our initial assessment) at risk. They were all seen during the early recovery phase, namely, one to eight weeks following the traumatic event. (The average time survivors were seen following the attack was five and a half weeks). We roughly divided the members of the survivor group with whom we worked using the TMR model into four subgroups: those who showed significant improvement, moderate improvement, slight improvement, and no improvement. This was not a scientific criterion but rather a subjective clinical measure that consisted of both symptomatology and coping. Accordingly, our results showed that sixteen (66.6 percent) of the twenty-four survivors showed significant improvement (and did not need additional therapy), five (20.8 percent) showed moderate improvements, two (8.4 percent) showed slight improvement (they needed additional help), and one (4.2 percent) did not improve at all and showed significant symptoms.

While our extensive clinical experience shows promise, we are quite aware that this approach needs further empirical evidence (a large empirical study is currently under planning), particularly by using randomized controlled trials. However, as we indicated in the preceding, the unprecedented demand for early intervention forced us to utilize early intervention methods even without a sufficient empirical base.

NOTE

1. We would like to acknowledge that many Palestinians were also killed or injured during the same period, a fact that unfortunately is ignored too often when one is exclusively engrossed in one's own pain.

REFERENCES

American Psychiatric Association. (1994). *Diagnostic and statistical manual of mental disorders*. (4th ed.). Washington, DC: Author.

Amir, N., Stafford, J., Freshman, M. S., and Foa, E. B. (1995). Relationship between trauma narratives and trauma pathology. *Journal of Traumatic Stress*, 11 (2): 385–91.

Bandler, R., and Grinder, J. (1975). *The structure of magic* (Vol. 1). Palo Alto, CA: Science and Behavior Books.

Bartmeir, L. H. (1946). Combatant exhaustion. *Journal of Nervous and Mental Diseases*, 104: 359–425.

Berger, R. (2001). *An ecological model for community-based intervention during traumatic stress: A manual.* Tel Aviv, Israel: Natal. (Hebrew).

Berger, R. (2002, May). *Society under siege: The impacts of terrorism on the Israeli society.* A paper presented at the conference of the Psychology of terror: Tackling the terrorist threat of the International Policy Institute for Counter-Terrorism, Jerusalem, Israel.

Berwin, C. R., Andrews, B., and Valentine, J. D. (2000). Meta-analysis of risk factors for posttraumatic stress disorder in trauma-exposed adults. *Journal of Consulting and Clinical Psychology,* 68 (5): 748–66.

Bisson, J. I., McFarlane, A. C., and Rose, S. (2000). Psychological debriefing. In E. B. Foa, T. M. Keane, and M. J. Friedman (Eds.). *Effective treatment for PTSD,* pp. 39–59. New York: Guilford.

Blanchard, E. B., Hickling, E. J., Barton, K. A., Taylor, A. E., Loos, W. R., and Jones-Alexander, J. (1996). One-year prospective follow-up of motor vehicle accident victims. *Behavior Research and Therapy,* 34: 775-86.

Bryant, R. A., and Harvey, A. G. (2000). *Acute stress disorder: A handbook of theory, assessment and treatment.* Washington, DC: American Psychological Association.

Bryant, R. A., Harvey, A. G., Dang, S., Sackville, T., and Basten, C. (1998). Treatment of acute stress disorder: A comparison of cognitive-behavioral therapy and supportive counseling. *Journal of Consulting and Clinical Psychology,* 66: 862, 866.

Damasio, A. (1999). *The feeling of what happens.* New York: Harcourt, Brace.

Dyregrov, A. (1989). Caring for helpers in disaster situations: Psychological debriefing. *Disaster Management,* 2: 25–30.

Ehlers, A., and Steil, R. (1995). Maintenance of intrusive memories in posttraumatic stress disorder: A cognitive approach. *Behavior and Cognitive Psychotherapy,* 23: 217–49.

Elklit, M. A. A. (2001). Effectiveness of psychological debriefing. *Acta Psychiatrica Scandinavia,* 104: 423–37.

Fisher, A. G., and Murray, E. A. (1991). Introduction to sensory integration theory. In A. G. Fisher, E. Murray, and A. Bundy (Eds.), *Sensory integration: Theory and practice,* pp. 3–26. Philadelphia: Davis.

Foa, E. B., Hembree, E. A., Riggs, D., Rauch, S., and Franklin, M. (2001, September). *Guidelines for mental health professionals' response to the recent tragic events in the U.S.* Center for the Treatment and Study of Anxiety, Department of Psychiatry, University of Pennsylvania, Retrieved on June 25, 2004, from www.ncptsd.org/facts/disasters/fs_foa_advice.html

Foa, E. B., Molnar, C., and Cashman, L. (1995). Change in rape narrative during exposure therapy for posttraumatic stress disorder. *Journal of Traumatic Stress,* 8: 675–90.

Foa, E. B., and Rothbaum, B. (1998). *Treating the trauma of rape: Cognitive-behavioral therapy for PTSD.* New York: Guilford.

Gidron, Y., Gal, R., Freedman, S., Twister, I., Lauden, A., Snir, Y., et al. (2001). Translating research finding to PTSD prevention: Results of a randomized-controlled pilot study. *Journal of Traumatic Stress,* 14 (4): 773–80.

Green, B. L., Grace, M. C., and Gleser, G. C. (1985). Identifying survivors at risk: Long term impairment following the Beverly Hills supper club fire. *Journal of Consulting and Clinical Psychology*, 53: 672–78.

Grinker, R. R., and Spiegel, J. P. (1945). Psychiatric disorders in combat crews overseas and in returnees. *Medical Clinics of North America*, 29: 729–39.

Gustafson, J. P. (1992). *Self-delight in a harsh world*. New York: Norton.

Harvey, A. G., and Bryant, R. A. (1998). Predictors of acute stress disorder following mild traumatic brain injury. *Brain Injury*, 12: 147–54.

——. (1999). Predictors of acute stress following motor vehicle accidents. *Journal of Traumatic Stress*, 12: 519–25.

——. (2001). Reconstructing trauma memories: A prospective study of "amnesic" trauma survivors. *Journal of Traumatic Stress*, 14: 277–82.

Hobfoll, S. E. (1989). Conservation of resources: A new attempt at conceptualizing stress. *American Psychologist*, 44: 513–21.

Hobson, J. A. (1994). *The chemistry of conscious states*. New York: Back Bay Books.

Janoff-Bulamn, R. (1992). *Shattered assumptions: Toward a new psychology of trauma*. New York: The Free Press.

Kessler, R. C., Sonnega, A., Bromet, E., Hughes, M., and Nelson, C. B. (1995). Post-traumatic stress disorder in National Comorbidity Survey. *Archives of General Psychiatry*, 52: 1048–60.

Koren, D., Arnon, I., and Klein, E. (1999). Acute stress response and posttraumatic stress disorder in traffic accident victims: A one-year prospective, follow-up study. *American Journal of Psychiatry*, 156: 369–73.

Lee, K. A., Valliant, G. E., Torrey, W. C., and Elder, G. H. (1995). A 50-year prospective study of psychological sequelae of World War II combat. *American Journal of Psychiatry*, 152: 516–22.

LeDoux, J. (1996). *The emotional brain*. New York: Simon & Schuster.

Lifton, R. J. (1967). *Death in life: Survivors of Hiroshima*. New York: Random House.

Litz, B., Gray, M., Bryant, R. A., and Adler, A. (2001). Early interventions for trauma: Current status and future direction. National Institute for PTSD. Retrieved on April 8, 2004, from www.ncptsd.org

McCann, I. L., and Pearlman, L. A. (1990). *Psychological trauma and the adult survivor: Theory, therapy and transformation*. New York: Brunner/Mazel.

McGaugh, J. L. (1989). Involvement of hormonal and neuromodulatory systems in regulation of memory storage. *Annual Review of Neuroscience*, 2: 255–87.

Mitchell, J. T. (1983). When disaster strikes: The critical incident stress debriefing process. *Journal of Emergency Medical Services*, 8: 36–39.

Mitchell, J. T., and Everly, G. (2000). Critical incident stress debriefing: Evolution, effects and outcomes. In B. Raphael and J. Wilson (Eds.). *Stress debriefing: Theory, practice and challenge*, pp. 71–90. London: Cambridge University Press.

Mitchell, J. T., and Everly, G. S., Jr. (1995). Critical Incident Stress Debriefing (CISD) and the prevention of work related traumatic stress among high-risk occupational groups. In G. Everly and J. Lating (Eds.), *Psychotraumatology: Key papers and core concepts in post-traumatic stress*, pp. 159–69. New York: Plenum Press.

National Institute of Mental Health. (2002). Mental health and massive violence: Evidence-based early psychological intervention for victims/survivors of mass violence. A workshop to reach consensus on best practices. NIMH Publication No.02-5138, Washington, DC: U.S. Government Printing Office.

Neria, Y., and Solomon, Z. (1999). Prevention of posttraumatic reactions: debriefing and frontline treatment. In P. A. Saigh and J. D. Bremner (Eds.), *Posttraumatic stress disorder: A comprehensive text*. Boston: Allyn and Bacon.

Netanyahu, B. (1997). *Fighting terrorism: How democracies can defeat domestic and international terrorists*. New York: Noonday Press.

Ogden, P., and Minton, K. (2000). Sensorimotor psychotherapy: One method for processing traumatic memory. *Traumatology*, 6 (3): 1–47.

Omer, H., and Alon, N. (1994). The continuity principle: A unified approach to disaster and trauma. *American Journal of Community Psychology*, 22: 273–87.

Omer, H., and Stenger, C. (1992). From the one true meaning to an infinity of constructed ones. *Psychotherapy*, 29: 253–61.

Panksepp, J. (1998). *Affective neuroscience: The foundations of human and animal emotions*. Oxford, England: Oxford University Press.

Parkes, C. M. (1975). What becomes of a redundant world model? A contribution to the study of adaptation to change. *British Journal of Medical Psychology*, 48: 131–37.

Pearlin, L. I., and Schooler, C. (1978). The structure of coping. *Journal of Health and Social Behavior*, 22: 337–56.

Pennebaker, J. W. (1993). Putting stress into words: Health, linguistic, and therapeutic implications. *Behavior Research and Therapy*, 31: 539–48.

Pennebaker, J. W., and Beall, S. K. (1986). Confronting a traumatic event: Toward an understanding of inhibition and disease. *Journal of Abnormal Psychology*, 95: 274–81.

Pennebaker, J. W., and Francis, M. E. (1996). Cognitive, emotional and language processes in disclosure. *Cognition and Emotion*, 10: 601–26.

Porges, S. (1995). Orienting in a defensive world: Mammalian modifications of our evolutionary heritage. A polyvagal theory. *Psychophysiology*, 32: 301–18.

Raphael, B., Meldrum, L., and McFarlane, A. C. (1995). Does debriefing after psychological trauma work? Time for randomized controlled trials. *British Medical Journal*, 310: 1479–80.

Rauch, S. L., van der Kolk, B. A., Fisler, R. E. A., Nathaniel, M., Orr, S. P., Savage, C., et al. (1996). A symptom provocation study of posttraumatic stress disorder using positron emission tomography and script-driven imagery. *Archives of General Psychiatry*, 53: 380–87.

Resick, P. A., and Schnicke, M. K. (1992). *Cognitive processing therapy for rape victims: A treatment manual*. Newbury Park, CA: Sage.

Riggs, D., Rothbaum, B., and Foa, E. B. (1995). A prospective examination of symptoms of posttraumatic stress disorder in victims of nonsexual assault. *Journal of Interpersonal Violence*, 10: 201–13.

Rose, S., Bisson, J., and Wessely, S. (2001). Psychological debriefing for preventing posttraumatic stress disorders (PTSD) (Cochrane Review). In *The Cochrane Library* (Vol. 4). Oxford, England: Update Software.

Rothbaum, B., Foa, E. B., Riggs, D., Murdock, T., and Walsh, W. (1992). A prospective examination of post-traumatic stress disorder in rape victims. *Journal of Traumatic Stress*, 5: 455–75.

Schachter, S., and Singer, J. E. (1962). Cognitive, social and physiological determinants of emotional state. *Psychological Review*, 69: 379–99.

Schafer, R. (1982). *The analytical attitude*. New York: Basic Books.

Schore, A. N. (1994). *Affect regulation and the origin of the self: The neurobiology of emotional development*. Hillsdale, NJ: Lawrence Erlbaum Associates.

Shalev, A. Y. (2002). Treating survivors in the immediate aftermath of traumatic events. In R. Yehuda (Ed.). *Treating trauma survivors with PTSD*, pp. 157–86. Washington, DC: American Psychiatric Press.

———. (2003).Psychobiological and neurochemical perspectives on early reactions to traumatic events. In R. Orner and U. Schnyder (Eds.). *Reconstructing early interventions after trauma.* Oxford, England: Oxford University Press.

Shalev, A. Y., Freedman, S., Peri, T., Brandes, D., Sahar, T., Orr, S. P., et al. (1998). Prospective study of posttraumatic stress disorder and depression following trauma, *American Journal of Psychiatry*, 155: 630–37.

Shalev, A. Y., Sahar, T., Freedman, S., Peri, T., Glick, N., Brandes, D., et al. (1998). A prospective study of heart rate responses following trauma and the subsequent development of PTSD. *Archives of General Psychiatry*, 55: 553–59.

Shalev, A. Y., and Ursano, R. J. (2003). Mapping the multidimensional picture of acute responses to traumatic stress: From diagnosis to treatment planning. In R. Orner and U. Schnyder (Eds.). *Reconstructing early interventions after trauma.* Oxford, England: Oxford University Press.

Shapiro, F. (1995). *Eye movement desensitization and reprocessing: Basic principles, protocols and procedures*. New York: Guilford.

Silver, S. M., and Rogers, S. (2002). *Light in the heart of darkness: EMDR and the treatment of war and terrorism survivors*. New York: Norton.

Solomon, Z. (1993). *Combat stress reaction: The enduring toll of war*. New York: Plenum Press.

Solomon, Z., Mikulincer, M., and Arad, R. (1991). Monitoring and blunting: Implications for combat-related post-traumatic stress disorder. *Journal of Traumatic Stress*, 4: 209–21.

Stern, D. (1985). *The interpersonal world of the infant: A view from psychoanalysis and developmental psychology*. New York: Basic Books.

Tromp, S., Koss, M., Figueredo, A. J., and Tharan, M. (1995). Are rape memories different? A comparison of rape, other unpleasant, and pleasant intense memories among employed women. *Journal of Traumatic Stress*, 8 (4): 607–27.

van der Kolk, B. A. (1996a). The complexity of adaptation to trauma: Self-regulation, stimulus discrimination, and characterological development. In B. A. van der Kolk, A. C. McFarlane, and L. Weisaeth (Eds.). *Traumatic stress: The effects of overwhelming experience on mind, body, and society*, pp. 182-213. New York: Guilford.

———. (1996b). Trauma and memory. In B. A. van der Kolk, A. C. McFarlane, and L. Weisaeth (Eds.). *Traumatic stress: The effects of overwhelming experience on mind, body, and society*, pp. 279–302. New York: Guilford.

van der Kolk, B. A., McFarlane, A. C., and van der Hart, O. (1996). A general approach to treatment of posttraumatic stress disorder. In B. A. van der Kolk, A. C. McFarlane, and L. Weisaeth (Eds.), *Traumatic stress: The effects of overwhelming experience on mind, body, and society*, pp. 417–40. New York: Guilford.

Van Emmerick, A. A. P., Kamphuis, J. H., and Hulsbosch, A. M. (2002). Single session debriefing after psychological trauma: A meta-analysis. *Lancet*, 360: 742–66.

Warda, G., and Bryant, R. A. (1998). Cognitive bias in acute stress disorder. *Behavior Research and Therapy*, 36: 1177–83.

White, M., and Epston, D. (1990). *Narrative means to therapeutic ends*. New York: Norton.

Chapter Thirteen

Posttraumatic Therapy in the Age of Neuroscience

Bessel van der Kolk

When people develop Post-Traumatic Stress Disorder (PTSD) in the wake of exposure to a traumatic event, the imprint of that trauma comes to dominate how they organize their way in the world. Verbalizing, making meaning, and putting the event in context may provide a means of feeling understood, rejoining the human race, and gaining perspective on the experience, but it may do little to reorganize the person to feel safe and focused on fulfilling the demands of the present. Given the subcortical nature of trauma imprints, effective therapy needs to help survivors tolerate the sensory reminders of the trauma and to physically experience efficacy and purpose in response to stimuli that once triggered feelings of helplessness and dependence.

Research on the impact of trauma on a variety of different victim populations has shown that a vast majority of people who are not immediately and personally affected by a horrible tragedy sustain no lasting damage. Most people who witness terrible events are able to find ways of going on with their lives with little change in their capacity to love, trust, and plan for a hopeful future. Those who are most directly exposed to the sensory realities of the traumatic events are at highest risk for developing psychological problems: those who are physically immobile and helpless while trying to escape from a disaster; those with first-hand experiences of the sounds, smells, and images of a calamity; those who directly witness the death and dismemberment of human beings; and those whose lives have been permanently altered by the death or injury of a loved one.

For most Americans trauma begins at home. The most common source of trauma for children and women is violence perpetrated by family members and intimate partners. Yet public disasters receive much more public concern than private traumas. Initially, communal tragedies tend to attract an enormous amount of attention and financial aid. Outpourings of social support, public acknowledgment, and practical help to restore functioning all have profound effects on helping victims recover. In contrast, lack of validation and public acknowledgment, such as usually occurs after an attack by acquaintances, tends to lead to shame, helplessness, secrecy, and preoccupation with maintaining one's emotional connections and financial security.

PTSD AS A DIAGNOSIS

When people fail to establish a new homeostasis in the wake of a traumatic event, they are likely to develop the symptom picture described in the *Diagnostic and Statistical Manual of Mental Disorders–Fourth Edition* (American Psychiatric Association, 1980) diagnosis of Post-Traumatic Stress Disorder (PTSD). At the core of PTSD lies the concept that the imprint of the traumatic event comes to dominate the total organism and how victims organize their lives—people with PTSD perceive most subsequent stressful life events in the light of their prior trauma. This focus on the past is likely to gradually rob their current lives of a sense of meaning and pleasure (van der Kolk and van der Hart, 1991).

In contrast to PTSD, which is characterized by intrusive sensory recollections of traumatic life experiences, ordinary events generally are not relived as images, smells, physical sensations, or sounds associated with that event. Ordinarily, the remembered aspects of experience coalesce into a story that captures the essence of what has happened. As people remember and tell others about an event, the *narrative* gradually changes with time and telling.

Since the last decades of the nineteenth century, it has been understood that extreme fear, terror, and helplessness during a traumatic event can overwhelm people's biological and psychological adaptive mechanisms. This breakdown makes them unable to assimilate the experience, that is, to integrate it as a personal event belonging to their past (Janet, 1889). Instead, memories of the trauma are "dissociated" and not only return as narrative memories of what has happened but replay in the form of intense emotional reactions, nightmares, images, aggressive behavior, physical pain, and bodily states that can all be understood as the return of elements of the mental imprints of the trauma.

Thus, the core pathology of PTSD is that certain sensations or emotions related to traumatic experiences are dissociated, keep returning in unbidden ways, and do not fade with time. That does not mean that the *stories* that traumatized people tell to *explain* what is going on do not change: narratives are a function of the interaction between speaker and listener. The problem with PTSD is that the images, sensations, and emotions related to the trauma do not change. Studies have shown that the traumatic imprints start changing, too, while people recover from their PTSD (Foa, Molnar, and Cashman, 1995; van der Kolk, Hopper, and Osterman, 2001).

Traumatized people often do not realize that their intense feelings and reactions are based on past experience. In fact, the traumatic experience itself may be largely forgotten. People have an infinite capacity to rationalize their feelings and blame their current surroundings for the way they feel. This capacity protects them from having to confront the helplessness and horror of their past. The mind has many different ways to hide its truths from its owners. Freud (1926) wrote: "If a person does not remember, he is likely to act out: he reproduces it not as a memory but as an action; he repeats it, without knowing, of course, that he is repeating, and in the end, we understand that *this is his way of remembering*" (p. 150). Most psychiatrists have come to accept that basic notion and, as a result, emphasize the need for traumatized people to verbalize and "own" their experiences. There is widespread agreement that without being able to put what happened into words traumatized people have a tendency to react to subsequent stress as if the trauma were still going on. If the problem with PTSD is *dissociation*, treatment should consist of *association*. As Freud (1914) put it, while the patient lives it through as something real and contemporary, we have to do our therapeutic work on it, which consists in large measure in tracing it back to the past (p. 152). As a result, in psychotherapy there always has been a major emphasis on trying to help patients give a full account of their trauma, in words, pictures, or other symbolic presentations.

THE NEUROBIOLOGY OF TRAUMA

Numerous studies (see van der Kolk, McFarlane, and Weisaeth, 1996) have shown that people with PTSD, when confronted with elements of the original trauma, have psychophysiological reactions and neuroendocrine responses that reflect their having developed a conditioned response to certain reminders of the trauma. When confronted with a sufficient number of sensory elements that match the imprints at the time of the original trauma (such as being touched in a particular way, being exposed to certain smells, or seeing visual reminders of the earlier event), patients with PTSD activate biological systems that make them react as if they were traumatized all over again: with fight or flight responses.

Studies during the past two decades have shown that people with PTSD develop abnormalities in the neurotransmitters that regulate arousal and attention. Normally, stress activates both principal stress hormones: catecholamines and cortisol. One of the most important findings in PTSD research has been that people with PTSD have low levels of cortisol. The effect of increased secretion of norepinephrine, combined with decreased cortisol, renders people with PTSD more reactive to arousing stimuli (Yehuda, 2002). The simultaneous activation of norepinephrine and cortisol stimulates active coping behaviors. Increased arousal in the presence of low cortisol levels, such as occurs in people with PTSD, provokes indiscriminate fight or flight reactions. In addition, because of a phenomenon called *state-dependent memory retrieval*, people in a state of high physiological arousal tend preferentially to access emotional memories that are related to memories that were laid down while they were in a state of high arousal, thus precipitating flashbacks and nightmares.

Recent advances in the neurosciences and the emerging ability to take images of the brain while a person is exposed to different challenges (e.g., Ledoux, 1996; Rauch et al., 1996) have made it possible to locate those areas of the brain that are involved in the processing of different experiences. Under ordinary conditions, the brain structures involved in interpreting what is going on outside the organism function in harmony. The subcortical areas of the brain, the evolutionarily more primitive parts that are not under conscious control and possess no language, have a different way of representing past experience than do the more recently evolved structures of the brain, located in the prefrontal cortex. These higher cortical structures allow people to use language and symbols to communicate about their personal past. However, when people are frightened or aroused, the frontal areas of the brain, which are responsible for the analysis of experience and associating it with other areas of knowledge, are deactivated (Arnsten, 1998).

Deactivation of the dorsolateral prefrontal cortex (which is responsible for executive function) in patients with PTSD interferes with their being able to formulate a measured response to threat. In addition, high levels of arousal also interfere with the adequate functioning of the brain region necessary to put one's feelings into words: Broca's area (Rauch et al., 1996). Thus, traumatized people are ill equipped to talk about their traumas in rational or analytical fashion.

Under conditions of intense arousal, the more primitive areas of the brain, the limbic system and brain stem, may generate sensations and emotions that contradict one's conscious attitudes and beliefs, thus causing traumatized people to behave "irrationally" in response to stimuli that are objectively neutral or merely stressful. One of the limbic structures that is centrally involved in traumatic reexperiencing is the amygdala, which serves as the "smoke detector" that interprets whether incoming sensory information is a threat. It creates "emotional memories" in response to particular sensations, sounds, images, and so forth, that are associated with threat to life and limb. When one is exposed to stimuli that represent danger, signals are passed to the rest of the organism to protect itself. These emotional interpretations are thought to be "indelible" (LeDoux, 1996): once the amygdala is "set" to remember particular sounds, smells, bodily sensations, and the like as dangerous, the person is likely to respond to these stimuli as a trigger for a fight or flight reaction.

THE SUBCORTICAL NATURE OF SELF-EXPERIENCE

The world of human infants initially is defined by their bodily sensations. As part of their becoming members of the human race, they come to interpret these sensations in the context of their physical interactions with their mothers. At that time, the only tool that a mother has to modulate emotional states of a baby is directly to change the infant's physical sensations by rocking, by feeding, by stroking, as well as by making soothing noises and engaging in other comforting physical interactions. The infant is a "subcortical creature . . . [who] lacks the means for modulation of behavior which is made possible by the development of cortical control" (Schore, 1994, p. 30). This is strikingly similar to the experience of traumatized people, who also appear to be at the mercy of their sensations, physical reactions, and emotions.

Once people are traumatized and develop PTSD, their ability to sooth themselves is compromised. Instead, they tend to rely on actions, such as fight or flight or on pathological self-soothing, such as self-mutilation, bingeing, starving, or the ingestion of alcohol and drugs, to regulate their internal balance. The degree to which these subcortical reactions can be inhibited depends, in part, on one's relative level of emotional arousal, which, in turn, depends both on the activation of brain stem arousal centers and on the activation of the prefrontal cortex. Under ordinary conditions, people can suppress their anger or irritation, even while the appropriate physiological processes associated with these states, such as increased blood pressure and contraction of stomach muscles, continue. This inhibition is called "top-down processing" (LeDoux, 1996, p. 272): higher (neocortical) levels of processing can, and often do, override, steer, or interrupt the lower levels, elaborating on, or interfering with, emotional and sensorimotor processing. As Damasio (1999) claims:

> We use our minds not to discover facts but to hide them. One of the things the screen hides most effectively is the body, our own body, by which I mean, the ins and outs of it, its interiors. Like a veil thrown over the skin to secure its modesty, the screen partially removes from the mind the inner states of the body, those that constitute the flow of life as it wanders in the journey of each day. . . . But this has a cost. It tends to prevent us from sensing the possible origin and nature of what we call self. (p. 28)

The usual regulatory system of adults uses top-down processing that is based on cognition and is operated by the neocortex. This process enables high-level executive functioning by observing, monitoring, integrating, and planning. It can function effectively only if it succeeds in inhibiting the input from lower brain levels. Traditional psychotherapy relies on top-down techniques to manage disruptive emotions and sensations. These are approached as unwanted disruptions of "normal" functioning that need to be harnessed by reason, rather than as reactivated unintegrated fragments of traumatic states. Top-down processing focuses on inhibiting rather than processing (integrating) unpleasant sensations and emotions.

THE TYRANNY OF LANGUAGE

In traditional, insight-oriented psychotherapy, people learn to *understand* that certain emotional or somatic reactions belong to the past and are irrelevant to their present lives. This understanding may help them *override* automatic physiological responses to traumatic reminders but not *abolish* them. While providing a deeper understanding of why they feel the way they do, insight of this nature is unlikely to allow the reconfiguring of the alarm systems of the brain. In a neuroimaging study using (PET) scans, Rauch et al. (1996) showed that when people relive their traumatic experiences, there is decreased activation of Broca's area and increased activation of the limbic system in the right hemisphere of the brain. This finding suggests that when people with PTSD relive their trauma, they have great difficulty putting that experience into words. Our finding of a relatively increased activation of the right hemisphere, compared with the left, implies that when people relive their trauma, they are imbedded in the experience: they are *having* the experience but cannot analyze what is going on in space and time. This explains why so many traumatized people attempt to avoid becoming aroused and losing control by facing what has happened to them. Instead, they tend to talk "around" the trauma rather than facing it.

THE THERAPEUTIC CHALLENGE

Experience shows that many traumatized people, when attempting to put their trauma into words, respond physically, as if they were traumatized all over again, rather than gaining relief. Reliving the trauma without being firmly anchored in the present often leaves people with PTSD more traumatized than they were before. Recalling the trauma can be so painful that many people with PTSD choose not to expose themselves to situations in which they are asked to do so. Hence, when one is treating PTSD, a central challenge is how to help people process and integrate their traumatic experiences without making them feel traumatized all over again or, in the language of neuroscience, how to process trauma so that it is quenched, rather than kindled.

Until the advent of modern psychological treatment methods, many societies made use of theater and ritual to deal with communal traumas. The Greek tragedies, as well as the rewriting of the tragedy of Vietnam in Hollywood movies, are good examples of this. In my own experience I have been astounded by the similarity between the communal healing rituals in various non-Western societies, from Kwa Zulu Natal to Laos. Over the past few years, our Trauma Center in Boston has collaborated with theater groups that work with traumatized inner-city children in the northeastern United States. Dramatic enactment is a way of dealing with, narrating, and transforming their traumatic experiences, by allowing the children both to share their personal experiences and to find action-oriented ways of coming to an alternative resolution to the once-inevitable outcome of the original traumatic event. This work is predicated on the idea that to overcome a traumatic experience, people require physical experiences that directly contradict the helplessness and the inevitability of defeat associated with the trauma.

In helping traumatized people process their traumatic memories, it is critical that they gain enough distance from their sensory imprints and trauma-related emotions so that they can observe these sensations and emotions without losing their ability to keep their wits about them or engaging in avoidance maneuvers. The Selective Serotonin Reuptake Inhibitors (SSRIs) often can facilitate that process. Studies in our laboratory have shown that SSRIs can be extremely helpful for PTSD patients to gain emotional distance from traumatic stimuli and stay calm enough to make sense of their traumatic intrusions (van der Kolk et al., 1994). After alleviating the most distressing symptoms, it is important to help people with PTSD find a language by which they can come to understand and communicate their experiences. To put the event(s) in perspective, the victim needs to relive it without feeling helpless. Traditionally, following Freud's notion that words can substitute for action to resolve a trauma (Breuer and Freud, 1893), this has been done by helping people talk about the entire traumatic experience (Herman, 1992; Resick and Schnicke, 1992; Foa, Dancu, Hembree, Jaycox, Meadows, and Street, 1999).

Victims are asked to articulate what happened and what led up to it; their own contributions to what happened, their thoughts and fantasies during the event, what was the worst part of it, and their reactions to the event in detail, including how it has affected their perceptions of themselves and others. Such exposure therapy is thought to promote symptom reduction by allowing patients to realize that remembering the trauma is not equivalent to experiencing it again; that the experience had a beginning, a middle, and an end; and that the event now belongs to one's personal history. If people can stick with exposure treatment and relive the trauma in words and feelings in a safe therapeutic context, there is a substantial likelihood that they will overcome their PTSD. However, these forms of treatment also have high dropout rates (Ford and Kidd, 1998), probably because patients feel too overstimulated reexperiencing the trauma without immediate relief.

Most traditional therapies have paid little attention to posttraumatic changes related to bodily experience: the sensate dimension of life. This neglect ignores that the origin of one's emotional states is the state of the body's chemical profile, the state of one's viscera, and the contraction of the striated muscles of the face, throat, trunk, and limbs (Damasio, 1999). Applying these lessons from modern neuroscience has made us realize that effective treatment of PTSD needs to involve promoting awareness, rather than avoidance of internal somatic states. Promoting awareness of the "felt sense" (Gendlin, 1988) allows feelings to be known, rather than to be sensed as harbingers of threats that need to be avoided. Mindfulness, awareness of one's inner experience, and a "felt sense" are necessary if one is to respond according to the current requirements for managing one's life, rather than reacting to certain somatic sensations as a return of the traumatic past. Such awareness allows people to introduce new options to solve problems and not merely to react reflexively. As Damasio (1999) writes: "Consciousness establishes a link between the world of automatic regulation and the world of imagination—the world in which images of different modalities (thoughts, feelings, and sensations) can be combined to produce novel images of situations that have not yet happened" (p. 258).

Imagining new possibilities, not merely the repeated retelling of the tragic past, is the essence of posttraumatic therapy. In recent years a variety of new techniques has been developed. These techniques have the potential for desensitizing patients with PTSD without fully engaging them in a verbal reliving of the traumatic experience. In this regard a relatively new and still somewhat controversial treatment for PTSD, Eye Movement and Desensitization and Reprocessing (EMDR) (Chemtob, Tolin, van der Kolk, and Pitman, 2000), is of particular interest. This treatment consists of having people remember (but not necessarily verbalize) their feelings, thoughts, and somatic sensations related to a traumatic event, while undergoing bilateral stimulation, usually by following the therapist's hand as it moves from side to side in front of the patient. In the vast majority of traumatized patients, this maneuver produces rapid mental associations to seemingly unrelated prior-life events and a gradual diminution of the emotional intensity of the memories of the trauma itself (van der Kolk, 2002). Aside from its remarkable therapeutic efficacy, this novel treatment challenges our most fundamental paradigms about how therapy changes psychological programs. Providing bilateral stimulation obviously does not directly affect consciousness; it is likely to work by means of its actions on subcortical processes that have little or nothing to do with insight and understanding.

CONCLUSION

The formulation of PTSD as the way the human mind responds to overwhelming trauma is only about twenty years old. Since then there has been an explosion of knowledge about how experience shapes the central nervous system and the formation of the self. Developments in the neurosciences have started to make significant contributions to our understanding of how the brain is shaped by experience and how life itself continues to transform the ways biology is organized. The study of trauma has probably been the single most fertile area within the disciplines of psychiatry and psychology in helping to develop a deeper understanding of the interrelationships between emotional, cognitive, social, and biological forces that shape human development.

Research in these areas has opened up entirely new insights into how extreme experiences throughout the life cycle can have profound effects on memory and affect regulation, biological stress modulation, and interpersonal relatedness. It promises to shed light on the fundamental question of how the mind comes to integrate experience in such a way that one is prepared for future threat, while being able to make a distinction between what belongs to the present and what belongs to the past. These findings, together with the development of a range of new therapy approaches, are beginning to open up entirely new perspectives on how traumatized people can be helped to overcome their past.

REFERENCES

This chapter is reproduced from Bessel van der Kolk, Posttraumatic Therapy in the Age of Neuroscience, *Psychoanalytic Dialogues*, 12 (3): 381–92. Copyright © 2002 by the Analytic Press. Reprinted with permission.

American Psychiatric Association. (1980). *Diagnostic and statistical manual of mental disorders* (4th ed.). Washington, DC: Author.

Arnsten, A. F. (1998). The biology of being frazzled. *Science*, 280: 1711–12.

Breuer, J., and Freud, S. (1893/1955). On the psychical mechanism of hysterical phenomena: Preliminary communication. *Standard Edition*, 2, pp. 1–18. London: Hogarth Press.

Chemtob, C. M., Tolin, D. F., van der Kolk, B. A., and Pitman, R. K. (2000). Eye movement desensitization and reprocessing. In E. B. Foa, T. M. Keane, and M. J. Friedman (Eds.), *Effective treatments for PTSD: Practice guidelines from the International Society for Traumatic Stress Studies*, 139–55, 333–35. New York: Guilford.

Damasio, A. (1999). *The feeling of what happens*. New York: Harcourt Brace Jovanovich.

Foa, E. B., Dancu, C. V., Hembree, E. A., Jaycox, L. H., Meadows, E. A., and Street, G. P. (1999). A comparison of exposure therapy, stress inoculation training, and their combination for reducing posttraumatic stress disorder in female assault victims. *Journal of Consulting and Clinical Psychology*, 67: 194–200.

Foa, E. B., Molnar, C., and Cashman, L. (1995). Change in rape narratives during exposure therapy for posttraumatic stress disorder. *Journal of Traumatic Stress*, 8: 675–90.

Ford, J., and Kidd, T. (1998). Early childhood trauma and disorders of extreme stress as predictors of treatment outcome with chronic posttraumatic stress disorder. *Journal of Traumatic Stress*, 11: 743–61.

Freud, S. (1914/1956). Remembering, repeating and working-through. *Standard Edition*, 12, pp. 147–56. London: Hogarth Press.

———. (1926/1956). Inhibitions, symptoms and anxiety. *Standard Edition*, 20, pp. 77–174. London: Hogarth Press.

Gendlin, E. (1988). *Focusing*. New York: Guilford.

Herman, J. L. (1992). *Trauma and recovery*. New York: Basic Books.

Janet, P. (1889). *L'Automatisme psychologique*. Paris: Alcan.

LeDoux, J. (1996). *The emotional brain*. New York: Simon & Schuster.

Rauch, S. L., van der Kolk, B. A., Fisler, R. E. A., Nathaniel, M., Orr, S. P., Savage, C., et al. (1996). A symptom provocation study of posttraumatic stress disorder using positron emission tomography and script-driven imagery. *Archives of General Psychiatry*, 53: 380–87.

Resick, P. A., and Schnicke, M. K. (1992). Cognitive processing therapy for sexual assault victims. *Journal of Consulting and Clinical Psychology*, 60: 748–56.

Schore, A. (1994). *Affect regulation and the origin of the self: The neurobiology of emotional development*. Hillsdale, NJ: Erlbaum.

van der Kolk, B. A. (2000). Post traumatic stress disorder and the nature of trauma. *Dialogues in Clinical Neuroscience*, 2: 7–22.

———. (2002). Beyond the talking cure. In F. Shapiro (Ed.), *EMDR: Towards a paradigm shift*. Washington, DC: American Psychiatric Press.

van der Kolk, B. A., Dreyfuss, D., Beckowitz, R., Saxe, G., Shera, D., and Michaels, M. (1994). Fluoxetine in post-traumatic stress. *Journal of Clinical Psychiatry*, 55: 517–22.

van der Kolk, B. A., Hopper, J. W., and Osterman, J. E. (2001). Exploring the nature of traumatic memory. *Journal of Aggression, Maltreatment and Trauma*, 4: 9–31.

van der Kolk, B. A., McFarlane, A. C., and Weisaeth, L. (Eds.). (1996). *Traumatic stress: The effects of overwhelming experience on mind, body and society*. New York: Guilford.

van der Kolk, B. A., and van der Hart, O. (1991). The intrusive past: The flexibility of memory and the engraving of trauma. *Imago*, 48: 425–54.

Yehuda, R. (2002). Post-traumatic stress disorder. *New England Journal of Medicine*, 346: 108–15.

Chapter Fourteen

Optimizing Affect Function in the Psychoanalytic Treatment of Trauma

Henry Krystal

Emotions undergo a developmental process to reach their mature form. Previously published studies of the genetic aspect of emotions indicate that affect maturation involves affect differentiation, verbalization, and desomatization. In their adult form, affects are suitable for information processing. The availability of such (adult) types of emotions is essential for analysands to benefit from the psychotherapeutic process. To use emotions effectively, one has to be able to tolerate emotions comfortably and to regulate them optimally.

This chapter strives to demonstrate how to evaluate a potential analysand's ability to use emotions for psychoanalysis. I describe patients who have disturbances in the functioning of their emotions. I discuss posttraumatic, psychosomatic, and addictive patients who often suffer from alexithymia, which represents a regression in affect form and function. This condition prevents patients from optimally benefiting from psychotherapy. I propose modifications in the technique necessary for making the emotions of these patients more adaptive for analytic treatment.

AFFECT COMPONENTS

Affects can be understood as having four dimensions or components, functioning in concert: cognitive, physiological, hedonic, and activating. The *cognitive* aspect of emotions is their meaning: for example, fear and anxiety are signals of impending avoidable danger. Fear signals external veridical danger, while anxiety signals danger of an intrapsychic, unconscious origin. Depression signals that something bad has happened, for which we tend to blame ourselves. Anger means that something bad has happened, for which we blame a person whom we are entitled to hate and punish.

The *physiological* aspect of emotions is not expressive, as we used to think. It is notable for its connection with psychosomatic disturbances. Since regressed emotions are somatic and minimally cognitive, bodily manifestations of affects are common. They do not, however, represent an enactment of a fantasy.

The *hedonic* aspect of emotions involves the quality of pleasure and displeasure. In order to understand this component, we must distinguish the idea of pleasure from gratification, as well as differentiate suffering from pain. The hedonic quality of experiences is greatly influenced by changes in the state of consciousness. Hence, dysphoric states represent a motivation for the use of consciousness-modifying drugs (Krystal, 1995).

The *activating* aspect of emotions involves the regulation of the arousal of the whole organism. This aspect of emotions is the bridge between psychology and neuroscience. The state of activation influences one's vitality and performance. It feeds back to modify the cognitive aspect. In severe depression, for example, cognitive disturbances occur just 20 percent less frequently than in schizophrenia (Krystal, 1988).

INFORMATION PROCESSING

The information-processing function of emotion involves the individual's ability to *recognize* the occurrence of an affect. If an individual experiences at least two aspects of emotions in a nondissociated fashion and the individual is capable of a certain degree of reflective self-awareness, he or she may recognize the occurrence of a *feeling*. A feeling is a subjective experience. If an individual is able to recognize that he or she is having a feeling, he is able to evaluate what portion of the intensity of the emotion is a response to the current event versus how much he or she derives from past memories and associations. This capacity is at the core of successful social behavior. It is in the best interest of an individual to be able to respond emotionally to each situation appropriately, with minimum intensification or blocking of the affect by emotional hangovers from the past.

When one recognizes the experience of a feeling with the intuitive recognition of one's absolute emotional self-continence, one may proceed to review the repertoire of possible responses. This is the most favorable way to select the course of action that is in one's best interest. Individuals who cannot do this are condemned to knee-jerk responses and to experience themselves as not being in charge of their own lives. Also, when in therapy they hear an interpretation, they do not respond with an emotional reaction that makes it an important, potentially self-modifying experience. Instead, they memorize what we say.

AFFECT TOLERANCE

We discussed the question of how we experience emotions—in other words, what we believe they are. Next is the matter of how we *react* to having the emotion. Affect tolerance is built up on the earlier-mentioned recognition of a feeling as our own personal experience. It is like color in perception. It makes life meaningful and exciting, even when it is painful. Patients with affect disorders have problems with affect tolerance. The ones who come for help usually do so at the end of a vicious cycle resulting from their maladaptive responses to *having* affects (Krystal, 1975).

THE GENETIC VIEW OF AFFECTS

Emotions in adults evolve from three affect precursor states (*ur-affects*) in the newborn: First, the emotions generally experienced as pleasurable evolve out of the state of well-being. Next, the unpleasant affects differentiate from the state of distress. The third affect precursor is not well known, because in the normal infant it disappears at about two months of age (Papousek and Papousek, 1975). It reappears in traumatic states, and expresses itself in trances and a variety of cataleptic dissociative responses.

The process of affect development is older than humankind. The differentiation of vocalization is also common in animals. A good-enough mother delights in recognizing that a specific kind of vocalization in the baby signals a particular need or demand and tries to fulfill it instantly. She thereby rewards the process of affect differentiation. As the child develops the use of words, the process of helping it to differentiate and to name specific feelings becomes a major part of the task of upbringing. The parent instructs the child about what he or she feels and about what the child should do about these feelings in a given situation. She demonstrates to the child that the more precise the naming of a more refined affect, the more effective its use as a signal, and the better it serves as a tool for the "art of living."

For example, enabling a child to recognize and tolerate shame is an important achievement. However, if the child is also able to recognize shadings and nuances of that affect such as chagrin, embarrassment, dishonor, ridicule, humiliation, disgust, and mortification, the child gains a chance to become familiar with, and better at, using the affect. Otherwise the affect can be deeply buried in the core of an "abscess" around which an addiction or psychosomatic disease may develop (Krystal, 1974).

The appreciation of the genetic development of affects and their potential for regression, which includes dedifferentiation, resomatization, and deverbalization, has important diagnostic and therapeutic consequences. Instead of thinking of psychosomatic disease as a product of the hyperactivity of an organ using models derived from conversion reactions, we need to keep in mind factors that relate to an interference with the desomatization of affect responses. As I will elaborate later, this change of orientation is essential for the consideration of effective analytic approaches to psychosomatic problems.

INFANTILE PSYCHIC TRAUMA

An important part of mothering in promoting the development of affect tolerance is not only to enable the young to bear increasing intensity and duration of affects but to step in before they overwhelm the child. There are definite limits to a child's resilience, especially early on. We need to consider the immaturity of the infant's general development and the nature of the affect precursors. If the mother is unable to relieve the baby within a short period of time, the affect precursors tend to snowball to the point that virtually every part of the mind, indeed the whole organism, is in a state of maximum excitement. The baby becomes virtually inconsolable. This state represents the onset of infantile psychic trauma. Severe, repetitive occurrences of this type result in failure to thrive or marasmus.

The consequences of infantile psychic trauma are severe. The tendency to experience intense fear, rage, shame, and guilt persists for life and has many repercussions. The one most pertinent to our concerns is a general dread of emotions, because they are experienced as heralds of an expected return of the infantile psychic trauma. It becomes a lifelong "doomsday orientation," seriously interfering with the normal development of affects. There is also an arrest in the genetic development of affects that prevents the differentiation, verbalization, and desomatization of emotions. These arrests, regressions, and impairments in affect vary greatly among individuals and even within the same person under a variety of influences.

The impairment of affect tolerance is not a matter of blocking disturbing or painful emotions. It must be clearly distinguished from defenses against emotions. In the most severe cases, where trust in the mothering parent has been undermined, we find a dread of potential "good objects." There is a fear of love. It is a most crippling, life-distorting problem. The consequence of this fear of love to the potential for a workable transference is self-evident.

As already mentioned, for the adult, it is important to keep one's emotions in bearable intensity. Otherwise, they can overwhelm one's judgment and self-control. In optimal circumstances, the subject is familiar with the appropriate intensity of emotions for most life situations and recognizes the exceptional situation when an event mobilizes memories that intensify current affect responses. A normal person becomes aware when such an overly excited (or deactivated) state would interfere with his or her optimal choice of the most adaptive response to the present situation. However, in families in which life consists of a constant battle between all the family members, the lesson learned is that nothing happens unless one maximizes one's affect responses. To put it plainly, unless one throws a fit, no one will take note of one's distress. People growing up in such families acquire the habit of maximizing rather than moderating their affect responses. The result is that they habitually produce emotional outbursts that tend to overwhelm their composure. They terrify themselves with their own affects.

ADULT CATASTROPHIC TRAUMA

In contrast to infantile psychic trauma, adult trauma is not brought on by intense emotions. Adult psychic trauma is initiated, as Freud (1926, pp. 71–115) indicated, "by the essence and meaning of the subject's estimation of his strength . . . and . . . his admission of helplessness . . . in the face of the 'Erlebte Situation,'" that is, the subjective helplessness in the face of what he experiences as unavoidable and inescapable danger and his surrender to it. With the surrender, the affect changes from fear, which is an activating affective signal of impending and avoidable danger, to another affect, the catatanoid reaction. This is the signal of unavoidable, unmodifiable danger to which one must surrender. The catatanoid reaction has certain commonalities with cataleptic responses—which in turn have the following attribute in common with trances: the more one submits, the more one obeys orders and feels as though one is unable to resist or escape, and the more one goes into a profound submission. This vicious circle is the initiation of the traumatic process. The traumatic process, once initiated, progresses along phylogenetically determined lines in a pattern established and common to the entire animal kingdom (Seligman, 1975). Kardiner (1941) and Zetzel (1949) had major parts of this process worked out. Bibring (1953) had a deep understanding of this process and its sequels, but the ego-psychology terminology was too limiting for him to be able to realize that what he was describing was psychic trauma.

On surrender, there is an automaton-like obedience that the SS commander Himmler liked to call "Kadaver Gehorchsamkeit." There sets in a progressively severe numbing of physical and psychological pain. Dissociations and self-representation splitting develop at an accelerating rate. Unless this process can be arrested at the "robot" state, the malignant phase of trauma sets in. It consists of a severe and progressive constriction and the closing off of all mental functions. One after the other—conation, problem solving, attention, perception, registration, recall, scanning, judgment, planning, evaluation of oneself and the environment, and all the rest, shut down. In rapid progression, all life-preserving functions are blocked, with merely a vestige of self-observation flickering until psychogenic death sets in, the heart stopping in diastole (Krystal, 1978a).

ALEXITHYMIA

For those individuals who manage to arrest the traumatic process in the robot state and have to live in it for a significant period of time, there are serious aftereffects that may last for the rest of their lives. Of all the aftereffects of trauma, it is relatively easy to identify the alexithymic characteristic in adult survivors of the Holocaust. As early as 1946, Minkowski described "emotional anesthesia" in these survivors. In alexithymia we find an affective disturbance: affect regression through dedifferentiation, deverbalization, and resomatization. Hence, instead of experiencing the "adult" type of emotions, which are mostly idea-like and in which action terms are predominant, alexithymic patients' affect responses consist mostly of physical reactions. Alexithymics cannot name their emotions and do not recognize that they are having a feeling. The alexithymic way of reacting is a direct continuation of some of the ways of functioning observable in the traumatic state. Psychosomatic and drug-dependent patients have a high rate of alexithymia (Sifneos, 1967; Krystal, 1971).

Analysands who do not have a history of trauma to relate to the interviewer will most likely suffer from the aftereffects of infantile psychic trauma. The finding of coexisting anhedonia establishes the certainty of the origin of both problems from trauma. Adult alexithymics who cannot use their emotions as signals to themselves tend to go in one of the following two directions: (1) Since their emotions become unwanted, useless burdens, they develop a stoicism, ignoring the affect signals from their minds and bodies. They become completely ruled by their intellectual self-control. Some alexithymics can be recognized by their stiff postures and wooden faces. (2) Alexithymic patients develop a fear and intolerance of all or some affective responses and tend to become addicted to a variety of things, especially and notably drugs, in order to block these responses. Their affects are regressed, and their affect tolerance is minimal. They become the kinds of patients who know all our interpretations by heart but remain unaffected.

This brings us to another aspect of alexithymia, which a group of Parisian psychoanalysts (Marty and de M'uzan, 1963; Marty, de M'uzan, and David,

1963) first reported. They realized that one simply could not successfully treat psychosomatic patients with psychoanalytic techniques devised for neurotics. The obstacle was a cognitive disturbance they named "operative thinking"—a thing-oriented, mechanical, impoverished, prosaic ideation. The loss of imagination and poetic attitude made free association impossible.

TRANSFERENCE

Posttraumatic, psychosomatic alexithymic patients' transferences are not the ones we know so well from working with "good neurotic" individuals. Alexithymic patients are cool and polite. They are quite willing to keep coming to analytic sessions and to wait patiently for the doctor to cure them. In the meantime, they repeatedly present the same kind of material: chronologically arranged details covering the period since the last session. A long-term diet of such material produces a countertransference of boredom. The occurrence of aggressive and sexual fantasies in the analyst's countertransference is an important clue to the nature of the patients' blocked associative powers and missing affects (Taylor, 1984a, 1984b).

Such patients hardly ever report dreams. When they do, they tend to be one-sentence productions, to which they cannot associate. If pressed, they may be able to squeeze out some additional details of the manifest contents of the dream. These patients are definitely not equipped for the psychoanalytic cooperative enterprise. Sifneos (1972–1973) cautioned that an accurate interpretation that would work well for a neurotic patient might produce a life-threatening exacerbation of the problem for a psychosomatic patient. In discussing these patients' transferences, the French group referred to them as "poorly libidinized." After many years of travail with such individuals, I concluded that we were dealing with an *idolatrous transference*. This transference represents a return to the infantile state in which all of one's vital and affective parts are attributed to the primal object. The authority to care for the subject's body is reserved to it too. In this orientation, all self-care may be carried out only under a "franchise" from an object of primal transference. The patients feel forbidden to exercise self-caring and self-soothing, or even self-regulating functions. They have a profound conviction, almost an unconscious creed, that a violation of this prohibition constitutes a Promethean transgression. These individuals believe that the violation of this fundamental taboo is punishable by a fate worse then death, that is, the return of the traumatic state (Krystal, 1978a, 1988, 1999).

A closely related alexithymic characteristic is an inhibition in wish-fulfillment fantasy, which I attribute to the traumatic interruption of the normal process of development of transitional object functions. This impairment is especially conspicuous in the wake of infantile trauma (Krystal, 1978b). In summary, all these problems are part of the posttraumatic inhibition in self-caring, self-soothing, and solacing functions (Horton, 1981). Clearly, all the just-mentioned characteristics constitute major obstacles to the progress and effectiveness of psychoanalysis.

CASE ILLUSTRATION

A middle-aged man, a concentration camp survivor, was brought in to see me by his wife because she was afraid that he would kill himself in a car accident. He was falling asleep while driving. He did in fact have a couple of near misses. An examination in the sleep clinic revealed sleep apnea due to a massive overgrowth of lymphatic tissue in his larynx. Surgery became necessary. While it was difficult to prove a psychosomatic origin of this hypertrophy, the patient did have a number of psychosomatic problems involving his gastrointestinal system. Moreover, he had an interesting problem—an inability to tolerate the cold. In temperatures in which most people felt comfortable, he felt unbearably cold.

He eventually came up with a solution to the problem that provided clues to its origin. One day he explained that finally he had found the means to react to the temperature like everyone else. He described that under his shirt he was wearing a paper garment of his own design and manufacture. It was fashioned from a paper sack by making three holes in it. In the concentration camp, where twice daily he was forced to stand a long time in the cold for prisoner counting, he survived by finding an empty cement sack and wearing the self-manufactured undergarment hidden under his striped jacket.

Mr. Blue was taken at age twelve with the entire Jewish population of his village in the Carpathian Mountains and shipped to Auschwitz in a cattle car. On arrival in Auschwitz, his family was killed in the gas chamber and cremated. Only he and his father were taken to the camp barracks. His father was with him until shortly before liberation, when he, too, was killed. The boy saw his father's body before it was sent to the crematorium. Although he related this part of his story several times, he made no comment about his emotional reaction to his father's death. He never spoke of his family's extermination. He was at the time of his father's death in the "Musulman" state, close to dying of psychogenic depletion, a state well known in the camps.

His most conspicuous presenting problem was his panic reactions. He had terrific heart pounding, chest pain, sweating, and other symptoms. He was in such a general state of distress that he was sure that he was dying or at the very least having a heart attack. He was seen in many hospital emergency rooms in this condition. Eventually (this was a matter of years), we were able to bring this condition into partial control with use of medication and psychotherapy. He never became completely free of the chest reaction, but he would come for an appointment a number of days later, describe the symptoms, indicate what triggered them, and discuss with me how he handled his reaction and how he managed the situation and dealt with the other person in the encounter. Through the years, we discovered that the affect that triggered this response could not be identified specifically. It would generally be an intense rage, but practically any other dysphoric reaction could be involved. The objects were usually family members, business associates, or, on occasion, incidental strangers although in many of the situations, he had the power or control of the situation or person, with the fear of helplessness frequently part of the mixture.

Although he was very cooperative, he was not capable of free associations or "uncovering" therapy. In the treatment, we maintained a "here and now" orientation. Very slowly we practiced affect recognition, verbalization, and tolerance. He did learn a lot about himself—for instance, that in situations of peril (public or private), he would freeze and go temporarily into the automaton state in which he had survived as a teenage prisoner of the death camp. As he became more comfortable with his emotions and experienced better self-control, he became a fairly well functioning person, able to withstand the normative "bad things" in life. He was, however, not too successful at enjoying things. For instance, he complained that he was not able to enjoy his grandchildren as he would like.

TREATMENT

Analytic approaches to the treatment of patients with posttraumatic problems who show various degrees of alexithymia and psychosomatic diseases or addictive problems or both cannot be done successfully with the principles of treatment developed for the neuroses alone. Intensive preparatory work is necessary, especially in the opening phases of the analysis. One needs to take every opportunity to show and explain the nature of the patient's emotional, affective, and cognitive disturbances (Krystal, 1982; Krystal and Raskin, 1970; McDougall, 1974).

CULTIVATING AFFECT TOLERANCE

We need to learn what the analysands' conceptions of their affects are and how they react to having emotions. The concept of affects as magical punishment, signs of weakness, or even stupidity have to be expected. The patient's "color blindness" about affects needs repeated attention. Next is the matter of their reaction to having an emotion, which may reveal deep-seated convictions about what should be done with affects. The most common conception is the wish-generated idea of the expressing of emotions as a means of getting rid of them, expelling them to the outside. Eventually, the analyst may be able to understand and demonstrate the regressions, deficiencies, and arrests that these patients have suffered in the genetic development of their affects. The problem is not a lack of expressiveness, but a resomatization.

Working on affect differentiation involves the naming of affects, interpreting the story behind the affects, and highlighting the differences between adaptive mature responses and the patient's infantile affective response. The patients gradually develop and increasingly improve their capacity for symbolic representation. Being able to accept a symbolic fulfillment of their needs and wishes instead of the concrete form they expect in the beginning establishes an essential component of the therapeutic effectiveness of the psychoanalytic process.

The message that the alexithymic patients need to receive, but which is very hard for them to register and feel, is that love is real and that it works. They have a difficult time seeing it that way. They cannot believe it and demand instant wish fulfillment. Having a very poor capacity for symbolic experience, they demand concrete gratification. They have a particular view on this matter: "If you loved me, then everything would feel perfect. Since it does not, then all you are offering is 'counterfeit nurturance.' So did everyone else, before now, whenever I needed and asked for loving!"

ACTIVATION OF DENIAL AND DEFENSES

When the patient is confronted with an anxiety-provoking situation, instant denial is activated. This in turn initiates a variety of defenses, including the kind designated against keeping the memory and affect object together (Dorpat, 1985). Defensive distortions of perception, cognition, and recall occur frequently when called up by painful affective signals. The traditional psychoanalytic idea that repressed contents are preserved intact is disproved by evidence that unconscious contents are continually reviewed and modified (Westerlund and Smith, 1983; H. Krystal and A. D. Krystal, 1994).

This discovery cautions us about the way reconstructed material must be handled. A basic principle must be reemphasized in this context: signal affects operate in information and perception processing like automatic switches (Bucci, 1988). Defenses against trauma (the updated version of the stimulus barrier) involve all the individual's mental and emotional functions, as well as all ego functions (Krystal, 1995). Posttraumatically, the responses to signal affects become rigid and assume an intensified, hyperalert state. Hypervigilance and emergency regimes persist for life and have to be dealt with as resistances. Trauma results in intrapsychic splitting, manifest in fixation on the past and various degrees of dissociation, progressing in severity to the point of producing identity dissociations (Brenner, 2001).

Impairment of the capacity to grieve successfully negates the potential of a successful outcome of the analysis. Only by being able to grieve and complete the grieving *successfully* can one achieve self-integration and the capacity for mutuality, interdependence, and intimacy (Wetmore, 1963; Krystal, 1999). In the preceding case, helping the patient to complete grieving for a current loss was a major task. Trauma throws one into the often-insoluble dilemma of an existence of connection versus separation, integrity versus disintegration, and activity versus stasis. Such conflicts demand our attention in therapy to a degree that is not as central or essential for "good neurotics" (Lifton, 1968). Stereotypic interpretations simply miss the point with such patients. Unlike average good candidates for analysis, these patients require the analyst's help in discovering that all affects are transformations of love, love being the model affect (Dorsey, 1971; Krystal, 1988, 1999). They need to practice recognizing that their rage represents their love outraged and that their shame is their love rejected and humiliated. It is this rejection and humiliation of their love that poisons their self-representation. Love is one's life power and all affects are modifications of it.

Although many such patients come prepared for a surgical solution, proposing that we "cut out" the bad part of them, we are oriented to the psychoanalytic endeavor of accepting lovingly every part of one's self-representation and all one's memories. Every mental construct, memory, object, and self-representation needs to be healed by a kindly, peaceful endowment of conscious self-recognition. Only then can mourning be completed and inner peace and harmony be achieved. If alexithymic patients stay in treatment long enough to be able to understand and feel what the therapist is talking about, it is then necessary to bring to their attention that they have severe inhibitions in self-care, self-soothing, transitional processes, and self-regulation. They treat themselves as robots and have no empathy for anyone. By this time it should be possible to interpret that their transference, dominated by the wish that the therapist take over the operation of all their vital and affective functions, is a version of an idolatrous transference. The patients have lived their lives submitting themselves to the substitutes for the primal object that they experience exactly as pagans do their idols.

However, to address ourselves to these transferences, we must remember that many aspects of them are preverbal, derived from pre-object relatedness.

Many clues to their meaning may be present not in the patients' words, but in their intonation, posture, and mien—all the kinds of communication derived from infancy (Kumin, 1996). Moreover, since in the traumatic state there is diminution of the sense of actuality and the symbolizing process, what we say may not be as important as how we say it, how we sound, and what emotion we convey. Consequently, for such patients it is necessary to view the therapist directly. In some situations it is desirable to admit to the patient that his or her perception of the analyst's reaction is accurate and to admit and explain a countertransference reaction or empathic failures or both (Maroda, 1999). Such a confirmatory admission will go a long way in enabling the patient to trust his or her feelings in key object relations, perhaps for the first time.

CONCLUSION

This discussion has reviewed the functions of emotions in general and the special challenges for psychoanalysis in the context of trauma and affect regression. Self-representation and psychosocial responses to significant others are markedly influenced by the status and availability of emotions. Psychodynamic psychotherapy cannot be effective unless the patient has adult-type emotions available and participates in the analysis emotionally. Without this capacity, it is not even clear to such individuals what is truly animate. The alexithymic answer to fantasy formation is that it has to be connected to immediate wish fulfillment—"otherwise what is the point of it?" This reaction is a direct effect of trauma: notably a repudiation of wishes and fantasies, giving up parts of self and object representations and replacing them with nothing. Analysis of these patients, to be successful, requires that the patients reintegrate every possible part of themselves, including the memory traces of the most terrible experiences, and that they consciously recognize that psychic representation is nothing but their own creation. This is the reason why in working with such people we must keep oriented to the idea that *psychic* reality is the only knowable reality.

We must enter the arena of infantile conflict in order to extend the scope of self-representation so that patients can feel empowered to exercise every form of self-care, including their prosodic and solacing competence. Historically, psychoanalysts worked with "psychoanalytically talented" patients without spending a great deal of time and effort examining the relationship of these patients' emotions to psychosomatic diseases, addictive mechanisms, issues of self-care, and self-esteem regulation. The expanding scope of psychoanalysis has required work with patients with whom it is imperative to pay attention to these issues.

Observations from analytic work with posttraumatic, alexithymic, and psychosomatic patients have a great deal to offer to everyday analytic treatment. No patients are free from some of these unpopular problems. When psychoanalytic theory postulated that the cause of neuroses was trauma, the understanding of the nature of trauma was at its incipience and not based on a broad perspective and long-term studies of the sequels of traumatization.

REFERENCES

The paper on which this chapter is based was presented at a panel on affect regulation at the International Congress of Psychoanalysis, Santiago, Chile, August 27, 1999.

Bibring, R. (1953). The mechanism of depression. In P. Greenacre (Ed.), *Affective disorders*, pp. 13–48. New York: International Universities Press.

Brenner, I. (2001). *Dissociation of trauma: Theory, phenomenology and technique*. Madison, CT: International Universities Press.

Bucci, W. (1988). Dual coding: A cognitive model for psychoanalytic research. *JAPA*, 33: 571–608.

Dorpat, T. (1985). *Denial and defense in the therapeutic situation*. Northvale, NJ: Jason Aronson.

Dorsey, J. (1971). *The psychology of emotions*. Detroit, MI: Wayne State University Press.

Freud, S. (1926/1961). Inhibitions, symptoms and anxiety. *Standard Edition*, 20, pp. 77–115. London: Hogarth Press.

Horton, P. L. (1981). *Solace, the missing dimension in psychiatry*. Chicago: University of Chicago Press.

Kardiner, A. (1941). *The traumatic neuroses of war*. New York: Hoeber.

Krystal, H. (1971). Trauma: Considerations of intensity and severity. In H. Krystal and W. G. Niederland (Eds.), *Psychic traumatization*. Boston: Little, Brown.

———. (1974). The genetic development of affects and affect regression. *Annual of Psychoanalysis*, 2: 98–126.

———. (1975). Affect tolerance. *Annual of Psychoanalysis*, 3: 179–210.

———. (1978a). Trauma and affect. *Psychoanalytic Study of the Child*, 33: 81–118.

———. (1978b). Self-representation and the capacity for self care. *Annual of Psychoanalysis*, 6: 209–47.

———. (1982). Psychotherapy with alexithymic patients. In A. J. Krakowski and C. P. Kimball (Eds.), *Psychosomatic medicine: Theoretical, clinical and transcultural aspects*, pp. 737–44. New York: Plenum Publishing.

———. (1988). *Integration and self-healing*. Hillsdale, NJ: Analytic Press.

———. (1995). Disorders of emotional development in addictive behavior. In S. Dowling (Ed.), *The psychology and treatment of addictive behavior*, pp. 65–100. Madison, CT: Universities Press.

———. (1999, May). Psychoanalytic approaches in trauma, alexithymia, psychosomatic and addictive problems. Paper presented at the meeting of The Michigan Psychoanalytic Society "Milestone Program."

Krystal, H., and Krystal, A. D. (1994). *Creativity and affect*, pp. 185–212. Norwood, NJ: Ablex.

Krystal, H., and Raskin, H. (1970). *Drug dependence*. Detroit, MI: Wayne State University Press.

Kumin, I. (1996). *Pre-object relatedness*. New York: Guilford.

Lifton, R. J. (1968). *Death in life: Survivors of Hiroshima*. New York: Random House.

Maroda, K. J. (1999). *Seduction, surrender and transformation*. Hillsdale, NJ: Analytic Press.

Marty, P., and de M'uzan, M. (1963). La Pensée operatoire. *Revue Psychanalytique*, 27: 345–56.

Marty, P., de M'uzan, M., and David, C. (1963). *L'investigation psychosomatique*. Paris: Presses Universitaires.

McDougall, J. (1974). The psychosoma and the psychoanalytic process. *International Review of Psychoanalysis*, 1: 437–54.

Minkowski, E. (1946). L'anesthesie affective. *Annal of Medicopsychology*, 104: 8–13.

Papousek, H., and Papousek, M. (1975). Cognitive aspects of preverbal social interactions between human infants and adults. In *Parent interactions* (Ciba symposia). New York: Associated Publishers.

Seligman, M. E. (1975). *Helplessness: On depression, development and death*. San Francisco: L. H. Freeman.

Sifneos, P. (1967, September 11–16). *Clinical observations on some patients suffering from a variety of psychosomatic diseases*. Proceedings of the 7th European Conference on Psychosomatic Research, *Acta Medica Psychosomatica*: 453–58.

———. (1972–1973). Is dynamic psychotherapy contraindicated for a large number of patients with psychosomatic diseases? *Psychotherapy and Psychosomatics*, 21: 133–36.

Taylor, G. J. (1984a). The boring patients. *Canadian Journal of Psychiatry*, 29: 217–222.

———. (1984b). Alexithymia: Concept, measurement, and application to psychotherapy. *American Journal of Psychiatry*, 141: 725–32.

Westerlund, B., and Smith, G. (1983). Perceptgenesis and the psychodynamics of perception. *Psychoanalysis and Contemporary Thought*, 6: 597–640.

Wetmore, B. J. (1963). The role of grief in psychoanalysis. *International Journal of Psychoanalysis*, 44: 97–103.

Zetzel, E. R. (1949). Anxiety and the capacity to bear it. *International Journal of Psychoanalysis*, 30: 1–12.

Chapter Fifteen

An Eye for an Eye: Fantasies of Revenge in the Aftermath of Trauma

Nina K. Thomas

Revenge has rarely commanded the attention of psychoanalysts except as an aspect of preoedipal and oedipal dynamics. This chapter addresses the intrapsychic significance of revenge in the aftermath of the kinds of catastrophic events that constitute traumas, be they war, ethnic conflict, political repression, or the like. It is proposed that revenge provides psychic stabilization by serving to shore up the individual who has experienced shame and humiliation, powerlessness, and helplessness because of traumatic events. Through the fantasy of inflicting equivalent pain and suffering on his torturer, the avenger is able to reverse the passivity of victimization and, by so doing, blunt the affect attendant to mourning. Furthermore, revenge creates a triadic relationship that links avenger and lost object through the necessary and persistent tie to the perpetrator. Attempts to disrupt fantasies of revenge potentially threaten "catastrophic grief" as a consequence. Other dimensions of the relational configurations of revenge are considered as well.

[M]en are unable to forgive what (they) cannot punish and (they) are unable to punish what had turned out to be unforgivable.

—Arendt, 1958, p. 241

One must, it is true, forgive one's enemies, but not before they have been hanged.

—Heine, as quoted in Freud, 1930, p. 110

When is punishment justice, and when is it revenge? That one shades readily into the other makes answering the question at best challenging. *The Random House English Dictionary* defines revenge as follows:

> To exact punishment or expiation for a wrong on behalf of, especially in a re-sentful or vindictive spirit. . . . Suggest a punishment, or injury inflicted in re-turn for one received. Revenge is the carrying out of a bitter desire to injure an-other for a wrong done to oneself or to those who are felt to be like oneself.

If punishment is the province of law and forgiveness the subject of theol-ogy, then to what discipline does vengeance belong? Social psychologists and cultural anthropologists, journalists, playwrights, and novelists more than psychoanalysts have focused on the subject of revenge. Psychoanalysis more often addresses the issues that underlie vengeance—memory, satiety, and mourning, among them.

With a handful of exceptions (e.g., Moss, 1986), psychoanalysts have paid scant attention to the subject of revenge itself and even less to revenge as a phenomenon that occurs apart from preoedipal and oedipal dynamics (Akhtar, 2002; Horney, 1948; Searles, 1965). What little attention has been paid embeds revenge in aggression and addresses it in that context or in terms of the vicissitudes of attachment (cf. Lichtenberg and Shapard, 2000).

As a by-product of trauma, however, fantasies of revenge rise to particular importance, especially in light of the significance of how mourning is or is not dealt with. Herman (1992) and others (particularly Searles, 1965) posit that re-venge is a form of resistance to mourning, implying that adequate mourning would obviate the need for revenge. Indeed, Volkan (2000) notes that the fail-ure of those generations that have experienced great traumas to mourn their losses consigns future generations to complete the mourning of the preceding ones. He proposes that much of the causes of cycles of interethnic violence can be accounted for by the unmourned losses of earlier generations.

This chapter addresses the intrapsychic significance of revenge in the after-math of the kinds of catastrophic events that constitute traumas, be they war, ethnic conflict, political repression, or the like. It will *not* consider the devel-opmental fault lines around attachment and separation but rather those exter-nal traumas experienced in the world of the child, adult, family, and commu-nity. It is my thesis that for some people, fantasies of revenge serve to maintain the memory of and link to the lost object, whether that be self-representation that has been lost or another. The fantasies become necessary to ward off cat-astrophic grief. For others, fantasies of revenge serve, as Hamber (2002) sug-gests, as a voice of protest particularly in the absence of what is experienced as adequate acknowledgment of what those seeking vengeance have endured.

It is more problematic when fantasies of revenge are enacted in reality, however. When such occurs, particularly on a group or national scale, the cycles of violence that Volkan (1997, 2000) discusses are unleashed.

REVENGE IN A RELATIONAL CONTEXT

> If you are looking for revenge you must first dig two graves. One for your enemy, the other for yourself. (Middle Eastern proverb).

That person-directed violence occurs within a relational context is self-evident. This relational configuration must be held in mind in thinking about how such traumas are metabolized by the survivor. The trauma of torture or other person-directed violence robs the victim of agency over his own body, of a sense of security and effectiveness in the world, and of his "beliefs in a fair and meaningful world" (Gorman, 2001, p. 444). Such a catastrophic experience also produces incomparable shame and humiliation, a sense of helplessness, powerlessness, and alienation. Survivors of the Rwandan genocide—eight hundred thousand people were massacred, most by machete attacks, within a one-hundred-day period—were extraordinarily relieved to learn that they were not alone in the experience of such brutality. They had envisioned that there was something uniquely shameful about them because they had been subjected to such a horrific experience (L. A. Pearlman, personal communication, February 2003). Such acts of unspeakable violence assail the most fundamental elements of a victim's sense of self, among them the ability to act with effect and meaning in the world. Revenge, however imperfectly, offers the fantasy of restitution of agency, self-determination, power, and order, a restoration of narcissistic intactness to use a psychoanalytic vocabulary.

Akhtar (2002) contends that "some *revenge* is actually good for the victim" (p. 179; emphasis in the original). He asserts that revenge animates the ego, counteracting the passivity wrought by victimization. In vengeful fantasies, the avenger reverses the dynamics of victim and victimizer, the victim *becomes* the victimizer, restoring a sense of power that had been lost in being the object of the perpetrator's hatred. It reverses the dominance-subjugation equation of victim and victimizer through the imagined reversal of roles between them.

But along with the reversal of roles, victim and victimizer are relentlessly joined to one another. This insistent presence of the victimizer makes him or her impossible to forget and, even more, makes it impossible to forget the trauma that occurred at the victimizer's hand. Boris (1990), writing from a very different though still relevant perspective, addresses the "obtrusiveness" of the bad object that makes it "impossible to become oblivious to." The quality of obtrusiveness, the impossibility of *not* remembering, is a hallmark of revenge.

In being tied to his victimizer, the victim trades being the *object* of the hatred projected by his tormentor to being the *subject* who holds that hatred within himself with all the potential for dehumanization as a subject who is entitled. "The dehumanization is what made me want revenge" (Blumenfeld, 2002, p. 167). Vitka Kovner, one of the "Avengers" in post–World War II Germany, had been a resistance fighter in Lithuania during the war. She blew up railroad tracks. After the war she helped to organize a plot against the Germans that would have poisoned the water of German towns, thereby inflicting collective punishment. When one of the leaders of the group was arrested, their plan shifted to poisoning the bread of German war prisoners. More than two thousand Nazi prisoners had to have their stomachs pumped of the arsenic with which their bread had been laced.

In contrast, Mario Villani, a prominent Argentine physicist who survived four years in Argentina's detention camps during the period of the "Dirty War" notes:

> [T]his torturer, this guy torturing me *now*, is a man like me. I mean I knew very well that I had never and would never use an electric prod on anyone. But it was important for me to realize that he was not a martian, not a cockroach, but a man like me. . . . Because if I looked at them like martians, I was doing the same thing they were. I was like them. So it helped me survive day to day, but even more importantly, I could inhabit my self. (Feitlowitz, 1998)

Villani's struggle against his torturer's splitting enables him to retain a coherent sense of himself rather than devolve into the "piece of shit" that would be the complement to the other's "Martian."

Fantasies of revenge not only enact identification between victim and victimizer but also threaten to launch the survivor into repeated images of violence that can, as Herman notes, "be as arousing, frightening and intrusive as images of the original trauma" (1992, p. 189). It is the potential for the trauma to be unleashed in experiences of reliving that makes clinical work so delicate an undertaking. Just as victim and victimizer can become indistinguishable, so, too, the boundaries that contain experience by dimensions of past, present, and future similarly can collapse into one another. For the clinician unfamiliar with such phenomena, the indeterminateness of when events being described occurred can be disorienting or, at the very least confusing. The inexperienced therapist may wind up focusing on a clarification of chronology as a defense against his or her own identification with both victim and perpetrator in the drama unfolding in the consulting room.

MEMORY AND REVENGE: THE FIGURATION OF TIME IN THE CONTEXT OF TRAUMA AND REVENGE

[W]hat seems apparent in the former Yugoslavia, in Rwanda, and in South Africa is that the past continues to torment because it is *not* the past. These places are not living in a serial order of time but in a simultaneous one, in which past and present are a continuous, agglutinated mass of fantasies, distortions, myths and lies. Reporters in the Balkan war often discovered, when they were told atrocity stories, that they were uncertain whether these stories had occurred yesterday or in 1941, 1841 or 1441. For the tellers of the tales, *yesterday and to-day were the same*. (Ignatieff, 1997, p. 186; emphasis added)

"Forgive and forget." "Let bygones be bygones." These are the often-invoked watchwords of communities in which survivors live in the aftermath of trauma. Such phrases capture the expectation that survivors of trauma will be silent about their suffering. Indeed, those facile clichés articulate the effective demand that whatever injury may have been suffered will be resolved speedily through repression or at the very least through denial. By contrast, some suggest that in the aftermath of such traumas as periods of political repression there is "too much memory." However, revenge defies the impetus to forget that otherwise characterizes periods following political violence, most particularly among bystanders to that violence.

Revenge is about remembering, or, rather, about being unable to not remember. Their inability to forget by virtue of the relentless remembering to which the intensity of their experience subjects them often results in survivors being ostracized by others in the community. The response of many in Israel to survivors of the Holocaust is one well-documented example (Moses, 1993). For the larger society, remembering the past is itself threatening, whether or not others have lived through the particular trauma. The risk is that they could themselves become potential victims, a threat warded off by the refusal to listen to the stories of suffering and survival.

For example, Argentina's Madres de la Plaza de Mayo, the mothers who every Thursday have marched in the square in Buenos Aires, a constant reproachful presence, their white scarves bearing photographs of their murdered or abducted family members, have been called by some "Las Locas." To the consternation of those who would prefer to forget, the mothers insist both on finding their "disappeared" of Argentina's Dirty War and on holding to account those responsible for the kidnapping, torture, and murder of their loved ones.[1] The mothers, as too the widows of the disappeared in Guatemala and the families of South Africa's apartheid victims, all struggle to find the "time" for their living. One brother of a Chilean victim remarked: "After they killed my brother, my father sat in a sofa to wait for death. We went to Argentina to a two-room apartment. My father continued sitting and my mother hanging photographs of my brother" (Berryman, 1993). It is commonly reported that one or more members of a family insists on maintaining the rooms of their disappeared loved ones as they were when they were abducted. Time is suspended with families remaining frozen in events that recur in memory without change.

In some cases of political repression, for example in Guatemala after the period of "La Violencia" or following the Dirty War in Argentina or the Pinochet years of military dictatorship in Chile, as, too, in Israel after the Holocaust, a readiness exists to blame the victim for failing to allow the larger community to relegate events to the past. The victim is thereby vaulted into conflict with a larger social group for failing to forget and for being rooted in the experience of the past.

MEMORY, MOURNING, AND REVENGE

The injury that has been forgiven should be forgotten, but the fact that it has been forgotten should be remembered. (Nootebaum, quoted in Akhtar, 2002, p. 178).

Nootebaum's paradox is both painful and difficult to negotiate. It speaks to the essential need for memorializing traumatic events. Ignatieff (1997) suggests that revenge is a way for the living to "keep faith with the dead" (what Hamber [2002] calls the "invisible pact") and to perpetuate their memory by continuing their project. Revenge may be said to memorialize the dead, taking the place of mourning. It becomes a "souvenir" of the lost loved one. What Gabbard (2000) says about hatred: "To hate is to hold onto an internal object in an unforgiving way," (p. 411) is equally applicable to revenge. What is held onto unforgivingly, the object of vengeance is the link to the lost loved one. A triadic relationship is thereby constructed. The relationship promises to revitalize the otherwise often emotionally dead trauma survivor by restoring a connection to the lost loved one (whether the loved one is the ideal self lost by the destructive dehumanizing effect of the particular trauma suffered or the lost "other") through the medium of revenge against the perpetrator. Relinquishing fantasies of revenge threatens the avenger with the loss of that connection, what revenge has, at least in part, served to avoid.

Renouncing revenge threatens what, in other contexts has been called a "catastrophic sense of grief" (Gabbard, 2000, p. 415), a confrontation with loss that the individual experiences as so potentially shattering to his world as to be impossible to get beyond. Imagining revenge may become psychically organizing for the avenger in a way similar to how some (Gabbard, 2000; Lichtenberg and Shapard, 2000) have described hatred. Gabbard (2000) writes that "the patient's identity may be organized around hatred, and the modification of the hating self-representation or of the hated object representation is often experienced as a form of annihilation" (p. 415). Revenge serves a similar function of shoring up the self against the collapse that can occur in the absence of such an energizing focus. For some patients, fantasies of revenge serve as the sandbags for levees against an impending flood. Threatened by memories of their traumas, patients may engage their vindictive imaginings to bolster themselves against the sense of degradation or loss of self-esteem attendant to the circumstances of their survival. Mourning, which requires a capacity to sustain a sense of self in the midst of profound loss, then is the opposite of revenge.

There is, however, an additional dimension, that is, the implicit violence whether in real or symbolic forms of revenge. Ignatieff (1997) offers that the discourse of violence in revenge can only be mitigated if alternative means of "reconciliation" offer commensurate respect and recognition of the dead as well as others who suffered.

There is a significant difference in the potential psychic outcome of fantasies of revenge as compared with acts of revenge. Fantasies of revenge leave the possibilities for completion open and continually available to revision, engaging the active imagination of the avenger, thereby enlivening him. To the extent that such fantasies are incomplete the victim-avenger can maintain an inequality, even a moral superiority between his victimizer and himself. When revenge is enacted, however, the equality between victim and victimizer becomes concretized. Such identity forces the newly minted victimizer to confront his own dehumanizing acts or to deny them in an equivalent manner to the original perpetrator.

ALTERNATIVES TO REVENGE

In the aftermath of decades of apartheid-era violence in South Africa, the Truth and Reconciliation Commission (TRC) was established. It took as its aim the "healing" of the country through the creation of an agreed on history of the events of the preceding period. A consensually established history, it was reasoned, would leave little room either to revise or to forget the human rights abuses of the past. With the slogan "revealing is healing" to promote its mission, the commission undertook the reconciliation of the nation in the interest of preempting the kind of vengeful violence that had characterized ethnic conflicts within Africa (as well as other regions) for a long time. Similar truth commissions have been undertaken in more than two dozen countries throughout the world.

Such political legal processes have adopted the understandable agenda of political stability. Doing so, however, can make the pursuit of forgiveness premature, as some have argued has been the case in South Africa. The "confession-amnesty-forgiveness" equation that was established in, for example, the South African TRC process, privileges "forgiveness" without recognizing the rage that still needs space for working through before revenge can yield to reconciliation (cf. Hamber [2002] for further elaboration of this point). The experience of one widow of apartheid-era violence serves as a counterweight to the forgiveness of others. One of the assassins of what came to be known as the Cradock Four sought her forgiveness, asking for a fifteen-minute meeting with her. "You have teased our grief for nearly twelve years . . . and you think you can reconcile in fifteen minutes," she said on meeting him (Meredith, 1999).

Another example is that of Marius Schoon, who, as a senior member of the African National Congress was, with his wife, active in the antiapartheid movement. Jeanette Schoon and her six-year-old daughter Katryn were murdered by a letter bomb sent to them by a South African security agent, Craig Williamson. Williamson had known the Schoons, even staying with them in their home at one point. During Williamson's amnesty hearing before the TRC, Schoon described his wife's and daughter's deaths: "On the wall just opposite the entrance door, there was blood from floor to ceiling, that had been Jenny, Sir. On the floor, there was a little pile of flesh and blood which had been Katryn." (South African Truth and Reconciliation Commission, 1998a).

Williamson's attorney then asked Schoon a series of questions:

Mr. Levine: Since Mr. Williamson's part in your personal tragedy for which he has come forward to seek amnesty, have you spoken to him?

Mr. Schoon: I have no intention of speaking to Mr. Williamson ever in my life, Sir.

Mr. Levine: Mr. Schoon, I would like to refer you to an article where I think you said that the only time you wish to see Mr. Williamson is down the sights of an A4 rifle.

Mr. Schoon: Sir, I said, over the sights of an AK47.

Mr. Levine: I tender Mr. Williamson to you at the next adjournment of these proceedings, in the spirit of reconciliation, do you accept this tender?

Mr. Schoon: No, Sir.

Finally, Schoon added that he found it "unfair and embarrassing" to be called on to reconcile with Williamson (South African Truth and Reconciliation Commission Hearings of the Amnesty Committee, 1998a).

VICTIM AND VICTIMIZER

Violence must be done to the self before it can be done to others. (Ignatieff, 1997, p. 54)

In being made the object of violence, the victim's humanity is erased. So, too, is that of the victimizer. Both victim and victimizer are reduced to one dimension. Perpetrator and victim each lay claim to all goodness in himself and badness in the other. The processes of externalization, projection, and projective identification work for both players in the trauma drama.

In the hearings for amnesty referred to earlier, Williamson remarked:

> On many occasions when we had discussions and I talked to (the) men and women that served under me, dehumanizing of the enemy occurred. . . . I don't believe that I or other people in the security forces involved in this type of war could have in fact done what was done if they saw the enemy as individual human beings. (South African Truth and Reconciliation Commission Hearings of the Amnesty Committee, 1998b)

It is difficult to know to what degree such testimony is genuine, particularly when receiving amnesty is uncertain. Even assuming its genuineness, still it is useful to unpack Williamson's remark: "I don't believe that I or other people in the security forces involved in this type of war could have in fact done what was done if they saw the enemy as individual human beings." First, the other has been made "the enemy," a container for the hated aspects that are disavowed in oneself and ascribed entirely to an "other." What then happens to the subject in the complementary processes to such "dehumanizing of the enemy?" Points of shared humanity are denied. The other serves an iconic role. The "despised," constructed entirely out of projections, becomes an object related to solely in terms of his symbolic function as the enemy. In constructing the enemy, however, one is similarly unidimensionally defined as a complementary enemy, thereby creating a paranoid universe.

Furthermore, any empathic regard for his victims is absent from Williamson's confession. If confession occurs without acknowledgment of the injury suffered by the victim then can it truly be regarded a confession? Recognizing the injury that has been done to another, acknowledging his or her humanity, seems the *sine qua non* of "confession." A capacity for guilt implies being able to see the other's wounds, to experience the other empathically. Absent such acknowledgment, perpetrator and victim continue to exist in a one-dimensional space.

REVENGE AS AN ATTEMPT AT ACKNOWLEDGMENT

In the face of the personal powerlessness experienced by victims of political abuses, revenge is often an attempt at achieving acknowledgment of what they have lived through. This is made more compelling in those circumstances where at least a partial intent is to undo the perpetrators' falsification of the victims' experiences. The Serbian denial of the massacre in Srebenica of more than seven thousand Muslim men and boys and the denial of the Holocaust are two of a score of dramatic examples. Postconflict recovery processes of truth commissions and war crimes trials afford victims the opportunity to have their stories heard and their experiences validated.

Two elements of the truth commission process have particular bearing for their impact on witnesses' recovery or resort to revenge—the provision of amnesty and the naming of names of perpetrators of human rights abuses. Amnesty, while politically expedient for reconstructing civil society, serves to effectively appropriate victims' stories to the sociopolitical aim of political stability. Thus, victims of the military juntas in South America remain vulnerable to coming on their torturers in the course of their daily lives on buses, in restaurants, and in the course of shopping (cf. Feitlowitz, 1998). The provision of blanket amnesty leaves victims with often little recourse but revenge as a way of achieving recognition of their experiences.

Equally, the legislation mandating the truth commissions in Argentina and Chile expressly prohibited the release of names of those held responsible for human rights abuses, though they might be, and were named, in victims' reports.[2] Although their stories were collected, victims were denied the opportunity to hold their perpetrators accountable by naming them in a public forum. Prohibiting the release of perpetrators' names subsumes the victim's experience to a presumed higher-order priority of national reconciliation, further denying victims the recognition of their experiences. Judicial concerns at times may have to trump individual psychological ones. But when the decision is made to do so, great care and due acknowledgment deserve to be made.

It is the victims' determination to wrest recognition of their humanity through holding the perpetrator to account that fuels their participation in such postconflict recovery processes as truth commissions and war crimes tribunals. Consciously and unconsciously, victims believe they can reinstate their narcissistic intactness by holding their victimizers publicly accountable. Many clinicians have seen something similar in those patients who have experienced sexual and physical abuse who often express the wish to "go public" by making their perpetrator's abuse a matter of public record. Such determination needs to be accounted for in the operation of truth commissions and tribunals since revenge can be an alternative strategy for winning acknowledgment of what the victim has experienced.

IMPLICATIONS FOR PSYCHOANALYSIS

It is often difficult to sit quietly with those patients whose wounds are so profound or who hold onto their wounds so tenaciously as to fuel vengeful fantasies. We are confronted with our patients' ideas of restitution through causing equivalent pain and suffering to their torturers. Such patients test our capacity to be neutral and to resist leaping to promoting "forgiveness" prematurely in denial of our own as well as our patients' sadism. The capacity to forgive is predicated on the ability to contain ambivalence, the both/and position: to see the self and other as both good and bad, both strong and weak, both threatening and fearful. Arriving at such a position involves mourning what has been lost, concretely as well as metaphorically. Among the things that make mourning problematic is the challenge to remember what has been lost without perpetually reliving that loss. We return to the Nootebaum paradox: "The injury that has been forgiven should be forgotten, but the fact that it has been forgotten should be remembered" (quoted in Akhtar, 2002, p. 178).

This chapter has taken as its focus the experiences of those who have survived unspeakable horrors of human rights abuses in the context of political upheaval. Primarily, the analyst must acknowledge the patient's capacity to survive so as to feed the restoration of healthy narcissistic self-regard. Fantasies of revenge shore up the patient's rent fabric of narcissism. To the extent that such fantasies retain the injury to the self as well as imagined injury to another, their maintenance contains a store of bitterness and pain. Invariably the analyst will become the recipient of that bitterness as the transference transforms her into the patient's perpetrator. The demanding task confronting the analyst is to survive such transformation. If something is to substitute for revenge, it can only do so to the extent that the patient no longer needs to activate his or her rage as a way of feeling whole.

Equally relevant for psychoanalytic work is that vengeful fantasies fill the space of uncertainty about whether the trauma will occur again. Bromberg (1996; cf. also Gabbard, 2000) addresses this issue in his consideration of how the patient's preparing for trauma serves to protect him against the unexpected. Anticipating misfortune magically installs a belief in being in control. By creating a dreadful scenario, the patient is neither subject to potential surprise nor unprepared when trauma occurs. Fantasies of revenge anticipate the trauma's repetition with a ready supply of justifiable rage in stock.

It is useful to distinguish between fantasies of revenge and acts of revenge. In part the distinction revolves around the intersubjective and relational configurations contained within each. Fantasies of revenge enliven an otherwise alienated and often affectively deadened person within an interpersonal universe in which she has impact and agency. The appeal of vindictive fantasies lies in how we are transformed. No longer weak or subservient, we are mighty and virtuous and fueled with the righteousness of redressing a wrong. The imagined revenge exacts suffering that, we tell ourselves, is only what the "other" is due. Thus, we are also morally vindicated by the punishment that we have accomplished. Equally, in the instance of revenge imagined, there is a triadic relationship constructed in which the perpetrator is the critical link between avenger and sufferer. Acts of revenge, however, risk precipitating the repetition of untamable cycles of violence and threaten the avenger with a similar dehumanizing effect as occurred in response to the original trauma.

There is some research evidence that both gender and culture influence the pursuit of revenge. For example, revenge appears to be significantly more prominent a component of Eurocentric cultures as compared with non-Eurocentric ones (Kadiangandu, Mullet, and Vinsonneau, 2001). This is not so surprising when we consider the reification of the individual as compared with the group in European cultures. By contrast, Central African tradition holds "penal sanctions . . . as a failure in the forgiveness process" (p. 505). The guiding principle of the justice processes in Central African cultures is the reintegration of the harm doer into society. "[I]t is bad for society to dismember itself" (p. 505).

What little attention has been paid to the role of gender has addressed forgiveness as opposed to revenge. There is some tendency for women to be less forgiving than men are, as reported in a study of those who came before the South African TRC (Kaminer, Stein, Mbanga, and Zungu-Dirwayi, 2001). However, another study comparing forgiveness amongst Congolese and French citizens found no such gender differences (Kadiangandu, Mullet, and Vinsonneau, 2001). It is difficult to extrapolate from the limited findings concerning gender differences in forgiveness to gender factors in revenge. Although more women came before the South African TRC than did men, their testimony was less often about abuses against them than against their husbands and sons. There was a notable lack of testimony about their own suffering. It is unclear if women more often than men would be likely to seek the restoration of the lost relationship through fantasies of revenge or if men have more authorization to pursue revenge as a justified means of accomplishing punishment. Certainly, the ability for women to express or enact rage for the injustices they experience against themselves is severely constrained in many cultures. How gender influences revenge fantasies remains unclear but would be valuable to examine further.

CONCLUSION

Most of what has been written from a psychoanalytic perspective addresses revenge in terms of developmental failures in the negotiation of preoedipal and oedipal challenges. My attention, however, has been to how revenge provides psychic stabilization in the aftermath of such catastrophic events as constitute traumas.

Revenge serves to shore up the individual who has experienced shame and humiliation, powerlessness, and helplessness as a consequence of traumatic events such as those that arise out of political repression and the events of war. Through the fantasy of inflicting equivalent pain and suffering on his torturer, the avenger is able to reverse the passivity of victimization and, by so doing, blunt the affect attendant to mourning. Equally, the intrapsychic implications of revenge for both victim and perpetrator have been elaborated, particularly as these relate to mourning. Revenge creates a triadic relationship that links avenger and lost object through the necessary and persistent tie to the perpetrator. Attempts to disrupt fantasies of revenge potentially threaten "catastrophic grief" as a consequence.

Revenge has been called a form of protest that restores a voice to victims (Hamber, 2002) and serves to memorialize their suffering. In the rush to "heal" nations recovering from periods of conflict, what is often overlooked is that survivors need and have the right to outrage. National efforts at reconciliation are intended to avert cycles of vengeance. Yet, recovery processes that privilege forgiveness prematurely can sow the seeds of instability by overlooking the need to express rage. The opportunity for survivors to achieve registration of their suffering is a prerequisite for defusing cycles of revenge. Being animated by anger as against the stance of passive victimization is a critical dimension of revenge. What constitutes a further challenge is finding a means for the anger of survivors to have a place for expression without the need for its being enacted. A challenge for psychoanalysts as well as the larger society lies in how to create a space safe enough for expressing the patient's rage, while enabling both participants and the process of analysis to survive.

NOTES

1. The issues played out in the demonstrations of Las Madres involve a complex combination of politics and psychology. The mothers became politicized by their search for an answer to what had happened to their loved ones in the face of continuous denials by the authorities about any knowledge of them at all. Family members were required to apply for death certificates to process estates and to go on with their lives, not unlike the situation facing surviving family members of the American September 11 tragedy. But to do so meant they were the effective "killers" of their sons, daughters, fathers, husbands, mothers, and wives. As Suarez-Orozco (1991) writes: "It is as if giving up hope is betraying their children."

2. This was not the case in the South African TRC where the legislation establishing the truth commission expressly provided for the release of names.

REFERENCES

Akhtar, S. (2002). Forgiveness: Origins, dynamics, psychopathology, and technical relevance. *Psychoanalytic Quarterly*, 71:175–212.

Arendt, H. (1958). *The human condition.* Chicago: University of Chicago Press.

Berryman, P. E. (Trans.). (1993). *Report of the Chilean National Commission on truth and reconciliation.* Notre Dame, IN: Notre Dame Law School.

Blumenfeld, L. (2002). *Revenge: A story of hope.* New York: Washington Square Press.

Boris, H. (1990). Identification with a vengeance. *International Journal of Psycho-Analysis*, 71: 127–40.

Bromberg, P. M. (1996). Hysteria, dissociation and cure: Emmy von N revisited. *Psychoanalytic Dialogues*, 6: 55–71.

Feitlowitz, M. (1998). Night and fog in Argentina. In M. Feitlowitz (Ed.), *A lexicon of terror*, 40–74. New York: Oxford University Press.

Freud, S. (1930/1961). Civilization and its discontents. *Standard Edition*, 21: 110. London: Hogarth Press.

Gabbard, G. (2000). Hatred and its rewards: A discussion. *Psychoanalytic Inquiry*, 20: 409–20.

Gorman, W. (2001). Refugee survivors of torture: Trauma and treatment. *Professional Psychology: Research and Practice*, 32: 443–51.

Hamber, B. (2002). Symbolic closure in post-conflict societies. *Journal of Human Rights*, 1: 35–53.

Herman, J. (1992). *Trauma and recovery.* New York: Basic Books.

Horney, K. (1948). The value of vindictiveness. *American Journal of Psychoanalysis*, 18: 3–12.

Ignatieff, M. (1997). *Warrior's honor: Ethnic war and the modern conscience.* New York: Henry Holt.

Kadiangandu, J. K., Mullet, E., and Vinsonneau, G. (2001). Forgivingness: A Congo–France comparison. *Journal of Cross-Cultural Psychology*, 32: 504–11.

Kaminer, D., Stein, D. J., Mbanga, I., and Zungu-Dirwayi, N. (2001). The truth and reconciliation commission in South Africa: Relation to psychiatric status and forgiveness among survivors of human rights abuses. *British Journal of Psychiatry*, 178: 373–77.

Lichtenberg, J., and Shapard, B. (2000). Hatred and its rewards: A motivational systems view. *Psychoanalytic Inquiry*, 20: 374–88.

Meredith, M. (1999). *Coming to terms: South Africa's search for truth.* New York: Public Affairs.

Moses, R. (Ed.). (1993). *Persistent shadows of the Holocaust: The meaning to those not directly affected.* Madison, CT: International Universities Press.

Moss, D. (1986). Revenge and forgiveness. *American Imago*, 43: 191–210.

Searles, H. (1965). *Collected papers on schizophrenia and related subjects.* New York: International Universities Press.

South African Truth and Reconciliation Commission, Hearings of the Amnesty Committee. (1998a). *Amnesty hearings, decisions and transcripts: On resumption.* 5

November 1988–Day 4. Pretoria, 2–6 November 1998, Part 4. Retrieved on June 29, 2004, from http://www.doj.gov.za/trc/amntrans/1998.htm

———. (1998b). *Amnesty hearings, decisions and transcripts: On resumption: 17 September 1998–Day 8*. Pretoria, 8–29 September 1998, Part 8. http://www.doj.gov.za/trc/amntrans/am1998.htm

Suarez-Orozco, M. (1991). The heritage of enduring a dirty war: Psychological aspects of terror in Argentina. *Journal of Psychohistory*, 18: 469–505.

Volkan, V. (1997). *Blood lines: From ethnic pride to ethnic terrorism*. Boulder, CO: Westview Press.

———. (2000). Traumatized societies and psychological care: Expanding the concept of preventive medicine. *Mind and Human Interaction*, 11: 177–93.

Chapter Sixteen

A Humanistic Approach to the Psychology of Trauma

Ilene Serlin and John T. Cannon

A humanistic approach to trauma focuses on the transformative therapeutic agents that help individuals move from "victim" to "survivor" and "thriver" in the face of trauma. A depth qualitative study of those transformative factors among participants identified as survivors or thrivers reveals themes of meaning and confrontation with death. Case vignettes illustrate how a humanistic clinician helps individuals find meaning in their lives and move beyond prior levels of functioning to transcendence.

And yet the day will come—I hope soon—when we shall understand that suffering can elevate man as well as diminish him. Neither ends nor means, it can bring him closer to his truth and his humanity.

—Elie Wiesel

How can suffering elevate us? How can it bring us closer to our truth and our humanity? These questions are at the heart of the humanistic psychological exploration of trauma. Humanistic psychology offers a philosophical and experiential perspective on how the experience of trauma can bring us closer to our humanity. This chapter will give a brief overview of humanistic psychology as it relates to trauma, followed by case illustrations. During the Loma Prieta earthquake in 1989 I (Ilene Serlin, coauthor of this chapter) volunteered at a San Francisco shelter that housed mostly elderly residents. I also participated with the Red Cross in their collaboration with the local psychological associations. After several days of being a participant-observer in the daily life of the shelter, I gathered the stories that I heard at the bedsides. My coauthor, John Cannon, then analyzed these stories for themes of psychological qualities that distinguished "thrivers" from "survivors" and "victims." These themes will form the basis for a humanistic approach to the psychology of trauma.

A HUMANISTIC PERSPECTIVE ON TRAUMA

What is trauma and why is it so disturbing? From a humanistic perspective, a traumatic event is a disruption so serious that it threatens our existence, shaking the foundation of who we are and who we once were. It makes us face our basic helplessness and mortality. Trauma confronts us with the reality of death, ripping through our sanitized lives and our monumental denial of death. Noted philosopher Ernest Becker (1973) says, "The idea of death, the fear of it, haunts the human animal like nothing else; it is a mainspring of human activity—activity designed largely to avoid the fatality of death, to overcome it by denying it in some way that is the final destiny for man" (p. ix).

Trauma is a wake-up call, reminding us that everyone dies. "To speak of 'the meaning of human life' is to speak also of death, for the fact that we all die is an inescapable part of our lives" (Gillman, 1997, p. 17). It is only by confronting death, however, that we can find the courage to create (May, 1975).

Every trauma that we experience shatters our sense of coherence and meaning. Since ancient times, rebuilding or creating new meaning from traumatic events has been central to all healing processes (Frank, 1963) and expressive therapies (Gersie, 1984; Moreno, 1977). Meaning is patterned as a story, inner narrative, or myth that provides a coherent explanation for why events happen and shows us the lessons that can be drawn from them.

How do we explain the recent spectacle of a flaming space shuttle hurtling through the air? It is incomprehensible to us; we have no current mythology to explain chariots of fire. Most traditional psychology and debriefing approaches to trauma do not help us either to confront death or to discover new meaning. The focus of these approaches is to restore a sense of normalcy and personal control in life. While restabilization is obviously necessary, it is not enough.

The humanistic approach to trauma encourages us to confront our death anxiety, to discover new meaning and identity, and to move from beyond prior levels of functioning to transcendence (Calhoun and Tedeschi, 1998; Carver, 1998; Decker, 1993; Egendorf, 1982; James, 1902; Parappully, Rosenbaum, van den Daele, and Nzewi, 2002; Updegraff and Taylor, 2000). According to Decker (1993, p. 41), "Trauma has demanded that we question our ordinary perspectives, search for a more expanded self-concept, and restructure our value hierarchy." Recent research shows that trauma can bring "growth and greater well-being" (Ickovics and Park, 1998, p. 238). This "better-off-afterward experience" (Carver, 1998, p. 247) is called "thriving" or rebirth. "Out of the ashes, at times literal ashes of loss and death . . . a phoenix-like process of internal restructuring may be set in motion which can have a liberating, regenerative effect upon the survivor" (Shabad and Dietrich, 1989, p. 467).

Humanistic psychology helps us deal more realistically with two central paradoxes of the human condition: freedom and fate (Schneider and May, 1995) and uniqueness and unity (Schneider, 1999) that are at the heart of the psychology of trauma. We struggle to understand with our rational senses and ask, Why was I in this place at this time? Why did I live and my neighbor did not? Did I do right? Did I do wrong? How could God allow such a terrible thing to happen? Is there evil? Is there a God?

These questions of meaning and faith take us inevitably to the realm of religion or spirit. Anthropologist Geertz (1973) observed that religion's role is to formulate "conceptions of a general order of existence" (p. 19). An ordered existence is coherent. Its opposite is chaos, which is intolerable.

Trauma plunges us directly into chaos. "To paraphrase Genesis, we would be exiled, and to be in exile is to tumble into chaos" (Geertz, 1973, p. 23). Chaos is associated with punishment for the original sin in the Garden of Eden, as well as a loss of innocence. The loss of innocence is one of the most pernicious effects of trauma, particularly after experiences such as the Holocaust, when basic faith in humanity or God is shattered. Moving beyond innocence and despair to a new way of knowing, called a "second naiveté" by Ricoeur (1967, 1976) and "radical amazement" by Martin Buber, Franz Rosenzweig, and Abraham Heschel, is a profound psychological and spiritual challenge. Psychologists working with this group have shown evidence of "vicarious traumatization," sometimes sharing the cynicism and hopelessness of the victim (Pearlman and Saakvitne, 1995), and sometimes demonstrating a "deep existential sense of shame" at what they see (Danieli, 1994). Some cope by relying on God or religious beliefs (Hood, Spilka, Hunsberger, and Gorsuch, 1996). Humanistic psychology, which has a strong philosophical and spiritual dimension, can help both victims and caregivers work directly with these issues.

When thrown into existential crisis, one's world crumbles. Nothing is what it appears to be. Trauma is experienced subjectively as the confrontation with nothingness, death, and terror. It can be terrifying to feel as though one is living in a universe with random death and suffering. How do we summon the courage to keep choosing life? How can psychologists help? (Serlin, Aanstoos, and Greening, 2000).

FROM DECONSTRUCTION TO RECONSTRUCTION

Human beings have always told stories. Telling stories helps us gain perspective on our lives. Narrative, as the psychological use of storytelling to rebuild coherence, has gained increasing attention as both a form of psychotherapy

(Epston, White, and Murray, 1992; Howard, 1991; Omer and Alon, 1997; Polkinghorne, 1988; Rotenberg, 1987; Sarbin, 1986; Schafer, 1983; Spence, 1986) and a method used in the human sciences (Polkinghorne, 1988; Howard, 1991; Erikson, Erikson, and Kivnick, 1986). Life stories of highly generative individuals show that they rewrite their narratives more optimistically (McAdams, Diamond, de St. Aubin, and Mansfield, 1997). Telling the story of the disruption and the reconstruction of a meaningful life can provide a narrative to deal with the existential sense of loss and help recover meaning, faith, and courage (Epting and Leitner, 1992; Feinstein and Krippner, 1988; Howard, 1991).

Humanistic psychologists have studied those transformative factors that help victims of natural and human-made disasters become survivors and finally thrivers (Cannon, 2002). While most of the psychological literature focuses on the pathology of trauma, Cannon and Serlin analyzed transcripts of survivors of the Loma Prieta earthquake for a clear understanding of those transformative moments in which survivors become thrivers. Analysis of the transcripts revealed themes that helped them transform disaster into meaning: work, courage, independence, relationships, family, and spirituality. Through reflecting on these themes, survivors were able to clarify their priorities and make changes in their lives (Cannon, 2002).

THE PRESENT NEED FOR HUMANISTIC PSYCHOLOGY

As we write, America in the midst of a new war in the Middle East. Despair, a sense of meaninglessness, and conduct disorders are increasing among high school students (Fox and Serlin, 1996). Use of psychological services and psychiatric medication at college counseling centers has increased significantly, with doubled rates of depression and suicide attempts (Goode, 2003) Consulting rooms are filled with driven thirty-year-olds having panic attacks (Serlin, personal communication, 2003). People are experiencing a new stress and vulnerability in almost all aspects of life. In response to the destruction of the Columbia space shuttle, one man said, "It was a wakeup call. . . . We're not perfect. Bad things happen to us." Another said, "So many Americans are delusional. . . . They think they are invincible. It's horrible what happened to the space shuttle. But maybe in the end, by reminding people in this country they are not all-powerful, it will do more good" (Gettleman, 2003, p. A21).

Trauma is pervasive; no one is immune. Not an isolated incident, trauma is a series of echoes and constant assaults on the nervous system. The presence of dread in everyday life has been described as "pre-traumatic stress." Trauma cannot be separated from dramatic social and political contexts and requires multidisciplinary understanding (Stewart and Fitzgerald, 2001). A psychological response to trauma must be respectful of the cultural context in which it occurs (Owusu-Bempah and Howitt, 1995). The psychology of trauma involves prevention as well as treatment. Helping others deal with the paradox of freedom and fate is a realistic preparation for the future. For example, some trauma preparation programs in Israel have brought death education classes into early school curriculum and use role-play and other experiential methods to teach children coping strategies (Ayalon, 1988). How do we live with trauma at this time, and how do we respond with psychological and spiritual maturity? The wake-up call that shattered our American innocence and destroyed our meaning systems on September 11 can hopefully prepare us for a changed world.

EXISTENTIAL AND HUMANISTIC PSYCHOLOGY

What gives us the courage to rebuild shattered lives? The philosophy of existentialism, influenced by the darkness of the war and the Holocaust, fully acknowledged the dark and tragic aspects of life (Binswanger, 1936; Kierkegaard, 1945). The ability to create despite death was, however, also part of the human condition, according to existentialist psychologist and psychoanalyst Rollo May. He bridged the more pessimistic European existential psychology and the more optimistic American humanistic psychology (Rogers, 1951).

While humanistic psychology acknowledges life's limitations, it also focuses on the potential for change. The "capacity to transcend the immediate boundaries of time, to see one's experience self-consciously in the light of the distant past and the future, to act and react in these dimensions, to learn from the past of a thousand years ago and to mold the long-time future, is the unique characteristic of human existence" (May, 1958, p. 67). Some humanistic psychologists choose to emphasize the capacity for free will (Allport, 1937; Murray, 1938; May, 1969; Wertz, 1994), and others emphasize the uniqueness of each human being. "Because each individual is a product of a unique genetic endowment, a singular history of meaningful experiences, and a never-repeated developmental progression, the totality of his or her personhood or the critical choices each makes will be unique" (Allport, p. 297).

Victor Frankl, the humanistic psychiatrist who was confined in four concentration camps during the Holocaust, found his own way to make meaning from his experience. He developed an approach called logotherapy, which was based on the fact that "in some way, suffering ceases to be suffering at the moment it finds a meaning, such as the meaning of a sacrifice" (Frankl, 1959).

Abraham Maslow, a founder of humanistic psychology and the past president of the American Psychological Association (APA), brought the study of transcendence into the field of psychology (Maslow, 1962, 1971), calling for a new kind of individual who could meet the challenges of the postwar era. "To put it bluntly, we need a different kind of human being . . . who is comfortable with change, who enjoys change, who is able to improvise, who is able to face with confidence, strength, and courage a situation with which he has absolutely no forewarning" (1962, p. 56). Maslow called this kind of individual a "self-actualizer." Long before the coaching or positive psychology movement became popular (Seligman, 1998), humanistic psychology used the language of self-actualization to describe how individuals transcend trauma.

Clinical Interventions

Given humanistic psychology's emphasis on the uniqueness of each individual and each encounter, the value of spontaneity (Perls, 1992) and personal ways of knowing (Polanyi, 1958; Serlin and Criswell, 2001; and Serlin, 1997), it follows that its clinical approach is nonprogrammatic. There are no manuals. Humanistic psychology is a process, a Socratic dialogue (Buber, 1958; Friedman, 1985) that resists quantification, manualization, and pathologizing of others people (Greening, 2001).

THE SURVIVOR OR THRIVER PERSONALITY

Research on the quality of thriving in adults and children is a recent phenomenon; the last ten years saw a shift in focus from "child survival" to "child survival and development." Child posttraumatic disorder was first named in the 1987 revised edition of the American Psychiatric Association, *Diagnostic and Statistical Manual of Mental Disorders–Third Edition*. Humanistic psychologists believe that this diagnosis is simplistic and does not identify the qualities of strength or coping that help psychologists foster these qualities in people who experience trauma. The qualities that differentiate a survivor from a victim have been described in terms of optimism, resilience, or hardiness. Optimism is a "generalized expectation of successful outcomes that is expressed in renewed efforts to attain goals, despite the disruption constituted by stressful circumstances" (p. 95). Resilience is defined as "Resourceful adaptation to changing circumstances and environmental contingencies" (J. H. Block and J. Block, 1980, p. 48). Hardiness (Kobasa, 1979; Maddi and Kobasa, 1981) is characterized by commitment, control, and challenge, and has been correlated with health (Maddi and Kobasa, 1994). The evidence suggests that hardiness protects physical and mental health, even as stressors mount. One critical aspect of hardiness is coherence, defined by Antonovsky (1979) as "confidence that . . . there is a high probability that things will work out as well as can be reasonably be expected."

Hardiness, optimism, and resiliency build what Siebert calls the survivor personality (1996). The survivor is one who "has survived a major crisis or challenge; surmounted the crisis through personal effort; emerged from the experience with previously unknown strengths and abilities; and afterwards find(s) value in the experience" (pp. 4–5).

THERAPIST TRAINING PRINCIPLES

According to humanistic theory, the most important agents of therapeutic change are the personality of the therapist and the therapist–client relationship (Bugental, 1987; May, 1989). The following are therapeutic guidelines that emphasize the development of the personal qualities of a healer in the therapist and the transformative potential of the healing relationship (Maslow 1965; Rogers, 1951). The ability to face mortality can lead to creativity and boldness in the face of death; life-changing events can be transformative; trauma involves the whole person; normalcy is socially constructed; and the human condition means living with uncertainty. Uncertainty is not a mental disorder for psychologists to treat. May (1975) described the leap of faith needed to deal with uncertainty and to leap into the unknown. Existentialists have called this the anxiety of nothingness.

A humanistic approach to trauma requires:

1. *The ability to confront one's own fears of death or darkness.* As therapists, we must ourselves confront death with a sense of inner peace. We can help others only to the extent that we can confront those fears ourselves.
2. *The ability to create life-affirming connections*: As therapeutic agents, humanistic psychologists strive to remain authentic and present with others (Bugental, 1989). Because their psychotherapeutic process is already a dialogue and mutually transformative, humanistic psychologists can move beyond traditional countertransferential problems such as "empathetic strain" (Lindy and Wilson, 1994) and "compassion fatigue" (Figley, 1995) to "posttraumatic growth" (Calhoun and Tedeschi, 1999). .
3. *Creativity and communication*: Humanistic psychotherapists draw on somatic or creative arts therapies to help participants find their voices (Elkins, 1999). The act of creativity is powerfully healing. After September 11, for example, children across the country expressed their feelings

through art. Making art objectifies experience and transforms raw feeling into image. It translates anguish into meaning and resiliency. Current research suggests that through the expression of stories of suffering, individuals may begin to organize, structure, and integrate emotionally charged experiences (Pennebaker, 1990). "Research in physiological psychology has shown that the visualization of a particular situation or action creates nearly as much neurological activity as actually encountering that situation" (Kolb, 1984, in Dodge, 2003). A recent study of eminent writers who had experienced existential crisis as an aspect of childhood abuse found that despite high incidences of depression, nervous disorders, anxiety, and dread, they were able to rework the trauma into autobiographical and literary narratives (Rivers-Norton, p. 292).

4. *Development of strengths in self and other.* Humanistic psychotherapists know their own strengths and weaknesses and can help others identify their unique coping skills. They are often self-disclosing or transparent in their clinical work with others. Their supportive expressive approach empowers clients to see options, create alternatives, and take concrete action steps.

5. *Personal psychological and spiritual maturity.* Humanistic psychologists support positive growth such as a greater appreciation of paradox (Calhoun and Tedeschi, 1998), an increased sense of faith (Pearlman and Saakvitne, 1995), and a spiritual well-being (Brady, Guy, Poelstra, and Brokaw, 1999) and have wrestled with the sense of meaning in their own lives and do not minimize the importance of it for their clients (Maslow, 1965). They are not resistant to conversations about God and may have a spiritual practice of their own. Humanistic psychologists can model a psychology which does not deny death and which respects the contributions of the elderly in our society.

CASE STUDIES

Margarita

This case was chosen because of its importantance to the new psychological challenges posed by globalization. Given the enormous loss of sense of place, culture, and traditional safety nets, people are increasingly disoriented and in states of chronic stress. Insurance code 309.29 lists Adjustment Reaction, Culture Shock, as a mental disorder. Psychotherapists who work with such displaced people may need to help them confront their pasts, which may include human-made trauma and death, and support them to create a meaningful new life and identity.

Margarita is a graduate student in her mid-thirties. She has been in the United States since she was an infant and left Nicaragua with her mother. Her mother is from a wealthy family in Nicaragua and her father is a Caribbean revolutionary "international terrorist" who fought with the Sandinista Revolution. Margarita struggled to understand herself, to establish her identity, and to assert her independence. To do this, she had to confront lingering shadows of death, meaninglessness, fate, and isolation.

Trauma haunts her. It is not a single event in her life, but an ongoing presence, containing echoes of earlier traumas. Her most recent traumatic shock is culture shock from a recent life-changing experience. Margarita went back to Nicaragua to come to terms with her past. She stayed three and one-half years, digging deeply into the culture of her family and village. The culture shock began as soon as she arrived. "My first experience began with assimilating to the farm life on the opposite side of the road of Sandino's hometown, called Niquinohomo (Masaya), where my granny is from. This area is very indigenous. After being an only child in San Francisco, I found myself feeding ten mouths, including family and plantation workers."

The most powerful moment came when she found her father. "I met my father for the first time when my mother visited and took me to him. Miguel was shot during the revolution by contras, while walking towards his tank. His troop got infiltrated and he was the only one to survive. Dad was trained in Spain, Brazil, and Bosnia in the areas of agriculture, ecology, biological and guerrilla warfare. Later, he would gain the title of 'international terrorist.' . . . found him at his mother's in Managua, unable to walk or speak coherently. 'I'm sorry I . . . I wasn't there.'"

Beginning to understand and carry her father's legacy, she now combined it with her own talents for poetry and drama as the activities director of a school back in the United States where she brought together black and Latino, elitist and poor children in an annual music contest. Empowering the youth was what she called "Doing Dreams." Being a conscious bridge between two worlds was "perturbing." It was, however, clearly her path and her calling. Asked what her legacy would be, she said that she would combine her mother's organizational abilities to make things happen with her father's socialist beliefs for a strong determination to make things "right by people."

The return to the United States was surreal and shocking. One thing that kept her sanity and gave her perspective was writing. She noted, "I didn't just need to deal with the present, but also had to accept my situation as a real part of life, realizing that so many others in my country had learned at infantile stages to adapt to harsh challenges of survival.

Seeing her legacy as the intricate blending of her mother's and father's projects and culture helped her make her own bridge to "doing [her] dreams" with "immense momentum of determination to make things happen." She left much stronger in her sense of self. "Nicaragua fully blessed me in gaining strong cultural identity, understanding my people and working through a sense of survival."

Discussion

This client confronted death on many levels and discovered renewed life in herself. She confronted absurdity in the form of the surreal culture clash and senseless killings and found meaning in her bridge-building work. She faced the tragic and heroic faces of her fate, but found freedom in her own life. Finally, she found her unique identity in the midst of a rich community and kept them all in balance. This therapeutic approach corresponds to the four challenges of existential psychotherapy as outlined by Yalom (1980): life (and death); meaning (and absurdity); freedom (and determinism); and community (and aloneness).

A humanistic psychotherapeutic approach helped her to find her own voice. Therapy was egalitarian and included mentoring. I (coauthor Ilene Serlin) connected her with graduate-student organizations specializing in multicultural agendas that gave her more support to transform her trauma into a vocation as a "wounded healer." Wounded healers represent an example of turning trauma into helping others. Margarita described it as "I bring my stuff here, but am learning life skills. . . . I do not leave this door feeling disempowered." For this student, that meant claiming her nonverbal, non-Western roots of the African Yoruba religion. Listening to tribal music, she danced and noted, "We make the magic at midnight—the world is calling out for us as healers, women, elders." She described how the immigrant experience deprived her of female role models, as her aunts and cousins "all went to school, worked, intermarried . . . had to show success, own a car, a home, individuate and live on their own."

She heard her grandmother's voice inside her urging her to marry a white man and reclaim an upper-class life in the United States. As the therapist, I joined her story, laughing and crying along with her. The connectedness was experiential. According to Margarita, the "feeling was immediate, there was an immediate commitment to her and to the space we created together. Therefore, I was able to make a commitment to myself." The commitment helped her feel "safe," which she "needed to be her authentic self, and encounter my own optimism and resilience." I shared stories of my own ancestors and their immigration experience and the common existential task of going back to one's roots for nourishment, while moving forward into a new identity in a new country. I became, in Margarita's words, a "bridge" helping her move through different worlds. Since trauma results in so many aspects of splitting, having a bridge is essential. It helped Margarita "transcend boundaries of what America puts here, and putting in place my own boundaries to survive." To do this, she learned to draw on psychological and spiritual resources, some from her own heritage: "In our traditions, we're spiritual people. The voice to navigate through the society and bridge has to come from there." Margarita's spirituality was not "up," but "down here, from the earth and the heart."

The dialogue was framed not as a therapist treating a disorder in another person, but as shared universal human experience. Through opening to a spiritual and archetypal perspective, we were both able to move beyond personal disruption into a transcendent experience.

Loma Prieta Earthquake

Natural disasters do not face us with problems of human evil, but they do confront us with other dilemmas of death, meaninglessness, fate, and isolation. Crisis intervention with survivors of the earthquake elicited the following stories of how they transformed trauma into thriving. These elderly residents were scared and were having difficulty sleeping. Because I (coauthor Ilene Serlin) helped them set up their sleeping cots, I talked to them as they went to sleep, developing a strong therapeutic rapport and trust. Being flexible allowed me to establish a context for the therapeutic conversation, as well as to have access to a time for effective use of relaxation and imagery. In contrast, a later program that was created by a local psychological association and the Red Cross set up counseling services far away from the area in a parking lot, with sign-up sheets on desks. Consequently, very few people attended.

Residents in the shelters freely shared their fears. All experienced danger and the potential of death. Some overcame this with altruism, by focusing on helping other people:

> I wasn't feeling emotionally scared. I was calculating the possibilities and it seemed quite possible that the house would fall apart, it was so violent. I was just trying to think what is the best place to go, where should I put this lady so that it's safest for her. I really was thinking what to do with her more than about me.

A shy student learned to reclaim life and be present in the here and now:

> I used to be really quiet and wouldn't say anything and if somebody bugged me I wouldn't say much. But now I just say what's on my mind. I don't think there's time to sit around and just get mad about stuff and not say anything. The time is here and now to speak your mind.

Another responded to death as a challenge: "And when the earthquake happened . . . felt ready to die. . . . I felt like I was being called to be as brave as I possibly could."

Cannon (2000, 2002) observed that "the survivors celebrated life. They understood that when it was their time to go, it was their time to go. In the meantime, they chose to celebrate life" (p. 145). The survivors also gained meaning from their experience. One survivor who had lost her husband was advised by authorities to evacuate her apartment. She responded by finding a meaningful alternative:

> I figured I'd go to O'Brien Army Hospital where I used to work. . . . I was a nurse there. And I'd help out there. . . . So I went there, and the guard screamed at me at the gate and says, "What do you want?" And I said, "I'm going to volunteer here. I worked here." So they let me in, and I went to my old unit.

Another survivor who was traveling from another country gave up her vacation and overcame bureaucratic obstacles to volunteer with the Red Cross:

> I didn't want to just sit around, you know, I came here for a vacation. . . . there was a lot of cleaning up . . . and things that needed to be done. . . . I was watching one of the news broadcasts and they had the phone numbers up for volunteers and so I called it. . . . Their phones were jammed so I just came down here anyway.

One student expressed the sense of meaning that commitment to self and others provided:

> I also have a little time left over. I'd like to help. I guess it's a feeling of purpose and accomplishment, that's why I'm here. Not because I feel like a saint or anything like that. Just give some purpose to my time that would otherwise be wasted.

Another student cried as he expressed how he drew a sense of meaning from the earthquake:

> Right now? What I feel is important is finding myself what . . . sort of comes from within me . . . rather than . . . being on the fast track treadmill. . . . what else is important is people . . . some of the most important things that I, I've seen this last week are the relationships that I've had with a few very, very special people. . . . the relationships are true treasures. . . . I'm doing a lot of reflecting about . . . what I want to do with my career . . also what I want to do about spirituality.

Some found and expressed meaning through religion, such as a renewed interest in church or God: "I thank God every night for taking care of me and letting me get through each day." Others found meaning through a personal sense of spirituality.

They also expressed their choice to live in terms of gratitude. Several of the elderly residents made comments like: "I had a full life. . . . Grateful I lasted this long"; "I was shook up, but you don't want to stay shook up. You're just grateful you're alive. You're all in one piece"; and "Well, I feel very fortunate because we were all together . . . and that was a real blessing."

The dilemma of freedom and fate was taken up by a student in a group discussion:

> We don't have control over certain things but we can make choices. . . . Its like we're a boat and we've got a rudder to steer our way. We don't have control over the tides, we don't have any control over the wind, but we have a responsibility and an ability to keep our hand on the rudder and at least try to keep the ship from sinking or steering it the right way. Or choosing to go places where, you know, the weather is OK to the best of our ability.

Some reached out to others at a time of crisis. One spoke of her commitment to self and others that helped her through the isolation:

> What struck me most was the attitude of the people in the building. Everybody came around. They were not only checking on me but they were checking on everybody else, and it was the first time since WWII that I have felt this same spirit of, we're all in it together to do the best we can. . . . So everything that I had I cut in half and we shared.

Some of these residents showed wisdom, transcending the dualities of trauma. They were able to experience the paradoxical loss and celebration of life simultaneously. "It's OK to feel lousy. Yes we're grateful but it's still lousy and that's OK." "This is real and vivid and poignant. . . . what happened to my home and my things has brought all of those . . . to life for me in a way that was never the case before. And I'm glad of that." Other expressions of transcendent moments were "kind of changed me into a better person. It may sound corny, but its true"; "I realized I had a soul"; and "I saw this really, really beautiful warm light and it was enveloping and healing. . . . I was really trembling and crying hard. . . . I just felt this wonderful love."

DISCUSSION

During the crisis of the Loma Prieta earthquake, humanistic psychologists who offered counseling observed survivors who were confronted with death, meaninglessness, fate, and isolation. Some, who were thrivers, were able to become more authentically themselves and create a more meaningful life.

Humanistic psychotherapy demonstrated a flexibility to therapeutic role and context that allowed people to feel respected as successful human beings, not as psychiatric disorders. In humanistic psychotherapy, the transference reaction is not analyzed, as much as lived consciously. In the earthquake shelter on dark evenings, I (coauthor Ilene Serlin) became the granddaughter listening to the elderly transmitting their stories, the family friend who might help someone place a call. All were neighbors, sharing stories about family and other memories, and caring about each other. More important than playing a role, I was present. Bugental says, "Presence is immensely more than just being there physically. . . Presence is being there in body, in emotions. It is being totally in the situation . . . in relating, in thoughts, in every way. Although fundamentally, presence is a unitary process or characteristic of a person in a situation, accessibility and expressiveness are its two chief aspects" (Bugental, 1978, pp. 36–37.) The conversation was client centered, as the flow of the narrative was established by the resident and no alienating forms or standardized questions were used. Questions of value and meaning were explored when initiated by the resident.

CONCLUSION

A humanistic psychology approach to trauma can bring human beings closer to truth and humanity. It does this by supporting trauma survivors in their confrontation with fundamental existential issues of death and meaning and by helping them move to new levels of psychological and spiritual growth. By transcending the trauma, survivors can become thrivers.

NOTE

Thanks to Moji Agha and students at Saybrook Graduate School and the University of Santa Cruz for helping with data collection. Special thanks to the elderly at the Loma Prieta shelter and the Red Cross volunteers for their inspiring stories.

REFERENCES

Allport, G. (1937). *Personality: A psychological interpretation.* New York: Henry Holt.
American Psychiatric Association. (1987). *Diagnostic and Statistical Manual of Mental Disorders* (3rd. ed., revised). Washington, DC: Author
Antonovsky, A. (1979). *Health, stress, and coping: New perspectives on physical well-being.* San Francisco: Jossey-Bass.

Ayalon, O. (1988). *Rescue!* Haifa, Israel: Nord Publications

Becker, E. (1973). *The denial of death.* New York: The Free Press.

Binswanger, L. (1936). *Being-in-the-world.* New York: Harper Torch Books.

Block, J. H., and Block, J. (1980). The role of ego-control and ego-resiliency in the organization of behavior. In W. A. Collins (Ed.), *Minnesota symposia on child psychology.* Hillsdale, NJ: Erlbaum.

Brady, J. L., Guy, J. D., Poelstra, P. L., and Brokaw, B. F. (1999). Vicarious traumatization, spirituality, and the treatment of sexual abuse survivors: A national survey of women psychotherapists. *Professional Psychology: Research and Practice*, 30: 386–93.

Buber, M. (1958). *I and Thou.* New York: Collier Books.

Bugental, J. (1978). *Psychotherapy and process.* New York: McGraw-Hill.

———. (1987). *The art of the psychotherapist.* New York: Norton.

———. (1989). *The search for existential identity.* San Francisco: Jossey-Bass.

Calhoun, L. G., and Tedeschi, R. G. (1998). Beyond recovery from trauma: Implications of clinical practice and research. *Journal of Social Issues*, 54: 357–71.

———. (1999). *Facilitating posttraumatic growth: A clinician's guide.* Mahwah, NJ: Erlbaum.

Cannon, J. (2002). *Personal experiences of the 1989 Loma Prieta earthquake.* Doctoral dissertation, Saybrook Graduate School, San Francisco, California.

Carver, C. S. (1998). Resilience and thriving: Issues, models, and linkages. *Journal of Social Issues*, 54: 245–66.

Danieli, Y. (1994). Countertransference, trauma, and training. In J. P. Wilson and J. D. Lindy (Eds.), *Countertransference in the treatment of PTSD*, pp. 368–88. New York: Guilford.

Decker, L. R., (1993). The role of trauma in spiritual development. *Journal of Humanistic Psychology*, 33 (4): 33–46.

Dodge, W. (2003). *An experiential vs. cognitive approach to treating oppositionally defiant adolescents with family therapy.* Unpublished doctoral dissertation, Saybrook Graduate School, San Francisco, California.

Egendorf, A. (1982). The postwar healing of Vietnamese veterans: Recent research. *Hospital and Community Psychiatry*, 33: 901–08.

Elkins, D. (1999). *Deep poetic soul: An alternative vision of psychotherapy.* Paper presented at meeting of Division 32, Presidential Address, American Psychological Association 107th Annual Convention, Boston, Massachusetts.

Epting, F., and Leitner, L. (1992). Humanistic psychology and personal construct theory. In F. Wertz (Ed.), *Humanistic Psychologist*, 20: 243–59.

Feinstein, D., and Krippner, S. (1988). *Personal mythology.* Los Angeles: Jeremy P. Tarcher.

Figley, C. R. (1995). Compassion fatigue as secondary traumatic stress disorder: An overview. In C. R. Figley (Ed.), *Compassion fatigue: Coping with secondary traumatic stress disorder in those who treat the traumatized*, pp. 1–20. New York: Brunner/Mazel.

Fox, K., and Serlin, I. (1996). High-risk youth and the transition to adulthood. In Lyons, A. (Ed.). *The Humanistic Psychologist* [special issue], 24: 349–63.

Frank, J. (1963). *Persuasion and healing*. New York: Schocken Books.

Frankl, V. (1959). *Man's search for meaning*. New York: Praeger.

Friedman, M. (1985). *The healing dialogue in psychotherapy*. New York: Jason Aronson.

Geertz, C. (1973). Religion as a cultural system. In *The interpretation of cultures*. New York: Basic Books.

Gersie, A. (1984, March). Have your dream of life come true: Myth-making in therapeutic practice. *Journal of Drama Therapy*.

Gettleman, J. (2003, February 3). As Iraq war looms, a new sense of vulnerability. *New York Times*, A21.

Gillman, N. (1997). *The death of death*. Woodstock, VT: Jewish Lights Publishing.

Goode, E. (2003, February 3). More in college seek help for psychological problems. *New York Times*, A11.

Greening, T. (2001). [Commentary by the editor]. *Journal of Humanistic Psychology*, 41: 4–6.

Hood, R. W., Spilka, B., Hunsberger, B., and Gorsuch, R. (1996). *The psychology of religion*. New York: Guilford.

Howard, G. (1991). Culture tales: A narrative approach to thinking, cross-cultural psychology, and psychotherapy. *American Psychologist*, 46: 187–97.

Ickovics, J. R., and Park, C. L. (1998). Paradigm shift: Why a focus on health is important. *Journal of Social Issues*, 54: 237–44.

James, W. (1902/1961). *Varieties of religious experience*. New York: Collier Books. Princeton, NJ: Princeton University Press.

Kierkegaard, S. (1945). *The sickness unto death* (Walter Lowrie, Trans.). New York: Doubleday Anchor Books.

Kolb, D. (1984). *Experiential learning: Experience as the source of learning and development*. Englewood Cliffs, NJ: Prentice-Hall.

Lindy, J. D., and Wilson, J. P. (1994). Empathetic strain and countertransference roles: Case illustrations. In J. P. Wilson and J. D. Lindy (Eds.), *Countertransference in the treatment of PTSD*, pp. 62–82. New York: Guilford.

Maddi, S., and Kobasa, S. (1981). Intrinsic motivation and health. In H. I. Day (Ed.), *Advances in intrinsic motivation and aesthetics*, pp. 120–33. New York: Plenum Press.

———. (1994). Hardiness and mental health. *Journal of Personality Assessment*, 63: 265–74.

Maslow, A. (1962). *Toward a psychology of being*. Princeton, NJ: D. Van Nostrand.

———. (1965). A philosophy of psychology: The need for a mature science of human nature. In R. Severin (Ed.), *Humanistic viewpoints in psychology*. New York: McGraw Hill.

———. (1971). *The farther reaches of human nature*. New York: Penguin Books.

May, R. (1953). *Man's search for himself*. New York: Norton.

———. (1975). *The courage to create*. New York: Bantam Books.

———. (1989). *The art of counseling*. New York: Gardner Press.

May, R., Angel, E., and Ellenberger, H. (1958). *Existence*. New York: Simon & Schuster.

McAdams, D. P., Diamond, A., de St. Aubin, E., and Mansfield, E. (1997). Stories of commitment: The psychosocial construction of generative lives. *Journal of Personality and Social Psychology*, 72: 678–94.

Moreno, J. (1977). *Psychodrama*. New York: Beacon House.

Parappully, J., Rosenbaum, R., van den Daele, L., and Nzewi, E. (2002, Winter). Thriving after trauma: The experience of parents of murdered children. *Journal of Humanistic Psychology* (Sage Publications), 42 (1): 33–71.

Pearlman, L. A., and Saakvitne, K. W. (1995). *Trauma and the therapist: Countertransference and vicarious traumatization in psychotherapy with incest survivors.* New York: Norton.

Pennebaker, J. (1990). *Opening up: The healing power of expressing emotions.* New York: Guilford.

Perls, L. (1992). *Living at the boundary* (J. Wysong, Ed.). Highland, NY: Center for Gestalt Advancement.

Polanyi, M. (1958). *Personal knowledge.* Chicago: University of Chicago Press.

Polkinghorne, D. (1988). *Narrative knowing and the human sciences.* New York: SUNY Press.

Ricoeur, P. (1967). *The symbolism of evil* (E. Buchanan, Trans.), pp. 351–52. Boston: Beacon Books.

———. (1976). *Interpretation theory: Discourse and the surplus of meaning.* Fort Worth: The Texas Christian University Press.

Rogers, C. (1951). *Client-centered therapy.* Boston: Houghton Mifflin.

———. (1961). *On becoming a person.* Boston: Houghton Mifflin.

Sarbin, T. (Ed.). (1986). *Narrative psychology: The storied nature of human conduct.* New York: Praeger.

Schneider, K. (1999). *The paradoxical self.* New York: Humanity Books.

Schneider, K. J., and May, R. (1995). *The psychology of existence: An integrative, clinical perspective.* New York: McGraw-Hill.

Seligman, M. (1999, August). The president's address. *American Psychologist*, 54: 559–62.

———. (1997). History and future of humanistic psychology: Presidential talk. Paper presented at the meeting of the American Psychological Association Convention, Chicago, Illinois.

Serlin, I. A. (2002, September). Psychologists working with trauma: A humanistic approach. *APA Monitor*, 33 (8): 40.

———. (2003, January–February). Fellow as mensch: A humanistic perspective. *The California Psychologist*: 25–28.

Serlin, I. A., Aanstoos, C., and Greening, T. (2000). History of Division 32. In D. Dewsbury (Ed.), *History of Divisions*, pp. 85–112. Washington, DC: American Psychological Association.

Serlin, I. A. and Criswell, E. (2001). Humanistic psychology and women: A criticalhistorical perspective. In K. Schneider, J. Bugental, and J. Pierson (Eds.), *Handbook of humanistic psychology: Leading edges of theory, research, and practice.* Thousand Oaks, CA: Sage.

Shabad, P. C., and Dietrich, D. R. (1989). Reflections on loss, mourning, and the unconscious process of recognition. In D. R. Dietrich and P. C. Shabad (Eds.), *The problem of loss and mourning: Psychoanalytic perspectives*, pp. 463–70. New York: International Universities Press.

Siebert, A. (1996). *The survivor personality.* New York: Berkley/Perigee Publishing.

Stewart, F., and Fitzgerald, V. (Eds.). (2001). *War and underdevelopment: The economic and social consequences of conflict.* Oxford, England: Oxford University Press.

Updegraff, J. A., and Taylor, S. E. (2000). From vulnerability to growth: Positive and negative effects of stressful life events. In J. H. Harvey and R. D. Miller (Eds.), *Loss and trauma: General and close relationship perspectives*, pp. 3–28. Philadelphia: Brunner-Routledge.

Wiesel, E. (1978). *A Jew today.* New York: Random House.

Wertz, F. (Ed.). (1994). *The humanistic movement: Rediscovering the person in psychology.* Fort Worth, TX: Gardner Press.

Chapter Seventeen

Empathic Strain, Compassion Fatigue, and Countertransference in the Treatment of Trauma and PTSD

John P. Wilson

This chapter explores the deep psychodynamic significance of empathy in the treatment of trauma-related syndromes. The themes of trauma-specific transmission are discussed, and encoded information that manifests in patients' transference reactions can be readily decoded through a process of empathic sustainment. New concepts are discussed, including modes of empathic attunement and empathic strain and identification of factors that facilitate successful treatment outcomes.

Listen to the voices of trauma. Can you hear their cry? Their pain exudes emotional blood from psychic pores. Nights are broken by frightening intrusions from ghosts of the past. Bodies hold memories, secrets and scars locked into sinew, glands and neurons. Weary souls of the abyss seeking peace in their souls.

—John P. Wilson (2003)

Trauma is part of the human condition and ever present in the lives of ordinary people throughout the world. Traumatic events punctuate recorded history in a manner parallel to momentous achievements that advance civilization. Traumatic events are the product of human intentions, the randomness of nature and acts of God. Traumatic experiences are *archetypal* in nature and have their own psychological structure and energy (Wilson 2002). Traumatic experiences vary along many different "stressor" dimensions and have simple and complex effects on the human psyche (Wilson and Lindy, 1994). Traumatic experiences not only are different qualitatively and quantitatively from each other but are subjectively experienced in individual ways through the life history of the person, the filters of culture, language, and the nature of injury produced to the organism in all its integrated wholeness. Trauma may strike at the surface or the deepest core of the self—the very "soul" and in-nermost identity of the person.

Traumatic experiences may lead to transformations of the personality, spirit and beliefs, and understanding of the meaning of life. In that same sense, trau-matic experience can alter life-course trajectories and have multigenerational legacies (Danieli, 1988). In a broader perspective, massive or catastrophic trauma may permanently alter, eradicate, or damage entire societies, cultures, and nations (Lifton, 1967, 1993). Indeed, as an *archetypal* form, trauma can be a psychic force of enormous power in the individual and collective uncon-scious of the species. Unmetabolized trauma of a violent nature caused by wars, terrorism, torture, genocide, ethnic cleansing, and the purposeful abuse of others may unleash destructive forces within the fabric of civilization (Freud, 1915–1917; Jung, 1929; Wilson, Friedman, and Lindy, 2001).

Trauma that is unhealed, unresolved, and unintegrated into a healthy balance within the self has the potential to be repeated, reenacted, acted out, projected, or externalized in relationships and give rise to destructive and self-destructive motivational forces. When we look at the "mandala" of trauma in archetypal forms, its presentation can be the vicissitudes of the demonic in its Mephistophelean forms, expressing the excruciating, depraved, unholy, sinister, vile, and evil elements of the Darkness of Being that intrusively invades the sanctity of human experiences and seraphic essence of loving relationships.

Listening and observing carefully one will see that the voices and faces of trauma are "snapshots" of the existential struggle to remain whole, to remain vital, and to restore that part of the self damaged by trauma. The stories of the survivors are inevitably universal variants on the archetypal abyss of the trauma complex (Wilson, 2002). However, for the therapist, counselor, and others in the healing role, the encounter with the voices and faces of the trauma patient is difficult and painful. Listening empathically to trauma sto-ries is taxing and stressful. To remain sensitive and finely attuned to the in-ternal experience of the individual's psychological injuries requires more than understanding that an event was traumatic—it requires skill and a capacity to use empathy to access the inner scars of the psyche and the organism. Effec-tive posttraumatic therapy or treatment is more than the application of a clin-ical technique; it is the capacity to facilitate self-healing by helping the pa-tient mobilize and transform the negative energies, memories, and emotions of Post-Traumatic Stress Disorder (PTSD) and associated conditions into a healthy self-synthesis that evolves into a positive integration of the trauma experience. However, in the role of a professional therapist, counselor, and so on, there is a significant and certain risk of empathic distress, compassion fa-tigue, "burn-out," and more technically (or traditionally), countertransference processes (CTRs).

EMPATHY, EMPATHIC ATTUNEMENT, AND EMPATHIC STRAINS IN TRAUMA WORK: THE VOICES AND FACES OF TRAUMA

Listen to the voices of trauma. They are like the top edge of a wave about to break over turbulent water, beneath which lies a potentially deadly rip curl ready to drag the person under the surface.

TRAUMA VIGNETTES: IMAGES OF THE ABYSS EXPERIENCE

FDNY

"All I could make out was his FDNY badge—*the rest was indescribable— crushed, burnt remains of a firefighter*" (Disaster Worker, World Trade Center, 2001, italics mine).

Crushed

"My best friend was crushed underneath a building and asked me for help, so I tried desperately to help her, but my efforts meant nothing, so I ran away with another friend. *I hear her voice even now; I'll never be able to forget it*" (Hiroshima, 1945, italics mine).

Frozen in Agony

"There were charred dead bodies scattered all over a burned-out field that once was a residential area. *Bodies frozen in agony reaching up toward the sky.* Unidentified bodies left like that for days" (Hiroshima, 1945, italics mine).

Innocent Brains

"Her [10-year-old] head was injured and *her brain stuck out of her fractured skull where she hit the hard concrete surface*. Her left eye popped out onto her cheekbone and blood was coming down her face. She was still alive but unconscious. I see that at night when I try to go to sleep" (Civil Disaster, Anonymous Patient, Wilson 1989, italics mine).

Skinned and Pinned

"We were on search and destroy patrol when we came across his body [American soldier]. *He had been captured, pinned to a tree and skinned alive*. His genitals were stuck in his mouth and his eyes were still wide open" (Vietnam Veteran, Bon Song, 1969, italics mine).

Rape Your Children or We Will for You

"I was given another choice: I rape my daughter or the guard does. I tried to reason with them, telling them that she was an innocent child. I pleaded with them not to humiliate her, not to hurt her, but instead to *rape me*, to do with me what they wanted. They laughed and repeated the two choices. I looked at my daughter hoping that she would tell me what to do—our eyes met and I knew that I could not save her from those wretched men. I lowered my eyes in *shame* to keep from seeing my daughter abused. One guard held my face up, forcing me to watch this horrible scene. *I watched, motionless, as she was raped before me and her little brother. When they were through, they forced me to do what they had done to her*. My own daughter, my son forced to watch it all. How could anyone do that? What kind of men are they? What kind of father am I?" (Ortiz, 2001, italics mine).

Death's Aroma

"I can still *smell those dead bodies in my nostrils even now*" (Buffalo Creek Dam Disaster, 1974, italics mine).

Human Rain

"It was his last day in Vietnam. He insisted on walking 'point' [first] man. We were near Cambodia—the Black Virgin Mountain area of Tay Ninh. He never saw the command detonated landmine as he stepped on it. *Pieces and parts of his body rained on us—like a shower in blood and pieces of flesh. It smelled horrible. We found what was left of his head and put it in a body bag*" (Vietnam Veteran, Tay Ninh, 1970, italics mine).

Footsteps

"I could tell by my stepfather's footsteps on the wooden hallway floor whether he was drunk when he came down the hallway to my room. When he started in on me [sexual abuse], *I left my body and went away* to a corner of the room, in the ceiling, with my teddy bear" (Sexual Abuse Victim, 1993, italics mine).

No Flesh, and Lots of Bones

"*I saw one woman—one corpse with the flesh removed from the bones . . .* then about 100 people, mostly women and children, none of them with clothes on, lying on the asphalt pleading for help" (Hiroshima, 1945, italics mine).

Eyes, Ears, Nose, and Mouth

"I went over and started taking pieces of wood from the woodpile, and I found a body. I picked up the back of her hair, what hair she had left. She didn't have no clothes on, and *I turned her over and the blood and mud and water came out of her eyes and nose and mouth and ears.* I had to go get clean" (Buffalo Creek Dam Disaster, 1974, italics mine).

Top Gun in Thailand

"We were on duty in Thailand and received a call that an F-4 Phantom jet was on fire. It landed burning and we [paramedics] responded. We put out the fire and opened the cockpit. The smoke was still pouring out. *I took off the pilot's helmet and blood ran out of his eyes and mouth from his burnt, black face.* He was dead. It was his birthday and he was my best friend. We had planned to party that night" (Vietnam Veteran, Thailand, 1968, italics mine).

Frankenstein or Freddy Kruger?

"When I woke up after surgery in the burn unit in Japan, they made me look at myself in the mirror. The nurse handed me a mirror and I threw up [vomited] when I saw the black deformed image that used to be me. I cried for days—it was like looking at a disfigured Halloween mask of a monster" (Vietnam Veteran, 1970, Army Burn Unit Hospital, Japan).

Blood on the Tracks

"The Serb snipers were active 24 hours a day. *My first hour in Sarajevo, I saw dead bodies on the tram line—women, children and old men—killed in the afternoon—blood on the railroad/tram tracks.* What kind of war is this? That was just the beginning—everyday some innocent person was killed by a sniper. There were so many killings that they began burying people in the city parks. Bosnia was an evil genocide and the senseless killing has never left me. *I still see the blood on the tracks and remember those innocent people*" (John P. Wilson, 1993, Sarajevo, italics mine).

Towering Inferno

"I still *hear the screams* and the sounds of the towers collapsing. *I wake up in a sweat, seeing the bodies falling from the tower*—it could have been me—I was on my way to work there [Tower I]. The next day, September 12, 2001, I couldn't feel much of anything. *I was just numb and completely overwhelmed.* New York seemed dead to me. I can still *smell* ground zero in my mind—*it won't ever go away*" (World Trade Center, 2001, italics mine).

POW's Crucifixion

"We were forced to watch as he [American POW] was tortured. They staked him to a pole and broke his bones with a metal rod, starting with his shins. *They inserted a sharp barb-hooked hanger in his belly into his liver and tugged on it until he screamed as if dying.* They shot him slowly, starting with his legs and worked their way up his body, one bullet at a time until the last one killed him . . . a shot in the forehead. *He had a look of horror in his eyes.* We were forced to watch and warned not to try to escape the camp in Cambodia, where we got caught. He tried to escape and we were given a lesson" (Vietnam Veteran, 1970, italics mine).

No Limits to Marquis de Sade

"During his first arrest 'L' tried to commit suicide, but he was shot in the leg and taken directly to a notorious prison. There he was immediately beaten brutally over his entire body, hooded, and subjected to falanga [beating the souls of the feet]. The torture continued and 'L' was forced to lick up blood from the floor. He was suspended on a cross, kicked over his entire body, and kept awake for days. Not broken by the physical torture, 'L' was subjected to psychological torture. He was placed in a room between a mother and a daughter. The mother was whipped and ordered not to make a sound or the daughter would be abused. He was subjected to mock execution several times; on one such occasion he was drenched with litres of petrol, and the torturers fumbled with matches in front of him.

"Threatened with homosexual rape and beaten to unconsciousness, he also received electrical torture around the ears. His nose was broken repeatedly, and he developed bleeding from the stomach and hemorrhagic vomiting. He was suspended both head up and feet up, and burned with cigarettes over his body. He could exhibit a multitude of scars from these burns. Subsequently, 'L' was isolated for about a year in a very small, completely barren cell. In this new prison he was also subjected to Russian roulette and deprivation of food. Later because of gangrene of the feet he was taken to a hospital outside the prison, and there he managed to escape" (Torture Victim, Rehabilitation Center for Torture Victims [RCT], 1992).

As we read these vignettes,[1] they evoke our own associations, images, feelings, and attempts to frame a context and perspective of understanding. Each voice is unique, real, and a part of history, past and present. These authentic vignettes are only excerpts of much more detailed trauma stories of some of my patients. Metaphorically, they are like the top edge of a wave breaking over the surf. The trauma therapist must "flow" with the wave or risk the currents of the rip curl forces beneath the surface.

EMPATHY, EMPATHIC ATTUNEMENT, AND EMPATHIC STRAIN IN TRAUMA WORK

Trauma work challenges the therapist's or professional's capacity to be empathic and effective when working with clients who suffer from PTSD. Seeing the faces of trauma clients and listening to their voices, their individual stories, is a form of traumatic encounter in itself that has been called secondary traumatization (Stamm, 1999), vicarious traumatization (Pearlman and Saakvitne, 1997), compassion fatigue (Figley, 1997), empathic strain (Wilson and Lindy, 1994), trauma-related affective reactions (Wilson and Lindy, 1994), and trauma-related CTRs. Trauma work and the role of the therapist require immersion into the phenomenal reality and ego-space of the person suffering from PTSD. *Empathic attunement* is the capacity to resonate efficiently and accurately to another's state of being; to match self-other understanding; and to have knowledge of the internal psychological ego-states of another who has suffered a trauma. Empathic capacity is the ability for empathic attunement and varies greatly among therapists working with PTSD patients. Effective posttraumatic therapy rests on the cornerstone of empathic ability and the capacity to sustain empathic attunement. Empathic capacity is a fundamental dimension of the psychobiology of empathy. In a sense, a good therapist or listener of a trauma victim has the ability to "decode" trauma stories and trauma-specific transference (TST) reactions (Wilson and Lindy, 1994).

Empathic attunement is part of the process of decoding, a "signal detection" of information flowing from the patient (sender) to the therapist who, in some basic respects, serves as a radio or satellite receiver that hones in on a signal being transmitted and decodes its message. Indeed, it is entirely possible to speak of TST reactions, the disclosure of the trauma story, and the "flow" of affect, cognition, and behaviors (including especially nonverbal actions) as multi-leveled messages being sent from the patient to the therapist. If visualized, one would see patterns or images of energy in waveform emanating from the trauma client and manifesting themselves in various amplitudes and frequencies as they flow in patterns toward the receptor site of the therapist's mind and consciousness. However, to adequately receive and decode the message without "noise" or "interference," the therapist must have the capacity for decoding, interpreting, and responding back with information to the client as part of the interactional communication sequence (Wilson and Lindy, 1994). Historically, Freud used a similar metaphor in one of his few writings on countertransference. In a paper written in 1912 to general medical practitioners, he stated:

> To put it into a formula: [the therapist] must turn his own unconscious like a *receptive organ toward the transmitting unconscious of the patient. He must adjust himself to the patient as a telephone receiver is adjusted to the transmitting microphone*. Just as the receiver converts back into sound waves the electric oscillations . . . so the doctor's unconscious is able, from the derivation of the unconscious which are communicated to him, to reconstruct the unconscious, which has determined the patient's free associations. (italics mine)

Thus, Freud understood that the interactional communication sequence in treatment was dynamic in nature and involved both the patient's and therapist's unconscious processes. However, he did not elaborate on the mechanisms of countertransference in detail. In his widely cited 1910 paper, Freud stated that it was critical for the analyst to

> recognize this counter-transference in himself and overcome it . . . we have noticed that no psychoanalyst goes further than his own complexes and resistances permit, and we consequently require that he shall begin activity with a self-analysis and continually carry it deeper while he is making his own observations on his patients. Anyone who fails to produce results in a self-analysis of this kind may at once give up any idea of being able to treat patients by analysis. (1910, pp. 141–42)

This passage illustrates that Freud believed that a therapist's self-knowledge of how his own unconscious thought processes were activated "by the transmitting unconscious of the patient" was central to successful treatment (1910). We can view the role of empathy as central to posttraumatic therapy; it is a vehicle to portals of entry in the interior space of the psyche. Like ancient pyramids, the ego has secret passageways into inner sanctums, rooms, and chambers that are rich in artifacts, valued objects, and elegant burial tombs.

Empathy is the psychological capacity to identify and to understand another person's psychological state of being (Wilson and Lindy, 1994). Empathic attunement allows access to the passageway and portals of the ego's pyramid. As defined fundamentally by Kohut (1959, 1977), empathy is a form of "knowing," information processing, and "data collection" about another or what is sometimes referred to as a "self-object." Rowe and MacIsaac (1991) state that "empathic immersion into the patient's experience focuses the analyst's attention upon what it is like to be the subject rather than the target of the patient's wishes and demands" (p. 18). In a similar manner they note that "the empathic process is employed solely as a scientific tool to enable the analyst eventually to make interpretations to the patient that are as accurate and complete as possible" (p. 64). Thus, we can view empathy as the primary tool by which to access the ego-state of the patient suffering from PTSD. Slatker (1987), in a review of empathy in analytic theory, states:

> Empathy is based on counter-identification; indeed, it is counter-identification that permits our empathy to be therapeutically useful. . . . the analyst's negative counter-transferential reactions can cause his empathy to diminish or even vanish altogether. When this happens, he may become vulnerable to additional negative counter-transference reactions. (p. 203)

The patient's ego-state, or ego-spatial configuration, includes the organization of experience into memory and function that governs attempts at adaptation to self, others, and the world. It represents the fluctuating dimensions of self-reference that include cognitive functions, affect regulation, ego-identity, and a sense of well-being (Wilson, Friedman, and Lindy, 2001). Moreover, there are at least five portals of entry into the ego-state of the PTSD client (2001) that are pathways created by PTSD symptoms organized into five clusters within the organism (i.e., PTSD triad: (1) re-experiencing, (2) avoidance, (3) hyperarousal, (4) ego-identity or self-processes, and (5) interpersonal attachment). These five portals of entry allow the therapist to understand the different symptom "channels," or manifestations, that comprise the information transmission being generated in specific forms of transference during treatment. Empathy, as one method of connecting to the ego-state and unconscious process of the trauma client, allows the therapist to creatively attune to *five* different channels of information transmission being generated by the patient.

INFORMATION TRANSMISSION OR "FLOW" IN THE TRANSFERENCE–COUNTERTRANSFERENCE MATRIX

When the patient and therapist are together in the safety of the clinician's office, an exchange of information occurs during the treatment. To an outside observer, not much appears to be happening except a verbal exchange for a brief period. Indeed, if videotaped and presented to viewers without sound content, it would appear that the two people talking could be anywhere—for example, at a restaurant, a residential living room, a hotel lobby, or a business office seated across a desk. Indeed, Freud (1915–1917) made a similar comment about the process of psychoanalysis:

> Nothing takes place in a psychoanalytic treatment but an interchange of words between the patient and the analyst. The patient talks, tells of his past experiences and present impressions, complains, confesses to his wishes and his emotional impulses. The doctor listens, tries to direct the patient's processes of thoughts, exhorts, forces his attention in certain directions, gives him explanations and observes the reactions of understanding or rejection which he in this way provokes in him. (pp. 19–20)

Freud's observation about "an interchange" of words and the role of the analyst as one who gently guides conversation and the process of free association is useful because it points to the active role of the therapist as one who observes, gathers information, and probes inquiries into different areas of the patient's past history. It is clear from his work that Freud (1912) understood that the therapist must use his unconscious as a receptive organ to the transmitting unconscious of the patient. The process of dynamic interchange between the patient and the analyst involves unconscious and conscious reception of information. In other words, *there are multiple channels of information being transmitted by the patient*: (1) words, (2) affect, (3) memories, (4) thoughts, (5) body posture, (6) voice modulations, (7) expression of their personality, and (8) here-and-now ego-state presentations or the saliency of their integrative consciousness during a period of time.

These dimensions of the patient, in the *context* of a therapeutic relationship, can be meaningfully thought of as forms of information transmission about their individual dynamics. They are *transference projections or transmissions* of psychological functioning. *The transmissions of data are different types of information flow emanating from the patient through encoded channels.* Figure 17.1 illustrates these mechanisms and reveals that the patient (sender) projects an information flow in a variety of forms, including transference dynamics. The analyst (receiver) is the object of the patient's information transmission and attempts clinically to decode the information encoded in the different channels.

When we think of posttraumatic therapy as an active process, it is possible to use words such as flow, wave, signal, energy, transmission, information gathering, and so forth, to characterize the nature of the transmitting unconscious of the patient. These defining concepts illustrate the features of a multichanneled process of verbal and nonverbal information transmission, which we have previously referred to as TST and which vary in their *intensity, frequency, amplitude*, and *modulation* in each channel of information transmission. In this regard, it is possible to conceptualize that at any given time there are seven

Figure 17.1.   Information Flow in Transference—Counter-Transference Matrix©.

"The transmitting unconscious of the patient" (S. Freud, 1912)

Defining Concepts: Flow, Energy, Transmission, Waves, Information, Channels, Signal Sending, Somatic Processes, and Unconscious Projection

Features: Multichannel Processes of Verbal, Non-Verbal and Somatic Information Transmission

Patient		**Therapist**
Ego-States	'Flow'	Ego-States
Affect	'Waves'	Affect
Defense	'Energy'	Defense
Prior History		Prior History
Trauma History	'Signals'	Trauma History
Personality Characteristics	'Information'	Personality Characteristics
Genetic Disposition	'Transmission'	Genetic Dispositions
Sender Variables		**Receiver Variables**

Patient	Signal Transmission	**Therapist**
Information Transmission*	Multichannel Process**	Information Reception & Decoding*
(Transferences & TST)	(frequency, amplitude, intensity)	(Affective Reactions/Counter-transference)
Encoded		**Decoded**
• Affect		• Affect
• Defense		• Defense
• Somatic States		• Somatic States
• Ego-States		• Ego-States
• Personality		• Personality
• Unconscious Memory		• Unconscious Thinking
• Cognition - Perception		• Cognition - Perception

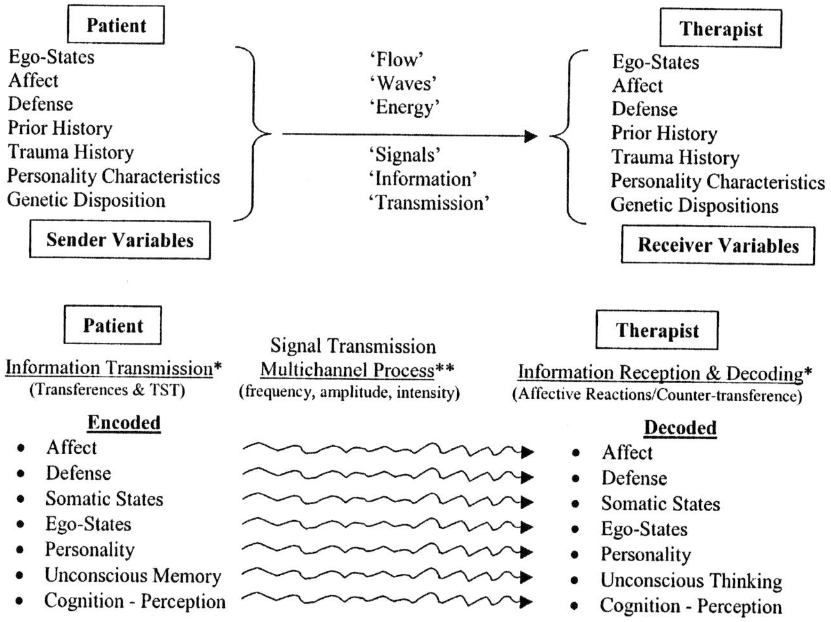

*In PTSD, information transmission is trauma specific transference (TST) projections.

**Multichannel process varies in frequency, amplitude, intensity modulation in each channel (e.g., affect, defense, somatic complaints)

Source: John P. Wilson and Rhiannon Thomas, 2004©

separate channels transmitting to the therapist (affect, defense, somatic state, ego-states, personality, unconscious memory, and cognitive processes). Furthermore, these same seven channels exist as potential receptor sites in the therapist. In a manner similar to a neuron, information flows, or is transmitted, from one part of the nerve across a synapse to an awaiting receptor location that receives the transmission, decodes it, and activates another process.

In essence then, encoded information is transmitted and decoded and capable of being processed for use in the treatment process. When construed in this way, we can see that empathic attunement is a vehicle for accurate reception of the information being generated by the patient. Therapeutic effectiveness requires accurate decoding of the channels and the ability and capacity to hold (i.e., store) the information without it overloading the capacities of the therapist channels (system overload). Transference and countertransference are old words used to describe the intricate and extraordinarily interesting process of human communication in the context of psychotherapy.

TRAUMA-SPECIFIC TRANSFERENCE TRANSMISSIONS: ORGANISMIC PROJECTIONS OF EMBEDDED PSYCHIC TRAUMA

Figure 17.1a illustrates how PTSD symptoms are transmitted during the process of psychotherapy. It is especially important to understand (TST) since it is always present during the treatment prior to resolution and integration of the trauma experience and the manifestation of PTSD. It is my belief, and clinically demonstrable in training work, that TST consists of a set of cues that are "leaked" out in subtle expressions in the seven channels shown in figure 17.1. More specifically, there are at least sixty-five distinct symptoms of PTSD (Wilson, Friedman, and Lindy, 2001) as well as unconscious projections of the trauma experience across the five clusters of PTSD symptoms: (1) re-experiencing, (2) avoidance or denial, (3) psychological hyperreactivity, (4) ego-states, and (5) interpersonal processes. In this regard, it is possible to speak of TST as omnipresent. It is as if the victim were speaking out saying, "see what happened to me—look at what the trauma did to change the way I used to be." Thus, the TST is an unconscious ego-state projection of the entire organism's response to traumatization and the changes induced at all levels of psychological functioning (i.e., allostatic changes—see Wilson, Friedman and Lindy [2001] for a discussion). Furthermore, the unconscious is a kind of "diplomatic spokesperson" who conveys messages to the therapist in this information transmission through the seven channels.

Unconscious projections require decoding and understanding; they are behavioral manifestations, sometimes symbolic, of that which the patient cannot express or recall by conscious effort. For example, a Vietnam War veteran patient used to pick at the soles of his boots with a pencil as he talked for years about his overwhelming combat experiences. He would repeatedly say "You know, doc, there is something missing about that night-long firefight" with a sad, tired forlorn expression. As it turned out, the unconscious memory of his picking at his boots was a reenactment of using a stick to pick out from the cleats in his boots the mashed brains of one of his buddies who died in the night-long firefight that killed all but three platoon members. This action of picking at his boots during treatment is a clear example of TST and repetition compulsion of the original postcombat reaction. It was as if his unconscious voice were transmitting the message: "Look here, doc, here is the clue to what I can't remember." Indeed, when his amnesia dissipated, the entire forgotten sequence of events returned to his memory about the night battle that changed his life forever as a nineteen-year-old soldier.

The terror, fear of annihilation, and immersion into human carnage was devastating to his ego and capacity to master the experience. However, he always recalled sitting on a log picking at the gray brain matter in the morning at "first light" as the sun broke through the clouds in the mountains of the central highlands of Vietnam in 1967. Thus, the image of a young soldier sitting alone, battle weary and totally exhausted, and picking human brains from the sole of his combat boots, encapsulated his current reality of being alone, divorced, isolated, alienated from others, and depressed. For him, the memories of war were both his link to the past, buddies killed, and his search for meaning. The unintegrated memories were bittersweet companions: they tortured him and sustained him at the same time. His unconscious fear was that to let go of the most powerful experience of his life was to let go of himself and his identity. The question for him, of course, centered on the issue of, "What's left, doc?" Indeed, we could say that he was "picking" at the meaning of his life after Vietnam.

The magnitude of the complexity of TST cannot be underestimated in the treatment of PTSD. It is one of the critically important features that differentiates PTSD treatment from that of therapeutic approaches to other disorders, including anxiety disorders. The clinician's ability to decode TST will be strongly associated with therapeutic outcome. Viewed in this way, the central role of empathic attunement takes on a clearer focus since it is one of the primary clinical skills by which to enter one of the portals of entry into the PTSD patient's ego-state. Conceptually, however, there is an advantage for this perspective, since knowledge that there are seven channels of information for five clusters of PTSD symptoms allows the therapist ways of knowing and approaching how to decode the TST and other transmissions. Furthermore, recognizing the universality of unconscious projections of the traumatic experience in any of the seven channels of the PTSD symptoms enables the therapist to formulate hypotheses and informed intuitions about the meaning and significance of any interactional sequence during treatment.

Figure 17.1a.   Trauma-Specific Transference Transmission (TST)©.

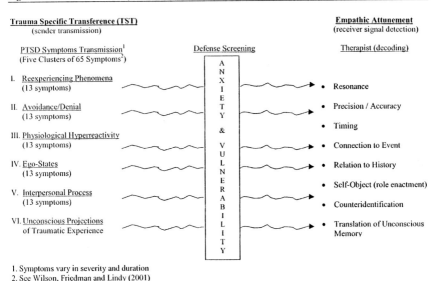

1. Symptoms vary in severity and duration
2. See Wilson, Friedman and Lindy (2001)

Source: John P. Wilson and Rhiannon Thomas, 2004©

In this regard, it is my belief that there is no randomness to the patterns of TST; they have meaning and significance at all times. Moreover, as figure 17.1a illustrates, ego-defenses serve as "screens," "filters," or "blocks" and control mechanisms to TST transmissions. The various defenses are control mechanisms directly concerned with anxiety and states of vulnerability. The greater the experienced (conscious or unconscious) anxiety and inner vulnerability, the more the defenses will be utilized to stave off threats (i.e., reexperienced traumatic memories) that were originally embedded in the trauma experience or that activate prior emotional trauma or conflicts from the patients' history. However, I wish to make it clear that what I am proposing is not the classic Freudian paradigm of trauma and ego-defense (Freud, 1915–1917, 1920). Rather it is a paradigm in which allostatic transformations caused by trauma alter organismic functioning in a holistic, dynamic manner.

These alterations produced by trauma have an impact on all levels of psychological functioning. *The organismic impacts are dynamically interrelated and express themselves in various channels of behavior. Traumatic encoding of experience is organismic; it is not an isolated subsystem of memory, affect, perception, or motivation.* TST reactions are direct manifestations of this set of organismic changes caused by trauma. Traumatic experiences, by definition, are forms of extreme stress with varying degrees of power to energize the organism's functioning and natural state of well-being. Traumatic experiences are not of the same type as normal development life experiences; they are beyond the line demarcating "usual" and "normal" from "unusual" and "abnormal."

Extreme trauma, especially catastrophic trauma involving the abyss experience (Wilson, 2002), can be thought of as Big Bang phenomena in a manner akin to the Big Bang theory of the universe. The Big Bang of profoundly catastrophic trauma rattles the organism to the core, rearranging its essential form but without destroying it completely. The result of the shake-up to organismic functioning is allostatic transformations of energy, which now has a program and life force of its own until treatment and healing restores organismic well-being, albeit in a new structural configuration than existed prior to the shattering caused by the trauma experience.

A MODEL OF EMPATHY IN TRAUMA WORK

By nature, the professional work with trauma patients presents many dilemmas to analysts, psychotherapists, counselors, medical personnel, and researchers. There is nothing ordinary or "normally" routine in attempting to understand the impact of trauma to an individual. As noted earlier, listening to, and encountering the faces and voices of, trauma patients is often stressful and difficult because traumatic experiences produce injuries to the spirit, body, and psyche that make it difficult to sustain empathy without losing concentration, losing attention to details of their trauma experiences, or feeling overwhelmed by the nature of a particular traumatic event. Traumatic events anchor the extreme point of the stressor continuum. Powerful affective reactions to trauma stories and the unfolding of the patients' history are normative and expectable (Wilson and Lindy, 1994). Similarly, it is empirically demonstrable that there are predictable patterns of psychological and physiological arousal when therapists, students, researchers, or others respond to the presentations of human distress, accounts of personal trauma, or the report of stressful life events (Wilson and Lindy, 1994; Ickes, 1997).

There is a psychobiological capacity for empathy, and elsewhere we have argued that it is an important adaptive function in human social interaction that potentially has profound consequences for the evolution of the species (Wilson and Lindy, 1994). Thus, understanding empathic processes in work with PTSD and victims of trauma in a variety of settings (e.g., medical triage, crisis intervention, emergency medicine, disaster responses, military defusings, critical incident debriefings, psychotherapy) is essential to successful treatment or intervention outcomes. Figure 17.2 presents an overall conceptual schema. However, space limitations preclude a full discussion of the schema and its dynamics and treatment.

Figure 17.2. Structure and Dynamics of Interpersonal Processes in Treatment of PTSD: Organismic Transmissions of the Patient[©].

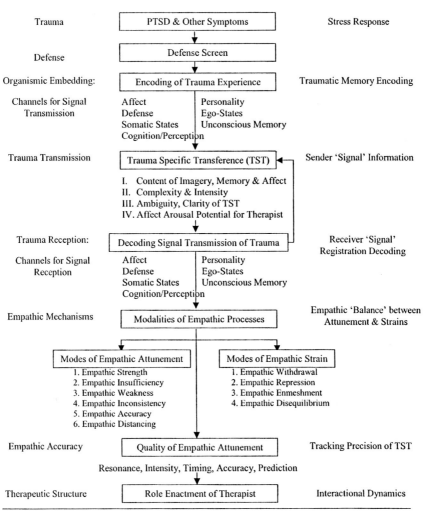

Source: John P. Wilson and Rhiannon Thomas, 2004[©]

PSYCHOBIOLOGICAL SYNCHRONY: THE BASES OF EMPATHIC ATTUNEMENT, MATCHING PHENOMENA, AND RESPONSE CONGRUENCE

In the treatment of PTSD and its associated co-morbidities (Wilson, Friedman, and Lindy, 2001), psychobiological synchrony simply means that the therapist is "in phase" with the client. However, to be in phase and synchronized with a patient can refer to various psychological and physiological phenomena. The study of psychological synchrony is not new, and experimental research (Levenson and Ruef, 1997) has examined the phenomena of therapists' reactions to their patients and found evidence for response matching of autonomic nervous system (ANS) functioning. Levenson and Ruef state:

> With the exception of those times when the therapist was said to be distracted by other concerns, they found that heart rate changes during these episodes were generally similar for both patient and therapist . . . the therapist's and patient's heart rate moved in similar directions as the levels of tension varied, but moved in opposite directions when the patient's antagonism was toward the therapist. (p. 48)

Consistent with my views of the role and significance of empathy to PTSD treatment, in particular, and trauma work more generally (i.e., emergency medicine, disaster response, acute intervention, and critical incident debriefing), Levenson and Ruef suggest that *empathic accuracy* involves a *parallelism* between two individuals in a variety of contexts, including psychotherapy: "[E]mpathic accuracy—a state in which one person (the subject) can accurately tell what another person (the target) is feeling—will be marked by psychological parallelism between the subject and target" (p. 62). *Thus, physiological parallelism can be thought of as part of the core mechanisms that govern empathic attunement, matching phenomena and response congruence in the treatment of trauma patients.* However, this is precisely where the potential difficulty lies because research evidence found that affective intensity (e.g., therapist exposure to the power of trauma stories and ultimate horror and hostility toward the therapist) was associated with distraction or a loss of empathic attunement. The receivers' capacity to sustain precise signal decoding was disrupted due to internal emotional states (e.g., fear, anxiety, uncertainty) and simultaneously activated dysynchronous, defensive security operations to quell the disrupted state of equilibrium or to reduce tension (empathic strain) created by the loss of synchrony.

Levenson and Ruef (1997) suggest a similar formulation from experimental research and state that *"high physiological arousal on the part of the sender is associated with low accuracy in the receivers' ratings of the targets' affect*" (p. 61, italics mine). This finding has direct relevance and application to the treatment of PTSD because, by definition, traumatic events constitute the extreme end of the continuum of stressful life events and the patients' reports of life-threatening, horrific, dangerous, or catastrophic experiences that contain the potential of *maximum affective arousal*.

The voices and faces of trauma patients confront therapists on a regular basis with emotionally laden, disturbing, and often-shameful accounts of human encounters with fragmenting effects of trauma (Wilson, 2002). Abyss experiences, in brief, present the therapists with reports of encounters with the darkest episodes of human existence and the specter of injury or death at the hands of fate or calculated, willful human malevolence. To sustain empathy effectively means that the therapists must open themselves to the uncomfortable parallelism of the patients' dysregulated affect, pain, and struggle to overcome their injuries. Empathic strains, strong affective reactions, and countertransference reactions are indigenous to PTSD treatment. The question is, how are they best managed in the service of maintaining empathic attunement to the inner reality of the patients' experiences?

DIMENSIONS OF EMPATHIC FUNCTIONING: A CONTINUUM OF ATTUNEMENT TO SEPARATION AND DETACHMENT

Empathic functioning exists on a continuum that ranges from minimal to optimal functioning in terms of empathic attunement. The continuum represents *qualities* of empathic functioning at any given time in the course of posttraumatic therapy (figure 17.3). The specific quality or adequacy of empathic attunement spans the spectrum from none (absent or disengaged) to partial to optimal connection and active engagement with the patient. A conceptualization of a continuum of empathic attunement is dynamic in nature and mirrors the reality that many factors influence the *disposition* to empathic functioning (detachment versus attunement), ranging from clinical experience in trauma work to personal history to fatigue and stress-related states, and the raw power of the trauma story of the patient to evoke strong affective reactions and CTRs in treatment.

The continuum of empathic functioning is a useful way to think about the adequacy of active therapeutic engagement with the patient. Minimal empathic functioning is the absence or only partial achievement of empathic attunement. There is a failure to relate to the client in a manner that manifests therapeutic congruency. On the other hand, therapeutic empathic congruency means that the therapist understands the distress by having knowledge of the internal ego-state of the trauma client, even if the client cannot verbalize all his

Figure 17.3.   Continuum of Empathic Functioning: Detachment Versus Attunement©.

Empathic Functioning

A Dynamic, Variable Process

Degrees of Empathic Attunement

Minimal ———————————————— Partial ————————————————— Optimal

Detachment / Disengagement	Withdrawal / Avoidance	Exploitative	Inadequate	Over-Identification	Attunement / Engagement

Empathic Continuum

Separation ◄————————— Modes of Empathic Attunement —————————► Connection

Noneffective / Nonfunctional Decoding Failure					Effective / Functional Decoding, Accuracy

Counter-transference Continuum

Type I (Avoidance) ◄————————— Modes of Empathic Strain —————————► Type II (Overidentification)

[Balance Point]

Source: John P. Wilson and Rhiannon Thomas, 2004©

or her inner thoughts, feelings, and memories. In this regard, the therapist decodes the flow of information emanating from the trauma client and receives it without distorting noises, signals, or defenses generated by their attempt to match understanding (i.e., congruent empathy) of the trauma experience of the client. The "matching" process of adequate signal detection and responsive communication includes both here-and-now processes and the traversing back in time into the patient's subjective reality of their trauma experience. In that regard, it is as if the therapist joins with the patient's memory and rides along like a fellow passenger on a journey of discovery in which the patient says— "look at this; experience this event or situation, and see what happened here long ago." Together, much like two persons seated together in an adventure park journey (i.e., a theme park), they *experience* the memories and emotions in a common flow that reveals the nidus of the trauma experience.

In sharing the re-living of the trauma together, the therapist exerts much energy and concentration to empathically attune to the client while at the same time maintaining a third-eye observation and protector of interpersonal boundaries. Clearly, this is among the reasons that Kohut (1977) thought of empathy as a process of knowing or data collection. However, to be an accurate recorder or collector, the trauma patients' data require four interrelated dimensions of empathic functioning: (1) empathic capacity, (2) empathic tolerance and sensitivity, (3) empathic endurance, and (4) empathic resistance. It is important to recognize that strains imposed on the process of attunement in posttraumatic therapy may cause *empathic breaks or ruptures*. A rupture, cessation, or sudden loss of empathic attunement reflects the inability to continuously track, understand, and accurately experience the ego-states and frame of reference of another person (Wilson and Lindy, 1994). Thus, understanding the factors that lead to a disruption in empathic functioning is necessary for identification of the traps, pitfalls, and potential trouble areas imposed by compassion fatigue, burn-out, overwhelming affective responses, and existence of disruptive countertransference (Wilson and Lindy, 1994; Figley, 2002).

MODES OF EMPATHIC STRAIN:
THERAPISTS' REACTIVE STYLES

The experience of empathic strain (table 17.1) occurs when empathic attunement gets challenged, overwhelmed, or rendered inadequate in the face of the patients' transference or self-presentation as part of the dyadic or group interactional sequence. Empathic strain may be experienced in a variety of ways that can result in complete countertransferential processes. However, empathic strain is typically manifest as increased tension, anxiety, problems of "focus" in concentration or attention, or increased ANS activity (heart rate, respiration, etc.). Empathic strain may also appear in somatic forms as muscle tension, sleepiness or drowsiness, gastric distress, headaches, and fatigue or more idiosyncratic reactions such as eye rubbing, localized muscle spasms, or urinary urgency. Furthermore, empathic strain may be conscious or unconscious in nature and potentially associated with rapid shifts in emotional states (e.g., anger, disdain, fear, horror) and cognitive processes (e.g., fantasies of escape, rescue, thoughts about nonclinical activity).

Empathic strain results from those interpersonal events in psychotherapy that weaken, injure, or force beyond reasonable limits a positive therapeutic response to the client. CTRs are only one source of empathic strain, yet we believe that in the treatment of PTSD, CTRs are perhaps the primary causes of treatment failure.

Building on the seminal works of Cohen (1952), Wolstein (1988), Tansey and Burke (1989), Slatker (1987), Danieli (1988), Lindy (1988), Parson (1988), Wilson (1989), Maroda (1991), Scurfield (1993), Wilson and Lindy (1994), and Dalenberg (2000a), it is possible to construct a schema for understanding modalities of empathic strain in the treatment of PTSD. Figure 17.4 illustrates these forms of empathic strain in a two-dimensional representation, based on Type I and Type II modes of CTRs crossed by the axis of objective and subjective CTRs.

Table 17.1. Modes of Empathic Strain©

I. EMPATHIC DISEQUILIBRIUM
    a) *Defining Conceptual Axis*: Normative, objective affective reactions and disposition to Type II—countertransference (Normative—Overidentification) associated with reactions to trauma story.
    b) *Features*: Empathic strain, experienced disequilibrium of personal states; shifts in well-being, uncertainty, vulnerability, and security.

II. EMPATHIC WITHDRAWAL
    a) *Defining Conceptual Axis*: Normative, objective affective reaction and disposition to Type I—countertransference (Normative—Avoidance) associated with personal reactions to trauma story.
    b) *Features*: Withdrawal from empathic attunement, separation, avoidance and security operations (i.e., unconscious defense processes), feelings of uncertainty and inadequacy; reliance on blank façade, misperceptions of transference.

III. EMPATHIC ENMESHMENT
    a) *Defining Conceptual Axis*: Personalized—idiosyncratic reactions to trauma story and disposition to Type II (overidentification) countertransference.
    b) *Features*: Personalized affective reactions; activation of personal issues; tendency to cross boundaries; overinvolvement with patient; excessive amplification of attunement responses; and reciprocal dependency.

IV. EMPATHIC REPRESSION
    a) *Defining Conceptual Axis*: Personalized—idiosyncratic reactions to trauma story and disposition to Type I (avoidance) countertransference.
    b) *Features*: Personal repression of memories, conflicts and unresolved problems aroused by the interactional sequence with patient. Loss of attunement may be severe and damaging to therapeutic outcome. Withdrawal, denial, and distancing are all defensive operations.

Source: John P. Wilson and Rhiannon Thomas, 2004©; John P. Wilson and Jacob Lindy, 1994

Objective CTRs are expectable affective and cognitive reactions experienced by the therapist in response to the personality, behavior, and trauma story of the client. Subjective CTRs are personal reactions that originate from the therapist's own personal conflicts, idiosyncracies, or unresolved issues from life-course development.

Type I and Type II modes of countertransference refer, respectively, to the primary tendencies of counterphobic avoidance, distancing, and detachment reactions as opposed to tendencies to overidentify and become enmeshed with the client. Type I CTRs typically include forms of denial, minimization, distortion, counterphobic reactions, avoidance, detachment, and withdrawal

Figure 17.4.   Reactive Style of Therapist©.

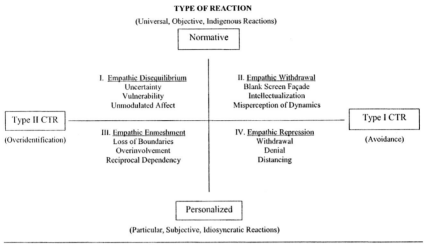

TYPE OF REACTION
(Universal, Objective, Indigenous Reactions)

Normative

I. Empathic Disequilibrium	II. Empathic Withdrawal
Uncertainty	Blank Screen Façade
Vulnerability	Intellectualization
Unmodulated Affect	Misperception of Dynamics

Type II CTR

(Overidentification)

III. Empathic Enmeshment	IV. Empathic Repression
Loss of Boundaries	Withdrawal
Overinvolvement	Denial
Reciprocal Dependency	Distancing

Type I CTR

(Avoidance)

Personalized

(Particular, Subjective, Idiosyncratic Reactions)

Source: John P. Wilson and Jacob Lindy, 1994©

from an empathic stance toward the client. Type II CTRs, in contrast, involve forms of overidentification, overidealization, enmeshment, and excessive advocacy for the client, as well as behaviors that elicit guilt reactions.

As figure 17.4 illustrates, the combination of the two axes of CTRs produces four distinct modes or styles of empathic strain that we have identified as (1) empathic withdrawal, (2) empathic repression, (3) empathic enmeshment, and (4) empathic disequilibrium. Although a therapist may experience one style or reaction pattern more than another, it is possible to experience any or all the modes of empathic strain during the course of treatment with a traumatized client (see Wilson and Lindy, 1994 for an extended discussion).

THE FOUR MODES OF EMPATHIC STRAIN (ES)

Empathic Withdrawal: ES Mode I

Empathic withdrawal is a mode of countertransference strain that occurs when the therapist experiences expected affective and cognitive reactions during treatment, and he or she is predisposed by defensive style and personality characteristics toward Type I avoidance and detachment responses. In this mode, a rupture occurs in the empathic stance toward the client. The result is often the loss of capacity for sustained empathic inquiry due to over-reliance on the "blank-screen" or on conventional or recently delegated or taught (for new therapist) therapeutic techniques. These reactions block the painful task of integrating the trauma experience and may lead the therapist to misperceive or misinterpret the behavior and psychodynamics of the client based on previous assumptions.

Empathic Repression: ES Mode II

A similar process occurs in *empathic repression*, in which the transference issues of the patient reactivate conflicts and unresolved personal concerns in the therapist's life. Thus, a personalized subjective reaction, combined with a disposition toward a Type I CTR, may be associated with repressive countermeasures by the therapist. His or her inward focus on areas of personal conflict is likely to be associated with an unwitting and unconscious withdrawal from the therapeutic role and denial of the full significance of the clinical issues being presented by the client.

Empathic Enmeshment: ES Mode III

The third mode of strain, *empathic enmeshment*, is the result of the therapist's tendency toward Type II CTRs coupled with subjective reactions during treatment. In this mode of empathic strain, the clinician leaves the therapeutic role by becoming over-involved and overidentified with the client. The most common consequence is pathological enmeshment and a loss of role boundaries in the context of treatment. In the treatment of PTSD, therapists with a personal history of trauma and victimization are especially vulnerable to this mode of empathic strain and may unconsciously attempt to rescue traumatized clients as an indirect way of dealing with their own unintegrated personal conflicts (Wilson and Thomas, 2004). Perhaps the greatest danger that occurs within this mode of empathic strain is the potential for the therapist to unconsciously reenact personal problems through pathological enmeshment. When this occurs it not only causes an abandonment of the empathic stance toward the person seeking help but may lead to secondary victimization or the intensification of transference themes that the patient brought to treatment in the first place.

Empathic Disequilibrium: ES Mode IV

Empathic disequilibrium, as figure 17.4 indicates, is characterized by a disposition to Type II CTRs and the experience of objective reactions during treatment, especially in work with patients suffering from PTSD and co-morbid conditions. This mode of strain is characterized by somatic discomfort, feelings of insecurity and uncertainty as to how to deal with the client, and more. It occurs commonly in therapists who experience either Type I or Type II CTRs. Consider the following case example:

> Teresa, a woman in her 20s, disclosed to her counselor the following trauma story regarding her internment in a South American prison for political dissenters. Her captors demeaned and abused her sexually, using rape in all its human forms. Next, they unleashed specially conditioned Alsatian dogs that intimidated, threatened, and bit her, drawing blood from her breasts. The dogs then had sexual intercourse with her. During these events the captors watched, laughed, and made humiliating and disparaging remarks. Next, her captors beheaded her two young children while forcing her to watch. They kicked her children's decapitated heads as "soccer balls." Finally they then placed her in an isolation cell and carried out a mock execution.

The counselor who was helping this client was badly shaken during the session when the trauma story was told, and she sought relief from the tension she experienced throughout the hour of treatment. Her reaction was such that she was overwhelmed by the content of the trauma story, which raised personal issues for her, as she was herself a woman in prime childbearing years. In the case example, the therapist indicated that she felt overwhelmed, tense, vulnerable, uncertain of her own capacity to bind anxiety, and she experienced increased physiological arousal. She stated that she felt somewhat insecure concerning her ability to adequately treat the torture victim, despite having worked quite successfully with other torture victims in the past. In particular, her objective CTR included vivid images of seeing the heads of the murdered children on the ground being sadistically abused by the victim's captors. These visual images and her natural identification with the woman as a mother and brutalized person were associated with an extreme state of ANS arousal (e.g., heart palpitations and intense anxiety). Her concern following the session was that if she could not more effectively modulate her affect, she would not be successful in her clinical efforts. An associated concern centered on her fear that the torture victim might become further isolated from sources of help or even worse, commit suicide.

This case illustration also indicates that empathic overarousal is associated with powerful affect reactions (e.g., anxiety and motor tension) and cognitive processes (e.g., images of sadistic torture) that extend beyond the therapy hour in distressing ways associated with feelings of self-doubt, feelings of vulnerability, and a need to discharge the therapist's hyperaroused state.

One interesting consequence of empathy is that the therapist may experience degrees of hyperarousal that are proportional to the level of hyperarousal that the patient manifests as part of their PTSD. Clearly, this is a type of dual unfolding in the dynamics of transference and countertransference. This is another example of parallelism in empathic congruence and matching phenomena.

Later in work of this nature, the client may begin to reexperience trauma-related feelings that he or she feels are activated in vivo during the therapy. Teresa, the torture survivor, for example, may feel that the therapist is failing to protect her from harsh, current political forces blocking immigration and thereby persecuting her anew. She may feel that the therapist is judging her for sacrificing her children to her political cause, irreverently dismissing her attachment to her dead children, or failing to hear her sadness and pain at now feeling inhibited sexually (thereby disrespecting her sexuality). As each of these elements in the trauma situation is partially reenacted and transferred onto the treatment, new trauma-based countertransferences may appear, impairing empathy by rupture, repression, enmeshment, or overarousal, until these processes are understood as part of the dual unfolding of the treatment.

Individual Variations in Modes of Empathic Strain

A two-dimensional model for a topology of countertransference has its limitations, and I am not suggesting that *all* relevant CTRs to PTSD fit into one of the four quadrants; for example, CTRs' reactions may also need to be categorized in terms of affect range and intensity, trauma role reenacted, defense cluster mobilized, symptom experienced by therapist, or segment of the treatment frame distorted. Neither do we wish to imply a static mode, one that confines CTR in a given treatment to one quadrant. Indeed, there is more likely a dynamic interplay among quadrants over time in a single case. Nevertheless, this model provides an important starting point, one that includes rather than excludes other dimensions and, for purposes of clinical use, establishes an important point of orientation. This dynamic model can be empirically demonstrated by critical analysis of videotaped "role-playing" of PTSD cases to see "in situ" the modes of empathic strain and countertransference.

THE IMPACT OF EMPATHIC STRAIN AND COUNTERTRANSFERENCE ON THE PSYCHOTHERAPY OF TRAUMA SURVIVORS

The understanding of empathic stress permits analysis of the factors that determine CTRs and how CTRs, in turn, affect the phases of stress recovery and potentially cause pathological results to the client. What happens to the treatment process and the phases of recovery when there is a loss of empathic attunement?

Figure 17.5 shows in a graphic form how the modes of empathic strain impact on the development of Type I and Type II CTRs. Elsewhere, we have presented a detailed discussion of these processes and dynamics in posttraumatic therapy. However, space restrictions enable only a condensed summary explanation here.

Figure 17.5. Counter-Transference (CF) Effects on Recovery from Trauma and Violence.

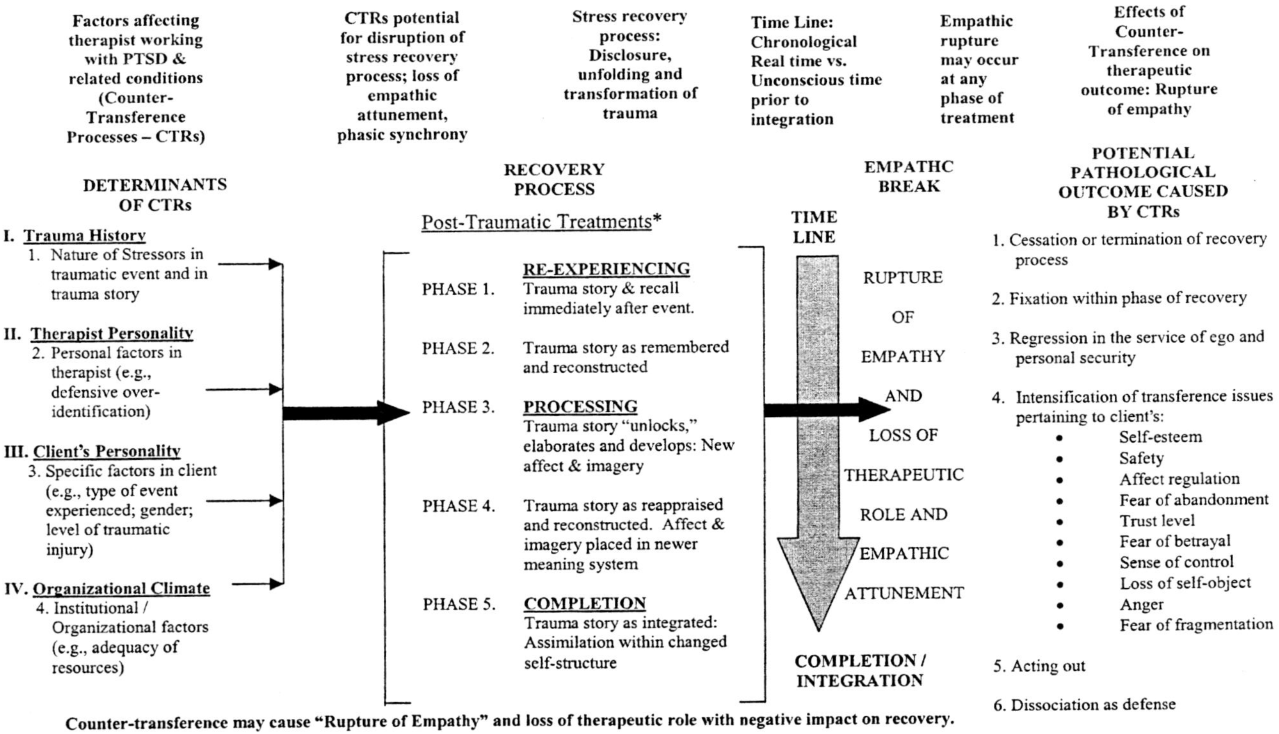

Factors affecting therapist working with PTSD & related conditions (Counter-Transference Processes – CTRs)

CTRs potential for disruption of stress recovery process; loss of empathic attunement, phasic synchrony

Stress recovery process: Disclosure, unfolding and transformation of trauma

Time Line: Chronological Real time vs. Unconscious time prior to integration

Empathic rupture may occur at any phase of treatment

Effects of Counter-Transference on therapeutic outcome: Rupture of empathy

DETERMINANTS OF CTRs

I. Trauma History
1. Nature of Stressors in traumatic event and in trauma story

II. Therapist Personality
2. Personal factors in therapist (e.g., defensive over-identification)

III. Client's Personality
3. Specific factors in client (e.g., type of event experienced; gender; level of traumatic injury)

IV. Organizational Climate
4. Institutional / Organizational factors (e.g., adequacy of resources)

RECOVERY PROCESS

Post-Traumatic Treatments*

PHASE 1. **RE-EXPERIENCING**
Trauma story & recall immediately after event.

PHASE 2. Trauma story as remembered and reconstructed

PHASE 3. **PROCESSING**
Trauma story "unlocks," elaborates and develops: New affect & imagery

PHASE 4. Trauma story is reappraised and reconstructed. Affect & imagery placed in newer meaning system

PHASE 5. **COMPLETION**
Trauma story as integrated: Assimilation within changed self-structure

TIME LINE

EMPATHIC BREAK

RUPTURE OF EMPATHY AND LOSS OF THERAPEUTIC ROLE AND EMPATHIC ATTUNEMENT

COMPLETION / INTEGRATION

POTENTIAL PATHOLOGICAL OUTCOME CAUSED BY CTRs

1. Cessation or termination of recovery process
2. Fixation within phase of recovery
3. Regression in the service of ego and personal security
4. Intensification of transference issues pertaining to client's:
   - Self-esteem
   - Safety
   - Affect regulation
   - Fear of abandonment
   - Trust level
   - Fear of betrayal
   - Sense of control
   - Loss of self-object
   - Anger
   - Fear of fragmentation
5. Acting out
6. Dissociation as defense

Counter-transference may cause "Rupture of Empathy" and loss of therapeutic role with negative impact on recovery.

Source: John P. Wilson and Jacob Lindy, 1994
*See Wilson, Friedman, and Lindy, 2001 for a discussion.

There are many determinants of CTRs in treatment. Figure 17.5 illustrates four major determinants of CTR in posttraumatic therapy, each of which singly or interactively can give birth to empathic strain. Empathic strain may result in one of many types of countertransference reactions and role enactments by the therapist (Wilson, Friedman, and Lindy, 2001). Moreover, a CTR may influence any phase of the recovery process, leading to a rupture of empathy and a loss of the therapeutic role function. When this occurs, as it inevitably does, a potentially pathological outcome may occur resulting in the following outcomes: (1) cessation or stasis in the recovery process; (2) fixation within a phase or stage in recovery; (3) indication of repression of behaviors; (4) intensification of transference issues; (5) acting out behaviors; and (6) dissociation.

ANXIETY AND DEFENSIVENESS IN THE ANALYST DURING TREATMENT OF THE PATIENT

Defensive behavior by the therapist is typically counterproductive to the successful treatment of PTSD. Similarly, the experience of anxiety and defensiveness during posttraumatic therapy is expectable and universal, especially given the context of the treatment focus. The idea that the analysts' level of anxiety and defensiveness is a potential problem in countertransference is not new and has been the subject of extensive investigation (Wolstein, 1988). In 1952, Cohen wrote a remarkable and insightful paper entitled "Countertransference and Anxiety" in which she proposed five therapeutic situations likely to produce anxiety and countertransference.

> The main situations in the doctor-patient relationship that undermine the therapeutic role and therapy may result in anxiety in the therapist and can be listed as follows: 1) when the doctor is *helpless* to affect the patients' memories; 2) when the doctor is treated continually as an *object of fear, hatred or contempt*; 3) when the patient calls on the doctor for advice or reassurance as evidence of his professional competence or interest in the patient; 4) when the patient attempts to establish a relationship of *romantic love* with the doctor; and 5) when the patient calls on the doctor for other intimacy. (1952 cited in Wolstein, 1988, p. 73, italics mine.)

This passage is germane to our focus on empathy and countertransference because it highlights the situations likely to produce anxiety; namely, when the patient expresses strong emotions of *fear, hatred* (anger, rage), *contempt* (hostility, disdain, degradation), or *romantic love* (sexualized feelings, demands for succorance, etc.). As applied to PTSD, many of the sequela of traumatic experiences involved those affects (fear, hatred, contempt, helplessness, love) that were prominent reactions to the stressors present in the event. Thus, TST transmission involves strong affects, which the patient typically finds difficult to properly modulate. The patient then transmits his or her anxiety, defensiveness, and fears to the therapist, often an unconscious transmission, as a request for help because of the feelings of insecurity, uncertainty, and confusion brought about by the trauma. The therapist receives this anxiety-based transmission and attempts to decode its meaning while sustaining empathy in the treatment process.

Cohen (1952) lists eighteen specific signs of anxiety and defensiveness in the analyst during treatment (table 17.2). These findings are particularly interesting for three basic reasons: First, the publication is fifty years old and still very relevant today to PTSD treatment approaches, although that was not her focus at the time. Second, it closely matches our description of Type I and Type II countertransference reactions. Third, recent empirical research confirms the presence of all eighteen signs of anxiety and defensiveness (Danieli, 1988, 1994b; Wilson and Thomas, 2004; Dalenberg, 2000a). Moreover, Wilson and Lindy (1994) in a previous study, listed four categories of information that constitute potential manifestations of countertransference reactions. Table 17.3 summarizes the factors, which parallel those found in other research (Danieli, 1988, 1994a; Dalenberg, 2000a; Figley, 2002; Wilson and Thomas, 2004).

Table 17.3 summarizes four sets of indicators of CTRs in the psychotherapy of trauma survivors: (1) physiological and physical reactions, (2) affective reactions, (3) psychological reactions, and (4) behavioral symptoms. These four categories were derived by talking extensively with colleagues in the field who work with trauma survivors (i.e., members of the International Society for Traumatic Stress Studies [ISTSS]). For example, nearly all stated that physical reactions were common (e.g., headaches, increased motor tension, flushing, sleeplessness, and increased ANS arousal), and were a salient clue that countertransference was at work. Notice how closely the symptom clusters match up to Cohen's (1952) formulation of anxiety and defense.

ORGANISMIC TUNING: THE POSITIVE THERAPEUTIC EFFECTS OF EMPATHIC ATTUNEMENT

Implicit in our analysis of the effects of empathic congruence in the treatment of psychological trauma and PTSD is the assumption that *phasic synchrony*, as a psychobiological phenomenon, is a process associated with natural healing. I am using the natural healing to describe positive allostatic readjustment following trauma; a recalibration of the organism's adaptation to stress and

Table 17.2. Anxiety and Defensiveness in Analyst During Treatment of Patient[1]

(A) Signs of Anxiety and Defensiveness in Analyst	Modes of Empathic Strain Type I or Type II (B)[2] Counter-transference Reactions (1994)	
	A	B
1. Unreasonable dislike for patient	III	I (disdain, repression)
2. Failure to identify with patient	III	I (detachment, withdrawal)
3. Non-responsiveness to emotional distress of patient	ii	I (distance, avoidance)
4. Overwhelmed by patient's problems	I	II (disequilibrium)
5. Excessive liking of patient	III	II (enmeshment)
6. Dreads therapy session/uncomfortable during session	II	I (fear, anxiety)
7. Preoccupation with patient outside office	III	II (overinvolvement)
8. Inattention, problems of concentration, drowsiness, sleepy	II	I (avoidance, denial, withdrawal)
9. Preoccupation with own (personal) affairs	II	I (avoidance, withdrawal)
10. Analyst has problems with time management (late to session)	II	I (avoidance, withdrawal)
11. Argumentative with patient	III	II (overinvolvement, defensive)
12. Defensive with patient; feels vulnerable	III	II (overidentification, defensive)
13. Counter-transference distortion	II	I (withdrawal, misperception of dynamics)
14. Analyst elicits affect; prods patient	III	II (enmeshment)
15. Overconcerned with confidentiality	III	II (enmeshment)
16. Oversympathetic due to mistreatment by authority of patient	III	II (overidentification)
17. Urge to help in acting	I	II (overidentification, prosocial disequilibrium)
18. Patient appears in analyst's dreams	III	II (overidentification)

Source: (John P. Wilson and Rhiannon Thomas, 2004), [1](M. B. Cohen, 1952) [2]and (John P. Wilson and Jacob Lindy, 1994).

Table 17.3. Factors Indicative of Counter-Transferences (CTRs) in Therapist/Helper

I.   PHYSIOLOGICAL AND PHYSICAL REACTIONS
   Symptoms of increased (ANS) arousal (e.g., heart palpitations and muscle tension)
   Somatic reactions to trauma story or therapy as a contextual process (e.g., stomach pain)
   Sleep disturbances; nightmares of patient's trauma
   Agitation, inability to relax, on edge, hypersensitivity
   Inattention, drowsiness, avoidance reactions, yawning, rubbing eyes
   Uncontrolled and unintended displays of emotion
   Isochronicity: physiological parallelism to affective state, client

II. EMOTIONAL REACTIONS
   Irritability, annoyance, disdain, or resentment toward client
   Anxiety and fear
   Depression and helplessness
   Anger, rage, hostility, passive aggression
   Detachment, denial, avoidance, numbing, or desires for aloneness and isolation
   Sadistic/masochistic feelings
   Voyeuristic and sexualized feelings
   Horror, disgust, dread, loathing, terror
   Confusion, psychic overload, overwhelmed, foggy after session
   Guilt, shame, and embarrassment
   Sadness, grief, sorrow
   Fatigue, exhaustion, feeling "drained," "spent," "wasted," "depleted"

III. PSYCHOLOGICAL REACTIONS
   Detachment reactions based on defenses of intellectualization, rationalization, isolation, denial, minimization, fantasy
   Overidentification based on defenses of projection, introjection, denial, altruism

IV. SIGNS AND BEHAVIORAL SYMPTOMS OF CTRs THAT MAY BE CONSCIOUS OR UNCONSCIOUS
   Preoccupation with patient's trauma history, dreams, or presentation during treatment
   Rescue fantasies: problem fixer, hero, rescuer, "dragon slayer," "white knight," good parent, etc.
   Forgetting, lapse of attention, parapraxes
   Leave therapeutic role stance of empathy
   Overhostility, anger toward client
   Relief when client misses appointment or wish that client not show for session
   Repeated scheduling problems by therapist
   Denial of feelings and/or denial of need for supervision/consultation
   Narcissistic belief in role of being specialist in Post-Traumatic Stress Disorder (PTSD)
   Excessive concern/identification with client (e.g., take trauma impact "home")
   Psychic numbing or emotional constriction; de-sexualization
   Self-medication as numbing (i.e., use of alcohol, etc., to reduce affect and pre-occupation)
   Loss of boundaries during therapy
   Pre-occupation with referring client or terminating treatment

Source: John P. Wilson and Rhiannon Thomas, 2004[©]; John P. Wilson and Jacob Lindy, 1994

movement toward a resolution of the unmetabolized psychic elements of the trauma experience (Wilson, Friedman, and Lindy, 2001). Positive allostasis is restabilization following change, which is a reorganization of the organism following the fragmenting impact of trauma. The configuration of organismic restructuring as positive allostasis has many variations that range on a continuum from minimal to radical transformation of the self and manifestations in behavior. However, it must be recognized that at this time we have no classification system of the phases, forms, or patterns of personality transformations that occur as part of positive allostatic reorganization. Neither do we have a handbook of typologies of the forms of posttraumatic self-integration that classify forms of the healthy personality while it emerges beyond the pathology of PTSD and its co-morbidities.

Considered in a broader perspective, we do not yet understand the positive organismic sources that are associated with resiliency, a sense of coherency and transformative integration of ego-space, and the structure of the self (Wilson and Raphael, 1993; Wilson, Friedman, and Lindy, 2001). *A dynamic theory of positive allostasis following trauma requires an understanding of the abyss experience of trauma and the trauma archetype and its complexes* (Wilson, 2002). The *trauma* complex, as part of the trauma archetype, conceptualizes posttraumatic impacts in a much broader perspective of PTSD than that of a stress-related anxiety disorder. Focusing clinical attention only on PTSD is like looking at a two-dimensional portrait of a person; it is missing a third dimension that embraces the totality of unconscious functioning of the trauma survivor.

Stated in simple terms, PTSD is a surface manifestation of a much deeper human phenomenon involving the universal archetype of trauma and the many constellations of the trauma complex that, in turn, articulate with all other archetypal experiences (Wilson, 2002). PTSD is only part of organismic change produced by trauma; a more dynamic understanding involving unconscious trauma complexes and other processes of the self is needed. And while PTSD is an important part of clinical focus, it is not the only dimension of central psychotherapeutic significance.

A shift in focus allows us now to examine how it is that empathic accuracy, as a qualitative phenomenon, relates to the successful treatment of psychological trauma and PTSD. Table 17.4 summarizes fifteen points of understanding how empathic congruence, phasic synchrony, and so on, facilitate the dynamic mechanisms that occur in the therapeutic encounter that are salutogenic. The following is an expanded explanation of these points:

1. *Empathy and the quantity of information*: Empathic congruence leads to the disclosure of a sufficient quantity of information. Because of phasic synchrony and isochronicity, the establishment of empathic congruence

Table 17.4.   Isochronicity and Organismic Tuning: The Positive Therapeutic Effects of Empathic Attunement©

1. Empathy and the Quantity of Information
2. Empathy and the Quality of Information
3. Trauma Linkage: Coupling the Elements Together
4. The Gestalt of Trauma
5. Precision and Accuracy of Decoding Trauma-Specific Information
6. The Role of Empathy in Informational Density and Cognitive Complexity
7. Empathy and Portals of Entry to Ego-Space Configuration
8. Trauma Disclosure and Reduction of Defensiveness
9. Clarity in Understanding: Ego-Defenses Built around Traumatization
10. Positive Allostasis: Restabilization Following Change Caused by Trauma
11. Threshold of Trauma Specific-Transference (TST) Recognition and Utilization in Treatment
12. Symbolization of Trauma Experience
13. Empathy and Information Storage: Future Stockpiles
14. Individual Therapist Awareness of Empathic Strain, Compassion Fatigue and Countertransference Processes
15. Isochronicity and Organismic Tuning: Holistic Healing through Positive Allostatic Restabilization

Source: John P. Wilson and Rhiannon Thomas, 2004©

facilitates the patient feeling understood, secure, and desirous of explaining how they have changed and been affected by the traumatic experience.

2. *Empathy and the quality of information*: By definition, phasic synchrony and empathic attunement with good resonance (precision) will generate accurate information flow from the patient. The ability of the therapist to stay phasically synchronized enhances the quality and detail of information about the trauma experience and its impact to the existing personality dynamics and history of the patient.

3. *Trauma linkage: coupling the trauma elements together*: Empathic attunement facilitates the therapist's ability to make the necessary links in the reconstruction of the patients' trauma history. Trauma linkage means that both the therapist and the patient can discover how the magnitude of trauma restructured the organism, altering the configuration of ego-space and the constellation of self-processes. Establishing trauma links to the various elements of the allostatic changes wrought by the trauma enables discovery of how the trauma complex was formed (Wilson, Friedman, and Lindy, 2001). In this way, both the patient and the therapist can "see" the entire picture of the trauma's impact in a manner similar to looking together at an X-ray, MRI, or PET scan of the body or brain. More specifically, once the structure of the trauma complex is evident, the process of

therapy becomes analogous to having a functional MRI image in real time to understand organismic functioning in a holistic manner. In other words, the dynamics of the process become transparent.

4. *The gestalt of trauma*: The establishment of the linkages in the trauma complex facilitates understanding the *gestalt of trauma* in the life of the patient. The gestalt of trauma means the ability to fit all the pieces of the puzzle together; to see the whole constellation as well as the individual parts in a manner not evident in their original state following the changes produced by traumatic impact.

5. *Precision and accuracy of decoding trauma-specific information*: Empathic attunement is synonymous with precision and accuracy in responding to the patient. Empathic congruence and phasic synchrony in therapeutic orientation enables the decoding of TST and the unconscious transmission of "leaked" information that the patient wishes to convey but may not be able to verbalize. Unconscious transmissions, especially in nonverbal body posture or somatic complaints, may represent condensed symbolic material with multiple meanings that have been warded off by defenses or transformed into symbolized communications.

6. *The role of empathy in informational density and cognitive complexity*: The treatment of trauma and PTSD is a dynamic dual-unfolding process (Wilson and Lindy, 1994). The patient and therapist have reciprocal effects on each other during the course of treatment. They are like fellow sojourners on a trip that encounters the unknown and, at times, frightened chasm of psychic uncertainty. However, the capacity for sustained empathic attunement yields these changes in the cognitive processes of the therapist: (1) information density and (2) cognitive complexity, which are related by-products of the encoding knowledge about the patient's psychodynamics (Aronoff and Wilson, 1985). Information density refers to the amount (density) of the elements configured in the ego-space of the patient's trauma complex, and cognitive complexity refers to the organizational differentiation of that material in the therapist. Thus, empathic accuracy facilitates greater cognitive complexity of information processing by the therapist.

7. *Empathy and portals of entry to ego-space configuration*: Empathic attunement enables the therapist to identify more easily the various portals of entry into the patient's ego-space and the nexus of the trauma complex. Wilson, Friedman, and Lindy (2001) have identified five portals of access to the interior sanctum of the PTSD processes—the five clusters of the PTSD symptom configurations. The creative therapist who is empathically attuned can quite readily enter these portals as avenues of gaining more information as to how the patient is processing the traumatic experience.

Trauma alters the organisms in synergistic ways—some subtle and others in intricately complicated ways. Furthermore, one implication of phasic synchrony is an ability to resonate with the organismic expressions of traumatic impacts; for example, to ego-defenses and areas of emotional vulnerability and injury; physiological hyperreactivity, dreams, affective lability, resistances, and areas of avoidance, denial, disavowal, and numbing. Since PTSD symptoms are transduced into seven channels of symptom transmission, access to the portals of entry into the ego-space of the patient is like walking down a dark passageway into the various chambers hidden by the façade of the patient's persona. Empathic congruence becomes a beacon of light that illuminates the pathways, focusing light in the necessary areas to properly traverse the hallway.

8. *Trauma disclosure and reduction of defensiveness*: Entry into the ego-space of the patient via empathic congruence and the mechanisms of phasic synchrony facilitates a more complete disclosure of the contents of the trauma narrative by the patient. Simultaneously, this process of disclosure will, over time, result in a reduction in the need for defensive guardedness. Genuine empathic attunement conveys the message from the therapist that they are the source of comfort and safety who will protect the patient from their fears and anxieties associated with organismic disequilibrium resulting from allostatic changes in the pre-trauma baseline of functioning.

9. *Clarity in understanding ego-defenses built around traumatization*: As a corollary to increased trauma disclosure and a reduction of defensiveness in the patient, the therapist naturally develops understanding and clarity as to the role of ego-defenses in protecting areas of vulnerability associated with traumatization. Authentic empathic attunement is one form of what Rogers (1951) termed unconditional positive regard for the patient. The process of sustained authentic attunement results in the therapist having a broader vista of the operation of the patient's defenses that, paradoxically, lessens their need for utilization in the *context* of a therapeutic sanctuary which can be experienced by the patient as a place of rock-solid safety amidst the inner turmoil of uncertainty and the search for meaning and purpose to the traumatic experience itself.

10. *Positive allostasis: restabilization following change caused by trauma*: Empathic attunement in its various permeations also serves to facilitate positive allostasis (Wilson, Friedman, and Lindy, 2001). As noted by McEwen (1998), allostasis refers to the body's effort to maintain stability through change when stress places demands on the organism's adaptive capacity. Positive allostasis refers to restabilization following change caused by trauma. However, it is not a return to the previous baseline of functioning. Rather, it is the creation of a new configuration of adapta-

tion. As noted by Horowitz (1986), a process of accommodation occurs in processing the trauma experience—what was ego-alien (trauma) is now assimilated into a new cognitive-affective structure in ego-processes and the self. Although positive allostasis is not the same as health, it is a central mechanism in the process of healing. In this regard, transformation of the trauma experience into an integrative, efficacious self-modality without debilitating symptoms of anxiety, depression, substance abuse, PTSD, and so on, may be regarded as the core of healing and organismic resilience.

11. *Threshold of TST recognition and utilization in treatment*: The therapist's capacity to recognize and properly utilize TST varies greatly in the treatment of PTSD. Empathic congruence and phasic synchrony enable a faster threshold of recognition of TST—ability to recognize and use this form of transference in the treatment process. As stated earlier, TST is considered present throughout the course of treatment and therefore empathic attunement enables recognition of its transmissions, dynamic significance, and critical importance as information "leakage" from the patient to the therapist.

12. *Symbolization of trauma experience*: The capacity of humans to symbolize experience has long been recognized in the psychodynamic literature (Freud, 1915–1917; Jung, 1929; Lindy, 1993). Traumatic experiences, as archetypal phenomena, are also symbolized to express the intrapsychic processes of the patient (Kalsched, 1996). Empathic accuracy serves as a vehicle by which to understand the idiosyncratic manifestation of the trauma experience. The symbolization of the trauma experience is yet another variation on the "information transmission" from the patient—it is their way of saying, "Look at this symbol—it contains representations of how I was affected by trauma—it is a clue for you to understand that which I cannot fully verbalize." We can also think of symbols of trauma as encapsulated information that contain categories of data that link elements of the trauma experience together in a unified manner. The symbols are generated by the unconscious architect of the patient who creates an object of expression. Interpretation of, or understanding, its meaning may be obscured to the patient's conscious awareness but, of course, unconsciously informative when accurately interpreted.

13. *Empathy and information storage: future stockpiles*: Empathic accuracy and congruence is associated with the capacity to receive, decode, and use information generated by the patient. In addition to the quantity and quality of information retrieved through the patient's multichanneled transmissions, such data can be stored by the therapist for future use in formulating the nature of psychodynamic functioning. Clearly, having more information about the patient is critically important in several ways. First, to formulate

hypotheses about the operation of allostatic mechanisms in PTSD and associated co-morbidities. Second, to use the stored information as an additional tool of sustained empathic attunement including, for example, hypothesis testing with the patient about their functioning. Third, to increase prediction through empathic accuracy, i.e., to anticipate patterns of behavior likely to be expressed by the patient in the course of "working through" the trauma (assimilation and accommodation of unmetabolized traumatic material).

14. *Increased therapist awareness of empathic strain, compassion fatigue, and CTRs*: As a natural consequence of sustained empathic attunement, empathic congruence, matching phenomenon, and so on, the therapist will develop greater self-awareness and insight into his or her own reactions to the work of treatment. Clearly, good empathic capacity implies awareness not only of the patient's internal psychological state but of the therapist's internal affective and psychological processes. Thus, self-directed empathic introspection (i.e., self-monitoring) is a way in which analysts identify their own reactions indicative of empathic strains, compassion fatigue, and CTRs.

15. *Isochronicity and organismic tuning: holistic healing through positive allostatic restabilization*: Organismic tuning refers to positive allostatic readjustment following a traumatic experience. Positive allostasis refers to restabilization in a holistic way that promotes growth, resilience, and efficacious functioning rather than stasis, fixation, fragmentation, and maladaptive psychopathology. *Organismic tuning*, or isochronicity, is a natural consequence of consistent, sustained, empathic inquiry. Organismic tuning also reflects holistic, synergistic interactive effects in the psychobiology of human stress response (Friedman, 2000a). Sustained, consistent, empathic congruence that accurately decodes the transference and trauma-specific transmissions of the patient facilitates positive allostatic restabilization, leading to organismic growth, health, optimal functioning, and movement toward the increased self-actualization of potentials (Wilson, Friedman, and Lindy, 2001).

NOTE

1. Abyss experience is the confrontation with the archetype of trauma; the demonic, and Darkness of Being (Wilson, 2002).

REFERENCES

Aronoff, J., and Wilson, J. P. (1985). *Personality in the social process*. Hillsdale, NJ: Lawrence Erlbaum.

Cohen, M. B. (1952). Countertransference and anxiety. *Psychiatry*, 15: 231–43.

Dalenberg, C. J. (2000a). *Countertransference and PTSD.* Washington, DC: American Psychological Association Press.

———. (2000b). *Countertransference in the treatment of trauma.* Washington, DC.: American Psychological Association Press.

Danieli, Y. (1988). Confronting the unimaginable: Psychotherapists' reactions to victims of the Nazi Holocaust. In J. P. Wilson, Z. Harel, and B. Kahana (Eds.), *Human adaptation and stress: From the Holocaust to Vietnam*, pp. 219–39. New York: Plenum Press.

———. (1994a). Countertransference and trauma: Self healing and training issues. In M. B. Williams and J. F. Sommer, Jr. (Eds.), *Handbook of posttraumatic therapy*, pp. 540–55. Westport, CT: Greenwood/Praeger.

———. (1994b). *International handbook of multigenerational legacies of trauma.* New York: Plenum Press.

Figley, C. R. (1997). *Compassion fatigue.* New York: Brunner/Mazel.

———. (2002). *Treating compassion fatigue.* New York: Brunner-Routledge.

Freud, S. (1910). The future prospects of psychoanalytic therapy. *Standard Edition*, 11: 141–42. London: Hogarth Press.

———. (1912). Recommendations to physicians practicing psychoanalysis. *Standard Edition*, 12: 111–20. London: Hogarth Press.

———. (1915–1917). Introductory lectures on psycho-analysis. *Standard Edition*, 15 and 16. London: Hogarth Press.

———. (1920). Beyond the pleasure principle. In *Standard Edition*, 18, pp. 3–64. London: Hogarth Press.

Friedman, M. J. (2000a). *Posttraumatic and acute stress disorders.* Kansas City, MO: Compact Clinicals.

———. (2000b). *Post-traumatic stress disorder: The latest assessment and treatment strategies.* Kansas City, MO: Compact Clinicals.

Horowitz, M. (1986). *Stress response syndromes.* Northvale, NJ: Jason Aronson.

Ickes, W. (1997). *Empathic accuracy.* New York: Guilford.

Jung, C. G. (1929). The collected works (Bollingen series XX, 20 vols.). In H. Read, M. Fordham, and G. Adler (Eds.), *The therapeutic value of abreaction* (CW 16) (R. F. C. Hull, Trans.). Princeton, NJ: Princeton University Press.

Kalsched, D. (1996). *The inner world of trauma: Archetypal defenses of the personal spirit.* London: Routledge.

Kohut, H. (1959). Introspection, empathy and psychoanalysis. *Journal of the American Psychoanalytic Association*, 7: 459–83.

———. (1977). *Restoration of the self.* New York: International University Press.

Levenson, R. W., and Ruef, A. M. (1997). Psychological aspects of emotional knowledge. In W. Ickes (Ed.), *Empathic accuracy.* New York: Guilford.

Lifton, R. J. (1967). *Death in life: The survivors of Hiroshima.* New York: Simon & Schuster.

———. (1993). From Hiroshima to the Nazi doctors: The evolution of psychoformative approaches to understanding traumatic stress syndromes. In J. P. Wilson and B. Raphael (Eds.), *International handbook of traumatic stress syndromes*, pp. 11–25. New York: Plenum Press.

Lindy, J. D. (1988). *Vietnam: A casebook*. New York: Brunner/Mazel.

———. (1993). Focal psychoanalytic psychotherapy of PTSD. In J. P. Wilson and B. Raphael (Eds.), *The international handbook of traumatic stress syndromes*, pp. 803–11. New York: Plenum Press.

Maroda, K. J. (1991). *The power of countertransference*. New York: Wiley.

McEwen, B. (1998). Protective and damaging effects of stress mediators. *Seminars of the Beth Israel Deaconess Medical Center*, 338 (3): 171–79.

Parson, E. (1988). Post-traumatic self-disorder: Theoretical and practical considerations for psychotherapy of Victim War veterans. In J. P. Wilson, Z. Harel, and B. Kahana (Eds.), *Human adaptation to extreme stress*, pp. 245–79. New York: Plenum Press.

Pearlman, L., and Saakvitne, K. (1997). *Trauma and the therapist*. New York: Norton.

Rogers, C. (1951). *Client-centered therapy*. New York: Houghton Mifflin.

Rowe, T., and MacIsaac, J. (1991). *Empathic attunement*. Northvale, NJ: Jason Aronson.

Scurfield, R. M. (1993). Treatment of posttraumatic syndrome disorder among Vietnam veterans. In J. P. Wilson and B. Raphael (Eds.), *The international handbook of traumatic stress syndromes*, pp. 879–89. New York: Plenum Press.

Slatker, E. (1987). *Countertransference*. Northvale, NJ: Jason Aronson.

Stamm, B. H. (1999). *Secondary traumatic stress: self-care for clinicians, researchers and educators*. Cutherville, MD: Sidran Press.

Tansey, M. J., and Burke, W. F. (1989). *Understanding countertransference*. Hillsdale, NJ: Erlbaum.

Thomas, R. B., and Wilson, J. P. (2004). Issues and controversies in the understanding and diagnosis of compassion fatigue, vicarious traumatization, and secondary traumatic stress disorder. *International Journal of Emergency Mental Health*.

Wilson, J. P. (1989). *Trauma, transformation and healing: An integrative approach to theory, research and post-traumatic therapy*. New York: Brunner/Mazel.

———. (2002, October 11). *The abyss experience and catastrophic stress*. Paper presented at the Conference on Terrorism and Weapons of Mass Destruction, St. Joseph's University, Philadelphia, Pennsylvania.

Wilson, J. P., and Lindy, J. (1994). *Counter-transference in the treatment of PTSD*. New York: Guilford.

Wilson, J. P., and Raphael, B. (1993). *The international handbook of traumatic stress syndromes*. New York: Plenum Press.

Wilson, J. P., and Thomas, R. (2004). *Empathy in the treatment of trauma and PTSD*. New York: Brunner-Routledge.

Wilson, J. P., Friedman, M., and Lindy, J. (2001). *Treating psychological trauma and PTSD*. New York: Guilford.

Wolstein, B. (1988). *Essential papers on countertransference*. New York: New York University Press.

Chapter Eighteen

The Complexities of Working with Terror

B. Hudnall Stamm, Craig Higson-Smith, and Amy C. Hudnall

This chapter discusses theory and research related to direct and indirect exposure to potentially traumatizing events brought about by working in terrifying situations. We posit that there are things that can be done—by the individual, the work group, the agency, and even a culture—that are protective for traumatic stress workers. The chapter begins with a review of the background literature on work-related indirect trauma, now conceptualized as a subfield of traumatic stress, most commonly labeled secondary or vicarious trauma. We then expand on some of the complexities of the experiences encountered by those who work in terrifying situations where workers may simultaneously be exposed to a malevolent environment of indirect (secondary or vicarious) or direct trauma. Using a person–event model, we present information on biological and psychological risks and protective factors that can influence an individual's work appraisal and competency, contributing to both positive and negative resiliency. Culture is examined as a contextual factor and a model of culture (part of culture, not part of culture) by exposure (direct, indirect) is presented. The chapter concludes with recommendations supporting the healthiest workplace possible in the face of terror.

A United Nations envoy had said that the devastation [in a refugee camp] is "horrific beyond belief. . . . I think I can speak for all in the UN delegation in saying that we are shocked."

> —Terje Roed-Larse to BBC News,
> April 18, 2002 (cited in Jenin Camp, 2002)

Upon hearing that five aid workers were freed from being taken hostage by warring forces, the IRC's president, George Rupp, said, "We are thankful that our colleagues are safe. Now we are focusing on bringing much needed assistance to the refugees and displaced people . . . who have been uprooted by the recent violence."

—International Rescue Committee, August 11, 2002

The next day . . . was probably the worst for us in terms of being in the middle of the fighting. For four hours that afternoon, there was shooting all around us and we were lying down on the floor, praying, comforting each other, and answering the phone, which was ringing about every 10 minutes.

—Karen Carr, personal communication, September 30, 2002

Living with terror changes you. It burrows into your soul. It pulls you apart thought by thought. It redirects the neurotransmitters of your brain. It writes its story into your hippocampus and your amygdala. It inhabits your sleep. It visits when you least expect it, even when you are miles or years from its home. It recreates you, unbidden, and unwelcomed.

The balance between hope and despair is fragile, yet repeatedly, the human spirit reveals its strength. It is about this strength that we write. It is also about recognizing the strength of terror and about calling its name. It is about engaging it in the dance. It is about naming life and choosing it over death.

We begin this chapter with the language of metaphor because it is impossible to speak directly of terror. The experience of terror falls beyond the capacities of our normal language. As Herman (1992, p. 1) so eloquently remarks:

The ordinary response to atrocities is to banish them from consciousness. Certain violations of the social compact are too terrible to utter aloud: this is the meaning of the word *unspeakable*.

Perhaps that is what makes terror so striking in our lives. Those of us who respond to human need in the face of horror struggle to know it and to articulate what we see it doing to others and what it does to us. As the authors of this chapter, we declare that the struggle may not always end in horror, though we may see horror along the way. It is our belief that when hope overcomes terror, even by the smallest margin, healing is present. We believe that there are things that can be done—by the individual, the work group, the agency, and even a culture—that are protective and that bolster the chance for hope to surmount terror. We have held these beliefs for some time and have learned from them in the field, through theory and through research. As a field of study, we are beginning to understand that caring when you yourself are afraid can be a substantially more complex task, psychologically, than caring from a position of safety.

In this chapter, we move from the clinic into the field, a change in venue that brings with it special circumstances for the mental health worker. In these field situations, many clinicians find that due to their expertise, they become the person to whom others look to make sense of chaos. This can be very difficult for the clinician. Because of their well-honed sense of empathy and professional knowledge, clinicians may be fully aware of the meaning of the chaos, even if it makes no sense to them. The clinician's work can transform from therapist to administrator, supervisor, planner, and even confidant. In this chapter, we examine the context of working in terrifying situations and offer suggestions for individuals and for the administration of workers who are managing in difficult situations such as humanitarian disasters, refugee camps, and other terror-initiated field operations.

LIVING AND WORKING WITH TERROR

Many events can produce extreme fear—some naturally occurring and others brought about by human action. Terrorism is brought about by human action. Events that violently put people's way of life at risk often leave individuals, families, and even entire populations in great distress. Terrorists, warlords, and other *ministers of chaos* (Seaquist, Forstenzer, and Quianzon, 1992) depend on this response in order to demoralize populations and thereby bring political power to bear on an enemy. The aim—and very often, the successful result—of terrorist attacks is to create widespread fear in the population. While we generally think to protect the "victims" of these events, those who help—aide workers, counselors, clergy, medical staff, graves registry personnel, engineers, and other kinds of helpers—are immersed in the same situation. The significance of protecting the caregivers becomes more prescient as we move into the twenty-first century.

According to the United Nations (UN), the number of nongovernmental organizations (NGOs) and their global networks almost doubled in eight years, from a total of 23,600 organizations in 1991 to 44,000 in 1999 (United Nations Development Programme, 2000). The International Committee of the Red Cross reported that the cost of human-made disasters, by the mid-nineties, had begun to overwhelm the world's ability to respond (Shawcross, 2000). In the 2000 UN General Assembly session for the twentieth century, Kofi Annan used as his theme "deliverance from evil" or the focus on support of humanitarian caregivers. Recognizing the tremendous emotional and physical risks for these caregivers, the UN further cited that one of its major goals for the next century is to ensure work safety for NGOs, the media, and workers' organizations (United Nations Development Programme, 2000). These figures have served to underscore the urgency of moving to a place of understanding that asks, How do we protect the helpers?

The daily business of living is interpreting our experiences. This person-event interaction is altered but not halted by being a helper. Helpers are not immune, by virtue of their work, to the fear. While helping does have some protective factors, other factors may leave helpers more vulnerable for a variety of reasons.

Often, helpers engage deeply with a person's or people's traumatic experiences, thereby increasing their personal exposure. It should be noted that it is misleading to compare the traumatic exposure of a helper with that of the person they are trying to help. We are not claiming that secondary exposure is the same as the primary victim's, but there are complexities in the dynamics of these relationships that bear consideration. Recounting the episode the trauma survivor has experienced is, at some level, processing the experience; thereby reducing its impact on further witnesses. Nevertheless, a helper working under emergency situations might engage with many similar traumatic stories every day for days on end. The cumulative effects of such exposure are often extremely distressing and difficult to manage.

Background Literature

The area linked to work-related indirect trauma, now conceptualized as a subfield of traumatic stress, is relatively new but has a rich history that parallels the general field of traumatic stress. This subarea came forward in the early 1990s, about a decade after the emergence of the current traumatic-stress literature, surging ahead in the mid-1990s (Figley, 1995; McCann and Pearlman, 1990; Paton and Violanti, 1996; Pearlman and Saakvitne, 1995; Stamm, 1995, 1999c; Wilson and Lindy, 1994). It quickly gained momentum in applied and research settings, generating literally hundreds of articles and numerous dissertations by the end of the decade (see Stamm, 1999c for analysis).

The precursor to the current understanding of work-related indirect trauma is generally acknowledged to be Haley's work describing therapists hearing from Vietnam veterans' reports of atrocities (1974). In reviewing the literature, it is possible to generally identify four threads that come together to feed into the current understanding of work-related indirect trauma.[1] These threads are (1) disasters, (2) war, (3) death studies, and (4) interpersonal violence. Viewed in retrospect, there are significant contributions that have a bearing on the current evolving literature around trauma.

The disaster literature was perhaps the first to routinely discuss the issues of the worker and the issues of the primary victims of the events simultaneously. Twenty-five years ago, the National Institute of Mental Health (NIMH) published one of the original operations manuals for the modern conceptualization of disaster responding (1978/1986). The 1985 manual by Hartsough and Myers expanded disaster-responding knowledge and included information on a training document for helping those working at disaster sites (Myers, 1985). At about the same time, research literature began to appear that reported negative consequences on workers working in disasters (Durham, McCammon, and Allison, 1985). In the late 1980s, Dunning (1988) commented on the multifaceted system impact of the work on emergency workers. She advocated for both prevention and intervention to reduce the negative effects of working in terrifying situations. This era of work is summarized in a review article by Shepherd and Hodgkinson (1990).

Along with the work on disasters, the literature on war is the most directly related to the current topic at hand. In fact, three papers were written in the early 1990s that addressed specifically the effects on helpers working with refugees. These include Van der Veer's (1992) discussion of the structural complexities of providing mental health interventions for refugees and Stearns's (1993) recommendation that disaster models be used to understand refugee situations. In 1993, Lansen wrote about the effect of working with torture survivors and Simon (1993) about the legal and other obstacles faced by human rights workers. Other papers that apply but are more directly related to war and even military operations include the effect of soldiers and their support personnel working in war zones (Bartone, Ursano, Wright, and Ingraham, 1989; Leach, 1994) as well as the problems associated with graves registry duty (Sutker, Uddo, Brailey, Vasterling, and Errera, 1994).

Literature also appears related to those who attended death. The effects of mass death and the consequences of postevent cleanup were compellingly addressed by Miles, Demi, and Mostyn-Aker (1984) in their discussion of the psychological impact of responding to the Kansas City Hyatt Regency skywalk collapse and in Raphael, Singh, Bradbury, and Lambert's (1983–1984) discussion of the Granville Rail Disaster. Vachon (1987) examined the effect of working around death during the dying process. The literature on interpersonal violence and the indirect effect on helpers is eloquently discussed in McCann and Pearlman's landmark 1990 paper that introduced the term *vicarious traumatization*.

CURRENT CONCEPTUALIZATIONS OF WORK-RELATED INDIRECT TRAUMA

Today it is widely accepted that interaction with victims of traumatic exposure places helpers at a high risk of secondary exposure. Various authors have grappled with this phenomenon in different ways. For example, classical burnout theory (Freudenberger, 1984; Maslach, 1986) tends to be closely linked with coping resources. Such coping resources are argued to be finite, and prolonged exposure to emotionally charged demands leads them to being chronically depleted. From this point of view, time away from the demands as well as work to build effective coping strategies is an appropriate intervention for people suffering from burnout.

However, Figley (1995) argued that some forms of stress, although themselves not life threatening, are so demanding on the witness and helper that they might induce emotional coping responses very similar to those of the traumatic stress response itself. For this response, Figley (1995) used the term "compassion fatigue." McCann and Pearlman's original theory of vicarious traumatization (1990) was expanded by Pearlman and Saakvitne (1995), who approached the study of work-related indirect trauma in terms of the relationship dynamics between trauma survivor and helper. Pearlman and Saakvitne recognized the special role of countertransference in the relationship, noting that particular forms of countertransference are linked to the emotional distress associated with work with trauma survivors.

The term "secondary traumatic stress" used by Stamm (1995, 1999c) makes explicit the close relationship between primary and secondary traumatic exposure. Primary exposure refers to those directly in harm's way while secondary exposure removes the person from the direct path, making their exposure secondary to the original victim (Stamm, 2002a). Recent work by Stamm and colleagues (Larsen, Stamm, and Davis, 2002) has conceptualized the difference between burnout and secondary or vicarious traumatic stress related to fear. These ideas generated from the revision of the Compassion Fatigue and Satisfaction test (Stamm and Figley, 1998) that is contained in the new Professional Quality of Life test (ProQOL) (Stamm, 2002b). Burnout is conceptualized as the gradual depletion of resources with the residual effect of inefficacy while compassion fatigue or secondary/vicarious traumatic stress is conceptualized as the rapid insertion of fear associated with the psychological material or others encountered in the work setting.

Beyond Secondary/Vicarious Trauma

Sometimes work-related trauma places one in the path of both direct and indirect trauma (Stamm, 2002a, 2002c). There are those who make themselves available to shore up the resources of those who have been traumatized, and they do this work in dangerous situations. The prima facie example of this would be those who respond to humanitarian disasters such as wars or terrorist attacks. Not only do the helpers find themselves dealing with the evidence of terror in the lives of others, they do so in day-to-day living conditions that are fundamentally unsafe. They often see grotesque or horrifying things in the line of duty. They may deal with general public health risks such as sanitation and overcrowding; food insufficiency; absence of medical assistance in the face of great need; poor to nonexistent housing; transportation crises; and poverty. In addition, they may be caught in the middle of exchanges of gunfire and shelling. They may be individually or collectively at risk due to political or cultural beliefs. They may be individually at risk of attack for personal gain of goods or supplies or at risk of physical or sexual attack motivated by the perpetrator's frustration, meanness, or revenge. All these things mingle with the altruistic desire and real fulfillment of being able to help make a positive difference in frightening situations.

Figure 18.1 represents some of the complexities of the experiences encountered by those who work in terrifying situations. The top row represents four broad theoretically and quantitatively derived categories of stressful experiences (see Stamm, 1999a and 1999b for a full explanation). The first broad category includes things like disasters, war, accidents, and so forth; what victims often describe as "bad things that happen" (bad things). These things come unexpectedly and have the capability to negatively affect a life but do not involve actual or narrowly escaped death. The next category of stressful experiences are all those that involve actual or threatened death. Sexual assault, the third category, is separated from the others due to both its relatively high prevalence and its unique personal characteristics. And last, problems in living refer to stressful events that lack the characteristic of extreme fear. Problems in living can range from mild such as worrying about the outcome of a meeting to severe such as following a major life change, for example, a divorce, that does not involve family violence. Taken together, these four broad categories can be used to generally classify stressful events that range from mild to severe day-to-day stressors (problems in living) that may not cause traumatic stress but have been shown to exacerbate negative reactions to extreme stress that can be a precursor to traumatic stress.

The diagram in figure 18.1 demonstrates the general types of events and their paths into direct and indirect exposure. As is demonstrated in the diagram, direct and indirect exposure has a strong bi-directional feature that can amplify or ameliorate the effect of the other. Humanitarian aide workers may experience direct or indirect exposure, often in a form that has elements of both combined. In some cases, aide workers have to make decisions with inadequate options or information and may affect future direct and indirect exposure. For example, aide workers may decide to move a refugee camp only to discover, to their horror, and with the best intentions, they chose a more rather than less dangerous location.

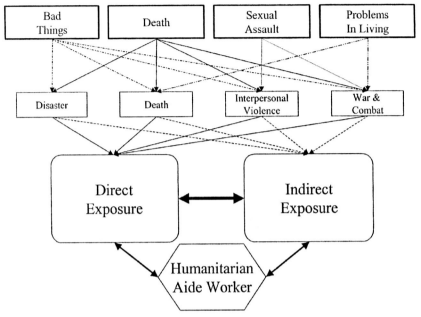

Figure 18.1.   Complexities of the Experiences Encountered by Those Who Work in Terrifying Situations.

Thus, those who work in these difficult situations may simultaneously be exposed to a malevolent environment (King, King, Keane, Fairbank, and Adams, 1998) of indirect (secondary or vicarious) trauma and direct trauma. The literature on this group of workers who are exposed directly and indirectly is only beginning to emerge. As noted in the preceding, this shared primary and secondary exposure is most akin to those working in emergency services but contains the additional element of intentional human malevolence associated with terrorism or war. Some of this literature is related to peacekeeping functions. Peacekeepers are all in a specific *militaresque* role but may come to the work from different backgrounds. Some peacekeepers are soldiers placed in the role of preventing fighting rather than participating in it. Others are police who have been recruited to prevent fighters from engaging each other.

The literature on peacekeepers is small and mixed. The early studies suggested that peacekeeping, like combat, had a devastating effect on at least some of those who did the work (Litz, King, King, Orsillo, and Friedman, 1997; Orsillo, Roemer, Litz, Ehlich, and Friedman, 1998). One of the key variables that differentiates combat from peacekeeping is the peacekeeper's enforced "helplessness" associated with not being able to "fight back" and defend oneself. Later research has shown that pre-event experiences and traits were strongly correlated with peacekeeper distress (Ballone, Valentino, Occhiolini, Di Mascio, Cannone, and Schioppa, 2000; Bramsen, Dirkzwager, and van der Ploeg, 2000; Bramsen, Dirkzwager, Van Esch, and van der Ploeg, 2001). Regardless of the precursors to negative reactions, the reactions seem to be moderate to long lasting (MacDonald, Chamberlain, Long, and Mirfin, 1999; Mehlum, 1999; Mehlum and Weisaeth, 2002). When helpers in war zones do not have extremely clear priorities, they themselves can become "ideal victims" (Eisenman, Bergner, and Cohen, 2000). Danieli (2002) has edited the most comprehensive work on the blended roles, and she aptly names those who do the work "protectors and providers."

BEING A HELPER CHANGES THE PERSON-EVENT INTERACTION

Working with Terror

Some helpers mistakenly believe that their role, training, and experience make them somehow immune to the effects of traumatic exposure. In so doing, they forget that the traumatic stress response is at least in part an autonomic biological response to danger (see Friedman, Charney, and Deutch, 1995, for a good introduction), and that although our theories and models might help us understand our response, they do not prevent those responses from happening. A great danger arises when helpers' deep assumptions of their own immunity allow them to put themselves at increased risk by continuing to work when they have exhausted their personal resources. They may not care properly for themselves even if they notice the early signs of secondary traumatic stress; sometimes helpers even conceal their pain behind masks of denial and avoidance because they (or others) feel that they are failing as helpers if they reveal their own distress.

In order to be effective in their work of connecting empathically to the direct victims of an event, helpers may try to avoid becoming desensitized to the violence around them. If they desensitize themselves or become numb to the situation in which they work, they might not be able to engage empathically with the distress of the people they aim to assist. They are not likely to have great success in their work. It is important that helpers remain aware, both cognitively and affectively, of the violence they seek to confront with healing. What is a positive coping skill for those living with an ongoing and extreme stressor is antithetical for the helper to be effective in his or her work.

As previously noted, in certain situations, helpers are confronted with direct traumatic exposure and secondary traumatic exposure simultaneously.

For example, in civil conflict situations many helpers work in communities that literally are war zones. In the last ten years, aide workers have increasingly been at risk for their personal safety. "In 1998, for the first time in history, more UN civilian workers were killed in the line of duty—twenty-four—than peacekeeping soldiers." The numbers were even worse by November 1999, with twenty-eight UN civilian aid workers killed in eleven months (Shawcross, 2000). The helper is forced to struggle with the emotional consequences of trying to care for others, while at the same time fearing for his or her own safety. Often, the helper lives with a sense of invulnerability, assuming "they are not the victims." We propose that this places the helper in an emotionally untenable situation; perhaps the rupture of a caregiver's invulnerability and sense of betrayal of trust leaves them with even fewer defenses than those people being helped who live with chronic tension and fear. Václav Havel, the former president of Czechoslovakia, provides an apt metaphor for how disarming this rupture can be, albeit in a different forum. He writes:

> Because I really was catapulted overnight into a world of fairy tales [translate as invulnerability], and then, . . . had to return to earth [vulnerable to the violence perpetrated on those for whom you are aiding] the better to realize that invulnerability is merely a projection of human archetypes and that the world is not at all structured like a fairy tale. . . . I was given no diplomatic immunity from that hard fall to earth. (Havel, 2002)

Here Havel is describing his move from author, poet, and activist to the Czechoslovakian presidency in 1990. But the surprise, the inadequacy of unanticipated change is apt. Although it has yet to be investigated rigorously, it may be that the psychological complexity of multiple direct and indirect exposure when one is in the role of protecting others is greater than either direct exposure or secondary exposure alone.

Helpers' perceived effectiveness is another aspect of their increased vulnerability. The importance of helplessness or powerlessness is a defining characteristic of some traumatic stress responses such as Post-Traumatic Stress Disorder (PTSD) and has been written about at length in the literature on traumatic stress. Its effects should not be forgotten when considering secondary traumatic stress (Stamm, 1999a). The emotional consequence of feeling powerless to assist people in need undermines the personal identity and meaning of many helpers, particularly when their job description and self-image defines them by their ability to help others. Factors such as the personal histories and cultural backgrounds of the client or the helper, the context within which help is being provided, and the nature of the traumatic experience all play a role in determining how much assistance is possible

(Weine, 1999; Danieli, 2002). These factors also play a role in determining what the helpers believe about their own competency in the situation, and how much they perceive themselves as being useful.

Helpers who have insufficient protection, either personal or institutional, from the deleterious emotional consequences of helping rapidly become ineffectual. Rather than seeing the helper as flawed, a deeper understanding of the person-event interaction in the context of culture as it relates to secondary traumatic stress is needed to enable the community of helpers to provide care in a way that does not ultimately destroy the helper or the community.

Components of the Person-Event Interaction

There is a broad range of responses that a person can experience and interpret, and those responses are particularly salient to understanding the effect of stressful events on those who find themselves helping in harm's way. Previously, one of us (Stamm) defined a stressful experience as "an individual's experience in relation to an event, such that elements of the event in combination with that specific individual create a situation whereby the experience itself is stress-producing and one's beliefs—of faith in life, in others, in self— are disorganized, restructured, or at least challenged" (Stamm, 1993, 1999a, 1999b). This definition recognizes that interpretation is idiosyncratic and that the challenge to one's beliefs and way of life can be slight or cataclysmic.

Until very recently, secondary traumatic stress has generally been treated in an undifferentiated way in the literature. Now trauma specialists are beginning to realize that this is a complex phenomenon, operating in different ways in different situations for different people. In order to grapple effectively with secondary traumatic stress, we need a more sophisticated and contextualized model of the person-event relationship. In this case, we perceive *context* to include both the organizational structure and the culture in which the helper functions.

Another important aspect in the development of a traumatic stress reaction is the number of highly stressful life events one is exposed to (Kessler, Sonnega, Bromet, Hughes, Nelson, and Breslau, 1995). One theory suggests that many of these highly stressful life events completely overwhelm our physical, mental, and social support mechanisms (Hobfoll, 1989). This drain on our resources challenges our ability to negotiate the world and leaves us vulnerable. Concurrently, the physical and psychological impact of these events can compromise a person's ability to work and maintain interpersonal relationships. One author suggests that these events are so powerful that they shatter our basic assumptions of the world, namely, that the self is worthy and the world is benevolent (Janoff-Bulman, 1992).

Because the disruption of these events is so severe, it can take a considerable amount of time to rebuild these support mechanisms. Given the potential impact of one event, the impact of multiple events on an individual is exponentially challenging. The triple impact of being affected by a second highly stressful event, having insufficient support mechanisms, and having limited financial and interpersonal resources leave the person more vulnerable to develop psychological problems. Furthermore, additional events are likely to irritate symptoms by bringing up memories of previous events. Taken together this literature suggests two important areas for research—the magnitude of an event and the resources of the person affected.

We take as a theoretical tool the Structural Approximation of Stressful Experiences, which expands on the organization of the person-event interaction posted by Stamm (1993, 1999a, 1999b; Stamm and Bieber, 1996), the Structural Approximation of Stressful Experiences (table 18.1). This model, which is based on data from one thousand people, suggests that the resources of the person interact with the magnitude of an event to render the person's understanding of the event. Resources are conceptualized as the ability to incorporate incoming information with one's conceptualization of the self, one's conceptualization of others, and one's goals. The event is conceptualized as a composite of the elements, which, if present, could make any event sufficiently novel for it to potentially change the individual's life path either in a

Table 18.1.   Structural Approximation of Stressful Experiences: Person–Event Interaction

Resources of the Person: A person's ability to incorporate incoming information with one's conception of the self, conception of others, and one's goals.	
Place in the World	An individual's perception of his or her worthiness and belongingness in the environment and the community.
Person to Person	An individual's understanding of others in relation to himself or herself.
Magnitude of the Event: A composite of the elements which, if present, could make any event sufficiently novel for it to potentially change the individual's life path either in a positive or negative direction.	
Abrogation of Reality	The gap between what one believes will happen and what is or has happened
Finiteness	The reality of death, desire for death, belief that someone has died, and life-after-death experiences
Person in Event	The person's feelings, beliefs, and actions during the event as the person perceives them at the time the measure is taken.

positive or in a negative direction (table 18.1). This theory is useful as it applies equally to those in primary and secondary positions concerning extremely stressful events. It also takes into account the current state of the person's resources, which include pre-event function, history, and traits as well as current strength of risk and protective factors, all of which have been shown to relate to the helper's professional quality of life and postduty function.

The Resources of the Person

At the most basic level, the resources of the person can be conceptualized as a person's ability to find a place in the world and to interact with others (Stamm, 1993, 1999a, 1999b; Stamm and Bieber, 1996). Disruptions in one's sense of self, which is one's place in the world, has been associated with poorer outcomes for both stressful and traumatically stressful events (Stamm, 1993, 1999b). Disruptions in one's sense of other, which is person-to-person interactions, are more negative when one has experienced traumatically stressful events. In extreme situations, the other is viewed as harmful and dangerous (Stamm, 1993, 1999b).

There is considerable literature on the nature of the person and what they do or do not bring to the traumatic experience, at least in terms of primary exposure. Demographic factors such as gender, class, racial and ethnic groups, level of education and income, and marital status have all been conclusively linked to the likelihood of a person developing PTSD (Kessler et al., 1995). Similarly, personality variables including introversion and neuroticism are predictive of PTSD following traumatic exposure (Schnurr and Vielhauer, 1999), not to speak of the genetic and neurobiological risk factors for which we are beginning to amass evidence (e.g., Friedman, Charney, and Deutch, 1995). While the research and theory on risk factors for traumatic stress reactions following direct exposure is useful as a guide to thinking about the consequences of secondary exposure, it is not appropriate simply to assume that the same factors operate in the same ways with respect to secondary traumatic stress.

Some work has been done on the factors that contribute to helpers' vulnerability to secondary exposure, but much of it is antidotal, theoretical, or retrospective survey with little attempt to separate secondary exposure from primary exposure (see Stamm, 1999c, for a bibliography). Even less is available on what supports resiliency in helpers. Our lack of empirical knowledge in this area highlights an important focus for future research. A better understanding of what assists helpers to survive the exposure implicit in their occupational choices would enable more responsible selection and training of helpers. What work has been done tends to focus on the characteristics that are most dangerous to helpers. Of these identified characteristics, the most commonly reported is a personal trauma history (cf. Ghahramanlou and Brodbeck, 2000).

The often ongoing and repetitive nature of secondary traumatic exposure arguably requires a slightly different approach to work on primary exposure, which is most commonly of limited duration. Where people's lives endure regular and predictable traumatic exposure, we need to look at the sources of endurance or resilience. Herman (1992, pp. 58–60) argues that approximately 10 percent of the general population appears to be naturally resilient to traumatic stress. She defines such resilience as the

> capacity to preserve social connection and active coping strategies, even in the face of extremity, [which] seems to protect people to some degree against the later development of post-traumatic syndromes. . . . [Resilient people remain] consciously focused on preserving their calm, their judgment, their connection with others, their moral values, and their sense of meaning, even in the most chaotic battlefield conditions.

Strumpfer (1995) coined the term *fortigenic* (literally, the origins of strength) in contrast with the more usual terms *pathogenic* (origins of illness) and *salutogenic* (origins of health). The fortigenic approach searches for traits and techniques which underlie resilience and which can be developed or taught. In fact, there is very little published work in this line, although the existing theory provides fertile ground for speculation. For example, why do people with better resources, people with better educations, and people from dominant social groups appear to be more resilient than others? A possible answer is that perceiving oneself to be able to take control while in challenging circumstances is critically important to resilience. This idea is not new to traumatic stress literature, and different ways have been suggested of conceptualizing a sense of control.

One very useful way of thinking about control is Sense of Coherence (SOC), a term introduced by Antonovsky (1979, 1987). SOC is made up of three distinct components: comprehensibility, manageability, and meaningfulness. Comprehensibility refers to the extent to which people experience their internal and external world as being ordered and consistent, and therefore predictable. Manageability is a person's sense of being able to mobilize sufficient resources to cope with stressful events. Finally, meaningfulness refers to the meaning that a person attaches to stressful events. SOC has been linked to traumatic stress in several studies including Frommberger and colleagues (Frommberger, Stieglitz, Straub, Nyberg, Schlickewei, Kuner, et al., 1999) who show a significant inverse relationship between SOC and the development of PTSD symptomatology. In a similar vein, Maercker, Schuetzwohl, Loebe, Eckhardt, and Mueller (1994) demonstrate that SOC mediates the degree to which a person will dissociate following a traumatic incident.

Current knowledge is limited around the factors that enable helpers to tolerate high levels of secondary exposure, but as the field develops, it is important that researchers identify those variables that result in some helpers' remaining resilient in the face of ongoing secondary trauma, as defined in the preceding.

The Magnitude of the Event

Of fundamental importance to understanding secondary traumatic stress is the nature of the stressor (Stamm, 1993, 1999b, 1999c, Stamm and Bieber, 1996). An unavoidable part of each person's coming to terms with their traumatic experiences is trying to explain the causes of his or her suffering, and sometimes to lay blame on the self, others, or some force outside of humanity. In the same way that people who have survived traumatic experiences question why it was that they had to endure that event, so, too, helpers ask themselves why bad things happen, and why they are the ones left trying to pick up the pieces.

Early in the understanding of traumatic stress, it became clear that it was impossible to assign the term "traumatizing" to one event and nontraumatizing to another. Clearly, events had elements, which for particular people, were overwhelming. The Structural Approximation of Traumatic Stress (table 18.1) attempted to understand what aspects of events feed into their potentially traumatizing character. Following this line of thinking, the magnitude of the event was defined as "a composite of the elements which, if present, could make any event sufficiently novel for it to potentially change the individual's life path either in a positive or in a negative direction" (Stamm, 1993). Structural analysis (factor analysis and longitudinal, multigroup factorial invariance) of narratives and survey data from over one thousand people yielded three factors, *abrogation of expected reality, finiteness, and person-in-event.* These three factors together described people's understanding of events. The abrogation of expected reality speaks to issues of betrayal of trust, specifically describing the gap between expectation and reality. Finiteness addresses both the sense of invulnerability and the recognition of the reality of death. Person-in-event is a complex composite of how people understand themselves during the event and the meaning they make of their own behavior as they analyze and, sometimes, reinterpret their behavior postevent.

Helpers are faced with this challenge in processing the experiences on multiple levels. Their work makes them witnesses and, in some cases, victim-participants or, in extreme cases, part of the traumatizing system. Imagine how the April 1994 massacre of Tutsi by Hutu extremists in Rwanda must haunt the United Nations Assistance Mission in Rwanda (UNAMIR) peace-keepers who watched, under orders to remain neutral. The nature of the traumatic exposure dictates, to a great extent, how difficult this is for helpers. Experience seems to show that a key aspect of the traumatic event's relationship to secondary traumatic stress of the helper is the extent to which the helper feels that they too are threatened. Thus, when we assist people who lost family members in a vehicle accident, which happened on a route that the helper travels frequently, the experience of personal threat is heightened. When we work with the war zone in our backyard, the threat is palpable.

For helpers in dangerous situations where they are trying to survive and to work, not only is there the ever-changing interpretation of rightness or wrongness of their own action in the event (person-in-event), but there is also the ongoing and growing awareness of the reality of death (finiteness). When this is mingled with a chronic reinterpreting or feeling of betrayal concerning the social contract or, in the case of workers, the contract they have with the organization for whom they work, the potential for distress, and even traumatic stress, is high.

The Work Environment

The person exists in the event. In the case of those working in the event, the work itself becomes part of the event and helps define the resources of the person. They may experience peri-traumatic reactions to the event (Marmar, Weiss, Metzler, and Delucchi, 1996; Marmar, Weiss, Metzler, Ronfeldt, and Foreman, 1996). Helpers who are themselves in danger or who lack adequate food and shelter must face the challenges of daily survival, over and above those of caring for traumatized people. Other important factors include the regulation of daily life activities, the reality of gender differences, the coping with extremes of climate, the presence of adequate technical support, the presence of supervision, the appropriate referral resources, the existence of skilled management, and so on.

A potential danger is the organization of help as highlighted by Friedman and Higson-Smith (2002) in their work with police. A primary function of police work is helping victims of crime and violence. In the course of their work, police officers endure high levels of direct and secondary traumatic exposure. This work suggests that early in police officers' careers they are made aware, by their colleagues and the system within which they work, that the honest communication of distress would result in negative judgments of them, both personally and professionally. This is referred to as "disenfranchised distress." It is argued that when helpers work within an environment that disenfranchises distress, a common alternative is to retreat into a complex state of denial, numbing, and dissociation. This state is described as negative resilience since, although intrinsically defensive, it allows helpers to survive, at least temporarily, the emotional impact of high levels of traumatic exposure. Sadly, negative resilience is ultimately associated with a loss of the ability to engage intimately with other human beings, poor conflict management, and increased abuse of alcohol and other substances (Friedman, 1996; Friedman and Higson-Smith, 2002; Friedman, Friedman, van der Kolk, McFarlane, and Higson-Smith, 2000).

If this model of police trauma has validity, it has important implications for the work environments in which helpers are discouraged from expressing the feelings of distress that arise from ongoing exposure to people in extreme difficulty. The various roles of those involved in environments of trauma each demand a unique set of responses. Each individual must evaluate his or her role and how best to support the victims while protecting themselves. For example, is the helper a therapist, an aide worker, a journalist, a peacekeeper, a teacher, a lawyer, or a logistician?

CULTURE AS CONTEXT

The person and the event both exist in the context of culture. Throughout the history of the human race, people have constructed societies in ways that facilitate communal and personal recovery from events that disrupt the life of the community. Our contemporary rituals of compassion, care and healing, and grief and remembrance have all evolved within our societies as ways of caring for our own. These rituals make up an important part of what we, somewhat loosely, refer to as "culture."

The social mechanisms of healing are as important to the health of helpers as they are to that of other members of society, even though most often the helpers are the ones who initiate and maintain the practices of care. Work in many different cultural contexts has shown how people with strong cultural identities are more resilient in the face of traumatic stress. Van de Put and Eisenbruch (2002, p. 151), writing about their work in Cambodia, report that "people in chronic- or postconflict situations do best if they keep a grip on their cultural identity." Higson-Smith (2002), writing about community work in South Africa, notes that African societies have survived many past challenges on the strength of communal healing rituals and systems, and that wherever possible, these culturally imbedded practices should be drawn on to promote healing in the modern and swiftly changing African context.

However, the nature of the world is such that the clear distinct historical boundaries between different cultural, religious, and linguistic groups are breaking down. One of the defining features of the nineteenth and twentieth centuries is the extent to which human beings began traveling across the globe. As we move into the twenty-first century, the enormous advances in communication technology have led to the globalization of societies. The migration of millions of people around the planet has resulted in cultures meeting and influencing each other. This cultural blending contains both opportunities and loss. While they may be enriched by a sharing of traditions, they may also feel their social identity is eroded as it is borrowed from other groups (Espín, 1999), and the differences between groups become less and less clear. This sense of cultural loss is an important variable in understanding many of the long-standing situations in the world today.

Because cultural and group differences are so unyielding and important during times of crises (Bar-Tal and Labin, 2001; Espín, 1999; Unger, 2002), the cultural match between helper and the community to be helped is of central importance and has not received sufficient attention in the psychological literature. Interviews of September 11 Red Cross Response workers in New York City serve to exemplify this issue. The extent to which the degree of cultural match or mismatch influences the helpers' resilience to secondary traumatic stress is mediated by two mechanisms: (1) the extent to which the helpers identify themselves as coming from the same group as their clients and (2) the extent to which helpers feel that they are effective in their work.

Shared Social Identity

Helpers and those they help share the same biological bases of fear (Stamm and Friedman, 2000). However, the interpretation of these biological reactions can be very different. Friedman and Marsella (1996) suggested that PTSD intrusion (B criterion) and arousal (D criterion) symptoms were biologically driven universal reactions and that expressions of avoidant or numbing (C criterion) were cultural. It is likely that the extent of a helper's identification with a particular culture is predictive of his or her resilience in the face of secondary traumatic stress and thus an ongoing ability to help. Helpers with strong, supportive links within their own community are far more likely to be able to persist in offering an effective service (Staub, 1989).

When a helper feels that he or she comes from the same social group as the helped, the extent to which the helper envisages himself or herself undergoing the same experiences will be increased (Cardozo and Salama, 2002; Power and Allison, 2000). Thus, for example, mothers with young children who work in the world of child abuse are in danger of becoming overly afraid and restrictive of their own children. The problem increases when the helper has survived the same experiences that they are working with the client to overcome. This is a common occurrence in situations where religious, ethnic, or cultural groups have been victimized for extensive periods. An overview of the historical trauma of African Americans in the United States helps this to become painfully apparent. African Americans who have felt strong enough to help within their culture have responded in a number of ways: by attempting to eliminate racism, by taking a militant Afrocentrist stand, or by focusing completely on racial difference (Cross, 1999). All these frames of reference are divisive and derive in some measure from the caregivers' inability to step outside of their situation and consider other alternatives.

There are, however, ways in which close social identity can also protect helpers in the face of secondary traumatic stress. Where helpers feel that their work is contributing to the greater good of their social group, for example, the helper who volunteers to treat those wounded in a revolutionary struggle, the broader meaning derived from this work may be a powerful source of resilience (Stamm, 2002a).

PLANNING FROM THE EXPOSURE
BY CULTURE PERSPECTIVE

Bringing together the preceding information, viewing all exposure as a person-event interaction, and recognizing the role of culture as context makes it possible to envision a planning method. At the risk of oversimplification, it is conceivable to conceptualize the problem from the perspective of the level of target for the event (being directly in harm's way versus secondary exposure) and the match between the culture of the helper and the environment in which they are helping (part of culture versus not part of culture). This yields a two by two matrix into which characteristics of the person-event interaction may be placed.

SUPPORTING THE HEALTHIEST WORKPLACE POSSIBLE

Sometimes the nature of the event is so horrific or the depletion of personal resources is so disastrous, it is impossible to describe working conditions as healthy no matter how much care and attention is provided by the individuals, the organizations, and the society. However, even under duress, a great deal can be done at the level of the organization to protect personnel from direct and indirect exposure and the negative effects of caregiving.

There are examples of NGOs beginning to recognize and automatically address the needs of their helpers. As mentioned earlier, the United Nations, on a global scale, is calling for the intentional and thoughtful support of aide workers. Organizations like Handicap International, World Vision International, and Médicins Sans Frontiéres are all creating divisions that focus solely on the emotional care and support of their aide workers. However, learning how to most effectively do this is still in its infancy. There is universal recognition, though, that an ability to predict the responses of aide workers will speed the process of healing (van Gelder and van den Berkhof, 2002; Cardozo and Salama, 2002). The Matrix of Helping (figure 18.2) is perhaps one move closer to such predictions.

What follows are recommendations for strengthening protective factors for workers who live day to day with horrifying risk factors.

1. *Educate personnel about secondary traumatic stress.* The key message here is that unless adequately managed, the high level of traumatic exposure experienced by personnel will inevitably result in secondary traumatic stress. Furthermore, secondary traumatic stress is extremely dis-

Matrix of Helping		
	Part of Culture (Language, Habits, Who Enemy Is, Etc.)	*Not Part of Culture*
Direct Exposure: Response as primary victim	• Culturally based attacks effective • Personally attacked • Can relax somewhat if get away—familiar soothing things	• Trauma from not knowing the culture and perhaps doing something that can get you hurt • Role strain and role confusion from not understanding, no rest from strangeness
Indirect Exposure: Response as helper	• Victims are like self, self is at risk • Victims may look for answers based on sameness, "why my family and not yours" • Familiarity of setting makes it easier to engage empathically, both benefit and risk for secondary effects	• Can distance self because victims are different • Victim may blame outsider for attack • May be easier to reach out to "poor victim" because they are strangers, altruism • May be more difficult to empathize, leading helper into self-doubt based on "why I cannot do this"

Figure 18.2.   Matrix of Helping.

tressing and debilitating and is more difficult to treat than other forms of traumatic stress.

2. *Ensure that people are never discouraged from expressing their distress.* It is important to develop a climate where staff can talk about their emotional responses without feeling as though it will in any way damage their standing in their colleagues' and supervisors' eyes.

3. *Assist staff in managing their emotions.* When staff members do not manage their emotions appropriately, it is important that this behavior be corrected in a supportive manner, sensitive to the difficulty of managing feelings in this context.

4. *Recognize the importance of cultural competence and respect.* Staff members should be assisted in developing "bi-cultural" characteristics that allow them to move fluidly in the culture in which they work but does not negate the culture from which they come.

5. *Address organizational health.* By putting the organization's health on the agenda of every meeting, an awareness of secondary traumatic stress grows within the agency. In most cases this is an item that is passed over with a "yes, we're all doing fine this week," but at other times asking the question can prevent supervisors from overburdening already vulnerable people.

6. *Make regulations and expectations clear.* It is important to have clear regulations to govern the work of staff members. The staff members of helping agencies are often deeply emotionally invested with the people with whom they are working, and so it is easy for work commitments to intrude on people's time away from work. Staff members do need to be able to leave their work at work sometimes.

While no list of recommendations will ameliorate the horror or chaos associated with ground zero for a humanitarian disaster, at least theoretically, the foregoing strengthens the person in the person-event interaction, thereby providing some small measure of support. Whatever can improve the balance between hope and despair, no matter how fragile, is a good thing. The goal of any mental health worker, as a clinician or as an administrator, must be to provide opportunities for the human spirit to reveal its strength and have the opportunity to choose to live as fully as possible even in the face of death, rather than standing in terror in the dark shadow of death.

NOTE

1. The literature in general was, and continues to be, dominated by articles related to psychotherapy. In this chapter, we shift our view slightly to examine the literature

more from the perspective of types of events than from the activity in which one is engaged in response to those events.

REFERENCES

Antonovsky, A. (1979). *Health, stress, and coping: New perspectives on mental and physical well-being*. San-Francisco: Jossey-Bass.

———. (1987). *Unraveling the mystery of health: How people manage stress and stay well*. San Francisco: Jossey-Bass.

Ballone, E., Valentino, M., Occhiolini, L., Di Mascio, C., Cannone, D., and Schioppa, F. S. (2000, December). Factors influencing psychological stress levels of Italian peacekeepers in Bosnia. *Military Medicine*, 165 (12): 911–15.

Bar-Tal, D., and Labin, D. (2001). The effect of a major event on stereotyping: Terrorist attacks in Israel and Israeli adolescents' perceptions of Palestinians, Jordanians and Arabs. *European Journal of Social Psychology*, 31: 265–80.

Bartone, P. T., Ursano, R. J., Wright, K. M., and Ingraham, L. H. (1989). The impact of a military air disaster on the health of assistance workers: a prospective study. *Journal of Nervous and Mental Disease*, 177 (6): 317–28.

Bramsen, I., Dirkzwager, A. J. E., van der Ploeg, H. M. (2000). Predeployment personality traits and exposure to trauma as predictors of posttraumatic stress symptoms: A prospective study of former peacekeepers. *American Journal of Psychiatry*, 157 (7): 1115–19.

Bramsen, I., Dirkzwager, A. J. E., Van Esch, S. C. M., and van der Ploeg, H. M. (2001). Consistency of self-reports of traumatic events in a population of Dutch peacekeepers: Reason for optimism? *Journal of Traumatic Stress*, 14: 733–40.

Cardozo, B. L., and Salama, P. (2002). Mental health of humanitarian aid workers in complex emergencies. In Y. Danieli (Ed.), *Sharing the front line and the back hills: Peacekeepers, humanitarian aid workers, and the media in the midst of crisis*, pp. 242–55. Amityville, NY: Baywood Publishing.

Cross, W. (1999, November). Multigenerational legacies of trauma: An interdisciplinary examination of persecution and genocide in various cultural contexts. Paper presented at the 15th Annual Meeting of the International Society for Traumatic Stress Studies, Miami, Florida.

Danieli, Y. (Ed.). (2002). *Sharing the front line and the back hills: peacekeepers, humanitarian aid workers, and the media in the midst of crisis*. Amityville, NY: Baywood Publishing.

Dunning, C. (1988). Intervention strategies for emergency workers. In M. Lystad (Ed.), *Mental health response to mass emergencies: Theory and practice*. New York: Brunner/Mazel.

Durham, T. W., McCammon, S. L., and Allison, E. J. (1985). The psychological impact of disaster on rescue personnel. *Annals of Emergency Medicine*, 14 (7): 664–68.

Eisenman, D. P., Bergner, S., and Cohen, I. (2000). An ideal victim: Idealizing trauma victims causes traumatic stress in human rights workers. *Human Rights Review*, 1 (4): 106–14.

Espín, O. M. (1999). *Women crossing boundaries: A psychology of immigration and transformation of sexuality*. New York: Routledge.

Figley, C. R. (Ed.). (1995). *Compassion fatigue: Coping with secondary traumatic stress disorder in those who treat the traumatized*. New York: Brunner/Mazel.

———. (Ed.) (2000). Treating Compassion Fatigue. Philadelphia: Brunner/Mazel.

Freudenberger, H. J. (1984). Burnout and job dissatisfaction. *Family therapy collections*. U.S. Aspen Systems Corporation.

Friedman, M. (1996). *Emergent self management for security and emergency personnel in situations of continuous traumatic exposure*. Paper presented at the European Conference: Stress in Emergency Services, Peacekeeping Operations, and Humanitarian Aid Organizations, Sheffield, England.

Friedman, M. J., Charney, D. S., and Deutch, A. Y. (Eds.). (1995). *Neurobiological and clinical consequences of stress: From normal adaptation to post-traumatic stress disorder*. Philadelphia: Lippincott-Raven.

Friedman, M., and Higson-Smith, C. (2002). Building psychological resilience: Learning from the South African Police Service. In D. Paton, J. M. Violanti, and L. M. Smith (Eds.), *Promoting capabilities to manage posttraumatic stress: Perspectives on resilience*, Springfield, IL: Charles C. Thomas.

Friedman, M., Friedman, M. J., van der Kolk, B., McFarlane, A., and Higson-Smith, R. C. (2000). *Resilience in the face of exposure to trauma*. Symposium conducted at the 16th Annual Conference of the International Society for Traumatic Stress Studies, San Antonio, Texas.

Friedman, M. J., and Marsella, A. J. (1996). Post-traumatic stress disorder: An overview of the concept. In A. J. Marsella, M. J. Friedman, E. T. Gerrity, and R. Scurfield (Eds.), *Ethnocultural aspects of post-traumatic stress disorder: Issues, research, and clinical applications*, pp. 11–32. Washington, DC: American Psychological Association Press.

Frommberger, U., Stieglitz, R., Straub, S., Nyberg, E., Schlickewei, W., Kuner, E., and Berger, M. (1999). The concept of "sense of coherence" and the development of posttraumatic stress disorder in traffic accident victims. *Journal of Psychosomatic Research*, 46 (4): 343–48.

Ghahramanlou, M., and Brodbeck, C. (2000). Predictors of secondary trauma in sexual assault trauma counselors. *International Journal of Emergency Mental Health*, 2: 229–40.

Haley, S. A. (1974). When the patient reports atrocities: Specific treatment considerations of the Vietnam veteran. *Archives of General Psychiatry*, 30 (2): 191–96.

Hartsough, D. M., and Myers, D. G. (1985). *Disaster work and mental health: Prevention and control of stress among workers* (DHHS Publication No. ADM 87-1422). Rockville, MD: National Institute of Mental Health.

Havel, V. (2002, October 24). A farewell to politics. *New York Review of Books*. October 24. Retrieved on January 3, 2003, from www.nybooks.com/articles/15750

Herman, J. L. (1992). *Trauma and recovery: The aftermath of violence from domestic abuse to political terror*. New York: Basic Books.

Higson-Smith, C. (2002). *Supporting communities affected by violence: A casebook from South Africa*. Oxford, England: Oxfam GB.

Hobfoll, S. E. (1989). Conservation of resources. *American Psychologist*, 44 (3): 513–24.

International Rescue Committee (2002, August 11). Uganda workers free five IRC aid workers. Retrieved on June 27, 2004, from www.theirc.org/index.cfm/www ID1583

Janoff-Bulman, R. (1992). *Shattered assumptions: Towards a new psychology of trauma*. New York: Free Press.

Jenin Camp "horrific beyond belief." (2002, April 18). BBC News. retrieved on June 27, 2004, from http://news.bbc.co.uk/2/hi/middle_east/1937387.stm

Kessler, R. C., Sonnega, A., Bromet, E., Hughes, M., Nelson, C. B., and Breslau, N. (1995). Epidemiological risk factors for trauma and PTSD. In R. Yehuda (Ed.), *Risk factors for posttraumatic stress disorder.* Washington, DC: American Psychiatric Press.

King, D., King, L., Keane, T., Fairbank, J., and Adams, N. (1998). Resilience-recovery factors in post-traumatic stress disorder among female and male Vietnam veterans: Hardiness, postwar social support, and additional stressful life events. *Journal of Personality and Social Psychology*, 74 (2): 420–34.

Lansen, J. (1993). Vicarious traumatization in therapists treating victims of torture and persecution. *Torture*, 3 (4): 138–40 (1993).

Larsen, D., Stamm, B. H., and Davis, K. (2002, Fall). Telehealth for prevention and in-tervention of the negative effects of caregiving. *Traumatic Stress Points*, 16 (4). Re-trieved on April 18, 2004, from www.istss.org/publications/TS/Fall02/telehealth.htm

Leach, J. (1994). *Survival psychology*. New York: New York University Press.

Litz, B. T., King, L. A., King, D. W., Orsillo, S. M., and Friedman, M. J. (1997). War-riors as peacekeepers: Features of the Somalia experience and PTSD. *Journal of Consulting and Clinical Psychology*, 65: 1001–10.

MacDonald, C., Chamberlain, K., Long, N., and Mirfin, K. (1999). Stress and mental health status associated with peacekeeping duty for New Zealand Defence Force personnel. *Stress Medicine*, 15: 235–41.

Maercker, A., Schuetzwohl, M., Loebe, K., Eckhardt, F., and Mueller, U. (1994). *Sense of coherence and dissociative experiences in victims of political persecution.* Paper presented at the 10th Annual Meeting of the International Society for Trau-matic Stress Studies, Chicago, Illinois.

Maslach, C. (1986). Burnout research in the social services: A critique. *Journal of So-cial Service Research*, 10: 95–105.

Marmar, C. R., Weiss, D. S., Metzler, T. J., and Delucchi, K. L. (1996). Characteris-tics of emergency service personnel related to peritraumatic dissociation during critical incident exposure. *American Journal of Psychiatry*, 153 (7) (Festschrift Supplement): 94–102.

Marmar, C. R., Weiss, D. S., Metzler, T. J., Ronfeldt, H. M., and Foreman, C. (1996). Stress responses of emergency service personnel to the Loma Prieta earthquake, In-terstate 880 freeway collapse and control traumatic incidents. *Journal of Traumatic Stress*, 9 (1): 63–85.

McCann, I. L., and Pearlman, L. A. (1990). Vicarious traumatization: A framework for understanding the psychological effects of working with victims. *Journal of Traumatic Stress*, 3 (1): 131–49.

Mehlum, L. (1999). Alcohol and stress in Norwegian United Nations peacekeepers. *Military Medicine*, 164: 720–24.

Mehlum, L., and Weisaeth, L. (2002). Predictors of posttraumatic stress reactions in Norwegian UN peacekeepers seven years after service. *Journal of Traumatic Stress*, 15 (6): 17–26.

Miles, M. S., Demi, A. S., and Mostyn-Aker, P. (1984). Rescue workers' reactions following the Hyatt Hotel disaster. *Death Education*, 8: 315–31.

Myers, D. G. (1985). Helping the helpers: A training manual. In D. M. Hartsough and D. G. Myers (Eds.), *Disaster work and mental health: Prevention and control of stress among workers*. Rockville, MD: National Institute of Mental Health.

National Institute of Mental Health. (1978/1986). *Training manual for human service workers in major disasters* (U.S. National Institute of Mental Health Disaster assistance and emergency Mental Health Section). Washington, DC: U.S. Government Printing Office.

Orsillo, S. M., Roemer, L., Litz, B. T., Ehlich, P., and Friedman, M. J. (1998). Psychiatric symptomatology associated with contemporary peacekeeping: An examination of post-mission functioning among peacekeepers in Somalia. *Journal of Traumatic Stress*, 11: 611–25.

Paton, D., and Violanti, J. M. (1996). *Traumatic stress in critical occupations: Recognition, consequences and treatment*. Springfield, IL: Charles C. Thomas.

Pearlman, L. A., and Saakvitne, K. W. (1995). *Trauma and the therapist: Countertransference and vicarious traumatization in psychotherapy with incest survivors*. New York: Norton.

Power, S., and Allison, G. (Eds.). (2000). *Realizing human rights: Moving from inspiration to impact*. New York: St. Martin's.

Raphael, B., Singh, B., Bradbury, L., and Lambert, F. (1983–1984).Who helps the helpers? The effects of a disaster on the rescue workers. *Omega*, 14 (1): 9–20.

Schnurr, P. P., and Vielhauer, M. J. (1999). Personality as a risk factor for PTSD. In R. Yehuda (Ed.), *Risk factors for posttraumatic stress disorder*. Washington, DC: American Psychiatric Press.

Seaquist, L., Forstenzer, T., and Quianzon, Y. K. (1992). *Professional peacebuilding. (The Venice Papers No. 3): A preliminary guide*. Paris: UNESCO.

Shawcross, W. (2000). *Deliver us from evil: Peacekeepers, warlords and a world of endless conflict*. New York: Simon & Schuster.

Shepherd, M., and Hodgkinson, P. E. (1990). The hidden victims of disaster: Helper stress. *Stress Medicine*, 6 (1): 29–35.

Simon, B. (1993). Obstacles in the path of mental health professionals who deal with traumatic violations of human rights. *International Journal of Law and Psychiatry*, 16 (3–4): 427–40.

Stamm, B. H. (1993). Conceptualizing traumatic stress: A metatheoretical structural approach. *Dissertation Abstracts International: Section B: The Sciences and Engineering*, 54: 3866.

———. (Ed.). (1995). *Secondary traumatic stress: Self-care issues for clinicians, researchers, and educators*. Lutherville, MD: Sidran Press.

———. (1999a). Empirical perspectives on contextualizing death and trauma. In C. R. Figley (Ed.), *Traumatology of grieving*, pp. 23–36. Philadelphia: Brunner/Mazel.

———. (1999b). Theoretical perspectives on contextualizing death and trauma. In C. R. Figley (Ed.), *Traumatology of grieving*, pp. 3–21. Philadelphia: Brunner/Mazel.

———. (Ed.) (1999c). *Secondary traumatic stress: Self-care issues for clinicians, researchers, and educators* (2nd ed.). Lutherville, MD: Sidran Press.

———. (2002a). Measuring compassion satisfaction as well as fatigue: Developmental history of the compassion fatigue and satisfaction test. In C. R. Figley (Ed.), *Treating compassion fatigue*, pp. 107–19. New York: Brunner/Rutledge.

———. (2002b). Professional quality of life: Compassion satisfaction and fatigue test, revision III. Retrieved on December 25, 2002, from www.isu.edu/~bhstamm/tests.htm

———. (2002c). Terrorism risks and responding in rural and frontier America. *Engineering in Medicine and Biology*, 21 (5): 100–111.

Stamm, B. H., and Bieber, S. L. (1996). Psychometric review of structural assessment of stressful experiences. In B. H. Stamm (Ed.), *Measurement of stress, trauma and adaptation*. Lutherville, MD: Sidran Press.

Stamm, B. H., and Figley, C. R. (1998). Compassion satisfaction and fatigue test. Retrieved on December 25, 2002, from www.isu.edu/~bhstamm/tests.htm

Stamm, B. H., and Friedman, M. J. (2000). Cultural diversity in the appraisal and expression of traumatic exposure. In A. Shalev, R. Yehuda, and A. McFarlane (Eds.), *International handbook of human response to trauma*, 69–85. New York: Plenum Press.

Staub, E. (1989). *The roots of evil: The origins of genocide and other group violence.* Cambridge, England: Cambridge University Press.

Stearns, S. D. (1993). Psychological distress and relief work: Who helps the helpers? *Refugee Participation Network*, 15: 3–8.

Strumpfer, D. J. W. (1995). The origins of health and strength: From "salutogenesis" to "fortigenesis." *South African Journal of Psychology*, 25 (2): 81–89.

Sutker, P. B., Uddo, M., Brailey, K., Vasterling, J. J., and Errera, P. (1994). Psychopathology in war-zone deployed and nondeployed Operation Desert Storm troops assigned graves registration duties. *Journal of Abnormal Psychology*, 103 (2): 383–90.

Unger, R. K. (2002). Them and us: Hidden ideologies—differences in degree or kind? *Analyses of Social Issues and Public Policy*, 2: 43–52.

United Nations Development Programme. *Human development report 2000*. New York: Oxford University Press.

Vachon, M. L. S. (1987). Team stress in palliative/hospice care. In L. F. Paradis (Ed.), *Stress and burnout among health care providers caring for the terminally ill and their families*. New York: Haworth Press.

Van de Put, W. A. C. M., and Eisenbruch, M. (2002). The Cambodian Experience. In J. T. V. M. de Jong (Ed.), *Trauma, war and violence: Public mental health in socio-cultural context*. New York: Kluwer/Plenum.

Van der Veer, G. (1992). The consequences of working with refugees for the helping professional. In G. Van der Veer (Ed.), *Counselling and therapy with refugees: psychological problems of victims of war, torture and repression*. Chichester, England: Wiley.

van Gelder, P., and van den Berkhof, R. (2002). Psychosocial care for humanitarian aid workers; The Médicins Sans Frontières Holland Experience. In Y. Danieli (Ed.),

Sharing the frontline and the back hills: Peacekeepers, humanitarian aid workers, and the media in the midst of crisis, pp. 179–85. Amityville, NY: Baywood Publishing.

Weine, S. M. (1999). *When history is a nightmare: Lives and memories of ethnic cleansing in Bosnia-Herzegovina*. New Brunswick, NJ: Rutgers University Press.

Wilson, J. P., and Lindy, J. D. (1994). *Countertransference in the treatment of PTSD*. New York: Guilford.

Part IV

SEPTEMBER 11

World Trade Center (September 11, 2001).

World Trade Center (September 11, 2001).

Hijacked

Ruth Knafo Setton

Hijacked: on the threshold
of spreading the word—new words:

cell phone, as in: "Tell the children,"

touch, as in: "Two who jumped, hand
    in hand,"

—the elevator smells of Old Spice and oranges,
the office boy rubbed pimple cream

over chin and nose,
so that when he moves to music we don't hear

arms flapping, wings

Hijacked, as in: "Don't ever wear those sunglasses when

you go out,"

cracked pink, still hissing

ash, as in: "A third of the city is under ash—
    ash on our flesh,"

Oh my God, as in:

Letter to a Suicide Bomber

Ruth Knafo Setton

Tell me this: before you detonate
the chubby girl on her way home
from school, the old man reading
Borges, the woman dressing
at the window, the boy
with shy eyes and spiked hair–

are the 70 virgins in purple?
your harem in heaven–as their blood bursts
beneath your pounding, as your fingertips
touch a charred page of Borges–the one

where he writes a story
that has already been written.

Chapter Nineteen

Reflections on September 11

Martin S. Bergmann

T*he tragedy of September 11 has imposed on the psychoanalytic community two broad tasks: first, to examine our heritage and see if our special
experience can contribute positively to the general problems our country
is struggling with; and second, to examine the effects this tragedy has had
on our work. This chapter views the clash of Islamic and Western cultures
through the lens of psychoanalytic thought and discusses the ability of psychoanalysis to deal with cultural and social change. It explores the ways
in which the attacks on the World Trade Center changed the balance between aggression and libido both on a personal and on a public level, nationally and internationally. Finally, it discusses the relationship between
public catastrophe and personal trauma in an effort to determine how we
can best help our patients cope with the new fear and uncertainty introduced into the American environment by the terror attacks.*

It is conceivable, although it is too early to know for certain, that September
11, 2001, will go down in history as one of those dates that changes the flow
of history; that it will rank with July 14, 1789—the storming of the Bastille
during the French Revolution—or with August 1, 1914, when Germany declared war on Russia, igniting World War I, an event that historians regard as
the true beginning of the twentieth century. Similarly, it is conceivable that
the twenty-first century began on September 11. It is too early to tell because
we do not know whether the current Muslim terrorism is an expression of a
small fanatical paranoid group, which can be liquidated within a reasonably
short amount of time, or that of a large segment of the Islamic world, fore-
shadowing a new conflict between Western pluralistic democracy and religious fundamentalism that will expand into a war comparable to the great religious wars of previous centuries.

Only a few years ago, the world celebrated the fact that after World War II we enjoyed half a century without a major war. Local conflicts abounded in Ireland, Israel, the Balkans, and Africa. But the major war between the United States and the Soviet Union was averted. Instead of a war with another state, what became clear after September 11 is that a hitherto unsuspected kind of enemy has emerged.

There is a consensus among historians that World War I was a mistake that could have been averted, but that World War II was inevitable given the nature of the Nazi regime. In the same way, it seems to me that a compromise between terrorism and Western democracy cannot be negotiated, and, therefore, this war is a necessary one. The culture of Islamic terrorism is paranoid, with all the inherent advantages and disadvantages of being paranoid. The advantages include the capacity to project aggression on the enemy, freeing the culture from inner conflict and conscious guilt. It is remarkable in having achieved an amalgam between destructive aggression and the sanction of the superego of that aggression. This is a new type of culture, in which libidinal ties, hate, and self-destructive tendencies are amalgamated to create a new psychic structure. In this culture, mothers raise children to die young as martyrs in a jihad. Abandoned youngsters in orphanages become members of a group bent on destroying a supposed enemy. Dedicating itself to death, it unites life and death in a new powerful combination. We have reasons to fear its emergence on the world scene.

However, a paranoid culture held together by aggression may also disintegrate from within because not enough libido is left to bind its members together. We can keep in mind that most cultures were once fanatic and rigid, and yet history shows that these rigid systems succumbed to an inner process of disintegration. The democratic religious pluralism represented by the United States is much more powerful, but it, too, has disadvantages. I would like to enumerate some of these:

1. We have a profound sense of guilt over our astonishing success and about the fact that we consume a disproportionate ratio of natural resources, not sharing our abundance with less fortunate cultures and nations.
2. We, being in a free country, are also free to express our anxieties. Having created a culture in which information is rapidly transmitted, any panic that appears anywhere, for whatever reason, has a tendency to become a panic shared by large masses.
3. We are a religious country. This fact creates difficulties in understanding that religion can also be a source of fanaticism and that there are fundamentalist tendencies in every religion. It may or may not be good propaganda to call terrorism a misunderstanding of Islam, but it does not repre-

sent the whole truth: jihad does play a role in Islamic thinking. Even if in the Koran it has a far wider meaning than currently used by the religious extremists, the religious obligation to convert the whole world to Islam cannot be simply ignored. At its core, every monotheistic religion believes that it alone is the "true" religion and that others are infidels, not on par with the adherence to the one and true religion. Every monotheistic religion is open to fanatic interpretation.

4. We are a highly individualistic society, and our tendency to look for individual solutions to problems that have no individual solutions is deeply ingrained. The buying of gas masks, keeping the car filled with gasoline, and buying medicine against mass biological warfare are all examples of futile efforts to find a personal solution to a public problem. In my view, such tendencies weaken the tie of the individual to the community and, being of limited usefulness, increase anxiety and loneliness.

5. We attempt to guess where the next attack will come from and to try to avoid any tall buildings, subways, and other parts of town considered dangerous, which represents a psychological coping mechanism. These are attempts to reach relative safety by differentiating between safe and unsafe places. They represent attempts to be active when no rational activity is available. We therapists must recognize that these irrational mechanisms do nevertheless offer a semblance of safety, but that they are the equivalent of phobic mechanisms.

6. We have an American culture that is a child-oriented culture, perhaps the first culture to put such an emphasis on its children. The American Dream assumes that every child will do better than his or her parent will, and this is particularly true when the parent is an immigrant. America spends much of its income on its children. An unspoken part of the American Dream is to protect the child from knowledge about human aggression. Paradoxically, we often let our children watch movies in which violence plays a major role. September 11 shattered our sense of security and many parents feel worse for their children than for themselves. Here, psychoanalytic knowledge may come to our aid. We know that the child is not free from aggression or even death wishes. Many children got scared on September 11, but so, too, did many adults. There are also parents who, when seeing their children playing at destroying the World Trade Center towers with an airplane, are horrified at the children's aggression, not realizing that to find an outlet in play is beneficial to the child and does not mean that the child will become a terrorist.

It so happens that Freud's writings contain hints and suggestions that are pertinent to the current situation, and more specifically, the following writings by Freud have become particularly interesting now. I will argue that in some of Freud's writings—particularly in *Thoughts for the Times on War and Death* (1915); *On Transience* (1916); *Group Psychology and Analysis of the Ego* (1921); *Civilization and Its Discontents* (1930); and "Why War?" (1933)—there is material that if judiciously applied to the current situation can help us to achieve a better understanding of the current crisis.

What Freud had to say in *Group Psychology and Analysis of the Ego* (1921) about crowds and the way the crowd is held together by libidinal ties to a leader and about how such ties disintegrate when the leader is defeated or dies has achieved new relevance. Freud pointed out that in crowds, as well as in military and religious groups, the relationship between the group members and their leader is characterized by the abrogation of the individual superego, replacing the individual superego with the authority of the leader. When this happens, what was previously prohibited becomes sanctioned. Derivatives of the aggressive instinct, normally prohibited, now find an outlet and are considered acts of heroism or martyrdom because they are sanctioned by the new ego ideal of the group. Freud further assumed that if the leader is eliminated or suffers a defeat, he loses the magic powers with which he was endowed and a sense of panic manifests. Panic, in turn, dissolves the libidinal ties of the group, and each individual seeks his or her own salvation; panic is contagious, spreading rapidly from one individual to another (p. 96). At the moment of this writing, there is no general panic in the United States, but there are signs of potential panic everywhere, and the government lacks the skill to combat it successfully. I will return to this problem later.

Freud further differentiated between crowds and organized groups like the church or the army: the first is loosely organized and the latter are groups that hold together over long stretches of time. Today we know much more about the interrelationship between these two types of groups. The attacks on Jewish shops during the *Kristallnacht* riots were a mob action, but the "final solution" of exterminating the Jews was accomplished within the framework of a permanent organization. We now know that to convert a crowd into a permanent group requires providing constant propaganda, blocking access to certain information, and utilizing a continuous secret service. Whether al Qaeda is a loosely organized group or one of those tight organizations remains to be seen.

Freud also wrote:

> [A] religion, even if it calls itself the religion of love, must be hard and unloving to those who do not belong to it. Fundamentally indeed every religion is in this same way a religion of love for all those whom it embraces; while cruelty and intolerance towards those who do not belong to it are natural to every religion. (p. 98)

If another group tie takes the place of the religious one—and the socialistic tie seems to be succeeding in doing so—then there will be the same intolerance towards outsiders as in the age of the Wars of Religion; and if differences between scientific opinions could ever attain a similar significance for groups, the same result would again be repeated with this new motivation. (p. 99)

Had Freud's book been written a decade later, he probably would have used National Socialism as an example. Today these observations remain valid.

In *Civilization and Its Discontents*, Freud (1930) reiterated this same idea in a somewhat different context:

When the Apostle Paul had posited universal love as the foundation of his Christian community, extreme intolerance on the part of Christendom towards those who remained outside it became the inevitable consequence. To the Romans, who had not founded their communal life as a State upon love, religious intolerance was something foreign.

Freud pointed out that civilization imposes a heavy burden on humanity in terms of curtailing the expression of both the sexual and the aggressive drives. A precarious balance exists between libido and aggression within every person; within every intimate relationship, be it that of parent and child or husband and wife; and within every society and between societies.

The exchange of letters between Einstein and Freud, which appears in Freud's writing under the title "Why War?" (1933), also gives rise to some new thoughts. Einstein asked Freud whether there was a way to deliver humankind from the menace of war. Einstein hoped that Freud's "far-reaching knowledge of man's instinctive life" would give him an answer not available to common sense. After a historical introduction, Freud reiterated to Einstein his dual-instinct theory:

When we read of the atrocities of the past, it sometimes seems as though the idealistic motives served only as an excuse for the destructive appetites; and sometimes—in the case, for instance, of the cruelties of the Inquisition—it seems as though the idealistic motives had pushed themselves forward in consciousness, while the destructive ones lent them an unconscious reinforcement. (p. 210)

Freud almost concluded the essay on a pessimistic note, that war and aggression are too deeply ingrained in human nature for us to hope that war can ever be avoided. But at the very end of the essay, he shied away from that conclusion.

The *psychical* modifications that go along with the process of civilization are striking and unambiguous. They consist in a progressive displacement of instinctual aims and a restriction of instinctual impulses. Sensations that were pleasurable to our ancestors have become indifferent or even intolerable to ourselves; there are organic grounds for the changes in our ethical and aesthetic ideals. Of the psychological characteristics of civilization two appear to be the most important: a strengthening of the intellect, which is beginning to govern instinctual life, and an internalization of the aggressive impulses, with all its consequent advantages and perils. Now war is in the crassest opposition to the psychical attitude imposed on us by the process of civilization, and for that reason we are bound to rebel against it; we simply cannot any longer put up with it. (pp. 214–15)

A year after this exchange took place, the Nazis came to power in Germany, and the circulation of this exchange was forbidden. Seventy years later we can ask, was Freud right in his optimism or was he right in his pessimistic attitude? The Holocaust showed that, if anything, human brutality had grown rather than diminished. On the other hand, he may not have been entirely wrong, for no major war has been fought for over fifty years. We can say that, in the civilized world, there is a new reluctance to wage war that was not there earlier. However, this gain has been offset by the rise of the new terrorism.

Freud never addressed the specific American contribution of the mixture of religion and religious institutions with ideas derived from the Enlightenment that were written into the Declaration of Independence. However, what he said about the fact that religious beliefs strongly demand an attack on the infidels has retained its sobering validity.

Kohut (1972) added to Freud's social psychology the concept of narcissistic rage. The aim of the Osama bin Laden propaganda is to fan this narcissistic rage among Muslim men, by continuously drawing their attention to the fact that their holy places have been violated by the entrance of infidels into Saudi Arabia—never mind that these infidels entered because one Arabic country, Iraq, attacked another. The unconscious appeal of the message is to the supposed violation and feminization of Muslim masculinity. Arabic honor has been restored by the destruction inflicted on the World Trade Center and the Pentagon. Whether al Qaeda aims at eliminating us or humiliating us is a matter of considerable importance in assessing the danger.

To appreciate the depth and originality of Freud's insight into the nature of culture should not obscure for us a serious limitation of the psychoanalytic vision. Psychoanalysis has not developed a theory to deal with cultural change. Freud, unlike some of his pupils, was not impressed by Soviet Communism and was never utopian in outlook. He asked what the Communists will do after they have eliminated the social classes that opposed their seizing power. Today we know that Stalin's terror was the answer. A theory of social change based on psychoanalytic principles has yet to be formulated.

When the environment changes as it did after September 11, we may expect that a previously existing balance between aggression and libido—between ego, id, and superego—will also change and that in certain people it will change radically. Both aggression and libido can be projected from within onto others, resulting in paranoia and erotomania, respectively. The massive attack on the towers changed this balance on all the levels mentioned. On one hand, there is a greater sense of mutual dependency within the community and within the Western world, but on the other, there is a release of individual aggression on the national and international level. The turning of aggression inward on the self creates a sense of guilt. In some cases, this guilt leads to humanitarian endeavors and social responsibility. But it can also become a weapon in the hands of an adversary. When this happens, we hear that the United States deserves the punishment it is receiving. As Hamlet, the Prince of Denmark put it, "Conscience makes cowards of us all/And thus the native hue of resolution/Is sicklied o'er with the pale cast of thought."

On September 11, there was a massive failure on the part of the Secret Services to protect us from a catastrophic event. This resulted in a sense of loss of authority. Some of the lost ground was later recovered when the president spoke to America after he himself regained his bearings. But a sense of helplessness and loss of confidence as well as not knowing what to do, prevails. America, although not in a state of panic, nevertheless shows many panic reactions. To counter acts of panic, psychoanalysis has taught us that the ego must be strengthened. I will now enumerate some of the ego functions that have to become activated:

1. An important ego function in the current crisis is to differentiate between what is possible and what is probable. This distinction is usually lost in a state of panic. An active ego can gain confidence by raising the question, "Is the high-rise, subway, train, or plane that I am afraid of taking a possible or a likely target?"

2. Another example of ego strength is the capacity to tolerate the unknown. This is true for individuals as well as the government. The government should help its citizens tolerate the fact that the future is unknown. In fact, the future was never predictable. We only operated with the assumption that it was; and now, the new reality forces us to give up this previously held certainty.

3. Among the many lessons Freud taught us was to recognize the power of the repetition compulsion, which in the present crisis manifests itself in equating the current trauma with past traumatic events. There are many Holocaust survivors and others who see the current catastrophe as a repetition of the Holocaust. Only the ego can use its powers to differentiate

between past and present and to limit the power of the repetition compulsion as determining current action.

I will now deal with the question regarding the effect of the catastrophe on our profession. It must be kept in mind that when Freud discovered the existence of psychic trauma, he thought only in terms of personal traumatic events that occur to an individual to which he or she reacts with the creation of hysteric and other neurotic symptoms. The first signs of neurosis that were the result of broader social conditions were encountered in the war neurosis. Reading that literature now suggests that at that time, the distinction between private and social neurosis was not yet made. It was the Holocaust, and the fact that Holocaust survivors underwent psychoanalysis and psychotherapy, that forced the therapeutic community to differentiate between social catastrophe and personal catastrophe. It was my good fortune to participate personally for ten years in studying this difference, and indeed it emerged only slowly and after considerable work. At first, psychoanalysts tended to make the mistake of translating the social catastrophe into personal terms and often in crude ways to deflect the survivors from talking about the Holocaust to talking about the Oedipus complex.

When a therapist deals with the personal trauma of the patient, he or she is, unless countertransference interferes, somewhat protected by being an observer. This protection is not available during the current catastrophe, because therapists, like patients, are experiencing it at the same time. Therapists need to make themselves available to the patient's needs even if their own anxiety is at a higher-than-normal level. In the last few years, there was a controversy initiated by Owen Renik as to how much of the therapist's personal life should be shared with the patient. Without entering into this controversy, it seems to me that because we wish to strengthen the sense of community, some disclosure as to whether we lost somebody personally or similar questions have to be answered, and answered with thanks for the interest of the patient.

Denial operates both ways. A public traumatic event can be used to deny psychic reality, and a psychic reality can be used to deny a realistically threatening situation. After September 11, both the inner reality of every person and the change in the national reality have received a jolt.

The patients who seek our help after September 11 will probably fall into two categories. In the first category are those who have been directly affected by the catastrophe, by the loss of someone who was vital to their life. These are the patients who will need our help to do their work of mourning. But there will be another group of patients: those who did not suffer a personal loss and yet require help after the catastrophe. These are patients who had earlier maintained a delicate personal balance between aggression and libido (defenses against and outbursts of symptoms of anxiety) and who barely managed to contain their aggression. The events of September 11 undid this equilibrium. In these cases, the task of the therapist will be to understand with the patient what kind of equilibrium was disrupted and to help the patient reach a new and more stable equilibrium.

Our main work has always been to establish connections that have been severed due to isolation. Much of the relief obtained in the course of psychoanalysis is through the reconnection of that which has been disconnected. However, in dealing with trauma, almost the opposite needs to be done. Trauma also makes connections between the social and personal realms, and if we help the sufferer to disconnect these two, the ego is strengthened. This can be done when the therapist succeeds in finding the bridge between the social catastrophe and the personal traumatic events that have become connected to it.

In a seminar about September 11, I heard a therapist quote her patient as saying, "The towers symbolized my father and my mother." The use of the word symbolize alerted me to the possibility that a public catastrophe can become a personal trauma only when the ability to symbolize has temporarily or permanently been lost. When we succeed in reconnecting September 11 to a personal trauma, the symbolic function of September 11 is restored and, almost by definition, the ability to symbolize is the antidote to trauma. Prior experience has demonstrated that it takes a special skill to know when to make genetic interpretations. They should not be made unless the patient is ready for them, and they should not be made in the face of a negative transference as long as the mourning process is still active or as long as anger is at a high level. Abreaction has to take place before insight can be reached.

At times this is easy to ascertain, but at other times it takes considerable work to establish. It is relatively easy to establish a connection between a trauma that a child suffered at the age of five when her house burned down with what happened on September 11. But it requires more subtlety to realize that somebody who has prohibited all signs of aggression now has difficulties in the post–September 11 period. In general, we can say that the social catastrophe has brought up in most of our patients deeper and earlier layers of anxiety that now demand attention.

It is conceivable that personal analysis has not prepared therapists for dealing with this social catastrophe. If therapists do not know their own personal connection to the catastrophe, their capacity to help can be severely curtailed. Therefore, self-analysis is imperative for most practicing therapists today. If self-analysis is incapable of dealing with the social trauma, a return to treatment may be indicated. Listening to anxious patients can be difficult when therapists themselves are anxious. It may even happen that the patient makes the therapist anxious rather than that the therapist is dealing with the patient's anxiety. On the opposite end of the scale, those patients who do not mention the September 11 catastrophe, because they are too isolated from a sense of community, can also be difficult because they do not satisfy the need of the therapist for sharing the experience. The changed situation has created new problems that we used to deal with under the rubric of countertransference. But the term may not be relevant here because we are dealing with a social catastrophe and a new term, perhaps "social countertransference," has to be coined.

Twice in the twentieth century Western democratic pluralism was challenged by totalitarianism. Robert Waelder (1960) differentiated between authoritarianism and totalitarianism. In authoritarian cultures, criticism of government is prohibited, but the population is not forced to say that they love and support the government. The population may be silenced, but not degraded. Both communism and national socialism were totalitarian societies. By contrast, the current crisis has its origin in a sector of a traditional culture that fears the encounter with American modernity. We have both to fight and to understand the new enemy. Either fighting without understanding or understanding without fighting will be detrimental.

Psychoanalysis has something to offer in the present crisis. We understand aggression and fanaticism and its relationship to the paranoid. We know the price of regression, and we understand how panic spreads. Our aggression has to be mobilized, but without losing our ego's capacity for judgment. As Shakespeare's *Henry V* told his soldiers before the Battle of Agincourt, "Every subject's duty is his king: Every subject's soul is his own."

I would like to go back to the question of whether we Freudian psychoanalysts have something unique to contribute to the mastery of the social trauma that took place in the United States because of September 11. The answer to that question is not simple. On one hand, I am convinced that we who have internalized Freud's *Civilization and Its Discontents* (1930) have an advantage over politicians and social scientists because we operate with the basic assumption that civilization itself, by imposing restrictions on our instinctual wishes, creates a hatred for civilization. Because there is in our unconscious a fifth columnist, who like the terrorists wishes to undo civilization, the terrorists who are unbridled in their hate for Western culture gain power they would not have had, had we only had to deal with outside forces.

However, in the seventy years that have passed since the publication of *Civilization and Its Discontents* (1930), certain weaknesses of that book have also become known. Freud, who emphasized the general hostility toward civilization, did not observe that this hatred is not equally distributed. There are men and women whose hostility to culture is particularly great because the balance between the libido and aggression is unfavorable to the libido. Already in 1972, Kohut published his paper, *Thoughts on Narcissism and Nar-*

cissistic Rage. More recently, Andre Green (2001) emphasized a particularly dangerous combination that can take place between the destructive drive and narcissism, which he called the "death narcissism." The psychology of terrorism is a particularly striking example of such a dangerous combination. It is particularly powerful because, when this grandiose distractive aim is to be achieved, the self can also be sacrificed without feeling any regard for the person. We can go even further and say that such a massive act of aggression is the equivalent in the aggressive drive of what sexual orgasm is for the libido. Whether or not we call it narcissistic rage or death narcissism, this combination sets the aggressive drive free from any restraint that results from inner conflict. Unlike war, the aim of this combination of narcissism and aggression is not victory nor conquest but sheer destruction.

In addition to differences in the amount of libido and aggression at the disposal of each individual, sociological differences, ignored by Freud, also play a role. The benefits of Western civilization are not equally distributed. Those who share little in these benefits can be sustained by hope for some time, but not for long. Modern technology, particularly television and films, have done a great deal to increase envy of the more affluent West.

There is an additional social force, which Freud was not aware of when he wrote *Civilization and Its Discontents* (1930). In the West, we may feel guilty for our relative success over other parts of the world. We may feel that we deserve the punishment because of our "arrogance" in not sharing our better economic level with the rest of the world. These guilt feelings are often associated with a type of naive Marxism, which maintains that Western prosperity is based on exploitation of the third world. Whatever justification that argument had in the nineteenth century, when the world was divided between industrialized countries and their colonies, is no longer valid. The West's success is based on its technology and not exploitation of the third world. Another accusation, however, is not so easily disposed of. The Western world is a dynamic society. When it encounters traditional societies with earlier customs and ways of living, it can often have a destructive influence, particularly with regard to the relationship between men and women sanctioned in the older societies. The West can therefore be accused of creating a sense of loss for many who cannot or do not wish to make the transition toward modernity.

There is still another problem psychoanalysis has to struggle with. Let us assume that our awareness of man's hostility toward culture would become widespread knowledge and its connection to terrorism acceptable. It may very well diminish the prevalent anxiety evoked by unconscious guilt. But until this massive social experiment is conducted, we cannot be sure that psychoanalytic knowledge will be assimilated well by the public. It may, for example, also evoke resistance. This resistance may increase the hostility toward psychoanalysis or further increase the guilt feelings about Western success.

As already stated, Freud, who was a child of the Enlightenment, was entirely confident that if psychoanalytic knowledge was more readily available, humanity would only profit from it (Freud, 1910). Today we cannot be equally sure that psychoanalytic knowledge is digestible by the public.

As mentioned earlier, Andre Green's (2001) introduction of the term "death narcissism," involves a particularly dangerous alliance between narcissism and the aggressive or death drive. The terrorism that confronts the West right now is an illustration of such a death narcissism because it aims only at destruction without receiving any benefit from this destruction. It is also ready to sacrifice the self for such a death, experienced as glorious beyond anything that life can offer.

Ordinary life, with its meager rewards, can easily appear paltry by comparison with the glory of death in mass destruction. Furthermore, when the aggressive drive can count on the approval of the superego, both ego and id find gratification in destruction, and any sign of intrapsychic conflict disappears. In a book that I wrote on the sacrifice of children and Western religions (Bergmann, 1992), I showed how martyrdom first appeared in the Jewish religion, only to be taken over later by Christianity and Islam. All monotheistic religions are, in their original form, hostile and ready to annihilate the infidels that are unwilling to accept the particular religion. Judaism and Christianity, however, were influenced by the ideas of Western enlightenment, which granted equality to all religions. A similar process has not taken place to the same extent in the world of Islam.

In retrospect it all makes grim sense. The enormous aggression released by World War II has not been overcome by the constructive forces of the Allies' victory. The enormous destructive power of the atomic bomb is with us, with or without terrorism to contend with. Terrorism has, at least in fantasy, made these weapons of mass destruction available for the very destruction of civilization. After Hiroshima, we all learned that civilization can destroy itself. For a while, we all thought that a war between the United States and the Soviet Union could make this nightmare come true. With the disappearance of communism, this danger subsided, but now terrorism has once more revived this fear. From a psychoanalytic perspective, the dangers of the destructive drive should not be underestimated or denied, but neither should we underestimate the desire of mankind to avoid self-destruction. The battle is on, and we are enlisted on the side of life and survival.

REFERENCES

The article on which this chapter is based was written immediately after September 11, 2001, and submitted to the *Journal of the American Psychoanalytic Association*. Because of the urgency and because it could not be incorporated in Vol. 49, No. 4, the editor, Arnold Richards, referred to it on the first page but published it online on *JAPA Psa-NETCAST*. The article appears here in print for the first time.

Dr. Knafo, the editor of this book, asked me to add some thoughts one year after the September 11, 2001, disaster. These reflections have been incorporated with the original ones.

Bergmann, M. S. (1992). *In the shadow of Morloch: The sacrifice of children and its impact on Western religions.* New York: Columbia University Press.

Freud, S. (1910). The future prospects of psycho-analytic therapy. *Standard Edition*, 11, pp. 139–51. London: Hogarth Press.

———. (1915). Thoughts for the times on war and death. *Standard Edition*, 14, pp. 273–302.

———. (1916). On transience. *Standard Edition*, 14, pp. 303–7. London: Hogarth Press.

———. (1921). Group psychology and the analysis of the ego. *Standard Edition*, 18, pp. 67–143. London: Hogarth Press.

———. (1930). Civilization and its discontents. *Standard Edition*, 21, pp. 59–145. London: Hogarth Press.

———. (1933). Why war? *Standard Edition*, 22, pp. 197–215. London: Hogarth Press.

Green, A. (2001). *Life narcissism, death narcissism.* New York: Free Association Books.

Kohut, H. (1972). Thoughts on narcissism and narcissistic rage. *Psychoanalytic Study of the Child*, 27: 360–400.

Waelder, R. (1960). Characteristics of totalitarianism. In *Psychoanalysis: observation, theory, applications: Selected papers by Robert Waelder*. New York: International Universities Press.

Chapter Twenty

Responses of the Mental Health Community to the World Trade Center Disaster

Charles B. Strozier and Katie Gentile

The extraordinary scale of the events of September 11 presented unique challenges to the many different mental health workers in the New York City area. This chapter reflects these challenges and is written from the standpoint of mental health volunteers as well as researchers in the midst of conducting an interview study of the experiences of people in and near the World Trade Center on September 11. Using data culled from interviews with survivors, we paint a particular picture of the events and the resulting traumatic experience. The narratives of two mental health volunteers are presented in order to speak to the confusion in developing systematic mental health response including organized service delivery and outreach after the occurrence of such a large trauma. This chapter integrates what we know about the pervasive effects of trauma with the experiences we have culled from our research with survivors and with our experiences volunteering and negotiating with the mental health services. We also discuss potential issues providers will have to address as well as ways in which services could be improved.

The extraordinary scale of the World Trade Center disaster created unique pressures on the mental health system in New York City to respond adequately to the intense psychological needs of victims and their families. Many were helped in a drama of epic proportions. And yet the frantic efforts after September 11 to establish an infrastructure of counseling and therapy were, in many respects, seriously muddled. The confusion was perhaps inevitable. The country had never experienced anything like these attacks, nor perhaps more importantly had anyone really imagined anything could happen on such a scale. At national and even international levels, that is, outside the areas of actual attack, the vicarious experience of the disaster through television generated its own kind of trauma. Many have come to feel there is a new malevolence in the world.

This chapter describes the ways in which the mental health community attempted to help those traumatized by the disaster, as well as draw some tentative conclusions and make some recommendations for the future. Written in fall 2002, this chapter is inevitably limited and cannot claim to be authoritative. For one thing, the trauma continues. No one would sensibly talk about it as over or in the past. But there is also no systematic data about the mental health response to the disaster, and it will be some time before the several studies underway are published.[1] This preliminary analysis is part of a larger psychological interview study of the World Trade Center disaster at John Jay College's Center on Terrorism and Public Safety under the direction of Charles B. Strozier. His colleague, Robert Jay Lifton, is also involved in the study, along with Katie Gentile, Michael Flynn, Cindy Ness, and Paula Glickman. The study method involves two two-hour interviews with each respondent (where possible) and follows a protocol developed by Lifton in his five important empirical studies (1961, 1968, 1973, 1985, and 1999). As of December 2002, the World Trade Center study has interviewed sixty-nine respondents and includes ninety-eight separate interviews and approximately 140 hours of interview data.

The unique character of the World Trade Center disaster itself cannot be sufficiently emphasized as a basis for understanding the mental health response, though of course it evokes other historical disasters (Erikson, 1995; Lifton, 1968; Barstow, 2000). Responses to the collapse of the towers can be distinguished within what can be called the different zones of sadness it created.[2] The zones are based on physical, emotional, and social proximity to the towers. The most intense was inside the fiery buildings. Virtually all those people above the floors where the planes hit perished in the flames. Thousands in the floors below, however, were evacuated in that precious hour or so before the collapse of the buildings themselves. Into the fiery buildings rushed the first responders, especially the thousands of firefighters, 343 of whom lost their lives. An impromptu triage center was set up inside the lobby of the north tower, which was the first tower hit but the second to collapse.

When the south tower collapsed and the entire complex was covered with debris, it was clear to the building engineers, the firefighters, and other helpers that the lobby had to be cleared. It was not immediately clear, however, where to go or how to get there. So many people were jumping by that point that the rain of bodies made it dangerous to leave, a detail evoked in three separate respondents in our World Trade Center study and captured visually by Jules and Gedeon Naudet in a documentary shown on CBS on March 10, 2002, and now generally available on the Internet.

Such a scene of carnage and chaos forces the self into a radically altered state (van der Kolk, 1987; van der Kolk, McFarlane, and Weisaeth, 1996;

Herman, 1992; Caruth, 1995; Strozier and Flynn, 1996a, 1996b; Lifton, 1968). One's immediate psychological response is a numbing, or a nearly complete closing down of feeling. The body still works and many sensations, especially those of fight and flight, remain effective. That focus in the moment of crisis can be highly adaptive, even though trauma forces the self into a dissociated state that is a kind of symbolic death. The mental health consequences for such an experience are likely to be enduring.

It is a mistake, however, to think the trauma was restricted to the first responders and those in the towers who survived. In the next immediate zone of sadness, extending for several blocks around the World Trade Center complex, were those direct witnesses of the event. Students, for example, at the nearby community college, workers in buildings nearby, and many thousands of pedestrians drawn to the scene watched in horror for the hour or so before the first tower collapsed as scores, perhaps hundreds, of people jumped to escape the scorching heat in the upper floors.[3]

In the next zone of sadness, from about Chambers Street to 14th Street, a typical witness was able to directly watch the fire and devastation but was just beyond sight of those jumping. Their reaction was mostly numbed horror that led to a closing down but without overt traumatic response. In varying degrees, that psychological generalization holds for the twenty-three respondents in the World Trade Center study for that zone of sadness. In the final zone, streets from the 20s north, one could no longer see the towers (with exceptions, of course, as in the southern exposures of tall buildings), but the day was filled with chaos, bomb threats and buildings evacuated, huge throngs fleeing across the bridges into Brooklyn and Queens, and a general sense of panic.

In this zone the nature and degree of trauma tended to blend with the much more distant and vicarious experience of those who watched the event on television. People were deeply affected but, for the most part, not traumatized in any clinical sense. In our work, we have found only one respondent from this zone who seemed traumatized in the strict sense of having enduring Post-Traumatic Stress Disorder (PTSD) symptoms. This respondent, a woman, was a special case in that she had worked in the north tower as recently as the Thursday before the Tuesday of September 11 and watched the disaster from the southern exposure of a tall Midtown Manhattan building as thirty-five of her former co-workers died.

And yet in an important respect, the New York experience of the disaster, even in geographically more remote zones of sadness had a unique character. That has to do with the smell, which united all. It was everywhere and nowhere, like death. Within the smell, of course, from the collapse of 220 floors, each about an acre, were all the incinerated computers and rugs and drapes and doors and mountains of cement and some asbestos and a lot of chemicals but also the bodies of thousands of people. The reason not many bodies have been found is that with the exception of firefighters in their protective gear or some caught in unusual pockets or those who jumped and were buried but not crushed, most do not exist in any corporeal form. They were not just burned but incinerated. At best, a body part remained. The rest floated into the air in that cloud and smoke. New Yorkers literally took them into their lungs and bodies and impacted them into their souls. The smell creates echoes of Auschwitz.

THE IMMEDIATE MENTAL HEALTH RESPONSE

What began to emerge within minutes of the attacks was an elaborate, if uncoordinated, mental health response. Institutions and governmental agencies familiar with and responsible for handling disasters sprang into action, but for the most part, what actually happened evolved empirically (and often with great confusion) and without overall planning. The mental health response took a number of forms: (1) a triage center was formed at Chelsea Piers between 20th and 23rd Streets on the West Side Highway; (2) later the Family Assistance Center was developed at Pier 94 (54th Street and 12th Avenue), along with the city's Department of Mental Health, Red Cross, and Disaster Psychiatric Outreach, while a section for children was created and at first headed by a psychiatrist, Desmond Heath[4]; (3) work proceeded at the Armory and at Bellevue DNA, as well as some counseling; (4) formal counseling programs were set up by managed care companies that negotiated contracts with companies directly affected; (5) ad hoc but important volunteer grief counseling was provided in a variety of settings; (6) arrangements of many kinds were made by psychoanalytic institutes and other training centers to provide counselors where needed; (7) pro bono work was provided by organizations such as the New York State Psychological Association, which claimed to have had three hundred members contributing their services[5]; (8) New York University's extensive use of its mental health center adapted to the special needs of many students in lower Manhattan[6]; and of course (9) ongoing individual counseling and psychotherapy sessions in the city that were addressing the trauma of the disaster were always present.

Some order began to emerge in those early, frantic days. The Compassion Center, for example, was originally set up in the New York Armory by the first weekend. The Compassion Center was designed to collect information from families of missing persons and to provide mental health services and general community resource referrals. Many people complained, however, that the Armory was depressing, dark, hot, and too small. The New York City Mayor's office and the City of New York solicited advice from the Red Cross on how to improve facilities to service families and victims. Those discussions led to the creation of the much larger and more appropriate facility on Pier 94.

The Red Cross also assumed increasing responsibility for the coordination of many of the mental health volunteers. The Red Cross organized many counseling sites, including the Compassion Center, Ground Zero, Chelsea Piers, and for a few days, Channel 13, where the telephone banks for the missing persons' lines were answered. In order to gain access to any of these sites, a volunteer had to go to a Red Cross office and register, a process that involved showing one's license. This seemingly sensible requirement, however, did not really fit the unusual situation in New York with its thousands of certified but unlicensed psychoanalysts and counselors. With the best of intentions, many qualified volunteers were turned away.

There were also serious problems with the actual availability of therapeutic services. We understand that crisis counseling was available and funded by FEMA, Project Liberty, and Safe Horizons, but the experiences represented by many of the respondents in the World Trade Center study, others whom we talked with more informally, and the men in my coauthor's (Gentile's) group were that the immense amount of red tape involved in such referrals was more than many people suffering from symptoms of PTSD could manage.

Nevertheless, a small army—some thirty-one thousand mental health workers, according to a Red Cross spokesperson (N. Rutherford, personal communication with Katie Gentile, Red Cross Public Relations, January 29, 2002)—volunteered their services between September 11, 2001, and January 2002. Of this astonishingly high and somewhat misleading figure, 84 percent or about twenty-six thousand, were what the Red Cross call "spontaneous volunteers," that is, people from the affected community or New York itself. How this number was arrived at and what it really means is unclear. The other five thousand volunteers for the Red Cross (again, according to their sources) were from all over the country who were flown in to provide their services. What either figure fails to reveal, however, is what these volunteers actually did, with whom, and for how long.

TWO ACTUAL EXPERIENCES FROM THE FIELD

Cindy Ness

There was a widespread desire to help on the part of New York's small army of therapists. For the most part, however, therapists were outside the loop of any helping structure and felt useless and frustrated. The evidence is mostly anecdotal in this regard, but the major topic of conversation whenever two or two hundred therapists have gathered anywhere in the city since September 11 has been what they were *unable* to accomplish. Few knew where to go, whom to talk with, where to volunteer, or what to really do. That helplessness was deeply confusing for many and is the subject of several studies in and of itself.[7]

But many therapists were involved, and some of their stories are quite illuminating. Cindy Ness worked in a structured setting established by a managed care company. Ness, a therapist herself and a resident of lower Manhattan who happened to be in Philadelphia when the disaster occurred, was asked to work for pay by a behavioral health company with which she had previously done trauma counseling. The behavioral health company had negotiated a contract with a corporation that had lost many of its employees in the disaster. Ness arrived in the city on the second day and immediately began debriefing groups of employees. Most of the people who came to talk were in a state of high alert. Many seemed unsure about what they should be doing—staying at home with their children or coming to work where they might be of some help, although none were really clear in what way. The two most common themes that emerged in the groups were the need to reestablish a sense of safety and the need to make meaning of the incident by doing something active.

On Friday, the third day after the attack, Ness was asked by the behavioral mental health firm to meet with employees who worked for an insurance company that had offices in both towers. The company had approximately eight floors of offices at the exact location where the first plane hit. Those employees who had arrived to work that morning when the plane hit were not accounted for and presumed to be dead. Most of the people she spoke with worked at another office of the company in Midtown. In general, this group seemed more at a distance from their emotions. They were waiting to hear if people they knew would be found. They had the same concerns about safety for themselves and family as the employees of the behavioral health firm, but in addition, almost all of them knew someone directly or of someone who was missing. The image of people who were trapped in the building was quite real to people in this group because they had a face to match the image.

On Sunday, Ness was asked to go over to the family center that the insurance company had set up in a Midtown hotel. The company had set up a twenty-four-hour crisis center and hotline that provided an array of services for family members or friends who were searching for loved ones. Many family members were from out of town and were put up by the company at the hotel. She was asked to be the clinician on the evening shift from 6 PM to 12 AM and then on call overnight. She lived at the hotel for three weeks, the first two while the operation was in full swing and then when she was the clinician assigned to handle mental health emergencies on the hotline.

The family crisis center coordinated the many different services under one roof that the people looking for loved ones would need—an updated list of people who were located, links to the Armory where DNA sampling was taking place, Pier 94, benefits information, mental health services, etc. While there were probably 150 people staying at the hotel, over the course of the day many more people would drop by to inquire after the missing.

Ness would frequently be called to speak with someone who was described by the volunteers (many employees of the company who were acting in the capacity as escorts and staffing the different tables) as "falling apart." Sometimes this would be precipitated by news that made it seem likely that the person being searched for was dead. Other times, the "falling apart" would occur at a point of exhaustion and often when they could no longer deny to themselves that there was a possibility of the worst materializing. Siblings had to take in that brothers and sisters were gone, wives and husbands that spouses were gone, parents that children were gone, and children that parents were gone.

Sometimes the reaction was sadness, other times terrible self-incrimination. One woman said repeatedly of her brother that it should have been her instead of him, that he was so good and she so bad, that he was so selfless and she so selfish. She lamented how they had wasted time arguing and said with great sorrow how they were just really getting to know each other. Another young man refused to acknowledge that there was any chance that his brother and sister-in-law were dead, even though they had been missing for nearly two weeks. He was sure he would kill himself if it turned out to be true that his brother was dead, as the brother was the one he leaned on, and he could not face the prospect of being alive without him. In his distraught state he even spoke about having to kill other family members because he could not let them suffer both his death and that of his brother.

Yet another family who flew in from Ukraine asked factual questions through a translator about what were likely the last minutes of their daughter's life. Then there was the husband who was trapped inside one of the towers of the World Trade Center along with seven or eight other people. Someone in the group had a skypager, and they were able to get a few calls out to loved ones telling them that they were loved. His wife never received a call but learned of the story through another employee. She was glad to have those words to hold onto since there would most likely not be a body to reclaim.

Katie Gentile

The second experience that we will relate involves me (Katie Gentile, co-author). I am a psychologist who heads the Women's Center at John Jay College where I teach counseling and women's studies courses. After September 11 I worked in four different settings: on the first weekend I volunteered with the Red Cross doing what is termed "callbacks"; for one day I volunteered with a financial firm; for two days I did paid work with an accounting firm; and for a few months from the beginning of October until the end of January, along with another psychologist, on a pro bono basis, we led a 3½ hour weekly psychotherapy group with maintenance machinists, who had worked in the World Trade Center in an arrangement negotiated through their union.

Callbacks with the Red Cross consisted of responding to people who had called in inquiring about their loved one and letting them know the missing person was not found in the hospital database. It was important in such conversations to make sure the Red Cross had a complete description of the person in question, explaining to the family about DNA samples, urging them to use LifeNet, and describing the location of the Armory and Pier 94. I worked next to a friend, and both of us alternately broke down, comforted each other, and called another family. There were often problems of a unique kind. The Red Cross workers were told to avoid any calls to Cantor Fitzgerald, which had its own table of workers. There were huge signs on the wall reminding volunteers not to deal with Cantor Fitzgerald. When a friend of Gentile accidentally called someone from Cantor, it caused a great scurry of activity and concern.

At the end of the first week Gentile volunteered her services through her psychoanalytic training institute, the Institute for Contemporary Psychotherapy (ICP). Therapists from ICP were quite well organized in their response to the World Trade Center disaster. They immediately were contacted by the Red Cross and then put on their list for mental health services. ICP also set up its own trauma response network on the computer for those with e-mail where they continually announced calls for mental health volunteers (i.e., doing callbacks, site visits with families and employees, assisting families when picking up death certificates, etc.). Through ICP Gentile worked briefly for two companies in hurried, even frantic, environments, where the corporate needs to do business and make money again pressed against dealing with some severely traumatized workers.

Just under a month after the attacks, Gentile was contacted by another ICP therapist and asked to accompany a group of maintenance workers on a site visit to Ground Zero. The workers were trying to go that night, but according to the rules, they needed to be accompanied by two therapists and two clergy; therefore, they were desperate to find therapists who would go with them on such short notice. These workers (they are all male) had helped maintain the building. In some respects, they kept the World Trade Center alive. Most of the group had worked there for at least fifteen years and some from the time the buildings opened. For this group, these buildings embodied their identities. Because they often had to spend entire weekends there and many nights, these buildings were at the very least a second home. They felt great pride in all they had done over the years to keep the towers effectively operating.

After this visit, Gentile's institute created a therapeutic group for the workers. It met weekly for three months and was led by Gentile and a colleague. The group was loosely framed. The men would saunter in between 10 and 11 AM and it might not end until 1:30 PM. The co-therapist began the group and Gentile ended it. Men came and went as their schedules allowed. Union representatives often came in to give announcements, and sometimes they stayed to participate, though sometimes these administrators interrupted the group process by admonishing the engineers to pull themselves up by their bootstraps. In general, it was difficult for the machinists to talk about their feelings, though they made some real progress in this regard over the months. The process was complicated. At times, the men tried to "protect" the (female) therapists from coarse language and obscene jokes. This protectiveness not only shielded them from discussing gruesome stories, it also allowed them to control the content of the group and shift it from focusing on their uncomfortable feelings of helplessness and vulnerability to being able to take control and protect the therapists.

The number in the group varied anywhere from seven to ten per week with some constant members and others attending more erratically, depending on their employment situations. Usually coffee and doughnuts were provided, and that seemed to make the engineers feel taken care of by the union. For these men, these sessions were a high point of the week because it was the only time they were able to talk with their co-workers who they had basically lived with for years. Furthermore, as became apparent within the first few groups, these men also survived the 1993 bombing. That bomb went off just down the hall from their offices. Many of them were wounded, one lost vision in his eye and has a long scar on his face. Two others were trapped by fire in an elevator shaft, and before their rescue were planning how to inhale enough smoke to be unconscious before they burned to death. Most suffered from severe PTSD symptoms afterwards. One said he has not slept more than three hours at a stretch since the first bombing. They all described knowing a second attack was coming. Each time there was a bomb threat (and there were many) or a loud noise, they jumped with fear. They were all already hypervigilant.

Humiliation was a central theme in this group. It was humiliating to need help, because they were the fixers. It was humiliating to be handicapped in functioning. It was humiliating not to be employed. It was humiliating that they were not asked to help in the recovery; thus, it was humiliating that their unique expertise in the buildings was not recognized, appreciated, and utilized, instead it went poof in the air, disappearing in the ashes. At the three-month mark (December 11), their nightmares actually got worse. They described waking each morning to the sounds of bodies splashing onto the sidewalks. They did not think they could face Christmas, after barely surviving the struggles with Thanksgiving.

Shopping was awful. They felt humiliated at their lack of an income and therefore the means to buy good gifts, as well as terror at the sight of all the packages that they saw as bombs.

The stories of their experiences did not come out all at once, nor was their narrative coherent. At first a couple of people dominated the meetings and told stories in a state of shock with blank stares. In time, however, the others joined in, and in general, members began to tell their stories with more affect. They would often get excited and speak over one another. One man told of being in the lobby of the north building when the south tower fell. He and a firefighter were dragging another injured firefighter to safety. But they were stuck in the lobby because outside it was raining people. They were afraid to leave the building because they could not find a clear spot where bodies were not falling onto the ground, and they thought if they ran out, a body would hit them for sure. When the first tower collapsed the wind from the falling building was incredible. One man described looking up to see pieces of building the size of cars and furniture flying above him across the lobby and out the other side of the building. He could also see firefighters in the air, which made them look like bats flying about.

Other men had similar stories of watching people jump and fall, of body parts littering the street, of the screams from the elevator shaft that initially alerted them to the magnitude of the attack, and of the pieces of the jet plane inexplicably lying on the sidewalk. One man was on the roof of one of the financial centers and swears the plane flew so close that he saw the pilot, and he cannot stop hearing the sound of the pilot gunning the engines as the plane approached the tower. Another expressed dismay because he had been procrastinating doing his job for the morning that required being on the roof of the north tower. Some watched with horror not knowing how to help some jumpers who seemed still to be alive after landing on the ground.

TOWARD THE FUTURE

It may be that there is an additional zone of continuing sadness among New York therapists listening to story after story of survival, death, and trauma. Therapists hold privileged information about the World Trade Center disaster, its horror, the recovery, the poisonous air, and the details that either were not in the news media or have been lost in the collective consciousness. Therapists, in working with survivors of the disaster, experience the horror in an ongoing way. That can make it difficult to process the stories and keep it from becoming toxic in their own lives as they reach out to heal others. Therapists in this sense themselves become witnesses to the trauma and to the zones of sadness, enveloped by them, not necessarily directly in the moment, but through time.

As we know about trauma, its effects linger, and as the focus of the community shifts, those people still struggling with PTSD can feel even more isolated and require more, not less, psychological help. A team of government interviewers from the New York City Department of Health six weeks after the event talked with 414 anonymous individuals in lower Manhattan and found that half were still experiencing physical symptoms, especially respiratory problems, and 40 percent had one or more PTSD symptoms, such as sleeplessness, depression, anxiety, guilt, anger, irritability, or emotional numbness.[8] Gentile's group of union workers who had been in the first zone of sadness barely made it through Thanksgiving and Christmas, and some may have psychological problems for years, if not the rest of their lives. Thousands of children lost a parent, mostly a father, the effects of which may last for generations.[9]

There are also severe indirect effects of trauma, which remain completely unaccounted for in the present structure. Researchers agree that disaster frequently results in a rise in substance abuse and belligerent acting-out behaviors in men with a marked increase in domestic violence (600 percent) and sexual assault (300 percent), while women often become depressed and anxious (Fothergill, 1996; Wilson, Phillips, and Neal, 1998; Barstow, 2000). Curiously, reactions to the World Trade Center, at least initially, have been somewhat counterintuitive in this regard, because there seems to have been a *decrease* in reports of domestic violence (Lewin, 2001; Winter, 2002). If true, such evidence is quite hopeful, but it may well be a reporting problem. Anecdotal evidence and the direct experience of Gentile with the Women's Center at John Jay College (a counseling context) suggests a marked increase in violence within intimate relationships since September 11.

Perhaps the explanation of this anomaly is that, unlike natural disasters, terrorism on a large scale makes women feel the danger within the home is more familiar and easier to deal with than the new and continuing dangers outside of the home. Certainly, U.S. policies toward immigrants after September 11 have made many women reticent to reach out for help from traditional and even neighborhood agencies. This in itself would cause a significant decrease in domestic violence reporting. In a way, that mirrors the shift in funding from social services to defense and military spending; women also may feel that domestic violence issues are not as important as those of national security. In that sense women may have lost their voice in the wake of the new dangers and the new militarism.

Nor, finally, can one ignore the subtle relationship between trauma and psychosomatic illness. The health care system itself may face rising and otherwise baffling costs in future years because of the World Trade Center disaster.

The concern of this chapter is with victims in New York. We are, however, a nation in mourning. Can mental health workers treat a country? Surely not in any traditional sense, but we might do well to think about ways in which the extremity of the attacks on the World Trade Center and the Pentagon continue to reverberate throughout the culture with psychological and political consequences we are just beginning to understand. Managed care companies driven by profits and determined to curtail expensive therapy significantly control the delivery of mental health services in the United States. The severe limits such companies place on treatment cannot begin to meet public needs. It is reasonable to urge that psychologists and therapists need to get more involved in the creation of public policy relating to disaster recovery, especially the new form of disaster represented by the World Trade Center. Their unique knowledge about the pervasive effects of trauma put them in a strong position to contribute to education, prevention, and treatment policies.

There is much to learn in this regard from the experience of other countries more familiar with terrorism. In Israel, for example, the mental health response to terrorist attacks is highly developed (Cohen, 2001). A special branch of the army deals solely with the traumatic effects of attacks on soldiers. Therapists themselves receive a great deal of supervision, and soldiers are helped through their trauma after any kind of attack. A large and complicated country such as the United States surely faces different problems and will need its own solutions. But it would seem that we have not fully recognized that the new terrorism and the cultural and political responses to it can have profound effects on mental health that can endure for years. That principle needs to be much more effectively integrated into public health policy if our hope is to find ways of healing a nation vulnerable to fear.

NOTES

1. The Solomon Asch Project of the Asch Center at the University of Pennsylvania, under a grant from the Mellon Foundation, is currently evaluating the mental health response to the World Trade Center disaster. There are undoubtedly many other studies underway. The Columbia Oral History Project will have data that in time could be culled for much useful information.

2. The image of "zones of sadness" is from Michael Flynn, personal communication, October 9, 2001.

3. The number of those who jumped remains unclear, in part because of the mostly self-imposed blackout on media coverage. For further details and quotes from some respondents in the World Trade Center study, see the preliminary report by Charles B. Strozier, 2002, "The World Trade Center Disaster and the Apocalyptic," *Psychoanalytic Dialogues* 12 (3): 361–80.

4. Desmond Heath talked about his experiences setting up this section on Saturday, October 13, 2001, at Robert Lifton's Wellfleet meetings. Alan E. Gross, Ph.D., who was active with Safe Horizon and was referred to Strozier by a contact in the Federal

Emergency Management Agency (FEMA), in an e-mail dated December 24, 2001, wrote to him with the information about the entities staffing Pier 94.

5. Gerald D'Alessio e-mail to Strozier, December 24, 2001.

6. Described in great detail by a respondent in the World Trade Center study.

7. Besides the work of the Asch Center, mentioned in the preceding, Doris Brothers of the Training and Research Institute in Self Psychology is conducting a small study with a questionnaire, and Paula Gluckman, a psychologist with a practice in New York City, is interviewing therapists on how the disaster has expressed itself in their patients (Strozier helped her develop her protocol).

8. Ground Zero: The impact; survey finds a community in anguish (2002, January 12), *New York Times* [Metropolitan Desk], p. 3. It was also reported at the International Academy of Cardiology meetings on November 20, 2002, in a study (Terrorist attacks increased dangerous irregular heartbeats) by A. Arshad, A. Kukar, V. Suma, M. Vloka, F. Ehiert, B. Herweg, et al., that heart rhythms more than doubled among New York heart patients in the month after September 11. Retrieved on May 4, 2004, from www.cardiologyonline.com. Note as well the special issue of *CNS Spectrums: The International Journal of Neuropsychiatric Medicine*, edited by Rachel Yehuda, August, 2002, "Assessing the Impact of Trauma and Loss One Year After September 11, 2002," pp. 39–42.

9. There was a huge gender gap in the victims, which has not been officially calculated but seems (from the *New York Times*, 2001, "Portraits of Grief") to be at least 80:20, men to women.

REFERENCES

Barstow, A. L. (Ed.). (2000). *War's dirty secret: Rape, prostitution, and other crimes against women*. Cleveland, OH: Pilgrim Press.

Caruth, C. (1995). *Trauma: Explorations in memory*. Baltimore: Johns Hopkins University Press.

Cohen, E. (2001). Interview with Charles Strozier, December 20 in his office as part of the WTC study. Transcripts are available on request to Strozier at chuck strozier@juno.com.

Erikson, K. (1995). *A new species of trouble: The human experience of modern disaster*. New York: Norton.

Fothergill, A. (1996). Gender, risk, and disaster. *International Journal of Mass Emergencies and Disasters*, 14 (1): 33–56.

Herman, J. (1992). *Trauma and recovery*. New York: Basic Books.

Johnson, K. (2002, January 1). PTST and the World Trade Center. *New York Times*, [Metropolitan Desk], pp. 1–2.

Lewin, T. (2001, October 21). Shelters have empty beds: Abused women stay home. *New York Times*, p. 20.

Lifton, R. (1961). *Thought reform and the psychology of totalism: A study of "brainwashing" in China*. New York: Norton.

———. (1968). *Death in life: Survivors of Hiroshima*. New York: Random House.

———. (1973). *Home from the war: Vietnam veterans, neither victims nor execution-ers*. New York: Simon & Schuster.

———. (1979). *The broken connection: On death and the continuity of life*. New York: Basic Books.

———. (1985). *The Nazi doctors: Medical killing and the psychology of genocide*. New York: Basic Books.

———. (1999). *Destroying the world to save it: Aum Shinrikyo, apocalyptic violence, and the new terrorism*. New York: Metropolitan Books.

Strozier, C. (1994). *Apocalypse: On the psychology of fundamentalism in America*. Boston: Beacon Press.

Strozier, C., and Flynn, M. (Eds.). (1996a). *Genocide, war, and human survival*. Lanham, MD: Rowman & Littlefield.

———. (1996b). *Trauma and self*. Lanham, MD: Rowman & Littlefield.

van der Kolk, B. (1987). *Psychological trauma*. Washington, DC: American Psychiatric Press.

van der Kolk, B., McFarlane, A., and Weisaeth, L. (Eds.). (1996). *Traumatic stress: The effects of overwhelming experience on mind, body, and society*. New York: Guilford.

Wilson, J., Phillips, B. D., and Neal, D. M. (1998). Domestic violence after disaster. In E. Enarson and B. H. Morrow (Eds.), *The gendered terrain of disaster: Through women's eyes*, pp. 115–22. Westport, CT: Praeger Publishers.

Winter, J. (2002, January 20–February 5). Shelter from the storm. *Village Voice*, pp. 17–18.

Chapter Twenty-one

Large Group Destruction: A Group Analyst at Ground Zero

Bennett Roth

Crisis groups following the September 11 attack on New York City were an opportunity to learn about how people managed their personal crises. The curative factors following the massive trauma to the World Trade Center (WTC) are complex: the products of whole constellations of factors in the ways and circumstances in which there was proximity to the site, what was seen and experienced, and the pre-traumatic personality. Diagnostic emphasis on Post-Traumatic Stress Disorder (PTSD) obscured individual and group dynamic complexity. The contributing elements may be in a variety of realms: genetic, developmental, psychological, perceptual, sociocultural, and structural. In general, group theory was ignored in discussion of the aftermath of this event. I have chosen to focus on large group theory because it is viewed as complementary to psychoanalytic "loosening of anxiety" usually bound in social contracts and other group structures.

World Trade Center (September 11, 2001).

429

Freud (1930) theorized that in reaction to extreme suffering, special mental devices are brought to bear, and this is the case within group behavior. As with all therapeutic efforts, resistance arises to stand in the path of therapeutic efforts and healing. In this case, two forms of specific group resistances are explicated that often thwarted therapeutic efforts.

Things fall apart; the centre cannot hold;
Mere anarchy is loosed upon the world,
The blood-dimmed tide is loosed, and everywhere
The ceremony of innocence is drowned;
The best lack all conviction, while the worst
Are full of passionate intensity.

—William Butler Yeats, "The Second Coming"

In the aftermath of the September 11 attacks in New York City and Washington, D.C., various therapy and crisis groups were created in an effort to assist the people traumatized by the sudden attacks. In retrospect, these groups afforded an unfortunate opportunity to learn about people in traumatic crisis within groups of various sizes. Many groups were formed to assist people in their return to work, schools, and home. Heterogeneous groups were formed around the mourning of people killed in the attack. This chapter uses a psychoanalytic group theoretical orientation as a frame of reference to clarify the effects of the attack and the impact on individuals of this sudden terrible traumatic crisis. In particular, it will focus on the psychoanalytic understanding of large groups and the use of psychoanalytically oriented groups to aid in the path to mastery and recovery.

In order to frame the following remarks concerning large groups, it is necessary to describe the current environment of analytic thinking in which these tragic events occurred. Within psychoanalytic theorizing in recent years there has been a continuous shift toward an emphasis on the ambiguous concept of relational theory accompanied by a related atrophy of the underlying understanding of, and interpretation of, destructive impulses. This drift is recognizable through the theoretical efforts of Mitchell and Greenberg and the historical emphasis on the theories of Ferenczi and Winnicott. Both historically and in current theories, the nurturing aspects of the analytic relationship have been emphasized while the drive derivative aspects have been diminished — in particular the destructive components of the drive theory that took decades to secure.

This relational—and U.S.—centric emphasis may be called into question by the obvious destructive aggression inherent in the terrorist attacks on New York City and Washington. As happened after World War I for Freud's theory, it is expected that there will be a return to a concern with destructive impulses (Grey, 2000). Psychoanalytic training programs have become insulated from the social environment since the experiments in the Berlin Free clinic. Within the current theoretical environment, psychoanalysts and psychoanalytic institutes seemed to suffer a paralysis of public response to the immediate psychological needs of people affected by the attacks.

Into this void those therapists following a cognitive approach responded first and most strongly to the victims. The helping community embraced the theoretical understanding of acute crisis intervention, stress-management strategies, and the diagnostic term "Post-Traumatic Stress Disorder (PTSD)." Such psychiatric nomenclature and symptom focus offered little help in understanding either group dynamics or individual behavior in groups. This narrow symptom approach generated competition for media attention and the funds offered to hospitals and relief programs. Advocates of the PTSD diagnosis shunned complex psychic motivations, structural understandings, and analytically oriented interventions. They also supported the illusion of the ability to control the long-term psychic effects on the personality of sudden trauma and loss of life.

In truth, a very small number of people developed PTSD, yet there was little theoretical opposition to advocates of the PTSD diagnosis. We know that psychic defenses and adaptations are not merely reactive. One recent study of the long-term effects of trauma suggests that character residues or persistent alterations in personality remain for considerably longer than anticipated (Honig, Grace, Lindy, Newman, and Titchener, 1993). Diagnostically, depression and phobic responses were equally manifested among those in proximity to the site of the attacks, at least as often as PTSD. The narrow symptom emphasis, with its strong media component, prevented many who would have benefited from seeking therapeutic help.

Rather than continue to argue the merits of a diagnostic category, it would be more productive to call for a comprehensive progressive strategy that encompasses an understanding of all reactions, psychic and symptomatic, to the terrorist attacks. Group analytic thinking offers a viable model to help observers and practitioners understand the various elements of the traumatic effects of the catastrophic attack. While at times it does so at the expense of a deeper understanding of individuals and symptoms, group analytic thinking is broad enough to allow us to study all aspects of human behavior. For current purposes, the study of these groups can be viewed from a psychoanalytic perspective and use a true psychic object-relational model while not ignoring the destructive elements that are essential to unconscious life.

It is possible to view a variety of large groups from a large group psychoanalytic perspective. To do so requires analysts comfortable with a dyadic hierarchical model, so that they can both distinguish and understand various complex group structures, multiple levels of participants, and various levels of group activities (i.e., subgroups) that usually function without notice. Like some automatic body or ego activities, group functions and the personality functions interacting within them are attended to only in crises or when they do not perform well. While it is well-accepted analytic truth that people hold various forms of group identifications and variable degrees of social adaptation, membership in groups, and roles within groups, all individuals are also dependent on and take for granted certain social and work group functions to support both daily life and a belief in the future. As Grey (2000) put it prior to the recent attacks, "the environment outside our consultation rooms is never completely free from danger" (p. 232). However, we rarely attend to that possible danger, because interconnecting layers of group functions and social contracts within society, interacting with our belief systems, values, and inner conflicts serve to protect us from any immediate sensation that there is an imminent danger or threat that would normally arouse anxiety or panic.

The average social and personal expectancy is that there is no possibility of being on the receiving end of destructive sadistic drives or actions. We also know that people function in both interpersonal and social reality with varying degrees of alert functions to danger in the background of their psyches and that disorders of this function are themselves well-known symptom groups. These primitive survival reactions are usually not aroused in daily social functioning. Such expectancies changed radically on September 11, and the effects of these changes will be described later in this chapter.

A deeper psychological understanding of large group behavior is derived from the works of Freud (1921), Bion (1959), Jacques (1955), and Turquet (1975). Coexistent with group identifications, individuals make unconscious use of institutions and social groups (with which they may identify) by cooperating with these large groups and, in doing so, unconsciously reinforce internal defenses against impulses, anxiety, and guilt. The intricate internal psychic processes that lead to distinctions between inside and outside, between "me" and "not me," must also be applied to the dynamics of belonging to a group, maintaining the boundaries of a group, and making distinctions between member, neighbor, and enemy both in and out of the group. In this complex identificatory process that impinges on the development of psychic identity and separateness, various types of large groups as entities (hordes or masses) marshal and use aggression (destructive and normal) to protect themselves and advance their own group goals.

These dynamics can be recognized when large groups and institutions are shared with others and used for common purposes, such as work. Existing groups become available for the psychic purposes of projection while fantasy relations through common conjoined projective identifications bond the group members together. In this manner, there is a continuous interplay of both introjective and projective identification within large groups. Perception and information in large groups and institutions are determined not only by their explicit and consciously agreed on reality work functions but also by their unrecognized fantasy functions in relation to unconscious needs. Jacques (1955) asserted that certain members of the large group are chosen to either accept the projections of the others or deflect them. By these mechanisms, the members of the institutions find relief from their own internal conflicts, maintain the structure of the large groups, and receive protection from other internal anxieties. Unlike the analytic situation, which is essentially private and limited in membership, large groups and institutional structures are subject to the dynamics of other large groups. They may partially function in a public/social environment, may be restructured by people leaving or changing roles, and may forcibly be changed when they no longer sufficiently serve to reinforce individual defenses.

Freud's (1921) original group paper, written from an oedipal perspective, suggests further functions of these large groups. An individual's projections are organized or channeled along certain social veins supplied by these specific artificial groups within our society. In that manner these institutions are designated not only to fulfill identificatory or defensive psychic functions but also to express unconscious aggressive/sadistic, protective, or magical functions. When we apply this insight to contemporary American values, it becomes recognizable that the designated artificial groups, including the military, political, and mystical-religious, serve distinctly important psychological functions: to absorb various levels of anxiety, to discharge the requisite drives "fairly" in reality, to absorb sufficient primitive anxiety while maintaining individual self-esteem regulation, and, when necessary, to specify a distinct boundary or external enemy. Each of these types of artificial groups may be studied separately and have their own types of leaders and specific psychic group-enhancing functions.

My interest in the problems posed by understanding the events of September 11 through a large group perspective is a result of my experiences with groups of various sizes in which I participated after the initial attack. The size and membership of these groups varied in their proximity to the attack site, as well as in the ethnicity, gender, and age of their members. The size of the groups varied from approximately five members to median groups of approximately thirty, to large groups of over one hundred. In some groups I was an observer, in some I shared a therapeutic role with other group therapists, and in others I was the group convener and consultant.

One group in particular aroused my interest. Ultimately, it was this group and my attempts to understand its focus and anxiety that both changed and enhanced my group perspective of these events. Elsewhere (Roth, 2002), I have described my impressions of the general themes that emerged in those groups and my understanding of some of the dynamics. Here I will convey a different perspective that emerged over a period of about ten months from the original attack. I reported:

> One group attended for a long period of time to their reactions when the first plane hit the North Tower. Everyone in the group fixated on remembering this exact time. This was obviously the first point when their stimulus barrier was overwhelmed, and when they experienced a splintering of the social/work group upon which they depended for support. They had a need to tell each other what happened to them or what they did at the moment that recognition of the scope of the attack set in. Some did nothing, some called supervisors, some called to people who were on fire, some went outside to watch, and some called loved ones. Significantly, their behavior shed some light on a frequently reported phenomenon. They all experienced the unreal quality associated with sudden stimulus barrier assault and horrific images of people being injured and killed, but were now in the group recalling individual differences under extreme reactions when their work group collapsed. The start of individual differentiation in reaction in the protection of empathic interactions in a non-critical environment established a space upon which others continued to talk to each other and continued to create their personal narrative. Doing so both builds memories and recovers suppressed memories evoked from listening to others. While memories were rebuilding there was the ongoing danger of disturbing denial and splitting defenses by such interactions that are associated with incomplete mourning and important reality testing deficits. Simultaneously, such defenses indicated a need to delay mourning and confrontation with a changed object world (Roth, 2002, p. 159–60).

Additional unreported information will help clarify the dramatic dynamics that were revealed in this group. Almost everyone in the group of about thirty people was psychologically stunned by both the sound of the plane hitting the first tower and the ensuing inferno, chaos, and debris. Their view, directly across from West Street on a low floor, allowed a clear line of vision to the immediate horrific aftermath—people being incinerated, physical and human debris falling to the street, the efforts of people to leave the building, and the beginning of police and fire department mobilization.

Highly idiosyncratic reactions to the stunning events were openly remembered and reported in the group in a variety of emotional contexts, ranging from bravado to shock. As people recalled, at the beginning of their recognition of the actual destructive events, most of their immediate behavior included attempts to contact people in authority and to call to people outside who were suffering. It was also revealed, as it had been in similar nearby groups, that a few people (three to five) were compelled to take a position themselves so that they could clearly view the unfolding disaster. Being compelled to view the carnage was a repeated phenomenon in all the bystander groups and coincided with two observations: some people inexplicably run toward danger, and over time, the people who saw the most devastation had a longer recovery period.

They continued looking out the windows, eventually fleeing the office down the stairs, which either took them to a place where they could not directly see the awful effects of the plane crash or took them directly onto West Street and in full view of the human suffering. Those who reported that they were afraid to look maintained that avoidant defense throughout the immediate phase of recovery. Their consistent emotions at this juncture, in a safe environment away from the actual site, were a mixture of awe, anxiety, and pride in having escaped and survived. There was also a curious absence of expressed empathy for the victims but they did for other survivors.

A small number of participants were still visibly anxious, and many revealed fearful expectancies concerning physically returning to their previously evacuated buildings, coming close to the attack site, traveling by subway or crossing bridges, or worrying about the effect of the air quality on their health. Almost all admitted to difficult relations with superiors in the return to work phase and felt that immediate supervisors were making harsh demands for productivity. Some directly raised trust issues, specifically whether supervisors could be trusted during the bomb scares then occurring. Elsewhere (Roth, 2002), I described that all the groups reported that some form of dynamic of a failure by "authority" was responsible for the attack. This seemed to be a milder form of that leader dynamic.

From the perspective of group cohesion, the degree to which people feel and act in an affiliated manner, act as a unit in a group, or share common projections, the reported act of fleeing the office seemed a highly individual event. About half of the fleeing members sought a "buddy" to leave with. This buddy was a positive friend before the attack. The most severely anxious and overwhelmed member of the group was a young woman who saw many horrible burn victims up close and somehow wound up separated from her buddies. Contacts made immediately after fleeing, communications of personal experiences, and contacts before the return to a different work site occurred along buddy configurations. Pairing in groups and outside of large groups is a well-recognized form of intense communication that partially offsets the isolation of being in a large group. In this case it supplied a group "residue."

From a dynamic view, it was evident that the groups readily talked with me without obvious reservation and seemingly without defense, a response I noted in almost all groups. This was likely the result of continuously felt mobile anxiety that was contagious in the groups and reported to be in the work environment. They also had not previously been given a "safe" time together, away from work-related authority figures. They used this time to tell their stories, not only to me as an outsider, but to each other. One result of this retelling was correction and addition to the stories, indicating that all the narratives had been subjected to secondary defensive processes.

It is important to distinguish group responses from individual reactions to the attacks. Individual reactions were dependent on proximity to the site of the attack, the threat and actuality of physical injury, and a prior history of trauma. The following are generalized statements taken from individual reports in the group settings. In reported individual crisis situations, the individual's stimulus barrier was suddenly overwhelmed or breached and caused not only psychic trauma throughout the personality structure but also primitive responses on a neurophysical and hormonal level. Most physiological responses that occurred were associated with the degree to which the individual experienced acute fear, fright, disgust, and the threat of death. Under these conditions, ego executive functions shut down, resulting in poor decision making and leaving the individual vulnerable to the contagion of fear, the influence of authority, and the emotional states of being overwhelmed. These emotional mood states persisted in varying degrees throughout the recovery period and were reexperienced in groups as uncontrollable, appearing as sudden surges of emotional discharge when regressively recalled.

The physical site itself became, as it was undergoing radical transformation, an object of transference attachment. The environment that had once been familiar and safe had been radically altered and damaged and became life threatening. This sudden and very unexpected change resulted in additional feelings of helplessness and hopelessness as well as fearfulness of the actual physical area that had been attacked. It was invested with extraordinary psychic power. Individual responses to having this experience varied, but almost all caught near and in the actual site maintained vivid snapshot-like memories with great emotional turbulence stored in this graphic.

After the attack and escape, many sought reassurance from authority figures as belief systems and superego identifications were challenged by the threat of physical annihilation of person and place, often leaving the participants vulnerable and confused. Part of this confusion was the result of the individual being forced out of his work group environment and identity and placed in a situation of isolation and loneliness. The ability to find authority figures or group leader models and the nature of those sought seemed determined by prior experiences and superego values. In acute crises viewed from a group perspective, as differentiated from individual crises, anxiety is loosened from its normal projective vanes, for example, paranoid anxiety, described by Ganzarain (2002) as appearing in so-called incest survivor groups. In these acute crisis groups, psychic paranoid anxiety combine with the real threat of annihilation to flood self and psychic systems with both real threat and psychic terror.

Once physically safe, in an effort to reduce anxiety and threat, a hierarchical chain was revealed in people's descriptions and reactions, in which there was a pyramid of belief that the authorities—teacher, police, priest, mayor, president—in whom good impulses have been projected, were saviors or omniscient parents. This projection seemed to be an attempt to internally or externally preserve in crises an external undamaged parental object as (group) symbolic leader and thereby alleviate residual psychic fears of annihilation, relieve anxiety, and defer individual decision making to an idealized leader. The immediately felt anxieties were simultaneously alleviated by locating the loosened paranoid feelings into the environment that had been attacked and altered until safety was achieved and, subsequently, projecting them onto an external enemy.

From a different perspective, during and after the attack, the fire department was a consistent projective recipient of the heroic fantasies and depressive anxieties that were loosened from their original sources. It was evident that in an effort to organize mourning reactions and channel depressive anxieties, fantasies, and responses to the fearful immolating fires, the unfortunate deaths of these men and women became a psychic location wherein which, hopefully, heroes could be found. To accomplish this was to avoid the experience of being overwhelmed with anger and helplessness at yet another protective group failure.

The returning workers who attended groups were often the first civilians to return to the attack sites now radically altered from their pre-attack physical structure. Those group members who were not able to find an idealized leader, those who projected their seemingly more powerful "bad parent impulses" onto authority figures, continued to believe more strongly that the authorities were "not doing their job" and that they "had to make their own decisions." Some of these conflicted people abandoned their jobs at the point of attack and fled immediately, only to suffer great anxiety in the following months as they were unable to reconstitute good relations with superiors. In crisis groups, they both offered and appealed to cynical phrases such as, "Why should we believe them? The people in Tower II believed them when they said it was safe and they died." Others sought reassurance and attempted to reconstitute protective idealizations from past good experiences or returned to religious services to seek calm explanation and alleviation of painful mourning reactions. Blos's (1976) earlier insights into the stabilizing effects of social groups directs our understanding to the idea that such people were using the group (work milieu) situation to modulate and synthesize their own barely and tenuously integrated split parental imago. With the large group disruption of the September attack on their work group, they could not overcome their inner sense of anxiety, divisiveness, and uncertainty, and therefore reverted to an increased need for hostile projections onto the leaders as a defense to maintain equilibrium.

Group behavior also revealed that cognitive processes were disrupted by acute crises. Individuals experienced breaks in attention, were unable to speak without becoming emotional, or experienced severe numbness. Repressors, those whose character defenses prevent expressing feelings in reality, while having intense psychosomatic reactions, were most likely to have prolonged physical reactions to the attacks and to a return to the physical site. For most group participants, the ability to put dangerous perceptions aside, that is forgetting, was disrupted in the short term after the attacks. This resulted in what appeared to be flashback memories containing the "snapshots," frequently reported nightmares, and other sleep disturbances. Loud sounds, alarm bells, and plane noises easily elicited alert arousal with sudden anxiety. The repeated false bomb reports and anthrax scares kept this alert functioning aroused.

A PSYCHOANALYTIC GROUP PERSPECTIVE

A psychoanalytic group perspective is not offered as a challenge to the traditional psychoanalytic perspective, which Turquet (1975) describes as a singular visual frame of reference. A group frame requires that the perceptual apparatus move and shift focus to other angles, sights, and human objects that present in the dyadic arrangement. A group perspective is meant not only to bring additional information to understanding the impact of catastrophe and mass trauma but also to offer direction as to how group structures have to be reconstructed in recovery attempts. There is very little in the analytic group literature that refers to the destruction on a scale that was witnessed at and near the World Trade Center. One term "disarroy" was useful (Turquet, 1975, p. 103) and refers to the actual experience of change within one's status in a group with an inherent notion of collapse and with a wish to return to status quo ante. This state of disarroy also carries with it various forms of defensive wishes, among them to disavow reality, and that what took place had never happened. Here, the term "violent group disarroy" may usefully be applied to the reports that describe reactions as "movie like" and unreal.

The following summary is taken from eyewitness responses presented in groups and reworked for the purposes of this chapter into a coherent framework. I report these mindful of the fact that this was an event of such stunning magnitude and destructiveness that it shattered all prior notions of human scale. From the moment that the extreme noise from the approaching planes was heard or as the planes were seen actually turning into the towers, the physical impact of the attack shattered the usual security assigned to the physical place and the function of the workplace. Safety was transformed into danger, security into physical threat, and the environment radically altered by unforeseen, and impossible to have been predicted, dangers and disintegration. Identification with place was shattered, with accompanying sound and extraordinary visual sights. While this was immediate, there were nearly simultaneous experiences of the frightful attacks on, and destruction of, the body integrity of fellow co-habitors of that space. From a group psychoanalytic perspective, the normal expectancy of continuous large group social safety was suddenly and instantly multiply fractured, accompanied by a kaleidoscopic bombardment of sensations requiring rapid visual surveying of the previously safe environment as it spasmodically underwent horrific transformations. Once shock subsided, there were rapid psychic changes as adaptive threat reactions drove people in vastly different directions. Safety and survival became paramount despite the fears evoked. These vulnerable and confused people were highly susceptible to authority and rumor while at the same time they often helped each other in remarkable and simple ways to get to safety.

Once safe, the required form of unconscious projection of individual protective aggressive wishes on those groups that protect us returned and focused, to varying degrees, on the leaders of these groups and the aggressive acts taken on our behalf. Immediately following the attack, it was both the perceived and real failure of those groups to prevent the attacks and hence the loss of life that was quickly questioned by some and loosened a psychic vulnerability in self-esteem and self-esteem regulation within the population nearest to the World Trade Center, in those who suffered immediate loss of life within their family and in the population in general. Directly after the local attacks there was a perceived threat to the country that was widely compensated for by the displaced use of the symbol of the American flag. Iconic support that focused on the flag seemed to offer a short-lived emotional rallying point to counteract group disarroy, however it did not deter anxieties resulting from the scope of the damage from such an unexpected attack.

As a result of the failed projection of protection, paranoid anxiety sought targets. The natural targets, the actual perpetrators, had deprived the public of a visible object of retaliatory fantasies. While seeking other secure attachments and group models (Turquet, 1975) to combat the loss of group structure, some people felt fearfully vulnerable while others remained vigilant to slights of any kind, half-truths or rumors, and previously repressed fears. In addition, failure of the groups and other leaders on whom our aggressive and protective wishes were projected (the army and air force), loosened feelings of personal vulnerability and the episodic return of older repressed annihilation anxiety activated by the attack. The repeated media representations of the events, showing American commercial jets flying into the buildings, added uncertainty and increased ambiguity for the people in the recovery groups by not allowing a designated enemy, an immediate recipient of vengeful fantasies.

One early result of this ambiguity, when coupled with the feeling of vulnerability, was the spread of paranoid anxiety seeking an external location on which to adhere. This spreading of anxiety took various forms—from the rumors of impending attacks on bridges and other areas where phobias might normally regressively reappear, to a general distrust of authority figures who may or may not have acted decisively immediately after the attack. When authority figures failed to assert authority in the period immediately following the attacks, there was a greater likelihood that fearfulness and depression would continue for a longer period. Without a clear visible target for retaliation, the loosened anxiety lasted longer and appeared frequently in the crisis groups, seeking some external attachment. One form it took was the anxious reporting of the rumors of more planes out there, of the bridges that were going to be blown up, and of a West Coast bridge that was next. There was also a heightened alertness to plane sounds in those closely affected by the attack, as the expectancy of continued assaults reactivated more alert anxiety and susceptibility to rumors and a distrust of the leader's concern.

Such a variety of immediate fears revealed a flow of mobile anxiety, which when it appeared in the group setting, was interpersonally very contagious. This anxiety often found regressive pathways, in and out of the groups, and easily evoked prior trauma and fantasies within the groups. In addition, following the attack, all forms of transportation were, in reality, affected and many anxious people were "held" in underground transportation; this event became a natural location for phobic displacements and much anxiety was displaced to this seemingly previously normalized and accepted means of transportation. As much as six months after the attack, delays on trains elicited fantasies of further attack incidents, and people in cars rushed across bridges and through tunnels.

Significantly, there was very little anger expressed in these groups, although in the mourning groups open anger was directed at the heads of companies and the highest officers in the city departments. The expression of this anger contained real complaints and additional psychic elements of the failure of leadership scapegoating seen in the other groups.

WORKING WITHIN NONANALYTIC
GROUP ENVIRONMENTS

From a large group perspective, it was within group environments that viewed anxiety and fear as foreign elements that crisis groups were organized for intervention. The numbers and kinds of groups that formed were quite varied, from large groups of over one hundred displaced employees to smaller, open-ended groups of people for whom anxiety was unmanageable and overflowing. Immediately following the attacks, executives and managers in work environments had to try to be leaders of a different sort of group than they had ever been trained for—one in which anxiety was spoken about, modes of adaptation had been compromised and were to be exposed, and where mourning was taking place. This was particularly true of teachers who had no training to hold discussion groups with children regarding anxiety and who may themselves have wanted to avoid coping with the mourning that follows the loss of a parent. Without work group leaders being first to reveal their anxiety and experience as models to the members of the group, there were powerful inhibitions to the sharing of fear and anxiety. Many people voiced fears of losing their jobs if they were revealing or spoke of their fears. In uniformed services groups and debriefing groups, there were additional fears (I did not lead any and was told of these)—fears of outsiders, psychoanalysts, of breaking with the codes of toughness, and fears of civilian strangers with different values. In almost all these groups, if the chief or vice president did not speak first of his fear, no ensuing group formation was possible.

All these kinds of groups required a profound psychological shift that was accomplished with varying degrees of success. They had to change from being work groups with productivity and performance goals, to being support groups that would contain anxiety, mourning, and fear. The therapeutic leader (group consultant) was an outsider, not only because he or she was not known to the organization but also because he or she held a totally different set of beliefs and ideas about anxiety and depression than those held by the human resource person or vice president. We were, as I often felt myself to be, analytic antibodies that aroused anxiety (defenses) in the group, and we were impeded in various subtle and obvious ways in reality.

Anxiety, spoken of and regressively felt, was not a welcome commodity in the environment in which the therapy groups took place. These conditions created many problems for the therapists in terms of having to work in unfamiliar or public environments and demonstrating their worth to people who did not share similar therapeutic models or values. In these environments, the therapeutic leader had to be sanctioned by the work group hierarchy for any viable treatment to occur. This sanctioning process maintained a hierarchy in which the therapeutic group leaders were made immediately subordinate. Often, the sanctions could be reversed and permission to do therapy could be withdrawn covertly by neglect or directly by refusal to allow permission. Whatever the environment, for the preceding reasons, it was unlikely that therapeutic leaders would be successful.

Many mistakes were made in initiating the crisis groups. Overly ideational presentations and approaches predominated as definitions and descriptions of PTSDs were frequently offered. And while there was some gain in channeling the group's responses along that informational line, the deeper questions regarding adaptation and mastery of anxiety and fear were not focused on or discussed in organizationally sanctioned opportunities. In addition, psychiatric symptom-based approaches served to avoid the problems of mobile anxiety and adaptation to stress frequently seen in private individual settings.

These errors may have occurred in an effort to establish some foothold in an unknown environment. Some of the errors arose from the leaders having to be active in their approach to overt symptoms while being dependent on others to gather people for the groups. Some occurred because of the uncertainty and lack of orientation, natural in this environment, in defining whom the "patients" were—the organization or the anxious survivors. In this manner, it was often unclear who had the power to sanction the group being formed and being allowed to continue and who had the power to bring sanctions against the group's formation and goals.

Paranoid thoughts loosened early in the attack became fixed on the air quality and anthrax-laden letters. It seemed that in all the locations these anxieties could not be alleviated by factual reports, whose authors themselves became the targets of suspicion.

In these crisis groups, the individual narratives revealed a latent content of a (failed) wish for a leader in the form of a healer of anxiety. This wish frequently extended beyond the time limit of the groups. This narrative ran counter to the "compensation by performance" speeches given by the non-therapeutic leaders in the work and school environments. The work leaders, in contrast to the therapeutic consultants, spoke repeatedly of compensation through industry and achievement—likely their own defense and adaptation. Most frequently, this was stated in large open meetings as "it's over" or "it's in the past" and "let's get going again." The group leaders remained silent during these speeches. To the extent that the work leaders were themselves anxious about criticism or offered the defense that enabled them to attain leadership, they feared any disruption of productivity goals, no matter what the goals were. This attitude prevailed in all the work environments.

Group leaders frequently had little control over how long they remained working with the groups and this resulted in many leaders "disappearing" before the work was done and leaving behind ambivalent responses to their interventions. For those who did not attend the groups, I could only speculate about their indifference or lack of need for therapeutic intervention at those intervals.

As events unfolded on a national level and the United States retaliated, there were continued fears of war, overt anxious responses to delays in transportation, and fears of being near the place in which so many died. There was continued interference in the physical area that surrounded the work environment. It is important to note that not all people suffered anxiety or crisis reactions. A small percentage, both male and female, reported no experience of anxiety. While some of these people were likely repressors, it seemed that many were caretaker or leader types who often responded to crises in a calm manner and assumed leadership positions to help those with anxiety.

Over time, there was a lessening of attention to anxiety among the workers and, eventually, reluctance to support further treatment. The intensification of anxiety at this time remained within a small percentage of the population directly affected by the attack or who had lost members of their family. Others seemed to accept slightly heightened vigilance or a vague suspicion of a second stage of attacks as a given, and the motto was clearly, "Let's put it behind us." In this climate, many organizations returned to normal operations and there was, as was expected, some loss of workers and staff. At one high school, only one student did not return at the resumption of school, while some auxiliary staff became anxious over exposure to toxic residues. For many parents of school schoolchildren and families of workers, anxiety was activated about the air quality and about returning to the attack site. The attack site itself became a target of fantasy, and many primitive fantasies could be elicited in groups regarding supernatural events occurring there. Interwoven with the primary and secondary experience of the attacks in the site itself, the physical location preserved all the force of its destruction and the capacity to arouse prior archaic conflicts.

During this time, the attitude changed markedly toward group interventions and attempts to foster group support. People who had prior anxiety conditions sought out or intensified their individual work. Few groups were sustained with people who were directly affected. Work and school returned to normal operations and anxiety projections were reattached. Productivity was again sought and rewarded. On occasion, an outburst of emotion was heard from someone who was distraught; however, events like these seemed to be taking place in private.

GROUP RESISTANCE

The problem of resistance from a group perspective operated at various levels through the organizations in which groups were convened. I have already alluded to the sanctioning dynamics of working at the group level, and I will clarify them here. Initially the work was done with the sanction of specific people in the organizations who sought help for their constituents—students, workers, parents, police, and fire department personnel. The people in the position of giving sanction were of variable familiarity with therapy in general and psychoanalytic thinking in particular. While certainly motivated by feelings of concern for their personnel, they also were in positions in which they functioned as work group leaders of organizations or units of organizations. Many were under personal pressure to return their organizations to both physical and psychological functioning as well as to accomplish physical restructuring of offices as soon as possible. No one was prepared for the events. Many leaders had been traumatized both by the suddenness of the attack and the scope of the new and immediate responsibility for the people under their auspices.

There was great variability in style of leadership among administrators. Almost all had little conceptualization of ongoing treatment or psychological needs. For many, even the most concerned and inviting of help, psychoanalytic perspectives were alien. Almost all operated with the attitude that if they "couldn't see it," it did not exist. This attitude short-circuited much of group treatment and put group leaders in the position of abandoning anxious workers or offering short-term interventions.

Another resistance was encountered, which was subtle, but perhaps even more destructive. This resistance emerged in two forms—the group analyst as enemy and masochistic interference. In the former, the usual fear of unconscious material came to the fore, as well as the fear of revealing in a group setting fears to people with whom one shared a work environment. Issues of confidentiality within groups became a cover for a fear of a change in values from productivity to understanding fears or anxiety. The value structures embedded in nonmedical, nontherapeutic group environments were at considerable odds with the culture and values of the therapeutic workplace. And significantly, the work site was the location in which the interventions took place.

The sanctions to help allocated by the executives could be turned into sanctions against the presence of therapeutic efforts. In particular, sanctions against groups occurred in response to viewing anxiety or people crying outside of group boundaries—emotional responses influencing the work environment. There was little understanding of the need to express emotions either following the terror attacks or during the subsequent real and imagined threats. Because the working group analyst has no political standing in this

environment, care has to be exercised to avoid being caught in historical conflicts present in the workplace.

The second form of resistance appeared as interference in the efforts to reform groups and build group trust within the framework of previously existing group structures. Within the working and planning groups appeared usually one person, who actively or covertly undermined all the therapeutic
group activities. Ganzarain (2000) has described the appearance of the "bad
mother group" in treating traumatized people in group settings, and on initial
inspection, this metaphoric description would seem to fit this person. In traumatized individuals, this metaphoric image has overdetermined and confused
psychic meanings derived from imaginary and real maternal failures. Among
the transference responses is a sadomasochistic style of relationship that is
dramatically intensified by the effects of the trauma and by being asked to
deal with other traumatized individuals.

However, this behavior seems to be a precursor to that mother-group phenomenon and to be specifically directed at the group therapeutic agent. In addition, the disruptive behavior occurred within the larger group setting and
not within a therapy group. Specifically, one person or a number of people
thwarted the attempts to create meaningful group therapy setups in blatant,
subtle, and masochistic ways. Examples include not convening the group, attempting to co-opt planned events, refusing steadfastly to abandon inappropriate activities, and attempting to undermine planned large group events.
While it may be possible to view these events within a current framework of
enactments, the fact that they occur within a large group situation in which
the therapeutic agent is often planning and convening groups makes the usual
forms of interpretation impossible. In other words, the behavior appeared as
a large group basic assumption in a completely work group situation.

I responded with feelings of despair, disgust, and helplessness to the actuality of the groups being prevented from forming. However thwarted I felt, I
tried, unsuccessfully at times, to control these feelings and to seek alternative
means of forming groups. As the person preventing the group from convening never fully entered the groups that were convened, there was no venue in
which to interpret behavior, nor do I believe, in reflection, that such an interpretation would have had any palliative effect. Likely, any interpretation outside of a working therapeutic relationship would have increased the destructive behavior. I have come to believe this kind of therapeutic interference is
actually a part of the large group experience of working with trauma.

It is possible to understand the behavior of the masochistic interferer from
an analytic group perspective. Within the large group structure, such a person
may be best understood as the unconscious partner in a pair that may be part
of large group experiences that occur around pervasive trauma. They pose a

real danger to therapeutic interventions in such situations. When the masochistic intervener is in a position of authority, he will mobilize unconscious forces against the therapeutic group leader. Tragically, as the therapeutic leader is frequently an outsider to the large group, there is great danger that the leader will become a scapegoat. Perhaps within this pair, hidden drive elements will find their unconscious expression. I believe that I have not understood this sufficiently, as I was often confronted by my own feeling of annoyance, helplessness, and anger at the creation of such obstacles. However, I think this behavior comes close to a basic assumption of annihilation anxiety, in which the enactor attempts to prevent treatment from taking place for others.

While Hopper (1997) and Turquet (1975) have previously described unconscious phenomena associated with large group behavior and annihilation anxiety, I do not believe that the attempts to rid the group of a therapeutic agent bear any similarity to their earlier descriptions. Rather, I think that in the service of an ongoing individual masochistic need and unusual projection, the group destructive individual attempts to annihilate or drive away the therapeutic agent, leaving the traumatized individuals untreated and abandoned.

In that way, he is duplicating his own experience by a dual projection and identification—being both the cause of the abandonment and the person abandoned. C. Chemtob (personal communication, 2002) confirmed having had similar experiences working within large social environments following disasters. In group psychoanalytic terms, there is a primal basic assumption pairing in the group—a life force versus annihilation anxiety and wishes. I believe this pairing may be elicited as a consequence of the interaction between the proximity to the actual attack, the appearance of group therapists, and the underlying dynamics within the individual and the large group.

CONCLUSION

Freud (1930) presciently described special mental protective devices that are brought into functioning in reaction to extreme suffering. Considering the scope of the terrorist attacks in New York City and Washington, D.C., and the amount of destruction involved, there is a likelihood that special group-related defenses were evoked. I have chosen to focus on large group structures in an effort to reveal behavior and dynamics that are usually ignored because of a preoccupation with individuals and symptoms (see, for example, Klein and Schermer, 2000).

Normal psychic functioning and development appear to follow a normal progression as long as the social and group background in which an individual functions, or grows up in, is preserved. The sudden collapse of various group structures and functions that provide security in everyday life and the loosening of anxiety bound by these group structures and functions affected both the individual survivors and the dynamics of the early acute phase crisis groups. It was remarkably easy for these groups to accept the presence of a therapeutic agent as a form of idealized leader who could "heal" their anxiety and fears for the future. Annihilation anxiety and psychic residuals of extreme vulnerability and fear that were previously aroused remained excited and intensified, yet they were held at the periphery of the groups' boundaries while the therapeutic leaders were accepted almost without ambivalence. Work group leaders were subjected to "negative evaluations" for having failed to protect the group, building, company, school, or country.

As time elapsed from the original attack and people became physically more secure, certain group themes emerged. These themes included the recalling of prior traumas, the return of prior phobias, the need to tell and recreate the traumatic experience, the need for a cognitive perspective of the meaning of the threat to existence, and the intensification of ambivalent reactions to work group leaders outside the therapeutic group. The groups were preoccupied with the same content as they moved to the six-month mark, although it became clear that certain members of the group were suffering greater anxiety and depression than others.

The lack of ambivalence to the therapeutic leader did not conform to the split good/bad parent images reported by Ganzarain (2001), nor did they result in any "massification" as suggested by Hopper (1997). However, it was abundantly clear from the narratives revealed in these early crisis groups that depending on the proximity to the site, when considered with what was actually seen, annihilation fears were responses to reality. The confluence of real physical threats of annihilation—seeing others die suddenly—resulted in the absence of the usual group experience of arousing psychic threat to survival. This combination of factors led to rather specific unequivocal concerns for both personal and group safety and reassurance in the form of careful listening and shared common experience. These crisis groups were effective, not in the usual sense of symptom removal, but in reducing the amount of experienced anxiety, reconstructing group support where it had been shattered, and allowing the emergence of a group structure as a base on which to rebuild anxiety-holding group structures at work.

Before closing, I would like to make one further large group observation, an abstraction from the experience of writing and researching this chapter. I have tried to convey the huge scope of the event that both bystanders and survivors were suddenly witness to and affected by. I am left with the irrevocable feeling that events of this magnitude characterized by such massive human destructiveness, like Hiroshima and the Holocaust, not only shatter existing group or social structures but become demarcation points for a larger shift in human social (large group) history.

REFERENCES

Bion, W. R. (1961). *Experiences in groups*. New York: Basic Books.

Blos, P. (1976). The split parental imago in adolescent social relations: An inquiry into group psychology. In A. J. Solnit, V. Schermer, P. B. Neubauer, S. Abrams, and A. S. Dowling (Eds.), *The psychoanalytic study of the child* (Vol. 31., pp. 7–33). New Haven, CT: Yale University Press.

Freud, S. (1930). Civilization and its discontents. *Standard Edition*, 21, pp. 64–145. London: Hogarth Press.

———. (1921). Group psychology and the analysis of the ego. *Standard Edition*, 18, pp. 65–184. London: Hogarth Press.

Ganzarain, R. (2000). Group as-a-whole dynamics in work with traumatized patients: Technical strategies, their rationales, and limitations. In R. Klein and V. Schermer (Eds.), *Group psychotherapy for psychological trauma*. New York: Guilford.

Grey, P. (2000). On the receiving end: Facilitating the analysis of conflicted drive derivatives of aggression. *Journal of the American Psychoanalytic Association*, 48: 219–36.

Honig, R. G., Grace, M. C., Lindy, J. D., Newman, C. J., and Titchener, J. L. (1993). Portraits of survival: A twenty year follow-up of the children of Buffalo Creek. *Psychoanalytic Study of the Child*, 48: 327–67.

Hopper, E. (1997). Traumatic experiences in the unconscious life of groups. *Group Analysis*, 30: 439–70.

Jacques, E. (1955). Social systems as a defense against persecutory and depressive anxiety. In M. Klein, P. Heineman, and R. Money-Kyrle (Eds.), *New directions in psychoanalysis*. New York: Basic Books.

Klein, R., and Schermer, V. (Eds.). (2000). *Group psychotherapy for psychological trauma*. New York: Guilford.

Roth, B. E. (2002). Some diagnostic observations of post-September 11, 2001 crises groups. *Group*, 26: 155–62.

Turquet, P. M. (1975). Threats to identity in the large group. In L. Kreeger (Ed.), *The large group: Dynamics and therapy*. Itasca, IL: F. E. Peacock Publishers.

Winnik, H. (1968). Contribution to symposium on psychic traumatization through social catastrophe. *International Journal of Psychoanalysis*, 49: 298–301.

Chapter Twenty-two

Terrorism on U.S. Soil: Remembering Past Trauma and Retraumatization

Maria V. Bergmann

Before the events of September 11, traumatic reliving in the transference would have been linked to a patient's own traumatic events from the past only. The attack of September 11 created both a social and a personal trauma. In many, it reawakened traumata that emerged from repression and therefore led to an experience of retraumatization. In some, traumata from the past could now be recalled and experienced with strong affect for the first time and could thus be analyzed.

The attack of September 11 was traumatic. Its violence mutilated America's self-image as an invulnerable world power. The experience of the sudden onslaught of destructiveness shared by everyone created a social trauma: A hitherto unknown feeling of vulnerability and a personal sense of insecurity now pervaded the population. As is well known, an unexpected terrorist attack, by virtue of the uncertainty of its potential repetitiveness, creates an additional powerful psychological weapon against its victims and constitutes a social trauma. The social trauma of September 11, shared by both analyst and patient, resulted in a new social and psychic reality and a need for different psychological techniques to modulate anxiety and enhance coping mechanisms within each person.

When Freud discovered the impact of trauma on psychic structure and development, he only had personal trauma in mind. Freud had thought that libido and aggression were in balance. In psychoanalytic work, we have been used to dealing only with internal psychic conflicts and personal traumata even if they were evoked by social traumata of major proportions. We attempt to establish connections between past and current internal conflicts: psychoanalysis connects issues that were previously separated. A trauma disrupts connections and isolates psychic continuity: it makes "false connections."

Under the impact of the current danger of a terrorist attack, we face a new psychoanalytic situation: our focus first needs to address the patient's capacity to function in the present and in current relationships—work or any other activity where psychic cohesion has been impaired. Because of the current crisis, reality-oriented thought and activity might be inhibited. Freud (1920) found that under the impact of the internal need of coping with a previous traumatic situation, traumata may be revived in the service of mastery. As we think of it today, such revival is motivated by the need to discharge anxiety stemming from a fear of retraumatization—the fear that previous traumatic experiences will be repeated, even if in disguise. What are the tools people have at their disposal to prevent such an impact and how can it be avoided? A sense of helplessness and overwhelming anxiety may lead to phobic reactions when such thinking is uppermost.

If traumata from the past have been revived, they inhibit reality-oriented thought and action, exacerbated by anxiety and confusion. When anxiety inhibits reality-oriented thought and action, it may lead to the revival of old traumata and new symptom formation. If earlier traumata have persevered and surfaced again, they burden current experiences. Current traumata may become fused with previously experienced traumatic states.

The current social trauma created a fear response to a *real* danger, which is different from past personally experienced private traumata, which evoked an internal anxiety reaction and muted the capacity to be verbal. Personal anxieties and survivor's guilt, which may have been reactivated from the personal past, can be faced more readily when separated from the present situation.

Under the impact of a traumatizing reaction to witnessing sudden violence an anticipatory capacity for an anxiety signal (Freud, 1926) might temporarily have been lost. In such a situation, an appropriate response arising from an internal capacity cannot assist in mitigating the social trauma until an anticipatory function is reestablished.

The intrapsychic meaning of the current crisis is not necessarily linked to earlier traumata with a purely personal meaning. The new trauma is part of a shared social reality. An analyst's readiness to deal with the present without necessarily linking it to the past, but with an acceptance of *justified* personal fear, may be a more convincing way of separating past from present and differentiating past anxieties from current or potential fears and dangers.

A patient may nevertheless link private traumatic pain of the past with the current social trauma. To assist with this differentiation comprises a hitherto not often encountered task in treatment. It is a new way of dealing with anxieties when they cannot be related to a personal past, but only to current social reality.

When private trauma is understood, social trauma remains. In the current situation, awareness of the unknown and living with it are not liberating: a real danger shared by everyone cannot be diminished. Patient and analyst alike share an unforeseen attack of terrorism. Such an event creates a psychoanalytic situation in which we are as helpless and as frightened as our patients.

REMEMBERING PAST TRAUMA AND RETRAUMATIZATION

Retraumatization takes place when a current event becomes connected with aspects of a past trauma that has not healed. When this takes place, the past returns affectively and experientially and fuses with the current traumatic feeling state. I call this conjunction of affect and the revival of previous traumatic experiences retraumatization. It is a reactivation or reawakening of the past fused with the present anxiety and panic-evoking occurrence.

There is an analogy to the dream in considering retraumatization: when the day residue relating to current events establishes contact with an unconscious wish, this merger of the two comprises a dream. In the same manner, past personal trauma and the current trauma creates an amalgam that the patient brings to the psychoanalytic situation. Freud (1920) held that the repetition compulsion is responsible for this phenomenon. We may consider retraumatization when past and present trauma occurs in conjunction of two events in the course of analysis. This merging may evoke a "Negative Therapeutic Reaction." When this occurs, the patient usually holds the analyst responsible for a revival of past painful experiences.

Themes from a personal past may have been displaced onto the current trauma. Whatever might have muted the patient's capacity to be verbal about the recent shock, and whatever from the personal past has been displaced onto the current trauma, might be linked to both the current psychic stress as well as to possible retraumatization.

A difference exists between patients relating a previous trauma and those who are retraumatized by remembering a past traumatic situation and those who reexperience a trauma in the present as if it were a new version of a trauma experienced in the past. A much stronger affective reliving is taking place in the present than if a trauma from the past is just being verbally remembered. Most importantly, a strong affect—agitation, anxiety, and psychic pain—surfaces in retraumatization as if the original trauma were happening again. There is a sharp difference then between remembering and reliving a trauma. I termed retraumatization the reliving or reexperiencing the original traumatic event with concomitant affect. During retraumatization the *internal landscape* includes the past although external circumstances might have greatly changed and defenses may have changed as well.

In a patient's narrative, we may be able to establish whether a person is dealing with an old trauma or an event that retraumatizes a patient: This depends on the strength of the patient's affect and the quality of reliving. On the other hand, this is also a matter of theory: Psychoanalytic theory puts the emphasis on the original trauma, but the trauma, when revived, continuously seeks access to events in the current reality which is the force that propels the original trauma forward. This is what Freud (1920) called a repetition compulsion.

In severe traumatization, repression is never complete, but some of it may remain dormant. This enables us to differentiate between a trauma that has been worked through and a trauma that can be restimulated. What has not been worked through will be subject to repetitious retraumatization.

For instance, a patient related in great detail how a woman helped her secretary, who was somewhat disabled, down the stairs of a tall office building across from the World Trade Center so she would not be left behind. This immediately led to associations of how the patient as a child was subjected to maternal depression and mourning because her mother had lost her parents in the Holocaust. The patient's grandparents had been "left behind": there was no one "to take them by the hand in time so they could flee from the Nazis as her parents had, and they perished in the Holocaust." For this patient, the parents' Holocaust experience took over; the feeling of helplessness and incapacity to move under the threat of Nazi domination became amalgamated with a fear of not being able to get out of an endangered building during the World Trade Center attack. The current possible danger combined with a previously imagined trauma and a fear of retraumatization. Patients may express anxiety more readily through the parents than through their own family. This is a repetition of a pattern constantly found among children of Holocaust survivors; their own concern is often pushed into the background in favor of the role of the parents and their Holocaust past. We may view this experience as an instance where remembering and retraumatization has been fused.

Patients with Holocaust experiences within their family of origin frequently asked when they first came for analytic consultation: "Have you personally experienced feelings connected to the Holocaust? The reason I ask is because if you have not, I don't believe you will understand what I mean." Patients need to understand that the analyst can fully appreciate their sense of internal terror although it could not be adequately verbalized. In such a situation, our task initially becomes one of assisting verbalization. Even when the children of the second generation have not experienced the Holocaust personally, they frequently absorb the traumata and anxiety of their parents within the family atmosphere.

The current situation and the Holocaust teach us how sudden massive destructiveness can temporarily wipe out or mute a belief in one's own libidinal capacities and those of others. Since the Holocaust, we have been aware that a massive traumatic onslaught may lead to a denial or numbing of affect or to excessive affective overstimulation. This may be discharged by acting out, by performing symbolic acts that have unconscious meaning, and by expressing overwhelming affect. Feelings of personal helplessness may cause narcissistic rage and may not be differentiated from past dangers. After Holocaust survivors became patients, psychoanalysts learned to assist in coping with social trauma. When Holocaust trauma was related in analysis either as having happened to parents, to grandparents, or to patients as small children, these could be worked with as traumatic impacts that affected a person's personal past that could be linked to a reliving in the present.

The following reports are from patient hours, told to me on September 12, 2001.

A patient admitted with great hesitation to admiring Osama bin Laden: "He is a strong, good-looking man who can get things done, even when this leads to massive destruction." The patient's father was the strong, good-looking man in the family, whereas her mother was "weak and depressed." The patient's only reliable object of identification and protection was her father, who was sometimes ruthless and brutal in order to "get things done." The patient admired and loved him and felt protected by him. Her current fantasies about the terrorist leader were linked to her father, who protected the family against actual social dangers by saving them from the Holocaust. He also was the only parent who could protect her from what she experienced as "personal dangers." Both parents had been Holocaust survivors. This patient dealt with her anxiety following the terrorist attack by denial and displacement.

The patient as a child lived through so many accounts of survival of loved ones while her family attempted to cope with the fallout of the Holocaust past, that she has always struggled not to join them in their depression. When she struggled not to succumb to depression, it helped her to go out and buy new clothes. This made her feel she was loved and had a future. As long as she could maintain these defenses, she was relatively free from anxiety; however, within a few days her denial of danger would shift to anxiety about her own body. A year before the terrorist attack, the patient had undergone potentially serious surgery. She was now reliving the traumatic effects of this realistic danger to her life. She said she was happy her children had not been in the city during the terrorist attack and her husband's work took him uptown.

For many people with traumatic Holocaust experiences, the anxiety following September 11 became overwhelming, and there was no sense of social communality. Such individuals do not feel better when there is an opportunity to help others, since their anxiety is not connected to realistic fears of a new social reality. It is primarily an internal private trauma from the past. When retraumatization occurs, it isolates the person from a sense of sharing. Distress and anxiety have to be discharged; however, no comfort can reach the person under the impact of reliving a trauma or phobic anxieties.

A patient whose family had rescued more than ten family members from a Nazi-occupied country and who had made an excellent adjustment to American culture and way of life was concerned about the psychological reaction — not of her children, who had been born here, but primarily about her mother, who had experienced bouts of depression since she had been rescued from the Nazis.

Another patient was afraid to board a subway train to come to her hour. On September 11 we talked on the telephone. The following day, the patient came to see me and was "less frightened than anticipated." Using the subway was related to "fumes penetrating her body." This patient had a history of allergies since childhood, clogging up her nasal passages and producing a cough when exposed to unexpected odors, even without fumes. She could not tolerate smelling an apartment being painted in her building, even if it was quite a distance away. The fear of fumes is related to a fear of penetration. The patient has a history of seductive sexual play with her father during childhood, potentiated by an ongoing loyalty conflict related to her closeness and love toward her mother. This conflict became revived and displaced onto a fear of odors.

The terror attack of September 11 reactivated body anxieties, most specifically a fear of being abused. She remembered some physical touching by her father when she was a little girl already in bed, and he said good night to her. She experienced this as an act of abuse. The "odors penetrating her body" stood for the revival of a familiar danger, namely the fear, but also an unconscious wish, of penetration by her father. In reality it seems no abuse occurred. The patient was terrified by her arousal when he touched her body. It appears that perhaps the patient's reliving served to tame the new trauma of attack by linking it to the past and thereby making it familiar.

Another patient who arrived to her session on September 12 dreamt on the previous night that a pilot was flying a plane by himself. The pilot had a bee's face, although he wore a big helmet. It was a bee nevertheless "because he had a stinger." Although the patient had previously discussed problems that contributed to her frigidity, such as extensive sexual play with an older brother toward the end of puberty and the beginning of adolescence, she did not discuss her fear of an erect penis with strong affect before September 11. The trauma of September 11 reactivated the patient's unconscious guilt about the sexual relationship with her brother and her fear of getting physically hurt. Although the patient had mentioned this event previously in analysis, but more in a narrative context, as "an event" during her growing years, it now emerged with greater clarity that "getting hurt" represented a conflict laden with affect and incestuous guilt. As the patient relived the incestuous experiences in analysis, her anxiety was displaced by fear of safety for her own children. She had come from a home in which children had experienced an insufficient amount of protection from either parent, and this was now clearly displacing her experience of lack of protection into anxiety about being unable to protect her own children in the case of a terrorist attack.

Associations to her dream indicated that the helmet was the protection of the head worn by firefighters as seen on television, working near the smoke of Ground Zero. Firefighters come after a fire has destroyed what was there before. The helmet that protects the head is like the protection offered by analysis—"head-shrinking"—but it cannot protect her, or her family, from an unforeseen attack or catastrophe. In this patient's unconscious, the destructive attack on American soil was put on the same footing as a feared hostile penetration into her body. The patient's associations have a transferencial message related to her body. She believes unconsciously that I am not protecting her from her husband's sexual wishes, which she does not share and which cause her some frustration and anguish.

The patient associates that the stinger represents the penis, erect and ready to hurt her. She was traumatized as a little girl by her brother's and her father's seductive, overstimulating play. Now she is afraid of the erect penis (the stinger) connected to her vaginal anesthesia, the result of overstimulation in childhood.

Following this communication in analysis, the patient went into an anxiety state related to her children. At first, she only wondered what she would tell them. She had told her oldest son that some "bad men" had hurt the two big towers, and the little boy asked her, "What are we going to do to punish them and to do something to them for what they did to us?" After dealing with the anxiety of two of her older children, she associated her own anxiety of what would happen if she was to lose a child in a terrorist attack; she would then relive the fate of her mother, who had lost the patient's younger sister in an accident.

On September 12, another patient related a dream about "a tower of books which were on fire" and something about a ruined cityscape. On awakening, she experienced a personal physical feeling of stomach pain and diarrhea. The patient associated the books with representing different ideologies that separated people. The fire related to emotion and to a feeling of vulnerability; the stomach pain underscored physical helplessness; and the burning of books by anti-Nazis who, on being discovered, would have been taken to a concentration camp, emphasized her own terror. The patient said: "A feeling of uncertainty emanated from the dream. You think you will be going to a building to work and then you wonder, is it going to be there, or will it have been blown up between today and tomorrow? There is uncertainty and inconsistency. Where will the fire strike? The towers were struck, not on top, but on a somewhat lower floor." This statement unconsciously referred to pain now located in her intestines. This patient is a creative artist who again started to work after many years of a "dry spell."

Unconsciously, these words related to her conflict, because the building where she does her creative work could have been damaged, and she could have had to "start all over again." If this were the case, it would have temporarily obliterated our work together, which significantly related to her capacity to again work creatively. She took a great deal of pride in her work. The destruction of the building where her studio is located also unconsciously referred to her hostile feelings against her creative self and toward me, who had helped her to overcome her work inhibition. There was continuous risk that the rise of hostility in the transference could affect her independent creative work and our work together, which then might have been in danger.

When differentiation between past and present and between internal and external dangers cannot be maintained affectively and cognitively, a crisis may occur in the analytic situation. Narcissistic hurt may attach itself to a current traumatic feeling-state and produce anger and a feeling of having been left helpless and unprotected. This may be experienced by the patient in the transference and expressed in various affective ways: silence, anger, or a general state of feeling, wanting and needing comfort. In order to diminish suffering and avoid a massive negative therapeutic reaction and lack of trust, the specific fantasy content and meaning of retraumatization in treatment is critical.

The experiences of September 11 created a new trauma, but for many it revived old traumata as well, and thereby the fusion of past and present comprised an experience of retraumatization. When a new trauma emerges, understanding it may be complicated by the fact that it is superimposed on one or two previous traumatic incidents or on a trauma-evoking atmosphere in which a patient might have lived during childhood.

A patient entered the analytic office on September 12 in a state of total fury. In her childhood the inconsistent, unpredictable behavior on the part of each of her parents had made their responses impossible to anticipate, even in very important issues of decision making that involved the patient. She experienced pervasive anxiety in situations where the outcome was uncertain. The unpredictability of a terrorist attack was unconsciously experienced as her parents attacking each other in a quarrel. In her outbreak of fury toward me, she was reliving some of these uncertainties. I had not anticipated or helped her cope quickly enough with an extremely traumatic situation two years earlier with a potentially serious illness. She added angrily that I had probably felt "we could just analyze this." The fantasy role of unpredictability and unprotectiveness represented for the patient the fusion of a past personal trauma with the current social trauma, in that instance one in which I was as helpless as the patient was, in the current terrorist attack. She felt she had been unsupported by me two years ago in what she had to do actively in the external world to combat her serious illness. I asked whether she knew why she had been unable to tell me so at the time. She said "it was unconscious." She probably had had no words to express those feelings.

I pointed out that the patient relived the unpredictability of an unforeseen attack in the outside world superimposed on her anxiety at the time when she experienced her illness as an unforeseen attack on her body. This was exacerbated by subsequently feeling unprotected by me. In her retraumatization, there was great anxiety. She had always been accident prone. She reported an actual "physical attack" in her parental home and underscored that what it meant to her had constituted a major personal injury. She ended by saying that after she learned of the September 11 attack, she tripped and fell down some stairs, reliving "being physically hurt." She could have been badly hurt, but fortunately escaped with a few bruises. I thought at the time that the patient's reliving and her response to her previous trauma was an example of "Nachtraeglichkeit (deferred action)," such as we frequently witness during a delayed affective reliving of a previous trauma. One may speculate that Nachtraeglichkeit may be related to avoiding the pain of retraumatization.

When the dysfunctional aspects within a person are related to the current crisis and are differentiated from past events when coping was impaired, the undoing of the linkage between past and present trauma improves the capacity to function better in the here and now. A personal sense of internal terror, if understood in treatment and separated from external danger, permits greater alertness to external danger without interference from anxieties stemming from past traumata. When the "self" becomes capable of separating past from present, self-protection has a better chance.

CONCLUSION

September 11 created an American social trauma in which patients and analysts were equally affected. The interaction between social trauma and personal traumatic events, and how to keep both in focus, presents a linkage that calls for help with mastery and management of anxiety in the face of massive external destructiveness that constitutes new challenges to therapeutic technique. Most analytic patients linked the physical, social, and psychological attack of September 11 to traumata in their own childhood.

I have found that new coping strategies for the management of personal anxiety vis-à-vis massive destructiveness in the *external* world are needed. It helps in many instances if the analyst asserts that the current traumatic reaction to terrorism is shared by both patient and analyst. When we can admit that we are as affected by the current trauma as our patients are, it becomes more acceptable for them to express fantasies of destruction and socially unacceptable affects, which may have been unleashed by witnessing massive public destructiveness.

Psychoanalytic technique can assist in separating the reliving of anxiety related to traumatic internal dangers from fears arising as a reaction to the uncertainties and destructive events in the current external world. When this differentiation is made, analytic strategies of helping with acute internal anxieties are possible. However, helping with the external situation is necessarily very limited or impossible in a terrorist attack.

The very unexpected aspect of this attack created a new trauma. On the other hand, for many, it evoked aspects of retraumatization, which became amalgamated with the terrorist events. For some, it brought about a lifting of repression and an experiencing of the affect of anxiety and horror about events in the external world for the first time. For others, it was a completely new experience, which was not linked to the past. The aura of certainty is gone not only from the American soil but also from the analytic situation that hitherto remained related primarily to internal anxieties caused by internal conflict.

Until September 11, we had not been called on to assist patients to differentiate current personal fears from phobic anxieties, which originated not only from internal psychic conflicts related to the personal past but also from a social fear that was shared by everyone. In the atmosphere of the current shared social uncertainty, this task has become more difficult, particularly for people who have been unable to master traumatic dangers in their past. Such people are likely to fuse past unmastered and current traumatic themes. Such fusion has the potential to create states of retraumatization. A patient's emergency responses, initiated by September 11, may initially be differentiated from genetic reconstructions of traumata. The meaning of previously internalized events and symptoms, as the result of traumatic experiences from the past, may eventually become integrated and shed light on the manner in which the terror of September 11 was experienced. As a rule, unconscious meanings are not immediately apparent. Like other serious traumas, Nach-traeglichkeit is an expectable delay. I believe it is necessary to develop new techniques for helping with the current social situation that has never before occurred in just this way on American soil.

REFERENCES

Freud, S. (1920). Beyond the pleasure principle. *Standard Edition*, 18, pp. 7–64. London: Hogarth Press.
———. (1926). Inhibitions, symptoms and anxiety. *Standard Edition*, 20, pp. 87–175. London: Hogarth Press.

World Trade Center (September 11, 2001).

Chapter Twenty-three

Skyscrapers and Bones: Memorials to Dead Objects in the Culture of Desire

Isaac Tylim

How does a culture immersed in technology and immediate gratification mourn? This chapter describes the ways in which technology is employed in the search for mother/paradise lost. It elaborates the underlying dynamics of cultural products that preserve or encapsulate the past by guarding against despair and intimations of mortality.

The city, for the first time in its long history, is destructible. A single flight of planes no bigger than a wedge of geese can quickly end this island fantasy, burn the towers, crumble the bridges, turn the underground passages into lethal chambers, cremate the millions. The intimation of mortality is part of New York in the sound of jets overhead, in the black headline of the latest edition.

—E. B. White, 1949

Who knows when some slight shock, disturbing the delicate balance between social order and thirsty aspiration, shall send the skyscrapers in our cities toppling? Does that sound fantastic?

—Richard Wright, 1940

CITY OF MEMORIALS: SKYSCRAPERS AND PLANES

Skyscrapers are sculptures of the contemporary urban scene. From New York to Kuala Lumpur and from Buenos Aires to Hong Kong, city landscapes are formed by towers of steel and glass. Skyscrapers are steel-skeleton buildings that seem to spring straight into the sky. In the 1900s, the photographer Alfred Stieglitz took the first photographs of the Flatiron building, New York

461

City's first skyscraper. Stieglitz regarded the Flatiron as a monument to American civilization—the Flatiron, the photographer declared, was to the United States what the Parthenon was to Greece.

By the turn of the nineteenth century, the Industrial Revolution, with its dramatic technological advances, rendered America the capital of Modernism. Modernization transformed culture at all levels, expanding the confines of time and space with unprecedented speed. The construction of skyscrapers in the New World became the modality of memorializing America's meteoric ascendance to the number-one world power. The revolution in construction and transportation turned air space into a commodity, as both skyscrapers and airplanes began to defy gravity. The conquest of new territories shifted from the ground to the open air. The aerial age was born (Douglas, 1995).

Modernity implied an acceptance of change as a fundamental fact. Writing about New York, Aldous Huxley (1991, pp. 315–16) declared that in America "most things in this modern land are provisional, made to last only till something better, or at any rate something newer, shall appear to take its place. . . . things, here, are built to be scrapped as soon as they have outworn their first youth."

Until the creation of the Preservation and Landmark commission, old buildings were destroyed so that new ones could be built. Construction, destruction, and reconstruction define not only America's fascination with movement and change but also the tempo of our culture's capacity for mourning and memorializing lost objects. The sculptor Gutzon Borglum lamented, "Our greatest buildings are ephemeral" (Douglas, 1995, p. 437). A *New York Times* editorial of October 26, 1926, remarked, "As for building for eternity, the need does not exist." In the popular imagination of America at the turn of the century, buildings appeared as practical structures not destined to last. The temporal quality of their existence seems to mirror the evanescent nature of flowers and candles, symbols that accompany mourning in many cultures.

The history of civilization is revealed through the ruins of surviving structures. The Greek Parthenon, the Egyptian pyramids, and the Angkor Wat temples in Cambodia, though differing in their functions, all share the quality of being memorials to lost worlds.

What about the building of memorials? Do memorials survive the passing of time or are they like most things in America, built to be scrapped as soon as they have outworn their youth? Cities around the world have built memorials to war, political leaders, military heroes, and victims of famine and epidemic. Memorials have tended to have short life spans, becoming forgotten markers of an urban landscape. One may speculate whether there is a correlation between the time a given society takes to erect a memorial and the time it takes for its meaning to fade in the collective memory of the population. Can it be inferred that the faster a memorial is created, the sooner it will fall into oblivion?

It took decades for memorials to the Holocaust and the Vietnam War to be erected. It took more than thirty years to make a military park at Gettysburg, and twenty to build a memorial at Pearl Harbor (Keller, 2001). In contrast to the slow pace of building these memorials, three months after the Oklahoma City bombing and less than two months after the destruction of the World Trade Center, respective committees were debating the question of memorializing the victims of the attacks. The slower, more thoughtful pace of subjectivity was challenged in an attempt to memorialize the tragedies in a fast and efficient manner, following the prescription of politicians and experts. This pressure to memorialize sooner rather than later mirrors the tempo of our high-tech world, where waiting thirty seconds for the unloading of an e-mail attachment begins to feel like an eternity.

MEMORIALS IN THE CULTURE OF DESIRE

In our consumer society, memorials are objects of desire destined to live a short life span. They are like fashions that last only a season or goods that are soon substituted by new commodities in the emporia of desire. Memorials do not sustain themselves. Culture has its way of affirming or negating memorials, either caring for them by maintaining them or diminishing them by scrawling graffiti on their eternal surfaces.

Why did Grant's Tomb, once a popular tourist attraction at the turn of the century (Miscone, 2001) lose its status? Who is familiar with the memorial to the American soldiers who died in British prison ships during the American Revolution or with the one dedicated to the more than one thousand passengers killed in the 1904 fire of the wooden excursion boat, General Slocum, on the East River?

Between 1776 and 1783, more Americans died on British prison ships anchored in New York Harbor than in all the years of the American Revolution. Numbering over eleven thousand, their bones were washed up by the East River tide for years (Miscone, 2001). The Prison Ship Martyrs' Monument, a memorial to those prisoners, was erected in 1907. Designed by Stanford White and built in Fort Greene Park, it is the tallest Doric column in New York City. Now forgotten by the public consciousness, it is covered with graffiti, a canvas for the anonymous artists of the inner city.

The *Encyclopedia of New York City* reports that the funerals for the victims of the General Slocum fire lasted more than a week (Jackson, 1995, p. 457).

One of the processions to the cemetery included 156 hearses that stretched for almost a mile. The thriving community known as *Kleindeutschland*, located on 6th Street, east of 2nd Avenue, did not survive the tragedy. The relatives of the survivors moved uptown to Yorkville on the Upper East Side. A memorial to the victims, mostly women and children, stands still in a remote corner of Tompkins Square Park. One cold December morning I searched for it and found it in a forsaken corner of the park. It was a humble display, a small rectangular marble structure, with the heads of women and children carved on it. I wondered whether my great, great grandchild on a cold December morning at the turn of the twenty-second century would discover the neglected memorial to the Twin Towers' victims in the same way.

THE TWIN TOWERS

The Twin Towers were the ultimate expression of America's conquest of aerial space. They were metallic sculptures built in downtown New York by the Japanese architect Minoru Yamasaki. The project, first presented in 1962, was completed in 1976. The "twins" and other smaller buildings surrounded an open plaza that according to *The Encyclopedia of New York City* (p. 1276) was modeled after St. Marks Square in Venice. The towers themselves evoked associations to the early Renaissance towers of San Geminiano in Tuscany. Although criticized as unimaginative by some, the purity of their lines pleased many classical, modern, and postmodern sensibilities.

SEPTEMBER 11, 2001

The Twin Towers fell in less than an hour, one collapsing within minutes of the other. No ruins comparable to the existing ruins of the Greek Parthenon, the Egyptian pyramids, or Cambodia's Angkor Wat temples, remained as memorials.

Soon after the World Trade Center attack, Mayor Giuliani urged New Yorkers to go out to restaurants and theaters and to engage in recreational activities. To counter terror, survivors were urged to seek refuge in theaters, restaurants, and analysts' offices, with a speed more appropriate to computer functioning than psychic functioning. The message encouraged a kind of "mourning-to-go," a *prêt-a-porter* model of working through trauma and loss.

America is the land of diversity, including people from many cultures and religions. Christians, Muslims, Jews, and Buddhists all rely on rituals of mourning that are not easily transferred to collective loss, less so to the urgency of cyberculture. Yet, despite the postmodern diversity of New York City, the rituals of mourning followed the rapid tempo of cyberspace. With the fire from the burning Twin Towers still raging, makeshift memorials, walls of prayers, reproductions of photographs of missing persons, and poems and notes posted on white canvases popped up around New York City. Technology imposed a new timetable on the mourning process, and the thousands of e-mails, photos, and objects that emerged almost immediately after the September 11 attack became the Parthenon of our times. The scanned photographs and photocopies of the missing loved ones, the candles blowing in the September breeze, the flowers that enveloped city corners and spots were spontaneous memorials created by individuals of all ethnic groups.

The most elaborate memorials were erected in downtown Manhattan in a matter of hours. They were living memorials, in constant flux. Union Square became the center of a spontaneous display of messages to the lost and the disappeared. Those unable to volunteer took pictures or used words to feel a part of history in the making. "Photos and text together have emerged for some people as the only response to the thought 'I cannot believe my eyes'" (Mandell, 2001). History rose on city streets out of tangible ashes one could smell for miles. The fragility of the makeshift memorials was recognized almost as soon as they were created—at the first sign of rain, the memorials were transported to shelters. The Union Square subway station offered them sanctuary, and by December, their remains were gathered by the Smithsonian for use in future exhibitions.

Mr. L

Mr. L is a survivor of the World Trade Center collapse. He entered the Tower at the moment the first plane hit the building. The doors of one of the elevators opened suddenly and a ball of fire rolled toward him. His hair caught fire, and he ran without looking back. Mr. L thought that if he were to turn his head to look, he might end up like Lot's wife, who was transformed into a pillar of salt when she attempted to flee Sodom.

> I was running in the lobby. . . . I felt fire on my head. My hair was burning, and small pieces of glass were cutting my arms. . . . I began to bleed. I heard someone asking for help. . . . I was unable to stop. . . . I felt as if different parts of my body were disintegrating in front of me. I thought I must be dying. Later I realized that those parts of my body were not really body parts but the papers and books that were sliding from my hands without me noticing it. . . . I was running to my grave . . . dying although running. Two months have passed since September 11th, yet I still smell the smell of burnt hair. Yesterday I had a dream. In

the dream there was a river, the Hudson I think. I look closely and I see body parts floating on the river. All seemed so tranquil and peaceful.

The word trauma derives from the Greek and means to make a puncture or hole. Indeed, in the experience of trauma, either the psyche or the body (or both) is punctured. The terror that follows a traumatic event creates a breach between the affect and the representation that is not easily overcome. A trauma is the by-product of an excess of excitation that breaks the ego's protective barrier.

Mr. L's internal disintegration may be compared with the external explosion he witnessed. Mr. L felt as if his body were breaking into pieces, falling apart while his hair was in flames. He thought he was dying. Was he being guided by the death instinct? The death instinct lacks psychic representation. The notion of death does not exist in the unconscious. However, one is capable of recognizing the presence of death in the dead body of the other, in the foul smell of decomposed bodies, in the spilling of human blood.

Mr. L became aware of the proximity of death when his hair caught fire and when he hallucinated pieces of his body—the papers and books—falling between his arms. His hair in flames is the equivalent of the ultimate castration. Mr. L was simultaneously embracing his death while denying it. This duality in confronting danger may be related to the perverse mechanisms that are at the core of fetishistic strategies.

For months Mr. L dreamed of body parts floating on the river. He also hallucinated the smell of burnt hair during sessions. Apocalyptic imagery was common in his associations. There were several references to the Holocaust, concentration camps, and crematoria.

In working with Mr. L, I became witness not only to his psychic pain but also to his bloody, carnal pain. My interventions tended to be minimal, as if I had to pay my respects to the body pieces floating on the river. Attempting to build a narrative of Mr. L's experiences of terror would have served me more than him. I learned that experiences of terror blurred the differences between psychic pain and bodily pain. Under these circumstances, the smell of death is disseminated in the consulting room. Indeed, the smell of burnt hair seems to have settled in the fabric of my analytic couch.

THE MATERIALIZATION OF LOST OBJECTS: BONES AND MEMORY

Segal (1991) has described two types of symbols. A quasi-symbol is one linked to concrete thinking. The symbol is equated with the object symbolized—the symbol and the symbolized are identical. In the other type of symbol, or true symbolism, the symbol represents the object but is not entirely equated with it. Segal claims that concrete symbolization or symbol equation is at the root of pathological mourning.

In the aftermath of loss, a proliferation of quasi-symbolic and symbolic objects seems to spontaneously grow out of the pool of psychic pain. The quasi-symbolic objects retain and incorporate material evidence of the lost objects into a symbolic creation. These concrete objects mingle with symbolic ones, with those objects that are removed from any physical connection to the lost or destroyed ones.

To Segal (1991) the aesthetic experience includes both the ugly and the beautiful because art embodies in its immutable stance the terrifying experience of depression and death. The memorial to the victims of the Khmer Rouge in Cambodia's Killing Fields is a tower of skulls. The concrete remains of the victims are the actual material used to build the memorial—a skyscraper of bones. While visiting Cambodia's Killing Fields, I accidentally stepped on a human bone, a rib. Back home, the memory of that bone continues to visit my mind as I stroll along the skyscraper canyons of the Western world.

One of the most striking sights greeting a visitor to the Auschwitz concentration camp museum in southern Poland are the hills of human hair and the mounds of shoes that are kept behind a glass wall. A reverse form of quasi-symbolic memorializing is practiced in a remote island of Indonesia. Women cut off their fingers when their husband or a male relative dies. The absent finger is the ultimate memorial, forever engraved on mutilated hands.

In Chile, an interdisciplinary team investigates common graves, trying to identify the remains of those *desaparecidos* abducted and murdered during the Pinochet regime. After conducting extensive research, including DNA laboratory studies, examination of dental records, and investigation of the history of fractures, the team is often able to establish the identity of the missing person. The skeleton of the victim is displayed on a bed—a posthumous dying bed. Following counseling sessions, the immediate family is invited to visit the arranged remains of their loved ones, reduced to the bones. This arrangement of bones is reminiscent of Cambodia's testimony. A community funeral is held, attended by friends, relatives, and families of other victims whose remains are still missing.

Urns containing the ashes of cremated loved ones rest on many fireplace mantles in Manhattan's apartments. During a ceremony that took place two months after September 11, the city offered ashes gathered from the ruins of the Twin Towers to those relatives willing to accept the quasi-symbolic substitute for the bodies of their loved ones lost during the attack.

Ms. D

Ms. D's husband died three years before she began her psychotherapy. She was married for over forty years. A retired teacher, she managed to live alone in a small apartment in uptown Manhattan after her husband's death. Following September 11, she developed insomnia and agoraphobia. A friend accompanied her to the initial consultation.

Ms. D was severely affected by the terrorist attack on the World Trade Center. She stated that although she lives far from Ground Zero "my windows are covered by dust . . . and I don't dare to clean them. I feel that the dust is really the remains of the cremated victims. We are surrounded by the dead . . . and I don't know how to stop thinking about them."

While recalling the wonderful years she spent with her deceased husband, Ms. D's associations led her to memories of her own father, a religious man, during World War II. Expanding on her religious upbringing, she began to entertain the thought of resolving her problem by performing a private ritual. On a sunny late September day, she decided to clean the windows of her apartment with a piece of clean, soft fabric. While performing this task, she was aware of the strong metallic smell in the air. On concluding the work, she placed the piece of fabric in a small bag. Then she went to her backyard, dug a hole in the dirt, and buried the bag.

I understood then that Ms. D was resuming her unresolved mourning for her beloved husband, precipitated by the collapse of the Twin Towers. At the time, I remember reading an article in the *New York Times* (Kimmelman, 2002, E 5, pp. 1–5) about a men's clothing store situated a few blocks away from the Twin Towers. The article described that the merchandise was shrouded by dust. The store's owner, just like Ms. D, hesitated in cleaning the goods. Perhaps he also perceived human remains in the dust. As a memorial to the lost lives, the owner decided to keep untouched a corner of his store where some Ralph Lauren sweaters rested. This corner became a makeshift altar, a humble, homemade, human-scale memorial to lost objects.

RUINS, ART, AND MEMORY

The material world, be it bones, stones, or wrecked metal, assists mourners in the process of working through depressive affects. In this manner, the psyche may symbolically restore that which was damaged or destroyed. The inability to restore or, in Kleinian terms, to repair the lost object may transform the fragmented pieces into persecutory objects. A regression to the schizo-paranoid position is then manifested by the prevalence of persecutory guilt rather than depressive guilt (Grinberg, 1973). Persecutory guilt is rooted in the death instinct, which leads to despair and impoverishment of the ego; depressive guilt leads to the affirmation of life and to the enrichment of the ego and its capacity for reparation.

Throughout the history of civilization, art has offered a medium through which to undo the pain of loss. Art harbors the potential to reverse despair, in its ability to highlight what is most relevant to the worlds it helps to unveil. Humanity as a whole is invested in maintaining those memorials for centuries to come. The conversion of physical structures into memorials of human tragedy is rooted in a conviction that monuments can soothe the wounds of the bereft while preserving the past for future generations.

The ruins of monuments across the world are major works of art that open the gates to the past through the perennial presence of their damaged integrity. Wounded yet beautiful, the ruins trigger in the viewer the capacity to integrate the good and the bad. This integration opens the door to reparation. The incomplete Parthenon, the pyramids, and the Angkor Wat temples force the tourist to complete the broken Gestalts, assisted by perception and imagination. Today visitors to Ground Zero may be enveloped and overwhelmed by the view, by the smell, and by the fragmented pieces of what once was and is not anymore. In the internal world, the remains of the Twin Towers gradually acquire the status of memorials to what once was. The integrity of the objects can be internally conjured. Bones and metal begin to unite in the building of the ultimate memorial to those who lost their lives in the Twin Towers.

How does art represent the dead? Finding a proper artistic language for memorial art is not a simple matter. Does Picasso's cubistic representation, *Guernica*, convey the pain of the urban victims of the Spanish Civil War? In an attempt to represent the trauma of the Vietnam War, the sculptor Michael Aschenbrenner created a series of glass sculptures entitled "Damage Bone." The medium, glass, becomes a metaphor for life and death. Glass suggests the strength of bone as well as its fragility. Rachel Whiteread's Holocaust memorial in Vienna is an inside-out room or library with shelves of books. A grid of chairs in Oklahoma City is a memorial to the victims of terrorism. From Maya Lin's wall-of-names Vietnam memorial in Washington, D.C., to the tower of skulls in Cambodia's Killing Fields, or the hills of hair in Auschwitz, all of these memorials use minimalist language to convey the pain of trauma.

Opposing arguments about what to do with the empty space left by the destruction of the Twin Towers rose soon after the attack. The question was whether to rebuild or to consecrate the site as a burial ground. Those that favored a park over a building claimed that an empty space visually evokes the emptiness left by the loss of lives; many wanted the names of the victims to be carved in stone. Esteemed architects took a strong stance in advocating building something new, perhaps even bigger than the original Twin Towers.

Taylor, a New York architect, described the World Trade Center as an introverted place. Its design was a self-contained one with no links to the external world. Self-contained and self-possessed, the visitor entered a maze of spaces and halls. Even the palm court, an atrium containing a row of palm trees, was indoors. Taylor suggested that in reconstructing the site, instead of replicating the inner-directness of the former design, an extroverted place should fill the fifteen blocks originally occupied by the Center (Riley, 2001).

Artists are inclined to build memorials in the sky or to build towers of remembrance. Ken Smith (2001) imagined a memorial on the roof of a new building, closer to the sky. "Just going all the way up there would be like a pilgrimage . . . in a sense, those people disappeared into the sky, into the emptiness, and this is one way to think about it, to experience the emptiness, see all those faces and feel the loss." Louise Bourgeois (Solomon, 2001) proposed a seven-story stone column topped by a star. The column stands for the Tower, and the names of the victims would be chiseled by hand in vertical rows. "The star looks inflated . . . and evokes the upward energy of a skyscraper. But its edges are dripping like wax on a candlestick."

THE REPARATIVE QUALITY OF ART

The work of art affords the integration of concrete, quasi-symbols and true symbols, part-objects into whole ones, facilitating the work of mourning and reparation. The lost object can be retrieved by strolling the Killing Fields or by revisiting the past through watching old videos on the VCR. The whole is in the part. One single rib in Cambodia's Killing Fields, a lock of hair behind a window glass in Auschwitz, one isolated stone in the acropolis in Athens, or a large piece of wretched metal from the Twin Towers harbors the potential to evoke both the terror of fragmentation and the comfort provided by the reparative power of the restored object.

ON VIRTUAL REPARATION

Technology (from the Greek *techne*, which refers to an art by which nature is transformed into artifice) has contributed to changing the way human beings go through the process of mourning. Since the Industrial Revolution, machines have become mediators of experience, expanding human actions in time and space. "Technology was originally designed to provide prosthesis to the human body. It was used as an external device to enhance and at times substitute for aspects of human functioning" (Tylim, 2000). The boundary between *techne* (artifice) and nature begins to blur with the advent of computers and the introduction of virtual or simulated processes.

Technology promises a union of the organic and the nonorganic (virtual/artificial) world. Humans possess the ability to create hybrid objects. The siege on culture led by technology challenges the very survival of subjectivity, threatening to overflow a kind of "Avenue of Memories." Technology is power. One either learns to adjust and to navigate the complex instruction manual of technology with its "how to" prescriptions or succumbs to the pain of being left behind.

How does a culture immersed in technology and accustomed to immediate online gratification manage to mourn destruction of such magnitude? What are the psychic transformations that must accompany the visions of collapsing towers so that mourning may take place?

In our techno-cyberworld, material reality and virtual reality collude in the manipulation of objects that, like the infant's transitional ones, may facilitate separation. In the choreography of presence and absence, those newly created products provide relief to the mourner, instilling hope in the power of the psyche to rebuild and repair.

Memorials to dead objects may be erected and words engraved on them like tattoos on the body; buildings may be constructed in memory of deceased patrons; and films or television reruns may be watched over and over again, like a trauma that must be repeated in order to be worked through. Virtually speaking, links may be established in cyberspace in a manic effort to deny loss through online e-chats. These diverse and ever-fluid memorials to dead objects allow the psyche to enter into a space where intimations of immortality offer a buffer against despair and hopelessness. The cyberworld manifests low tolerance of time and history building. In the material/technological world, the present is a construction of a memorial to the past that is not yet the past. Every individual in America seems to be in possession of a gadget capable of delivering memorials-to-go, while museum curators rushed to incorporate two-month-old World Trade Center memorabilia into retrospectives. The hurry to memorialize reveals the underlying dynamics of a culture that favors objectivity over subjectivity, action over reflection.

While the Twin Towers were burning, cellular phones were for many the means by which last rites were performed. Good-byes from a high floor on one of the tallest skyscrapers in the world were sent into the air. In the midst of disintegration, the potential for reparation still breathed in the power of these last words. Witnesses took photographs or videorecorded the chaos, while a sea of e-mails forged virtual communities. Virtual *shivas*[1] gathered around the World Wide Web, this "whole" wide world that seemed to be virtually whole only in the global domain of cyberspace.

Mr. B

Mr. B is a forty-four-year old manager at a company in lower Manhattan. The following is an excerpt from a session in which he recounts his whereabouts on September 11, 2001.

> The time was about 8:45 A.M. I was walking on Fulton Street toward my favorite place, where every morning I get a cup of coffee before heading west to my office. Suddenly, I heard a big bang coming from outside. I ignored it and kept walking as usual. As soon as I entered the coffee shop, I noticed that the small TV was on with no sound. I waited in line for a few minutes. My turn came and I placed my order. Suddenly, one of the workers began screaming (Mr. B's voice gets louder at this point): "The Tower is on fire . . . a plane hit the World Trade Center. . . . The Tower is on fire!" I stood still, not knowing what to do, holding the cup of hot coffee in one hand and the *New York Times* in the other. People started pouring out into the street from inside the coffee shop and from other stores. I stood still, unable to move. I was mesmerized by the images on the small TV screen. I couldn't believe it. I thought that it must be a trailer for a new movie scheduled to be released sometime around the holiday season. Yet I was watching the Towers burning. . . . I mean I was watching the images of the burning Towers on a small TV screen set firmly installed on a high shelf behind the counter. The sound was off. Imagine, no sounds, just images. At home I remained glued to the TV for days, eager to be fed that piece of filtered reality I was unable to confront face to face. I didn't want to admit that at Ground Zero everything was lost forever.

For Mr. B, the mediation provided by the televised images served as a buffer against the terrible reality happening on the streets of his native city. Although leaving the coffee shop for the street would have offered Mr. B a perfect, albeit terrifying, view of the burning Twin Towers, he felt compelled to witness the disaster from the distance afforded by a miracle of twentieth-century technology. For him, the firmly mounted television on a high shelf was juxtaposed with the image of the collapsing Twin Towers on the screen. Deprived of a reporter's voice-over to organize the events of the day into a story, Mr. B felt lost amidst the chaos that was erupting internally and externally. He then proceeded to soothe himself by declaring that the horror scene he was privy to was the announcement of another Hollywood blockbuster.

It would seem as if Mr. B fell for the allure of the images. Seduced by the gloss and the colors of the unscheduled morning news, he was rendered passive in front of a telereality that was being created simultaneously with the events that were unfolding on the streets while he was sipping coffee.

Several months later, while analyzing his reactions on that infamous Tuesday morning at the downtown coffee shop, Mr. B's associations led him to compare himself with "those tourists I encountered over the summer while traveling in France. They appeared more inclined to take pictures of the sites they visited than to experience the moment . . . like my friend's wedding that seemed put together for the making of the video instead of the spontaneity of the dancing guests. . . . Maybe these people are just like me. They, as I, are not strong enough to face losses. In watching TV, I am trying desperately to hold on to what is escaping me at the same time as I am holding on to it."

Mr. B gained insight into the meaning of his freezing in front of the television set. Dealing with images of the "hyperreal," which affirms the death of the real, was for him safer than facing the tragedy directly. Mr. B was gradually able to process painful facts by holding on to the conviction that pictures or images ultimately endure and survive memory. Pictures and images are indeed entrusted with the task of carrying a version of those destroyed Tower/objects whose lost integrity seems restored and repaired in the immutability of their bidimensional presence. Moreover, the repetitive images yield intimations of immortality against the background of Ground Zero where, in Mr. B's words, "everything seemed lost forever."

REFLECTIONS ON MR. L, MR. B, AND MS. D

The clinical vignettes presented in the preceding remind us that terror belongs to a class of primitive affects that tend to disorganize the ego. As the cases illustrate, terror may be induced from within or from without, re-establishing that which Freud referred to as the "imperishable" (Freud, 1913), those early stages of development that are bound to co-exist with more advanced ones.

The experience of terror mobilizes unconscious residues of past traumas. The Freudian notion of *Nachtraglichkeit* (*après coup*, deferred action, or retroactive attribution of meaning) describes the psychic tendency to reconstruct or reinterpret psychic events as if they were intrinsic elements of reality. Overall terror transports the individual to a place that is mysterious and uncanny, yet familiar and already known. The *unheimlich* (mysterious, uncanny) is the opposite of that which is *heimish* (domestic). Freud (1919) reminds us that the term *unheimlich* is an ambivalent one, since that which is familiar is also that which remains hidden.

What are the reasons for this ambivalence? The mysterious and uncanny elements in the experience of terror are due to the process of repression or rather to a failure of the repression, since that which should have been kept hidden is uncovered. Human reactions to corpses or mutilated bodies evoke the experience of terror since the corpses or body pieces elude the repressive barrier. The result is something obscene (obscene in the sense of being off scene), in other words, "the pornography of death."

In facing the pornography of death, what might be required for Mr. L, Mr. B, and Ms. D to be able to complete their respective work of mourning? Mr. L, Mr. B., and Ms. D are residents of a country and city not used to foreign terrorist attacks. For them, the work of mourning explores unknown dimensions partially due to the impact of the trauma but also due to their culture's attitude toward death.

Mr. L, Mr. B, and Ms. D grew up in a culture that sanitizes death. Fifty years ago, people dealt with the raw reality of death inherent in home-based funerals. Today in America's big cities, the contact with death has been relegated to sporadic visits to funeral parlors. In a culture of desire, vanity seems to have no limits. Some groups dress up their dead and apply makeup to them before their display in an open casket. Black limousines, sympathy cards, and monetary contributions have all become prescribed and commercialized rituals.

A tension between the need to remember and the need to forget dominates the American landscape of memorialization. Technology, the media, and cyberspace threaten to take over the individual's subjective capacity to mourn. Under these circumstances, as in the case of Mr. B, in-vivo mourning may be replaced by virtual mourning. Perhaps September 11 fostered a desanitization of death, evoking the psychological need to deal with the concreteness of death in corpses, dust, bones, and smell of burnt hair.

NOTE

1. *Shiva* in Hebrew, comes from the root *shev* meaning to sit down. It refers to the seven days of mourning following the death of a loved one. The mourners are expected to sit on a low chair during that period. Family and friends visit during this week or pay a shiva call, a "mitzvah" in itself.

REFERENCES

Douglas, A. (1995). *Terrible honesty: Mongrel Manhattan in the 1920s*. New York: Farrar, Straus and Giroux.
Freud, S. (1913). Totem and taboo. *Standard Edition*, 13, pp. 1–162. London: Hogarth Press.
———. (1919). The "uncanny." *Standard Edition*, 17, pp. 217–52. London: Hogarth Press.
Huxley, A. (1991). *Jesting pilate*. New York: Paragon House.
Jackson, K. T. (Ed.). (1995). *The encyclopedia of New York City*. New Haven, CT: Yale University Press.

Keller, B. (2001, November 22). Remembering and forgetting. *New York Times* [Op-Ed], A25.

Kimmelman, M. (2002, January 13). Out of minimalism, monuments of memory. *New York Times*, sec. 2, pp. 1, 37 and E5, pp. 1–5.

Mandell, J. (2001, November 18). History is impatient to embrace September 11. *New York Times*, sec. 2, p. 38.

Miscione, M. (2001, December 23). The forgotten. New York memorials fade from memory. Can the Trade Center be different? *New York Times*, sec. 14, p. 11.

Riley, T. (2001, November 11). What to build. *New York Times Magazine*, p. 92.

Solomon, D. (2001, September 30). From the rubble, ideas for rebirth. *New York Times*, sec. 2, p. 37.

Segal, H. (1991). *Dream, fantasy and art*. London: Tavistock/Routledge.

Smith, K. (2001, November 11). What to build. *New York Times Magazine*, p. 96.

Tylim, I. (2000). eXistenZ: The blurring of the organic and the high-tech world in Cronenberg's films. *Psychoanalytic Review*, 87: 455–61.

Part V

LOOKING TOWARD THE FUTURE

Ash City *by Joshua Neustein (2000).*

Chapter Twenty-four

Traumatized Societies and Psychological Care: Expanding the Concept of Preventive Medicine

Vamik D. Volkan

This chapter examines the psychological repercussions of shared catastrophes on both an individual and societal level. Shared catastrophes are divided into subgroups: natural causes, human-made disasters, and ethnic or other large group conflicts, each of which may trigger its own distinct set of psychological consequences and ethnic, national, or religious identity issues. Nongovernmental organizations (NGOs) and the mental health professionals who work with traumatized societies need to understand the maladaptive societal changes that result from experiencing a catastrophe and how they may lead to future conflict through the process of transgenerational transmission. Besides caring for people with individual Post-Traumatic Stress Disorder (PTSD) and working through their own responses to trauma, indigenous mental health workers may be able to develop and enact strategies to interrupt the vicious cycle of transgenerational transmission, administering "preventive medicine" to societies recovering from shared trauma.

When a massive disaster occurs, those who are affected may experience its psychological impact in several ways. First, many individuals will suffer from various forms of Post-Traumatic Stress Disorder (PTSD). Second, new social processes and shared behaviors may appear throughout the affected community or communities, initiated by changes in the shared psychological states of the affected people. And third, traumatized people, may, mostly unconsciously, oblige their progeny to resolve the directly traumatized generation's own unfinished psychological tasks related to the shared trauma, such as mourning various losses. This chapter focuses on the latter two expressions of the psychological impact of disaster. In particular, it addresses the impact of trauma resulting from conflict between large groups. In this context, a large group consists of thousands or millions of people, most of whom will never

meet one another, who share a sense of national, religious, or ethnic same-
ness—in spite of family and professional subgroupings, societal status, and
gender divisions—while also sharing certain characteristics with neighboring
or "enemy" groups (Volkan, 1999a, 1999b).

TYPES OF DISASTERS

Shared catastrophes are of various types. Some are from natural causes, such
as tropical storms, floods, volcanic eruptions, forest fires, or earthquakes.
Some are accidental human-made disasters, such as the 1986 Chernobyl accident that spewed tons of radioactive dust into the atmosphere. Sometimes,
the death of a leader, or of a person who functions as a "transference figure"
for many members of the society, provokes individualized as well as societal
responses—as did the assassinations of John F. Kennedy in the United States
(Wolfenstein and Kliman, 1965) and Yitzhak Rabin in Israel (Erlich, 1998;
Raviv, Sadeh, Raviv, Silberstein, and Diver, 2000) or the deaths of the American astronauts and teacher Christa McAuliffe in the 1986 space shuttle *Chal-
lenger* explosion (Volkan, 1997). Other shared experiences of disaster are due
to the deliberate actions of an enemy group, as in ethnic, national, or religious
conflicts. Such intentional catastrophes themselves range from terrorist attacks to genocide and from the traumatized group actively fighting its enemy
to the traumatized group rendered passive and helpless.

A recent study by Goenjian, Steinberg, Najarian, Fairbanks, Tashjian, and
Pynoos (2000) compared Armenians directly affected by the 1988 Armenian
earthquake with Armenians traumatized as a result of Armenian-Azerbaijan
ethnic enmities during the same year. It concluded that, after eighteen months
and again after fifty-four months, there were no significant differences in individual "PTSD severity, profile, or course . . . between subjects exposed to
severe earthquake trauma versus those exposed to severe violence" (p. 911).
Such statistical studies measuring observable manifestations of a trauma's
lasting effects (anxiety, depression, or other signs of PTSD) are misleading,
however, insofar as they do not tell us much about individual minds or hidden, internal psychological processes; apparent symptomatic uniformity may
hide significant qualitative differences. Furthermore, such studies do not tell
us about societal processes that may result from catastrophes and their long-
term (transgenerational) effects. For instance, the fact that many injured Armenians refused to accept blood donated by Azerbaijanis after the earthquake
indicates that the tragedy had in fact enhanced ethnic sentiments, including
resistance to "mixing blood" with the enemy.

Even though they may cause societal grief, anxiety, and change as well as
massive environmental destruction, natural or accidental disasters should

generally be differentiated from those in which the catastrophe is due to ethnic or other large group conflicts. When nature shows its fury and people suffer, victims tend ultimately to accept the event as fate or as the will of God (Lifton and Olson, 1976). After human-made accidental disasters, survivors may blame a small number of individuals or governmental organizations for their carelessness; even then, though, there are no "others" who have *intentionally* sought to hurt the victims. When a trauma results from war or other ethnic, national, or religious conflict, however, there is an identifiable enemy group who has deliberately inflicted pain, suffering, and helplessness on its victims. Such trauma affects large group (i.e., ethnic, national, or religious) identity issues in ways entirely different from the effects of natural or accidental disasters.

A closer look suggests that it is sometimes difficult to discriminate between different types of disasters. For instance, the massive August 1999 earthquake in Turkey that killed an estimated twenty thousand people was obviously a natural disaster. But it is also an example of a human-made accidental catastrophe: many of the structures that collapsed during the earthquake had not been built according to appropriate standards. Furthermore, it became known after the quake that builders had bribed certain local authorities to construct cheaper, unsafe buildings.

Incidentally, among the most interesting effects of that earthquake was that the disaster stimulated changes in heretofore durable ethnic sentiments. After the earthquake, rescue workers from many nations rushed to Turkey to help— among them Greeks. By publishing pictures and stories of Greek rescue workers, Turkish newspapers helped to "humanize" the Greeks as a group, who for decades had generally been perceived as an enemy. Indeed, only a few years before the quake, Turkey and Greece had almost gone to war in a dispute over some rocks (Kardak/Imia) near the Turkish coast (Volkan, 1997). The Turkish disaster and the earthquake in Greece the following month actually initiated a new relationship between the two nations—what is now referred to as "earthquake diplomacy" in many diplomatic circles.

A closer look at this softening of the relationship between Turkey and Greece after the earthquakes shows that it is motivated by deep, mostly unnoticed, psychological dynamics. The shared aggressive fantasies that go along with enmity or opposition have not gone away, rather they are covered over by an apparent shared-reaction formation—at the large group level, the generosity provoked by the death of thousands of members of the enemy group is actually at root a defense mechanism. This seemingly negative unconscious motivation does not take away from the reality of this new closeness, however. The crucial issue is whether this closeness can be sublimated. Some recent events indicate that the brotherly feelings engendered by the earthquakes may be threatened, but only time will tell to what extent this "togetherness" can be institutionalized. (For more details on what I call the "accordion phenomenon," see Volkan, 1999d.)

Although massive disasters like the Turkish earthquake may sometimes fall into several categories at once, it remains useful to differentiate between them because those that are due to ethnic, national, or religious conflicts—including wars and war-like situations—are the only ones that can trigger a particular large group identity process. This process is perhaps most easily imagined as a cycle: Disasters deliberately caused by other groups lead to massive medical/psychological problems. When the affected group cannot mourn its losses or reverse its feelings of helplessness and humiliation, it obligates subsequent generation(s) to complete these unfinished psychological processes. These transgenerationally transmitted psychological tasks in turn shape future political/military ideological development or decision making or both. Under certain conditions, an ideology of entitlement to revenge develops, initiating or contributing (or both) to new societal traumas: the circle is, sadly, completed. Diplomatic efforts, political revolutions, and changes in the identity of the large group may all contribute to interrupting this sequence; later in this chapter, I will suggest a special role for mental health workers in breaking the cycle of the traumatized—and traumatizing—society.

SOCIETAL PROCESSES AFTER DISASTERS CAUSED BY "OTHERS"

All types of massive disaster have psychological repercussions beyond individual PTSD. Indeed, the fact that natural or human-made disasters evoke societal responses has long been known. If the "tissue" of the community (Erikson, 1975) is not broken, however, the society eventually recovers in what Williams and Parkes (1975) refer to as a process of "biosocial regeneration" (p. 304). For example, for five years following the deaths of 116 children and 28 adults in an avalanche of coal slurry in the Welsh village of Aberfan, there was a significant increase in the birthrate among women who had not themselves lost a child.

The impact of some accidental human-made disasters is much wider. Again, the nuclear accident at Chernobyl, with at least 8,000 deaths (including 31 killed instantly), provides a representative example. Anxiety about radiation contamination lasted many years, and with good reason. But these fears exercised a considerable impact on the social fabric of communities in and around Chernobyl. Thousands in neighboring Belarus, for example, considered themselves contaminated with radiation and did not wish to have children, fearing birth defects. Thus, the existing norms for finding a mate, marrying, and planning a family were significantly disrupted. Those who did have children often remained continually anxious that something "bad" would appear in their children's health. Here, instead of an adaptive biosocial regeneration, society reacted with what might be termed a "biosocial degeneration."

Biosocial regeneration and degeneration are also observable after disasters due to ethnic or other large group hostilities. A somewhat *indirect* biosocial regeneration occurred among Cypriot Turks during the six-year period (1963–1968) in which they were forced by Cypriot Greeks to live in isolated enclaves under subhuman conditions. Though they were massively traumatized, their "backbone" was not broken because of the hope that the motherland, Turkey, would come to their aid. Instead of bearing increased numbers of children like the inhabitants of Aberfan, they raised hundreds and hundreds of parakeets in cages (parakeets are not native birds in Cyprus)—representing the "imprisoned" Cypriot Turks. As long as the birds sang and reproduced, the Cypriot Turks' anxiety remained under control (Volkan, 1979). The art and literature stemming from the Hiroshima tragedy (Lifton, 1968) might also be considered a form of symbolic biosocial regeneration. In the case of Hiroshima, however, the society also exhibited biosocial degeneration and showed "death imprints" for decades after the catastrophe; the society's backbone was in fact broken, and biosocial regeneration could only be limited and sporadic.

What primarily differentiates catastrophes due to ethnic conflict from natural or human-made disasters is that, in the former, societal responses can last in *particular, uniquely damaging* ways for generations: the mental representation of the disastrous historical event may develop into a "chosen trauma" for the group (Volkan, 1997, 1999a, 1999b). The "memories," perceptions, expectations, wishes, fears, and other emotions related to shared images of the historical catastrophe and the defenses against them—in other words, the *mental representation* of the shared event—may become an important identity marker of the affected large group. Years, even centuries, later, when the large group faces new conflicts with new enemies, it reactivates its chosen trauma in order to consolidate and enhance the threatened large group identity. The mental representation of the past disaster becomes condensed with the issues surrounding current conflicts, magnifying enemy images and distorting realistic considerations in peace negotiation processes. I will return to these mechanisms of transgenerational transmission and reactivation of chosen trauma later in this chapter.

Initially, when a large group's conflict with a neighboring group becomes inflamed, the bonding between members belonging to the same group intensifies. There is a shift in members' investment in their large group identity; under stressful conditions, large group identity may supersede individual identity. This movement exaggerates the usual rituals differentiating one group from the other. As the two groups enter "hot" conflict, the relationships between people in each group become governed by two obligatory principles: (1) keeping the large group identity separate from the identity of the enemy and (2) maintaining a psychological border between the two large groups at any cost (for details see Volkan, 1988, 1997, 1999c). When large groups are not the "same," each can project more effectively its unwanted aspects onto the enemy, thereby "dehumanizing" (Bernard, Ottonberg, and Redl, 1973) that enemy to varying degrees.

After the acute phase of the catastrophe ends, however, these two principles may remain operational for years or decades to come. Anything that disturbs them brings massive anxiety, and groups may feel entitled to do anything to preserve the principles of absolute differentiation—which, in turn, protects their large group identity. Thus hostile interactions are perpetuated. When one group victimizes another, those who are traumatized do not typically turn to "fate" or "God" (Lifton and Olson, 1976) to understand and assimilate the effects of the tragedy, as in a natural disaster. Instead, they may experience an increased sense of rage and entitlement to revenge. If circumstances do not allow them to express their rage, it may turn into a "helpless rage"—a sense of victimization that links members of the group and enhances their sense of "we-ness." We see the tragic results of this cycle across the globe.

DIAGNOSING SOCIETAL PROCESSES
AFTER LARGE GROUP HOSTILITIES

The methodology for diagnosing societal shifts resulting from a population's shared psychological changes after large group hostilities is relatively new; I first began developing it during work in Northern Cyprus after the Turkish Army divided the island of Cyprus into *de facto* Northern/Turkish and Southern/Greek sectors in 1974 (Volkan, 1979). Diagnostic work carried out by members of the Center for the Study of Mind and Human Interaction (CSMHI) in Kuwait three years after that country's liberation from Iraqi occupation provides a more recent and refined example of the methodology (Thomson, 2000: Howell, 1993, 1995; Saathoff, 1995, 1996; Volkan, 1997, 1999a).

In 1993, a CSMHI team made three diagnostic visits to Kuwait under the directorship of Ambassador W. Nathaniel Howell (Ret.), who, as U.S. ambassador to Kuwait during the Iraqi invasion of 1990, kept the Embassy open for seven months during the occupation of Kuwait City. Ambassador Howell and other CSMHI faculty members interviewed more than 150 people from diverse social backgrounds and age groups to learn how the mental representation of the shared disaster echoed in the subjects' internal worlds. The technique of these interviews was based on psychoanalytic clinical diagnostic interviews, in which the analyst "hears" the subject's internal conflicts, defenses, and adaptations. As the subject reports fantasies and dreams, this material adds to the interviewer's understanding of his or her internal world. As can easily be imagined, we found that many Kuwaitis suffered from undiagnosed individual PTSD. Nevertheless, our emphasis in these interviews was not on individual diagnosis but on discovering shifts in societal conventions and processes.

After interview data were collected, we looked for common themes in the interviews indicating shared perceptions, expectations, and defenses against conflicts created by the traumatic event. These "common themes" may not register in the public consciousness as represented in news, cultural production, and so on, but come to light when we observe them in many interviewees. We learned, for example, that young Kuwaiti men's perceptions of Iraqi rapes of Kuwaiti women during the occupation had become generalized. This meant that on some level, they perceived all Kuwaiti women to be tainted. We found, as well, that many young men who were engaged to be married now wanted to postpone their marriages and that those who were not yet engaged wanted to put off seriously seeking a mate. Because women who have been raped are traditionally devalued in Kuwaiti culture, the generalization of perception was threatening conventions about the age of marriage. While this shift did not pose an actual danger, it did create a measure of societal anxiety.

We found even more direct expressions of societal "maladaptation" in postliberation Kuwait. During the invasion and occupation many Kuwaiti fathers were humiliated in front of their children by Iraqi soldiers, who sometimes spat on them, beat them, or otherwise rendered them helpless before their children's eyes. In cases where humiliation or torture had occurred away from their children's view, the fathers often wanted to hide what had happened to them. Without necessarily being aware of it, fathers began to distance themselves from certain crucial emotional interactions with their children, especially with their sons, in order to hide or to deny their sense of shame. Most children and adolescents, though, "knew" what had happened to their fathers, whether or not they had personally witnessed these events.

Many school buildings in Kuwait City were used as torture chambers during the Iraqi occupation. When I visited Kuwait City during this project, however, it was hard to believe from looking at schools and other buildings that catastrophe had struck there only three years earlier. Except for a few buildings with bullet holes that were intentionally left as "memorials" and the highway heading north toward Iraq still lined with destroyed military vehicles, the city appeared completely renovated. Adults did not speak to children about what had happened in the schools during the invasion, but the children knew; when they returned to their renovated schools, that "secret" quite naturally caused them psychological problems.

The very young—without, of course, knowing why—began to identify with Saddam Hussein instead of with their own fathers. In one telling instance, at an elementary school play staging the story of the Iraqi invasion, the children applauded most vociferously for the youngster who played the role of Saddam Hussein (Saathoff, 1996). "Identification with the aggressor" is the psychoanalytic term for a period in which a child identifies himself or herself with the parent of the same sex with whom the child has been involved in a competition for the affection of the parent of the opposite sex (A. Freud, 1936). In childhood, this process results in a child's emotional growth. A little boy, for example, through identification with his father, whom he perceives as an "aggressor," makes a kind of entrance into manhood himself. In other situations, however, like those of many Kuwaiti elementary school children, identification with the aggressor—in this case, Saddam Hussein—can obviously create problems.

The reiteration of the "distant father" scenario in Kuwaiti families thus set in motion new processes across Kuwaiti society. Many male children, who needed to identify with their fathers on the way to developing their own manhood, responded poorly to the distance between themselves and their fathers—resulting, for example, in "gang" formations among teenagers. Frustrated by the distant and humiliated fathers (and mothers) who would not talk to their sons about the traumas of the invasion, they linked themselves together and expressed their frustrations in gangs. Of course, some degree of gang formation is normal in the adolescent passage, as youngsters loosen their internal ties to the images of important people of their childhood and expand their social and internal lives through investment in "new" object images as well as in members of their peer group.

In the ordinary course of events, however, this "second individuation" (Blos, 1979) maintains an internal continuity with the youngster's childhood investments. For example, the new investment in the image of a movie star is unconsciously connected with the old investment in the image of the oedipal mother or a new investment in a friend remains somewhat connected to the "old" image of a sibling or other relative. Humiliated and helpless parent images necessarily complicated the unconscious relationship between the Kuwaiti youngsters' new and old investments. Indeed, as we have found in other situations as well, when many parents are affected by a catastrophe inflicted by others, the adolescent gangs that form after the acute phase of the shared trauma tend to be more pathological. In Kuwait, the new gangs were heavily involved in car theft—a new social process involving the emergence of a crime that essentially had not existed in pre-invasion Kuwait.

The CSMHI team made some suggestions to Kuwaiti authorities based on this research. We proposed a number of political and educational strategies to help the society mourn its losses and changes and to speak openly about the helplessness and humiliation of the occupation in a way that would heal splits between generations as well as between subgroups within Kuwaiti society — such as between those who fought against the Iraqis directly and those who escaped from Kuwait and returned after the invasion was over. When we tactfully presented our findings about children and adolescents to the authorities, however, no action was taken.

Since we now have a technique for evaluating posttraumatic societies (for details, see: Volkan, 1999d), this is an arena in which psychodynamic insights can be useful for nongovernmental organizations (NGOs) and the mental health workers associated with them. NGOs that deal with traumatized societies after ethnic or other large group conflicts need to recognize the shared psychological problems and maladaptive societal changes that may lead to future conflict because of transgenerational transmission.

TRANSGENERATIONAL TRANSMISSIONS

During recent decades, the mental health community has learned much about the transgenerational transmission of shared trauma and its relation to the mental health of future generations. This development owes a great deal to studies of the second and third generations of Holocaust survivors and others directly traumatized under the Third Reich (since there are so many studies on this topic, I will mention only two with which I am extremely familiar: Kestenberg and Brenner, 1996; Volkan, Ast, and Greer, 2002). Nevertheless, this mental health issue has not received sufficient consideration from those official international organizations and NGOs who deal with the psychological well-being of refugees, internally displaced individuals, and others who have experienced the horrors of war or war-like conditions. For example, the official joint manual of the World Health Organization (WHO) and the Office of the United Nations High Commissioner for Refugees (UNHCR) (1996) on the mental health of refugees mentions only crisis intervention methods, relaxation techniques, alcohol and drug problems, and professional conduct toward rape victims.

Of course, after a disaster, the crisis takes precedence over other considerations, but, when the crisis is over, crucial psychological processes continue in full force. The WHO/UNHCR report does not refer at all to the serious issues of societal response and transgenerational transmission following ethnic, national, and religious conflicts. And my own professional experience with the WHO and UNHCR at various troubled locations around the world suggests that these organizations have not yet seriously considered these issues and do not yet plan to develop strategies for preventive efforts to break this cycle of trauma and transmission.

If we want to understand the tenacity of large group conflict, we must first understand the mechanisms of transgenerational transmission. One of the best-known examples of a relatively simple form of transgenerational transmission comes from A. Freud and Burlingham's (1942) observations of women and children during the Nazi attacks on London. Freud and Burlingham noted that infants under the age of three did not become anxious during the bombings unless their mothers were afraid. There is, as later studies have established, fluidity between a child's "psychic borders" and those of his or her mother and other caretakers (see, for example, Mahler, 1968), and the child-mother/caretaker experiences generally function as a kind of "incubator" for the child's developing mind. Besides growth-initiating elements, however, the caretaker from the older generation can also transmit undesirable psychological elements to the child. The same fluidity also occurs in drastic ways among adults under certain conditions of regression, such as after massive shared catastrophes—even after the crisis ends and life as refugees, for example, begins.

In Tbilisi, Georgia, I examined a Georgian woman from Abkhazia and her sixteen-year-old daughter who had been refugees for over four years. The two were living under miserable conditions with other family members in a refugee camp near Tbilisi. Every night the mother went to bed worrying about how to feed her three teenaged children the next day. She never spoke to her only daughter about her concerns, but the girl sensed her mother's worry and unconsciously developed a behavior to respond to and to alleviate her mother's pain. The daughter refused to exercise, became somewhat obese, and continuously wore a frozen smile on her face. As our team interviewed both of them, we learned that the daughter, through her bodily symptoms, was trying to send her mother this message: "Mother, don't worry about finding food for your children. See, I am already overfed and happy!"

But there are many forms of transgenerational transmission. Besides anxiety, depression, elation, or worries such as those the Georgian woman from Abkhazia presented, there are various psychological tasks that one person may assign to another. This transgenerational conveyance of long-lasting tasks is the one that perpetuates the cycle of societal trauma described in the preceding. The well-known phenomenon of the "replacement child" (Poznanski, 1972; A. Cain and B. Cain, 1964) illustrates this form of transmission. A child dies; soon after, the mother becomes pregnant again, and the second child lives. The mother "deposits" (Volkan, 1987) her image of the dead child—

including her affective relationship with him or her—into the developing identity of her second child. The second child now has the task of keeping this deposited identity within himself or herself, and there are different ways for the child to respond to this task. The child may adapt to being a replacement child by successfully absorbing what has been deposited in him or her.

Alternately, he or she may develop a "double identity," experiencing what we call a "borderline personality organization." Or the second child may be doomed to try to live up to the idealized image of the dead sibling within himself or herself, becoming obsessively driven to excel. Similarly, adults who are drastically traumatized may deposit their traumatized self-images into the developing identities of their children. A Holocaust survivor who appears well adjusted may be able to behave normally because he has deposited aspects of his traumatized self-images into his children's selves (Brenner, 1999). His children, then, are the ones now responding to the horror of the Holocaust, freeing the older victim from his burden. As with replacement children, such children's own responses to becoming carriers of injured parental self-images vary because of each child's individual psychological makeup apart from the deposited images.

After experiencing a group catastrophe inflicted by an enemy group, affected individuals are left with self-images similarly (though not identically) traumatized by the shared event. As these hundreds, thousands, or millions of individuals deposit their similarly traumatized images into their children, the cumulative effects influence the shape and content of the large group identity. Though each child in the second generation has his or her own individualized personality, all share similar links to the trauma's mental representation and similar unconscious tasks for coping with that representation. The shared task may be to keep the memory of the parents' trauma alive, to mourn their losses, to reverse their humiliation, or to take revenge on their behalf. If the next generation cannot effectively fulfill their shared tasks—and this is usually the case—they will pass these tasks on to the third generation, and so on. Such conditions create a powerful unseen network among hundreds, thousands, or millions of people.

Depending on external conditions, shared tasks may change function from generation to generation (Apprey, 1993; Volkan, 1987, 1997, 1999a, 1999b). For example, in one generation the shared task is to grieve the ancestors' loss and to feel their victimization. In the following generation, the shared task may be to express a sense of revenge for that loss and victimization. Whatever its expression in a given generation, though, keeping alive the mental representation of the ancestors' trauma remains the core task. Furthermore, since the task is shared, each new generation's burden reinforces the large group identity. As indicated earlier in this chapter, I term such mental representations the large group's "chosen trauma." In open or in dormant fashion or in both alternately, a chosen trauma can continue to exist for years or centuries: whenever a new ethnic, national, or religious crisis develops for the large group, its leaders intuitively re-kindle memories of past chosen traumas in order to consolidate the group emotionally and ideologically.

The behavior of Slobodan Miloševik and his entourage before the Serbs' war with Bosnian Muslims in 1990–1991 and again before the conflict with Kosovar Albanians in 1998 exemplifies this leadership function. By reactivating the Serbs' chosen trauma, the memory of the Battle of Kosovo (June 28, 1389), Miloševik and his supporters created an environment in which whole groups of people with whom Serbs had lived in relative peace as fellow Yugoslavians became "legitimate" targets of Serb violence. As the six-hundredth anniversary of the Battle of Kosovo approached, the remains of Prince Lazar, the Serbian leader captured and killed at the Battle of Kosovo, were exhumed. For a whole year before the atrocities began, the coffin traveled from one Serbian village to another, and at each stop a kind of funeral ceremony took place. This tour created a time collapse. Serbs tended to react as if Lazar had been killed just the day before, rather than six hundred years earlier.

Feelings, perceptions, and anxieties about the past event were condensed into feelings, perceptions, and anxieties surrounding current events, especially economic and political uncertainty in the wake of Soviet Communism's decline and collapse. Since Lazar had been killed by Ottoman Muslims, present-day Bosnian Muslims—and later present-day Kosovar Albanians (also Muslims)—came to be seen as an extension of the Ottomans, giving the Serbian people, as a group, the opportunity to exact revenge in the present from the group who had humiliated their large group so many centuries before. In this context, many Serbs felt entitled to rape and murder Bosnian Muslims and Kosovar Albanians. (For further details of the reactivation of the Serbian chosen trauma and its consequences, see Volkan 1997, 1999a).

THERAPEUTIC INTERVENTIONS AND THE NEED FOR "PSYCHOPOLITICAL DIALOGUES"

When a catastrophe is in its crisis phase, what international organizations, such as UNHCR, WHO, the Red Cross, and Red Crescent, can do for the people who are affected depends, of course, on the conditions on the ground. It may be dangerous for foreign mental health workers to enter certain zones until a necessary level of safety is ensured, which may take some time. Once security has been established and foreign mental health experts arrive on the scene, how they approach traumatized people is well documented in the WHO/UNHCR manual (1996) mentioned in the preceding.

But security issues, searches for relatives, and military, paramilitary, and propaganda interests sometimes take unnecessary precedence over direct psychological health concerns. When Finnish psychiatrist Henrik Wahlberg, representing WHO, arrived in Macedonia to assist Kosovar refugees following the NATO bombings in 1998, he found that since the bombing had stopped, refugees were ready to return to Kosovo en masse. They wanted to return to their homes, to find out what had happened to their lost relatives and to houses, farms, and businesses left behind. They gave little or no thought, at this point, to seeking psychiatric help. When the road from Skopje, Macedonia, to Pristina, Kosovo, had been secured, Dr. Wahlberg visited a mental hospital in the Kosovo capital that was still manned by Serbian psychiatrists and staff—but there were no patients in residence. When Dr. Wahlberg revisited the hospital the next day, he found that the Serbian doctors and staff had been forcibly replaced by Kosovar Albanian doctors who sat in locked offices, protected by armed guards. But still no one was being treated there.

I believe that NGOs—and those foreign psychiatrists, psychologists, or social workers associated with such organizations—can help indigenous mental health workers in two ways. First, they can train these local caregivers through lectures, seminars, and workshops. In the course of CSMHI's work in traumatized societies such as Northern Cyprus, Kuwait, the former Yugoslavia, and the Republic of Georgia, we have seen evidence that NGOs have been very effective and helpful in providing this intellectual, consultative, and supervisory help to local health care workers. This is no small task indeed, since in a given crisis area there may be only a few previously trained psychiatrists, psychologists, or similar professionals—or none at all. We found just such a situation in South Ossetia (within the legal boundaries of the Republic of Georgia), where foreign mental health care workers—some of whom, in fact, belonged to the former enemy ethnic group—had come to help teachers and parents understand the concept of psychological trauma.

Providing intellectual support, however, is *not* enough. I propose that to be truly helpful, foreign psychiatrists, psychologists, and social workers must consider a second, concurrent approach, one that is often bypassed in war-torn areas: Outside experts must, from the first, pay attention to local mental health workers' own psychological needs. Without working out their own internal conflicts concerning ethnic or other large group conflicts, indigenous workers will not be fully able to help their own people, however high the quality of the consultative and supervisory aid they receive from foreign workers.

I met one Bosnian psychiatrist who, having survived the 1993 siege of Sarajevo, found herself "paralyzed" in the work of treating the PTSD population when peace finally arrived. The months-long siege by Bosnian Serbs was a massive catastrophe in itself. About eleven thousand residents of Sarajevo were killed, and an estimated sixty-one thousand were wounded. Everyone, including mental health workers, was traumatized. Three years before I met her, this psychiatrist had begun to experience a symptom that was still with her when our paths crossed: before going to sleep or on awakening, she would check her legs to see if they were still attached to her body. When I examined the meaning of the symptom with her, we discovered that it was connected to an incident during the siege: She had rushed to the hospital one night, fearing that she might be shot any moment by a stray bullet, and had seen there a young Bosnian man whom she had known before the ethnic troubles began.

The young man's legs had been smashed in a bomb explosion, and they had to be amputated, an operation that she witnessed. This incident, for personal psychological reasons, came to symbolize the tragedy of Sarajevo for her. Unconsciously, she identified with this young man. Instead of recalling the tragedy by experiencing appropriate emotions, she was remembering only her own horror of being under enemy attack day after day. Because of her unconscious fear of experiencing these terrible feelings, she could not fully help her patients experience their emotions in the therapeutic setting or relieve them of maladaptively repressing or denying what had happened to them. A few months after I brought the connection between her symptom and her identification with the young man to her attention, however, her symptoms disappeared.

In bloody ethnic or other large group conflicts, those who are not directly physically affected are nevertheless psychologically affected by the group's trauma. As mentioned previously, the eruption of large group conflict strengthens the emotional links among individuals who belong to the same group. Under these circumstances, even a person who was not directly affected tends to experience feelings—ranging from group pride and a sense of revenge-entitlement to group shame and humiliation and helplessness—in common with the other members of the group; these are inherently collective feelings. The loss of people, land, and prestige affects everyone—including indigenous mental health caretakers—in a victimized large group.

A young Croatian psychiatrist who was not directly traumatized during the Croatian-Serbian war was assigned to work in a hospital in Vukovar, a border city between today's Croatia and Serbia, after peace was established. During the war the Serbs had sacked Vukovar as residents of Croatian origin fled inland; today Vukovar is a Croatian city, though most of its residents are of Serbian ethnicity. Thus, the young Croatian psychiatrist was proud to be assigned by his Health Ministry to work in Vukovar, and he thought it his national duty to help to change the emotional atmosphere of the city so that Croatian former residents would want to return. His sense of ethnicity was thus highly intensified, though not in any specifically prejudicial way, when he arrived in Vukovar.

His colleagues, who were of Serbian origin, also wanted to demonstrate their good will toward the newcomer, and so addressed him by his first name. Soon, however, working daily with colleagues who spoke to him as if nothing had happened between their ethnic group and his began to infuriate the young Croatian psychiatrist. Furthermore, he believed that one of them had been involved in making an "extermination" list of Croatian hospital patients when Serbian forces were attacking the city; he felt like a traitor for working with this person. Therefore, when treating his PTSD patients in the Vukovar hospital—most of whom were Serbian, and only a small number Croatian— he found himself confounded, largely, in his function as a mental health caretaker. Though not personally traumatized during the conflict, this doctor needed to work through his feelings associated with belonging to the traumatized group in order to further, in his professional work, the task of reconciliation he consciously so much wanted to support.

But it is not enough to help a traumatized large group's mental health professionals to work through personal ethnic sentiments that interfere with constructive, realistic interaction with patients. Besides taking care of people with individual PTSD and working through their own responses to trauma, indigenous mental health workers may also play a very important role (when politics permit) in helping their societies to confront the societal effects of shared psychological response to large group trauma. Indeed, indigenous psychiatrists, psychologists, and social workers may even be able to develop and to enact strategies to interrupt the vicious cycle of transgenerational transmission.

CSMHI-sponsored conversations between prominent Estonians and Russians resulted in a variety of concrete actions. After the dialogues, participants became involved in such activities as writing psychologically informed, tension-reducing articles for local newspapers, revising schoolbooks to change images of the enemy group, cultivating realistic public debate, and so on. NGOs and associated foreign mental health workers can similarly help indigenous professionals to find psychologically useful and politically tactful strategies to bring their newly gained insights to the public arena (Apprey, 1996, 2000; Volkan, 1999d).

At present, the possibilities for engaging indigenous mental health workers in such activities remain mostly theoretical—perhaps, indeed, mostly wishful thinking. Nevertheless, CSMHI has recently participated in a promising experiment in the Republic of Georgia. For more than two years, we have been collaborating with Georgian psychiatrists and psychologists who belong to the Tbilisi-based Foundation for the Development of Human Resources (FDHR) and with South Ossetian teachers and psychologists at the Tskhinvali-based Youth Palace in a project of "preventive medicine" for their traumatized societies.

Soon after the Republic of Georgia regained its independence from the Soviet Union, civil war erupted between Georgians and South Ossetians as the latter group began to take steps toward its own independence. Since the cease-fire in 1992, there has been little further violence between Georgians and South Ossetians, but no political solution has yet emerged. Our program was intended to help indigenous child-care workers to explore their own traumas so that they could be better caregivers and perhaps help to prevent the children from carrying the trauma's influence into adulthood and transmitting it to future generations. Ninety traumatized South Ossetian children in Tskhinvali (capital of South Ossetia), ranging in age from eight to fifteen, met weekly in small groups of twenty with teachers and caretakers to explore their responses to trauma through a technique resembling play therapy.

The need for the teachers and psychologists to address their own responses to the trauma was particularly evident in a session that CSMHI observed in which the South Ossetian children were asked to draw pictures. One of the children drew a small island in the middle of blue water with a tree on it. On the highest point of the island, a stick figure stood shouting, "Help! Help!" Although this would have been an opening for one of the teachers to ask why the figure was calling for help or otherwise probe what appeared to be an expression of helplessness, no one did so. Another drawing, illustrating a story that the children were inventing, depicted a person who arrives on an island, sees a boatload of other people, and wants to fight them. Such a reference to aggression provoked another child to exclaim, "Even though it is hard to make friends after war, we want peace!" and the group moved on to other topics without exploring the subject further. Throughout the session, difficult feelings were either ignored or suppressed. Later, in a debriefing after the children had left, one of the instructors admitted that she was afraid to touch on painful topics such as aggression and helplessness. When a CSMHI team member inquired as to what happened to the children's aggressive feelings, the instructor responded, "It is too much for the teachers to talk about painful things, so we do not let the children talk about them either."

I later learned the story of this young South Ossetian teacher/psychologist and how her own experience in the war both motivated and paralyzed her. During the conflict in Tskhinvali, Lia (not her real name) was among twenty children and teenagers sent away from the fighting to safety in Russia as part of a humanitarian aid program sponsored by an international organization. When the organization representatives approached her mother, they said she could only send one of her children. The fact that Lia was chosen by her mother to be "saved" caused her a type of survival guilt both during the war and long after it. All during her four-month "exile," she was acutely aware that her mother had chosen her over her sister, and she fantasized that her mother and sister were both killed in the conflict. Although both mother and sister lived through the war unharmed, Lia's guilt, now internalized, was all consuming and eventually transformed into a feeling that no one would like her.

She again "abandoned" her family to attend a university in Russia. Now, Lia returned to Tskhinvali once again and still convinced that she was unlikeable, she was driven to help others, especially to help the children. Paradoxically though, if the children she was working with talked about their experiences of helplessness and terror (which they needed to do to recover from the trauma), Lia's guilt over having been chosen to be spared the dangers of the war became overwhelming. Consequently, she, and other helpers too, could not bear to encourage the children to discuss openly their painful experiences. This outpouring of her story to me was the first time she had unburdened herself of the guilt that plagued her. After that, whenever I went to Tskhinvali, we discussed ways in which she could begin to let go of it, begin to make peace with her sister and family, and become better able to help others deal with such painful feelings.

Despite the teachers' own challenges, the South Ossetian youth program was a success for the children who participated in it. Its impact is reflected in that no youngster who participated in the program fell victim to prostitution or criminality, two of the major new societal processes particularly affecting youth in South Ossetia since the conflict.

Our program went one step further, however: we sought to develop the Georgian and South Ossetian caregivers with whom we were working into "core groups" working to break the cycle of enmity between the two groups from within each community. Using the concept of "psychopolitical dialogue," a technique developed by CSMHI in work with parliamentarians, political leaders, and other influential members of traumatized societies, CSMHI faculty organized small group meetings in which the caregivers explored their own ethnic sentiments, rituals, and perceptions of the enemy and began to differentiate fantasied expectations of themselves and their enemies from realistic ones. Whenever possible, we also brought together mental health workers from the antagonist groups in small groups for a series of similar dialogues. Though I will not detail here the technique (see Apprey, 1996; Volkan, 1997, 1999a, and, in particular, Volkan, 1999d), we believe that such dialogues may succeed in generating psychological and emotional healing between the two groups from within each.

After less than three years, it is difficult to say yet whether we can significantly affect societal processes and potential transgenerational transmissions in Georgia; "preventive medicine" for traumatized societies is by necessity long-term work. Whether this or any experiment will proceed depends on the continued availability of funds as well as on political considerations and "permissions." Unfortunately, the lack of response that our work in Kuwait received from local authorities is not an isolated instance, and this is one of the major obstacles to the sort of "treatment" for traumatized societies that I would like to encourage. But we know too well the costs of not having the courage to re-open large group psychological wounds in a therapeutic way before they can develop into what I call chosen traumas. Societal responses to a war or war-like situation may not appear for years after the shared trauma, and the connection of present problem to past cause is often lost. Societies are often puzzled by the symptoms that emerge, and may develop incorrect or inadequate (or both) explanations. Since the actual cause remains unknown, attempts to counter its effects are easily frustrated or may even worsen the situation. Involving indigenous mental health workers as "healers" of maladaptive results of societal changes and transgenerational transmissions theoretically makes a great deal of sense. But the appropriate international organizations must sanction and support the practice for it to receive the methodological development and scale of field testing it richly deserves.

CONCLUSION

While we have amassed a great deal of knowledge about individual PTSD, we need to remember that after ethnic, national, or religious hostilities, whole societies change too. Though postconflict societal changes "piggyback" on physical destruction, economic collapse, and political constrictions, the shared psychological causes also need to be thoroughly explored. The mental health professional should be aware that the help he or she can provide needs to go beyond treatment of individual cases of PTSD. Foreign and indigenous mental health professionals alike can seek a role in developing strategies to break the transgenerational transmissions of trauma and their malignant consequences. Besides being healers of traumatized individuals, we, as psychiatrists, psychologists, or other mental health workers, can also look for ways to help administer "preventive medicine" to societies recovering from ethnic, national, and religious conflicts.

REFERENCES

This chapter is reproduced from Vamik D. Volkan (2000), Traumatized societies and psychological care: Expanding the concept of preventive medicine. *Mind and Human Interaction*, 11 (3): 177–94. Earlier versions of this chapter were presented as a paper at the Eighth International Conference on Health and Environment at the United Nations in New York, April 23, 1999, and at a conference entitled "Crossing the Border" sponsored by the Dutch Adolescent Psychotherapy Organization in Amsterdam, May 18, 2000.

Apprey, M. (1993). The African-American experience: Transgenerational trauma and forced immigration. *Mind and Human Interaction*, 4: 70–75.

———. (1996). Heuristic steps for negotiating ethno-national conflicts: Vignettes from Estonia. *New Literary History: Journal of Theory and Interpretation*, 27: 199–212.

———. (2000). From the heuristic to the empirical: Integrating interethnic kindergartens. *Mind and Human Interaction*, 11: 195–207.

Bernard, V., Ottenberg, P., and Redl, F. (1973). Dehumanization: A composite psychological defense in relation to modern war. In N. Sanford and C. Comstock (Eds.), *Sanctions for evil: Sources of social destructiveness*, pp. 102–24. San Francisco: Jossey-Bass.

Blos, P. (1979). *The adolescent passage*. New York: International Universities Press.

Brenner, I. (1999). Returning to the fire: Surviving the Holocaust and "going back." *Journal of Applied Psychoanalytic Studies*, 1: 145–62.

Cain, A. C., and Cain, B. S. (1964). On replacing a child. *Journal of the American Academy of Child Psychiatry*, 3: 443–56.

Erikson, K. T. (1975). Loss of communality at Buffalo Creek. *American Journal of Psychiatry*, 133: 302–25.

Erlich, H. S. (1998). Adolescents' reactions to Rabin's assassination: A case of patricide? In A. Esman (Ed.), *Adolescent psychiatry: Developmental and clinical studies*, chap. 22, pp. 189–205. London: The Analytic Press.

Freud, A. (1936). The ego and the mechanisms of defense. In *The writings of Anna Freud*, Vol. 2. New York: International Universities Press, 1966.

Freud, A., and Burlingham, D. (1942). *War and children*. New York: International Universities Press.

Goenjian, A. K., Steinberg, A. M., Najarian, L. M., Fairbanks, L. A., Tashjian, M., and Pynoos, R. S. (2000). Prospective study of posttraumatic stress, anxiety, and depressive reactions after earthquake and political violence. *American Journal of Psychiatry*, 157: 911–16.

Howell, W. N. (1993). Tragedy, trauma and triumph: Reclaiming integrity and initiative from victimization. *Mind and Human Interaction*, 4: 111–19.

———. (1995). "The evil that men do . . . ": Societal effects of the Iraqi occupation of Kuwait. *Mind and Human Interaction*, 6: 150–69.

Kestenberg, J., and Brenner, I. (1996). *The last witness: The child survivor of the Holocaust*. Washington, DC: American Psychiatric Press.

Lifton, R. J. (1968). *Death in life: Survivors of Hiroshima*. New York: Random House.

Lifton, R. J., and Olson, E. (1976). The human meaning of total disaster: The Buffalo Creek experience. *Psychiatry*, 39: 1–18.

Mahler, M. S. (1968). *On human symbiosis and the vicissitudes of individuation*. New York: International Universities Press.

Poznanski, E. O. (1972). The "replacement child": A saga of unresolved parental grief. *Behavioral Pediatrics*, 81: 1190–93.

Raviv, A., Sadeh, A., Raviv, A., Silberstein, O., and Diver, O. (2000). Young Israelis' reactions to national trauma: The Rabin assassination and terror attacks. *Political Psychology*, 21: 299–322.

Saathoff, G. (1995). In the hall of mirrors: One Kuwaiti's captive memories. *Mind and Human Interaction*, 6: 170–78.

———. (1996). Kuwait's children: Identity in the shadow of the storm. *Mind and Human Interaction*, 7: 181–91.

Thomson, J. A. (2000). Terror, tears, and timelessness: Individual and group responses to trauma. *Mind and Human Interaction*, 11: 162–76.

Volkan, V. D. (1979). *Cyprus—war and adaptation: A psychoanalytic history of two ethnic groups in conflict*. Charlottesville: University Press of Virginia.

———. (1987). *Six steps in the treatment of borderline personality organization*. Northvale, NJ: Jason Aronson.

———. (1988). *The need to have enemies and allies: From clinical practice to international relationships*. Northvale, NJ: Jason Aronson.

———. (1997). *Bloodlines: From ethnic pride to ethnic terrorism*. New York: Farrar, Straus and Giroux.

———. (1999a). *Das Versagen der Diplomatie: Zur Psychoanalyse nationaler, etnischer und religiöser Konflikte*. Giessen, Germany: Psycho-sozial Verlag.

———. (1999b). Psychoanalysis and diplomacy, part I: Individual and large-group identity. *Journal of Applied Psychoanalytic Studies*, 1: 29–55.

———. (1999c). Psychoanalysis and diplomacy, part II: Large-group rituals. *Journal of Applied Psychoanalytic Studies*, 1: 223–47.

———. (1999d). The tree model: A comprehensive psychopolitical approach to unofficial diplomacy and the reduction of ethnic tension. *Mind and Human Interaction*, 3: 142–210.

Volkan, V. D., Ast, G., and Greer, W. F. (2002). *The Third Reich in the unconscious: Transgenerational transmission and its consequences*. New York: Brunner-Routledge.

Williams, R. M., and Parkes, C. M. (1975). Psychosocial effects of disaster: Birth rate in Aberfan. *British Medical Journal*, 2: 303–4.

Wolfenstein, M., and Kliman, G. (Eds.). (1965). *Children and the death of a president: Multi-disciplinary studies*. Garden City, NY: Doubleday.

World Health Organization and United Nations High Commissioner for Refugees. (1996). *Mental health of refugees*. Geneva, Switzerland: World Health Organization.

Chapter Twenty-five

Storytelling as a Way to Work Through Intractable Conflicts: The TRT German-Jewish Experience and Its Relevance to the Palestinian-Israeli Context

Dan Bar-On and Fattma Kassem

This chapter demonstrates how storytelling can be used to work through intractable conflicts in intergroup activities. The storytelling approach will be defined within other approaches to small group interventions. The To Reflect and Trust (TRT) group that originally employed the storytelling approach will be discussed in detail. The group was initially composed of German descendants of Nazi perpetrators and Jewish descendants of Holocaust survivors. Later, practitioners working in current conflicts from Northern Ireland and South Africa, and Palestinians and Israelis joined its sessions. The storytelling method was also applied in a yearlong Jewish-Palestinian workshop at Ben Gurion University from 2000 to 2001. This program will be described here. The discussion will focus on the way personal storytelling facilitated working through processes in intractable conflicts.

SMALL GROUP INTERVENTIONS TO WORK THROUGH INTRACTABLE CONFLICTS—A TYPOLOGY

One can classify small group processes[1] whose purpose is to attempt a resolution of ethnic conflicts into three main approaches of intervention:

1. *Human relations groups*: These groups are based primarily on Contact Hypothesis (Allport, 1954; Pettigrew, 1998). These groups try to create personal relationships between the participants. The assumption is that getting to know each other contributes to change in stereotypic perceptions, attitudes, and relations. The problem with this approach is that it tends to disregard the historical background and the current political reality of asymmetric power relations. While this approach may have advantages in the

short run, it usually has little long-term impact, as the external power relations and the hostile environment may erase the positive effect created by the small group process.

2. *The confrontational model*: This model was developed at Neve Shalom and Givat Havivah as a critical response to coexistence models based on the Contact Hypothesis (see Maoz, 2004). This approach focuses on collective identities and the asymmetric power relations between the parties at the expense of diminishing opportunities to create close personal relationships of trust and friendship among participants of the group. This strategy attempts to achieve the goals of empowering members of the minority group and helping the dominant group develop new insights into their own identity ambivalence and their power orientation (Maoz, 2000a; 2000b; Sonnenschein, Halabi, and Friedman, 1998; Suleiman, 1997). Helms (1990) viewed the problem that arose in the encounter between majority and minority as one of vagueness in the definition of self among the people of the majority (the white majority in the case of the United States).

This vagueness stands out in the face of clearly strengthening identity among the oppressed minority (black minority in the case of the United States). Moscovici (1976) and Mugny and Perez (1991) similarly maintained that in the encounter between the hegemonic group and the minority group, there is an advantage in the latter's social self-representations. The minority knows how to differentiate between their self-representation and that of the majority with whom they are often in disaccord, while the hegemonic group usually has no similar clear representation, but merely a vague self-representation. This is because they do not need the representation of the minority group for their own survival. Therefore, during the first stages of the confrontational encounter, the minority group will strive to use its relative advantage, and it is the hegemonic group that must reexamine the vagueness and marked internal contradictions in their self-definition (Maoz, Bar-On, Steinberg, and Farkhadeen, 2002).

An observer of the process sometimes feels that both groups come to a workshop as if they were walking along ethnocentric independent axes with no meeting point (Steinberg and Bar-On, 2002). One can describe the initial "absence of a meeting point" in the following way: the Jews are trying to preserve the status quo and approach the Palestinians on an individual basis; the Palestinians are trying to change the status quo and reproach the Jews on a collective level. These are the forces motivating various subjects in the group: each side tries to tip the scales toward its own axis, thus keeping its identity "intact," as before the encounter, so that it will not have to examine its validity, discover internal contradictions and tensions, and make cardinal changes.

3. *Developing a third option: Group encounters focusing on family stories.* A new design of the current workshop was developed to address some of the shortcomings of the previous intervention models. In this model family stories are produced by members of both groups and shared in the group encounters (Zehavi-Verete, 2000). The family stories represent the emotional personal and collective history of the conflict from both perspectives, on the one hand, but, on the other hand, enable the processing of emotional ties and allow more complex representations of the self and "other" to evolve in the course of the group process. This model was developed within the Jewish-German context by me (Bar-On, coauthor), in the framework of a group process that brought together children of Holocaust survivors and descendants of Nazi perpetrators (Bar-On, 1995a). This group later expanded to include practitioners from Northern Ireland, South Africa, and Palestinians and Israelis (Bar-On, 2000). This approach has now been applied to a group process of Jewish and Palestinian students in Israel.

STORYTELLING AS A WAY TO WORK THROUGH THE HOLOCAUST

Here, an assumption is made that one has to work through the unresolved pain and anger related to the past through interpersonal encounters between the parties. The concept of working through, initially developed in relation to individual therapy, has been used to explain the laborious psychological process that an individual must go through and that demands more than a one-time "insight," as the individual confronts repressed childhood experiences. In absence of this process, the repressed content may continually interfere in relating one's feelings, attitudes, and behavior to the changing reality (Novey, 1962). The concept was developed by Freud to describe the process between patient and therapist, but it was widened to apply to social traumatic experiences and Post-Traumatic Stress Disorder (PTSD) (Danieli, 1988). The original goal of the process of working through—letting go of the influence of the repressed content—was later replaced by a more modest goal—the ability to "live with" the painful traumatic event in better terms (Lehman, Wortman, and Williams, 1987).

After World War II, therapists borrowed the concept of working through to describe survivors coping with the traumas originating from the Holocaust and its intergenerational aftereffects. Later, the concept was used to understand the processing of distress after the Holocaust as "normal" delayed reactions to the abnormal circumstances and terrible loss the survivors suffered from during and after the Holocaust (Danieli, 1988). The same concept also served those who wished to conceptualize the possibility of living with the loss and helplessness stemming from that period, in an ever-changing reality. It helped explain why many survivors succeeded in normalizing their lives, not showing any pathological signs for many years. Still, the repressed contents could suddenly surface, thereby threatening the survivors even if their functioning had been "normal" for years (Davidson, 1980).

Children were sensitive to their parents' silencing, and a sort of "double wall" was erected between the two generations (Bar-On, 1995b). Parents did not talk about their experiences and their children did not ask. Even when one side wished to open up a "window" in their wall, they were confronted with the other's wall. We have found very few spontaneous incidences in which both parties opened up windows in their walls, simultaneously having feelings mutually delivered and accepted.

There exists only a beginning of a psychological literature concerning the intergenerational effects of the Holocaust on the descendants of the Nazi perpetrators: Can one speak of working through where descendants of perpetrators are concerned (Bar-On, 1990)? To what extent have the atrocities that their fathers committed been transmitted to the children through a "conspiracy of silence" of their parents (developed for very different reasons than that of the survivors' silencing)? How did the children start to confront and work through this silence (Hardtmann, 1991; Rosenthal, 1998)?

The possibility to acknowledge such questions by professionals was suppressed mainly through the assumption of *psychological symmetry*: presenting both groups of descendants as burdened by the Nazi era, psychologically speaking, could interfere with the *moral superiority* of the victim over their victimizer (Bar-On, 1995a). This could account for the fact that almost no attempt had been made to discuss these issues simultaneously or to try to bring members of the two "sides" of this human-made catastrophe together into a dialogical, semitherapeutic context. We will now describe an example of how the working-through concept was applied to a group process, bringing together descendants of Holocaust survivors and descendants of Nazi perpetrators.

SHARING STORYTELLING BETWEEN PARTIES IN CONFLICT: ACKNOWLEDGMENT AND WORKING THROUGH

A micro setting of a group process will be presented here that tried to address and work through the various levels of the conflicts and the painful memories between Germans and Jews and later also between Jews and Palestinians. The To Reflect and Trust (TRT) group initially brought together descendants of Holocaust survivors from the United States and Israel and descendants of

Nazi perpetrators from Germany in 1992 (Bar-On, 1993). The group process that evolved was based on the participants sharing their personal stories. This helped them work through the collective and personal abyss that still existed between them so many years after the Holocaust. The TRT group process will be described, as it evolved from 1992 to 1998.

Developing a Common Emotional and Conceptual Language across the Abyss

After some years of intensive work with descendants of survivors in Israel (Bar-On, 1995b), and after interviewing descendants of Nazi perpetrators in Germany (Bar-On, 1989), a group setting was formed in which both these groups faced one another and initiated an open dialogue. The questions addressed were as follows: Could they face each other genuinely? Could this encounter help each party work through aspects that they could not work through in their separate "tribal ego" setting? Through such an encounter, would a common agenda emerge over and beyond the separate agendas of each side (Clay, 1993)?

Six encounters between a group of eight descendants of Holocaust perpetrators and a group of five American and four Israeli descendants of Holocaust survivors took place over six years, rotating between Germany, Israel, and the United States. The meetings usually lasted four to five days. Except for the first encounter, which was devoted to getting acquainted mainly by listening to each other's personal accounts and stories (Bar-On, 1993), the scheduling was done by the group itself, and the content of the meetings continued to focus on reflecting on those stories from the first Dan Bar-On and Fattma Kassem meeting.

During this joint working-through process, a kind of a common emotional and conceptual language developed, beyond the separate languages that characterized the communities from which these people had originated. This development also created a dilemma for the two groups of descendants. They had to struggle with the question: "Shall we become an isolated sect, as the communities we belong to cannot cope yet with our new mutual experience, or will we have to give up our common experience in order to remain active members of our original communities?" Even if this situation was not discussed openly in the group at that early stage, the important point about this group was that they chose to go in neither of these directions. They were willing to pay the price of containing the tension between these options, using the group's support and hoping that their communities would slowly move closer to each other, to where the group created its own new "space." This may account for the fact that the TRT group process was a relatively slow process and was acknowledged by parts of the German and Jewish communities only after several years.[2]

How did the process unfold? It was my role (Bar-On, coauthor) (as an initiator of the group, even though I clearly belonged to the Jewish group) to present questions and suggest conceptualizations about where the group was heading in its process. Though these were my formulations, I tried to offer ideas that members of both groups could identify with and associate the construction of their personal and collective experiences with these formulations. Clearly, everyone did not always agree with these formulations, and they have also been changed as a result of the discussion in the group. In the following paragraphs, some of these formulations will be discussed.

At the beginning, members of both groups shared their own stories—how, when, and in what ways they could trace the aftereffects of the Holocaust within their own lives. For some it was a daily struggle that was accompanied by sleeplessness, fears, and uncontrollable reactions. Often these were associated with the silence, the repression, or other difficult reactions of their parents and their social surroundings. In many cases, the acknowledgment of a personal relationship to the Holocaust was accompanied by a feeling of estrangement, internal (from oneself) as well as external (from one's social surroundings). It took many years to clarify and comprehend how these aspects of estrangement were associated with addressing one's personal relationship to the Holocaust.

The Jewish members of the group suffered from physical uprootedness, as their parents had immigrated to the United States or to Israel after the Holocaust. This physical uprootedness was usually accompanied by psychological uprootedness, associated with the fact that their parents could not overcome the loss of so many family members and had difficulty integrating themselves into the new society. The German members of the group did not go through physical uprootedness as their families usually continued to live in their original surroundings. Still, they shared the feeling of psychological uprootedness, but for other reasons than the descendants of survivors: The German members felt that due to the atrocities committed by their parents, their roots had been poisoned and they could no longer use them as a base for their own identity. They had to develop new roots, similar to the descendants of the survivors.

Struggling with the feelings of estrangement and uprootedness brought up new questions that the members of the group addressed: Can I allow myself to live my own life, neither dependent nor counterdependent on my parents? This was a major issue for members of both groups. The Jewish descendants' separation from their parents was more difficult (as the latter leaned on them, emotionally, especially at the later stages of their lives). The descendants of Nazi perpetrators tended to counterreact and distance themselves from their Nazi parents, thereby suffering from an emotional void (A. Berger and

N. Berger, 2001). This problem became more severe over time, especially when the parents aged and the objective justification for caring for them became a daily reality and necessity.

In many ways, members of both groups struggle daily with dreaming of death, bearing names of dead people (especially among Jewish descendants of survivors), and of having fantasies of sacrificing themselves for a human cause (especially among the descendants of Nazi perpetrators). As one member of the group mentioned: "We talk about our feelings, emotions and ideas, but they all concern the dead people who are in the back of our minds." Perhaps, not by coincidence, some members of the group belong to the helping professions. Are they trying to give a special meaning to their lives under the shadow of death?

Members of the group could, quite easily, establish an open dialogue with the victim in themselves. This was easy for both descendants of Jewish victims and descendants of Nazi victimizers. But it was much more difficult for both groups to identify and enter into an open dialogue with the victimizer within oneself and to let the two "figures" talk to each other. Eventually it became clear that we also have this potential role within ourselves. Only by openly acknowledging and entering into a dialogue with that role may its uncontrolled potential be reduced in future, unexpected situations. After this realization, a new issue was defined: once we accept and let go of these two roles of victim and victimizers within ourselves—what is left? Who are we if not defined through these roles? This understanding actually suggested the beginning of a new process of identity construction, one that was based neither on negation of the "other" nor on the role of the victim within oneself (Bar-On, 1999).

The issues associated with identity construction brought up the question of "who suffered more?" This was a new issue that included the scaling of suffering. In the group context, it became evident that we tend to create a subjective scale of suffering. We were told that there are families of survivors in which only the members who have been in Auschwitz were "allowed" to talk about their suffering in family gatherings. In the group this issue came up in relation to the BBC filming: We asked ourselves if certain German participants were more important because their father had been a prominent figure in the Nazi regime? Or was it associated with the fact that they had to work harder through the prominent role of their fathers (Bar-On, 1995a). Perhaps, in the light of extreme suffering that causes us to feel helplessness, we tend to feel in control by rating it. As some people cannot grasp the experiences their parents had during the Holocaust, the rating helps us make sense of it. It is much more difficult to relate to the experiences of the other as just being *different*, not *more or less*. It became an issue for the group—how to maintain the legitimacy of grasping the difference without rating it, as this in itself creates additional pain and humiliation.

It was important to bear in mind that members of the group developed a feeling of mutual trust and respect, suggesting a new symmetry between parties in the dialogue. However, this by no means erased the asymmetry that still existed in people's minds concerning their parents during the Holocaust— there were the victimizers and the victims. Although it was very difficult maintaining these two types of relationships simultaneously, it was very important to find a way to navigate between them. This process was associated with the relationship between the past and the present and how to manage them simultaneously.

Through the group experience, it became clear that the outcome of the process was not to forget or to be done with the past, once and for all, but to find new ways to live with it, perhaps in ways that are more conscious but also that are less threatening and self-destructive. This suggests that by working through such massive trauma, one does not end it or let it go but can find new *ways to live with it*. The Holocaust will always be there, and descendants of survivors and of perpetrators will still have to struggle with its aftereffects. One German member said: "The day we will feel that it is done with will mean that we went off our course." Still, the negative impact of the Holocaust on their lives and the lives of others can be reduced through conscious working-through processes with groups as well as with individuals. Perhaps these issues were the group's main "product" that could be presented as its own way of working through by doing forgiveness and reconciliation, rather than talking about it.

Hamburg 1998: Bringing in Practitioners from Current Conflicts

In 1998 the group decided to invite practitioners who work with victims and victimizers of atrocities in current conflicts (South Africa, Northern Ireland, and Palestinians and Israelis) to participate in a joint meeting. The purpose was to see whether the TRT group process of storytelling, and reflections on the stories in a trustful atmosphere, would also be relevant for these other settings.

It was clear to the organizers of these TRT encounters that each conflict setting had its own "biography" that had to be carefully studied and taken into consideration. In addition, the TRT dealt with the Holocaust that had happened many years ago and had a clear-cut division between victims and victimizers. Their descendants had no current agenda except for what was still burdening their minds and hearts. Still, we wanted to see whether the TRT storytelling approach had any relevance for practitioners who struggle with the peace-building process in the regions noted in the preceding. We assumed that this sort of dialogue between members of the opposing sides could be a necessary step toward reaching the deeper underlying issues that political, legal, or financial steps, or even time alone, may not help to heal and comprehend. The

TRT experience also suggested that the process of working through the past into the present is an intergenerational process. The full account and the evaluation of the seminar can be found elsewhere (Maoz and Bar-On, 2002).[3] In the following years the storytelling approach of the TRT group has been translated into programs implemented in the various current conflict settings. We will now describe one workshop that took place in Israel in 2000–2001.

DIALOGUE UNDER FIRE: JEWISH AND PALESTINIAN STUDENTS ENCOUNTER THEIR FAMILIES' LIFE STORIES

As a consequence of their participation in the TRT encounters, we decided to develop a workshop for Jewish and Palestinian[4] Israeli students, based on the TRT approach of storytelling. The workshop was called "Life Stories in the Service of Coexistence." Students were asked to interview members of their parents' and grandparents' generations and to present some of these interviews in the classroom. Based on theoretical materials, the students analyzed their respective interviews in mixed couples and wrote a final joint paper based on that analysis.

I (Bar-On, coauthor) observed, by watching behind a one-way mirror, four Jewish and Palestinian students' yearly intergroup processes at Ben Gurion University in Israel, facilitated by practitioners from Neve Shalom. These group processes were based on the confrontational model. My coauthor (Kassem) participated and facilitated many educational programs for Israeli Jews and Arabs, trying to promote coexistence and dialogue. The workshop described here was a new attempt to work though the painful past and confront each other's reality in a constructive way, using the method of storytelling.

In October 2000, severe violence broke out between Jewish Israelis and Palestinians, within Israel and in the Occupied Territories, the latter known today as the Al-Aqsa Intifada.[5] The workshop was scheduled to begin at Ben Gurion University at the end of that month. For this program, we recruited thirteen Jewish students out of the twenty-four who had applied and twelve Palestinian students. There was a real threat (and a lot of talking among the students) that the Palestinian students would not show up, because of the events of October 2000 in which the police had killed thirteen Israeli Palestinians. Therefore, we decided to start the group process with a few separate uninational meetings, in which the Palestinian group met with my coauthor (Kassem), speaking in Arabic, and the Jewish group met with me, speaking Hebrew. We decided to avoid recording the sessions because we assumed that this might cause apprehension, mainly on the Palestinian side. However, the students were told that they should keep a personal log in which they would describe, in one page, what happened in the group process at each meeting. On the other page, they were asked to write down their own reactions to these events.

During the initial two uninational sessions, members of both groups were asked to share some of their family background, before conducting any interviews. However, the students also expressed their tension and concern regarding the events that had happened outside the classroom, especially if the fatal outcomes would limit the willingness of the Palestinians to encounter the Jewish participants ("Will they be willing to listen to my family story?" asked a Jewish student). The binational encounters started during the third week. After a short round of getting acquainted, the students were instructed to conduct interviews with their family members, transcribe these interviews, and bring them to the seminar.[6] Twelve sessions were held during the first semester, four of which were uninational, and twelve sessions were held during the second semester, one of which was uninational. In the binational meetings, Jewish students and Palestinian students shared fourteen (seven from each side) of their interviews that they conducted with their family members (one of their grandparents' generation and one of the parents' generation). Students were given two additional assignments to be conducted in mixed Jewish-Palestinian couples:

1. To read and summarize one article from the course syllabus and jointly present it in the class during the last part of the second semester.
2. To jointly write a final paper, comparing their interviews, using their own personal logs, and linking them with the theoretical models.

The group process that evolved was powerful. The fact that the students' perceptions of themselves and of each other were mediated through the family stories contributed to the their ability to listen to each other and construct a more complex image of the "other" than the one conveyed through the media. The Jewish students learned for the first time some of what had happened to Palestinians in Israel throughout its history. Some of the Palestinians told stories of family members who were refugees during the 1948 war. Others described the period under the military regime in the fifties and sixties and still others emphasized the current daily life of an underprivileged minority in Israeli society. Jewish stories were told of grandparents who went through the Holocaust, of others who immigrated to Israel; some stories were based on their Zionist ideology, others out of necessity and hardship: they covered the difficulties of both in adjusting to a new society and of wars and heroism of other family members.

The Palestinian students started by criticizing some of the Jewish stories as being "biased." According to their perception, the Jewish students were emphasizing their own family suffering, excluding the Palestinians' suffering from their stories. "We have heard so much about your Holocaust, but where are our grandparents' stories of suffering caused by some Israeli Jews? Why do these aspects of the past not appear in your stories?" But they also listened to the Jewish stories with which they could identify and feel more empathetic toward. For example, when a Jewish participant told the story of her father, who had emigrated from France and still does not fully feel at home in Israel, a Palestinian student reacted by saying that this is also the problem that she has in this country (of not feeling at home). Though the background may have been different for the two participants (emigration versus persecution), the common image of rootlessness elicited feelings of empathy and openness on both sides. Or when a Palestinian student described how her family avoided evacuation from their hometown and was later forced to live in a "Ghetto" there.[7] A Jewish participant responded that her father had grown up near that "Ghetto" and used to describe it very vividly in a positive way. The Jewish student had to reexamine some of her father's stories and the reasons for the discrepancies in the construction of the past in the memories of her father and that of the Palestinian student.

This group process did not happen in a vacuum: There was a war outside and sometimes events happened that disrupted the processes and made listening to the stories quite impossible. Therefore, storytelling was only part of the process. Several meetings were actually devoted to political clashes of an ethnocentric nature (Steinberg and Bar-On, 2002), during which each group tried to obtain control over what is just, true, and relevant. As a rule, the facilitators tried to bring the group back to the storytelling mode, but several students felt that by doing so, they were trying to stop the "real thing" from happening: meaning that one group will finally win in this kind of power struggle. In a way, the ethnocentric discourse also had a positive function for the group: it clarified how far apart the positions were and that there was no way to win, but that this power struggle only brought about a kind of group fatigue. This, in its own way, may have led these students finally to search for other ways. In this group, the search could always materialize into a new family story. But also other aspects of the process, such as the lectures given by experts[8] or the presentations of the papers, had their own impact. These more intellectual interventions provided some concepts that could be used to reflect on what had happened earlier in the process or what was going on in the here and now.

When the memorial days of both the Jews and the Palestinians arrived in April–May, new difficulties arose. It reached a peak when the Palestinian group asked the Jewish group to stand with them for a moment of silence as part of their new Al-Naqba ritual (thereby actually imitating the Jewish ritual of the Holocaust memorial day). The Jews did not join in, and this created a traumatic experience for the Palestinians in the group. Questions such as the following arose: Do the Jews only talk of what they learned but are not willing to implement it? Did we only imagine that we became closer through our storytelling? There was a severe conflict for some of the Jewish members between their dominant collective Zionist norm (not willing to accept Al-Naqba [the Catastrophe] as a day of mourning) and the new intergroup solidarity that started to develop as a result of the group process. They did not find a way to resolve that conflict at that moment. Still, the two groups worked through this crisis during the following joint sessions. A few Palestinian participants had an opportunity to voice their anger, never before verbalized in the group so clearly. Some of the members of the Jewish group apologized and said that they believe that in the future they would join the Palestinians in their mourning.

Also in other cases, external events and internal voices became interwoven and created interruptions of communication in the group (Zupnik, 2000). When a Palestinian participant made his initial declaration ("I do not believe in coexistence"), it represented for some of the Jews their fear of what was going on outside the room, in daily life: the fear that the Palestinians have returned to an earlier total refusal of accepting a Jewish State. There were other moments of fear and despair. Some Palestinian participants expressed their fear when listening to Jews in the media shouting "death to Arabs" after a suicide bombing killed about twenty youngsters near the Tel Aviv Dolphinarium. On the other hand, a Jewish student spoke after the same event of her total regression "back to where I was at the first encounter."

But there were also encouraging expressions. Some Jewish participants said that the group meetings encouraged them to read more about the roots of the conflict and to listen more intently to the news. Some tended to present more "dovish" views outside the group, in contrast to the more "hawkish" views that they represented in the group discussions.

For the two facilitators, the events outside the seminar were difficult to manage. Sometimes their weekly pre-seminar planning started by sharing feelings of anger and frustration about the violence happening daily. The TRT experience helped the facilitators take into account emotional needs of their students in this delicate process of storytelling. For example, both of them felt a great responsibility in caring for the participants of the other group. Therefore, at some points, it was my coauthor (Kassem) who took care of a Jewish participant who felt under attack, while I tried to contain a radical anti-Jewish position held by a Palestinian student, that was hard even for certain Palestinian students to accept. As a result, more intergroup diversity was exhibited, within both the Jewish as well as the Palestinian group than is usually seen in similar encounters. The uninational meetings also contributed to this aspect. Especially the Palestinian group that had some opportunities to discuss its internal differences and needed to decide if these should be voiced in front of the Jewish group.

DISCUSSION: STORYTELLING AS A GROUP PROCESS THAT CAN ENHANCE WORKING THROUGH

Two very different group processes were described that are both based on a storytelling method. The TRT group dealt with a human-made catastrophe that happened many years ago, still vibrating in the souls of the descendants of both the survivors and the perpetrators, but with no continuous, everyday agenda. The differentiation between victims and victimizers was clear-cut and common knowledge. The storytelling enabled members of Jewish and German groups to come closer to each other, bridging the gap over the abyss that has continued to exist between their communities since the Holocaust. Members of the group could see themselves as missionaries of a new way to work through the past, releasing energies to confront the present with less burdened perspectives (Maoz and Bar-On, 2002).

The German people who chose to participate in this group were a highly self-selected group (only 10 percent of my original German interviewees joined the TRT group). In that sense, one could claim that they were initially more advanced in their working-through process, when relating to their parents' atrocities during the Nazi era (Bar-On, 1990). But there is firm basis to claim that the group process assisted them, and helped them support each other, in continuing this working-through process, which seems to be endless (as one of the German members of the group defined it). Though some of this working through happened already in the German self-help group, before the TRT group was established, the encounter with the Jewish members added new dimensions to the working-through process, especially in terms of acknowledgment and legitimation. But also the Jewish members of the group expressed their own gains from the group process: their ability to move out of the black and white dichotomy of "we the victims" and "they the perpetrators," understanding that the world is more complex, and also their ability to accept that some of the descendants of the victimizers suffer from the atrocities their parents had committed.

When practitioners from current conflicts were exposed to the TRT process, they first had to learn how their own conflicts were different from that of the original TRT context and from each other (Bar-On, 2000). In their current contexts, the conflict was still ongoing and had real agendas of dispute, partially still unresolved. The differentiation between victim and victimizer was often blurred. Actually, both sides felt that they were being victimized by the other, unable to take responsibility for their own victimizing role. In addition, there was a power asymmetry, creating two different agendas of coexistence between the parties: that of maintaining the status quo versus that of changing it (Maoz, 2000b). Issues of justice making (punishing the perpetrators) and compensations (for the victims) were partially unresolved. But even when considering these differences, the storytelling approach of the TRT had relevance for the current conflict groups. One could learn from the TRT experience how to bring in the past without disrupting the present; how to create trust that will enable people to listen to others, even identify with them. It highlighted the intergenerational aspect of the conflict; the tension between the micro-sheltered process and the macro social processes. The development of the residential[9] in Northern Ireland was one possible expression of implementing that relevance (Hetherington, Deanne, Irvine, O'Neill, and Lindsay, 2000).

The possibility to adapt the TRT process, even in its second phase of the current conflicts, into an educational program with young Jewish and Palestinian Israeli students was another step away from the original TRT group. Now, young students were involved, not practitioners or middle-aged descendants of the Holocaust. Although they volunteered to participate in the workshop (such as the TRT members), many of them had no previous experience in working with people involved in the Palestinian-Israeli conflict. They were still at the stage of constructing their individual and collective identity (Litvak-Hirsch, n.d.); perhaps, therefore, they were less able to reflect on that process and its relation to the conflict (Bar-On, 1999) or to similar or different processes of the other group. For the students, working through the past meant first to acknowledge and listen to stories of the other side and develop an ability to contain them. Instead of seeing only their own pain (e.g., for the Jewish students—the Memorial day of the Holocaust), they are able to address some of the pain of the Palestinian students on their Memorial day of 1948, which they call Al-Naqba. No doubt that the ongoing violent conflict between Israel and Palestine made such containment of the "Other's" pain extremely difficult.

Finally, a different time span of the process was involved: the process had to be adjusted to a university seminar of two semesters, with no further obligation or commitment on the part of the participants, unlike the multiyear process of the TRT group. This seminar also included academic requirements, such as maintaining certain standards of formal learning, writing papers, presenting theoretical material, and earning grades. Still, even these aspects could be translated into part of the learning process, after additional opportunities were created to analyze the stories and to encounter one another on the level of "how to write a paper together on our interviews."

The Ben Gurion Jewish-Palestinian workshop was an interesting implementation of the TRT process. It enabled some students to learn about their own families and about the origins of their own identity construction. Most of the Jewish students emphasized the importance of learning about the "Other" less known to them until now, and through that process, clarifying some of the more ambiguous aspects of their own identity construction (Helms, 1990; Bar-On, 1999). Some of the Palestinian students described another process: they had learned more about their own family, and this strengthened their ties and identification with their collective. Only from that perspective could they contain unknown or difficult aspects of the stories of the Jewish side. The negotiation around what is a "good story to tell" and the fear of the other side's inability to listen to one's stories, preoccupied the minds of participants throughout this process. Only certain stories created the impact of opening up a more emotional and empathic dialogue. This was especially true of the stories that presented shortcomings or internal human dilemmas of the dominant Jewish side (such as the issue of rootlessness) and the more personal experiences of the oppressed Palestinian side (e.g., the experiences of refugees during and after the 1948 war).

In that sense, the storytelling proved to bring together certain aspects of the other two intervention methods: creating emotional ties among participants (as in the contact-coexistence model) and introducing the external conflict and asymmetry into the microgroup process (as practiced in the confrontational model). The internal differences expressed by members of the Jewish as well as the Palestinian groups, mentioned in the preceding, was a positive outcome, difficult to achieve in such encounter groups. The storytelling process had the virtue of developing a deeper emotional involvement that perhaps made it more difficult to stick to only collective group identities and thereby allowed these internal group differences to surface. But according to the participants' summary, a larger time span should be provided when designing such a seminar, in order to work through this involvement and bring about a long-lasting effect of the group process.

One may assume that the facilitators leaned on their TRT experience and that this experience helped them foresee and manage situations in the group (especially around certain critical moments) that other facilitators would be less prepared for. To a certain extent, the TRT experience helped the facilitators demonstrate how stories from both sides could be contained in an atmosphere of trust and acceptance that helped internalize these stories and reflect on them. Still, a lot of unlearning had to be done in order not to expect the students to follow in the footsteps of the TRT group. Comparing the learning process in the original TRT group and in the Jewish-Palestinian students' group shows that many of the issues were context related and could not be transferred from one context to the other.

Still, issues such as the concerns of rootlessness, the difficulty of confronting the victimizer within oneself, or the tension between the group process and the external hostile reality seemed to be universal and surfaced through the process of telling family stories in almost every conflict setting. On the other hand, the Jewish-Palestinian students' group also had its own specific characteristics: it needed its own time to warm up, to delve into political discussions, to develop crisis situations (such as Al-Naqba day), and to find ways to come back from them. One should not forget that this group had its special timing. It started at a moment of crisis and violent outbreak, in which it was difficult just to tell and listen to family stories. But this timing also motivated the members of both groups to look for and find ways to work through the threatening external reality.

In summary, the present chapter described a new way to approach intractable conflicts through small group work based on storytelling. This can be seen as a transformative process of building relationships between groups in conflict. It is the beginning of a way that should be tested further rather than a well-ridden path that can be formulated and taught extensively. Still, its width of applicability is promising if the original German-Jewish TRT, its inclusion of current conflict groups from South Africa, Northern Ireland, and Palestinians and Israelis, and the application to a Jewish-Palestinian students' group at the Ben Gurion University are considered.

NOTES

This analysis is partially based on previous reports of the TRT group process (Bar-On, 2000; Maoz and Bar-On, 2002). I wish to thank Dr. Schmidt and Ms. Kutz from the Koerber foundation and Dr. Farris, the President of Stockton College of New Jersey, and Dr. Jan Colijn, the Dean of General Studies at Stockton College, for their help in funding the last few TRT encounters.

1. We are thankful to Dr. Ifat Maoz of the Hebrew University, Jerusalem, for her help in structuring this typology.

2. The German Federal Government gave the author the "Cross of Merit" in 2001, among others, for initiating this group. Yad Vashem (The Israeli Memorial Institute of the Holocaust) invited the author to be a fellow of its international seminar in 1999, thereby also addressing his work in Germany with descendants of Nazi perpetrators. The BBC documentary was shown on Israeli television in 1999 and repeatedly since then.

3. Two additional wider TRT group processes have taken place since the Hamburg seminar: in Bethlehem, Palestinian National Authority (PNA), in October 1999 (Adwan and Bar-On, 2001) and at Stockton College of New Jersey, in July 2000. Another workshop took place in Northern Ireland, in August 2002.

4. Both groups were Israeli. We will refer to them here as Palestinian and Jewish. The naming of the groups plays a role in the conflict. Sometimes people are named Israelis, when actually referring to Jewish Israelis (thereby excluding the Palestinian-

Israelis). Palestinian Israelis are named Israeli Arabs by certain Jews though most of the former see this as a negation of their self-determination as Palestinians.

5. The Al-Aqsa Intifada broke out at the end of September 2000, as a result of Sharon's provocative visit to Temple Mount. In Israel, the demonstrations lasted a couple of weeks. The Al-Aqsa Intifada of the Palestinian of the PNA against Israeli Jews has not yet ended.

6. The students were instructed to conduct the interviews using the biographical method of Rosenthal (1998). They were supposed to encourage their interviewees to tell their life story with as little interference as possible and to ask questions only after the main narration. A short demonstration was facilitated in the seminar in which they interviewed each other in triads, rotating the roles of interviewee, interviewer, and observer and reflecting on some aspects of these different roles.

7. The Israeli army gave this name to the quarter into which the remaining Arab citizens of the town were forced into, after the 1948 war ended, and most of the Arab population had been forced to leave or run away.

8. Marc Ross (2000) of Bryn Mawr College, Bryn Mawr, Pennsylvania, gave a presentation of his studies and observations of ethnic conflicts in France and Northern Ireland. Steinberg presented the typology she has developed while analyzing Neve Shalom Jewish-Palestinian workshops, showing how the groups move from ethnocentric discourse through several categories to dialogical moments (Steinberg and Bar-On, 2002).

9. In such a residential area, some of the TRT North Irish participants brought together for a weekend British ex-militaries with people from Northern Ireland (Catholic and Protestant) who have been involved in the "Troubles."

REFERENCES

Adwan, S., and Bar-On, D. (Eds.). (2001). *Victimhood and beyond*. Beit Jala, Israel. PNA: PRIME.

Allport, G. W. (1954). *The nature of prejudice*. Reading, MA: Addison-Wesley.

Bar-On, D. (1989). *Legacy of silence: Encounters with descendants of the Third Reich*. Cambridge, MA: Harvard University Press.

———. (1990). Children of perpetrators of the Holocaust: Working through one's moral self. *Psychiatry*, 53: 229–45.

———. (1993). First encounter between children of survivors and children of perpetrators of the Holocaust. *Journal of Humanistic Psychology*, 33: 6–14.

———. (1995a). Encounters between descendants of Nazi perpetrators and descendants of Holocaust survivors. *Psychiatry*, 58: 225–45.

———. (1995b). *Fear and hope*. Cambridge, MA: Harvard University Press.

———. (1999). *The "other" within us: Changes in the Israeli identity from a psychosocial perspective*. Jerusalem: Ben Gurion University with Mosad Bialik. (Hebrew).

———. (Ed.). (2000). *Bridging the gap*. Hamburg, Germany: Korber-Stiftung.

———. (2001). Who counts as a Holocaust survivor? Who suffered more? Why did the Jews not take revenge on the Germans after the war. *Freie Assoziazionen*, 4: 155–87. (German).

———. (2004). Will the parties conciliate or refuse? The triangle of Jews, Germans and Palestinians. In Y. Bar-Siman-Tov (Ed.), *From conflict resolution to reconciliation*. Oxford, pp. 239–54. Oxford, England: Oxford University Press.

Bar-On, D., and Charny, I. W. (1992). The logic of moral argumentation of children of the Nazi era. *International Journal of Group Tensions*, 22: 3–20.

Berger, A., and Berger, N. (2001). *Second generation voices*. Syracuse, NY: Syracuse University Press.

Danieli, Y. (1988). Confronting the unimaginable: Psychotherapists' reactions to victims of the Nazi Holocaust. In J. P. Wilson, Z. Harel, and B. Kahana (Eds.), *Human adaptation to extreme stress: From the Holocaust to Vietnam*, pp. 219–38. New York: Plenum Press.

Davidson, S. (1980). The clinical effect of massive psychic trauma in families of Holocaust survivors. *Journal of Marital and Family Therapy*, 1: 11–21.

Hardtmann, G. (1991). *Partial relevance of the Holocaust: Comparing interviews of German and Israeli students*. Report to the GIF, Jerusalem, Israel.

Helms, J. (1990). *Black and white racial identity*. Westport, CT: Greenwood Press.

Hetherington, M., Deanne, E., Irvine, T., O'Neill, J., and Lindsay, J. (2000). *Toward understanding and healing*: An evaluation report of the lusty bag residential. Derry/Londonderry: Derry City Council.

Lehman, D. R., Wortman, C. B., and Williams, A. F. (1987). Long-term effects of losing a spouse or child in a motor vehicle crash. *Journal of Personality and Social Psychology*, 52: 218–31.

Litvak-Hirsch, T. (n.d.). Who does this house belong to? Dilemmas of Israeli identity construction. Unpublished doctoral dissertation, Ben Gurion University, Beer Sheva.

Maoz, I. (2000a). Multiple conflicts and competing agendas: A framework for conceptualizing structured encounters between groups in conflict: The case of a coexistence project of Jews and Palestinians in Israel. *Peace and Conflict: Journal of Peace Psychology*, 6: 135–56.

———. (2000b). Power relations in intergroup encounters: A case study of Jewish–Arab encounters in Israel. *International Journal of Intercultural Relations*, 24: 259–77.

———. (2004). Coexistence is in the eye of the beholder: Evaluating intergroup encounter interventions between Jews and Arabs in Israel. *Journal of Social Issues*, 60: 404–18.

Maoz, I., and Bar-On, D. (2002). From working through the Holocaust to current ethnic conflicts: Evaluating the TRT group workshop in Hamburg. *Group*, 26: 29–48.

Maoz, I., Bar-On, D., Steinberg, S., and Farkhadeen, M. (2002). The dialogue between the "Self" and the "Other": A process analysis of Palestinian-Jewish encounters in Israel. *Human Relations*, 55: 931–962.

Moscovici, S. (1976). *Social influence and social change*. London: Academic Press.

Mugny, G., and Perez, J. A. (1991). *The social psychology of minority influence.* London: Cambridge University Press.

Novey, S. (1962). The principle of "working through" in psychoanalysis. *Journal of the American Psychoanalytic Association*, 10: 658–76.

Pettigrew, T. F. (1998). Intergroup contact theory. *Annual Review of Psychology*, 49: 65–85.

Rosenthal, G. (Ed.). (1998). *The Holocaust in three-generations: Families of victims and perpetrators of the Nazi regime.* London: Cassell.

Ross, M. H. (2000). "Good enough" is not so bad: Thinking about success and failure in ethnic conflict management. *Peace and Conflict: Journal of Peace Psychology*, 6: 27–47.

Sonnenschein, N., Halabi, R., and Friedman, A. (1998). Legitimization of national identity and the change in power relationships in workshops dealing with the Israeli/Palestinian conflict. In *The handbook of interethnic coexistence.* New York: Continuum.

Steinberg, S., and Bar-On, D. (2002). An analysis of the group process in encounters between Jews and Palestinians using a typology for discourse classification. *International Journal of Intercultural Relations*, 26: 199–214.

Suleiman, R. (1997). The planned encounter between Israeli Jews and Palestinians as a microcosm: A social-psychological perspective. *Iyunim Bechinuch*, 1: 71–85. (Hebrew).

Time Watch. (1993). [Television series episode]. In C. Clay (producer), *Children of the Third Reich* [Documentary on the encounter at Nveh Shalom of the TRT group of children of Holocaust survivors with children of Nazi perpetrators.] London: BBC production.

Zehavi-Verete, T. (2000). Mutual exposure to the "family album"—a helping device for Jewish-Arab dialogue. *Dapim*, 30: 5–64. (Hebrew).

Zupnik, Y. J. (2000). Conversational interruptions in Israeli-Palestinian "dialogue" events. *Discourse Studies*, 2: 85–110.

Chapter Twenty-six

No Amount of Suffering

Michael Eigen

*Different kinds of relationships with suffering are explored in connection
with the ambivalence toward destructiveness that permeates our world.
Denial of suffering and its counterpart and addiction to suffering are
traced through struggles of individuals working with life's traumatizing
impacts, with an eye toward general problems humanity faces.*

The notion that suffering is redemptive has lost much of its appeal, although it
is far from extinct. We bear witness to the cruelty of suffering, so much need-
less, pointless pain—from disease (mental and physical), murder, torture,
predatory actions, and unwanted acts of nature. Terrorism is present from
within or outside the systems and selves we inhabit. What good can come of
it? Often precious little, as pain feeds pain, suffering begets suffering.

Yet there are individuals for whom suffering plays a role in opening, as
well as closing, worlds. Perhaps it would be better if this were not so. But it
is so and we had best pay attention. In our world, suffering is a fact, in every
social system, in every human being. It will never be eliminated. But it can
be addressed. It can be listened to. To some extent, we can speak with it,
speak from it. We can cry, scream, touch, look into each other's eyes, and feel
one another. We can learn to breathe together.

There is suffering and there is suffering. Ordinary, everyday suffering is
usually taken for granted. One gets through it and then goes on with one's life.
Indeed, one's life is premised on getting through it. One does not look too
hard or long at pains that streak the moments throughout a day, or one could
not get through the day. To sit and stare at injury and wonder what to make
of it is, in most instances, a luxury.

To some it is a necessity. Daily pains are not simply daily pains. They are
world pains, soul pains, pains that touch lives and one's own life. They stop

one short, floor one. They must be thought about. As Freud (1900; Eigen 1996, chap. 12) depicted, injury unites injury, spreading through psychic time dimensions, wounds linking together from early to late, late to early, symphonies of injury, creating vast seas of suffering drawn together in one insistent pain point. Trickles of pain unite with other trickles, forming networks of suffering through the psychic body and often in the body itself. Trauma hits soul and body in one blow, in many blows.

The person standing next to you may be dying. May be dead and gone for many years, waiting for life. She goes on speaking, dancing, and laughing. You come closer and cannot find this person. She was never there. Or she was there one moment, not the next. Invisible explosive waves made her a shell. No one noticed. You could not see it. An invisible suicide bomber exploded, and while your attention was riveted by torn bodies, blood everywhere, and ghastly devastation for all to see—you did not realize that the intact woman standing next to you was nowhere to be found. She vacated her house before she lived in it.

"I remember the moment," she tells you. Each time I remember the moment it could be any other moment. It is all moments. Like the report of an Israeli doctor who has to decide whether to treat someone or not. Who gets care in an emergency? The mutilated ones, of course. The bleeding bodies. They are obvious. Everyone knows they must be cared for if they have a chance of living. The aids were passing over a lady shaking, crying for help. She did not feel anything except something wrong. Something was wrong and she didn't know what. No visible wounds, no signs. The doctor took one look and said, "Treat her!" She, too, must be included. No one could tell that the force of explosive waves knocked her lungs out. Quaking air passing through her destroyed her lungs.

My patient, Leila, paused to let her words sink in. I saw a child in a house of important (certainly, self-important) people. She looked alive. She looked like a person. How could they know she was not there? It would take a special doctor, a special person, to see insides blown away by invisible forces. She had become that special kind of person who can see feelings that are not there. Almost as a response to deficit, she developed a very special psychic sensitivity. If you were dead, wounded, or hollowed out and standing next to her, she might notice. She knows the explosive force of invisible waves and has the touch a person sometimes needs.

It is difficult to notice or know what to do. She was sent to therapists as a child, but they tried to pressure her into life. They did not dwell on the fact that she was "gone." They built on her "thereness." Natural enough, but "gone" was left out. Perhaps they played for time, hoping she would outgrow it. How could a house of love create an emotional vacuum? Perhaps the best thing to do if a child feels bad is to pretend not to notice and let things slide, hoping they will change. But the vacuum settles into place, a vanished place eating life's insides. It was a relief, long into adulthood, to find a therapy that did not torment her into life, so that her special kind of sensitivity found breathing room.

Vance, too, was relentless in documenting emotional abuse. "My mother said I was somber. I felt a blackness in her pores, in her vagina, a poison." He could not get over the feeling of having sex with her, although there was little evidence this literally happened. The feeling was vivid—an intense fantasy feeling that consumed his body, filled his pores, as if his cells fed on images of her sickness. She was beautiful in face and body but not there. Another bombed-out being, gone. Were corpses in beautiful bodies being invisibly warehoused and injected into mothers after they gave birth? Where are all these gone people coming from? Were they always there? We just did not notice? We noticed but did not want to see? We could not see because we dare not feel such helplessness?

"My father tried to hide my dysphoria. *You* could be filled with compassion but I have no feeling for it. It's too scary to be attached to you. You're too scary, not attentive enough. Do you know how to carry a person in your body?

"My mother stared with vacant eyes. Her emptiness did not rise to the level of contempt. Others had contempt when it came to emotional things. My father pretended to be interested but he wanted things to be OK. He did not want to know or feel what I felt. My feelings were so much drama, window dressing, not serious enough to count. He dismissed them. His final judgment, 'You're too sensitive.' Implying I had it easy, he had it hard. *He* knew life and rose to meet it. He toughed it out. My pain was child's play. *He* had the feelings that counted."

There were broad, rough parallels between Vance's and Leila's backgrounds: holes in mothering, floods in fathering. Leila's mother was ill, dying slowly throughout her childhood. In a photo of her holding Leila in infancy, her eyes were glazed, not quite seeing, not merely self-referential or uncomfortable, but somehow stopping at some invisible barrier before they met the infant's gaze. Her father filled the hole with emotional storms, intermittent morning rages, rushes of affect, love, sudden caring, erotic streamings, and jokes—everything was funny. He tried to be related every moment he was not working. Everything was tears. Tears were funny too. He was as filled with life as her mother was with death. But it was the wrong kind of fullness, to match the wrong kind of emptiness. The baby and child was lost in a space that vanished and filled with noise. Emotional tumult blotted her out, could not find her in the dying. Her family was gifted. She was gifted too. Gifts filled with worms, and inside the worms, creative treasures. For Vance and Leila everything was organized and collapsed around the mother's illness and filled out and inflated, around the father's energy, self-importance, self-centered outpourings, and depressive exuberance; a balloon that never was fully inflated and another always about to pop.

Vance and Leila were galled by the father's lie-infested energy, as if lying made him strong or vitality gave a right to lie. Lying was an ego thing but went deeper. Vance discovered his father lied about everything, could not help it. He lied about the truth. Perhaps what galled Vance most was that his father's picture of himself was a ghastly lie, a lie that made living possible, in a life that made lying necessary. He talked as if life mattered, people mattered, and feelings mattered. But what really mattered were *his* feelings, *his* use of life and people. He did as he liked and made believe he was thinking of others. Vance could not stomach this fundamental dishonesty. It made him a satellite of his father's ego. He could not stomach worshipping a god that did not see him, a god that insistently missed the mark, nearly totally egocentric and self-excusing. Whatever god did was right; what Vance did was wrong.

Yet Vance worshipped him with a love that tore Vance to pieces. His father was beautiful in his eyes. A beauty that ripped his heart out. Primal devotion — where can it go? In Leila it found its way to God. She had a lifelong love affair with God, a love–hate relation, to be sure. But it made her more forgiving of others, if not herself. No such luxury for Vance. He was stuck on his father and his father's betrayal of the god-image, an image both played roles in creating. What happens when you discover there is no difference between God and the golden calf? That neither exists or both are everywhere?

What happened to Vance was he became a high achiever who swallowed the hook of severity. Not only was nothing good enough, but "goodness" itself was a theory, a construct he knew but could not feel. He tried his best to be good and to live a good life. But what he felt most was being bad, the rage, the terror, the hate, the dread. The lie in everything scratched his eyes out. He could not let it go, and he did not know what use to make of it, except self-torment. He knew he should take pleasure in life. Pleasure existed, joy existed (his father's overt message?). But what he actually felt was evil everywhere. His father lived by looking away from anything bad in himself, justifying it. Vance could not look away from the destroying, destroyed self. As if atoning for his father's psychopathy, it was as if he could not give in until all psychopathy in the world disappeared.

Any opening of his heart was intensely painful. It has taken years, but there *are* openings. They close fast enough, but cannot be denied. They are there (too), these moments of opening. And they are valued, even if devaluation catches up with them. "Heart feels," he says. "My heart — a little node on an organic, venous column, and it hurts so badly sometimes. Little moments of love." Five minutes later he spoke about the importance of integrity, how corruption kills, and how integrity kills. Someone at a meeting told him he acted like "an incorruptible judge. Stainless steel." Immediately Vance saw corrosion behind the steel. He fell quiet and in a little while a moment of recovery came. "I'm just learning to talk with people. It's the last part of my life and I'm just learning to talk with someone who disagrees with me. To speak with someone who disagrees and not break off, not disconnect or try to win. To listen, to speak." Here is a moment that escaped the father's knife, escaped Abraham's blade, but not soon enough to escape the posttraumatic shock that followed the sons of Isaac. A new kind of burning bush, corrosion eating good moments that totally vanish yet endure. To listen, to speak—a new kind of life, a life of moments.

Leila lives a gifted spiritual life with friends, fellow seekers, and family. Most of her hate is directed against herself. She is ill like her mother, but unlike her mother, she is up and around, living as fully as her frame allows and living beyond her frame. She is rich in life. But, like Vance, severe. There is a devil that accuses her, that gives no rest. Everything is a sign that something is wrong with her essentially, that she is miscreated. It is a drill that goes deeper and strikes no oil. She could be singing, praying, and talking with her partner, and it tightens in the background, defeats her.

In their different ways, Vance and Leila share this severity, this drill, this devil. What is it? How does it work? In O'Connor's (1971) writings, destroyers aim at phoniness, especially phony goodness. Not just vices, but anything off, taints in virtues, any false move or tone or use of a function—a destroyer gets it. As I suggest in an earlier work (Eigen 1998, chap. 6), her destroyers are like sharks cleaning psychic garbage. No end to psychic garbage, no end to destruction. This destructive force works in a seek and destroy mode, attracted to lies.

Is this not different from the traditional Devil, the father of lies? The devil, too, is a destructive force. Its work is not cleaning up goodness but the latter's destruction. It nourishes itself by destroying goodness. There are variations, substories. Satan (Kluger, 1967; Eigen, 1993, pp. 200–208) was initially an accuser, like a prosecutor in a court of law. Satan, as a special kind of lawyer, served a legal function. He used law to prove fault. He exposed flaws, failings, and hypocrisies—like O'Connor's destroyer, like Vance's, like Leila's, whether directed at others or self. He sought to prove souls unworthy of God's love. He sought to prove goodness spurious, no man good.

Christianity made Satan's job a little tougher, insofar as law no longer was a conclusive arbiter. A pivot point was grace. Accusation and destruction struck deeper. It was not enough to prove a soul guilty of sin or crime or black mark. The soul itself was sinful and dependent on God's grace for redemption. Satan cut into the heart of the soul, and only faith in the mystery of

God's free work at such a depth could make a difference. However, as time goes on, the destroyer makes inroads in each new playground.

As often happens in the mind of man, one age's villain becomes another's hero. Satan, the envious angel, brought low by prideful rebellion, began to be recognized as an important source of energy, linked with the power of his "faults." Pride, envy, ambition, sexuality, the will to power, destructive force—signs of vitality, partly re-worked by Blake, Nietzsche, and Freud. For Blake, reason became a tyrant, a force of severity, reducing reality to reason's limits, needing to be qualified by other dimensions, other worlds, and other functions. The work of destruction continues, sliding through fashions.

In our present age of ambiguity, irony, and equivocation, any tendency can function many ways: destructively or generatively, both. Alchemical and mystical models invite us to mix opposites, sublimate lower to higher (now also, higher to lower), and value contributions diverse capacities make in acts of transformation. Bringing together, mixing, transcending opposites, and valuing capacities—sounds good, is important. But is the daily life of a Vance or Leila caught in a destructive spin? A torment, perhaps a mockery. Good for those who can, sometimes good for moments for those who cannot. But missing—a little like their parents and most of the adult world—where Vance and Leila live, where they must go.

Bion touches the substrate these people gravitate toward, dwell in, when he writes of a "force that continues after . . . it destroys existence, time, and space" (1965, p. 101). This is an amplification or extension of Freud's "force against recovery" (1937) and Klein's "destructive force within" (1946). I think he pins the issue. He is stating directly what these people feel. He is describing exactly what they are up against, what they say they are subject to, and what they report over and over with the greatest anguish and chagrin, because no one sees it or believes them. No one sees it as it is.

Vance and Leila may live full lives, although Vance does not connect with his and Leila is constantly under self-attack. Not just the externals are there. Vance and Leila are extremely sensitive beings; sensitivity filled with riches. They undergo experiences few are aware of or can take. They survive the worst repeatedly. They are taking medication, which provides some relief, but does not stop the process they must undergo. They know Bion's description (1965) inside their guts and fear it will never end.

Trauma plays a role in the initial shock. It gets things rolling, and then destruction takes on a momentum of its own. The cardinal player now is their own natures. Will they ever recover from themselves? Vance holds on to the evil his parents inflicted. Leila mainly annihilates herself, looking for proof of shame, degradation, or banishment. She fears she is beyond the place where humanity lives; no one can find her. No matter how emotionally, spiritually full her life—she fears she is not seen or valued. Not only is she invisible but somehow maimed and warped beyond the human. She and Vance have discovered inner monstrosity, although to most people they look fine.

A sick, deranged id seeks a monstrous ego. Damage, warp, and something twisted runs through us. A trauma world is a permanent part of the psyche, and we do the best we can with it. It does not go away. We have an eye on it and an eye on health, a special sort of binocularity. Images of health and illness fuse and split. We are stuck between being unable to distinguish between them, getting the distinctions wrong, or dividing them in so extreme a way that we further alienate ourselves, increasing a sense of exile.

Vance and Leila feel monstrous, feel monstrous things happened to them, feel they emerged from a family of monsters. Monsters they love; monsters they hate. The latter, more so Vance. Leila felt monstrous by contrast with the great people around her. An atmosphere of gifted, self-important people drove her into the ground. Abuse takes many forms, endless unseen variations of disaster. Leila felt grateful if someone noticed that she felt something or, miracle (nearly never), came close to noticing with some precision (even in a generic way) what it might be. For Vance, feelings were something exploited by others. For Leila, they were a pipeline to God or an SOS to people who looked the other way.

Deranged ids seeking monstrous egos turned into psychopathic/depressive shells by omnivorously murderous superegos (a great "paradox"—superegos devoid of ethics): destructive waves. The living soul breathes in an atmosphere made of annihilating forces and breathes in a sense of catastrophe. Catastrophe becomes part of the cement that binds personality, links it to others. Nothing is more binding than damaged bonds or more mesmerizing than toxic nourishment, especially when ecstasy merges with rage and terror. (Eigen 1999, 2001a, 2001b, 2002; for Bion's sense of catastrophe as link, see Eigen 1998, chaps. 3–6 and 1996, chaps. 1, 2, 4–6, 12, 16).

One of the great secrets of trauma is that it trades in radiance. And it is not simply that radiance and black hole mirror, filter, and mix with each other, which they do. Pain and something beatific inextricably fuse, creating a more intense, endurable bond than either alone. One becomes bonded to one's own deranged structures, self as one knows it, as well as to warps of others. Early writings on masochism and attachment to suffering are helpful but do not do the trick.

Freud (1937, pp. 240–47) recognized a certain helplessness in face of a destructive force he could not fathom. Blake (1790–1793) recognized Satan's radiance. There are heavenly and hellish ecstasies and everything between. Radiance is not limited to goodness. Demonic glows captivate, enthrall. People come alive through demonic orgasms, even when intensity of aliveness reverses into agonizing deadness.

Proof of the power of a destructive force (Freud, 1937; Klein, 1946; Bion, 1965) is that it never lets go. There is no final victory over it, although it sometimes claims a final victory for itself. If you are a rager and fight your rage, you will have to continue fighting it your whole life long. Let down your guard, and the flash takes you by surprise. In a blink, you traumatized someone and yourself once more. It takes less than a moment to become a terror, and recovery may take a lifetime. Reactive, incendiary rage is only one example. On the other side of the coin, if you are a self-decimator, your work is endless too. Again, no final victory. This tendency can run you into the ground, even make you ill in an instant. Either way (out or in), you place yourself or others in danger. Danger—disaster—is a constant in the background.

Destructive power is relentless. It never stops grinding one down. Vance and Leila have beautiful experiences, love moments, erotic breakthroughs, heart openings, love of learning, and rich experiences with friends, loved ones. Leila has felt God many times. Vance has visions of goodness and love that he admits are authentic, even if destruction washes them away. He cannot say if he has never had these tastes, more than tastes. All the more tormenting that hate and terror decimate them, an unknown annihilating force mocks them. Vance and Leila get through their days as best they can. They do not give in. They try to stay the course and undergo what must be undergone. They do their best and feel their best cannot be good enough. They struggle with themselves and may die in the struggle.

Freud made real inroads, inferring important consequences from the infant's period of dependence on parental might, good will, skill, and kindliness, especially emphasizing paternal protection and maternal nourishment. Fusions of hostile pushing away, taking in, hostile and loving dependence, satisfaction, and assertion form an affective background marked by a multiplicity of tendencies. The mother plays a special role in regulating distress.

Of special importance is the infant's sense of helplessness, which feeds idealization of helpers (Freud, 1921). The other must do for the infant what the infant cannot do for itself. There must be someone somewhere who can do it better. Helplessness fuses with rage, terror, idealization, and love. Other researchers qualify infantile helplessness. After all, helplessness is an adult construction read into the infant. The infant does what it is able, plays a role in mutual adaptation, seeks the nipple, adjusts its body, and helps regulate stimulation. It feels its oats and its way, enjoying activity and the mutual play of energies. Again, the infant may seem to be helpless yet feel omnipotent and boundless, possibly identifying with the other's capacities. In clinical work, a sense of helplessness and being controlling go together.

Klein's (1946, 1957; Eigen 1996, chaps. 1–3) formulations emphasize the use of good feelings to offset bad ones. Libido defends against the death drive. Life-affirming feelings play down destructive ones, especially difficult when destructive urges increase aliveness. Idealization is used as a defense against hostile anxiety, ultimately against the destructive urge within, yet often becoming part of it. The ego tries to save a sense of goodness in a psyche awash in annihilation dread. Idealizing goodness is one precarious, if often rigid, gambit. Goodness itself may become suffocating.

Helplessness tends to get lost in Klein's (1946) account, buried in drive or ego activity, the warrior attempts to offset anxieties concerning destruction. Psyche is inherently active, as life is, but gains extra impetus defending against helplessness. Helplessness acts as a kind of rocket launcher, although it never is sloughed off. Helplessness may be helpful in generating cultural activity, but it remains a living undercurrent, an essential part of our reality that we pay a price for. We propel ourselves away from feeling helpless, but we cannot escape it in the end.

Our culture is phobic about helplessness. Helplessness is bad, associated with being a victim, getting poor health care, being poor in general, and being subject to disasters one could protect against if one were more active. One should be proactive, fix things, work to make things better, redress injury and wrong, and be an active agent of choice and desire. Emphasis on control spins out of control, like the recent rash and crash of corporate greed, getting high on money and letting the rest of reality go to hell. Such heady greed runs through our world, a hypertrophy of "I can and will and have a right to." Why not milk the economy and political system for all its worth? A sickly version of following one's dream, with desire degraded to material terms. One feels shame and guilt at not being an inflated-enough version of oneself. One feels shame and guilt if one is not a successful enough psychopath.

Psychopathic hypocrisy is precisely what Vance hated in his father. His father performed fatherly duties by initiating his son into the ways of the world. Vance found what he was expected to take in revolting and clung to the underside of life, yet established a niche that worked. He did not lie down and die in the face of the lying nature of life. But the lie stuck in his gut, and he could not digest it. The rape of goodness or pretense of goodness left him desolate. He saw the rage at helplessness everywhere, and helpless rage mounted.

Freud cataloged aspects of helplessness: birth anxiety, sexual and aggressive anxieties, intrusion, separation, abandonment anxieties, castration anxiety, death anxiety, mortifications associated with ambition and work and everyday interchanges, as well as wounds of all sorts, wounds to sensitivity, and sensitivity in danger of being flooded, going under, going into shock, numbing, going dead, dreading the onset of aliveness again. Baffled but trying to learn something about recovery. Freud wrote about our struggles to defend against anxieties associated with one or another form of helplessness, only to become imprisoned by our personality, the fortress we work so hard to maintain.

Vance rages at the prison, the crime of making believe personality is worth inhabiting, when it really is a killing machine. He hears that personality opens avenues of experience closed to him, not simply closed so much as not believable. He believes there are others who love, who are true, and who care. But he sees the lies of life like flies blanketing his eyes, stuffing his ears and insides. He can not laugh or take it lightly. I have never heard Vance laugh. He is serious about pain. Every lie grows from, is attached to, bears witness to, and promotes pain. Where he sees lies, he sees trauma. People should stop and look and listen, admit they are killing machines, admit they are helpless. He wants the world to care. If it did, he would not believe it, but he would long to believe.

Bion (1965, 1970; Eigen, 1998, chap. 3) pulled on threads of Freud and Klein and made an art of helplessness. He saw that precocious activity often made matters worse and suggested that passivity in the face of evil could be more effective. This was not a matter of nonresistance but more a waiting on reality, letting impacts build and transform, becoming familiar with what one is up against, and opening to unknown possibilities. In therapy, what one confronts is the disaster of personality, disaster that binds personality together, and disaster that personality binds. What one confronts are ways personality responds to its traumatic plight. One finds ways to squeeze the sense of disaster into controllable packets, even if one creates simulacra of disaster to control. Very much like the psychotic who thinks he can stop going crazy only to find out he cannot—we try to control what we cannot control and settle for what we can (usually another delusion).

Catastrophe plays a major role in Bion's picture. A new thought shakes, if not shatters, a person. New feelings make one tremble. Two people meeting create impacts neither is equipped to handle. Emotional big bangs are everywhere, and we keep growing to try to endure and process them. We grow or get worse but cannot stay the same. Bion calls the attitude of openness to experience faith. He calls the unknowable reality that impacts "O." Openness to O-impacts, faith in the unknowable, catastrophic O. There is not much one can do except try to be available to the impact and the processing of impacts and grow with the processing as it grows with you. This reaching toward openness, faith in O, is an ethics and a practice. It is unlike the self-aggrandizing practice of the dominant culture (Vance's and Leila's fathers), but a challenge to do right by experience.

Few authors express this kind of openness to sensitivity as fully as Rilke (1977) (*Duino Elegies*). He seems wholly bent on letting experience speak, holding on to nothing, giving himself to the impact of moment as it builds, transforms, opens, and shatters. He stays close to terror. Even beauty is terrible when it does its work, when one cannot shut out the feel of things, insofar as one can bear, past what one can bear. Rilke opens the lid and speaks from the opening more than most. Every angel is terrible, he says, and one must open through this terror to find the place of poetry. The moment of helplessness arrives when experience sears, stings, festers, ripples, and vibrates. One lives for it. Without terror of opening, what sort of being could we be? Experience strikes us dumb; then poetry comes.

Is this one reason why Vance and Leila hold terror for us? Because we cling to terror as it clings to them? Adhesive terror that rips beyond pieces. They cling to traumatic impacts no one wants to know about and which no one can do anything about. Impacts that make one helpless, that reveal one's helplessness. Are they the failed poets of helplessness, or is the torment of their lives that poetry? Their torment is a revelation of what our successful world cannot leave behind. Our high-flying world cannot shake off the sense of catastrophe that marks us. Its solutions exacerbate the terror and rage, even as it makes living easier, better (longer life expectancy, higher material, educational level for many, more money, power, freedom, choice, etc.). Annihilation creeps through good feelings meant to wipe it out. We use good feelings to annihilate annihilation and are surprised when good feelings explode. For a moment, helplessness is revealed, but only for a moment. Recovery begins, mastery regroups, but dread does not end. It is difficult to take in that good feelings are not always good, certainly not identical with goodness, and that hate can be more powerful. Are Vance and Leila ahead of us? They have no doubt that terror and hate are real. They will not be bought off by programs meant to enforce a sense of power.

Rilke opens to anguish, terror, and beauty, to the trauma of sensitivity, to the impact of love/no love, to the impact of time, to presence/absence, and to the impact of sensitivity itself. He is so sensitive to sensitivity. He alerts us to give the world to itself by transforming it—precisely by letting it have an impact inside us, letting impact incubate, visible become invisible, swirling, dropping into dream-work, poet-work, alpha function[1]—passing through psychic digestive systems, tasting, transmuting experience, with psychical beings working like new kinds of worms.

Bion is open to destruction, catastrophe, disaster, how life undoes life, and how life frightens life. This is his faith discipline, his moment of transformation, his opening to the world. He does not let it go, any more than Vance or Leila do. Mixtures of rapture, hate, terror, rage, rupture. He never budges. He stays and stays and lets the worst speak. He tells us this trauma world is real; it is part of the real world, the regular world. It is even part of the dominant culture, with its lust for mastery and confidence. Winning will not make it go away. Neither winning nor losing is decisive in this realm. He keeps sensitivity open to forces which make one insensitive, which make one scream, which make one stop screaming as one tries to shut everything out, especially the sound of one's life. He keeps sensitivity open to what happens as it begins to go under. He supports the individual's journey through being murdered and enduring a process of recovery, acknowledging helplessness as a dimension of repair. The work of helplessness—helplessness does work too.

I suspect Rilke's murder may be more exquisite than Bion's, no less dreadful, but more exquisite. Deliciousness is not too far away, if one stays with the trembling, the blackout, the resonance. His poetry opens places we have been too scared to believe in; precious places we need, where we live an inner life like bird wings fluttering, shaking sparks of water in the fiery air. Bion keeps his eye on desolation and explosiveness and how we attack the process Rilke discovers. We best not make believe we are not explosive or that we know what to do with this part of our nature. A measure of acknowledged helplessness may aid the quality of approach.

I am not speaking against feeling one's oats, crowing about one's successes, living one's vital nature, or enjoying one's active aliveness. I know ambition, power, social interchange, and give and take—the stuff of life. I am saying, though, give helplessness a chance. Do not leave helplessness behind. Not just because Vance and Leila will not let us, although that is true enough. There are many kinds of Vances and Leilas in this world, many levels, qualities, tones, and situations. Many sorts of abuse exist around us: the terror in families, in oneself, as well as between groups, nations, peoples; and God's terrors.

There is a moment of helplessness that stops our breath, a quick shock, before we jump into action. I propose we do more tasting of that moment, sifting it, letting our faith muscle grow, as building tolerance for the fleeting shock begins to transform us. We are a race—the human race—of soul terrors. Righting economic, political, social, familial, military wrongs helps, helps a lot. But soul terrors, fragility, vulnerability do not end. It is a utopian fantasy to think they will. We ought not live our whole lives in terms of our fears, and certainly not our hates. But we cannot leave them behind. We need to open up and try to learn what we can do with them, with ourselves. Experts tell us all sorts of things. Sometimes they are helpful, sometimes not. Human nature is not something anyone is expert about, and medicine will not solve the problem, short of medicating much of humanity (which may be happening).[2]

Society has not left Vance and Leila behind. They do well in life. They live the fullest life they can, given their talents, abilities, disabilities. But each is caught by a downside they cannot shake out of, not with therapy, nor medication. Seeking help has helped. They make richer, fuller use of themselves than they could without it. They have a wider range of experiences. I honestly think without help they could have died. Still, what feels most real, most true to Vance is his terror and rage. He believes in love and truth, wants to believe in it. But his truth is trauma and emotional abuse. That is what he sees when he looks around, covered with good will, good feelings, and the will to power. He sees egos exploiting souls. He knows there is love in his home, the home he built, his family, his friends, and his colleagues, and in the world he helped create. He acts as if he were loving, hoping the feeling will take. But his truth is elsewhere: misery, suicidal sense of being a monster, killer in a race of killers, states of terror, helplessness and rage. He wishes therapy would transform him, free him, but given that he is who he is, the next best thing is bearing witness, so the world knows that such things exist and that normalizing ideas do not make it better.

Leila believes in radiance, the beauty in life. It is real for her. God is real. Spirit is real, the life of the senses deliciously real. Her crises of faith are elsewhere. What kind of God permits the useless agonies people undergo, ghastly illness, a psyche subject to every nuance of fragility, every dreadful whisper and agony magnified? How has she endured such suffering and survived? How could she have been so unseen, dropped, empty, so stuffed with emotional noise and peoples' egos as a child? She could not help but feel ashamed. Her pain was a signal of failure. God must think she is awful. She *is* awful. Hate fills her pores but she barely feels it. It seeps into her like poison. She pulls back, rigid, tries to hide but she cannot make her insides go away. Hate is a judgment, a condemnation. She can never be a human being. To be merely wooden like Pinocchio would be a blessing.

Vances and Leilas will exist as long as traumatized sensitivity exists, as long as we wound each other and make believe we know what to do about it. To be helpless in face of our predicament is no shame. To struggle with it is no shame either.

NOTES

1. Alpha function—Bion's term for whatever work is done to begin digesting life's impact, including our impact on ourselves. It overlaps with "primary process" and "dream-work," which help initiate the processing of affect. He said he chose such a term to keep things open, to remind us we do not know very much about how we digest experience and make life real. In one talk, he described alpha as a nest where birds of meaning might alight (Bion, 1980; Eigen, 2001a, chaps. 1–4, and 2004, chaps. 2–4).

2. For discussion of what is left after everything is "fixed," see Eigen, *Rage* (2002), pp. 170–79.

REFERENCES

Bion, W. R. (1965). *Transformations*. London: Heinemann.

———. (1970). *Attention and interpretation*. London: Tavistock.

———. (1980). *Bion in New York and Sao Paulo*. Perthshire: Clunie Press.

Blake, W. (n.p., 1790–1793). *The marriage of heaven and hell.*

Eigen, M. (1993). *The electrified tightrope.* A. Phillips (Ed.), Northvale, NJ: Jason Aronson.

———. (1996). *Psychic deadness.* Northvale, NJ: Jason Aronson.

———. (1998). *The psychoanalytic mystic.* London: Free Association Books.

———. (1999). *Toxic nourishment.* London: Karnac Books.

———. (2001a). *Damaged bonds.* London: Karnac Books.

———. (2001b). *Ecstasy.* Middletown, CT: Wesleyan University Press.

———. (2002). *Rage.* Middletown, CT: Wesleyan University Press.

———. (2004). *The sensitive self.* Middletown, CT: Wesleyan University Press.

Freud, S. (1900). The interpretation of dreams. *Standard Edition*, 4/5, pp. 1–361. London: Hogarth Press.

———. (1921). Group psychology and the analysis of the ego. *Standard Edition*, 19, pp. 65–143. London: Hogarth Press.

———. (1937). Analysis terminable and interminable. *Standard Edition*, 23, pp. 216–53. London: Hogarth Press.

Klein, M. (1946/1952). Notes on some schizoid mechanisms. In M. Klein, P. Heinemann, S. Isaacs, and J. Riviere (Eds.), *Developments in psychoanalysis*, pp. 292–320. London: Hogarth Press.

———. (1957). *Envy and gratitude.* London: Tavistock.

Kluger, R. S. (1967). *Satan in the Old Testament.* Evanston, IL: Northwestern University Press.

O'Connor, F. (1971) *The complete stories.* New York: Farrar, Straus and Giroux.

Rilke, M. R. (1977). *Duino Elegies* (David Young, Trans.). New York: Norton.

Chapter Twenty-seven

Terror and Forgiveness

Robert Karen

Terrorism is a trauma for the group, much as it is for individuals. Primitive defenses, such as splitting and projective identification, are a normal response to trauma, but they generate a pernicious style of group functioning, often including a fixation on purity, purges, and revenge. Such defenses are contagious and rapidly incorporate many people within the group. They also elicit parallel defensive strategies in adversary groups, thereby promoting escalation and the likelihood of more trauma. I argue that for the group, as for the individual, mourning is a necessary antidote to primitive defenses and to the obsessions that typically accompany them; that forgiveness, when extracted from the realm of piety, has an important role to play in mobilizing a response to terror; that monotheism, often a force for polarization, can also be understood developmentally as the basis for tolerance and complexity. I ask: Can a society bring to the international arena a level of maturity that is only rarely exercised interpersonally? Can understanding the psychotic potential in group functioning help innoculate a society against the extremes of herd mentality and behavior, both at home and abroad? A psychoanalytic view of a nation's response to terror is discussed.

One week after September 11, Susan Stamberg conducted a strained and solemn interview with three clergymen on National Public Radio concerning their religion's response to terrorism. The ten-minute segment ended on the subject of forgiveness. The three men, a Christian, a Jew, and a Muslim, all favored it ("Christ forgave those who crucified him," etc.), with the Muslim alone insisting on the added necessity of punishment. Few in the audience, let alone in the studio, could have had much interest at that moment in their common humanity with people who had just murdered thousands of their countrymen. But nobody on the panel said the obvious human thing: "I'm not ready to talk about forgiveness when we're still breathing in the air of our dead; I'm too full of rage." So instead we heard a reasonable sermon about the importance of forgiving even those things that are most difficult to forgive, and I think most people promptly forgot it.

I remembered it because I had just written a book about forgiveness and was wondering whether and how forgiveness might be seen as relevant to a nation in mourning from a terrorist attack and mobilizing itself for war. What I heard that day not only felt unreassuring on this point but disappointingly lifeless, a condition that I attributed to defensive processes, mainly splitting and dissociation.

The clergymen said nothing about their own hatred of the terrorists or their wishes for revenge. They did not talk about how hard it might be for them to live up to their faith's expectations, not to mention their doubts, if they had any, about whether forgiveness even made sense. So to that extent they were splitting off some piece of their own experience and, perhaps, inadvertently suggesting the world itself is split—into those who embody higher ideals and those who do not—a kind of reductionism and loss of complexity that often accompanies the splitting process. The three were present that day because National Public Radio (NPR) wanted them to be the voice of their religions within days of the greatest massacre of civilians in American history, a seductive expectation. It seemed, maybe as a result, as if they were unconsciously determined to embody a purity that did not allow for unkind feelings. So they dissociated themselves from those feelings, as if they did not exist, and, thus, did not feel them. A related process of splitting and dissociation—and a similar quest for purity—is emblematic of the psychology of the terrorist.

Terrorists split off their human concern rather than their rage, which enables them to do terrible things to those they perceive as enemies (Segal, 2003). They also view the world as split into good and evil, which makes them feel entitled to a hatred and aggression undiluted by doubt. Their passion and certainty, their woundedness and fixation on righteous revenge can be contagious among people who experience themselves as downtrodden. The pious ideal of forgiveness, in contrast, has very little appeal to anyone, especially in times of strife, and is quietly dismissed as preachy and irrelevant. Bland compassion and piety are no match for paranoia and resentment, which are hard to beat in the best of circumstances. It is rare that a leader like Mahatma Gandhi emerges who can even temporarily turn this equation on its head.

Is there a more Gandhian approach to our current dilemma? One that offers a way out of dissociation, splitting, and escalation? One that is not a disguised form of masochism, that does not induce paralysis, but that emerges from the secure self? People tend to associate Gandhi with nonviolence, but Gandhi was a relentless fighter who was able to preserve the humanity of his adversary. In this sense he also stood for the preservation of wholeness and complexity.

Because forgiveness is almost always conceptualized in pious terms, its fate since September 11 has not been a happy one: to be spoken about in platitudes and tossed aside as wholly irrelevant to the sort of person one actually is or to life as one actually lives it. And yet, the subject—"Can we forgive?"—does keep popping up, as if there is an itch in the body politic that keeps needing a scratch. I think the itch is important, but the conceptualization is wrong.

The question is not—"Can we forgive Osama bin Laden?"—but how do we preserve our own wholeness and complexity? How do we keep from succumbing to a traumatic environment, which by its very nature forces dangerous splits and simplifications? The drift toward splitting and projection creates an atmosphere in which people cannot bear nuance, ambiguity, or doubt. They come to hold narrower and narrower points of view, while those they dismiss as irrational, softheaded, or insidious are seen as rigidly adhering to other views they can no longer tolerate in themselves.

If the ability to live with ambiguity and difference is a key marker of maturity in individuals, as Erikson held (1968), the same standard seems to apply to groups. But as splitting and projection accelerate, this tolerance, never huge to begin with, rapidly erodes. It might have a better chance of holding its ground if more of the population, including those in power, were aware of, and prepared to deal with, the irrational processes unleashed in times of conflict. Unfortunately, these processes, although well known in psychoanalysis and dealt with daily by people in clinical practice, are rarely considered in social or political contexts.

Retaining complexity also calls for expansion of the idea of forgiveness itself. Forgiveness needs to be understood not so much as a final act, where all sense of anger and resentment is erased and replaced by warm regard, but as a whole set of internal processes, states of mind, and creative measures that emanate from the secure self and that form a resistance to splitting and projection. These capacities, far from promoting a bland "do-gooderism," are really the foundation of nuanced thinking. They enable one to keep one's head in the face of irrational hatred; to thoughtfully consider criticism, even hostile criticism; and to make positive gestures even when one feels unfairly afflicted. They represent the sort of strength and self-confidence we recognize in good parents and good therapists, both of whom need to almost literally clamp themselves together, to keep their love and aggression from becoming dissociated, in the service of maintaining a connection with a child or patient who is consumed by rage.

In a political leader or diplomat, these strengths optimize the possibility that he[1] will become neither inflamed by insults nor cowed by threats but deal effectively with other regimes, even those with manipulative, bellicose, or irrational leaders, and will build rapprochements that leave his country in a more lastingly secure position. The part of the self from which forgiveness emanates can, thus, be understood as essential for the exercise of foreign policy, which must always be able to encompass both aggression and reconciliation and cannot afford to be held hostage to either.

So here, too, we have a subtle, critical, far more pressing question than "Can we forgive the terrorists?" In this case: How in times like these do we hold onto the forgiving aspects of the self, which are associated with our most mature responses?

If comprehended this way—as critical to the preservation of complexity, a resistance to the dumbing-down mechanisms that run wild in states of conflict, and the retention of mature elements of the self—forgiveness has a fateful role to play in a society's mobilization to face an external challenge. But it must be talked about and understood. It needs a constituency.

Obviously, to begin with, no one wants to forgive mass murderers. We want to catch them, bring them to justice, see them dead, and so forth. We are not particularly concerned about them as people, at least not when they are on the loose. It would be good and healthy if we could "recognize the humanity of the perpetrator[s]," as Desmond Tutu recommends (Simpkinson, 2001), but most of us cannot honestly do that. We make them into objects, and we do not care because of the damage they have done and their capacity to do more. Talk of forgiving them when their crimes are still fresh and unpunished is revolting, not least of all because it interferes with the side of the self that is concerned with immediate survival and the need to act efficaciously. (Splitting and dissociation do have positive uses.) But we are not just in the business of catching criminals but also of making friends and forging alliances, and some of the friends we want to make are people who have some pretty nasty feelings and attitudes about us. If we are to beckon them out of those positions, we need to be able to tolerate, to live with, and to *forgive* that they have taken them. Otherwise, we become the insecure bully who will show the world what he can do to people who do not like us.

Even with those like bin Laden, whose humanity is difficult to grasp, this issue is not entirely irrelevant. If we imagine bin Laden in captivity, with all that he represents no longer a threat; if we imagine him in a pitiful state; or if we imagine him going through some sort of transformation or conversion that leaves him genuinely repentant and weeping as he voluntarily donates all his funds for the reconstruction of lower Manhattan—we might alter how we view him. *Just knowing this*—that we are capable of splitting, of demonizing our enemies, but that there is at least a jot of contingency to it, and that it is within us to retract that demonization—represents both a preservation of complexity as well as a shift toward the forgiving end of the spectrum. It softens our tendency to view the world in good-versus-evil terms and moves us, however slightly, toward recognition of the humanity in those we fight, even if it is a humanity that at the moment we would prefer to ignore. Such a shift, small as it is, has policy implications.

The ability to retain complexity would also enable us to resist spreading the demonization too widely—to refrain from equating all of al Qaeda with its leadership, to feel concern for some of its young fighters and their families, to not equate all of fundamentalist Islam with al Qaeda, to be on the alert for receptivity and common ground in a population we might be too inclined to think of as one hating mass. It would show up in how we conduct ourselves in conflict, in attempts to reach out to those who can be reached, in our willingness to think about our own wrongs, and, where possible, to rectify or apologize for them. Inhabiting this larger emotional space might improve our position with a world whose sympathy we owned on September 11 and have largely squandered since.

SPLITTING AND THE QUESTION OF EVIL

The people who planned and executed the attack on the World Trade Center and the Pentagon see the U.S. government and perhaps the American people as demonic and worthy of destruction (*Frontline*, 2001). In response, we wish not only to protest our goodness but to annihilate them in return. The "we" I am talking about here, as well as the "they," is a complex issue in itself. There are many "wes" and many "theys," and the multiplicity exists within each person as well as within each group. That multiplicity, like all forms of complexity, is at risk in a traumatic environment. We can learn something about this oscillation between binary and complex thinking by looking at how the capacity to tolerate complexity and ambiguity arises in human beings to begin with.

It is widely held in the psychoanalytic world that the baby maintains separate universes for the good and the bad, such that each person, himself included, is experienced in two almost entirely disconnected ways—wonderful and beloved or evil and persecutory—depending on the moment. Mom is beatific when the baby feels good, persecuting and hateful when it has gas pains, when it is overtired, or when its cries are unheeded, with no sense in the earliest days that the person or thing it is loving now is the same one it was hating two minutes ago. In the 1930s and 1940s, analyst Melanie Klein argued that the infant, beset by primitive fantasies, by fears of persecution, of the destruction of the good object, and of the rudimentary self, relies on splitting as a defense. She also held that the simple moral division into good and bad is the newborn's only possible mode of organization, of sorting out the bad from the good and keeping the bad from contaminating the good (Klein, 1935, 1946, 1957).

Thus, in Klein's view, through one template every object is imbued with a positive glow that automatically includes feelings of love, idealization, and adoration. Through the other, the baby experiences danger, persecution, hatred, and envy (Klein, 1946). The result of this sorting process is not just a black-and-white universe, but a split universe in the sense that everything and everybody has two incarnations—each with its own history and associations—that can only be known one at a time.

Continued splitting helps the developing infant and young child to hold onto its own sense of goodness by projecting all its aggression into the bad, persecuting parent, so that, again, there are two pure entities, but now coexisting and in opposition.

This tendency toward idealization and demonization—an aspect of what Klein called the paranoid-schizoid position—is never abandoned and plays a big part in the worshipfulness and ardor, the feuds and grudges of later life. We see this same process at work in our waking and dreaming lives where there is a felt experience of persecution by a force much greater than oneself. Through certain compelling unconscious processes, we transform a complicated struggle into a simple one in which there is the powerless, victimized innocent on one side and a cruel, uncaring, very nearly omnipotent figure on the other. Getting even can then become the just revenge of the wounded. When bin Laden giggles over the destruction and loss of life at the World Trade Center, as he was seen to do in a notorious videotape, he is revealing not only a horrifying contempt for human life, but also, I think, a sense of persecution by a force so large and so bad that all aggressive acts against it are justified and all wounds inflicted, even including the deaths of 2,800 civilians, a source of delight. This position, in which hatred and persecutory rage are condensed into a cool state of ideological disregard for life has been described by many commentators as "evil" (*Frontline*, 2002).

The word evil in this context seems perfectly apt; but it becomes problematic when used as a blanket adjective for individuals. Serious thinkers have become cautious about how they apply this term because of the history of persecution and extermination of populations associated with it, especially in the context of twentieth century nationalist movements and ideologies, but not without a sidelong glance at Christianity's prolonged mistreatment of Jews, heretics, and others. Colloquially, and in our rage, bin Laden, like Hitler, Stalin, Pol Pot, or Saddam Hussein, are the embodiment of evil. But the stamp of evil, when applied to a person or a group, is a kind of excommunication from the human race. It bends us back toward the sorting process of infancy in which the universe is composed of pure, uncomplicated forces of good and bad, where those who perceive themselves as wholly good jettison all responsibility to look at their own failings or even to know that they, too, have it within them to do bad. Worse, by labeling someone evil we have entered the terrorist mindset where certain people are no longer people.

Nevertheless, the tendency to think this way is inherent in human psychology. The binary, black-and-white mentality is a huge and constant temptation. Under splitting's sheltering simplicity, there are good behaviors, bad behaviors; good people, bad people; right thinking, wrong thinking; righteous nations, wicked nations. The potential to live there not only is never lost, but it represents a significant part of our psychic life, for many people the most significant part. It is associated with blaming and revenge seeking and bedevils the conflicts of daily life. It gathers force in group functioning in the form of scapegoating, xenophobia, warmongering, witch-hunting, the draconian treatment of prisoners, and, ultimately, genocide. It is also at work in idol worship, cult phenomena, and religions of the one true faith, typically monotheistic religions, which presents a paradox I address shortly.

MOURNING

Splitting also undermines the health of the self, in part through the impoverishment of mourning. Carrying a torch for a hated enemy can divert one from experiencing and honoring one's losses, and if losses are not adequately attended to, the individual is never made whole. Much of psychotherapy consists of helping the patient to mourn early losses that were too much for him to process as a child and instead became incorporated as depression and defenses against it.

The intersection of politics and personal loss has often been portrayed in literature and film. *Prisoner of the Mountains*, a Russian movie based on a Tolstoy story, is a recent example with particular relevance to the problem of terrorism. Two Russian soldiers in a Caucasus region like Chechnya are captured by local rebels and held in a mountain village. Their captor is an aging guerilla whose son, also a rebel fighter, has been imprisoned by the Russian forces. Although the father has devoted his life to combating the Russians, one senses that, absent the occupying army and its oppression, this old man would still need a focus of his hate and might still be beyond human reach. A preoccupation with revenge can often make one appear well functioning; but beneath the surface may be a pathological organization that contains a primitive destructiveness, an unworked-through traumatization, or an inability to mourn (Steiner, 1993).

The old man is a widower. Nothing is said about how or when his wife died, but one suspects that he never recovered from that loss and perhaps some earlier loss that it echoed. Whatever his grievances, they are displaced onto the Russians and organized around them with such a fixity that no warmth escapes him, not even toward his adolescent daughter. She helps care for his two Russian captors and develops an affectionate attachment to the younger one, a sweet boy not much older than she.

Toward the end of the movie, there are two botched escapes: one by the two Russian prisoners that ends in the older soldier's death and one by the rebels that ends in the death of the old man's son. The father now plans to execute his remaining captive, whom his daughter loves. He marches him off to the hills and tells him to stop. With his back to his captor, the soldier waits for his death. The gun is fired. He feels nothing. He turns to see the old man lowering the rifle, having shot it into the air. The old man turns sadly and walks back to the village.

The moment the old rebel forsakes the execution and seems to accept that the Russian boy is just a symbol, he appears, at least for the moment, to abandon the splitting and projections that have supported him psychologically and the hatred that has governed his life. A sadness seems to engulf him, as if he is drawing closer to himself and his suffering. This could be the end of life for him; without his obsession with revenge, he may destroy himself. But depending on the strength of his resources and his ability to reach out, this could also be the beginning of a mourning process—for his lost son, for his wife, for some aspect of his childhood, for the years lost to obsession.

Successful mourning, as Freud implied (1917), is the antidote to depression, especially because, in Klein's rethinking, mourning does not end one's connection with the lost person but renews it, so that one regains the sense of having that loving relationship securely within oneself again (Klein, 1940). Mourning is often incomplete, and one doubts that the old guerilla will ever be free of depression. And yet one leaves the movie able to imagine that at least a small renewal may be dawning for him, perhaps in the form of increased wisdom and humanity and something better between his daughter and him.

When mourning fails, as it often does, it is usually because too many barriers stand in the way. At best—that is, in the nonpsychotic individual—one is too angry or too full of guilt or too unable to deal with one's own ambivalence toward those who have been lost to go through all the necessary feelings and arrive at a true sadness and then a stable love. A ready solution is available, however, in the form of idealization: denying the complexity of the lost person and the complexity and ambivalence of one's feelings for him. My dead wife was an angel; the terrorist who blew up the bus she was on is a monster whom I will hate and pursue and feel persecuted by forever. But, ironically, if this is the direction my psychic energies take me, I end up internally enmeshed with the killer, while the love of my wife is lost to me.

People generally need help in mourning, much as children do when they have lost a parent. Typically, the child is overcome with anger, guilt, persecution, and a sense of his own badness—much of it the result of negative feelings he harbored toward the lost parent that he cannot shake; much of it because he feels that he was abandoned and deserved it. He needs to be held; he needs another point of view; he needs to be patiently understood while he enacts his rage, including often rage at the remaining parent; he needs to be encouraged to express his awful feelings in words in order for the healing aspects of mourning to take hold (see, for example, Furman, 1974; Bowlby, 1980). If he has all this, his chance of being able to digest the loss, in all its complexity, well enough to move on is much improved. He is bathed in the caring of the person who stays and supports him; and, gradually, he can be bathed in his own caring because of his identification with that person.

Successful mourning can, thus, be understood as an aspect of self-love, and like all self-love, it is learned in relation to a loving other. In the process, the child can get beyond his sense of being broken and diminished, get beyond the guilt he naturally feels about having ill thoughts of the dead, understand that his anger or hatred was and is okay, and, that, even if the relationship was not perfect, that fact does not invalidate his love. He is able to reconnect in a good way with the full range of his feelings and, in the end, retrieve the loving connection with the lost parent. Mommy left me, but mommy loved me, and I still love mommy. Mourning is, therefore, an important element of the building and retention of complexity, and, in that sense, can be seen as a bulwark against states of splitting and obsessive revenge.

Laura Blumenfeld (2002) addresses this issue in her book about her wish to avenge an attack on her father, who was shot in the head by a young Palestinian while visiting Jerusalem. Although her father was not killed, Blumenfeld found herself obsessed with revenge and went through a long process that included in the end meeting with the gunman's family and, ultimately, with the gunman himself. In *Revenge: A Story of Hope*, she writes that in letting go of her preoccupation with vengeance, she gave herself the chance to come to terms with personal losses that she had bypassed before.

The crisis of mourning versus vengeance and what weight to give to each relates in a societal crisis as well. The direction a nation takes in its response to a terrorist attack will have important implications for its psychological functioning. A loss of wholeness and surrender to mechanisms of defense is always a threat, perhaps especially in group behavior, and can be inferred whenever the flags go up too quickly. In the United States since September 11, there have not been enough efforts to make sense of things, not just regarding the terrible loss of life, not just about how bad it feels to be so hated and so savagely attacked, but about the loss that we feel, as citizens of this nation, and of our sense of power and invulnerability. Suddenly, we are as vulnerable as everyone else. More so, in some ways, because our society is wide open and because with all our power and flaws and the expectations we excite, we are a natural target for grudges.

If we were more fully committed to absorbing this, or at least making the effort, then the terrorist attacks would open up a broader public discussion—

about how to minister to ourselves in the wake of this trauma, about how to adapt to the new world it reflects, about how to live maturely with the images and expectations others have of us, about how to assume broad new precautions at home, diplomatic initiatives abroad, and more restrained and carefully limited military operations. The alternative is to try to deny the loss, to try to retain our sense of omnipotence, to believe we can crush the demon in its nests: no one is going to threaten us; no one is going to make us question who we are or where we stand.

THE CHILD'S MONOTHEISM

At an early age—Klein believed in the second or third month (1957)—it begins to dawn on the child that the mom he loves is the same person as the mom he hates, and as he awakens to this, he experiences the crises that represent a preliminary push toward maturity and what I will call monotheism. If the witch he wants to destroy, whom he has wished every vile thing upon, and has hurt, literally, with his biting, scratching, and kicking, is the very person he loves and needs beyond measure, he has made an error that could cost him everything. Thus Klein proposed what she called the "depressive position," a psychological state characterized by guilt and remorse, and, inevitably, a wish to repair the damage one feels one has done. If all goes well, repeated experiences of such anguish and efforts to repair and—if his parents are receptive—success in repair will gradually lift the child out of this depressive state. They help usher him into another state of being where he takes people in in a new way. Perhaps most profoundly, he is able to perceive good and bad in the same person simultaneously, which means his very love is a different sort of thing than it was before.

Positive experiences with the depressive position in the next few years will constitute the child's first encounters with a number of critical psychological processes, including mourning (not just regarding the damage he may have done, but also over the loss of the idealized parents, the idealized self, and the Eden that they had inhabited); separation (in the sense of having the security to explore the world on one's own); the taking back of negative projections and thereby knowing oneself and others in a more complex, nuanced way; taking responsibility, which is a corollary to this knowledge; and letting go of narcissistic grandiosity and omnipotence, which are inherent in the child's early psychology. All these aspects of maturity are just the barest glimmer at first. They only truly take root—to the extent they do—by being nourished and encouraged in the family; and they are easily lost in a traumatic environment.

The child's more unified internal world takes time to coalesce, is never fully built, and does not replace the earlier binary world, which both the child and the adult may live in much of the time or slip into when under pressure. Indeed Klein believed there is a natural oscillation between the two psychic positions (1935, 1940). But a positive experience with the depressive position brings the child to the essence of its forgiving self, for it represents the ability to accept the difficult, sometimes troubling ambiguity that is life, where frailty and error, even betrayal and cruelty, can in some sense be tolerated and recognized as human. Ideally, one returns to the depressive position repeatedly in life, feeling remorse, concern, and the wish to repair some damage one has done. It acts as a counterweight to one's inevitable narcissism and callousness about the feelings of others and also as a spur to the deepening of the personality—or of society as a whole (consider the soul-searching of many white Americans in response to the civil rights movement).

For the child in this increasingly shades-of-gray world, love and hate still exist. But they no longer exist separately, at least not all the time, the love being directed toward a perfect, idealized parent, the hatred directed at a fiend who cares only about herself and devours her young. The child has achieved the ability to transcend the binary state; he can to some extent bring the love and hate together. There is now an imperfect parent, who can lose her temper, who can make a lousy meal, who can talk too long on the phone, yet remain a good and loved person. In addition to love and concern, the child is ideally able to feel a range of negative feelings toward this integrated parent, including fury and hatred, but all within an envelope of love. I am hurt precisely because I love you and because I need you to love me. I am angry because I love you. I criticize you because I love you. I hate you because I love you. I want you to be different—to be more of the good things I know you can be—because I love you.

In this new dimension, love is the final word. It is a much less perfect-looking place than the Eden that preceded it. But it is stabler, more real, and the child does not have to slip into the hell of total hatred, persecution, and fantasies of revenge in order to experience such feelings in a more moderate and contained way or to be on the receiving end when others are in such states. A kind of emotional monotheism has developed. All things, good and bad, are possible in this unified world. It represents the most profound sort of security and connectedness. But it is a fragile state that is easily lost and one may require considerable effort (and frequently help) to regain it.

THE SPIRITUAL CORE OF MONOTHEISM

What we normally think of as monotheism—the institutional monotheism of organized religions—arose for many purposes, some of them political, related to group cohesion, the establishment of law and maintenance of authority, and nation building. Monotheistic religions have been the most pernicious in their behavior toward nonbelievers, in the past a tool of conquest, today the battle shroud of the terrorist.

But monotheism has a spiritual core that has also inspired great good. I use the metaphor of monotheism (and for me it is only a metaphor) because of its implication that God is one, God is love, God runs through and emanates from all people, whether they are believers or not, whether they behave badly or not, whether they are one of us or not. From this perspective, it is radically egalitarian and radically forgiving. It is, in fact, very like the envelope of love discussed earlier, an envelope that can contain all that is within us no matter how bad or negative it is or seems to be. A people's attainment of monotheism—that is, as a concept that is widely grasped and advocated—might therefore be fairly understood as a significant milestone in the development of the human spirit, even if that attainment is only partial and inconsistent. It strikes me as parallel and perhaps related to an individual's capacity to love in the presence of ambivalence.

The temptation of splitting is great, however, both within us as individuals and among us in the form of those whose psychologies require such simple divisions or those who have something to gain by creating and playing on them. "Let's not forget our vulnerability, let's not forget where we came from ('we were once slaves in Egypt'), let's not forget the vulnerability of others less fortunate than we"—is not an easy position to take or to hold. One experiences an almost irresistible urge to dissociate and forget. Blaming or refusing to see the victim is a necessary corollary, often yielding to the smug entitlement of the comfortable.

So at the inception of monotheism we find not only universalism but exclusion, and both going by the same name. In monotheistic religions, believers or those with a particular vision may set themselves up as closer to God than others. Nonbelievers, wrongdoers, and those with a threatening point of view have been demonized, and the concept of the devil has been used to suggest a dark other, a pure evil, and those who do his work. In this negative monotheism, the container is broken, and there now exists a realm outside of humanity, outside of God's creation, outside the envelope of love where the not-us reside (the first-born males of Egypt). This position has its own logic and appeal and makes possible certain cohesions and compromises (a selective monotheism) that the human psyche demands.

Transitions from a universalist to an exclusionary monotheism are smooth and seamless. Note, for instance, how "the temptations of splitting," which I eluded to earlier, can easily assimilate this to the metaphor of the devil: The devil tempts us toward a black and white view. He is the source of all splitting. He creates divisions; he sows conflict. Those who succumb to his way of thinking are in his sway. They are dangerous and must be denounced or eradicated. And suddenly the split is recreated in the name of its opposite. It is hard to be sure at times where the splitting lies. Is it in your hatred? Or is it my hatred of you for your hatred? Locating responsibility for splitting is, at times, like trying to locate Moses's grave, which according to biblical legend always shifted positions when one tried to approach it. True monotheism, therefore, implies a humiliation, an openness to the possibility of error, the ability to move forward while holding at least a seed of doubt about one's stances.

But monotheism is an inherently unstable concept—oscillating much as the individual does between Klein's positions of paranoia and trust—and it transmutes into its opposite when it is overly certain of itself. This mutation often takes place for defensive reasons, when some combination of psychic forces pushes one toward the needed comfort of feeling victimized, self-righteous, grandiose, chosen.[2]

In the words of orthodox rabbi Brad Hirschfield, vice president of the National Jewish Center for Learning and Leadership, "If you really think you're in contact with a God who speaks to you, you'd better be very careful . . . because where are the correctives?" (*Frontline*, 2002).

The ease with which the universalist aspect of monotheism is lost is apparent in the contagiousness of paranoia. When I hurt you because of something cruel or selfish I have done and you experience me suddenly as an enemy, I am drawn to hate you back in the same black-and-white way. Like you, I now forget any goodness in our connection. Suddenly, and with crazed conviction, I experience you as an enemy as well, and I want to kill.

We are all prone to this paranoiac contagion, although to different degrees. The more strongly monotheistic integration has been established in us psychologically, the less susceptible we are to the paranoia and projections of others and the better able we are to hold on to our connectedness even in the face of a hatred that stirs in us a persecutory rage. But no one is ever perfect at this, and perhaps only a very few are very good.

In psychoanalysis what I have called monotheistic integration might be considered the core of the secure or the forgiving self and is related to well-known processes and states of being that have become understood as signposts of healthy emotional development: Erikson's "basic trust," Bowlby and Ainsworth's "secure attachment," Klein's "internalization of the good breast" and resolution of the depressive crisis in childhood (Karen, 1998).

In Kleinian thinking the term "depressive position" is used to describe a truly depressed place, where one feels guilty and overcome with a loss that does not seem reparable. Unfortunately, the same term is used to describe the resolution of that condition. What does one emerge into when depressive functioning has taken a successful course? The felt sense of secure attachment—where one is able to maintain the love of one's inner objects while in contact with one's goodness and badness—captures one aspect of the expanded psychic space one finds oneself in. The related idea of monotheism, with its implication of an elevated human spirit—including freedom, tolerance, a respect for the subjectivity of others, and some degree of ease with both conflict and ambiguity—captures another. Both suggest a link between the processing and resolving of depressive crises and the relational creativity, including parental creativity, that emerges from that on the other.

For the developing child it makes new things possible in relationships, which may be metaphorically likened to relationships between and within groups. He can now say, "You hurt me, Mommy," or "I hate you, Daddy," without feeling that he will lose their love. And he can grow up to be a person who can hear such pronouncements from his children and others—even when these pronouncements are loaded with victim's rage, which can feel horribly victimizing in itself—without being jarred out of his love. In this we see the emergence of both healthy, confident protest and the ability to take in protest even in its less mature forms.

But, again, it is never perfect and often not that good, which means that every life is a crazy quilt of splitting and paranoia, of terrible feelings of guilt and badness that seem as if they cannot be dispelled, of hopelessness over the prospect of repair, of idealization and escapist fantasies of perfection, but, hopefully, also of the monotheism that enables us to stay in the zone of creativity, nuance, and connectedness with oneself and others, a force for keeping relationships intact. At its apex, monotheism allows the greatest of all freedoms: the freedom to be. Along with that capacity comes the suppleness that allows us to tolerate and forgive much of what bothers or afflicts us in others and to beckon them, when necessary, away from splitting and acting out by empathically responding to their primitive, unvoiced needs.

BECKONING

Child development gives us a useful window through which to see and understand much of what is at stake emotionally in dealing with terrorist atrocities and the psychological response to them. The metaphor of the parent and child is always strained as it moves farther from that context, and yet it may be useful when describing the relationship between a great power and those who are in a state of demonizing rage against it. We all have it within us to slip into this state, and the steadfastness of the good-enough parent (or psychotherapist) provides a model for what to look for in ourselves and our leaders when facing it in others. By saying this, I do not mean to infantilize the enemies of the United States. Rather, I am talking about terrorism and of the responses to it, both of which often contain an infantile component. Indeed, parents themselves are often infantile, especially when dealing with a child's rage. The beckoning aspect of monotheistic creativity, what Bion (1959) discussed in terms of containment and what has been culturally recognized as an aspect of sensitive maturity, can emerge from either side in a conflictual relationship. Everyone needs this type of empathic containment at times.

In childhood the development of a healthy, integrated monotheism in childhood depends on the parent's mature love. The parent invites the child away from splitting and toward monotheism not by preaching or hammering but by living monotheistically with the child, by demonstrating and reestablishing an acceptance of complexity and ambiguity, that all feelings are allowed, even hateful feelings; that they do not destroy love; that the two can coexist. This does not mean that the parent never gets angry, never punishes unfairly, never wants to throw the child against the wall, never succumbs to splitting by plunging into some form of self-righteous verbal brutality. No parent is perfect and we would not want one who was. What is important is that the parent's capacity to tolerate aggression and negative feelings, the child's and his own, be relatively strong. This helps the child develop some ease with aggression, his own and others, which leads to both mastery and modulation.

Parents need access to their aggression, but their use of it must be tempered by concern and empathy. When a parent is too neglectful, scary, or rejecting, the child has a hard time holding onto a monotheistic integration. He is unable to see mom as a combination of good and bad because her badness is too much for him to cope with and integrate into a larger picture of someone he loves—a risk with obvious parallels for a powerful nation facing those who feel oppressed by it. In cases like this, the child may have to dissociate from his love for the mother because it hurts too much to stay open to her. That is a situation in which splits become deeply ingrained and sometimes last a lifetime, so that not even in old age, when the parent is being laid in her grave, is the grown child able to feel any loss.

Like parents, psychotherapists must deal with irrational hatred and aggression, and they, too, must have the strength and creativity to protect themselves when under assault without losing the message of the patient's hatred or denying the possibility—no matter how irrational the patient's accusations may be—of their own role in the conflict. Perhaps most important, they must not be so overcome with their own inflamed reactions that they abandon their role as a guardian of the underlying connection.

As a nation, we may need to pursue our interests in ways that others find egregious at times, but we need to be careful lest others experience us, in all our power, as uncaring, omnipotent bulldozers. We have much good to offer, but in our relations to people who already have grievances and already feel subjugated or ignored, we can easily encourage a splitting such that it becomes hard for them to remember the good that is in us.

Alongside of defensive and military responses, there also needs to be a kind of openness: What is the message in al Qaeda's hatred? Can we understand what makes so many young Muslims attracted to them? Can we grasp what it means to be angry and envious, to feel overpowered and lacking in options, to feel that one's cultural heritage is being stomped on by the happy-go-lucky tank of American social freedoms, cultural exports, financial and military muscle? Can we acknowledge that we understand this without feeling as if we are losing our own legitimacy as a people, condoning crimes against us, or becoming paralyzed in response to them?

When Bush gave his address to the nation two months after the terror attacks on September 11, he asked, why do they hate us? And he responded, "They hate us because of what you see here. . . . They hate our freedoms," and so on. It was a lost opportunity to seed a more complex view by acknowledging that there are some in the Islamic world with understandable gripes against us, that we need, perhaps, to better understand what they are, that a fraction of that group feels so enraged and powerless that they are drawn to a camp of malignant and violent haters, and that we will make it our business to reach out to the disaffected even as we pursue and disable those who attack us. Many in the Islamic world who heard what he said that night felt bitterly misunderstood (see, for example, Ford, 2001).

PROJECTIVE IDENTIFICATION

There is a kind of magic at work in the parent's beckoning and eliciting from the child. By acting as if it is already so, the parent brings into being aspects of the child that were not quite there before or only present in nascent or minimally developed form. A similar process can take place between analyst and patient and in other intimate relationships. It is part of the creativity by which we are sometimes able to help each other to grow. We may notice this capacity in people we consider mentors, who bring out qualities in us when we relate to them that we did not know we had. To illustrate in simple terms, by believing that another person is honorable and treating him accordingly, one may elicit an honorableness that he might not otherwise have exhibited. This was one of the principles that guided Gandhi in his dealings with the British, even as he applied pressure through nonviolent assaults.

It is fair to assume that some of the respect the British accorded him, often despite initial reactions of hatred or contempt, came about because he behaved respectfully toward them and acted as if they would do the same. He was able to elicit something from his antagonists by acting as if it was there all along, almost as if he had put it into them. In psychoanalysis this magnetic transmission, this eliciting of a nascent quality, is recognized as an aspect of projective identification, one of the most powerful unconscious communicative processes in human relations. It can feel generous, manipulative, guilt provoking, or invasive; it is a protean force with great potential for good and for ill.

The idea of projective identification was introduced by Klein in 1946 but would take decades to attain its current status. Far from viewing it as a positive force, Klein initially saw projective identification strictly as a defensive process, and a very primitive one at that, as the prototype of aggression, a way of purging oneself of contact with the contents of one's own mind and relating to others not as separate people but as expelled aspects of oneself.

It was similar to Freud's idea of projection, introduced in 1895, which, like so many of Freud's concepts, is now a part of our common lexicon. Freud described projection as attributing one's own thoughts to someone else, which can lead to a paranoid reaction. The famous example concerned cases of latent homosexuality: I feel a strange and powerful desire for him. But it cannot be—I must not desire another man. So, these feelings, they must mean *he* desires me. Yikes! He thinks I am a fag! He is stalking me and wants to fuck me! And this makes me unbearably anxious because it threatens to awaken me to my own forbidden wish (Freud, 1895). But in Freud's projection, everything happened inside the projector. What happened inside the other person was not necessarily an issue. Klein suggested a much stronger interpersonal component.

For Klein, projective identification is an essential ingredient of the infant's primitive fantasy life, the infant's way of ridding itself of anxiety and badness, metaphorically equivalent to the body's ridding itself of uncomfortable contents through excretion. But just as the child's refusing to defecate can be an act of defiance and defecating explosively a primitive form of attack, so, too, the baby's use of projective identification goes beyond its initial evacuative function (Feldman, 1992). Through her work with small children in play therapy, where she saw them enact destructive fantasies, Klein came to believe that the baby imagines that through its power to project out unwanted feelings and pieces of itself, it is able to dominate and control the mother and thus avoid any sense of being separate from her. At other times, it projects in a state of rage and imagines damaging or destroying her (Joseph, 1988).

At this point we are still in the realm of classical projection. But Klein and her followers recognized that the baby lives its projective fantasies in such a way that the mother often comes to feel these unwanted things that the baby seemingly puts into her. Projective identification thus has an uncanny, potentially very disturbing quality to it, as if, somehow, a real transfusion has taken place, which is partly what can make dealing with psychotic and borderline patients, who lean heavily on this defense, so potentially unnerving.

"Identification" became a part of the term because, insofar as the baby projects harmful parts of itself into the mother, the mother then becomes identified in the baby's mind with the bad parts of the baby (just as doctors, policemen, spouses, passersby can come to represent elements, often terrifying elements, of the psychotic's mind). Gradually, as the baby matures, it has less need for this defense and largely abandons it as a primary mode of operating interpersonally (Joseph, 1988).

Wilfred Bion broadened the idea of projective identification in the 1950s by emphasizing that it is a fundamental aspect of interpersonal connection, with certain benign and healthy aspects, and that it is the foundation of empathy. The baby's projections, he wrote, are not just a matter of attacking and controlling the mother, but rather the baby put things into the mother's mind in order to get them back in more digestible form. In other words, its projections are a primitive form of communication and part of the baby's involvement in its own nurturing process, as fundamental as crying or following. The baby needs the mother to understand and interpret its experience, much as the patient needs the analyst. Bion argued that the mother acts as a "container" for the baby's projections, that she is able to tolerate feelings that the baby cannot. Unless her own psychology is compromised, rather than deny entry to her child's projections or fling them back, she works with what the small child has put into her and returns it in a way he can use it (Hinshelwood, 1989). Thus, the baby may be feeling annihilation anxiety, which it transmits to the mother to the point where she finds his squalls making her feel on the verge of coming apart. But she is able to digest and make sense of what he has put into her. So she soothes him, tells him he is hungry or overtired, and assures him he will be all right. Bion did observe that some mothers cannot tolerate the child's projections, tend to dissociate in such a way as to not notice them, or, worse, criticize or reject the child for its irritability or neediness, thereby compounding the child's distress and escalating its projective efforts (Bion, 1959).

The terrorist's use of projective identification is linked with a good-versus-evil division of the world. All badness, including the badness one feels unconsciously to exist in oneself, is exported to the other and reacted against: The enemy is arrogant, the enemy is power hungry, the enemy is violent, the enemy has no concern for me or my people—but I remain a good-hearted person who only kills in self-defense. Although I am engaged in killing, I am not a killer. *He* is the killer. And because I identify him now with the scariest and most ruthless parts of myself, he becomes a source of dread. But this way of thinking is not the sole province of megalomaniacs.

In 1982 Brad Hirschfield, a young American Jew, moved to Hebron, a critical town on the West Bank, which until the occupation, was closed to Jews.

(There has been now, for many years, a small and militant Jewish enclave there amidst a hostile Arab population, an explosive condition with a history of violence on both sides, the most notorious incident, in 1994, the murder of twenty-nine Palestinians in a mosque by an unbalanced Jewish extremist). In a remarkable testimony, a version of which first appeared on PBS's *Frontline*, Hirschfield relates his own absorption in the feelings of exultation and omnipotence that can accompany group identification and splitting:

> Hebron is traditionally understood to be one of the four holiest cities in the land of Israel," says Hirschfield. "It's the burial place of the matriarchs and the patriarchs—of Abraham and Isaac and Jacob and Sarah and Rebecca and Leah. . . . To be able to go back to a place where, in 1929, Jews were run out of town in a pogrom is unbelievable. To be able to say, at the age of eighteen or nineteen, 'This is where I belong,' is intoxicating after thousands of years of exile. . . . It's like you get drunk on messianism. You believe anything is possible, because you have all the answers. . . . I don't think I thought for a minute about the impact of my beliefs on other human beings who didn't share them. . . . I don't know if it would have changed for me if it hadn't gotten so out of control that it led to a Jewish underground that committed murder. I don't know that I would have noticed. No. I know I didn't notice when it was at the level of intimation or beatings. . . . You lose any reference point except your own internal world, and my own internal world was the whole world. . . . The worst part of it is until it rose to the level of murder, I don't think I thought of it as violence. That's why there are no easy answers about what those guys did in those airplanes. You have to imagine being in a place where what other people see as violent behavior, you don't. You actually see it as redemptive" (*Frontline*, 2002).

Hirschfield says he does not believe there is a moral equivalence between the extremist Jewish settlers and the September 11 hijackers. "It's just that when I look at those terrorists, I don't see something wholly other, because I know from my own life experience what it means to allow your most deeply felt beliefs to motivate you to do violent things to other people" (*Frontline*, 2002).

Projective identification seems to take hold more readily and more extremely under the influence of group identifications. In a classical study of the nursing service of a general hospital, published in 1959, Menzies Lyth describes how nurses, in an unconscious effort to defeat anxiety, subtly adapt their own defenses to those commonly used by others in the institution, thereby taking on the institution's values, its projections, its scapegoating, its prejudices (often paranoid) about patients, patients' families, doctors, and so on. Under the influence of group-think, a person's psychology can thus acquire a rigidity that is more extreme than what he might exhibit in other aspects of his life, and his capacity to think for himself is impoverished. The group defenses are incorporated by each individual and projected back into the group in a kind of endless feedback loop, which progressively erodes complexity and difference. These intensified defenses, Menzies Lyth writes, "inhibit the capacity for creative, symbolic thought, for abstract thought, and for conceptualization. They inhibit the full development of the individual's understanding, knowledge and skills that enable reality to be handled effectively and pathological anxiety mastered" (Menzies Lyth, 1988, pp. 74–75).

Bion (1961) famously argues that groups often operate at a psychically primitive level, with primitive fantasies and psychotic anxieties similar to what is experienced in early infancy. He saw irrational group processes wrapped around certain "basic assumptions." Of these, the basic assumption of fight/flight is most dominated by concerns about loyalty and treachery and a tendency toward idealization and demonization (1961). Bion believed that such processes could have an adaptive value. If used in a sophisticated manner they "can provide the basis for action, commitment, and loyal followership in the service of task performance, as well as the basis for appropriate defensive measures when a group is faced with realistic external threats" (Gould, 1997). But such sophistication is often wanting. Echoing Bion, Segal writes:

> All groups tend to be self-centered, narcissistic, and paranoid. . . . On the whole it does not do much harm that the French think they are the cleverest in the world, the British that they are the fairest or the Americans that they are just "great." But if the group becomes dominated by those mad premises, the situation becomes dangerous. . . . The post-Hiroshima world was acting on a psychotic premise, with the USSR and the US-led West . . . each viewing the other as an evil empire and threatening total annihilation. (2003)

Where there is a state of aggravated conflict, groups are capable of descending rapidly to astonishingly primitive levels of information processing where extreme people, statements, and actions from within the adversary group are reacted to with paranoia as if representative of the whole. Conversely, angry threats or characterizations meant for a certain element are picked up by, and enrage, the entire world of which it is a part. And, again, individuals within the group are sucked along almost helplessly. They get caught up in the fear for their survival; there are plenty of Iagos to make the most of treacherous interpretations; and anyone with a contrary view risks being denounced as soft on the enemy now seen as a monster without complexity, without differences among us individuals.

RUNAWAY SPLITTING

One of the anxieties that group identification and merger protects the individual from is anxiety over expulsion, abandonment, excommunication. For the infant excommunication means annihilation, the most primitive anxiety and one that no one is ever entirely free of. And groups do excommunicate, engaging in purges and splits whenever internal dissent is experienced as threatening to the majority: if one's fellow citizen does not agree that a particular enemy is evil, if he holds out for a more nuanced view, then there is something suspect about him, and perhaps he partakes of that evil. Not only does one project into the enemy the violence and hatred one cannot countenance in oneself, but one projects into one's compatriot one's own doubts, regrets, and internal warnings and turns him into the enemy within. The paranoid instincts and the capacity to detach from the feelings of others that characterizes states of splitting are perhaps most useful on the battlefield. But they can be like a pestilence in ordinary life, subtly infusing a social condition that had previously been one of substantial warmth and solidarity. During and just after the destruction of the World Trade Center there was an outpouring of selflessness, generosity, and altruism, not only at the site, where ordinary people became heroes, but all over the country.

The flags we hung and the candlelight vigils we attended were meant to express solidarity with the dead, with those they left behind, and with each other in a time of loss. But the half-dozen sticker flags pasted on the mirror in my building lobby by a superintendent who often exhibited a narrow, bullying character did not feel like an act of mourning or solidarity. It felt more like the middle finger of revenge stuck high in the air. And yet it was difficult for anyone to suggest that they be taken down. The blithe acceptance of splitting and the fear of opposing it came into play quickly and with force. One can imagine the pressures the average person felt in Yugoslavia after Tito's death, when opportunists were denouncing and spreading panic about the intentions of other ethnic groups, or in 1930s Germany where brown shirts stood ready to crush anyone who questioned their treatment of the Jews.

Whatever evil is, it seems to gather strength in the presence of splitting. And as splitting gathers strength, it has several characteristic effects: it unleashes tremendous rage, giving every victim a cause and every bully a target; it cows internal opposition, inducing fear, silence, and acquiescence; and it engenders more splitting, drawing to it those who get caught in its web or who relish its power. In certain contexts, like the paranoid atmosphere in revolutionary France, the splitting and projective identification can cause a people to devour itself.

The Communist Party of Stalin's era typified this process. As purges and splits grew ever more extreme, people were excommunicated or murdered for all sorts of "deviations," while split-off groups like the Trotskyists devised their own splinters, deviations, and excommunications. With each split new demons were manufactured. In the late twenties and early thirties when Stalin ordered the dissolution of the popular front, the Communists denounced the socialists as "social fascists" and in New York and elsewhere violently attacked and broke up their meetings. In Germany, where the popular front had not only included political unity among the left-wing groups but shared social institutions as well, a new cry went up among the German party members: "Kick the little social fascists out of the kindergarten!" In Spain militarized party members systematically assassinated their anarchist allies, helping to pave the way for Franco's victory (see, for example, Orwell, 1962). While this represented a cold calculation on Stalin's part (everyone was his enemy), many party members believed that they were performing a necessary purge of elements that would be dangerous to the workers' future. As Menzies Lyth's research suggests, they were in some sense powerless to think otherwise.

In the United States in the fifties, we witnessed a similar self-devouring phenomenon in response to Stalin, as rightists accused liberals of being "soft on Communism." People who opposed McCarthy, even including President Eisenhower, were termed "witting or unwitting tools" of the Communist conspiracy.

The more one has participated in such acts of bad faith—the vicious name-calling, the in-fighting, as well as the ex-communications and the hatreds that grow out of them—the more one becomes committed to the logic of polarization. There can be no room for trust, mutual respect, or common ground with those who do not toe the line. We face some of that danger now, for September 11 and the war against Iraq has provided new opportunities for splitting. As Didion (2003) reported in the *New York Review of Books*, people who have tried to make sense of the attacks in terms of what motivates such hatred against the United States or who have questioned a predominantly militarist response have been referred to as the "Blame America First crowd." They have been charged with lacking "moral clarity" (William Bennett), dismissed as part of "the liberal left tendency to 'rationalize' the aggression of September 11" (Christopher Hitchens), even likened to a potential "fifth column" (Andrew Sullivan). This corruption of dialogue can be difficult to reverse, partly because of the kinds of responses it elicits, until a national dialogue deteriorates to a point where all that is heard are extreme statements.

What I earlier called paranoiac contagion can be understood in terms of the play of projective identification. Clinical experience has confirmed repeatedly that projective identification is powerful not only because of the effect it has on the person making the projections but because it works on the target person as well. The radiant love of the infant has the capacity to lift and swell the parent's sense of himself, much as the adulation of the crowd swells the performer or the dictator, while the angry accusations of the four-year-old reduce the parent to his worst image of himself.

One's identity as a member of a group, as an American, is also susceptible. We can absorb the negative projections directed at us to the extent that they corrupt our view of who we are. Denounced rationally and irrationally and viciously attacked, we may involuntarily and without conscious awareness, experience our Americanness as hateful and bad, feel compelled to deny it, and counterattack with our own splitting and projections, such that we now see ourselves as a wholly good, with nothing to apologize for in our behavior; while we see the terrorists, their sympathizers, and anyone who raises a critical word as wholly bad, with no cause for grievance or anger against us. This very way of being not only terrifies others, but it depletes and debilitates the self (in this case, the metaphorical group self), emptying it of complexity and vitality. Meanwhile, each side, in its self-righteous certainty, behaves in ways so as to confirm the negative caricature held by the other. Projective identification can thus become like virus growing in strength as it is passed back and forth between hosts.

Once violence enters the picture, there is almost no way to prevent this contagious migration to the extremes. We have seen this polarization again and again, between Catholic and Protestant in Northern Ireland and between Hindu and Muslim on the subcontinent. How do you argue with someone whose child had been killed by the IRA and wants to see all Catholic activists put to death? Israelis and Palestinians were within inches of a landmark settlement a few years ago when Israel elected Ehud Barak prime minister; but after monstrous acts on both sides, majorities on both sides now seem wedded to the views of their most bellicose leaders.

Where there is demonization, there is usually idealization as well. That is inherent in splitting, even if it seems fantastic in the current crisis. Any world superpower, but perhaps especially the United States, given its history of democracy, individual freedom, opportunity, and good deeds, as well as the hope it has represented to the world, is prone to idealization. In some respects those who demonize us, who see us as pure evil, may also unconsciously be waiting for us to drop the devil's mask and become who we really are—not a nation with selfish interests, humanitarian and bullying impulses, wishes to do well combined with blindness and insensitivities about the outside world—but solely a force for freedom, human dignity, and the righting of all wrongs. This, too, is an aspect of splitting that needs to be appreciated if we are not to sink further into a simplified view of ourselves and others. Evidence for this may be seen in the Middle East where there was a huge burst of Israeli tourism to Egypt after the two countries made an official peace in 1979 and a largely warm response from the Egyptians they met. As implausible as it may seem, buried in the long-standing hatred the two peoples had for each other seemed to be a dormant yet powerful love. This love affair ended for various reasons, including, quite possibly, an idealization that could not be sustained, given the fact that people are people.

Whether a nation's leaders are able to dampen chauvinist splitting in times of crisis and promote a more nuanced approach to real or potential adversaries is often, at least to some extent, a matter of luck. South Africa was lucky to have F. W. de Klerk, the last white president, who began the dismantling of the apartheid regime, and the shockingly reconciliatory Nelson Mandela as its first black president; it could have had much worse. The United States was lucky to have had Abraham Lincoln beckoning the nation to heal, to forgive, to think more deeply and spiritually about what it had gone through and was unlucky to have lost him.

But, of course, it is not just luck, and we could improve our luck in any case by making a deeper understanding of psychological processes a part of our national consciousness. The discoveries of two great fields—psychoanalysis and social psychology—about how human nature works, about the primitive and irrational mechanisms that often rule us, and our capacity to attenuate and transform them through comprehension, attention, and concern, have been sequestered in professional circles. They should be part of our education for citizenship, taught to children from the earliest grades. If done well, that teaching could be both an aid to critical, independent thinking and at least a partial inoculation against the dangers of splitting, of group-think, of demagoguery, and of the many forms of mass manipulation to which democracy becomes more vulnerable as subtler methods of mass communication are more widely used.

Only a fraction of the population will ever grasp the meaning of projective identification or the implications of monotheism, and we will always have fundamentalists pushing debate toward the primitive end. But there is a significant body of knowledge indicating that a person's reflective capacity, his ability to think about something that has been largely unconscious before, what Bion called "alpha functioning" and Peter Fonagy "mentalization" (Fonagy, 1991), is catalytic in itself and attenuates the extremes of infantile, unconsciously motivated behavior. Analogously, we are in a better position as a political culture if a significant fraction of educated people recognize primitive group processing and its antidotes and know they will be understood by some if they speak about it publicly.

The contribution that creative political leadership might offer in a crisis like ours is to help the nation preserve the complexity of its thinking. By example, through reminders, the leader can provide for the nation something along the lines of what Bion envisioned for the group therapist—to interest the group in seeing itself in more complexity and depth (Billow, 2003). In a volatile environment, someone needs to make the case that each of us is more than we imagine; that hate and love can operate independently of each other; that anger and aggressive acts may contain the wish for deeper connection; that flaws, limitations, and bad behavior are universal; and that repair is possible. It is particularly important, I think, to try not only to beckon our own society toward a greater monotheism in the psychological sense but to teach it about the processes by which monotheism is instilled and lost and, in particular, the role that a more powerful society can play in dealing with the grievances of those enraged against it. When such leadership is not provided adequately by the president and other elected officials, it falls more heavily on psychologists, social scientists, writers, and others.

CONTAINMENT AND REPAIR

On this last point, Bion's idea of the parent as container and transformer of the child's projections (Bion, 1959) is particularly meaningful—presenting creative possibilities in dealing with the splitting and projections of aggrieved populations. The key thing is not passivity or piety, but operating out of a self that has not lost itself—that is, has not succumbed to projections and counterprojections. It is a self that is cognizant of the psychological forces acting on it and that is able to read beneath the angry words and act without discarding complexity.

Part of the creativity of parenthood is the ability to handle being experienced by one's child as bad. If that is too threatening, if it destabilizes the parent's own sense of goodness, then the child is put in an untenable position. He not only is thwarted in his efforts to use projective identification and get help managing his anxieties, but his tendency to idealize and demonize is reinforced. Badness, he learns, cannot, after all, be tolerated. It kills goodness, kills love, damages those we love. Mom's hostility proves it. Meanwhile, his sense of his own badness is strengthened, as is his desperate need to get rid of it by projecting it onto mom. And so a vicious cycle develops.

It takes a lot for parents to resist this. They have their own insecurities and self-doubts that the child inflames. But, ideally, the parent is able to stay lovingly connected frequently enough regardless of where the child goes. Or if he does not stay so connected, he can notice it, be concerned about it, understand it, and pull himself back from the impulse to retaliate. He also knows enough of the time that the child, in all his ire, is still ardently in love with him, even if the child himself has lost touch with that. So he does not succumb to the child's projections, and he does not live in fear of an unbearable loss, which might make him alternatively clinging and rageful. When the parent operates out of this secure place a good enough percentage of the time, he is able to empathically contain the child's projections.

Parents feel constrained by their love, by their responsibility, by the undeniable permanence of the relationship with the child. They may be stirred to hatred and defensiveness and the wish to attack, but there is some wish to resist surrendering to destructive responses, more so at least than among political groups or people in almost any other relationship. And yet it is fair to say that this capacity, this triumph of creativity over reactivity, this commitment to connectedness, is applicable to group relationships—indeed, we celebrate it as brilliant and sensitive diplomacy. It would certainly be helpful in dealing with enraged elements of the Arab and Muslim worlds.

No matter what we do as a nation, some will remained hardened against us. Many of them have been brought up in schools that teach our demonization. We have to use every bit of muscle and arm-twisting to prevent funding such institutions. Military steps need to be taken to track down actual terrorists. Bin Laden, fused to his megalomania and frightening moral positions, and others like him have too much at stake to be reached by any kind of working out of grievances. But they swim in a world that supplies them with power, and much of that world is reachable. Many there do not have personal reasons to be committed to revenge. Their hearts have not yet been rent; their hands are not yet bloody. How effectively are we speaking to them? How welcome have we made the communications they may wish to address to us?

Finally, an important aspect of monotheism is its loss. No one is monotheistic all the time; it is not human. There is a constant coming and going from it that needs to be honored—both with a readiness to repair and to welcome repair, as well as a healthy degree of self-doubt that keeps one open to criticism and complaints. Much of the ability to do this has its roots in childhood, particularly in the grace with which parents handle their own transgressions, and it is codified in religion through concepts like forgiveness and atonement.

Repair is inherent in the new monotheism of the developing child's emotional life. It can be seen as the beginnings of both forgiveness and apology. Throughout our lives we eject people from the loving circle, and then, in forgiving, apologizing, owning up, or just reconnecting with our own connectedness, our hearts go out to them. Each return to depressive functioning, if it includes some successful mourning, has the capacity to shrink our dependency on idealization and demonization and thus to both replenish and enlarge our monotheism. The confidence to repair and believe that our efforts will be accepted suggests a knowledge that even at our worst, even after we have lost faith and returned to a binary state, we still have a right to love and to feel okay about ourselves and to know that if we make amends our love will be accepted and returned.

We do see facets of monotheistic repair at times in group functioning. Our nation has its own proud history of repair in the form of the help we have given defeated nations in rebuilding, where we have had to retract our demonizations in order to accept former enemy peoples in a new light. Some of the most striking recent examples of group repair are a number of social experiments, many pioneered by Dan Bar-On (see chapter 25 in this book), where victim and perpetrator are brought face to face in an effort to enable each to move beyond frozen positions that are unhealthy for them and for the larger social milieu. The most ambitious recent example may be the Truth and Reconciliation Commission in South Africa where those whose family members had been slain and those responsible were able to confront each other in open court (Reid and Hoffmann, 2000). Results were mixed, but something of emotional value took place, a much-needed opportunity to express one's rage or regret in some cases and at times a softening, such that there was a greater ability on each side to see humanity on the other.

Child therapists are often aware of this desperate human need for expression, which is so evident in the child's craving to voice his rage at his parents; it is one of the enduring frustrations and hurts of childhood that this need is so frequently squashed. In clinical situations, where parent and child are brought together, much can be accomplished simply by allowing the child to have his voice no matter how outrageous it may sound.

If we as a nation wished to encourage such expression, this would be a time to invite Muslim leaders, including those we do not like, to speak to us about the sources of rage against us. It could show that we are willing to learn; it would give them an opportunity to bomb us with words and release some of the frustration they feel, even if it seems to us overly blaming or irrational; and it could create opportunities for understanding on both sides. Such a dialogue could also be a great propaganda tool for us if we use it wisely. Let those who are enraged at us see their rage reaching its target. Let those who can grasp it also take note that we are listening. Efforts like this to reach out to the Arab and Muslim world would constitute a more sophisticated propaganda campaign than we have been able to muster thus far. Other elements might include working with moderate Muslim clergy worldwide to combat the extremist message and enlisting our own (strangely quiet) Muslim population to speak out more forcefully on the same theme.

Apology is another aspect of both propaganda and repair. Even the simple acknowledgment of or expression of concern about previous insensitivity or harm done can be a powerful tool in reaching out to disaffected people. Groups—which is to say, individuals experiencing themselves through a group identification—have a hunger for such acknowledgment much as people do in more intimate realms. Pope John Paul's apology to the Jews for centuries of persecution was inadequate. His main failing was in taking no institutional responsibility for Catholic anti-Semitism, attributing it solely to the behavior of errant individuals. He was under substantial pressure from within the Vatican to not go even as far as he went for fear that he would tarnish the Church's image, a fear that would no doubt restrain an American president from speaking openly of such things as our misguided support of the Shah in Iran, our abandonment of the Shi'ites who rose against Saddam in 1991 at our urging, our bungled handling of the Iraq occupation, or the horrible prisoner abuse at Abu Graib.

But even the Pope's inadequate apology had a softening effect on many Jews who harbored an abiding hatred for the church. President Clinton's apology to the victims of the infamous Tuskegee experiment (in which federal health officials intentionally allowed poor black sharecroppers with syphilis to go untreated for decades in order to study the effects) had a similar impact on many of the survivors and their families.

Even the grown child who feels no conscious love for a parent often unconsciously harbors the fantasy that the parent will at last be able to take in his protests, be affected by them, and direct toward the hardened child a loving sorrow and concern. In such fantasies, when drawn out in therapy, the story sometimes ends (much to the grown child's own surprise) with an outpouring of tears and love on both sides. That does not mean anything like that will happen in real life, but the buried passion that the child has for the parent seems to be metaphorically related to hidden wells of attraction and interest within hostile populations.

In the Muslim world at the current time, there is enough sense of grievance toward the United States, enough feeling of persecution, real and imagined, to have created the conditions where large numbers are susceptible to the demonizing trends, feverishly promoted by some well-funded fundamentalist groups, that feed the impulse toward terror among the powerless. Ideally, this might cause us to ask certain questions that emanate from a mature consciousness: Can we engage in the beckoning process that seeks to make the best of a difficult situation? Can we do it without losing our ability to respond strongly, even militarily, when needed? Can we demonstrate a concern for what we have done in the past and what we continue to do that causes understandable resentments against us?

But even if enough critical mass of political and intellectual interest gathers around such questions to make them a part of the social agenda, they are not easily answered, and they raise other, more difficult, questions. To cite one of the most obvious: in a mature society, some can be counted on to understand that apologizing, even for the grossest insensitivities and exploitations, is not equivalent to self-denigration or groveling. To have been too much for ourselves, to have looked the other way when others suffered, to have carelessly caused suffering are aspects of the corruption of power to which all people and peoples are susceptible and prone. To acknowledge it is not to be masochistic or bad but human and sorry. But how can an American president apologize for past insensitivities to the Muslim world without being accused of desecrating the dead of September 11 and risking a public relations debacle that could destroy him? How does he respond to such accusations without being drawn into the vortex of splitting and projective identification? How does he show respect to those who revert to splitting and the desire for revenge as a necessary defense and comfort in traumatic circumstances even as he opposes turning their pain into policy? And these are just the first of the challenges, internal and external, that would confront him.

Gandhi's model may still teach us a lot, but it was a strategy for the downtrodden, not the powerful, and although it brilliantly dampened the potential for demonizing and polarization between English and Indian, it did not prevent the splitting between Hindu and Muslim that tore his country apart. It is possible to envision a powerful nation exhibiting some of the wisdom that Gandhi displayed in insurgency. It is possible to envision an America—I think it is instructive to do so—that, like the good enough parent, can contain projections, repair and welcome repair, and encourage a healthy monotheism. But how to move a nation to that place, and what qualities of leadership are needed? How to present a monotheistic face to the world without suppressing or denying or inflaming internal divisions? How to develop a consciousness that acts as a counterforce to primitive defenses, the longing for omnipotence, the natural resistance to mourning, the grieving widow bent on revenge, and those who would ride to power on her grief? This challenge, which stands before us like the Himalayas, perhaps requires a new contingent of Gandhis to map and to scale it.

NOTES

This chapter is reproduced under a different title from Robert Karen, Two faces of monotheism, *Contemporary Psychoanalysis*, 39 (4): 637–63. Reprinted with permission from *Contemporary Psychoanalysis*.

1. As Jonathan Lear did in *Love and Its Place in Nature* (1998), I would like to quote David Velleman (1989) to explain my use of pronouns in this chapter:

> Some readers may take offense at my use of "he" to denote the arbitrary person. Let me assure these readers that I share their goal of inclusiveness in language and differ with them only about the means to that goal. My view is that traditional usage in this case makes English more inclusive, not less.
>
> The rule governing traditional usage is that when "he" denotes the arbitrary person, its gender is purely grammatical, not semantic, and hence carries no implications as to the referent's sex. So understood, "he" no more denotes a man, because of being masculine,

than the German "die Person" or the French "la personne" denotes a woman, because of being feminine.

The alternate practices that are currently recommended as inclusive—such as saying " 'he or she' or alternating 'he' with 'she'—actually threaten to rob the language of its capacity for gender-neutral reference to persons" (From *Practical Reflection*, Velleman, 1989).

2. Even the idea of chosen has been understood in two ways: chosen to spread the word, which can still include others as equal children of God, or chosen in the sense of being superior or being favored with a direct line to God, which, of course, would contradict the word.

REFERENCES

Billow, R. M. (2003). *Relational group psychotherapy: From basic assumptions to passion*. New York: Jessica Kingsley.

Bion, W. R. (1959). Attacks on linking. *International Journal of Psycho-Analysis*, 30: 308–15. (Reprinted in *Melanie Klein today: Developments in theory and practice*, E. B. Spillius (Ed.), 1988, London: Routledge)

———. (1961). *Experiences in groups*. New York: Basic Books.

Blumenfeld, L. (2002). *Revenge: A story of hope*. New York: Simon & Schuster.

Bowlby, J. (1980). *Loss: sadness and depression*, Vol. 3 of *Attachment and Loss*. London: Hogarth Press; New York: Basic Books.

Didion, J. (2003). Fixed opinions, or the hinge of history. *New York Review of Books*, 50 (1): 54–59.

Erikson, E. H. (1968). *Identity: Youth and crisis*. New York: Norton.

Feldman, M. (1992). Splitting and projective identification. In R. Anderson (Ed.), *Clinical lectures on Klein and Bion*. London: Routledge.

Fonagy, P. (1991). Thinking about thinking: Some clinical and theoretical consideration in the treatment of a borderline patient. *International Journal of Psycho-Analysis*, 72: 1–18.

Ford, P. (2001, September 27). Why do they hate us? *Christian Science Monitor*. Retrieved May 2, 2004, from csmonitor.com

Freud, S. (1895). Draft H—paranoia. In James Strachey (Ed.), *Standard Edition of the complete psychological works of Sigmund Freud*. 24 vols. London: Hogarth Press (1953–1973), Vol. 1, pp. 206–12.

———. (1917). Mourning and melancholia. *Standard Edition*, 14: 237–58. (Reprinted in *Essential papers on object loss*, by R. V. Frankiel (Ed.), 1994, New York: New York University Press)

Frontline. (2001). Hunting bin Laden: Osama bin Laden v. the U.S.: Edicts and Statements. *PBS Online*. Retrieved May 2, 2004, from http://pbs.org/frontline

———. (2002). Faith and doubt at ground zero. Source notes. *PBS Online*. Retrieved on May 2, 2004, from http://pbs.org/frontline

Furman, E. (1974). Some effects of the parent's death on the child's personality development. In R. Frankiel (Ed.), *Essential papers on object loss*. New York: New York University Press.

Gould, L. (1997). Correspondences between Bion's basic assumption theory and Klein's developmental positions: An outline. *Free Associations*, 15 (1): 15–30.

Hinshelwood, R. D. (1989). *A dictionary of Kleinian thought*. London: Free Association.

Joseph, B. (1988). Projective identification: Some clinical aspects. In E. B. Spillius (Ed.), *Melanie Klein today: Developments in theory and practice*. London: Routledge.

Karen, R. (1998). *Becoming attached: First relationships and how they shape our capacity to love*. New York: Oxford.

Klein, M. (1935). A contribution to the psychogenesis of manic depressive states. *International Journal of Psycho-Analysis*, 16: 145–74. (Reprinted in *The selected Melanie Klein*, by J. Mitchell, Ed., 1986, New York: Free Press)

———. (1940). Mourning and its relation to manic depressive states. *International Journal of Psycho-Analysis*, 21: 125–53. (Reprinted in *The selected Melanie Klein*, by J. Mitchell, Ed., 1986, New York: Free Press)

———. (1946/1975). Notes on some schizoid mechanisms. In *Envy and gratitude and other works, 1946–1963*, pp. 1–24. New York: Delacorte.

———. (1957/1975). Envy and gratitude. In *Envy and gratitude and other works, 1946–1963*. New York: Delacorte.

Lear, J. (1998). *Love and its interpretation*. New Haven, CT: Yale University Press.

Menzies Lyth, I. (1959). The functions of socials systems as a defense against anxiety: A report on a study of the nursing service of a general hospital. *Human Relations* 13: 95–121. Cited in Young, R. M. (1998). Benign and virulent projective identification in groups and institutions. Retrieved on May 3, 2004, from human-nature.com

———. (1988). The functioning of social systems as a defence against anxiety. In *Containing anxiety in institutions*. London: Free Association Books.

Orwell, G. (1962). *Homage to Catalonia*. Boston, MA: Beacon Press.

Reid, F., and Hoffmann, D. (2000). *Long night's journey into day*. Berkeley, CA: Iris Films.

Segal, H. (2003). The mind of the fundamentalist/terrorist. *News & Events* [annual issue]. London: Institute of Psychoanalysis.

Simpkinson, A. (2001). Are we ready to forgive? Interview with Desmond M. Tutu. Retrieved on May 3, 2004, from www.beliefnet.com/story/88/story_8880_1.html

Steiner, J. (1993). *Psychic retreats: Pathological organizations in psychotic, neurotic and borderline patients*. London: Routledge.

Velleman, J. D. (1989). *Practical reflection*. New Jersey: Princeton University Press.

Young, R. M. (1992). Benign and virulent projective identification in groups and institutions. *Human Nature Review*. Retrieved on May 3, 2004, from human-nature.com

Chapter Twenty-eight

Creative and Clinical Transformations of Trauma: Private Pain in the Public Domain

Danielle Knafo

This chapter considers the ways in which some artists convert their private trauma into public works of art. It aims to show how these works provide meaning, connection, and continuity in times of social turmoil and rupture. The oeuvres of Michal Heiman, a contemporary Israeli artist, and Charlotte Salomon, a German-born artist killed in Auschwitz, exemplify the creative solutions to personal and political tragedy. A case illustration is also presented to demonstrate ways creative techniques can be employed to master trauma in the analytic space.

Picasso once said that "Art is not Truth. Art is a lie to make us realize truth" (quoted in Chipp, 1968, p. 264). One can say something similar about psychoanalysis. Psychoanalysis is not life but through the illusion of transference one learns to better appreciate what life is about. In this chapter, I will address how both art and psychoanalysis, largely born from trauma, help us to better realize truth and appreciate life. This will be accomplished by considering both art and psychoanalysis as processes that function in the service of survival by overcoming the imprint of death, survivor guilt, death anxiety, and the psychic numbing associated with them.

The human condition is ironic because, on the one hand, we all possess a very powerful need to deny our mortality and the anxiety of death and annihilation. On the other hand, the more we free ourselves of these emotions and truths, the more restricted our consciousness and activities become and the less we allow ourselves to be fully alive. Freud (1915) acknowledged the importance of allotting death its proper place when he wrote "Would it not be better to give death the place in reality and in our thoughts which is its due, and to give a little more prominence to the unconscious attitude towards death which we have hitherto so carefully suppressed?" (p. 299).

I agree with Lifton (1987) who claims that artists who do not shy away from the subject of death or near death offer us ways in which to recognize death, to touch it, to enter into it, and to expand the limits of our imagination to imagine the real in order to survive and live in a world such as ours. It is my belief that clinicians can learn from artists who are adept at finding ways to combine reality and fantasy in a playful engagement with their pasts, all the while creating a transformational object of art, an object that synthesizes loss and attempts to repair it at one and the same time (Knafo, 2002; Segal, 1991). An important objective in the treatment of individuals who have experienced trauma, then, is the provision of creative, rather than mutually destructive, outlets for the expression of aggression.

MICHAL HEIMAN: MAKING
ART BETWEEN BOMBARDMENTS

Heiman glances in the small screen of her video camera as she films herself. She wants to see her face. She needs to see her face. She seeks the mirroring validation of the many fear reactions she experiences as she drives in a car on

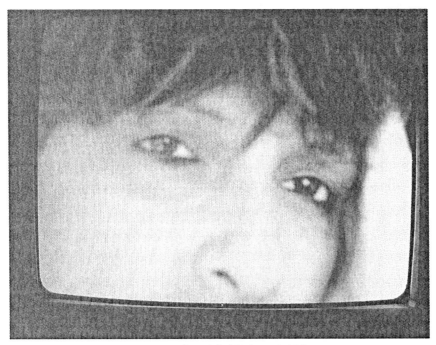

Mirror Test *by Michal Heiman (2001).*

her way to Jerusalem from Tel Aviv to teach at Bezalel Academy of Art. The car winds through streets that, over the last three years, have become perilous sites inviting numerous attacks by suicide bombers. Heiman wishes to document her fear as well as create a womb-like protective cell against external menace. She wishes to block out the danger by replacing her rearview mirror with a camera that mirrors herself, her emotions. Ironically, in her attempt to protect herself, she endangers herself because while thus preoccupied she might ignore external road signs that are intended to preserve her life.

Heiman (born 1954), a prominent contemporary Israeli artist, transforms her private pain in the public domain. Rather than focus on visions of external damage and ruin, she conveys what life under terror is about from the inside, hence her title for the piece, *Fish Bowl*.

Having been an analysand for over a decade herself, Heiman incorporates her interest in projective techniques for personality assessment as well as her awe of psychoanalysis into her art. She intends to screen these films in a museum space containing six couches. Audiences will watch as six people view the film for the duration of a fifty-minute hour. These six people must come up with one story; they must agree. Is it possible for her films to elicit only one story? Is it possible for different minds to give up one view of reality for another? The projective quality of Heiman's work, as well as the fact that no one "story" exists about the land of Israel, a land forever changing, renders such a task daunting.

Heiman does not merely create from the present-day trauma and turmoil she experiences and witnesses. As a young adolescent, she entered a closet she shared with her brother only to find her uncle who had hanged himself among her clothes. Because the family's public account of the uncle's sudden death involved his having suffered a heart attack, Heiman was asked to keep her version of the event silent, which meant keeping her trauma to herself, doubting its veracity, and struggling with feelings of guilt and confusion that it had aroused in her. Heiman vows to this day that a mirror in the closet saved her sanity. Rather than remain trapped in a restricted space with the dangling body of her uncle, she instead saw her own image reflected in the optically expanded room behind her.

It is interesting that the significance of Heiman's car mirror recalls the mirror that "saved" her in the confined closet of her youth. In both situations, she succeeds in overcoming the threat of death and self-annihilation by literally expanding the space beyond that of death's imprint and by reasserting her sense of self. Unsurprisingly, then, the mirror—whether real or figurative— has become an essential component of her art. Heiman looks into the mirror of her video camera as she drives to Jerusalem and has us look into the mirrors of our souls.

Artists like Heiman respond directly to the political tension and violence they are forced to live with. Making art in an age of terror, as she does, requires a curious amalgamation of the traumatic and the life affirming: a claustrophobic reality is transformed into a realm involving multiple possibilities. Yet, as in life, the artist does not allow for all possibilities, once elicited, to be actualized. Forcing her respondents to overcome the impossibility of interpretive closure places them in situations not unlike that of political leaders in the Middle East. For Heiman, the personal is political and the political personal. Both the personal and the political are subject to analysis. And, in the end, it all becomes fodder for her art.

Heiman had encountered difficult times when she embarked on her personal analysis.[1] She was administered projective tests to aid in her diagnosis. Later she used these very tests as raw material for her creative endeavors. Transforming passive into active is one of the things artists do best. Heiman (1997) created her own projective test, the *Michal Heiman Test* (M.H.T.), first exhibited as *Documenta X* in Kassel, Germany (curated by Catherine David) in 1997. The M.H.T. is modeled after the Thematic Aperception Test (TAT), a psychological test composed of black and white drawings to which the subject makes up stories.[2] By replacing the drawings with photographs and adding several images in color, Heiman plainly states that the Israeli external reality—replete with its imagery of war, soldiers, and occupation—is so compelling and oppressively omnipresent that one cannot avoid its influence on the inner life of her subjects. Thus, her photographs consist primarily of people posing in front of "sites where battles were fought and memorial monuments were erected to the fallen, places of national heritage, of grief where blood was spilled" (Agassi, 1997, p. 10).

Heiman's version of the TAT is clearly more personal and deliberately political than the original. Furthermore, by having art spectators sit and volunteer to be "tested" in the space of a gallery or museum, Heiman brings her projective technique into a collective cultural space. How can one, she asks implicitly through her art, ever truly separate the private from the public, the personal from the collective, and the past from the present? How can art not reflect reality? The foreshortening that takes place between reality and the imagination emerges in spectators' reactions to images of a young girl pointing to the ever-changing map of Israel; two hands holding the mangled face of a corpse; an Israeli soldier with a rifle and a club staring at the back of a Palestinian man standing with his face to the wall in a refugee camp; a group of Egyptian prisoners with their arms in the air; a group of young Israelis posing atop an enemy tank; a family (Heiman's) posing in front of the Tel Hai monument; a stone pedestal whose inscription reads: "It is good to die for our country." Heiman's test is clearly one that fills in for most psychological tests' cultural blind spots. It is a test that highlights the ways in which Israeli identity is composed of sacred places, tourist sites, evasive borders, heroic myths, and states of anxiety, emergency, and terror (Katz-Frieman, 1996, p. 10). Through her art, Heiman creatively plays with the dual struggle of surmounting trauma associated with being terrorized and that of being forced into the role of occupier and aggressor.

More recently, Heiman has been creating art in response to the Second Intifada (Palestinian uprising, begun in 2000). Continuing her interest in projective techniques, she has produced a new version of the Rorschach inkblot test that she calls *Blood Test*. Heiman replaces ink with blood taken from newspaper clippings—blood from victims of terrorist attacks; the blood of former prime minister Yitsak Rabin after his assassination, and blood from Arabs, Jews, and foreign workers.

In all these works, Heiman addresses the issue of repeated exposure to sensationalist images of atrocity. In our time and especially in Israel over the last three years, daily newspapers assail their readers with image after image of violence, blood, carnage, and destruction. It is known that viewing these images on a daily basis eventually inhibits their inherent shock value as well as one's interest in the personal suffering of those depicted. One suicide bomber's portrait begins to resemble another, and one victim's body becomes indistinguishable from the next. Heiman's aesthetic recycling of these horrific images compels us to undo our numbing defense so that we no longer remain indifferent (Sontag, 2003). We are forced to notice, contemplate, learn, and study the reasons for mass affliction. Heiman's focus on enlarged and close-up images of bloody hands and wounds divorced from personal signifiers additionally has us personalize these politically motivated acts. The crimson blood we all have in common when brutally injured or killed eliminates all differences between Arab and Jew. Thus, we all become would-be victims, and we all potentially have blood on our hands.

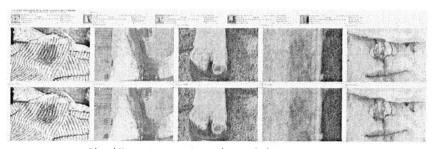

Blood Test, No. 4 *(series A) by Michal Heiman (2002).*

Today Heiman collects photographs of homes, buses, and vehicles that have been blown up and ripped apart. Photographers do not knock on doors in order to request permission to photograph. What was once a private enclosed space, privy to a select few, is transformed into public ruin for anyone to observe and even walk through. Photographers invade these spaces, just as the Palestinian bombers or the Israeli military already has. Her horror at the intrusiveness of photography in these cases has led Heiman to title her latest exhibition *Photo Rape*, a title that raises ethical questions regarding the rights and privacy denied the subjects whose interior homes and private selves lie ravaged and exposed. Heiman transforms these images into works of art that juxtapose emotion and history, public and private, outside and inside.

The photographs are mounted onto enormous canvases, and their realistic yet strangely lit atmospheres create a Vermeer-like impression that succeeds in offsetting the grim subject matter. The tension between the erotic pleasure of color and the thanatopsistic scene results in an uncanny attractiveness. Placing the photographs on walls as backdrops for her spectators, Heiman poses the ultimate psychoanalytic question: "WHAT'S ON YOUR MIND?" She thus forces her audience to concede a personal connection to what it sees. Heiman also elevates the effect of witnessing brutal raw images that are potentially traumatizing when left alone by inviting symbolic, verbalized accounts. By having her spectators/patients associate to what is seen or attempt to provide meaningful formulations for their reactions, Heiman becomes the artist/analyst who provides the structure in which to reexperience their trauma in order to help them work through the effects of that trauma.

Unlike Winnicott's (1951) transitional space, which is meant to soothe the child by living in this in-between realm bridging the inside and outside worlds, these images rip apart any illusion of safety and emphasize the very transitory nature of life and connectedness to people, places, and objects. Children, like victims of bombings, are helpless and unable to survive on their own. Indeed, Heiman is acutely sensitive to such juxtapositions. In one series of photographs, baby carriages and children's wagons are strewn adjacent to dead bodies and ruins from bombsites. There is no safe haven. Childhood illusions evaporate in the carnage. Mothers cannot guarantee safety and neither can museums or therapy. Yet, all is not hopeless in Heiman's world because her transformation of trauma into artistic expression reflects her ability to transcend what would otherwise be an overwhelming and unbearable situation. Surviving trauma, according to Robert J. Lifton (1987), involves being able to continuously imagine the encounter with death "in order to create past it, stay in it, and use it, yet move beyond it" (p. 258).

Heiman, like other artists (e.g., Otto Dix, George Grosz, Käthe Kollwitz) who create in an age of terror, does so by engaging, and having us engage, in an ongoing dialogue with death. The traumatic reaction to terrorist events involves the dissolution of connection to social structures and people as well as a disintegration of the illusions that are needed to make a more or less tolerable fabric of life (Benyakar and Knafo, see chapter 5 in this book). The art object attempts to restore these broken connections and impose form onto the destruction if only by representing it within a new structure: the structure of art. The art object, by inviting dialogue with its spectators, also acts to restore threatened social connections (Rose, 1995).

A debate exists about the artistic representation of atrocities that reflects the hierarchical opposition between history and imagination (Van-Alphen, 1997). Adorno (1962) proposed his now famous dictum that "after Auschwitz it is barbaric to continue writing poetry," a statement that set up the tone for tremendous distrust of literary or artistic representation of the Holocaust. He and others concluded that although it is necessary to record and remember—that is, to be historians—one must not exploit the pain of the victims by creating anything that might allow others to derive aesthetic pleasure—that is, to be artists. The brouhaha surrounding a 2002 exhibition at the Jewish Museum, *Mirroring Evil*, on art of Nazi aesthetics, confirms this point.

Beyond the morally ambiguous terrain this type of art deals with lies the claim that the very nature of such trauma does not lend itself to artistic expression. Steiner (1967), for instance, argued that language has been demolished by the Holocaust and that "The world of Auschwitz lies outside speech as it lies outside reason" (p. 123). Yet, despite many allegations that one cannot use language after having been traumatized, there are equal claims that one *must* use language in order to master these traumas. Elie Wiesel, when writing about the Holocaust, describes the irresolvable paradox: "How is one to speak of it? How is one not to speak of it?" (quoted in Bohm-Duchen, 1995, p. 103). Milosz (1983) declares that, after horror, "people's attitude toward language . . . changes. It recovers the simplest function and is again an instrument serving a purpose; no one doubts that the language must name reality, which exists objectively, massive, tangible, and terrifying in its concreteness" (p. 80). Indeed, art born of trauma is quite concrete and literal as is the play of children who have been traumatized. After author and Holocaust survivor Primo Levi complained of no longer being able to write, he continued to author seven books replete with powerful, desperate explorations of the essence of a human being in a world that stripped Jews of their humanity. Lifton (1987) argues that we need Hiroshima, Auschwitz, and Vietnam in order "to deepen and free . . . imagination for the leaps it must make" (p. 256). Laub and Podell (1995) provocatively assert that survival itself can be viewed as an art of trauma.

It is not a coincidence that many of these authors refer to the nearly impossible task of putting traumatic experience into words, a task recognized

by researchers who find that trauma is apparently not processed symbolically (e.g., van der Kolk, 1997). Clinicians who treat severe trauma are well
aware that verbalization, the very tool of psychoanalytic therapy, is far from
easy in such cases. Along with the challenge of employing language for
something that is deemed impossible to put into words is that of working
within a human relationship after it has been proven that human beings cannot be relied on. This is why clinicians need not be too disheartened when
faced with the finding that every intervention we make in these treatments
is, of necessity, largely incomplete and ineffective, because nothing we say
can erase the memories or bring back lost loved ones and nothing we do can
make the world a safe place or guarantee that demonic events will never
again be repeated.

This is not to say that as analysts we have nothing to offer. We can be
there with our patients, share their pain, and bear witness to the events that
caused it. We can help them express their feelings so as not to choke on
them and give words to their thoughts so as not to be mute or vocal solely
through the body. Most of all, we can assist our patients to find meaning in
their suffering, the only thing that ultimately helps them bear it. I sometimes find it useful to recall Ernest Becker's view on the essence of transference as "a taming of terror" (1973, p. 145). In the analysis of one who
has suffered trauma, one tries to find a way of helping the traumatized person change from being, or perceiving oneself as, a victim, with its concomitant passivity and dependence, to being a survivor, a person capable of
taking action to control one's destiny.

I believe that analysts can help their patients achieve this state by providing a creatively flexible analytic space, a space that at times may even come
to resemble a torture chamber. The analyst might also assume the roles of victim, tormentor, and helpless bystander, as needed. Transference in these cases
often entails a destruction of the therapist's preferred role as help giver. I am
reminded of a patient who consciously identified with Palestinian suicide
bombers as she perceived herself as destroying the treatment, herself, and me
in one massive wave of aggressive acting out. In such cases, one of the challenges is to try to transform the immense rage and need for revenge into self-
assertiveness, play, humor, and, if lucky, a creative product. Creativity and
humor should not be considered mere peripheral or defensive activities because they allow us to appreciate the ridiculous and absurd in life all the while
embracing the most important of human conditions.

An excellent example of this is Heiman's 2002 series, *Holding*. Modeled
after the famous movie poster from *Gone with the Wind* of Clark Gable holding Vivien Leigh in his strong, masculine arms, Heiman juxtaposes endless
images of bombing victims being carried in the arms of their saviors. Mirror-

ing the exact pose of the cinema's romantic couple, Heiman's acerbic humor has us witness the passing (*gone* with the wind) of romantic fantasies of love and Eros, only to be replaced by desperate couples — both Palestinians and Israelis — scrambling for cover or medical assistance in a life or death situation. This is the new pairing, she seems to be saying. This is sadly today's form of human contact.

The images of terrorized couples are horrific not only because they are bloody but, more importantly, because they show the terror, confusion, and desperation in the eyes of the people who run from death and, at the same time, run for their lives. Yet, as she documents the human state of emergency and alarm, Heiman masterfully creates a literal "holding environment" in them. The gesture of having one's fears and wounds physically and symbolically held reflects the artist's ability to contain her audience's most primal emotions and provide a safe space in which to express them.

Holding, No. 3 *by Michal Heiman (2003–2004).*
(Photograph by Moti Kimchi for Ha'Aretz, June 3,
2001, Tel-Aviv, Israel).

K: PSYCHOANALYSIS IN CHAINS

I shall refer to a patient whom I saw in analysis as K, in honor of Franz Kafka who wrote of the terror of being subjugated to inexplicable human horror. K was a woman in her thirties and the product of a forced immigration from post–World War II Eastern Europe. She was born in the land of the lost and the dispossessed: a DP camp. K's father had been blinded in an "experiment" in a concentration camp during the Holocaust (Knafo, 1998). K's most prominent childhood memories involved suffering and abuse at the hands of her survivor father whose "nerves were shot." Mr. K. was a powerful and influential man in the immigrant Eastern European community to which they belonged. At the same time, he was blind, the victim of oppression, and he worked a menial job. Mrs. K, a career woman, was not at home much of the time, a fact that reinforced the inordinate attachment that developed between K and her father.

Mr. K was a strict man who did not hesitate to use corporal punishment. K often described the manner in which she provoked her father to administer harsher beatings by hiding from him, compelling him to aimlessly flail and thrash about the house until he found her. This "battle of wills" evolved into a "game" of mutual torture in which each party alternatively took turns playing the roles of victim and victimizer, but always ended with the father "ripping into" K.

K's choice of vocation was a subject filled with ambivalence and conflict. Whereas she viewed herself as a photographer, she associated photography with luxury, selfishness, and neglect of her Eastern European/father tie. She knew that photography was self-expressive and therefore had difficulty with the exhibition of these feelings in a nonabusive, nonaltruistic mode. As a result, she experienced severe creative inhibition and hung her photographs with the picture side facing the wall. K thus expressed the ambivalence she felt regarding her father's blindness. Whereas she had become his eyes and offered to capture the visual world for him, she simultaneously symbolically "blinded" herself by depriving herself of the ability to view and portray the world from which he was excluded. As a result, she reduced her visual voice to that of "speaking to the walls."

Psychoanalysis became associated, in K's mind, with photography, self-expression, self-indulgence, aggression, and assimilation. Consequently, all the conflicts she experienced with her ethnic identity and her art were also experienced in relation to her treatment. Consciously, she appreciated that my background was different from her own and expressed relief at the fantasy that I was therefore in a better position to regard her objectively. Unconsciously, I believe that she was hoping to avoid the sadomasochism associated with her world by being in treatment with someone whom she viewed as outside of it. In the end, her feelings were too powerful, and they seeped into the treatment and even took it over.

K's self-perception as a victim was so deeply ingrained that it had become an integral part of her character. Life to her was a prison; trauma and pain were even idealized in her worldview. Her verbal expressions conveyed the sense she had of herself as a martyr. She employed very vivid language to communicate her profound feelings of persecution. K shouted at the top of her lungs for the duration of most sessions, as she related, in sadomasochistic terms, her experiences of being "spit on," "beat over the head," and "pinned against the wall." She was initially capable only of perceiving herself as the slave in relationships, a helpless prey of torture and cruelty. Nevertheless, in the transference, K acted out primarily by missing sessions or coming late and delaying the payment of her bills. She did not call to cancel her sessions and thus recreated the hide-and-seek game she had once played with her father. Like her blind father, I could not see her, did not know where she was, and felt angry at being treated so disrespectfully. And as with her father, K confessed her expectation/wish that I hit her and, ultimately, kick her out of treatment.

Coming face-to-face with the intensity of her aggression was extremely disconcerting for K and for me. However, as her life events and acting out behaviors were mirrored and interpreted, and her intense pain contained and held, she began to recognize and accept the pervasiveness of her sadomasochistic view of life. This was accomplished first by analyzing her relationships outside of the treatment and then by analyzing the transference and her acting out behaviors. Transference analysis proved the most effective but necessitated our temporarily allowing the analytic space to be transformed into a concentration camp of her own making, wherein either she or I was cast in the role of prisoner and held in bondage. This was not always easy because it evoked powerful feelings in me as well (e.g., fight-flight), yet I knew it was essential to enter K's world of torture and violence in order to help her move beyond it. K's analogy of analysis with a concentration camp was a very somber matter, yet by casting me in whatever role she wished and watching me survive her repeated attacks, this world ultimately became a less threatening one.

My being a woman, I believe, was also a significant factor in K's treatment. K's mother was absent much of the time and, when she was present, K developed a disrespect for her that generalized to all matters feminine. Her overattachment and overidentification with her father prevented her from incorporating softer, more maternal, elements into her personality. Instead, she viewed reality as an arena in which she needed to fight for her life. And fight she did. Fighting with me and against me in the analytic space without being attacked in return gradually led K to allow herself to be "held" by me, which, in turn, allowed for a degree of internalization of my nurturing behaviors toward her. As she became gentler toward herself, the world became a friendlier and less persecutory place in which to live. One outcome of this change was her marriage to her longtime boyfriend with whom she established a home.

It was at times difficult to reconcile K's world of misery and torture with her artistic world. Much of her emotional life was unsublimated, raw, powerful, and angry. Photography was psychologically loaded and guilt inducing due to its connection to her father's blindness, resulting in K's experiencing acute bouts of creative inhibition. At these times, I directed her to experiment in a medium other than photography, and she chose clay. Because making art with clay involved tactile sensations more than visual ones and could easily be performed by a blind person, K's guilt was alleviated and her creative impulses liberated, which then allowed her to return to photography, her artistic medium of choice.

It is important to note that during the entire time that the analytic space took the form of a torture chamber, this milieu simultaneously became an artist's studio, a place where K imaginatively created images that would ultimately set her free. It was in this third space (Winnicott, 1951; Ogden, 1994), a space that bridged the past with the present and external and internal worlds, that K and I finally sculpted a new self, a self both angry and free. Accepting this change was inevitably fraught with conflict because it represented Americanization and the possibility of getting her needs met and of being treated with dignity and respect.

As K gradually relinquished her masochistic stance, she began to take on more assertive roles in her life. Although photography did not entirely disappear, it receded into the background. In its place, K's political activity, initially employed in defensive identification with her father, eventually became an area to which she brought her creativity and in which she took charge and legitimately sublimated and expressed her angry feelings. Her activism required multiple public speaking engagements in which she came to excel, which is significant since she began treatment with a phobia of public speaking. K had finally found her voice.

CHARLOTTE SALOMON: SUICIDAL ART

Charlotte Salomon (1917–1943), like Heiman and K, experienced childhood trauma (a family history of multiple suicides) that assumed a new form in the context of social tragedy (Nazi persecution).[3] Before she was murdered in Auschwitz in 1943, twenty-six years old and five months pregnant, Salomon completed a barely veiled autobiographical picture novel titled *Leben? oder Theater?* (Life? or Theater?), a brave life-confirming artistic document that prevailed over the somberness of its inspiration and content. Salomon crafted this amazing work of art because, in her words, "I have a feeling the whole world has to be put back together again." Rather than follow in the footsteps of the women in her family—her mother, grandmother, and aunt—all of whom had committed suicide, Salomon chose instead to transform her private trauma into a work of art, a work that has become a noble testimony to the power of spiritual preservation.

"*C'est toute ma vie!*" Salomon exclaimed to Georges Moridis, a doctor and friend in the Resistance to whom she entrusted her oeuvre before being ushered to her death. Indeed, the work she had frantically produced between 1940 and 1942, while exiled in France's Cote d'Azur, was her life and more. In addition to being a poignant coming-of-age story set among increasing Nazi oppression, it was the way she found to stay alive, to choose life over death, and to become immortal through her art.

If we appreciate the full value of her statement to Dr. Moridis, then the bookends of this masterpiece are highly significant. Salomon chose to open her musical theater with the suicide of her aunt Charlotte, after whom she was named. Although her aunt's suicide took place four years before Salomon's birth, the artist considered this event an apt one to begin the story of *her* life. Born into a legacy of willful death, her blood tie was one against which she would struggle for the remainder of her life.

The work concludes in Nice where she was exiled along with her maternal grandparents. While there, her grandmother, unable to bear life anymore, made a suicide gesture. As if to speak both to her grandmother and herself, Salomon desperately draws attention to the sun, flowers, and mountains. Finally, she states that her grandmother has a choice: to write or die. The grandmother chose death. Not long afterward, it became inevitable that Salomon confront the same choice: to take her life or to undertake something, as she put it, "wildly eccentric." *She* chose the latter. Salomon chose the path of creativity. "I will create a story so as not to lose my mind," she announced. Indeed, between her bookends of death, Salomon created a space for mourning—mourning the many losses she had had, mourning the future she would never have. In the end, Salomon's *Gesamtkunstwerk* can be considered a type of memorial.

Salomon *knew* the essence of trauma. She strove to make sense of the trail of family suicides under conditions in which she found herself increasingly isolated and endangered as a Jew. Unsurprisingly, then, her work came to reflect the familiar discontinuity, disruption, and fragmentation associated with traumatic experiencing. Although the entire oeuvre (1,325 gouaches each measuring roughly 13" x 10"; 784 were numbered into a final version by the author) was completed using only the three primary colors, indicating a strong life force, the pictures themselves reveal an intensity that belies psychological and realistic danger (Salomon, 1981). It is a work of urgency, a work that suggests impending doom. Its images are at once intimate and claustrophobic.

More than twenty characters speak in soliloquies and dialogues in thousands of scenes from Salomon's external and internal life. Images alternately present close-ups, long shots, flashbacks, and montages, winding from one person to another and from one angle to another, in a serpentine composition. Sometimes, the artist employs multiple angles to suggest the passage of time, placing the most recent events in the foreground and earlier incidents in receding

*Life? or Theatre?: A Play With Music by Charlotte Salomon (1940–1942). Collection
Jewish Historical Museum, Amsterdam. Copyright Charlotte Salomon Foundation.*

planes. At other times, she applies an aerial perspective, dispensing with ceil-
ings in order to peer into the rooms of a house. In yet others, she sets the images swirling about the page with no discernible order. Finally, she sometimes
breaks up scenes in a comic-book style. It is often difficult to know where one
scene ends and the next begins. At times, her use of multiple selves in one

frame is dizzying. Whereas many pages depict one or two characters, it is not uncommon for a page to be inhabited by dozens of characters or for the same scene to be portrayed a dozen times or more. Although Salomon thereby attempted to achieve cinematic effects, she often created a whirlwind of text, color, and image that must have reflected the confused and terrified state of mind in which she found herself.

The clustering of images also reflects the combination of memory and fantasy, from whose archives she drew the content of her stories. Some occurrences are pure fictional representations. Her mother's death, which took place when she was a child of eight, for instance, was not an event Salomon actually witnessed or even knew about (she was informed that her mother died of influenza). In fact, she was told of the family suicide trail only after her grandmother tried to hang herself in Nice. Her grandfather, apparently upset by his wife's suicide attempt and the encroaching war, callously confronted Salomon with the family birthright (four women and two men had committed suicide) and even prodded her to take her own life. It is not difficult to understand why her grandmother's suicide attempt served as a pivotal catalyst for Salomon's creative endeavor. She simultaneously witnessed the suicide of her grandmother and was told about the suicide of her mother for the first time, both suicides involving women who jumped from an open window to their deaths. Salomon depicts the two suicides in her work, one witnessed and one imagined, condensing the important women in her life and thus combining adult pain with childhood longing.

Salomon's strong need to imagine how the event of her mother's suicide took place has her depicting the episode from both inner and outer perspectives. In one frame, we look directly into the mother's face, which is attached to profiles of her husband and daughter. Then we see her dreamily looking out of the window. As the coloring becomes darker and more ominous, we observe her from behind. And, finally, all that remains is a stark empty window frame. The next frame is a close-up of her dead face. Before the death, we witness a child who was very attached to her mother and who empathically watched as her mother became increasingly depressed and disinterested in life. Intimate conversations take place in bed during which mother enlightens daughter about how beautiful it is in heaven and that she would like to go there and become an angel. She promises to write from heaven, and after her death, Salomon repeatedly checks the mail for the letter that never arrived. Endless repetitions reflect her attempts to master a life that was quickly spinning out of her control.

The relationship between image, text, and music are very intricately interwoven in *Leben? oder Theater?* Although Salomon's work is visual, it is also highly texted. Scenes are additionally escorted by suggestions for musical accompaniment culled from opera and other sources. In the first part of the

Life? or Theatre?: A Play With Music *by Charlotte Salomon (1940–1942). Collection
Jewish Historical Museum, Amsterdam. Copyright Charlotte Salomon Foundation*

work, Salomon added text onto tracing paper, which was superimposed onto
the painted pages. It is not coincidental that she dispensed with the tracing paper and began to include text directly on the painted pages at the point at
which she meets Alfred Wolfsohn (renamed Amadeus Daberlohn in the play).

She also has Wolfsohn/Daberlohn comically enter her tale to the tune of the toreador's song from *Carmen*.

Wolfsohn was a kind of voice therapist, called in to help Salomon's stepmother, singer Paula Lindberg (renamed Paulinka Bimbam), with her voice. The entrance of Lindberg and Wolfsohn into Salomon's life was radical. Salomon idolized Lindberg and received much love, warmth, and attention from this extremely positive maternal figure. Adolescent idealization swings back and forth between her stepmother and her Svengali-like mentor, both recipients of serious crushes, creating palpable and shifting oedipal tension. One painting pictorially illustrates Salomon's primal scene tableau: she is in the lower right corner facing the viewer while, in the background, Wolfsohn and Lindberg are literally making beautiful music together.

Salomon met with Wolfsohn, often in secret, and absorbed many of his ideas, which are evident in her oeuvre. Wolfsohn's theories, clearly influenced by psychoanalysis, are allotted a great deal of space. His axiom, "You must first go into yourself—into your childhood—to be able to get out of yourself" is quoted four times. Page after page exists of text that winds around his disembodied head floating in space. Indeed, at one point, Salomon drew Wolfsohn/Daberlohn's figure 191 times above each phrase of a rather lengthy pontification. Wolfsohn believed that geniuses are made, not born, and that one becomes an artist only by getting in touch with one's inner self. He also preached that creativity was born of trauma and suffering. "The emotional life of the singer," he said, "must suffer a great upheaval to enable that singer to achieve exceptional results." When reading these words, it is impossible not to think of the exceptional results achieved by Salomon in her musical masterpiece.

Salomon's epic, although heavily influenced by the political conditions under which she lived, allots little space to the actual depiction of these events. Nonetheless, she does chronicle the Nazi attacks on the Jews that accelerated in 1938 and culminated in Kristallnacht, November 9, 1938. Her father was arrested and sent to Sachsenhausen, a labor camp. Salomon depicts with brutal clarity scenes of Nazis marching and a guard standing over the bowed shadow of a figure her imprisoned father had become in the camp.

As the work proceeds, Salomon's images become more sloppily produced and text assumes a more central place. This is partly because Salomon shifts her focus from actual memories to psychological complexities. Toward the end of her oeuvre, Salomon's text progressively crowds out image until it completely takes over. It is clear that Salomon was feverishly trying to complete her work as she sensed that time was running out. Irregularly sized letters and disembodied words become bolder and demand more room, often with barely a space between them. Her last words are: "And with dream-

Life? or Theatre?: A Play With Music *by Charlotte Salomon (1940–1942). Collection Jewish Historical Museum, Amsterdam. Copyright Charlotte Salomon Foundation.*

awakened eyes she saw all the beauty around her, saw the sea, felt the sun, and knew, she had to vanish for a while from the human plane in order to create her world anew out of the depths. And from that came *Life or Theater?*" Her final image is one of herself seated at the beach in her bathing suit, paintbrush in hand. She looks out to sea and contemplates her death, a death that she willingly embraces but a death not caused by suicide. In large letters printed across her back are the words "LEBEN ODER THEATER." In the end, Salomon chose *both* life *and* theater.

Although Salomon's work did not succeed in saving her life, it seems to have given her life a purpose. It allowed her to visit her past, no matter how painful, in the context of a terrifying present and future. It brought to life her youthful passion and creative spirit. It connected her, in her isolated exiled state, to those most dear to her and breathed life back into the dead, in blatant refusal to accept their disappearance from her life. It helped her battle the death forces in her by facing the truth about her family and the world. It helped her to find herself. She wrote: "The war raged on and I sat by the sea and saw deep into the heart of humankind. I was my mother my grandmother indeed I was all the characters in the play. I learned to walk all paths and became myself."

CONCLUSION

Creative Repair: The Art of Trauma

The art discussed in this chapter is an art created at the intersection of personal, aesthetic, social, and political experience. It is art made in the service of survival. The creation of art when facing death involves the aesthetic response to human emergency. It represents an attempt to shift the power relations by handing power to the weak and helpless, to those most in need of safety and support. It is a warning system as well as a form of resistance against destructive forces (Stiles, 1992). Kristine Stiles (1992) has given the label "destruction art" to works that "situate the body in the center of the question of destruction and survival" (p. 75). Paradoxically, although the content of this art is destruction, its purpose seems to be aimed at preventing trauma from destroying the survivor's power to fantasize and diminish her spontaneity and individuality. Instead, this art is in the service of mastery over destruction, loss, numbing, and mourning.

Freud realized the relevance of mastery in such phenomena when he wrote *Beyond the Pleasure Principle* (1920). There, he observed that nightmares of shell-shocked soldiers challenged his theory positing that all dreams are representations of the fulfillment of ungratified wishes. Freud came to regard such dreams as constituting a violent attempt to master and overcome trauma. Childrens' games (e.g., *fort da*), played in the shadow of loss, were understood as serving a similar function. In their play, children repeat everything that has made a great impression on them in real life, and in doing so, they abreact the strength of the impression and, as one might put it, make themselves masters of the situation (pp. 16–17). Freud extended this argument to artists, especially as it concerned creativity related to trauma. Unsurprisingly, then, the works of both Heiman and Salomon involve endless repetitions as they compulsively attempt to master a situation veering out of control. Their aesthetic repetitions assault viewers and induce in them sensations felt by the artists themselves, and thereby have them share the psychological burden, as well as the ethical responsibility, of containing them.

Although it is definitely possible for us to feel traumatized by witnessing repeated scenes of bombings or suicides, the aesthetic response to such art is far from simple. Despite the difficult content of the artworks discussed here, there also exists a clear attempt to discover and communicate truth—truth about humankind and truth about one's inner world. This attempt is not unlike the task facing psychoanalysts. We, too, embark on a joint journey with our patients, a journey that takes us to the depths of the human spirit. Sometimes, we do not like what we see or recoil from the intensity of emotion and experience. Nonetheless, we know that it is truth that ultimately sets people free from their pain and symptoms. That truth, often relentlessly pursued by artists, is a truth often avoided by most. Although Heiman and Salomon clearly struggle to deal with their personal and collective trauma, their art compels us to acknowledge, if only through unconscious identification, that we are all survivors of devastation from wars, holocausts, and nuclear disasters, and we all live with the imprint of death and the guilt that surrounds it. Artists possess the gift of using aesthetic form to present us with these unpalatable truths in order to help us digest them.

In addition to their heightened sense of inner and outer reality (Greenacre, 1957), artists also have a strong need to repair the bleak and damaged world they see before them. According to Melanie Klein's theory, creativity is born of the depressive position. It is the infant's wish to repair the destroyed harmony with the mother that propels it toward a creative solution: the restoration and recreation of a lost world. "True reparation," writes Segal, "must include an acknowledgement of aggression and its effect" (1991, p. 92). Art, therefore, involves the balancing of ugly (aggressive) and beautiful (reparative) elements because it takes into account the reality of separateness and loss.

In certain ways, Klein's theory reminds me of the response found in the Jewish mystical tradition of the Kabbalah to people who question why there is evil in the world or how a benevolent God can allow evil to exist. The Kabbalah teaches that because God made humans his partner, Creation remains unfinished. It is only through *Tikkun Olam*, acts of healing and repair, that Creation is completed and the world restored. Indeed, artists possess the singular ability to restore life from the most broken and damaged pieces. Thus, Michal Heiman takes a world shattered by human bombs and uses embraces and blood to glue the shards back together again, and Charlotte Salomon adds color and humor to the tune of suicide and mass annihilation in her epic tale.

The artist, like the mother in Bion's theory, becomes the container of malignant projections from the environment and gives them back to spectators in a form they can handle. This does not mean that art born of terror is easy to look at. It simply means that such art may render our reality easier to look at and our lives easier to bear.

Psychoanalytic treatment of trauma offers the patient similar avenues of repair. Although K captured the world in her photography, she was initially unable to look at that world or have others look at it. Only after transforming the analytic space into a cruel and sadomasochistic play arena was K able to confront her darker side, the side that was passed onto her by family tragedy. The psychoanalytic space, with its continuity and lack of judgment, created a structured and accepting setting in which to play with and play out the most horrific of experiences. Psychoanalysis, then, offers its traumatized patients the ultimate creative experience: the possibility of creating a survivor who is strengthened rather than destroyed by trauma. If analysts succeed in achieving this, then they too participate in the creative process, a process that ultimately embraces life while unflinchingly staring death in the eye.

NOTES

This chapter is reproduced from Danielle Knafo, Creative and clinical transformations of trauma, *Israel Journal of Psychoanalysis*, 2003, 1 (4): 537–63. Reprinted with permission from the *Israel Journal of Psychoanalysis*.

1. All information about Michal Heiman's life and career are taken from interviews and conversations with the artist over the last several years. She has read and given permission to print this chapter as is.

2. In 1998, Heiman created a second "test" modeled after the TAT. Her *M.H.T no. 2, Ma belle-mere, Test pour femmes* (My mother-in-law, test for women), includes sixty-seven cards with photographs of Heiman's mother-in-law at the time.

3. All biographical information on Salomon's life is taken from Felstiner's 1994 biography of the artist.

REFERENCES

Adorno, T. (1992). Engagement (1962). In Rolf Tiedemann (Ed.), Sherry Weber Nicholsen (Trans.), *Notes on literature*, pp. 76–94. New York: Columbia University Press.

Agassi, M. (1997). M. H. T.: Looking as a test or the test of looking. In *Michal Heiman Test (M. H. T.) Supplement*. Israel.

Becker, E. (1973). *The denial of death*. New York: Free Press.

Bohm-Duchen, M. (1995). Fifty years on. In *After Auschwitz: Responses to the Holocaust in contemporary art*, pp. 103–45. Sunderland, England: Northern Centre for Contemporary Art.

Chipp, H. (1968). *Theories of art*. Berkeley: University of California Press.

Felstiner, M. L. (1994). *To paint her life: Charlotte Salomon in the Nazi Era*. New York: HarperCollins.

Freud, S. (1915/1957). Thoughts for the times on war and death. *Standard Edition*, 14, pp. 275–300. London: Hogarth Press.

———. (1920/1955). Beyond the pleasure principle. *Standard Edition*, 18, pp. 7–64. London: Hogarth Press.

Greenacre, P. (1957/1971). The childhood of the artist. In *Emotional growth*, Vol. 2. New York: International Universities Press.

Heiman, M. (1997). *Michal Heiman Test (M.H.T.)*. Givatayim, Israel: Eli Meir.

Katz-Freiman, T. (1996). A matter of distance. In *Desert cliché: Israel now—local images*, exhibit catalog, p.10. The Israeli Forum of Art Museums and the Bass Museum of Art, Miami Beach, Florida.

Knafo, D. (1998). Transitional space in the treatment of immigrants. *Israel Journal of Psychiatry*, 35: 48–55.

———. (2002). Revisiting Ernst Kris' concept of regression in the service of the ego. *Psychoanalytic Psychology*, 19: 24–49.

Laub, D., and Podell, D. (1995). Art and trauma. *International Journal of Psycho-Analysis*, 76: 991–1005.

Lifton, R. J. (1987). *The future of immortality and other essays for a nuclear age*. New York: Basic Books.

Milosz, C. (1983). *The witness of poetry*. Cambridge, MA: Harvard University Press.

Ogden, T. (1994). The analytic third: Working with intersubjective clinical facts. In *Subjects of analysis*. Northvale, NJ: Jason Aronson.

Rose, G. (1995). *Necessary illusions: Art as "witness."* New York: International Universities Press.

Salomon, C. (1981). Leila Vennewitz (Trans.), *Life or theater? An autobiographical play by Charlotte Salomon*. New York: Viking.

Segal. H. (1991). Art and the depressive position. In *Dream, phantasy and art*, pp. 85–100. London: Tavistock/Routledge.

Sontag, S. (2003). *Regarding the pain of others*. New York: Farrar, Straus and Giroux.

Steiner, G. (1967). *Language and silence: Essays on language, literature, and the inhuman*. New York: Atheneum.

Stiles, K. (1992). Survival ethos and destruction art. *Discourse: Journal for Theoretical Studies in Media and Culture*, 14: 74–102.

Van-Alphen, E. (1997). *Caught by history: Holocaust effects in contemporary art, literature, and theory*. Stanford, CA: Stanford University Press.

van der Kolk, B. A. (1997). The psychobiology of post-traumatic stress disorder. *Journal of Clinical Psychiatry*, 58: 16–24.

Winnicott, D. W. (1951/1975). Transitional objects and transitional phenomena. In *Through pediatrics to psycho-analysis*, pp. 229–42. New York: Basic Books.

Carbon Reflection *by Joshua Neustein (1992).*

Index

About the Contributors

Karen Alkalay-Gut, Ph.D., was born in London on the last night of the Blitz. Since 1972, she has been living in Israel where she teaches poetry at Tel Aviv University. She chairs the Israel Association of Writers in English and is vice chair of the Federation of Writers Union in Israel. She is the coeditor of *Pen Israel Anthology 1997*. Recent poetry books include *The Love of Clothes and Nakedness*, *In My Skin*, and *High Maintenance*.

Elia Awwad, Ph.D., is currently the director of the Palestinian Red Crescent Society's Mental Health Department where he works on several projects addressing the psychological trauma experienced by children and their families in the Palestinian West Bank and Gaza Strip. He provides counseling and training services for emergency medical service teams, schoolteachers, refugees, women, and youth. His work includes joint Palestinian-Israeli efforts pertaining to drug addiction, peace education, reconciliation, trauma training, and research. He has written extensively on his work with victims of violence and trauma in the Palestinian-Israeli context.

Ofra Ayalon, Ph.D., is an Israeli psychologist and family therapist as well as an internationally renowned traumatologist, author, and trainer in the field of trauma and coping with terrorism. She is currently the director of Nord COPE Center and Senior Consultant at the Community Stress Prevention Center in Kiriat Shmona-Tel Hai College, Israel. Dr. Ayalon has published extensively on the impact of domestic violence, trauma, stress, major disasters, war, terrorism, and bereavement in children. She authored the book *Rescue: Community Oriented Prevention Education for Coping* and has devised a comprehensive method for a crisis intervention program widely used to enhance coping skills for survivors and rescue workers during and after major disasters.

Dan Bar-On, Ph.D., is professor of psychology in the Department of Behavioral Science at Ben-Gurion University in Beer Sheva, Israel. Dr. Bar-On's pioneering field research in Germany focused on the psychological and moral aftereffects of the Holocaust on the children of the perpetrators. He is author of *Legacy of Silence: Encounters with Children of the Third Reich* and *Fear and Hope: Three Generations of Holocaust Survivors' Families*. Dr. Bar-On is known for bringing together descendents of Holocaust survivors and perpetrators described in his book *The Indescribable and the Undiscussable*, as well as Israelis and Palestinians. He is the director of a new Center for the Dialogue between Populations in Conflict and the codirector (with Professor Sami Adwan) of Peace Research Institute in the Middle East (PRIME).

Mordechai Benyakar, M.D., Ph.D., is president-elect of the Section of Military Psychiatry and Disaster Interventions of the World Psychiatric Association (WPA). He is also the director of the International Training Program on Stress Trauma and Disaster Intervention. He is a supervisor at the Center of Psychic Trauma of the Faculty of Medicine of Buenos Aires and an invited professor at the Medical School of Buenos Aires University (UBA). He is a professor at the Sackler Medical School in Tel Aviv University and was director of the Mental Health Program in Tel Aviv and Ramat-Gan, Israel, during the Gulf War and in Argentina during the terrorist attack on the Jewish Community of Buenos Aires. Dr. Benyakar has published over four hundred articles on disaster, stress, and trauma and recently published a book (in Spanish) titled *Disruption/Individual and Collective Threats: The Psyche Facing War, Terrorism, and Social Catastrophes*.

Rony Berger, Psy.D., is the director of Community Services for Natal, the Israel Trauma Center for Victims of Terror and War. He is an internationally recognized expert in dealing with the psychological preparation and aftermath of terrorist attacks. He is also a researcher at the Harry Truman Center for the Advancement of Peace at Hebrew University in Jerusalem. Dr. Berger is completing two books: *Parents and Children in the Shadow of Terror* and *Transcending Trauma: A Mind-Body Self-Healing Approach*.

Maria V. Bergmann is a practicing psychoanalyst in New York. She is a training and supervising analyst of the New York Freudian Society. Her psychoanalytic papers and teaching activities in the United States and abroad have centered on issues of feminine development, creativity, trauma, the Holocaust, problems of technique, and treatment of perversions. She is the author of *What I Heard in the Silence: Role Reversal, Trauma, and Creativity in the Lives of Women*.

Martin S. Bergmann is clinical professor of psychology at New York University's Postdoctoral Program in Psychoanalysis and an honorary member of the American Psychoanalytic Society, as well as a member of the New York Freudian Society and the International Psychoanalytic Society. He is the author and editor of many books, including *The Evolution of Psychoanalytic Technique*, *Generations of the Holocaust*, *Anatomy of Loving*, *In the Shadow of Moloch*, and *The Hartmann Era*.

Harold P. Blum, M.D., is clinical professor of psychiatry and training analyst at New York University's School of Medicine, Department of Psychiatry. He is the executive director of the Sigmund Freud Archives. Dr. Blum is past editor in chief of the *Journal of the American Psychoanalytic Association* and past vice president of the International Psychoanalytical Association. He is the author of several books and more than 150 psychoanalytic papers.

John T. Cannon, Ph.D., wrote his dissertation on experiences of the 1989 Loma Prieta earthquake. He has worked for the Alegent Health Behavioral Services for the past ten years. One of his special interests is the recovery and relapse of trauma victims and survivors.

Michael Eigen, Ph.D., is the author of ten books, including *Rage*, *Damaged Bonds*, *Ecstasy*, *The Psychoanalytic Mystic*, and *The Electrified Tightrope*. He is on the faculty of, and a training analyst at, the National Psychological Association for Psychoanalysis and associate clinical professor of psychology at New York University's Postdoctoral Program in Psychotherapy and Psychoanalysis.

Kiki Elefant is a contemporary Israeli artist who has exhibited at the Israel Museum of Art, the Artist House in Jerusalem, and the Limbus Gallery in Tel Aviv. She lives and works in Hertzilia, Israel.

Bracha Ettinger is a very influential contemporary artist whose work has gained historical significance. She is also a major theorist in the field of psychoanalysis, aesthetics, and feminism. Among her publications are *The Matrixial Gaze* and *The Matrixial Border Space*. Her paintings have been exhibited in major museums including the Pompidou Center and Stedelijk Museum, the Drawing Center of New York, and the Palais des Beaux-Arts, Brussels. Many art historians and philosophers, among them Griselda Pollock, Jean-Francois Lyotard, and Felix Guattari, have written about her work.

Ettinger's artwork deals with the relationship between memory-traces and the Holocaust and with the working through of grief and trauma through art.

Katie Gentile, Ph.D., is an assistant professor and the director of the Women's Center at John Jay College of Criminal Justice. She has presented at conferences and written articles on the effects of trauma on the creation of time, and sexual abuse, dissociation, and eating problems. She is also a psychoanalyst in private practice in New York City.

Ann Pollinger Haas, Ph.D., is research director of the American Foundation for Suicide Prevention and Professor of Health Services at Lehman College of The City University of New York. Together with Herbert Hendin, she has coauthored numerous peer-reviewed articles on Post-Traumatic Stress Disorders (PTSDs) in Vietnam veterans as well as a book, *Wounds of War*, on the psychological aftermath of the Vietnam War. The relation of PTSD to suicide was the subject of a study they published in the *American Journal of Psychiatry*, "Suicide and Guilt as Manifestations of Posttraumatic Disorder in Vietnam Veterans."

Michal Heiman lives in Tel-Aviv, Israel, and teaches photography and critical studies at Bezalel's Academy of Art and the Sam Spiegel School of Film and Television in Jerusalem. Her art underscores her understanding of the intimate tie that exists between art, psychology, therapy, and politics. She has had many solo and group exhibitions and has gained an impressive reputation on the local as well as international art scenes. She is a recipient of the Israel Museum prize for photography.

Herbert Hendin, M.D., is medical director of the American Foundation for Suicide Prevention and professor of psychiatry at New York Medical College. While director of the Center for Psychosocial Studies, he was the principal investigator on a five-year study of Post-Traumatic Stress Disorder (PTSD) in Vietnam veterans. In addition to more than fifty professional articles and five books on suicide, Dr. Hendin coauthored with Professor Ann Haas ten articles on PTSD as well as a book *Wounds of War: The Psychological Aftermath of Combat in Vietnam*.

Judith Lewis Herman, M.D., is professor of clinical psychiatry at Harvard University's Medical School and the director of training at the Victims of Violence Program in the Department of Psychiatry at Cambridge Hospital. She is well known for her research in the areas of child abuse, domestic violence, and posttraumatic disorders. Her books *Trauma and Recovery* and *Father-Daughter Incest* are landmarks in the field.

Craig Higson-Smith, M.A., is a senior research specialist in the Human Sciences Research Council of South Africa, a director of the South African Institute for Traumatic Stress, and a private consultant to various South African industries. His interests are in the fields of violence, traumatic stress, and community psychology.

Amy C. Hudnall, M.A., is an adjunct professor in the history department at Appalachian State University. Her work focuses on cross-cultural trauma and genocide from an historical frame of reference. She is also the managing editor for the *NWSA Journal*, the flagship journal of the National Women's Studies Association.

Marvin Hurvich, Ph.D., is a training and supervisory analyst at the Institute for Psychoanalytic Training and Research, The New York Freudian Society, and New York University's Postdoctoral Program in Psychoanalysis and Psychotherapy. He is a professor of psychology at Long Island University, Brooklyn Center, a diplomate in Psychoanalysis, American Board of Professional Psychology, and a member of the International Psychoanalytic Association. His major current area of interest involves the theoretical, clinical, and empirical aspects of annihilation anxiety.

Robert Karen, Ph.D., is a psychologist in private practice in New York City. His most recent books are *Becoming Attached: First Relationships and How They Shape Our Capacity to Love* and *The Forgiving Self: The Road from Resentment to Connection*. His work has appeared in *The Psychoanalytic Review*, *Readings*, *The Yale Review*, *The Atlantic Monthly*, *New York Magazine*, *The Nation*, and elsewhere. He is an associate clinical professor at the Derner Institute of Advanced Psychological Studies at Adelphi University.

Fattma Kassem is a doctoral student at the Ben-Gurion University in Israel. She has worked as a lecturer and facilitator on the project "Two Conflicts, Four Countries" (participants were history teachers from Turkey, Greece, Israel, and Palestine) and a facilitator at the Unit of Democracy and Coexistence, a project that brings together Israeli and Palestinian students.

J. David Kinzie, M.D., is professor of psychiatry at Oregon Health & Science University, Portland, Oregon. He has served as a general physician in Vietnam and Malaysia and as a psychiatrist in Malaysia. Dr. Kinzie started the Indochinese Psychiatric Program (now the Intercultural Psychiatric Program) in 1977. He is director of the Torture Treatment Center of Oregon and of the Child Traumatic Stress Center of Oregon and is the author of over one hundred articles on the subject of trauma. He currently treats Cambodian-, Somali-, and Spanish-speaking patients.

Danielle Knafo, Ph.D., is associate professor in the Clinical Psychology Doctoral Program at Long Island University's C.W. Post Campus. She is a member of faculty and a supervisor at Derner's Postdoctoral Program in Psychotherapy and Psychoanalysis. Dr. Knafo is the author of *Egon Schiele: A Self in Creation*, as well as numerous publications on psychoanalysis and creativity. She maintains a private practice in Great Neck, New York.

Ruth Knafo Setton, Ph.D., is the author of the novel *The Road to Fez* and the recipient of awards from the National Endowment for the Arts, PEN, and the PA Council on the Arts. She is the writer-in-residence at the Berman Center for Jewish Studies at Lehigh University and the fiction editor of the literary journal *Arts and Letters: A Journal of Contemporary Culture*. She has just completed a new novel and a collection of poetry.

Henry Krystal, M.D., is professor emeritus of psychiatry at Michigan State University and a member of faculty at the Michigan Psychoanalytic Institute and the Michigan Psychoanalytic Council. He is recognized as an authority on affect, theory, substance abuse, and trauma. Dr. Krystal is the author of numerous publications, including *Massive Psychic Trauma, Drug Dependence* (with Herbert Raskin), and *Integration and Self Healing: Affect, Trauma, and Alexithymia*.

Wlodzimierz Ksiazek was born in Poland and has lived in the United States since 1982. He is represented by Kouros Gallery in New York City and Alpha Gallery in Boston. He has had many one-man shows and group exhibitions in the United States and abroad, as well as numerous monographs dedicated to his work with essays by the likes of Donald Kuspit, Robert Morgan, and Dominique Nahas.

Robert J. Lifton, M.D., is a visiting professor of psychiatry at Harvard Medical School. He is the internationally renowned author of numerous books that combine the social, psychological, and political. They include *Death in Life: Survivors of Hiroshima; The Nazi Doctors; Home from the War: Vietnam Veterans: Neither Executioners nor Victims; Destroying the World to Save It: Aum Shinrikyo; and Apocalyptic Violence and the New Global Terrorism*.

Joshua Neustein is an artist who helped pioneer environmental, conceptual, and political art in the 1970s. He has exhibited in American, European, and Israeli museums. His work is in the collections of the MOMA, Metropolitan, and Guggenheim Museums, New York; Gropius-Bau and Jewish Museum (Liebeskind), Berlin; Zachenta, Warsaw; Albright Gallery, Tel-Aviv; Hertzilia Museum, Stedelijk, Amsterdam; and more. He has received the Jerusalem Prize, Sandberg Prize, Guggenheim Fellowship, and Pollock Krasner Grant.

Bennett Roth, Ph.D., is in private practice in New York City. He is a fellow and member of faculty at IPTAR, a fellow of the American Group Psychotherapy Association, and a fellow in psychoanalysis of the psychoanalytic division of the American Psychological Association. Dr. Roth is a faculty member of the Adelphi Postdoctoral Program in Psychoanalysis. He is the senior editor of *The Difficult Patient in Group*. Dr. Roth worked under the New York Times Neediest Cases grant, assisting both corporations and New York City schools recover from the effects of being in close proximity to the World Trade Center site.

Carolee Schneemann is a multidisciplinary artist whose work has been extremely influential in transforming the very definition of art, especially with regard to discourse on the body, sexuality, and gender. Her video and installation pieces have been shown at the Los Angeles Museum of Contemporary Art; the New Museum of Contemporary Art, New York City; as well as in Europe. Published books include *Imaging Her Erotics—Essays, Interviews, Projects* and *More Than Meat Joy: Complete Performance Work and Selected Writing*. She lives and works in New Paltz, New York.

Ilene Serlin, Ph.D., ADTR, is a fellow of the American Psychological Association (APA), Council Representative and past president of Division 32 (Humanistic Psychology) of the APA, and member of the newly established APA Task Force on the Psychological Effects of Efforts to Prevent Terrorism. Dr. Serlin served on the Disaster Team of the Loma Prieta earthquake, for which she received recognition by the American Red Cross. She has taught in the United States, Russia, Europe, and Israel.

B. Hudnall Stamm, Ph.D., is a research professor and director of Telehealth at the Idaho State University Institute of Rural Health. Working primarily with rural and underserved peoples, Dr. Stamm focuses on cultural trauma, telehealth, and secondary traumatic stress. She is editor of the book *Secondary Stress*.

Charles B. Strozier, Ph.D., is a professor of history at John Jay College where he also directs the Center on Terrorism and Public Safety. He is a practicing psychoanalyst and a training and supervising analyst at the Training and Research Institute in Self Psychology in New York. Dr. Strozier is the author of

Heinz Kohut: The Making of a Psychoanalyst and the editor (with Michael Flynn) of *Trauma and Self* and *Genocide, War, and Human Survival*, in addition to numerous other books and articles on history and psychoanalysis. He was the founding editor for fourteen years of *The Psychohistory Review*.

Nina K. Thomas, Ph.D., ABPP, is a psychoanalyst in private practice in New York City and Morristown, New Jersey. She has been involved in work with trauma both nationally and internationally for more than fifteen years. A supervisor in the relational orientation of the New York University's Postdoctoral Program in Psychotherapy and Psychoanalysis, she is also a faculty member and senior supervisor of the Contemporary Center for Advanced Psychoanalytic Studies in Livingston, New Jersey. Dr. Thomas is at work on a research project studying the psychological implications of victim-witness testimony in the aftermath of political violence, war, and ethnic conflict.

Isaac Tylim, Psy.D., ABPP, is a training analyst of the International Psychoanalytic Association and a member of faculty and supervisor at the Institute for Psychoanalytic Training and Research (IPTAR), and at New York University's Postdoctoral Program in Psychotherapy and Psychoanalysis. Dr. Tylim is coordinator of inpatient psychology at Maimonides Medical Center and clinical assistant professor of psychiatry at Downstate Medical Center. He is the secretary of the International Psychoanalytic Association's Committee on the United Nations. He is the coeditor of *Terrorism and the Psychoanalytic Space: Perspectives from Ground Zero*.

Bessel van der Kolk, M.D., is a well-known teacher, researcher, and clinician in the area of posttraumatic stress. He is a professor of psychiatry at Boston University and Medical Director of the HRI Trauma Center in Boston. He is past president of the International Society for Traumatic Stress Studies. Dr. van der Kolk is the author of over a hundred publications on trauma, including *Psychological Trauma* and the coeditor of *Traumatic Stress: The Effects of Overwhelming Experience on Mind, Body, and Society*.

Vamik D. Volkan, M.D., is professor emeritus and founder of the Center for the Study of the Mind and Human Interaction (CSMHI) at the University of Virginia, Charlottesville, Virginia. He is also a founder and a former president of the International Society for Political Psychology. Dr. Volkan is a training and supervising analyst at the Washington Psychoanalytic Institute and the author and editor of over thirty books, including *Bloodlines: From Ethnic Pride to Ethnic Terrorism* and *The Third Reich in the Unconscious: Transgenerational Transmission and Its Consequences*.

John P. Wilson, Ph.D., is professor of psychology at Cleveland State University. He is cofounder and past president of the International Society for Traumatic Stress Studies. Dr. Wilson is an internationally recognized expert in Post-Traumatic Stress Disorder (PTSD) and currently serves as the international director of the Institute for Psychotraumatology in Dubrovnik, Croatia. Dr. Wilson is the author or editor of thirteen books on trauma and PTSD, including *Treating Psychological Trauma and PTSD* and *Broken Spirits: The Treatment of PTSD in Asylum Seekers and Refugees* (with Boris Drozdek).